THE GIANT BOOK OF

SUPERNATURAL

THE GIANT BOOK OF
SUPERNATURAL

Edited by
Colin Wilson

This edition published and distributed by
Parragon Book Service Ltd in 1995
Unit 13-17 Avonbridge Trading Estate
Atlantic Road
Avonmouth
Bristol BS11 9QD

Produced by Magpie Books Ltd, London

First published as The Mammoth Book of the Supernatural
by Robinson Publishing 1991 © Colin and Damon Wilson

ISBN 0 75250 137 2

A copy of the British Library Cataloguing in Publication
Data is available from the British Library.

Printed in Great Britain.

Colin Wilson was born in Leicester in 1931. He left school at sixteen and spent several years working in a wool warehouse, a laboratory, a plastics factory and a coffee bar before *The Outsider* was published in 1956 to outstanding critical acclaim. Since then he has written many books on philosophy, the occult, crime and sexual deviance plus a number of successful novels. His work includes *The Mind Parasites, New Pathways in Psychology* and *The Occult*. Mr Wilson is well known as a lecturer and radio and television personality. He lives in Cornwall.

Damon Wilson was born in 1965 in St Austell, Cornwall. He inherited his father's interest in the subject of human potentiality, and has recently had years researching the paranormal. After working as a journalist, he received an honours degree in Cultural Studies in 1988. He has collaborated with his father Colin Wilson on *The Encyclopaedia of Unsolved Mysteries*, and has edited the *Second Mammoth Book of True Crime* and *The Mammoth Book of the Supernatural*.

Contents

Foreword by Damon Wilson

Race reads Puységur's mind under hypnosis. Lavoisier declares that meteorites cannot exist. Charcot rediscovers hypnotism. Freud learns from his discovery. Does hypnosis involve the will of the hypnotist? The story of the wicked magician Thimotheus. The Heidelberg case—a woman is hypnotised into becoming a sex slave. The case of the Notting Hill hypnotists. Doctor who raped his patient under hypnosis. Robert Temple on hypnosis. J.B. Priestley makes a woman wink at him. Wolf Messing hypnotises a bank clerk into handing over a fortune. Janet's case of Leonie. Thomson Jay Hudson and 'man's two selves'. The subjective mind and the objective mind. Maeterlinck and the 'unknown guest'. The Borodino case. Man's two brains. Völgyesi on animal hypnosis. The 'will-beam'.

of Nandor Fodor. Fodor's first seance. The Lajos Pap case. The case of Aldborough Manor. The Chelsea poltergeist. The ghost of Ash Manor. Eileen Garrett's seance. Fodor's investigation of the talking mongoose. The case of Mrs Fielding.

9. The Spirit Mafia 257
Modern theories of the poltergeist. The case of Philip, the invented ghost. Guy Playfair in Rio de Janeiro. Playfair undergoes 'psychic surgery'. How Edivaldo became a psychic surgeon. Laboratory analysis of poltergeist noises. Are poltergeists caused by black magic? The case of Maria Ferreira. The case of Marcia and the statue of the sea goddess. David St Clair's experience of a black magic curse. Guy Playfair investigates the Enfield poltergeist.

10. The Power of the Witch 284
Montague Summers causes a scandal. The witchcraft craze in Europe. Angéle de la Barthe. The moon goddess Diana. 'Thou shalt not suffer a witch to live.' The Devil. The Cathar heresy. The Knights Templars. The case of Jehanne de Brigue. The Papal Bull denouncing witchcraft. The *Malleus Maleficarum*. Witchcraft in Germany. The North Berwick case. Did the North Berwick witches possess genuine magical powers? The case of Isobel Gowdie. The career of Matthew Hopkins. The case of the Salem witches. The Chambre Ardente affair. African witch-doctors and rain-making. The case of the band-saw. Charles Leland and the English Gypsies. Leland's *Aradia*. The Witchcraft Act is finally repealed in Britain. Gerald Gardner and modern wicca. The case of the Jersey rapist.

11. Possession: Illusion or Reality? 327
Kardec on possession. Oesterreich's book on possession. Janet's case of Achille. Wickland's *Thirty Years Among the Dead*. Wickland's possessed patients. Is possession due to infected tonsils? The spirit from the dissection room. Ghosts who believe they are still alive. The case of Minnie Morgan. Anita Gregory on Wickland. The case of Lurancy Vennum. The Devils of Loudun. The possessed priests. Madeleine de la Palud is seduced by her confessor. Fornication among the

clergy. Possession of the Louviers nuns. Max Freedom Long and his theory of the 'three selves'. William James and Doctor Titus Bull on possession. The Thompson case. Doctor Adam Crabtree and 'voices in the head'. The case of Sarah Worthington. The case of Art. Julian Jaynes's theory of the 'bicameral mind'. The case of Anna Ecklund. Ralph Allison and the case of Janette. Is possession 'multiple personality'? The case of Elise. The case of Douglass Deen. A note on reincarnation. The case of Shanti Devi. The case of Jasbir. *The Search for Bridey Murphy*. Arnall Bloxham and hypnotic regression. Doctor Arthur Guirdham and the Cathars. The scepticism of Ian Wilson. The case of the Pollock twins.

16. The Expansion of Consciousness   525

The career of Ouspensky. Ouspensky and mystical consciousness. The discovery of laughing gas. The nitrous oxide trance. The 'Connectedness' of consciousness. A world of mathematical relations. Foreseeing the future. 'Coming down to earth.' Raskolnikov on his narrow ledge. 'Upside-downness.' The passivity of human consciousness. The Robot. The seven levels of consciousness. Why man is on the point of an evolutionary breakthrough. The problem of negative feedback. My experience in Tokyo. The billiard balls. Man's hidden powers.

Appendix: Why I changed my view of poltergeists.

Foreword
by Damon Wilson

IN THE winter of 1969, when I was 4 years old, our family spent most of the winter in Deya, in Majorca. My memories of the place are not very clear: I chiefly recall the small boy called Pedro, who lived next door and who drew pictures in the dust of the courtyard with a stick, and a tall man in a cloak and an odd-shaped hat who walked into the house one day and showed my mother how to split a banana into three with his thumb-nail. From the fact that he presented me with one of his books—a children's story called *The Poor Boy Who Followed His Star*—I gathered that he was a writer like my father. Years later, when I became an avid fan of the *I, Claudius* series on television, I was impressed to realise that I knew its author.

What I did not know was that my father had asked Robert Graves's advice on writing a book about 'the occult', and that that advice had been 'don't'. It was as well he ignored it, for the book and its consequences became an important part of our lives during the next few years. It led—to begin with—to a BBC television series called '*A Leap in the Dark*', in which my father was the presenter. We bought our first video machine to record them—the early kind whose tapes played for a maximum of one hour—and so videos became a part of our lives long before they became as common as televisions. One result was that I was able to watch the 'Leap in the Dark' series as often as I liked. The 'creepiest' was the Edgar Vandy case, in which a dead man 'came back' to describe his accidental drowning through the mouth of a medium. The point of the programme was to try to show that only the dead man could have provided the information, and that telepathy by the medium could not account for the complex data she was able to provide. But the one I remember most was the case of a girl called Christine Beauchamp, who suffered from 'multiple personality'—she periodically turned into a scatterbrained and mischievous child who called herself Sally, and who embarrassed

Christine by doing mischievous things that landed her in all kinds of trouble. Then there was the account of the poltergeist which wrecked the office of a German lawyer in Rosenheim, and which subsided only when a shy, nervous girl called Anne-Marie was sacked. I was intrigued to learn that this was not a real 'ghost', but some kind of manifestation of Anne-Marie's unconscious frustrations.

All this meant that, by the age of 10, I had a fairly good working knowledge of the paranormal, which I accepted in the same matter-of-fact way that I accepted all the books and magazines about true murder cases that lay about the house. Like any normal 10-year-old, I would not have wanted to meet a ghost; but I was intrigued to learn that they could be explained by a science called 'parapsychology'.

One day I learned that it was not quite as simple as that. A man called Mike Delaney came to stay with us, and I learned that he was a publican who had been driven out of his pub by a poltergeist that smashed rows of bottles and glasses, and made the electronic tills go haywire—Mike was still suffering from nervous strain. My father was writing a book about poltergeists—and had been to Croydon to look into the case. There were apparently no 'disturbed adolescents' associated with the pub, and Mike himself had no doubt that the culprit was a spirit. I talked to Mike for hours, and noted that he preferred not to discuss the haunting—it was obvious that he was still deeply disturbed by it. In fact, he went to see our doctor, and took his advice to commit himself to our local mental home in Bodmin. (That quickly proved to him that there was nothing wrong with him, and he discharged himself and went off to Africa to become a mercenary.)

My father also went to Yorkshire to look into the case of a 'spirit' that had wrecked every breakable object in the house (see Appendix). When he came back, he was finally convinced that poltergeists are real spirits, and not just the unconscious energies of frustrated adolescents. Obviously, it was possible to be too 'scientific'.

But another experience of the time also demonstrated that it was possible to be too credulous. When my mother was going to Bodmin one day, my father asked her to go and look at St Mark's Church, and see if she could find out anything about a poltergeist haunting there. A journalist called John Macklin, well-known for his 'believe it or not' stories, had described how a coffin had risen up off its trestles and floated down the aisle. The man in the coffin, a Liskard builder called Pencarrow, objected to being buried near his estranged wife, and his spirit caused poltergeist disturbances until his son decided to bury him elsewhere. There was even a bare patch on the lawn of the churchyard, where Pencarrow's coffin had rested before being taken away—no grass had grown there since. My mother was asked to try and get a photograph of the bare patch.

In fact, she found that there was no St Mark's Church in Bodmin, or even in Cornwall. The vicar, the Rev. Basil Bradley, had never lived in Bodmin. And no builder called James Pencarrow had lived in Liskard either.

Another story by John Macklin—about a 'cursed' field in North Cornwall—proved to be equally unfactual. When my father wrote to Macklin asking for an explanation, he got an angry letter in reply protesting that no one had ever questioned his accuracy, but offering no other explanation. All of which seemed to demonstrate that the science of parapsychology had to tread an extremely wary path between scepticism and credulity.

In fact, what tends to happen is that the positions become polarised; the sceptics attack the believers as gullible idiots; the believers attack the sceptics as dogmatic materialists. Both seem incapable of moderation or objectivity. The career of the French statistician Michel Gauquelin illustrates both positions. By the age of 7 he was a total convert to astrology, and could rattle off the character-types associated with each sign of the zodiac; his friends called him Nostradamus. While studying at the Sorbonne, he learned of the earlier researches of 'Hitler's astrologer' Karl Ernst Krafft, who had tried to 'prove' astrology by statistical means. Krafft had studied the horoscopes of thousands of professional men, mostly musicians, and announced that he had proved that individuals are cast in the mould of their 'sun sign' (i.e. Aries are pioneers, Geminis changeable, Cancers home-loving, etc.) Gauquelin, who was studying statistics and psychology, decided to put Krafft's results through a computer. That convinced him—as he had suspected—that Krafft was deceiving himself. His reaction was to become a determined opponent of astrology who missed no opportunity to denounce it as nonsense. He even went so far as to ignore the occasional fact that supported astrology. But since he was a statistician, he continued with his research. And when he looked into the question of 'rising signs' (the 'planet' that is coming up over the horizon at the moment of birth) he was startled to realise that the evidence was no longer negative. In a group of 576 doctors, he discovered that a significant proportion were born under Saturn—as astrology predicts. Similar researches into actors showed that Jupiter was their rising sign, while sportsmen tended to be born under Mars. He also investigated the notion that people born under the 'even' signs (Taurus, Cancer, Virgo etc) are introverts while those born under the odd signs are extraverts; again he was surprised to find that his statistics supported this view.

He announced his findings in 1955, in *The Influence of the Stars—A Critical and Experimental Study*. He expected to be attacked by scientists; in fact, they ignored him. It was the astrologers who assumed they were under attack, and responded with scathing criticisms.

But another sceptic, Professor Hans Eysenck, who checked Gauquelin's results, was courageous enough to invite the derision of his fellow psychologists when he wrote: 'The results were extremely clear-cut and so significant statistically that there is no question whatsoever that the effects were not produced by chance.'

By 1976, Gauquelin's findings had become increasingly influential, and parapsychology had acquired a new respectability through the researches of Dr Andrija Puharich and the Stanford Research Institute into the powers of the Israeli metal-bender Uri Geller. It had also acquired widespread popularity, so that books like von Daniken's *Chariots of the Gods* and Castaneda's *Teachings of Don Juan* became bestsellers. Orthodox scientists felt it was time to act. They formed a Committee for the Scientific Investigation of the Claims of the Paranormal (CSICOP), apparently unaware that the Society for Psychical Research (founded in 1882) had been founded for exactly that purpose.

Unfortunately, CSICOP differed from the SPR in starting out from a position of hard-line scepticism —in fact, of downright hostility to the very notion of the paranormal. Its basic position seemed to be that anyone who reported paranormal events must be either a fool or a liar. At a meeting of the American Association for the Advancement of Science in 1979, the eminent physicist John Wheeler was applauded for his battle-cry: 'Drive the pseudos out of the workshop of science.' Oddly enough, it was the same John Wheeler who created his own version of the 'anthropic principle' (the notion that man has, in some respects, a 'priveleged position' in the universe), in which he asserted that man may be creating the universe by observing it.

I was surprised to learn that one of the founders of CSICOP, the scientific journalist Martin Gardner, had been a friend of my father's. He is the author of a book called *Fads and Fallacies in the Name of Science*, an amusing attack on various 'crank theories', such as the view that the earth is flat, and he and my father had been in correspondence for some years when they finally met (at Gardner's home) and found one another sympathetic—one of my father's science fiction stories has an affectionate portrait of him as a mediaeval monk called Martin the Gardener. But when he came to write a biography of Wilhelm Reich in the late '70s, my father re-read the chapter in *Fads and Fallacies* about Reich and concluded that it was biased and inaccurate. In *The Quest for Wilhelm Reich*, he commented on Gardner's book: 'He writes about various kinds of cranks with the conscious superiority of the scientist, and in most cases one can share his sense of the victory of reason. But after half a dozen chapters, this non-stop superiority begins to irritate; you begin to wonder about the standards that make him so certain he is always right.' Gardner took this to be a declaration of war, and launched attacks on my father's 'credulity' in his books *Science: Good, Bad and Bogus* and *The New Age*. He also wrote a letter to the *New York Review of Books* protesting that articles by my father (on astrology and paranormal phenomena) had been included in *The Oxford Companion to the Mind*. His general tone makes it clear that he regards anyone who can defend the paranormal as a dangerous maniac.

In 1981, CSICOP was shaken by rumours of scandal. One of its members, Dr Dennis Rawlins, discovered that a refutation of Gauquelin's 'Mars effect' was based on inaccurate research; among other things, it based its findings on 303 sports champions instead of Gauquelin's 2,088. When the mistakes had been corrected, the report tended to confirm Gauquelin. When he pointed this out to this fellow members on the executive council, he found them unresponsive—they seemed to feel he was splitting hairs—and he was not allowed to print a letter on the subject in the CSICOP journal *The Zetetic Inquirer*, even though he was an associate editor. In fact, Rawlins made his own follow-up study of the Mars effect which concluded that Gauquelin was wrong after all. This he was allowed to publish in the magazine on condition that the section that revealed the truth about the first debunking report was edited out. He insisted that a note be printed to the effect that part of the article had been censored, and this was agreed; but when the article appeared, the note had been removed.

Rawlins now insisted that the dispute be judged by a team of impartial referees. The council agreed, but insisted that they should choose the referees. When, in fact, the referees agreed with Rawlins that the first report had been based on faulty data, the council declined to print the referees' report. In 1979 Rawlins tried to speak out at a CSICOP press conference; the council stopped the conference before he could finish, and then met in closed session and voted him off the executive. When the *Zetetic Inquirer* continued to refuse to publish the correction (in spite of the fact that Rawlins remained an associate editor), he finally resigned, and told the whole story in a pamphlet called *STARBABY*. Its cover states: 'They call themselves the Committee for the Investigation of Claims of the Paranormal. In fact they are a group of would-be debunkers who bungled their major investigation, falsified the results, covered up their errors, and gave the boot to a colleague who threatened to tell the truth.' In 1980, Marcello Truzzi, founder and editor of the *Zetetic Inquirer* (and an old friend of my father), resigned when the council refused to agree that if you print an attack on someone, it is only fair to print their reply.

CSICOP was embarrassed but unrepentant; they obviously felt that, in spite of their misdeeds, they were right to take an uncompromising stand against the 'black tide of occultism' (Freud's phrase). Since then, CSICOP has expanded, and now has branches all over the world.

My own attitude to the dispute is obviously influenced by the fact that I am an interested party. But when I recently read large parts of Gardner's *The New Age: Notes of a Fringe Watcher*, I think my reaction had little to do with its sideswipes at my father. It was a feeling of sadness that a mind as brilliant as Gardner's (and I still reread his *Fads and Fallacies* with pleasure) should remain so relentlessly *negative*. There is a passage in Shaw's *Man and Superman* where the president of the brigands insists on reading aloud verses of sentimental poetry about a girl who jilted him. The hero slaps him on the shoulder and says: 'Put them in the fire, president. You are sacrificing your career to a monomania.' The president replies sadly: 'I know it.' Mr Gardner does not know it. He is like a man who wants to tell you his grievances at length, unaware that you do not find them as fascinating as he does.

What seems so odd is that a committee for the investigation of claims of the paranormal does so little actual investigating. It seems to prefer appeals to 'reason' that are actually restatements of its basic prejudice—that paranormal phenomena do not and cannot exist. It seems that no one in this organisation of scientists can recognise the purely logical objection to the 'debunking' method, the objection that William James stated in a single sentence: 'If you wish to upset the law that all crows are black, you must not seek to show that no crows are; it is enough if you prove one single crow to be white.' In other words, it would not make the slightest difference if 99% of claims of the paranormal were exploded, if just 1% stood up to the most rigorous investigation.

This book is full of flocks of white crows. But since my father has omitted it, perhaps I can offer my own favourite example—the odd story of Frederick Bligh Bond and the excavations at Glastonbury Abbey.

In 1907 the Church of England bought Glastonbury Abbey—which had been destroyed by Henry VIII—for £36,000, and chose Bond, who was an architect, to excavate the ruins. What the Church did not know was that Bond was keenly interested in Spiritualism and telepathy.

There was one minor problem—there was no money to organise a full-scale dig. So Bond decided to try a short cut. He asked a psychic friend, John Allen Bartlett, to try 'automatic writing'. On the afternoon of November 7, 1907, Bartlett and Bond sat facing one another, Bartlett holding a pencil and Bond resting his hand gently on it. Bond asked: 'Can you tell us anything about Glastonbury?', and the pencil wrote: 'All knowledge is eternal and open to mental sympathy. I was not in sympathy with the monks—I cannot find a monk yet.' This, it seemed, must be Bartlett's 'guide'. Bond suggested that he knew a few living monks who might form a sympathetic link. Soon after, the pencil traced an outline that they recognised as the abbey, but with a long rectangle —which they did not recognise—stuck on its eastern end. The sketch was signed 'Gulielmus Monachus' —William the Monk. And when Bond asked for more details, he obliged with a more precise sketch of the rectangle—which was obviously a chapel—and added two smaller rectangles—probably towers—to the north. Another monk who called himself Johannes Bryant the Lapidator (stonemason) added more details. Other monks, including the Abbot Bere, Ambrosius the Cellarer and Peter Lightfoot the Clockmaker provided more information in Latin and Old English.

By the time the money was finally available to start excavations —in 1908—Bond had accumulated remarkably detailed information about the abbey from his ghostly informants. In May 1909 the workmen began to dig trenches along the lines indicated by William the Monk. Bond's rival Caroe came to look, and must have been mystified by their apparently random arrangement. A few days later, Bond proved he knew exactly what he was doing when the digging revealed an immense and unsuspected wall running north and south for 31 feet—the east chapel. Digging at the other end revealed two towers. From then on, discovery followed discovery. The monks told Bond of a door in the east wall leading into the street; this sounded unlikely, because east doorways are rare it proved to be exactly where they said it was. Bond was slightly sceptical when they told him that the chapel was 90 feet long—that seemed too big; but it proved to be 87 feet, and the wall and plinth added the extra three feet. They even told him that he would find the remains of azure-coloured windows, although most of the stained glass of that period was white and gold; but the azure glass was duly found. When a skeleton was uncovered, with its damaged skull between its legs, the monks explained that it was one Radulphus Cancellarius, Radulphus the Treasurer, who had slain in fair fight an earl called Eawulf of

Edgarley. No one had ever heard of an earldom in Edgarley (a nearby village), but ancient records unearthed a nobleman called Eanwulf of Somerton, very close to Edgarley. . .

After nine years of non-stop success, Bond decided that it would now be safe to tell the true story of the 'Company of Avalon' (as the monks called themselves). In 1918, he did so in a book called *The Gate of Remembrance*. The effect was instantaneous and disastrous. Budgets were cut; Bond was obstructed by red tape, and in 1922 was dismissed. He lived on, a lonely and embittered man, for another quarter of a century. While the abbey became a tourist attraction that brought the Church a satisfactory return for its investment, Bond's book was not even sold in the abbey bookshop.

Oddly enough, Bond himself did not believe that his information came from dead monks; he thought it probably originated in the 'racial unconscious'. That made no difference; the Church of England was not only opposed to Spiritualism, but to anything that sounded 'supernatural'. Fourteen years after Bond's dismissal, Archbishop Cosmo Lang recognised the absurdity of this position, and appointed a committee to look into the claims of Spiritualism. The committee sat for three years, and finally concluded that the claims of Spiritualism were probably true, and that, in any case, there is nothing in the idea of communication with the dead that contradicts Christian doctrine. Embarrassed by this report, the Church decided to drop it into a drawer, where it remained for another forty years, until its publication in 1979.

The problem remains: why is it that CSICOP and the Church of England can both take up the same uncompromising position on the paranormal? On one level, the answer is obvious. Coping with this complex material world requires a down-to-earth attitude, and the most successful copers will be the down-to-earth materialists. We all want to be successful copers, therefore we are all inclined to be impatient with anyone who seems to live in a world of ideals and abstractions. We all agree that ideals and abstractions are important for the progress of humanity; but we would like to keep them at bay until they have proved their worth. Shaw's Andrew Undershaft remarks: 'That is what is wrong with the world at present. It scraps its obsolete steam engines and dynamos; but it won't scrap its old prejudices and its old moralities and its old religions and its old political constitutions. What's the result? In machinery it does very well; but in morals and religion and politics it is working at a loss that brings it nearer bankrupcy every year.'

In 1962, Thomas S. Kuhn's book *The Structure of Scientific Revolutions* set out to investigate this reluctance to scrap old prejudices. He points out that when scientists have accepted a theory as satisfactory, they are deeply unwilling to admit that there might be anything wrong with it. They ignore small contradictions, but get furious if the contradictory facts grow larger. They are unaware that there is anything wrong about this reaction; they feel that it is the natural attitude of a reasonable man in the face of time-wasting absurdities. New 'paradigms' are always seen as time-wasting absurdities.

All this is as natural as the urge to self- preservation; in fact, it *is* a part of the urge to self-preservation. William James made the same point in an essay called 'On a Certain Blindness in Human Beings'. Cart-horses used to be blinkered to stop them from shying in the traffic; human beings need blinkers to keep them relaxed and sane. Kuhn tells a story of an experiment using playing cards, in which some of the cards were deliberate 'freaks'—black hearts and red spades. Subjects were asked to call out the suits as the cards were shown to them. When the 'freak' card was shown only for a moment, nobody noticed anything wrong. But if the exposure was slightly longer, they became puzzled and upset; they knew there was something wrong, but didn't know what it was. Some suffered 'acute personal distress'. When they fathomed what was wrong, the distress was replaced by relief. But a few failed to spot the deliberate mistake, and suffered an increasing build-up of anxiety. According to Kuhn, the demand to introduce new factors into our belief systems causes the same distress and anxiety—and encounters the same resistance.

What we are talking about, of course, is preconceptions. What is a preconception? It is a kind of mental map that enables you to find your way around, and saves you a great deal of trouble and anxiety—and no anxiety is worse than the anxiety of not knowing where you are and where you are going. Once we have gone to the trouble of acquiring a map, we are naturally anxious not to have to alter it. Small changes are not too difficult to accept. But large changes produce a sensation like the ground quaking under your feet.

The psychologist Abraham Maslow described an experiment that takes this argument a stage further. The subjects this time were baby pigs. The most timid pigs wanted to stay close to their mother in the sty. More enterprising ones explored the sty, and, if the door was left open, went outside. If the door was then closed, they squealed pitifully until let in. Next time the door was left open, they hesitated about venturing out. Then curiosity overcame them, and they decided to take the risk. These 'explorers' were, in fact, the most dominant and healthy among the piglets.

I shall not press the comparison too far, since the members of CSICOP may be offended at being compared to non-dominant piglets. Besides, some of the most obstructive conservatives in the history of science have been highly dominant. I simply want to plead my point that CSICOP is not furthering the progress of science by shouting abuse at scientists who are engaged in paranormal research and demanding that they be driven out of the workshop of science (which means suspending their grants). By trying to repress research into the paranormal they are striking at the very essence of science. And in telling the rest of us to stop thinking about the frontiers of science and leave it to the professionals (i.e themselves), they are ignoring the fact that anyone who applies his intelligence to the solution of a problem is, by definition, a scientist. And that includes all the readers of this book.

I am not trying to argue that we should drop all standards, and give serious consideration to every crank theory. But when I look at the number of fairly well-authenticated white crows in the field of paranormal research—telepathy, dowsing, psychometry, precognition—the attitude of CSICOP seems akin to Nelson clapping his telescope to his blind eye and declaring that he could see nothing.

In a chapter of *The New Age* entitled 'PK (Psycho-Krap)', Martin Gardner remarks that 'most professional parapsychologists will be embarrassed by . . . the scribblings of such irresponsible journalists of the occult as Colin Wilson, Lyall Watson and D. Scott Rogo'. Whether my father's work on the paranormal amounts to embarrassing scribbling I leave to the reader to decide; you are undoubtedly less biased than I am.

1.
The Rebirth of Magic

IN PARIS in the year 1960 there appeared on the bookstalls a volume with the euphonious title *Le Matin des Magiciens* (*The Morning of the Magicians*). The authors were an oddly assorted pair—a flamboyant journalist named Louis Pauwels, and Jacques Bergier, an atomic physicist who was also a practising alchemist. It is a curious hodgepodge of a book, as the authors themselves recognised, for they wrote in the first chapter: 'Skip chapters if you want to; begin where you like, and read in any direction; this book is a multiple-use tool, like the knives campers use . . .' To everyone's astonishment, it became a best-seller, running through edition after edition in France. Serious critics were irritated and baffled by its success; they pointed out that the book was merely a series of wild speculations on magic, alchemy, telepathy, prophecy, strange cults, the Great Pyramid, Hitler's astrologers, the Cabala, flying saucers, and a thousand other topics. This mass of eccentricity was held together by one simple theme: that the world is a stranger and richer place than science is willing to recognise.

It was a message that apparently had a wide appeal in France, especially to the young. They were less interested in the book's argument about the narrowness of science than in the imaginative appeal of its magical wonders. Other writers saw that there was money to be made out of the occult, and as books on astrology, reincarnation and visitors from outer space rolled off the presses there was no sign of any loss of interest. The craze spread to the United States, Britain, Spain, Italy, Germany, France and South America. In 1968, a German book called *Memories of the Future* made a fortune and a reputation for its author Erich von Daniken, and sold more copies than any other book except the Bible. Daniken's thesis was that the earth was visited thousands of years ago by spacemen, who left behind signs of their presence such as the statues of Easter Island and the pyramids. Stanley Kubrick's film *2001, A Space Odyssey*, was based on the same idea. It became a kind of cult, and its admirers went to see it again and again, just as they might attend a religious ceremony. The great occult boom had arrived.

I had bought *The Morning of the Magicians* when it appeared in England in 1963 (under the title *The Dawn of Magic*), but although I enjoyed it, had not taken it too seriously; it struck me as a little too wild and undisciplined. Besides, it was full of errors. It talked, for example, about the remarkable maps which, it declared, had been presented to the Library of Congress in the mid-19th century by a Turkish naval officer called Piri Reis, the oldest of which dates from the 1st century AD, yet *which shows Antarctica*, which was not discovered until 1818—and which, moreover, seems to show its shape as it was before it was covered with ice. Another map shows a land bridge across the Bering Strait, between Siberia and Alaska, which has not existed for at least 12,000 years. All this seems to argue that civilisation is far older than we realise—or possibly that the world was visited in the remote past by aliens from other planets.

The authors were right about the maps, but they had spoiled an interesting and exciting argument by being wrong about Piri Reis, who was actually a Greek pirate who was beheaded in 1554. And although I was not aware of this particular error when I first read the book, I sensed a general atmosphere of carelessness that I found irritating. This is why I felt no temptation to join in the 'Occult Revival' that seemed to be going on all around me.

Not that I was indifferent to the subject of the 'supernatural'— otherwise I would not have bought the book in the first place. When I was about 10 years old, I had been deeply impressed by a series of articles in a Sunday newspaper that purported to be the after-death experiences of an airman who had died in the Battle of

Britain, as received through a 'spirit medium'. He described what it was like to die in considerable detail, and how the 'next world' was a marvellous place with emerald-green grass and perpetually flowering trees—I remember being particularly impressed by his account of going to swim in water that was like warm cotton wool, and didn't get up your nose. I hurried to the local library, and located various books on Spiritualism, including Harry Price's *Most Haunted House in England*, an account of the haunting of Borley rectory (see pp. 233ff). This so impressed me that I read my way right through every book they had on ghosts, poltergeists and life after death. For the next month or so I kept my schoolfriends in a state of astonishment with weird tales of the occult.

My enthusiasm soon waned when an uncle presented me with a book called *The Marvels and Mysteries of Science*, and my mother bought me a chemistry set for Christmas. Science filled me with an ecstatic excitement that was as magical as any fairy tale, and the fascination with 'the occult' seemed to vanish like a dream at cockcrow. Yet it revived in flashes over the years: for example, when, at the age of 20, I was living in London, and came upon a strange work called the *I Ching* in the local library—newly translated by Jung's friend Richard Wilhelm. Like everybody else who has ever acquired the *I Ching*, I immediately consulted the oracle on my own future, and was gratified when the result was the first hexagram in the book: Ch'ien, The Creative, with a judgement:

> 'The creative works supreme success,
> Furthering through perseverance.'

This led me on to a study of ritual magic and witchcraft, as well as to the work of Gurdjieff and Ouspensky. I was particularly struck by a passage in the introduction to Ouspensky's *New Model of the Universe*:

'It is the year 1906 or 1907. The editorial office of the Moscow daily paper *The Morning*. I have just received the foreign papers and I have to write an article on the forthcoming Hague Conference. French, German, English, Italian papers. Phrases, phrases, sympathetic, critical, ironical, blatant, pompous, lying and, worst of all, utterly automatic phrases which have been used a thousand times and will be used again on entirely different, perhaps contradictory, occasions. I have to make a survey of all these words and opinions, pretending to take them seriously, and then, just as seriously, to write something on my own account. But what can I say? It is all so tedious. Diplomats and all kinds of statesmen will gather together and talk, papers will approve or disapprove, sympathise or not sympathise. Then everything will be as it was, or even worse.

'It is still early, I say to myself; perhaps something will come into my head later.

'Pushing aside the papers, I open a drawer in my desk. The whole desk is crammed with books with strange titles, *The Occult World*, *Life After Death*, *Atlantis and Lemuria*, *Dogme et Rituel de la Haute Magie*, *Le Temple de Satan*, *The Sincere Narrations of a Pilgrim*, and the like. These books and I have been inseparable for a whole month, and the world of the Hague Conference and leading articles becomes more and more vague and unreal to me.

'I open one of the books at random, feeling that my article will not be written today. Well, it can go to the devil. Humanity will lose nothing if there is one article less on the Hague Conference.'

All this was a faithful reflection of my own state of mind at the time. At the age of 20 I was already a father, and was living in South Wimbledon, in the home of an old invalid who had hired my wife as a nurse. Since my marriage I had made a living by working in a series of plastics factories. It was hard to find landladies who would put up with babies, and we had moved four times in the course of one year. Within a few months our present landlord would die, and my wife would take on a job as the nurse of a half-insane virago who lived in Earls Court; she would prove to be our worst trial so far, and she exhausted us both so much that when we separated—to try and find yet another home—we concluded that we were sick of marriage, and drifted apart.

During the next three years I worked at a series of temporary jobs—in offices, factories, coffee bars—and tried to write a novel about an 'outsider' who feels as Ouspensky did about modern civilisation. I had always been fascinated by rebels and 'outsiders', social misfits who loathe what the philosopher Heidegger called 'the triviality of everydayness'. And it was while working as a dishwasher in a London coffee bar in the mid-1950s that I decided to lay aside the novel and try to express my frustrations in a more straightforward manner by writing a book about 'outsiders'.

It proved to be a good decision. *The Outsider* happened to be accepted by the first publisher to whom I sent a dozen or so pages, and, when it appeared in 1956, became an immediate bestseller. This was partly because it was a book that had something new to say—I am neither stupid nor modest enough to regard its success as a fluke. But it was also because the English literary scene had been singularly devoid of new talent since the end of the war. And the journalists who wrote about me made much of my publisher's admission that I was only 24, and that I had written it in the Reading Room of the British Museum, while sleeping during the nights on Hampstead Heath to save rent.

The result, at all events, was an explosion of international notoriety and more money than I had ever dreamed of. But fame, I soon discovered, also had its negative side. The British are not—to put it mildly—a nation of intellectuals. Unlike the French, the Germans—even the Americans—they take no interest in the world of ideas. They were impressed by *The Outsider* because it had been written by a 24-year-old who had not been to a university. But they were not really in the least interested in romantic rebels with foreign names like Novalis, Nietzsche, Dostoevsky and Ouspensky. Moreover, it soon became clear that the popular press resented the publicity for which they themselves were responsible, and which had helped to make the book such a success. In the following year, 1957, they seized the first opportunity to announce their complete loss of interest in the whole Outsider phenomenon. This happened to be after the publication of my second book, *Religion and the Rebel*, which was hatcheted. The Americans, always delighted to see a success-bubble explode, followed suit. (*Time* ran a headline 'Scrambled Egghead'.)

I found it a traumatic experience. But at least I was infinitely better off than when I was working for £5 a week in a plastic factory or coffee bar. Ever since I had been a small boy, I had dreamed of living in a tub, like Diogenes, or in some tiny room under the earth, rather like one of Tolkien's Hobbit holes—a warm, comfortable retreat stocked with food and books. I didn't really much care for being 'famous' and going to literary parties; mixing too much with people bewildered me and gave me a sensation I called 'people-poisoning'. I wanted to be allowed to spend my days reading and thinking. So, together with my girlfriend Joy—whom I had met soon after my marriage broke up—I moved to a remote area of Cornwall, into an old cottage that was a fairly good imitation of a Hobbit hole, and went back with relief to reading, writing and thinking about the ideas that interested me so much.

What were these ideas? Well, to begin with, I had a deep conviction that man is on the point of an evolutionary break-through to a higher stage. These strange ecstasies that filled the romantics with an odd sense of power and certainty were not illusions: they were, in fact, glimpses of the unknown powers of the human mind. H.G. Wells once remarked that the world has changed more in the past sixty years than in the previous 60 centuries. He meant, of course, in technology. Yet it seemed to me that man himself has also changed more in the past 2 centuries than in the whole of his previous evolution, and that he is now close to the stage at which a new creature will emerge like a butterfly from a chrysalis.

The Morning of the Magicians had also talked about a 'new kind of man', and the possibility that human beings may be about to achieve an 'awakened state'. The authors had even made the important comment that what is now needed is an Einstein of psychology who can understand the hidden powers of the mind. Yet it was hard to see how these important ideas connected up with their talk about the Hollow Earth, vanished civilisations and aliens from outer space. Which is why I continued to feel that the 'occult revival' was something I could safely ignore. Yet on lecture tours of America—which I made at intervals in an effort to keep my bank-manager happy—I frequently bought paperbacks with titles like *Famous American Hauntings* or *Exorcism—Fact not Fiction* to read on the plane. And, like Ouspensky, I continued to find something oddly fascinating in this strange if occasionally lunatic world of speculation.

It was in 1969 that my American literary agent wrote to ask me if I would be interested in writing a book about 'the occult'. I accepted because I needed the money; besides, I felt I probably knew as much about it as anybody. But I found it hard to take the commission seriously—I only had to re-read that passage in

Ouspensky about *Atlantis and Lemuria* and *The Temple of Satan* to feel that I was going to have to write it with my tongue firmly wedged in my cheek. That winter—1969—I took the family to a small village in Majorca, where I was supposed to be a 'visiting professor' in the extramural department of an American college. There I met the writer Robert Graves, whose book *The White Goddess* had given me severe headaches many years before, and I asked his advice on writing a book about the occult. He gave it in one word: 'Don't.' And I have to admit that, if I had not already received half the advance, I would probably have taken his advice.

It is difficult to say at which point I began to change my mind. I think it was the day Joy read aloud to me a passage from Osbert Sitwell's autobiography *Left Hand, Right Hand*, in which he tells a story of how, just before the First World War, he and a group of brother officers went to see a famous palmist 'as a lark'. What happened dismayed him. The palmist kept looking at hand after hand and saying: 'I don't understand it. I can see nothing . . .' The explanation came a few months later when the war broke out, and the men whose palms had been 'blank' were killed . . .

Now it seems clear from Sitwell's other works that he was not a 'believer' in the supernatural—in that respect he seems to have shared the attitude of his father, Sir George Sitwell, who once grabbed a 'spirit' that was walking around at a seance, and revealed it to be the medium in her underwear. And the more I studied this subject of the paranormal, the more I discovered that some of the most convincing witnesses were not spiritualists or occultists, but unbelievers who had had just one odd experience.

Charles Dickens is another example. In a letter of May 30, 1863, he decribes how, the previous Thursday, he had had a dream in which he saw a lady in red, who stood with her back towards him. He thought he recognised her as someone he knew, but when she turned round, saw that she was, in fact, a stranger. The lady remarked 'I am Miss Napier'. And as he was dressing that morning, he thought: 'What a preposterous thing to have such a distinct dream about nothing. And why Miss Napier?'

That same evening Dickens gave one of his famous public readings, and some friends walked into his dressing-room with the lady in red, who was introduced to him as Miss Napier . . .

This story raises perhaps the most difficult of all questions about the 'supernatural'. It should be *totally impossible* to know about an event before it takes place, except as some kind of vague guess. Time is a one-way street, and the future has not yet happened. We may choose to believe in all kinds of strange things: spontaneous combustion, telepathy, out-of-the-body experiences, haunted houses, phantom hitch hikers . . . But each one of these might well have some more-or-less rational explanation. In the case of foreseeing an event that has not yet happened, there is no 'rational' explanation: it seems to defy the laws of reason. Yet, as I was soon to discover, there are hundreds of well-authenticated cases of people who have foreseen the future.

What fascinated me was that this was not really so remote from my interest in 'outsiders'. Because what these cases seemed to prove beyond all doubt was that human beings possess strange *powers* of which they are normally unaware. And this is precisely the intuition that had excited so many of the great poets and musicians of the 19th century. In *The Prelude*, for example, Wordsworth decribes how, one moonlit evening, he borrowed a small boat he found moored on the edge of Lake Windermere, and how, as he rowed out into the middle of the lake, a huge black peak seemed to tower above him like a living creature. For days afterwards, he says:

> ' . . . . my brain
> Worked with a dim and undetermined sense
> Of unknown modes of being',

and his dreams were troubled by 'huge and mighty forms that do not live'.

Is that mere 'poetic imagination'? Or had he actually *seen* something that the rest of us do not see because our senses are too narrow and practical, in the same way that some people can see ghosts?

Here is an example that brings home the point even more clearly. Richard Church was a poet who was born in London in 1893, the son of a post office worker. Life was hard; his mother, whom he adored, destroyed her health by working as a schoolteacher to help support the family. Church himself suffered from such poor health that at one point he was sent

away to spend some months in a convalescent home. He felt
miserable and sick with longing for his mother. And then there
came a strange experience that, in some ways, transformed the
rest of his life. He describes how:

'. . . one heavy morning, when the outside world was iron-
bound with frost, I stood at a long French window in the play-
room waiting to go down to breakfast. The sun was just risen
beyond the ground, and stood above the lawns, his great red
disk etched with naked twigs of the bushes. Under these bushes
a gardener was chopping down a dead tree. I watched him. The
axe flashed red, and fell. It rose again. The movement, steady
and sure, fascinated me. Suddenly I realised that the sound
of the blows did not synchronise with what I saw. The thud
came when the axe was on an upstroke, ready for the next
blow.

'I disbelieved the evidence of my eyes. Then I thought my
spectacles (those miracle workers) must have betrayed me; or
that my illness had begun to affect my vision. I stared intently,
screwing up the eye-muscles against any possible intrusion of light
or irrelevant image. But the picture I saw and the sound I heard
remained disparate.

'Then, while I stared, knowledge came to me; the knowledge
that follows a recognition of fact, of concrete experience, bringing
with it a widening both of the universe and of the individual's
understanding of it. These moments are rare, and they are wholly
vital. For a flash, the recogniser is a god, who can say 'I am', as
Jehovah said in the Old Testament.

'On that frosty winter morning, between getting up and going
down to breakfast, in an antiseptic, varnished institution where
the inmates and staff were so dehumanised that they were little
more than parts of the mechanism of the place, leaving me in a
murmurous solitude, day after day bemused and lonely, elated by
the very dreariness of things, there I stood transfigured . . .

'I had found that time and space are not absolute. Their power
was *not* law. They were not even unanimous; they quarrelled with
each other; and through their schism the human imagination, the
hope, the faith, could slip, to further exploration where intuition
had formerly hinted, but where logic and fatal common sense had
denied.

'I felt both power and exultation flooding my veins. The blood glowed warm within me, rising to my brain and pulsing there, like a crowd roaring some racial acclamation. I had found out the cheat of time and space; and if that were so, then other seemingly stable laws of nature might be questioned, to the advantage of this fettered and hoodwinked spirit, this hidden and oppressed self, locked in the dungeon of my body.

'I looked again, and still the evidence wrote itself upon the frosty air, against the disk of the sun who had now risen an inch or two higher, like the minute-hand of a giant clock, jerking itself up toward the hour, invisibly visible in its motion. The beauty of this syncopation between sight and sound released me from so much, from the mass of daily life, the burden of the flesh and its strict locality, from the drag of earth.

'That last was my most hated foe. The drag of earth, the weight that would pull me day and night, making every movement, even the smooth gestures which we throw in sleep, a labour too heavy to be borne; the putting on of clothes, the passage from chair to chair, the endless travel from one room to another, and that final torture, the treadmill of the tandem, during those Sunday rides behind my brother, as I tried to do my share of the pedalling, under the goad of his tongue, lashing me to it.

'But now I was free. Since time and space were deceivers, openly contradicting each other, and at best offering a compromise in place of a law, I was at liberty to doubt further, to carry on my exploration of the horizons of freedom. Still conscious of the warm blood whispering in my veins, I looked down at my wrist and saw the transparent flesh, the bird-bones, the channels of blue beneath the skin. All this was substance as fragile as a plant. It could not possibly outweigh the solid earth under my feet, where I and the rest of duped mankind walked with such docility.

'The sun had brightened to a liquid fire that dazzled my sight, reducing the woodman and his brief moment of revelation to a penumbral figure under the shadow of the bushes in the dead grey frost. I stared at the light, and the stuff of life within my body began to increase its speed of flow. I sensed, with a benignancy deeper and more assured than reason, that my limbs and trunk were lighter than they seemed, and that I had only to reduce them by an act of will, perhaps by a mere change of physical mechanics, to command them off the ground, out of the tyranny of gravitation.

'I exerted that will, visualising my hands and feet pressing downwards upon the centre of the earth. It was no surprise to me that I left the ground, and glided about the room (which was empty) some twelve or eighteen inches above the parquet floor. At first I was afraid of collapsing, of tumbling and hurting myself. But I had only to draw in a deep breath, and to command the air through the heavy portions of my anatomy, *watching* it flow and dilute the solid bone and flesh through the helpful chemistry of the blood, this new, released and knowledgeable blood, and I soared higher, half-way to the ceiling. This thoroughly frightened me, and I allowed myself to subside, coming to ground with a gentleness that was itself a sensuous delight.

'I could not leave the matter there. I must put my discovery to the test again, and accordingly I drew in a deep breath and was just about to visualise that downward pressure of will upon body, when the door opened, and a nurse came in.

'"Why, little boy?" she said. "Haven't you heard the breakfast bell?"

'Then she took a second glance at me, stooped and peered into my face, "Is anything wrong? Are you feeling poorly this morning?"

'I was almost indignant, and disclaimed the suggestion that I might have a temperature, for that would mean going to bed in the large ward where a pail stood conspicuously in the middle, on a sheet of mackintosh; an improvisation which disgusted me.

'I hurried away without replying, leaving the nurse looking after me with some inquiry in her manner. The corridor and staircase were empty, for everybody was at breakfast in the vast dining-room below. Here was another opportunity! I drew my breath again, I scorned the liars of time and space, I took the presence of Christ into my hollow, featherweight bones, and I floated down the staircase without touching either tread or baluster. Alighting outside the dining-room door, I entered and took my seat, content now to live incognito amongst these wingless mortals.'

This is surely one of the most remarkable passages ever written by a poet. His other references to the experience—in his auto-biography *Over the Bridge*—make it clear that he is telling of something that actually happened; this is not some childish fantasy or daydream. Did he actually float through the air in a physical sense, as he seems to be claiming? Or was he having what is known as an 'out-of-the-body experience'? His account seems to make it quite clear that it was his physical body that floated clear of the ground. And his case is far from unique. Dozens of children have been quite convinced that they have floated downstairs without touching the stairs. In her book *The Decline and Fall of Science*, the researcher Celia Green quotes a letter from a woman who claims to have had the experience as a 17-year-old schoolgirl:

'Each girl took her turn lying on a long wooden table . . . with the others gathered *tightly* around her, so that there were no gaps . . . As one lay there, the girls chanted a rhyme—the actual words of which I have forgotten, but which referred to the person on the table as looking white, ill and then dead. It was spoken quite slowly and in unison so that its drone-like tone had great depth and was very penetrating.

'Several girls took part before me without much success . . . Some . . . did admit to feeling a strange sensation . . . and it was this plus the declaration of a friend that encouraged me to try it.

'I have absolutely no explanation why I was able to rise approximately three feet from the table surface. I was perfectly conscious that I was rising and might even have uttered an exclamation of surprise . . . The rapidity of the rise and indeed the fact that I had risen at all caused me to jerk my body out of the lying position, and with much commotion the girls cushioned my fall.'

I, on the other hand, *do* have a kind of explanation of what happened. It is quite clear that a sceptic would claim that it was all auto-suggestion: the low chanting, the suggestion that the person was becoming pale, then dead, would induce a certain mood like hypnosis. And, the sceptic would assert, this then produced the illusion of floating up into the air. My own explanation is that the 'mood' simply triggered some unknown power that we all possess, just as Richard Church's mood of exultation somehow showed him how to float off the ground. And if this sounds absurd, then consider the well-authenticated case of Joseph of Copertino, the 'flying monk' whose feats of levitation were witnessed by dozens of famous men of learning, including the philosopher Leibniz. Born in Apulia, Italy, in 1603, Giuseppe Desa was—like Richard Church—a sickly boy; and, like Church, he was subject to sudden moods of ecstasy. He was one of those persons who feel dissatisfied with the sheer weight of the flesh that they have to carry around with them, and mortified it with fasting and flagellation. He became a priest at the age of 25. And one day when he was saying mass in his own church of St Gregory of Armenia, he uttered a cry and, in the upright position, flew with his hands outstretched to the cross above the altar. The nuns who were present thought he would catch fire on the candles, but moments later he flew back down into the church and began to dance and sing as he chanted the name of the Virgin. Later, when seeing the pope, he was again seized with ecstasy and rose into the air. And he continued to do so for the remainder of his life—he lived to be 60—witnessed by hundreds of people. He seems to have been a simple, happy soul, who did not resent the envy with which he was regarded by his fellow Franciscan monks, and who rose into the air like a balloon every time he was overwhelmed by sudden joy.

But if we want to understand more about these 'hidden powers', it is worth looking more closely at Richard Church's experience. And the first thing that is important to note is that until he was 7, he was appallingly short-sighted. When this was finally noticed by the school doctor, he was taken along to an optician who tested his eyes. He was amazed when the optician dropped lenses into a frame on his nose, and the small letters on an illuminated card suddenly became clear. But this was nothing to his amazement when he first wore the glasses, and realised that he could suddenly see everything with incredible sharpness and clarity. For the first time he could see the pupils of his mother's eyes, the hairs on his father's moustache. When he stepped out onto the pavement, it 'came up and hit me', so he had to grab hold of his father:

'The lamplight! I looked in wonder at the diminishing crystals of gas-flame strung down the hill. Clapham was hung with necklaces of light, and the horses pulling the glittering omnibuses struck the granite road with hooves of iron and ebony. I could see the skeletons inside the flesh and blood of the Saturday-night shoppers. The garments they wore were made of separate threads. In this new world sound as well as sight was changed. It took on hardness and definition, forcing itself upon my hearing, so that I was besieged simultaneously through the eye and through the ear.

'How willingly I surrendered! I went out to meet this blazing and trumpeting invasion. I trembled with the excitement, and had to cling to mother's arm to prevent myself being carried away in the flood as the pavements rushed at me, and people loomed up with their teeth like tusks, their lips luscious, their eyes bolting out of their heads, bearing down on me as they threw out spears of conversation that whizzed loudly past my ears and bewildered my wits.

'"Is it any different?" asked Jack . . .

'"It makes things clearer," I replied, knowing that I had no hope of telling him what was happening to me.'

If you can read this passage with indifference, then you are missing the point. It is about far more than a boy's first pair of spectacles. To grasp its real significance, ask yourself the following question: was his new vision of the world more or less true than his old one of a few minutes earlier? The answer has to be: truer, for blurred vision is obviously less accurate than clear vision. And the implications of this reply are tremendous. For it means that the rest of us are normally blind to the reality around us.

How can this be? After all, few of us are as short-sighted as Church was, and, in these days of Social Security, no one need be without spectacles. Yet we are, in effect, just as short-sighted as the young Church, for we take the world for granted. We have a kind of robot inside us, who does things for us. You learn to read slowly and painfully, then the robot does it so fast that you are not even aware of 'reading' these words: they seem to be speaking to you from the page. The robot is typing this book. He drives my car and sometimes even gives lectures for me. But he also takes over all kinds of other things which I would prefer to do myself. I take my dogs for a walk on the cliffs, but they enjoy it much more than I do because their robot is less efficient. Mine makes me take too much 'for granted'. He glances at something, says 'Oh yes, we know all about that . . .', and *prevents me from really seeing it*. It is just as if I spent my life wearing a dark pair of sun-glasses.

But does this really matter? In some ways, no. I get just as much exercise whether I walk 'robotically' or not, and a meal supplies me with just as much energy whether I eat mechanically or not. The real trouble arises if I begin to feel depressed or discouraged. These sun-glasses make the world so much darker. But my vitality—and therefore my health—depends upon *enthusiasm*. It depends upon a certain eagerness. It depends upon *noticing differences*.

Ouspensky tells a story that makes the same point. He describes how he and a friend were crossing the River Neva in St Petersburg.

'We had been talking, but both fell silent as we approached the [Peter and Paul] fortress, gazing up at its walls and making probably the same reflection. "In there are also factory chimneys," said A. Behind the walls of the fortress indeed appeared some brick chimneys blackened by smoke.

'On his saying this, I too sensed the *difference between* the chimneys and the prison walls with *unusual clearness* and like an electric shock. I realised *the difference between the very bricks themselves*. . . .

'Later in conversation with A, I recalled this episode, and he told me that not only then, but *always*, he sensed these differences and was deeply convinced of their reality.'

And Ouspensky goes on to say that the wood of a gallows, a crucifix, the mast of a ship is, in fact, a *quite different material* in each case. Chemical analysis could not detect it; but then, chemical analysis cannot detect the difference between two twins, who are nevertheless quite different personalities. Ouspensky begins this important chapter with a paragraph that ought to be written in letters 20 feet high:

'It seems to us that we see something and understand something. But in reality all that proceeds around us we sense only very confusedly, just as a snail senses confusedly the sunlight, the darkness and the rain.'[1]

A similar experience was reported by the American psychologist Abraham Maslow, who had been told of it by a marine who had been stationed in the Pacific for several years and had not seen a woman. When he came back to base, he saw a

---

1. *Tertium Organum*, Chapter 14.

nurse, and immediately had a 'peak experience'—an experience of sudden overwhelming delight—as it suddenly struck him with a kind of shock that *women are different from men*. We say 'Of course women are different from men', yet these words disguise the fact that we have allowed the robot to obliterate the real difference. We do not see it with that sense of shock and amazement experienced by the marine—although it is true that a man might experience something similar if he walked past an open doorway and caught a glimpse of a woman removing her clothes. And this example makes us aware that we have simply allowed our senses to collapse. You could compare them to a tent that has been blown flat, so it is no longer of much use as a shelter. Because of this collapse of our senses, they cannot do their proper work, *which is to show us the differences between things*.

In short, I am suggesting that it is the 'robot' who destroys our 'magical' powers, and prevents us all from being able to float through the air like Richard Church or Joseph of Copertino.

Let us look more closely into this fascinating problem.

You may feel that the idea of floating through the air is just a little too much to swallow. Yet there is another odd faculty which seems to be closely related to it, and which thousands of people have reported: I mean the odd ability to be in two places at once.

When the Society for Psychical Research was formed in London in 1882, it received hundreds of reports of people who had 'seen' other people who were not actually in the room. In many of these cases, the person who appeared was about to die, or had just died, and the person who saw him (or her) was a close relative. So such 'apparitions' could be explained either as ghosts, or—if you did not believe in ghosts—as some kind of telepathy. In a typical case, a man sitting in his room in Dublin awoke in the night and saw his father—who was on his deathbed in Wales—sitting in a chair with his face covered by his hands; a moment later, he vanished. The man was so impressed that he rushed over to Wales, and found that his father had been delirious for two days. And when he entered the room, his father remarked that he had been to see him the day before . . . [1]

1. Quoted in my *Beyond the Occult*, p. 187, and in *Phantasms of the Living*, by Gurney, Myers and Podmore, Volume 2, p. 461.

But the Society also received hundreds of reports of people who were not ill or in any danger being seen in other places. These they called 'phantasms of the living", and the case cited above is from one of its earliest and most impressive compilations. The following typical case is recounted by the poet W.B. Yeats:

'One afternoon . . . I was thinking very intently of a fellow student for whom I had a message, which I hesitated about writing. In a couple of days I got a letter from a place some hundreds of miles away where the student was. On the afternoon when I had been thinking so intently I had suddenly appeared there amid a crowd of people in a hotel and seeming as solid as if in the flesh. My fellow student had seen me, but no one else, and had asked me to come again when the people had gone. I had vanished, but had come again in the middle of the night and given him the message. I had myself no knowledge of either apparition.'[1]

What seems to have happened here is that Yeats's anxiety to deliver the message somehow caused him to 'project' his image several hundred miles, where it apparently behaved like a normal person. And in the case of the man who was dying in Wales, we may again surmise that the father's anxiety (in fact, he wanted to tell his son the whereabouts of an overcoat) again caused him to 'project' himself to Dublin. And it is a plausible hypothesis that when people are on the point of dying, they are able to tap some unconscious power which allows them to 'show themselves' to some close relative about whom they are anxious. (In the same way, there is strong evidence that people who are drowning, or in some great physical danger, really *do* see their past lives flashing in front of their eyes within a second or two.)

But there are other cases in which people seem to have used this power more or less deliberately. One evening in the the late 1920s, the novelist John Cowper Powys had spent the evening dining with the great American writer Theodore Dreiser. Powys suddenly looked at his watch: 'I must hurry.' But as he left Dreiser's New York apartment he remarked: 'I'll appear before you later this evening.' Then he rushed off to catch his train to upstate New York. Dreiser assumed the comment was a

1. Yeats: *Essays and Introductions*, p. 37.

joke. But two hours later, as he sat reading, he looked up and found Powys standing by the door. He stood up, saying: 'John, come in and tell me how you did it.' At that moment, Powys vanished. Dreiser rushed to the telephone and rang Powys's home. Powys answered, and, when Dreiser told him what had happened, replied: 'I told you I'd be there.'

Dreiser adds that Powys later declined to discuss how he had done it. But that may not be because Powys wanted to be secretive. It may be, quite simply, that he did not know. He probably 'felt it coming on' during the evening, an odd state of mind which he recognised as the ability to 'project' himself. And it is almost certain that he did not know he had done it until Dreiser rang him up.

Perhaps the strangest case on record is that of an attractive French schoolmistress named Emilie Sagée who lost 18 jobs in sixteen years because of her peculiar habit of being in two places at once. The way she lost her eighteenth job is typical. In 1845, she was a teacher at a school for young ladies at Neuwelcke, near Wolmar, on the shores of the Baltic. One day as she was writing on the blackboard, a second Emilie appeared standing beside her. As she turned to see what the pupils were murmuring about, her 'double' vanished. On another occasion, she was on her knees beside a girl called Antoinette von Wrangel, pinning her dress, and as the girl looked in the wardrobe mirror, she saw two Emilies, and fainted.

The last straw was when another teacher had left her pupils alone for five minutes. Suddenly, they were astonished to see Emilie seated in the teacher's chair. Stranger still, there was another Emilie out in the garden. Two of the bolder pupils tried to touch the apparition, and said it felt like muslin. One of them even walked through her. Then the apparition vanished, although the other Emilie could still be seen in the garden. Later, a friendly pupil asked Emilie what had happened. She explained that she had looked into the classroom through the garden window, seen that the teacher was absent, and felt worried that the girls would misbehave. It seems that, in some strange way, her worry had projected her 'double' into the room.

When parents heard these stories they began withdrawing their children from the school, and Emilie was sacked. She then went to live with her sister-in-law, and everyone in the family got used to seeing her double wandering around the house. But the strain seems to have been too much for her; one day she left the house and vanished, never to be seen again. The likeliest explanation is that she drowned herself.

One of the most famous cases recorded by the Society for Psychical Research concerns a young student named S.H. Beard, who was engaged to a girl named Miss Verity. In November 1881, Beard was sitting in his room in London reading a book about the power of the will. It suddenly entered his head that he would like to 'appear' to Miss Verity, who lived at 22 Hogarth Road, Kensington. He concentrated his mind and tried to visualise the house, and the bedroom on the second floor where his fiancée slept. Suddenly he became aware that he could not move his limbs; he felt 'frozen'. And at that moment, in Hogarth Road, Miss Verity woke up and found him standing by her bed. She screamed, and it awoke her 11-year-old sister. As the two girls stared at the apparition, it vanished. Beard himself did not know he had succeeded until Miss Verity told him about it next time he saw her.

A month later he decided to try it again. By now Miss Verity and her sister had moved to Kew. Once again he made the attempt, writing later: 'I also put forth an effort which I cannot find words to describe. I was conscious of a mysterious influence of some sort permeating my body, and had a distinct impression that I was exercising some force with which I had been hitherto unacquainted, but which I can now at certain times set in motion at will.' Half an hour later he 'came to' and realised he had been asleep—or in a trance. The next day he discovered once again that he had been successful. But it was not Miss Verity who had seen him this time, but her married sister. She had seen him walking from one room to another, and later he had walked into her bedroom, touched her hair, taken her hand in his own and stared intently at the palm before he vanished. The sister woke Miss Verity, who was in the same bed, to tell her what had happened.

All these stories seem to make the same point made by Richard Church. We take it for granted that we live in a 'solid' world of space and time, advancing from moment to moment according to unchangeable laws, and that we are stuck in the place where we happen to be at the moment. We are, in a sense, 'trapped'. We feel this particularly strongly when we are bored or miserable—that we are helplessly at the mercy of this physical world into which we happen to have been born. Yet these odd experiences all seem to show that this is untrue. The 'real you' is not trapped in space and time. With a certain kind of effort of will it can rise above space and time, and be 'elsewhere'. Later in this book we shall discuss the strange fact that human beings have *two* brains, and that we all have two different 'selves' who live one in each of them (see page Pp. 60ff). Brain physiologists have no idea of why we need two more-or-less identical brains in our heads—one tongue-in-cheek suggestion is that one of them is a 'spare' in case the other gets damaged. My own belief is that we have two brains, *so we can be in two places at the same time*. Human beings are *supposed* to be capable of being in two places at the same time. Yet we have not quite discovered the 'trick'. When we do, we shall be a completely different kind of creature—no longer the same kind of human being who lives out his life so incompetently on this long-suffering planet, but something far more powerful and purposeful. This is what I mean when I say that I believe man is on the point of an evolutionary leap.

But, as I have already explained, I had arrived at this conviction long before I began to take an interest in 'the occult'. It was already the foundation of my first book *The Outsider*, written almost twenty years earlier. What convinced me was the curious change in human consciousness that began to take place around the year 1750. What happened, quite simply, was that man suddenly learned to *daydream*. He began to use his imagination in a completely new way. In fact, you could almost say that the human beings who existed before 1750 had very little imagination at all.

You probably believe that, if you could take a time machine back to the age of Shakespeare, you would find life far more fascinating than today. In fact, you would find it incredibly boring and depressing. The streets would have stunk of dung, urine, dead rats and rotting vegetation—an open sewer ran down the middle of most of them, and rich people wore high platforms on their shoes to keep them from getting their feet dirty in the thick mud. But what would really have depressed you would have been the people themselves. We think of the modern New Yorker or Londoner as a fairly unlovely product of our technological civilisation. But he is a noble and sensitive soul compared to the average Elizabethan. As reflected in the literature of the period, the Elizabethan was self-centred, stupid—most of them were illiterate—and utterly materialistic. He was also appallingly cruel; a mother starving with a child at her breast meant nothing to him, and his favourite entertainment was to attend a public execution, in which a man was often branded with hot irons, then half-hanged, then taken down while still alive and torn open so his intestines spilled out. The Elizabethans also loved to attend the playhouse, and their favourite plays were full of blood and violence—like Marlowe's *Tamburlaine the Great* or Kyd's *Spanish Tragedy*—which ended with the stage piled with corpses.

It would be pointless to blame them for this—when life is an endless struggle, people become hard and ruthless. But it is important to recognise that these people were very different from ourselves in one basic respect—that they lacked what we would call imagination. Most of us have learned the trick of 'putting ourselves in other people's shoes', of imagining what it would be like to be someone else. So newspapers can always guarantee a large sale if they have some 'human' story about a child who has lost his dog, a baby in need of a heart transplant, a 'tug of love' between divorced parents. The Elizabethans would have found this baffling; to hold their attention, a story had to be either farcical or cruel. *Don Quixote*, one of the most popular novels of the following century, kept its readers in a state of delight by showing its hero being beaten unconscious in every other chapter.

The 'great change' began in the middle of the 18th century—or, to be more precise, in the year 1740. A year earlier, a 50-year-old printer named Samuel Richardson had been asked by a publisher to write a kind of Teach Yourself book about the art of letter-writing. Being a natural preacher, Richardson decided to write letters that would teach his readers about religion and morality as well as paragraphing and punctuation, so he interspersed business letters and character references with letters full of reproach, good advice and moral observations. And as he was writing, he recalled a story he had heard twenty years before, about a pretty 'lady's companion' named Pamela who had been driven to the point of suicide by the determined efforts of her employer's son to seduce her, but ended by marrying him. The young man's relatives had at first regarded her with extreme disapproval, but her 'dignity, sweetness and humility' had at last won their hearts.

The story of Pamela was at first intended to form part of the *Familiar Letters*, but Richardson's wife and a young lady guest found it so fascinating that he soon decided to turn it into a separate book. *Pamela, or Virtue Rewarded*, appeared—anonymously—on London bookstalls on November 6, 1740, and quickly became the literary sensation of the season. The reason is simple: although Richardson had intended it as a kind of sermon on the importance of chastity, its readers were more interested by the young master's attempts to deprive Pamela of her virginity—as, for example, when he hides in a cupboard as she gets undressed, then leaps on her and throws her on the bed. (She is saved by the intervention of the housekeeper.) Or later, when he tries to rape her as a brothel madame holds her hands, but is deterred when she has a kind of seizure. This kind of thing kept them reading breathlessly through 800 or so pages.

In effect, *Pamela* was a kind of magic carpet that transported the reader into the lives of its characters. In our age of the television soap opera, this has become a commonplace; in the 1740s it seemed stunningly original. There had been plenty of novels about faraway places with strange-sounding names, of which *Robinson Crusoe* is still far and away the best. But no one had thought of writing about the kind of people who might live next door. Moreover, unlike most of the novels of the period, *Pamela* was a long book; the reader could get lost in it for days at a time. It was, in effect, a *kind of holiday from being yourself.*

The *Pamela* craze swept across Europe. It produced an immense appetite for novels, and lending libraries sprang up in every town in the same way that cinemas sprang up in the first decade of the 20th century. Europe became a nation of readers. And sensitive young people made the interesting discovery that if you found the real world boring and disappointing, there was nothing to stop you from turning your back on it and spending your days living other people's lives.

And it was at this point that the young Wordsworth rowed out into the middle of the lake and was overwhelmed by a sense of 'huge and mighty forms that do not live'. If he had been born half a century earlier—at about the time Richardson was writing *Pamela*—that experience would have been impossible: he would have beheld the hills of the Lake District with the same practical eye as the local farmhands. But half a century of novel-reading had taught people to use the imagination, and it was because he possessed a lively imagination that Wordsworth could experience these strange moods of total freedom and of 'unknown modes of being'.

There was, of course, one basic problem about these magical excursions into 'other worlds'—they made the real world seem so appallingly dull. Every young person has experienced this feeling after an hour or so absorbed in a favourite book—or videotape. It is like walking out into a cold wind after a hot bath. The reaction of many of these 'romantics'—as they called themselves—was to spend still more time in the magic world of books. And this inevitably made them hate the real world even more. Many committed suicide; many more died tragically of illnesses like tuberculosis, brought on by misery and deprivation. And many simply plodded on sadly, accepting that life is one long disappointment, yet dreaming of better things. One of the most moving episodes in Richard Church's *Over the Bridge* describes how a long-haired young man with dirty nails came to tune their piano. He smoked continuously as he worked. When he had finished, Richard's brother Jack asked him if he could give him a few hints on how to play a Beethoven piano sonata—Jack had been wrestling unsuccessfully with it for weeks. 'The result was like the opening of a weir.' The scrawny musician tossed back his hair, cracked his knuckles, and proceeded to play. And the two boys listened in rapt silence as the magnificent music flowed through the room. When it was over, the musician wiped his face with a dirty handkerchief. He was sweating, and emitting an odour of mice or bats. And Jack, too moved even to thank him, hurried from the room to ask his father if he could have piano lessons.

This picture of the musician, with his unwashed hands and dirty handkerchief, seems to me to capture the essence of the Outsider tragedy. Inside him he carries around the magnificent world of Beethoven, even a touch of Beethoven's genius. How must he have felt as he sat on a crowded bus, jammed between workmen and housewives, wondering whether he had enough money for another packet of cigarettes? It must have seemed to him that he was a kind of changeling, condemned to a life of servitude by some malicious enchanter. And this, I felt, was one of the major problems of our world: that there are thousands of people who are intelligent enough to make some real contribution to modern life, yet who are condemned to remain permanently unknown.

It was because I was fascinated by this problem of the 'Outsider', the intelligent misfit, that I wrote my first book. What seemed so paradoxical was that these people were not dying because they hated life. On the contrary, they wanted *more life*. You could say that they were on strike for a more interesting way of life. The problem was summarised by the great romantic writer Hoffmann in his novel *Murr the Tomcat*, in which the mad musician Kreisler tells the Princess: 'You seem, your highness, not to be very interested in dreams, and yet it is really in dreams that we grow butterfly wings so that we can esape this narrow, tight prison, and fly, like glittering moths, up to the sky, to the highest heaven.' And he adds, with typical humour: 'Every man really has an innate inclination to fly, and I have known serious, respectable people who in the late evening fill themselves up with champagne, as a gas useful for ascending to the heights, as balloon and passenger at the same time.'

'As balloon and passenger at the same time.' That was the great romantic dream. But he adds elsewhere in the book: 'Is it not eternally true that our flight is impeded by leaden weights that we cannot identify—nor do we know where they come from, or who attached them to us.' Hoffmann himself made heroic attempts to fly, both by writing his famous Tales, and by drinking vast quantities of German wine, which ended by ruining his health so he died in the greatest misery.

All this explains why I came to believe that man is on the point of an evolutionary breakthrough to a higher stage. He obviously *wants* to fly—not in the physical sense, but on the wings of the mind. And, as Bernard Shaw once remarked: 'The brain will not fail when the will is in earnest.'

So long before I wrote *The Occult*, I was convinced that we all possess unknown powers of which we are only dimly aware. But how do we become aware of them? How do we learn to make use of them? One thing was obvious to me: that the first step is to learn to *sink inside ourselves*. Imagine that someone has offered you a rare wine to taste, a wine that was made while Napoleon was still alive. The first thing you do is to raise it to your lips, and then *sink inside yourself*, until you are aware of nothing but the smell and taste of the wine. Most of us can remember doing something of the sort as a child, listening to the rain pattering on the windows, and perhaps rolling up into a ball in the warm bed, totally happy and relaxed. (I knew a girl who told me that whenever she did this as a child, she used to murmur to herself: 'Isn't it nice to be me?')

It is significant that John Cowper Powys, whom we have already encountered, attached great importance to this 'trick' of sinking inside himself. He described it for the first time in a novel called *Wolf Solent*, which was published in 1929—that is, at the same time as the incident when he 'appeared' to Theodore Dreiser. And this coincidence is enough in itself to make us wonder whether there might not be some connection between the two. Let us look a little more closely at *Wolf Solent*.

The novel opens with a long chapter that is typical of Powys—a description of a train journey. The opening paragraph sets the tone:

'From Waterloo Station to the small country town of Ramsgard in Dorset is a journey of not more than three or four hours, but having by good luck found a compartment to himself, Wolf Solent was able to indulge in such an orgy of concentrated thought, that these three or four hours lengthened themselves out into something beyond all human measurement . . .'

The first thing you feel is that Powys is in no hurry. You can almost sense him chortling to himself as he settles down—imaginatively—into that railway compartment and prepares to indulge in his 'orgy' of thinking. So let us try to follow his example—that is, relax deeply, and forget all impatience. Unless you can place yourself in that mood of peaceful abandonment, of not caring how long this takes, you will miss the point of what Powys is saying.

'A bluebottle fly buzzed up and down above his head, every now and then settling on one of the coloured advertisement of seaside resorts—Weymouth, Swanage, Lulworth and Poole—cleaning its front legs upon the masts of painted ships or upon the sands of impossibly cerulean waters.

'Through the open window near which he sat, facing the engine, the sweet airs of an unusually relaxed March morning visited his nostrils, carrying fragrances of young green shoots, of wet muddy ditches, of hazel copses full of damp moss, and of primroses on warm grassy hedge-banks.'

All this is intended to hypnotise the reader: the buzzing bluebottle, the 'sweet airs of an unusally relaxed March morning', the fragrance of green shoots.

After introducing us to his hero, and explaining that he is on his way to Dorset to take a job as a squire's literary adviser, Powys tells us how much Wolf hates London, with its unending rush, and how much he detests all the barbarous mechanicalness of modern civilisation. In an image that would have far more appeal now than it had in 1929, he tells us that Wolf sees the whole earth as looking like a helpless, vivisected frog, 'scooped and gouged and harrowed'.

'And then', says Powys, 'stretching out his legs still further and leaning back against the dusty cushions, he set himself to measure the resources of his spirit against these accursed mechanisms. He did this quite gravely, with no comic uneasiness at the arrogance of such a proceeding. Why should he not pit his individual magnetic strength against the tyrannous machinery invented by other men?

'In fact, the thrill of malicious exultation that passed through his nerves as he thought of these things had a curious resemblance to the strange ecstasy he used to derive from certain godlike mythological legends. He would never have confessed to any living person the godlike intoxication of personality that used to come to him from imagining himself a sort of demiurgic force, drawing its power from the heart of Nature herself.'

And as he sits there, watching the telegraph poles flashing past, Wolf imagines himself to be a prehistoric giant 'who, with an effortless ease, ran along by the side of the train, leaping over hedges, ditches, lanes and ponds, and easily rivalled, in natural born silent speed, the noisy mechanism of all those pistons and cog-wheels.'

Two pages later—Powys is nothing if not leisurely—he tries to analyse this 'mental device' that gives him so much peculiar strength.

'This was a certain trick he had of doing what he called "sinking into his soul". This trick had been a furtive custom with him from very early days. In his childhood his mother had often rallied him about it in her light-hearted way, and had applied to these trances, or these fits of absent-mindedness, an amusing but rather indecent nursery name. His father, on the other hand, had encouraged hm in these moods, taking them very gravely, and treating him, when under their spell, as if he were some sort of infant magician.'

Wolf calls this peculiar habit 'mythology' or 'mythologising', an oddly disappointing name for a concept of such momentous importance. And he admits that it makes him feel 'as if he had been a changeling from a different planet, a planet where the issues of life—the great dualistic struggle between life and death—never emerged from the charmed circle of the individual's private consciousness.'

In other words, the trouble with our planet is that it keeps us entangled in *triviality*, so we never get a chance to confront these great issues.

What is so interesting about this whole passage is that strange sense of *power* that it expresses. Wolf knows that, when he sinks deep inside himself, he has the strength and the ability to 'measure the resources of his spirit against these accursed mechanisms'. He becomes a kind of magician. We can, of course, dismiss this as pure wishful thinking—until we remember how he was able to 'project' himself back to Dreiser's apartment in New York.

In a later novel *Porius*, Powys invents an even more unwieldy name for this habit of withdrawing deep inside himself; his young hero has christened it 'cavoseniargizing'—which suggests withdrawing into a cave. What he means is that there are certain moments in which the gulf between his body and his soul is somehow bridged, 'so that his soul found itself able to follow every curve and ripple of his bodily sensations, *and yet remain suspended above them*.' We normally have the sense that the body is a rather unwilling servant that obeys us only reluctantly; yet in moods such as *Porius* describes, the sense of unwillingness vanishes, and it seems that the body is simply the visible part of the soul. Racing drivers speeding at 200 miles an hour have occasionally described the same odd sensation of being suspended above themselves while nevertheless wholly in control. It is the sensation that convinced the Romantics that man is really a god.

At this point, let us return for a moment to those remarks made by Hoffmann's mad musician Kreisler: that 'it is in dreams that we grow butterfly wings by which we can escape our prison and ascend to the highest heavens', and that 'every man has an innate inclination to fly'. The first remark takes on new significance when we think of Dickens' lady in red, Miss Napier, and the second when we recall Church's description of the morning he suddenly realised he could fly. 'I felt both power and exultation flooding my veins. The blood glowed warm within me, rising to my brain and pulsing there . . . I had found out the cheat of time and space . . .' In short, Church was unconsciously doing what Wolf Solent does on the train: he was 'cavoseniargizing'. And a few moments later, he was literally flying. Cavoseniargizing seems to be the key to 'magical' powers—the key, for example, to those preposterous coincidences that Jung called 'synchronicities', and which he believed were somehow *caused* by the unconscious mind.

In other words, Powys is really suggesting that *we* control this curious power over space and time, and if we knew the trick, could exercise it when we like. Think again of the experience of tasting a very rare wine: the way that you try to induce what Shaw called 'the seventh degree of concentration', and descend inside yourself.

I recognise that words like 'cavoseniargizing', or even 'mythologising', are unlikely to achieve wide popularity: both are too clumsy. But I am not sure my own substitute is any better. I have always called this deliberate 'self-absorption' subjectivising, bearing in mind Kierkegaard's remark: 'Truth is subjectivity.' He obviously meant this descent into ourselves, as if we were stepping into a lift and pressing the button labelled 'Basement—7th level'.

The romantics saw the answer, but they went about it in the wrong way. Their problem, quite simply, was immaturity. If you asked a 5-year-old child to imagine what would make him happiest, he would probably describe some endless Christmas party with slabs of iced cake and sherry trifles. If you asked a teenage youth what would make him happiest, he would probably describe some charming girl who would look at him with adoring eyes. The romantics were still thinking in terms of iced cake and pretty girls.

At the beginning of the 19th century, the most famous romantic novelist was a German called Richter, known as Jean Paul, whose novels are full of his own equivalent of Christmas cakes and pretty girls. A glance at his most famous novel *Titan* will give us the essence of romanticism in a nutshell. In the opening chapter, its young hero, Count Albano, is returning to Isola Bella (Beautiful Island), the island where he was born, and which he left as a baby. His mother is dead, and he has never seen his own father; now he is returning to meet his father—an Austrian knight—for the first time. Two friends transport him in a boat to the island during the night, then lead him, blindfolded, up to the top of the ten garden terraces. As the first rays of the sun gleam on the horizon, his friend Dian—a Greek painter—pulls off the blindfold:

"'Oh god!" cried Albano with a shriek of ecstasy, as all the gates of the new heaven flew open, and the Olympus of nature, with its thousand reposing gods, stood around him.

'What a world! There stood the Alps, like brother giants of the Old World, linked together, far away in the past, holding high up over against the sun the shining shields of the glaciers. The giants wore blue girdles of forest, and at their feet lay hills and vineyards, and through the aisles and arches of grape-clusters, the morning winds played with cascades as with watered silk ribbons, and the liquid brimming mirror of the lake hung down as if suspended by the ribbons from the mountains, and they fluttered down into the mirror, and a carved work of chestnut woods formed its frame.

'Albano turned slowly round and round, looked into the heights, into the depths, into the sun, into the blossoms; and on all summits burned the alarm fires of mighty Nature, and in all depths lay their reflections. A creative earthquake beat like a heart under the earth and sent forth mountains and seas. Oh then, when he saw on the bosom of the infinite mother the little swarming children, as they darted by under every wave and every cloud—and when the morning breeze drove distant ships in between the Alps—and when the *Isola Madre* towered up opposite him, with her seven gardens, and tempted him to lean upon the air and be wafted on a level sweep from his summit to her own—and when he saw the pheasants darting down from the *Madre* into the waves—then did he seem to stand like a storm bird with ruffled plumage on his blooming nest, his arms were lifted like wings by the morning wind, and he longed to throw himself off the terrace after the pheasants, and to cool his heart in the tide of Nature.'

Here we have a kind of verbal equivalent of Van Gogh's painting *The Starry Night*, with its flame-like trees and its sky that seethes like a whirlpool with sheer vitality.

In fact, Jean Paul does not always write on this ecstatic level; many of his works are about humble schoolmasters who live quietly in some small country village, and marry a local girl, and spend their lives peacefully teaching children the three Rs, and writing poetry which they never try to publish. But whether he is writing of magnificent landscapes or idyllic little villages, we can see why thousands of young people read Jean Paul with tears in their eyes, and regarded him as the greatest writer since Shakespeare. It seems absurdly ironic that he is now totally forgotten.

But what is so interesting here is how much things have changed in the sixty years since *Pamela*. Richardson was a realist; people read him because he wrote about the sort of people they knew. But if you are going to be carried away by a writer, rather like Sinbad the Sailor being carried up into the air by the roc, you may as well go for stories about young counts with mysterious fathers, which take place in the midst of magnificent scenery. If, like most of Jean Paul's readers, you had never been outside your native town or village, then why not also have the benefits of a technicolour travelogue?

But as you read Jean Paul's splendid description of Isola Bella, you will notice that the mood it attempts to induce is one of *abandonment*. Like Albano, you are supposed to cry 'Oh God!', and feel as if you want to fling yourself off the terrace and swoop like a bird over the sea. Jean Paul is trying to persuade you to *give yourself* to this wonderful landscape, like a girl giving herself to a lover. And here we encounter the greatest problem of the romantics. They may have intuitions of hidden powers, of the ability to fly or to float into the air like a balloon. But it is all basically Christmas cake and pretty girls. You sit back *passively* and wait for it to be handed to you on a plate. Church, on the other hand, is excited by his insight to make a sudden effort:

'I exerted that will, visualising my hands and pressing downwards upon the centre of the earth. It was no surprise to me that I left the ground . . .'

And the student Beard, we may recall, had been reading a book about the power of the will when he decided to try to 'appear' to his fiancée Miss Verity.

These 'hidden powers' we are speaking about demand a certain effort, a non-passive attitude—something like Powys's 'thrill of malicious exultation', the feeling that he is a 'demiurgic force', not a passive creature waiting to be swept off his feet.

In the following chapter I want to look more closely at some of these 'hidden powers', and the methods by which we can contact them. But it is important, above all, to remember that the method for contacting these powers consists in 'subjectivising', withdrawing inside yourself. *This* is the basic secret of 'magic'.

2.
The Powers of
the Hidden Self

SIX YEARS BEFORE the publication of *Pamela*, the wife of a gamekeeper on the shores of Lake Constance, in Austria, gave birth to a male child whose influence would be as tremendous and far-reaching as that of Samuel Richardson. Unfortunately for Franz Anton Mesmer, he was not a novelist but a scientist and a philosopher—I say unfortunately because everybody loves a good story, but few people like being asked to think. Even clever people are inclined to react to original ideas with indifference or hostility. So Mesmer's amazing contribution brought him little but trouble, and when he died in 1815, he was virtually forgotten. Yet his ideas, as we shall see, are virtually the intellectual cornerstone of modern psychology.

Mesmer grew up amidst peaceful mountain scenery, and it left its mark on him for a lifetime. His naturally religious temperament inclined him towards the priesthood, but after attending a Jesuit university at Dillingen, he came to realise that his immense curiosity pointed to a career in science and philosophy. So he studied philosophy, then law, and ended up at the age of 32 with a medical degree as well. Interestingly enough, his doctoral thesis was called 'The Influence of the Planets Upon the Human Body'.

But its thesis was less absurd than it sounds. Mesmer believed that nature is pervaded by invisible energies—the force of gravitation is an example—and that when we are in tune with these energies, we are healthy. When the energies are blocked, either by physical problems or negative mental attitudes, we become unhealthy. If the energies can become unblocked, we become healthy again.

This cheerful attitude brought him success, and within two years he had married one of his wealthy patients, a widow von Posch, and moved into a magnificent house in Vienna, where he counted the Mozarts among his many friends. It looked as if nothing could stand in the way of a lifetime of good fortune and respectability.

But how can the 'vital energies' be unblocked? One obvious way is to induce a crisis—we recognise this when we take aspirin to get rid of a cold by making us perspire. In Mesmer's day, most doctors tried to induce a crisis by bleeding the patient, which, amazingly enough, often seemed to work. But there should surely be easier ways? In 1773, he thought he might have stumbled on the solution. His friend Father Maximilian Hell, the Professor of Astronomy at Vienna University, had been experimenting with magnets, and was inclined to believe that they could unblock the vital fluids—he even designed specially shaped magnets that would fit over various parts of the body. Mesmer tried it out on a patient in 1773, taking with him his friend Leopold Mozart. 29-year-old Franziska Oesterlein lay in bed suffering from general debilitation. Mesmer tried applying some of Hell's powerful magnets, moving them from her stomach down to her feet. After an hour or so, Frau Oesterlein reported strange currents moving around her body. These built up to a crisis, and she ended by feeling much better. Repeated doses of the magnetic treatment soon cured her.

Father Hell was naturally inclined to claim the credit, and at first Mesmer was inclined to give it generously. Then he noticed something rather odd. One day when he was bleeding a patient, he noticed that the flow of blood increased when he moved close, and decreased when he moved away. It looked as if his own body was producing the same effect as the magnets. Instead of using magnets, he began passing his hands lightly over the patient. This seemed to work just as well. And as he tried the method on more patients, Mesmer decided that he had discovered the basic principle of healing: not ordinary 'magnetic' magnetism, but *animal* magnetism. In 1779 he published a pamphlet on his discovery. To his astonishment, it aroused general hositility instead of the acclaim he had expected from his colleagues in the medical profession. They insisted that Mesmer was a charlatan who cured his patients by mere suggestion—a notion in which there was obviously a certain amount of truth. They also suggested that Mesmer's motives in passing his hands over the bodies of female patients were not as pure as they should be.

As rich patients talked about spectacular cures, the hostility grew. Mesmer spent a week at the estate of Baron Haresky de Horka, who suffered from unaccountable 'spasms' and fits, and he persisted throughout a disappointing week when it looked as though the baron was failing to respond to treatment. It took six days before the baron began to shudder with asthmatic paroxysms. When Mesmer held the baron's foot, they stopped; when he held his hand, they started again. Clearly, Mesmer was controlling the baron's vital fluids and making them flow at will. With enough of this, he reasoned, all the blockages should be cleared away, like masses of twigs and leaves in a stream, and the energies should flow unimpeded. So they did; when Mesmer returned to Vienna, the baron was cured.

Undeterred by mounting hostility, Mesmer thought of new ways of distributing the magnetic fluid: he 'magnetised' jars of water, connected up the jars with metal bands, and placed the apparatus in a large wooden tub half-filled with iron filings and water. Patients sat with their feet in the water, or sat with their backs against magnetised trees. The results were remarkable—but his colleagues pointed out that leaving scantily clad men and women in close contact with one another would probably stimulate their vital fluids anyway . . .

Mesmer's good angel was off-duty on the day he agreed to treat a blind young pianist named Maria Theresa Paradies, a protégée of the Empress. He was unaware that her blindness was due to a detached retina. Oddly enough, after a few weeks of treatment in Mesmer's house, the girl became convinced she could see dimly. A Profesor Barth was sent to examine her, and he admitted privately to Mesmer that she seemed to have improved. But his report stated that she was still blind—which was undoubtedly true. The girl had be be dragged away from Mesmer's house by force. And Mesmer, tired of insults and threats, decided to move to Paris in 1778.

Here he met with the same mixture of acclaim and vilification. Dr Charles D'Eslon, personal physician to the king's brother, became an ardent admirer, and lectured on Mesmer's ideas to the Society of Medicine on September 18, 1790. Mesmer's mixed-group cures continued to attract dozens of wealthy patients, who would sit with their feet in the wooden tub or *baquet*, and form a chain and press their bodies together to facilitate the flow of vital fluid. One patient, Major Charles du Hussay, was cured of the after-effects of typhus, which had turned him into a trembling wreck, by a 'crisis' that made his teeth chatter for a month, but which left him perfectly restored. Cases like this so impressed the king that he offered Mesmer a lifelong pension to remain in France; Mesmer demanded half a million francs for research. When the king refused, he left France—on the same day that D'Eslon was lecturing to the medical faculty—and returned only when his patients contributed 350,000 gold louis, many times more than what he had asked for. But Mesmer had made an enemy of the king, who appointed a 'commission' of scientists to look into Mesmer's ideas. It included the great American Benjamin Franklin, the chemist Lavoisier (who was to lose his head in the Revolution) and the inventor of a new decapitation machine, a certain Dr Guillotin. It is an episode that reflects discredit on Franklin, who was much prejudiced against Mesmer. He was also ill, so that he did not actually attend any of the 'experiments'. But he signed the report which dismissed 'animal magnetism' as mere imagination. Mesmer was actually absent from France at the time (1794) and was not even consulted. He returned, but nothing could restore his fortunes. A hostile doctor introduced himself as a patient, allowed Mesmer to 'cure' him, then wrote a report denouncing him as a quack. This kind of thing was unanswerable. After the Revolution (during which he lost all his money) Mesmer fled. The Austrian police prevented him from returning to Vienna. He spent his last quarter of a century living quietly in Constance, not far from his birthplace.

Now it may seem to many open-minded readers that Mesmer's critics were by no means incorrect: that his theories *were* absurd, and that his cures were, indeed, due to 'suggestion'. Yet this is really to miss the point. We must remember, to begin with, that medicine in the time of Mesmer was completely 'materialistic', in the sense that it was firmly believed that all medical problems are physical in origin, (to which they added as a corollary: 'and can be cured by bleeding'.) Even if we take the least sympathetic view of Mesmer, we have to recognise that he had stumbled on a recognition of tremendous importance: that the mind plays as much a part in illness as the body. If his sceptical colleagues had been open-minded enough to study his cures, instead of attacking them as quackery, they would have found themselves asking questions that would have created a science of psychology a century before Freud.

Second, our conviction that Mesmer's ideas about magnetism and 'animal magnetism' are based on pure ignorance may well be incorrect. Well into the late 19th century, many doctors were still conducting serious experiments with magnets, and producing some extremely interesting results—for example, causing paralysis to move from one side of the body to the other. We have forgotten all this, and our descendants may well shake their heads at our complacency.

Moreover, in the 20th century, another remarkable rebel, Wilhelm Reich, came independently to the conclusion that health is governed by 'tides' of vital fluid; he called this 'orgone energy'. Reich *was*, in many ways, a crank; he was more Freudian than Freud, and believed that all illness can be explained in terms of sexual neurosis. Yet his indifference to current scientific dogmas led him to some interesting discoveries which may well be one day considered as an important contribution to modern science.

It may also be mentioned in passing that it has now been scientifically established that the human body possesses an 'aura' or 'life-field', which seems to be electrical in nature. A young biologist named Hans Driesch divided a sea urchin's egg into two and killed off one half; the other half did not turn into half a sea urchin embryo; to his surprise, it turned into a perfect but smaller embryo. When he pressed two embryos together they turned into a double-size embryo. Driesch realised that there must be a kind of invisible blueprint, like a mágnetic field, which 'shapes' living things, just as a magnet can shape iron filings on a sheet of paper.

A later experimenter, Harold Saxton Burr, discovered that he could measure this 'life-field' with a voltmeter, and diagnose illness from its fluctuations. In effect, he has placed what occultists call 'the human aura' on a scientific basis. *This* is almost certainly what Mesmer was affecting with his magnetic fields.

But Mesmer is the father of modern psychology in a far more important sense.

One of his wealthier disciples in Paris was a marquis named Armand Marie-Jacques de Chastenet, surnamed Puységur, and he and his two younger brothers had paid Mesmer the vast sum of 400 louis for training in his techniques. He then proceeded to apply them with enthusiasm to the servants and tenants on his estate at Buzancy, near Soissons, his first step being to 'magnetise' a lime tree in the park. One of the servants was a 20-year-old shepherd named Victor Race, and Puységur proceeded to tie him to the lime tree, and to make 'magnetic' gestures in front of his face. After a few 'passes', Victor closed his eyes and fell asleep. The marquis ordered him to wake up and untie himself. To his surprise, Victor untied himself without opening his eyes. Then he went wandering off across the park. Puységur was baffled; he knew he had induced some kind of a trance, but had no idea of its nature. More than 2 centuries later, science is still in roughly the same position.

What Puységur had done, of course, was to stumble upon hypnosis—a technique that later came to be called (incorrectly) 'mesmerism'. (Mesmer himself preferred to call it somnambulism—the word hypnotism was invented in 1843 by James Braid.) And as he continued to practise on Victor, Puységur made some baffling discoveries—for example, that he could give Victor *mental* orders, and the shepherd would respond just as if they were spoken aloud. Moreover, Puységur could hold conversations with Victor in which his own part was unspoken, and Victor would reply just as if he had spoken aloud. Victor could even be made to stop speaking in the middle of a word. Puységur describes in his *Memoirs in Aid of a History of Animal Magnetism* (1809) how he even got Victor to repeat the words of a song which he—the marquis—was singing mentally. What was equally interesting was that Victor was normally a rather stupid young man, but that when hypnotised, *he became far more intelligent and perceptive*.

That this was no fluke was proved in experiments with another subject named Madeleine. In front of an audience, Puységur would place her in a trance, give her various mental orders—which she would carry out—then invite members of the audience to transmit to her their own mental orders—for example, asking her to pick up a certain object. Again and again, without hesitation, Madeleine went straight to the object and picked it up. To demonstrate that Madeleine was not simply wide-awake and peeping (in spite of having her eyes closed), he would blindfold her with a thick piece of cloth; it made no difference to her immediate response to mental suggestions. One sceptic—a baron—suspected that Puységur had some code by which he communicated with Madeleine, and asked for the experiment to be conducted in the home of a mutual friend, M. Mitonard. Puységur agreed, and in Mitonard's home, lost no time in hypnotising Madeleine and placing her 'in rapport' with Mitonard. Mitonard when gave her various mental orders, and watched her carry them out. Suddenly, Mitonard stood as if lost in thought. After a moment, Madeleine reached into his pocket, and brought out three small screws she found there; Mitonard admitted that he had put them there for that purpose, and that now he was totally convinced. So was another sceptic called Fournel, who had stated that nine-tenths of these strange 'magnetic' phenomena were due to fraud; but when Fournel himself was able to 'mentally' order a hypnotised subject—with blindfolded eyes—to go to a table, select a hat from a number of other objects, and put it on his head, he had to admit that fraud had to be ruled out.

Now quite clearly these experiments were among the most important ever conducted in the history of scientific research. It obviously makes no difference if Fournel was correct in saying that nine-tenths of the people who performed such tricks in public were frauds; it is the other tenth that matters. What Puységur had demonstrated beyond all doubt was that telepathy exists (although the word would not be invented for another century). He, of course, thought it was 'magnetism'—that his own magnetic current was influencing the hypnotised subject just as a magnet influences a compass needle. Perhaps he was not entirely wrong. Whatever the explanation, Puységur had virtually demonstrated 'magic' in public. He had also totally undermined the kind of materialism that was becoming so fashionable at the time, and which asserted that man is a machine, and that the mind is a mere product of the body, just as heat and light are products of burning coal. Puységur had proved that mind is in some way independent of the body and *higher* than the body.

His demonstrations should have caused the greatest sensation since the invention of the wheel. Why did they not? Because of the unfortunate accident of being associated with the highly suspect name of Mesmer. Mesmer was a fraud. 'Magnetism' was really due to suggestion. Therefore hypnotism was also a fraud, and all the demonstrations in the world failed to prove otherwise. The hostility was so tremendous that 'mesmerism' was made illegal in France (and much the same in Austria), and a doctor who even expressed his support for the ideas of Mesmer—let alone practised them—could lose his license. The medical profession was in a state of near-hysteria, determined to stamp it out, if necessary, with fire and sword. Mesmerism remained—scientifically speaking—a pariah throughout most of the 19th century, and any doctor who became interested in it did well to keep silent.

The storm had still not blown itself out by 1809, when Puységur published his first book on hypnotism. Anything to do with Mesmer was still regarded with the deepest hostility. But many doctors took to heart Jussieu's comment that the phenomena deserved further investigation, and conducted their own experiments. D'Eslon—Mesmer's original French advocate—recorded a case of a man who could play cards with his eyes closed. A Dutch experimenter described a case of a hypnotised boy who could read with his fingertips and a girl who could read his mind and describe people and places he knew (but she didn't). A German experimenter described an epileptic boy who could distinguish colours with the soles of his feet, even when he had stockings on. In Baden, a hypnotised girl correctly read a message in a sealed envelope—even though the hypnotist himself did not know what it was. In Sweden, a professor described a girl who was able to read a book when it was placed open on her stomach, while her eyes were blindfolded. This particular phenomenon was observed again and again with 'sensitives'. In England, a young schoolteacher named Alfred Russel Wallace—who was later to share with Darwin the honour of 'discovering' evolution—found that one of his pupils, under hypnosis, could share his own sense of taste and smell; when Wallace tasted salt, he grimaced; when Wallace tasted sugar, he made delighted sucking motions. When Wallace stuck a pin in himself, the boy jumped and rubbed the appropriate part of his body.

What all this clearly demonstrated was that human beings have 'unknown powers' which are not generally recognised. But since they are so easy to demonstrate in the laboratory, they obviously ought to be recognised. Then why were they ignored? Let us not be too harsh on those doctors and scientists who denounced Mesmer. It was not pure stupidity and wickedness. Science was simply not ready for these discoveries. It was plodding along at its own slow pace, discovering electricity, atoms, meteorites. (In 1768, the great chemist Lavoisier—who reported unfavourably on Mesmer—was asked by the French Academy of Sciences to go and investigate a great 'stone' that had fallen from the sky at a place called Luce. His report stated that all the witnesses had to be mistaken, for 'stones' did not and could not fall out of the sky; it was not until the following century that the existence of meteorites was acknowledged by science.) If science had rushed on much faster, it might have been led into all kinds of untrue assumptions—as Mesmer was.

On the other hand, there can be no doubt that Mesmer and Puységur would have shaken their heads in amazement if told that, *two centuries* after their discoveries, science still refuses to acknowledge them. That is carrying conservatism to the point of sheer mulishness.

Of course, we now accept hypnosis as a reality. That came about in the last decades of the 19th century, mostly through the researches of the great French doctor Jean-Martin Charcot, who ran the Salpêtrière Hospital (mostly for very poor patients) in Paris. Charcot was puzzled by the phenomenon of hysteria—how a woman could believe she was pregnant, and her stomach swell up, or a man believe his arm was paralysed, and be unable to move it. He soon discovered that he could induce exactly the same effects by hypnosis, and he gave amazing demonstrations in which people would drop on all fours and bark like dogs, or flap their arms when told they were birds, or even eat a lump of charcoal with relish when told it was chocolate. Because Charcot was practising on poor down-and-outs, his rich medical colleagues did not feel threatened as Mesmer's colleagues had. And they were completely won over when Charcot announced his conclusion that hypnosis was just *another form of hysteria*. That made it perfectly all right. Of course, Charcot was mistaken. We can see perfectly well that, in fact, hysteria is a form of hypnosis; the hysterically pregnant woman has, in effect, hypnotised herself—convinced her unconscious mind that she is pregnant, so it causes her stomach to swell. However, Charcot's error had one excellent effect, in that it made hypnotism more-or-less respectable again. And a young doctor called Freud, who had come from Vienna to study under Charcot, was deeply impressed by the phenomena of hypnosis, and reasoned that it must be caused by *some part of the mind which is far more powerful than our everyday consciousness*. So Mesmer's discovery had led, in a roundabout way, to the foundation of modern psychology.

But Freud's interpretation of hypnosis—that it merely demonstrates the enormous hidden powers of the unconscious—only confirmed the view that was originally held by Mesmer's colleagues: that it was all a matter of 'suggestion'. If you tell a hypnotised man that you are about to touch his arm with a red-hot poker, and in fact you touch it with an icicle, he screams with pain, and will develop a blister. This is merely a demonstration of the immense powers of the unconscious mind. But it is not a case of 'mind over matter', for the unconscious is really a kind of gigantic machine—far bigger and more powerful than the puny mechanisms of the conscious mind. Freud won over the scientists so easily because his view was so determinedly realistic.

But what if someone had asked Freud—or Charcot, for that matter—how a hypnotised girl could read a book placed open on her stomach, or obey orders given to her mentally? How could *this* be explained in terms of 'unconscious suggestion?' The answer of course, is that it cannot be. Which means that, as far as modern science is concerned, some of the most important findings of Mesmer, Puységur, D'Eslon, Alfred Russel Wallace and the rest, are still ignored. Hypnosis is 'suggestion', and that is that.

It follows, of course, that no one can be induced to do something under hypnosis that he—or she—would not do when normally awake. And yet, as we shall see, this is a highly questionable assertion. Consider, for example, 'the Story of the Wicked Magician Thimotheus', as described by Professor Heinz E. Hammerschlag in his book *Hypnose und Verbrechen* (*Hypnotism and Crime*):

'One March evening in the year 1865, there was a knock at the door of an honest workman in the village of Solliès-Farliede (Bar). He lived in the house together with his two children, a boy of fifteen and a girl called Josephine, aged twenty-six. Josephine opened the door and was deeply frightened, without knowing what there was about the man standing there that could awaken such a feeling of terror. Certainly he was ugly, unkempt, and club-footed; and he gave her to understand by a sign that he was a deaf-mute. In addition, there was something about this terribly neglected man which filled her with fear, so that she would gladly have turned him away. But her father had compassion for the pitiful state of the beggar; and he allowed him to come into their living-room and to join them at supper which was ready on the table. During the meal Josephine had a chance of more closely watching this man, whose long black hair and untidy beard filled her with revulsion. A cold shudder passed down her spine when she saw his strange habits while he ate. When he poured out some wine for himself, he did not, for example, fill his glass at one time but usually put it down three times before it was filled, and never took a sip from the glass without first making a sign of the cross over it.

'Later in the evening, some neighbours who had heard about the peculiar stranger called at the house. The conversation was carried on very painfully with paper and pencil. It emerged that the deaf-mute stranger was a cork-cutter named Thimotheus Castellan who had had to give up his occupation because of an injury to his hand and who now travelled through the country as a healer, magnetizer and water-diviner. His signs and his mysterious behaviour made a great impression on the simple peasants. Only Josephine, out of fear, remained silent. When the stranger was later brought to the haystack for the night, she remained on the bed in her room fully dressed and for many hours could not fall asleep. Nevertheless, the night passed without anything unusual happening. The following morning, her brother was the first to leave the house to go to work. He was followed afterwards by her father and the stranger.

'Before some minutes had passed the beggar returned by himself to the house where he found Josephine occupied with her work. She dared not turn him away, although the same feeling of anxiety overcame her as on the previous day. He sat in silence near the hearth and watched the girl at her work. Their silence was repeatedly interrupted by visits from neighbours who evidently regarded the stranger as someone endowed with unusual powers. They observed him with astonishment and even brought him articles of food as presents. Just as one of the neighbours, without being noticed, entered the kitchen he saw the stranger making mysterious signs with his hand behind the girl's back. Josephine herself seemed restless and excited and was obviously very glad to see any visitor who interrupted her isolation with the beggar, the cause of so much anxiety. But towards noon she could no longer avoid being alone with him. For they sat together at the mid-day meal, which she provided for him so as not to let him go away hungry.

'And now the incomprehensible happened: Josephine had just begun to eat, when the man stretched out his hand and made a movement with two fingers as if he were going to put something into the spoon which she was taking to her mouth. At the same moment she felt that she was becoming unconscious. She came to as the man was standing in front of her and sprinkling her with cold water. Then, so she later reported, he took her in his arms, carried her into her room and there violated her. While this took place she was fully conscious, but in spite of all her efforts she could not ward off the fiend nor could she, by knocking on the wall, draw the attention of neighbours; she could not even answer a relative who knocked at the door and called for her.

'Early in the evening the neighbours, to their astonishment, saw Josephine leave the house in the company of the lame beggar. She gave the impression of being very disturbed, and called out to her acquaintances unintelligently and incoherently. No one understood how the girl, whose reputation was unstained, could follow the man on the road; yet no one tried to prevent her or ask her what was the cause of her behaviour.

'For two days the unusual pair roamed about in the surrounding area. At night they found refuge with a farmer who took pity on the girl without, however, being able to persuade her to return home. On the third day, they came to the village of La Cappelude and stayed at a farmhouse. Here a most unusual scene was soon enacted. Josephine fell from one extreme to the other: at one moment she smothered her companion with tenderness, at the next she pushed him away in fear and disgust. Here as well, the neighbours came running as soon as they heard of the unusual visitor.

'In the evening Josephine asked a girl from a neighbouring house to let her stay there for the night. But her companion forbade her to leave him, and as she wanted to go in spite of that, he made some mysterious signs over her body. Whereupon Josephine fell into his arms and remained as if paralysed for nearly an hour. The beggar then asked a neighbour, 'Shall I make her laugh?' and she immediately burst into a mad, yelling laughter. 'Now I will bring her back to herself,' he said, and slapped her face violently three times. Soon Josephine seemed to awaken from a deep sleep without having felt any mistreatment; she laughed and said she felt very well. They were given a room in the house for the night. When everyone in the house was asleep, a dreadful noise was heard coming from their room. The farmer armed himself with a stick, intending to throw the beggar out of the house as quickly as he could, but Josephine refused to follow the farmer's advice not to go with the beggar, so they were allowed to remain in the house. The next morning, in the presence of the members of the household and neighbours, the man made Josephine crawl about the room like an animal. This enraged the onlookers and they threw him out of the house. He had hardly left the room when the girl got into a dreadful state; suddenly she could neither speak nor move her arms; a stark and confused expression came over her face. Those present could think of no other way of helping her than by calling the beggar back. Scarcely had he stepped into the room, when the girl's fixed gaze left her. Murmuring some unintelligible words, he got her out of her fearful state by using his strange methods, at the same time once more giving her three slaps in the face. Then they both left the house.

'On the following day, they met some hunters who spoke to them. While the beggar, who had suddenly recovered his speech, was talking to them, the girl succeeded in getting away unnoticed. By hiding under a hill she eluded pursuit and, after a long search, found her way to the village she had left in the morning. There she met some kind-hearted men who took her home. On the way back, she was repeatedly overcome by states of excitement which sometimes seemed like attacks of rage. A doctor was brought and Josephine was given a thorough medical examination. The doctor found that the girl was suffering from fever and nervous strain; according to his opinion there was no mental disturbance. After about six weeks of rest she was well again; at any rate the excitement and attacks of anxiety stopped.

'In the meantime Thimotheus Castellan was arrested for vagrancy and begging. During the enquiry the court considered the question whether the young girl's will-power was so weakened by the "magnetic influences" exerted by the accused that the intimate relations between them constituted rape.

'Two physicians were charged to express their expert opinion on this question. In their report they stated:

'We the undersigned declare . . .:
(1) That by the so-called magnetic effect on the will of any person who is disposed to it by nervous temperament, an influence can be exerted such that the person's moral freedom is completely perverted or more or less destroyed.
(2) That if one puts a young girl into magnetic sleep one can have intimate relations with her of which, when she awakens, she has no knowledge.
(3) That it is possible, by the effect of magnetism, to blunt the feelings so much and to weaken the will of a young girl to such an extent that, without her being completely asleep, she no longer has the necessary moral freedom to resist intimacy, or to give her consent to it with full understanding.'

'On the basis of this report and the confirmation of its outcome by three other doctors, Castellan was sentenced by the court to twelve years' hard labour.'

Here it seems clear that the doctors were correct, and that Josephine 'no longer had the necessary moral freedom' to prevent her rape or abduction. Perhaps the most interesting part of the narrative is the neighbour's description of seeing Castellan make 'mysterious signs with his hand' behind her back, and Josephine's subsequent deposition that he stretched out his hand and made a movement with two fingers, which had the effect of causing her to become unconscious. It sounds as if Castellan hypnotised Josephine without any of the normal preliminaries of hypnotic induction—in fact, simply by an exercise of will power.

This also appears to be true in another celebrated criminal case reported by Hammerschlag, which he describes as 'a case of criminal exploitation of hypnosis unique in the history of criminology and hypnotism'.

In the late summer of 1934, a Heidelberg official (Hammerschlag calls him H.E.) reported to the local police that his wife had been swindled out of 3,000 marks. The swindler, he thought, was a man who posed as a doctor, and he even believed that he had been sexually abusing Mrs E. The lady herself remembered that the 'doctor' had often sent her to sleep by placing his hand on her head, but to all other questions answered: 'I can't remember.' Mrs E. had no history of mental illness—in fact, she came of healthy farming stock.

The police turned the case over to Dr Ludwig Mayer, who found that he was able to place Mrs E. under hypnosis. But she seemed unable to answer any questions about her 'illness'. Eventually, she was able to make a preliminary statement:

'Before I was married I was once travelling from home to Heidelberg wishing to go to a doctor because I had stomach pains. On the way a man got into my compartment and seated himself opposite me. He had a conversation with me, we began to talk about my sickness and he said that he could see immediately that I was ill. He said that he was a nature healer and homeopath, presenting himself as Dr Bergen from Karlsruhe-Daxlanden, and explained that it was just the kind of illness that I had that he could treat very well. When the train stopped at Graben he invited me to join him in a cup of coffee. I didn't want to because I felt so insecure. But he was very helpful as I got out of the train

and carried my case. Suddenly, he took hold of my hand and it
seemed to me as if I no longer had a will of my own. I felt so
strange and giddy. Later he ordered me verbally and by letter to
come to Karlsruhe or even to Heidelberg, at the station, where he
always met me. I no longer know the place in which he treated me.

'I was often in a room at Heidelberg but I no longer know
where. He met me at Tiefburg, took my hand and said that it was
very dark around me. After a long walk we went up two steps, he
opened the door and then it became light again. The room was
small and simple, with a couch and a table . . . he placed his hand
on my forehead and said: 'You are getting calmer and calmer!' I do
not know what he did to me. I cannot remember any more. . . .'

Soon after this, a swindler named Franz Walter was arrested
for other crimes; his description sounded so much like that of
'Dr Bergen' that Mrs E. was asked to identify him. She thought it
was the same man, but he denied it. But Dr Mayer was convinced
he was lying. He began the long and painful process of 'unlocking'
Mrs E's memory. Little by little, an amazing story emerged. After
causing Mrs E. to fall into a trance on that first day, Walter had
taken her to his room, made her lie on a couch, then placed her
arms behind her and told her that she could not move. After that,
he had raped her. He had then ordered her to lose all memory of
this event.

Later, Walter had ordered her to become a prostitute. The men
to whom he sold her were taught a 'magic word', 'Combarus',
which would make her do whatever they asked. Walter took all
the money she earned.

But after her marriage, her husband became suspicious about
the amount of money she was spending. She told Walter that her
husband was thinking of going to the police. He then told her that
the best thing she could do would be to 'get rid of him'. She was
ordered to buy poison and put it in his food. This plan failed when
her husband ordered her not to go out that evening. Next she was
told to take a pistol out of the drawer, shoot him in the head, then
place it in his hands as if he had committed suicide. She actually
pointed the gun at her husband's head when he was asleep and
pulled the trigger; but he had taken the precaution of removing
all the bullets. Walter next ordered her to pick poison mushrooms

and to feed them to her husband with ordinary edible ones; he did not like the taste, and pushed them away after a mouthful. Even so, he was stricken with diarrhoea and vomiting. She gave him a white powder that Walter had ordered her to slip into his coffee; but she had spilt most of it in her pocket, and the small amount she used only gave him stomach-ache.

Walter's next—and fortunately his last—scheme was to kill the husband by tampering with the brakes on his motor-cycle. On the first occasion he came close to crashing into a moving train at a level crossing; on the second, he injured an arm and a knee.

Having failed in his attempts to kill her husband, Walter now ordered her to kill herself. His first instruction was to take an overdose of sleeping tablets on an empty stomach; but her own doctor refused to prescribe the tablets. After this Walter ordered her to jump out of a moving train; but she fell into conversation with a comforting elderly lady who drove all thoughts of suicide from her head. Walter now assured her that her husband was in love with another woman and meant to leave her; he ordered her to drown herself in the Rhine. Fortunately, her housekeeper noticed her distress and followed her, preventing her from jumping.

And so, finally, the husband went to the police, Franz Walter was arrested on another charge, and Ludwig Mayer solved the case by 'unblocking' the hypnotic suggestions by which Walter had tried to prevent her from recalling what had happened. Franz Walter was found guilty, and received ten years in jail.

The most obviously striking thing about this story is that Walter did not hypnotise her by saying 'Look into my eyes' and making mesmeric passes with his fingers. He simply took her hand. How could that happen? The advocates of 'suggestivism' would argue that he had already made suggestions that placed her in his power, and that taking her hand—with its 'invasion of her personal space'—merely confirmed it. But there is nothing in her account to suggest that this is so. Here, as in the case of the wicked magician Thimotheus, it looks as if hypnosis was induced by the direct influence of one mind on another.

The same conclusion seems to emerge from a more recent case, described by the science journalist Robert Temple, in his monumental book *Open to Suggestion* (1989).

In January 1985, Maria Malheiras, a Portuguese woman living in London, was accosted by a Portuguese man who seemed to be in some distress, and who asked her if she knew of a clinic in the Notting Hill area of London. He introduced himself as Manuel, and went on to explain that his father had once worked at the clinic, and had found an envelope containing £3,000 under a pillow. Now the old man was on his deathbed, and could not rest in peace unless the money was restored . . . He waved a fat envelope under Maria's nose.

Maria said she knew of no such clinic, although she had been familiar with Notting Hill for many years. As they stood talking, Manuel stopped another passer-by and asked him if he knew of the clinic. This passer-by—a younger man—who also happened to be Portuguese (and was also called Manuel) said he was unable to help, but he joined in the conversation. And as he introduced himself and took her hand, Maria experienced a strange cold feeling, and felt disoriented. And as she stood talking, she began to experience a dreamlike sense of unreality, a kind of amnesia.

The newcomer now told her to go home, collect her jewellery and her building society savings book, and go and draw out all her savings. She did as she was told, and returned to Notting Hill Gate, where the two men were waiting. (She had, in the meantime, spoken to her husband on the telephone and been uncharacteristically rude, hanging up on him.) They now asked her to go to the post office to buy a stamp, and told her they would hold her handbag. They were, of course, gone when she returned. She had lost a total of £1,141.

The swindlers were caught by accident. A Portuguese hairdresser happened to overhear one of her customers telephoning someone and agreeing to cash a cheque and hand over £8,000. The hairdresser had heard of the two swindlers, and she persuaded the woman to tell her why she was about to give away such a large sum of money. Her story proved to be almost identical to Maria's. The police were notified, and arrested the two Manuels as the money was being handed over. It emerged subsequently that another victim had given them £1,500, while yet another had handed over his life's savings of £6,000. The swindlers were each sentenced to eighteen months in prison and deported back to Portugal.

Here it seems clear that the younger of the two swindlers—his name proved to be Manuel de Matos Amaro—was the hypnotist; the role of the elder was merely to lull her into a state of trust. (The fat envelope later proved to be stuffed with a wad of newspaper.) But it seems clear that here, once again, the hypnotist induced a 'trance' merely by touching her hand.

Temple goes on to demolish the notion that (a) people cannot be hypnotised against their will, and (b) that people under hypnosis will not commit acts that they would not commit in their normal state—he cites many cases of people who have been prepared to commit crimes or acts of violence under hypnosis. And a chapter on rape discusses once more the question raised by the Heidelberg case: whether a woman who is raped under hypnosis is really submitting because she secretly wants to. In a case cited by Magnus Hirschfeld, this is obviously so:

'A good many years ago I was consulted in a case where a doctor had assaulted a woman patient while she was in a hypnotic state—many such occurrences are recorded in scientific literature. The patient was a married woman who suffered from weak nerves, irritability, and hysterical "spasms." As is the case with many hysterical women, she had unlimited confidence in her doctor, who had commenced a course of hypnotism for various neuralgic complaints, heartburn, and insomnia. The patient was an excellent subject for hypnosis. It was sufficient for the doctor to lower his upraised hand for the woman to shut her eyes immediately. At the court hearing of the action, instituted against the doctor by the husband, the doctor made a full confession and described the suggestions he made and to which the woman automatically yielded, as follows: He ordered her to raise her skirt, lie down, spread her legs, take out his penis, introduce it into her vagina, then, during the act, perform parallel movements until mutual orgasm occurred, which in her case took place in the same way as in the waking state. The woman became pregnant. The impotent husband, who had long suspected the doctor, engaged a detective who was able to prove his suspicions. The doctor alleged that he had used the woman for therapeutic reasons. She had, he said, an unhappy life with her husband, and her depression had finally become so intense that she decided to kill herself; sexual intercourse with him had cured her both physically and mentally. He was rewarded for his "therapeutic conscientiousness" with one year in prison.'

In this case, it is clear that the woman herself was a more-or-less willing participant, and that the induction of hypnotic trance was intended to allow her to feel totally guiltless.

On the other hand, a case cited by Erik Hoencamp clearly involves more than a game of make-believe:

'He said I should not be afraid of him and kept talking to me. While he was saying that, he started to caress my lower body in the area of my genitals. I just let that happen, did not feel like, nor had the power to say no. He asked me if I liked it. Although I did not like it, I said yes. Only I did not have any fear which normally would have been there.

'Then he started to rub my breasts. He told me I should not be scared and he kept going and pulled up my bra and caressed my bare breasts. At the end of the session we made a new appointment. When the time of the appointment came near, I still trusted him, hoping that he would not touch me in that way.

'He started as usual again, but talked directly to me. I felt heavy, like the other time. He told me that I would like to unbutton my blouse and pants. I didn't do it, but then he said that I would like to prove and show that the first treatment sessions really had helped me. He caressed my breast again and after a while pulled down my pants and panties and he even put his hand in my vagina. I heard him say "You will go deeper and deeper and become more excited." I just said yes to everything, he kept on going and wanted me to take his genitals in my hands. I said no, I would rather not, I'm scared. I was very scared. After a while I held his penis, he caressed me and rubbed his lower body against the inside of my legs. He said I had to go on. I would have liked to have knocked him away, but one way or another I couldn't do it. I felt as if I was paralyzed and was very scared. He kept saying to me, you will go deeper and deeper. He started to get closer with his genitals, I started to panic and cried.'

It seems here very clear that the girl had no basic wish to submit.

In another case cited by Temple, a girl met a man on a train, and he touched her forehead and blew into her ears. When they met by chance on another train two weeks later, he repeated this behaviour, then went to the girl's room and made love to her. She wanted to resist, but felt powerless. The next day she felt that she had been forced against her will, and went to the police to report it.

But if the girl was wide-awake, could she really be made to do something against her will? Temple describes one of his own experiences that helps to explain how this is possible.

'Moving about while in a trance is a strange experience, and I have done it once myself. Having been hypnotized several times by my medical doctor, there was one occasion when I left his office while still hypnotized. He hypnotizes patients after hours, and on this occasion we had taken rather a long time over it and I could sense that he was becoming very anxious to get home to see his wife about some matter which had arisen. I worried about detaining him, and so when he counted me out of the trance and I did not awaken, I did nevertheless open my eyes and simulate being awake in order to fool him. This is an ironical twist, for it is usually the other way round in hypnosis: people simulate being hypnotized when they are still awake. In my case, the tables were turned. He scrutinized me and I convinced him I was out of the trance. We then parted company and I joined my wife, who always waited for me because I didn't trust myself driving after hypnosis. When we got into the car I confessed to her that I was not really awakened from the trance, and told her to blow on my face. This is generally a foolproof way to waken some one. But it did not work, partly because my wife found it a ridiculous thing to do and could not help laughing. The more sternly I insisted that she blow on my face, the more uncontrollable did her mirth become. She found it impossible to believe I was still hypnotized. We began to drive home and after a time I ordered her to stop. I had seen a beautiful old tree and, being very fond of old trees, and being very emotional while in the trance, I got out of the car and ran across a field to see the tree. I embraced the trunk and sobbed, telling the tree how beautiful it was, and crying generally at the beauty of everything in the world in the way a maudlin drunk might do. I then reeled backwards and fell flat on my back on the grass. I remember looking dreamily up at the night sky and admiring its beauty and uttering maudlin remarks about the grandeur of the cosmos. By this time my wife had caught up with me and helped me to my feet, and she dragged me back to the car. I kept insisting, "Blow in my face! Blow in my face!" This time she did so earnestly, but it didn't work. I then mumbled to her that in extreme circumstances like this there was only one sure-fire method to wake me up, and that was to take me home and give me some neat gin. (I should add that I hate neat gin, and this was not a ploy!) That was precisely what happened: moments after I drank the neat gin I woke up from the trance completely.'

This fascinating instance provides an important insight into hypnosis. It is clear that, in a certain sense, Temple was 'drunk'. He was wide-awake, and yet aware that he had not achieved the normal level of *focused* attention that characterises the waking state. It was as if a certain level of his being remained asleep. It becomes possible to see how a girl could be wide-awake and yet feel powerless to resist the hypnotist's orders.

Now according to the suggestion theory, hypnosis is merely a matter of inducing a certain kind of 'self-consciousness'—the kind that causes teenagers to blush. Temple tells a story of a girl who was told that she would forget the combination of the safe while she was actually turning the dial. She was unable to recall it until the suggestion was discontinued. What happened is clear. At the suggestion that she might not be able to remember, she began to *doubt herself*, and went into a state of confusion that prevented her from recalling the combination.

This is certainly a plausible theory of how hypnotism works— yet it obviously fails to explain how hypnosis could be induced merely by a squeeze of the hand.

The alternative view—suggested by the experiments of Puységur—is that hypnosis involves some kind of telepathic contact or 'thought pressure'. The writer J.B.Priestley has a story that seems to support this. In *Outcries and Asides*, under the title 'True Strange Story', he tells how he attended a Poetry Society banquet in New York. Priestley remarked to his neighbour and he admits he has no idea why he did so—'I propose to make one of those poets wink at me, and I'll try the fifth one from the left, that dark heavy-set sombre woman, obviously no winker.' 'After concentrating on her for a minute or two, it seemed to me that she winked at me, and I cried triumphantly, 'She did it . . .' But my neighbour did not believe me, and I really was not sure myself . . . However, after the speeches and awards had been made . . . the dark, sombre woman poet . . . came up to me. 'You're Mr Priestley, aren't you? Well I must apologise for winking at you. I've never done such a thing before and I can't imagine what made me do it then. Just a silly sudden impulse . . .'

Again, according to *Psi; Psychic Discoveries Behind the Iron Curtain* by Lynn Schroeder and Sheila Ostrander, the Polish 'mind reader' Wolf Messing had even greater abilities in this direction. Forced to flee to Russia at the beginning of the Second World War because he had predicted Hitler's death if the dictator 'turned towards the East', Messing captured the interest of Joseph Stalin, who ordered a series of experiments. In the first of these, Messing walked into the bank, presented the teller with a 'note' (actually a blank sheet of paper), and asked for 10,000 roubles. The cashier handed these over, and Messing packed them into his briefcase and left. Then, with the two observers who had witnessed the experiment, he re-entered the bank and handed back the money. The cashier collapsed with a heart attack when he realised what he had done.

The supreme test set by Stalin was to enter his country-house—bristling with guards—without a pass. And one day, as Stalin sat working in his office, Messing walked coolly into the grounds and into the house. The guards and servants stood back respectfully. Stalin looked up with astonishment as Messing walked into his room. The mind reader explained that he had simply sent out a mental suggestion that he was Lavrenti Beria, the much-feared head of the secret police, and the guards had actually *seen* him as Beria.

But long before Messing was born, the part played by telepathy in hypnosis had been demonstrated beyond all doubt in 1885 by a French doctor, J.H.A. Gibert, who invited the eminent psychologist Pierre Janet to Le Havre to witness some of his experiments. Janet had a patient called Leonie, a peasant woman

who was an example of the condition known as multiple personality (which we shall study in a later chapter). Leonie was
normally rather dull and stolid, but during her attacks of 'somnambulism' (to which she had been subject since childhood) she
became a completely different person, lively, gay and sarcastic.
This secondary personality denied that she *was* Leonie, whom
she regarded with some contempt. Finally, a third personality
emerged, who was more mature and balanced than either of the
others.

Leonie was easy to hypnotise—Gibert could do it simply by
touching her hand. What interested Janet was that if Gibert tried
to do this without concentrating, it did not work. Eventually,
Gibert was able to hypnotise Leonie solely by concentrating his
mind—he could even do so when she was on the other side of
Le Havre. Several scientists came to Le Havre to observe these
experiments, including Frederic Myers, one of the founders
of the Society for Psychical Research. On one occasion they
witnessed Gibert standing outside the house where Leonie was
staying, mentally ordering her to appear. Three minutes later she
came out, and walked across the town to Gibert's house.

On the same evening, Gibert sent out a suggestion that Leonie
should go down into the drawing-room of the house, where she
was staying, at eleven o'clock the next morning, and open a
photograph album. The doctors were watching in the garden at
eleven when Leonie came into the drawing-room. She seemed
confused, and touched several objects. Then she opened the
photograph album, and was looking through it when the doctors
entered the room.

Janet's paper describing all this caused a sensation in the
following year, but was quickly forgotten; it failed to fit into
the 'scientific' theories of the time, which were dominated by
Charcot's 'hysteria' theory of hypnosis. But in America at about
this time, another investigator was pursuing the mystery of
hypnosis with total indifference to what the scientists thought. His
name was Thomson Jay Hudson, and he was a Detroit newspaper
editor and an official of the Patent Office.

Hudson's interest began as a result of a lecture he attended
in Washington D.C.; it was given by the eminent physiologist
William B. Carpenter. The audience of 'highly cultivated ladies

and gentlemen' included a young college graduate to whom Hudson refers as C.

C. was placed under hypnosis, then asked by Carpenter if he would like to meet Socrates. He replied that he would esteem it a great privilege if Socrates were still alive. Carpenter explained that he had the power to invoke the spirit of Socrates, and pointing to a corner of the room exclaimed, 'There he is.' C. looked at the place indicated, and his face took on an expression of awe and reverence. Carpenter performed the introductions, and C. looked speechless with embarrassment, although he still retained his wits enough to offer Socrates a chair. Carpenter then explained that Socrates was willing to answer any questions, and C. proceeded with some hesitation to open a conversation. Since Carpenter had explained that he was unable to overhear the philosopher's replies, C. acted as intermediary and repeated everything Socrates said. For two hours this amazing 'conversation' continued, and the answers were so brilliant and plausible that some of the audience began to wonder whether there really *was* an invisible spirit in the room.

Later Carpenter offered to introduce C. to the spirits of more modern philosophers, and with most of these he felt a great deal more at ease than with Socrates. What emerged from these conversations was a 'wonderful system of spiritual philosophy . . . so clear, so plausible, so perfectly consistent with itself and the known laws of Nature that the company sat spellbound.' With each new philosopher C.'s manner changed, exactly as if he were speaking to a series of real people, and the language and style of the invisible philosophers changed too: it was all so weirdly real that the audience felt as if they were watching a play.

Hudson watched the demonstrations with baffled amazement. Hudson knew that C. was a total sceptic on the question of 'spirits'—as was Hudson himself. Under hypnosis he accepted the existence of the spirits of the great philosophers because he could obviously *see* them. What seemed most surprising was that the 'spiritual philosophy' expressed was not that of C. himself—he frequently expressed his astonishment at some of the statements of the dead philosophers. Yet the whole philosophy was such a coherent system that according to Hudson, it could have been printed in a book verbatim and would have 'formed one of the grandest and most coherent systems of spiritual philosophy ever conceived by the brain of man'.

There happened to be a number of spiritualists present in the audience, and many of them were inclined to the hypothesis that real spirits were present, until Carpenter disillusioned them by summoning up the spirit of a philosophical pig which discoursed learnedly on the subject of the Hindu doctrine of reincarnation.

Hudson explained these extraordinary powers by suggesting that human beings possess two minds, which he calls the subjective and the objective mind. The 'objective mind' is the part of us that deals with everyday life and copes with practical matters; the subjective mind is concerned with our inner powers and energies. It is as if the mind had two faces; one turned towards the outside world, the other turned towards the inner worlds of memory and intuition. For practical purposes they are rather like a husband and wife; the husband—the objective mind—assertive and aggressive, the wife shy and taciturn, inclined to doubt her own judgement in the face of her husband's superior forcefulness. Under hypnosis, the husband is put to sleep, and the wife, no longer tongue-tied with self-doubt, can exercise her powers of intuition without fear of criticism. As a result, she can perform far more considerable feats than when her domineering partner is awake. She seems to have remarkable powers over the body, so that a man under hypnosis can not only have a tooth extracted without pain, but will even obey an order not to bleed. He becomes capable of feats of strength that would be impossible if he were awake—an old favourite of stage hypnotists is to tell a man that he is about to become as stiff as a board, then make him lie between two chairs while someone jumps up and down on his stomach.

Hudson is fascinated by these powers of the subjective mind. He cites a case of an illiterate girl who, when in a fever, began to speak Greek, Latin and Hebrew. A young doctor was so intrigued by this that he investigated the girl's past life, and discovered that, at the age of 9, she had lived with a Protestant pastor who used to walk around the house reading aloud in these languages. Consciously, the girl had not assimilated a single word; but some hidden tape recorded in the brain had preserved everything.

Hudson discusses the mystery of calculating prodigies—usually young boys of no particular talent or intelligence who can perform astonishing feats of calculation within seconds—like 5-year-old Zerah Colburn, who once snapped out the answer to the square root of 106,929 before the questioner had finished speaking. He also discusses the curious power of 'eidetic imagery'—and describes an artist friend who could conjure up a scene at will and then see it projected in detail on a blank canvas.

Genius, says Hudson, is simply a perfect balance between the objective and subjective minds—as if a husband and wife are in such deep sympathy that the wife has lost all her shyness and pours out her intuitions in the certainty that they will be understood. When this happens, the subjective mind can actually take over, and the result is known as inspiration, a spontaneous outpouring of insights. Hudson cites the example of the great political orator Henry Clay, who was once called upon to answer an opponent in the Senate when he was feeling sick and exhausted. Clay asked the man sitting next to him to tug on his coat-tails when he had been speaking for ten minutes. Two hours later, after a magnificent speech, Clay sank down exhausted, and asked his friend reproachfully why he had failed to interrupt. In fact, the friend had not only tugged his coat-tails; he had nudged and pinched him, and even jabbed a pin deep into his leg. This aspect of the 'subjective mind' seems to be what the Spaniards call the *duende*, the 'demon' that sometimes takes over great singers or dancers so they seem to be possessed by a force greater than themselves. They *are*, in fact, 'greater than themselves', for the ego—as we have seen—is a left-brain entity.

Yet the limitations of the subjective mind are as odd as its talents. Hudson observed that it can reason deductively—from the general to the particular—but not vice versa. Induction is the ability to leap from a collection of facts to the laws underlying them. The subjective mind can be shown any number of trees without noticing that they add up to a wood. It leaves 'leaping to conclusions' to its more enterprising and aggressive partner. In fact, the subjective mind is oddly short-sighted and passive. This also explains why it tends to be bad at argument, which involves selecting and reasoning—making choices. Right-brain people—'subjective-minders'—usually become tongue-tied when someone tells them something in an authoritative voice, even when they can see it is nonsense; they find it hard to put their perceptions into words. This also explains, says Hudson, why psychic powers often evaporate when confronted with scepticism. The subjective mind is intensely suggestive, so a mere hint that it is a fraud turns it into a nervous wreck. Hudson cites the case of a clairvoyant named Bishop, who demonstrated again and again his power to read people's minds and decipher the contents of sealed envelopes. But when the well-known journalist Henry Labouchere denounced him as a fake, and challenged him to read the number of a bank note sealed in an envelope, he failed miserably. He had done the same thing successfully a thousand times; but the aggressive self-confidence of a left-brainer was enough to shatter his self-confidence and paralyze the powers of the subjective mind.

This brings us to what Hudson considered the most important thing about the subjective mind: that it is responsible for all so-called psychic phenomena—including ghosts and poltergeists. This suggestion naturally infuriated the spiritualists; but Hudson argued his case with impressive skill and conviction. He points out that a hypnotist can induce a blister in a good hypnotic subject by suggesting that he had been burnt by a hot iron, and argues convincingly that the stigmata of the saints—bleeding nail holes and wounds—can be explained in the same way. He discusses some of the remarkable cures that have been brought about by hypnosis, and concludes that the subjective mind has immense healing powers. In fact, he became convinced that the miracles of the New Testament were a manifestation of these powers. By way of testing this hypothesis, he decided to try to cure a relative who suffered from rheumatism and nervous convulsions. The method, apparently, was to persuade his own subjective mind that it *could* be done, even though the relative lived a thousand miles away. He informed two friends that he intended to begin the treatment—so that they could bear witness if it worked—and started on May 15, 1890. He decided to try to communicate the healing suggestions by an effort of will just as he was on the point of going to sleep. Some months later, one of the two 'witnesses' met the relative, whose health had improved remarkably; the improvement had started, he said, in mid-May. Hudson claimed that he and close associates had made more than a hundred similar experiments, and that not one of them had been a failure.

Hudson explained these theories in a book called *The Law of Psychic Phenomena*, which appeared in 1893 and became an immediate bestseller—by 1925 it had gone through forty-seven printings. It was Hudson's sheer bad luck that, within ten years of its publication, Sigmund Freud's theory of the unconscious mind had become even more celebrated.

Just before the outbreak of the First World War, the Belgian dramatist Maurice Maeterlinck made another highly creditable attempt to explain the nature and origin of man's 'hidden powers'; the title of his book, *The Unknown Guest*, is a three-word summary of his answer. Inside every one of us, says Maeterlinck, there is an unknown entity that lives 'in a sort of invisible and perhaps eternal palace, like a casual guest, dropped in from another planet, whose interests, habits, ideas, passions, have nothing in common with ours'. In fact, the 'unknown guest' is a kind of 'second self'—like Hudson's subjective mind. Maeterlinck recognised that the 'unknown guest' is not only responsible for telepathy and premonitions of danger, but for such inexplicable powers as precognition of the future. He cites the case of the wife of the Russian general Toutschkoff, who woke up one night dreaming that she was at an inn in an unknown town, and that her father came into the room to tell her: 'Your husband has been killed at Borodino.' When the dream had been repeated a third time, she woke her husband to ask: 'Where is Borodino?' He had no idea, and they had to look it up on a map. But later that year, Napoleon invaded Russia, and her husband was killed at Borodino. Her father came into the room, just as in the dream, to tell her the news.

Now in fact modern scientific research has placed this notion of 'the unknown guest' on a scientific basis.

For some reason that no physiologist yet understands, human beings have two brains. Or rather, the brain they possess is 'double'—almost as if a mirror had been placed down the middle, so that one half reflects the other. We seem to have two hearing centres, two visual centres, two muscle-control centres, even two memories. Why this should be so is baffling—one guess being that one of the brains is a 'spare' in case the other gets damaged. What seems even odder is that the left half of the brain controls the right side of the body, and vice versa.

From our point of view, the most interesting part of the brain is the bit at the top—the cerebral cortex. This is the most specifically human part; it has developed at an incredible speed over the past million or so years—so fast (in geological time) that some scientists like to speak of 'the brain explosion'.

If you could lift off the top of the skull and look down on the cerebral cortex, you would see something resembling a walnut, with two wrinkled halves. The bridge between them is a mass of nerve fibres called the *corpus callosum* or commissure.

This mass of millions of nerve fibres is obviously important. Which is why brain specialists were puzzled when they came across freaks who possessed no commissure, and appeared to function perfectly well without it. In the 1930s, brain surgeons wondered if they could prevent epileptic attacks by severing the *corpus callosum*, and so preventing the spread of the 'electrical storm' from one hemisphere to the other. They tried severing the commissure in monkeys and it seemed to do no harm. So they tried it on epileptic patients, and it seemed to work. The fits were greatly reduced—and the patient seemed much the same as before. One scientist remarked ironically that the only purpose of the commissure appeared to be to transmit epileptic seizures. Another suggested that it might be to prevent the brain from sagging in the middle.

In 1950, Roger W. Sperry, of the University of Chicago (and later of Cal Tech) began investigating the problem. He discovered that severing the commissure appeared to have no noticeable effect on cats and monkeys. But it *would* prevent one half of the brain learning what the other half knew. So if a cat was taught some trick with one eye covered up, and then asked to do it with the other eye covered, it was baffled. It could even be taught two different solutions to the same problem (say, pressing a lever to get food) with each side of the brain. There could be no doubt about it; we literally have two brains.

Sperry and his associate Michael Gazzaniga then studied a human patient whose brain had been split to prevent epileptic attacks. He seemed to be perfectly normal, except for one oddity—which they expected anyway. He could read with his right eye, but not with his left. It had been known since the 19th century that, in human beings, the two halves of the brain seem to have different functions: 'right for recognition, left for language'. People who had damage to the right cerebral hemisphere were unable to recognise simple patterns, or enjoy music, but they could still speak normally. People with left-brain damage were able to recognise patterns, but their speech was impaired. Obviously, then, the left deals with language, and you would expect a split-brain patient to be unable to read with his right eye (connected, remember, to the opposite side of the brain). Sperry's patient was also unable to write anything meaningful (i.e. complicated) with his left hand.

They noticed another oddity. If the patient bumped into something with his left side, he did not notice. And the implications here were very odd indeed. Not only did the split-brain operation give the patient *two separate minds*; it also seemed to restrict his identity, or ego, to the left side. When they placed an object in his left hand, and asked him what he was holding, he had no idea. Further experiments underlined the point. If a split-brain patient is shown two different symbols—say a circle and a square—with each eye, and is asked to say what he has just seen, he replies 'A square'. Asked to draw with his left hand what he has seen, and he draws a circle. Asked what he has just drawn, he replies: 'A square'. And when one split-brain patient was shown a picture of a nude male with the right-brain, she blushed; asked why she was blushing, she replied truthfully: 'I don't know.'

One 'split-brain' patient tried to hit his wife with one hand while the other defended her. Another tried to unzip his flies with one hand while the other tried to do them up. A patient who was given some wooden blocks to arrange into a pattern tried to do it with his right hand, and the left hand continually tried to interrupt him; finally, he had to sit on his left hand to make it behave.

The implications are clearly staggering. The person you call 'you' *lives in the left cerebral hemisphere*. This is the half of the cerebrum that deals with language and logic. It could be regarded as a scientist. The right half seems to work in terms of patterns and insights; it is basically an artist. And it seems to be a 'second self'. It was natural for the patient to try to solve the wooden block pattern with his right hand (connected to the left brain), because the doctor had asked *him* to do the puzzle, and the conscious, everyday self lives in the left brain. If he had not been a split-brain patient, the right brain would have quietly helped him to solve the puzzle by 'putting ideas into his head', and he would not even have been aware of it.

So what is it like to be a split-brain patient? The unexpected answer is that most of them do not even notice it. And if we reflect for a moment, we can see that this makes sense. If I try to solve some puzzle—say a Rubik cube—after a few glasses of alcohol, my 'insight' refuses to function. This is because alcohol seems to interfere with the connection between right and left. It has, in fact, given me a kind of instant split-brain operation. Yet I hardly notice this. My conscious self is so accustomed to coping with reality that it hardly notices when the 'other self' withdraws its help. But if I attempted to write this book after several glasses of alcohol—or when I was so tired that the 'two selves' had lost contact—I would instantly realize that something was wrong. For writing is an act of close co-operation between the two selves. The right takes a 'bird's eye view', surveying all the possibilities; the left chooses between them and decides which of them to turn into words. If the right fails to do its half of the job, the left stares blankly at the sheet of paper and wonders what to say.

Is the right cerebral hemisphere 'the unknown guest'? That might be going too far. We still know so little about the brain and its working that it would be better to preserve an open mind. But we can safely say that the right hemisphere is the entrance to the 'invisible palace' of the unknown guest.

There is another point of vital importance to be made. All mental illness is caused by the conflict between 'the two selves'. The left ego is the master of consciousness, the right is the master of the unconscious. And the relation between the two is not unlike the relation between Laurel and Hardy in the old movies. Ollie is the left-brain, the boss. Stan takes his cues from Ollie. When Ollie is in a good mood, Stan is delighted. When

Ollie is depressed, Stan is plunged into the depths of gloom. Stan is inclined to *over-react*.

When Ollie wakes up on a wet Monday morning, he thinks: 'Damn, it's raining, and I've got a particularly dreary day in front of me . . .' Stan overhears this and sinks into depression. And—since he controls the energy supply—Ollie has that 'sinking feeling', and feels drained of energy. This makes him feel worse than ever. As he walks out of the gate he bumps into a man who tells him to look where he's going, then trips over a crack in the pavement, then misses a bus just as he arrives at the stop, and thinks: 'This is going to be one of those days . . .' And again, Stan overhears, and feels worse than ever. And once more, Ollie feels that sinking feeling. By the end of the day, he may be feeling suicidal—not because things have been really bad, but because of a continual 'negative feedback' of gloom between the right and left.

Consider, on the other hand, what happens to a child on Christmas Day. He wakes up full of pleasurable anticipation; Stan instantly sends up a flood of energy. When he goes downstairs, everything reinforces the feeling of delight—Christmas carols on the radio, the Christmas tree with its lights, the smell of mince pies in the oven. Each new stimulus causes a new rush of delight; each new rush of delight deepens the feeling that 'all is well', and that the world is a wonderful and exciting place after all.

What, then, *is* hypnosis? The first thing we have to recognise is that all creatures are, to a large extent, machines. The body is an elaborate machine; so is the brain. But a machine can be operated by anyone who has access to it and knows how it works. It seems fairly obvious that the hypnotist somehow puts the left brain—Ollie—to sleep, and gains direct access to Stan. And Stan can make the machine do some remarkable things. If the hypnotist tells him that he will become as stiff as a board, and will lie on two chairs, with his head on one and his heels on the other, while a heavy man jumps up and down on his stomach, he will do it without hesitation.

Which raises an interesting question: if Stan possesses these powers, why will he not exercise them when Ollie tells him to do so? The answer is that he knows Ollie too well, and does not trust him as he trusts the hypnotist. Yet it should also be obvious that if we *could* somehow persuade Stan to trust Ollie, we would gain access to all the 'hidden powers' that Stan controls. And man would suddenly become a kind of superman. *This* is why it is so important for us to understand the basic mechanisms of hypnosis . . .

Robert Temple's story about how he wanted to embrace a tree reminds us that most of us spend a great deal of time in a semi-hypnotised condition. Our 'everyday consciousness' is only half-awake. It becomes fully awake only when we are full of excitement or sense of purpose. (Doctor Johnson said: 'When a man knows he is to be hanged in a fortnight it concentrates his mind wonderfully.') As soon as our attention begins to flag, we sink into a kind of light hypnosis. And when our minds 'go blank', we are virtually in a trance.

All this was known long before Mesmer. In 1636, a mathematician called Daniel Schwenter observed that if a small bent piece of wood is fastened on a hen's beak, the hen fixes its eyes on it and goes into a trance. Similarly, if the hen's beak is held against the ground and a chalk line is drawn away from the point of its beak, it lies immobilized. Ten years later, a Jesuit priest, Fr Athanasius Kircher, described similar experiments on hens. All that is necessary is to tuck the hen's head under its wing and then give it a few gentle swings through the air; it will then lie still. (French peasants still use this method when they buy live hens in the market.) A doctor named Golsch discovered that frogs can be hypnotized by turning them on their backs and lightly tapping the stomach with the finger. Snapping the fingers above the frog is just as effective. Crabs can be hypnotized by gently stroking the shell from head to tail, and unhypnotized by reversing the motion. In *Hypnosis of Men and Animals* (published in 1963), Ferenc András Völgyesi describes how Africans hypnotize wild elephants. The elephant is chained to a tree, where it thrashes about savagely. The natives then wave leafy boughs to and fro in front of it and chant monotonously; eventually, its eyes blink, close, and the elephant becomes docile. It can then be teamed with a trained elephant and worked into various tasks. If it becomes unmanageable, the treatment is repeated, and usually works almost immediately.

Nothing in all this contradicts the Freudian 'suggestion' theory of hypnosis. But Völgyesi also discusses the way that snakes 'fascinate' their victims. Far from being an old wives' tale, this has been observed by many scientists. Toads, frogs, rabbits and other creatures can be 'transfixed' by the snake's gaze—which involves expansion of its pupils—and by its hiss. But Völgyesi observed—and photographed—a large toad winning a 'battle of hypnosis' with a snake. Völgyesi observed two lizards confronting each other for about ten minutes, both quite rigid; then one slowly and deliberately ate the other, starting at the head. It was again, apparently, a battle of hypnosis. What seems to happen in such cases is that one creature subdues the will of the other. Völgyesi observed that hypnosis can also be effected by a sudden shock—by grabbing a bird violently, or making a loud noise. He observes penetratingly that hypnosis seems to have something in common with stage fright—that is, so much adrenalin is released into the bloodstream that, instead of stimulating the creature, it virtually paralyses it. (We have all had the experience of feeling weakened by fear.)

All this supports the observations made by Puységur, Gibert, Messing and Hammerschlag: that hypnosis often involves a 'beam of will' directed from one person to another.

And now, at last, we can see the basic obstacle that separates us from our 'hidden powers'. *We are unaware that we possess this 'will-beam'.* We are always allowing it to 'switch off', so we fall into a passive condition, like a blank television screen. You could compare us to a person with amnesia, who goes out shopping with a wallet full of money, then suddenly 'goes blank' and returns home without his shopping or his wallet. If you had such a person in your family, you would obviously not allow him to go shopping alone. Yet most of us are subject to this kind of amnesia. When we are full of energy, we fulfil our daily tasks with a sense of determination and purpose. But as soon as we grow tired, the energy switches off, and life seems oddly boring and meaningless. If a sudden problem arises, we groan with boredom and feel that it is 'not worth doing'. We have, in fact, fallen into a hypnotic condition, exactly like Schwenter's hen with the wood on its beak. The 'hidden will' switches off; the 'unknown guest' falls asleep; we become, in effect, robots.

If we wish to evolve to the next stage in human development, we must learn to grasp the meaning of the discoveries of Mesmer, Puységur and Maeterlinck. It is true that the 'unknown guest' lives in an invisible palace. But he is nonetheless real. And if we wish to learn to make use of his powers, we must train ourselves to recognise his reality as clearly as we recognise the reality of the material world around us.

3.
Visions of the Past

PERHAPS THE MOST remarkable of all the now-forgotten explorers of Maeterlinck's 'invisible palace' was another American, Joseph Rodes Buchanan, whose discoveries were, in their way, even more astonishing than those of Mesmer. Buchanan came to believe that every object in the universe has its whole history 'recorded' on it—rather like a videotape recording—and that the human mind has the power to 'play back' this recording.

But before we proceed any further, let us consider a practical example.

In the winter of 1921, a number of people had come together in a room of the Metapsychic Institute—the French version of the Society for Psychical Research—in Paris, to test a clairvoyant, Madame De B-. Dr Gustav Geley, a leading French investigator, and director of the Institute, asked someone to pass a letter to her. A painter and novelist called Pascal Forthuny grabbed it. 'It can't be difficult to invent something that applies to anybody!' He began to improvise jokingly. 'Ah yes, I see a crime . . . a murder . . .' When he had finished, Dr Geley said: 'That letter was from Henri Landru.' Landru was at the time on trial for the murder of eleven women—crimes for which he was guillotined in the following year.

No one was very impressed by Forthuny's performance; after all, Landru's trail was the chief news-event of the day, so murder was an obvious topic to come into Forthuny's mind. Geley's wife picked up a fan from the table. 'Let's see if that was just luck. Try this.'

Still light-hearted, Forthuny ran his fingers over the fan in a professional matter and looked solemnly into space. 'I have the impression of being suffocated. And I hear a name being called: Elisa!'

Madame Geley looked at him in stupefaction. The fan had belonged to an old lady who had died seven years earlier from congestion of the lungs; the companion of her last days had been called Elisa.

Now it was Forthuny's turn to suspect a joke. But Madame Geley insisted on another experiment. She handed him an officer's cane. This time Forthuny looked serious as he let his fingers stray over it. He began to describe army manoeuvres, somewhere in the Orient. He spoke of the young French officer who had owned the cane, of his return to France by sea, and of how the ship was torpedoed. He went on to say that the officer was rescued, but developed an illness and died two years later. Madame Geley verified that he was right in every particular.

This curious faculty—which so amazed Forthuny—had first been discovered more than sixty years earlier by Joseph Rodes Buchanan. He had labelled it 'psychometry'.

Buchanan was born in Frankfort, Kentucky, on December 11, 1814, three months before the death of Mesmer (who died on March 5, 1815, at the age of 81). His father was a doctor and an author, and Buchanan was something of an infant prodigy, studying geometry and astronomy at the age of 6, and taking up law when he was 12. When his father died in the following year, Buchanan supported himself as a printer, then as a schoolteacher. And at some time during his teens, he came upon the theories of Mesmer, and was fascinated by the notion that the universe is permeated by some 'magnetic fluid', and that the stars and the planets cause 'tides' in this fluid. As we have seen, Mesmer believed that these 'tides' cause sickness and health in human beings, for we are also full of a kind of magnetic fluid generated by the nerves. When this fluid becomes blocked or stagnant, we become ill. When it is unblocked—by magnets, or by the doctor's own 'animal magnetism'—we become well again.

All this excited the young Buchanan, who was convinced

that the world was on the brink of some tremendous medical discoveries. He recognised, of course, that the secret of the 'nerve aura' lies in the brain, not in the nervous system, for the brain is its central control box. But in the 1830s, almost nothing was known about the anatomy of the brain. What *was* known was that different parts of the brain seem to govern our instincts—protectiveness, tenderness, aggression, selfishness, and so on. The great physiologist Joseph Gall discovered the basic structures of the brain in the late 18th century, and his pupil J. K. Spurzheim went on to try to locate various areas of the brain that were connected with human emotions—destructiveness, love, acquisitiveness, cheerfulness, egotism, and more than twenty others. Spurzheim was convinced that when any of these areas becomes highly developed it causes a bump on the skull, which can be felt with the fingertips. The science of these 'bumps' was called phrenology, and it soon became the happy hunting-ground of all kinds of quacks and charlatans.

When Buchanan went to study medicine at the University of Louisville in 1835, he was disappointed to discover that no one seemed to have heard of Gall or Spurzheim. However, he did not allow this to dampen his enthusiasm, and flung himself into the study of the brain, devising experiments to test their theories. Nowadays a man who held his beliefs would be shunned by his colleagues as a crank; but in that less sophisticated—and less narrow-minded—era, he was simply regarded as a brilliant young experimenter. He was excited to discover that when a patient was hypnotized, he would respond with the appropriate emotion if various 'bumps' were gently touched—anger, love, joy, grief and so on. This notion became known as 'phreno-mesmerism' and Buchanan claimed to be its discoverer—with some opposition from other followers of Mesmer and Spurzheim. He was only 24 years old when he located what he believed to be the 'region of sensibility' in the brain. And it was in this region that he later decided that the power of psychometry resided.

Three years later, Buchanan had a fateful meeting that was to determine the course of his whole life. It was with a newly consecrated bishop of the Episcopal Church named Leonidas Polk, who had abandoned the army in favour of the church, and whose diocese included practically the whole of the American south. (He later became a Civil War general, and was killed at Marietta in 1864.) The bishop happened to mention casually that he could instantly detect brass when he touched it—even in the dark—because it produced an offensive metallic taste in his mouth. Polk allowed Buchanan to feel his 'bumps,' and Buchanan was delighted to discover that his region of sensibility—governing the physical senses—was abnormally developed. (It is important to note that phrenology—usually dismissed as a pseudo-science—could be astonishingly accurate, and that modern science has verified some of its claims.)

The bishop was so transparently honest that it never occurred to Buchanan to doubt his word—but neither, apparently, did he ask Polk to submit to scientific tests. Instead, he decided to test others and see whether they might also have the same highly developed sensibilities. Any one of his students whose head showed an unusual bump of sensibility was roped in, and Buchanan was gratified to discover that this faculty of 'sensing' brass through the fingers was relatively common. In fact, his subjects could distinguish various metals, and substances like sugar, salt, pepper and vinegar.

There was nothing very odd about this, as far as Buchanan was concerned. After all, the tongue has precisely this power—so why not the finger-ends, which are equally important for sensing objects? Besides, as we have seen in the last chapter, scientists of the nineteenth century were aware of a power that modern science has forgotten—that of 'seeing' with other parts of the body beside the eyes. This sounds absurd, yet precise descriptions of scientific experiments leave no doubt that it happened, and that it could still happen. Dr Justinus Kerner, whose book *The Seeress of Prevorst* was a 19th century best-seller, described how the 'seeress,' Friederike Hauffe, could read with her stomach; he made her lie down with closed eyes, placed documents on her bare midriff, and listened to her reading fluently from them. Later in the century, Professor Cesare Lombroso, the founder of scientific criminology, carefully tested a girl who was able to see through the tip of her nose and her left ear, and who could smell through her chin and—later—through her heel.[1] Modern

1. For a longer account of both cases see chapters 4 and 7.

paranormal research has identified people who can 'see' colours through their fingertips, but modern science still regards the case as nonproven. In Buchanan's day it was regarded as a perfectly normal possibility.

Buchanan also observed that people in warm climates could 'sense' metals and other substances better than those in cold ones. That was also logical, for in warm climates, we sweat more, and sweat-dampened skin is more sensitive—for example, to wind—than a dry skin. This, says Buchanan, is 'a fact which I now consider as well settled and familiar as any other in medical science'. And when he imparted this fact to his students, he took care to disarm scepticism by an immediate demonstration. Various chemicals were carefully wrapped in paper, and given to the students to hold. Some of the substances were strong stimulants or narcotics, some emetics, some even cathartics. Out of a class of 86, half the students experienced definite effects from the substances they held—some holding the emetic had to put it down hastily to avoid being sick. (He does not mention what happened to those holding laxatives.) Buchanan got the 43 who experienced these effects to sign a testimonial, which he includes in his book.

His next thought was that if a mere substance could affect a 'sensitive' so strongly, then living people would produce an even stronger effect. He selected his best sensitives, and asked them to try placing the hand on the head or body of another person, then to concentrate on the effect. Again, his sensitives showed by their reaction that they were somehow picking up the feelings of the other person. When the hand was placed on the stomach of a person suffering from a disease of that region, a 'morbid impression' was produced. Buchanan claims that he himself became so good at sensing the diseases of patients in this way that he would feel ill after a few minutes and have to break the contact.

One of Buchanan's best sensitives was a man named Charles Inman. He could experience the mental states of patients by lightly running his fingers over their 'bumps'. But could it have been telepathy? Or even mere auto-suggestion? Buchanan decided to try a simple experiment. He selected from his correspondence files four letters written by people with strong characters, and asked Inman if he could discover anything about the character of the writers by merely holding their letters. The result, he says, surpassed all his expectations; Inman began to talk about the letter-writers with as much insight as if he had known them personally.

Two of the letters were from a ʌurgeon named J. B. Flint and a doctor, Charles Caldwell, who had founded the college at Louisville. These men had once been friends, but had become bitter enemies. Inman immediately sensed their mutual detestation, and their negative emotions affected him so powerfully that he had to put the letters down. Buchanan asked him which of the two he thought would win in a conflict; Inman held up Caldwell's letter and said: 'This one would crush the other.' It was, in fact, true—Caldwell's efforts had resulted in Flint being removed from his chair of surgery.

One of the other letters was from an eminent politician, and Inman was able to say that he was a man of considerable mental and physical power. What could happen, asked Buchanan, if Dr Caldwell and the politician met in a head-on collision? Inman shook his head. That would be highly unlikely, he said, because both were too courteous and dignified. Buchanan insisted—suppose the unthinkable happened and they *did* clash? Reluctantly, Inman gave his opinion. The two men would never reach the stage of open hostility, but if some disagreement *did* break out, the politician would probably handle the situation by some tactful rebuke that would immediately check the doctor. Since Buchanan had seen that precise event take place, he was deeply impressed.

But what did it all mean? For a 'sensitive' to identify a metal or a chemical—or even someone's illness—was one thing; but surely to pick up someone's character from a letter was quite another? Buchanan did not think so. Photography was a fairly recent invention—the photographs of the period were known as daguerreotypes, after the inventor Daguerre. A daguerreotype, Buchanan reasoned, is nothing more or less than a 'light painting', a painting made on sensitive chemicals by the light reflected from its subject. Well, human beings seem to emanate 'nerve aura', and this seems to vary according to their strength of character. So why should a sensitive not be able to pick up the nerve aura from letters?

If this reasoning strikes us as specious, it is mainly because Buchanan has missed out a step in the argument. A bloodhound can tell the difference between two human beings by the scent on their clothes. Buchanan regarded sensitives like Charles Inman as human bloodhounds who can pick up the 'scent' of the nerve aura. And if his precise character-readings sound improbable, we have to reflect that such processes as sound-recording and television transmission seem equally unlikely. A gramophone record is a series of bumps on a disc of plastic or wax; when a needle travels over these bumps, it reproduces the sounds that originally made the bumps. But any bright child will immediately raise the question: how can a few bumps record *all* the instruments of the orchestra? Surely at least there ought to be a separate row of bumps for each instrument? Sound recording is a preposterous miracle which, in any well-ordered universe, ought not to be allowed to happen. And any scientist in 1842—the year Buchanan performed these experiments with Inman—would have stated with certainty that it *could* not happen. Buchanan's nerve aura daguerreotypes are no more or less absurd than a long-playing record or compact disc.

We may, of course, feel that Buchanan was deceiving himself with his own enthusiasm and excitement. But reading his careful and precise accounts of his experiments, it is hard not to feel that any reasonable person would have found them just as exciting and just as convincing. He describes, for example, how he called upon a clergyman in Boston, the Rev. Kent, whom he describes as having an active mind but a feeble constitution. (Many later experimenters discovered that sick people made the best 'sensitives'.) Kent thought the whole idea preposterous, but agreed to co-operate. Buchanan tried handing him a letter that had been written to him 'by a gentleman of strong character and ardent emotions, immediately after the death of his wife'. The Rev. Kent described his sensations in an account of the experiment. After placing his right hand on the folded letter: 'I felt nothing in my frame at the moment, but very soon an increasing, unusual heat in the palm of my hand; this was followed by a prickling sensation, commencing in my fingers' ends and passing gradually over the top of my hand, and up the outside of my arm. I felt for nearly a minute no change in my mental condition, and stated this. Dr Buchanan had given no hint of the nature or author of any letter he had with him—and I had no bias or subject on my mind from the day's experience to influence me. A rush of sadness, solemnity and distress suddenly came over me; my thoughts were confused and yet rapid—and I mentioned, there is trouble and sorrow here . . .'

Buchanan next handed Mr Kent a letter by General 'Stonewall' Jackson, written to Buchanan's father-in-law during an election campaign 'in a spirited style': 'My first sensations were sharper and stronger than before, passing up in the same manner from my finger's ends. In less than a minute my whole arm became violently agitated, and I yielded to an irresistible impulse to give utterance to my thoughts and feelings. A determined, self-confident, daring and triumphant feeling, suggested the language I used, and it seemed to me that I could have gone on triumphantly to the accomplishment of any purpose, however subtle or strong might be the opposition to be overcome. My whole frame was shaken, my strength wrought up to the highest tension, my face and arm burned, and . . . when I retouched the letter, after repeated removals of my hand by Dr B., in consequence of my great excitement, it was like touching fire, which ran to my very toes.'

We can see why Buchanan, watching the clergyman's mood change from scepticism to intense excitement, should have been totally convinced. Further experiments—he carried out literally hundreds in those first two years—deepened his certainty that he had made one of the major scientific discoveries of the age. In his 'Original Sketch' of psychometry, written in 1848, he wrote exultantly: 'If, then, man, in every act, leaves the impression or daguerreotype of his mental being upon the scenes of his life and subjects of his action, we are by this law furnished with a new clue to the history of our race; and I think it highly probable that, by the application of this principle, the chasms of history may be supplied, and a glimpse may be obtained of unrecorded ages and nations whose early history is lost in darkness. The ancient manuscripts, paintings and other works of art . . . are doubtless still instinct with the spirit that produced them, and capable of revealing to psychometric exploration the living realities with which they were once connected. At present these relics are barren of significance. Their hidden meaning lies waiting for the future explorer, as the hieroglyphics of Egypt awaited the arrival of Champollion . . .

'*The Past is entombed in the Present!* The world is its own enduring monument; and that which is true of its physical, is likewise true of its mental career. The discoveries of psychometry will enable us to explore the history of man, as those of geology enable us to explore the history of the earth. There are mental fossils for the psychologist, as well as mineral fossils for the geologist . . . Aye, the mental telescope is now discovered, which may pierce the depths of the past, and bring us in full view of all the grand and tragic passages of history . . .'

It is easy to sympathize with his excitement. He was no mad enthusiast or religious crank, but a respectable man of science. If he was correct, as he had not the slightest doubt that he was, then his name would rank with the greatest discoverers and explorers in human history. It was surely impossible that his findings could fail to arouse wide interest . . .

They did precisely that, as the *National Cyclopedia of American Biography* tells us: 'His lectures and experiments attracted much attention in the United States and Europe, and he received many encouraging endorsements from physicians. But he realised that the medical profession was then extremely conservative, and he gave up the labours of propagandism and united with other physicians in establishing, in 1845–46, in Cincinnatti, Ohio, the Eclectic Medical Institute, an institution fundamentally devoted to independent thought and progress. He was professor of physiology in the college in 1846–56, and dean of the faculty in 1851–56. He retired from the college in 1856.'

Buchanan was fortunate to establish a haven for himself. It would protect him from the coming storm—the storm caused by the rise of the movement called Spiritualism, which made every respectable doctor and scientist in the United States the sworn enemy of anything that sounded like 'occultism'. But that is a story that must be told in the next chapter.

Meanwhile, before we proceed with the story of psychometry, it is important to consider an interesting parallel development on the other side of the Atlantic; an idea that, by that revolutionary year 1848, had already made its discoverer famous. It was called the Odic force.

Karl Reichenbach was one of those dynamos who seem born for wealth and success. Born in 1788, he had flung himself into the bold and venturesome spirit of the age, and built his first ironworks when he was 26. A sugar-beet factory followed; then there were blast furnaces in Moravia and a steelworks at Ternitz in Austria. He purchased vast estates, including a castle. Turning to the study of tar derivatives, he discovered paraffin, creosote and a blue aniline dye.

He was approaching 50 when his business partner, Count Hugo zu Salm, died, and Reichenbach found himself involved in tiresome legal battles with the count's sons. He won; but the litigation filled him with longing to turn his back on the world of quarrelsome human beings. When, in 1839, he was created a baron (*Freiherr*), he decided to retire to his castle at Reisenberg, near Vienna, and plunge into the peace of scientific research. But he was no longer concerned with organic chemistry. He now felt free to pursue an old dream, which was connected with the mysteries of the human mind.

When he was in his early 20s, Reichenbach had been excited by the researches of the poet Goethe into the nature of light. Goethe had decided that Newton was wrong in believing that white light is made up of the seven colours of the spectrum—a conclusion he reached by looking at a white wall through a prism and observing that the rainbow colours only appeared around its edges. If white light was really multicoloured, why did not the whole wall turn into a rainbow? Goethe decided that colours are created by the mechanism of the eye, pointing out that if you rub your eyes vigorously in the dark, you see vivid flashes of colour. Goethe's results had been dismissed by scientists as muddle-headed; but Reichenbach suspected he might be right after all. If so, it would be one more proof that the human mind is more complex than we think. And it was this possibility that fascinated Reichenbach.

Like most other scientists in Europe in 1839, he was interested in mesmerism and hypnotism (usually known as 'somnambulism'). It is also certain that he was aware of a mystery that was still causing speculation all over Europe: that of the youth called Caspar Hauser, who had been murdered by an unknown assailant a mere seven years earlier. Hauser had first walked into the town of Nuremberg on Whit-Monday 1828, apparently unable to speak a work. His feet were bleeding, and proved to be so white and tender that it was obvious he had never walked on them. A letter he was carrying, addressed to an army captain, stated that he was a foundling who wished to serve his king and country. He wrote his name on a piece of paper in crude and childish letters: Caspar Hauser. And it soon became clear that the unfortunate youth—who seemed to be about sixteen—had spent his whole life in darkness, chained to a bed in some unknown dungeon. He had no memory of who he was; his mind was totally unformed. Yet he proved to be intelligent and, under the tutelage of a local schoolmaster, soon learned to speak.

Because he had been raised under such abnormal conditions, Caspar proved to have an extraordinary sensitivity. His sight and hearing were abnormally acute; he could see in the dark, and demonstrated his ability by reading aloud from the Bible in a completely black room. His sense of smell was so keen that he began to vomit if coffee, beer or any other strong drink was in the same room. The mere smell of wine literally made him drunk. The static electricity in the air during a thunderstorm caused him intense suffering. His teacher, Dr Daumer, soon discovered that Hauser could instantly detect copper or brass as soon as he came into a room, even if it had been carefully hidden. Moreover, he could distinguish between various metals—exactly like Buchanan's subjects—simply by holding his hands above the cloth that concealed them.

Hauser was also something of a human magnet—another phenomenon that has never been explained by science. Some people can build up such a powerful electric charge that anyone who touches them receives a severe shock. Hauser was not actually 'electric', but he attracted metal, and when he was on a horse, the stirrups stuck to his feet. He responded strongly to magnets; the north pole gave him a different sensation from the south pole, and he seemed to perceive different colours at either end.

In 1829 an unknown man entered Daumer's house when Hauser was alone and stabbed him. He recovered; but in 1832, the same man stabbed him again in the public gardens, and this time it proved fatal. The criminologist Anselm von Feuerbach published a paper in which he argued convincingly that Hauser was a prince of the house of Baden, a brother of the queen of Sweden who, for reasons of political intrigue, had been kept alive by those who were ordered to murder him. (His brothers, Feuerbach maintains, *were* murdered soon after birth.) Feuerbach was bitterly attacked for his views—for in those days of petty princelings, royalty was regarded as above criticism—and died soon after Caspar Hauser's murder. The mystery still remains unsolved.

Whether because of the Hauser case, or because of some more general interest in abnormal sensitivity, Reichenbach began to repeat some of Mesmer's experiments with magnets—which, according to Mesmer, could cause small tides in the universal ether, and move it around the body. Then, in 1844, he heard about a girl named Mary Novotny, daughter of a tax collector in Vienna, who suffered from general debility and cataleptic attacks—like Justinus Kerner's famous patient, Friederike Hauffe, 'the Seeress of Prevorst'. Herr Novotny was asked if he would take a large magnet—no doubt supplied by Reichenbach—into his daughter's bedroom in the middle of the night, and see if she responded to it. The results were far more striking than he had expected. Around the poles of the magnet, the girl saw a fiery glow, a kind of aurora borealis, reddish-yellow from the south pole and bluish-green from the north. Could this have been auto-suggestion? Reichenbach got his assistant to go into the next room and point the magnet at her through the wall; she immediately detected its presence. Blindfolded, she could tell when the armature was moved from the end of the magnet. And, like Caspar Hauser, Miss Novotny proved to be a kind of magnet herself—at least, her hand stuck to the magnet as if her skin was made of iron.

Two months later, Reichenbach heard about another sick girl, Angelica Sturmann. He had, meanwhile, been experimenting with 'magnetized' crystals, and found that they also affected sensitives. But for his first experiment with Miss Sturmann, he took a large piece of ordinary mountain crystal. He hid this in a dark room, then asked for the girl to be brought in. Within moments she had pointed out the crystal; she said that it was glowing and emitting sparks, and that a blue light was streaming out of its peak. When Reichenbach turned it upside down, she saw a kind of red and yellow smoke around the bottom.

His tests with sensitives revealed that they enjoyed holding their fingers in the blue light, which they found cool and pleasant, while the reddish-yellow light produced a warm, slightly nauseating, sensation. Metals like brass and copper produced this same unpleasant sensation; so did quicksilver, which seemed to explain why many of his 'sick sensitives' could not stand mirrors. When he threw a spectrum on a wall with a prism, and placed glasses of water in the blue and the yellow light, the sensitives could tell the difference; the 'blue' water tasted faintly lemony, the 'yellow' bitter and sickly—one sensitive vomited after tasting it.

His sensitives could also see plants and flowers in the dark— they seemed to be surrounded by a dim light. In fact, so were animals and human beings. And when a bell was rung, its vibrations produced a colour which gradually died away. The light from human beings was dim and smoky, except around the hands. These had clear colours streaming from the fingertips—blue from the right hand, yellowy-red from the left. A blindfolded sensitive could tell which hand he was touching her with according to whether it produced a cool or a warm sensation. 'You see,' remarks Reichenbach, 'that a man is polarized from right to left . . . in the same way as a crystal'—anticipating one of the most interesting discoveries of modern brain physiology.

All this seemed to support Mesmer's conclusions about animal magnetism; but, oddly enough, Reichenbach disagreed. This was surely not some 'etheric' fluid that pervaded all space, but some mysterious energy that was common to magnets, crystals and living creatures. Reichenbach called this energy 'Od' or 'Odyle', and it became generally known as the 'Odic force'.

Here it becomes possible to see the error in Reichenbach's reasoning. Our senses are all tuned to different kinds of energy; our ears vibrate to sound, our eyes to colour, our skins to warmth. The range of our senses is limited, apparently by survival needs; it would be of no particular use to us to be able to see the sun's ultra-violet rays, or the infra-red radiation from a hot stove. It sounds very much as if Caspar Hauser's years in darkness developed his senses to a point where he could perceive far beyond the normal range, just as some of Reichenbach's sick sensitives could see the vibration of a bell or a violin. They were not perceiving 'Od', but ordinary energy. The force that animates living beings seems to have little in common with heat and light, although we now know that all living creatures generate a weak electric field—which its discoverer, Harold Burr, called the 'L-field'. Whatever the nature of this life-force, it is certainly not Reichenbach's 'Od'. Reichenbach, like Goethe, had been led astray by his enthusiasm and his desire to find some simple uniting principle behind all phenomena. He would have done better to be contented with multiplicity.

Nevertheless, by the year 1848 Reichenbach had achieved European celebrity. His 'Od' theory was regarded as the latest scientific advance, and most scientists were willing to preserve an open mind about it—Reichenbach's descriptions of the precautions he took against auto-suggestion were so impressive. Others were beginning to take up his ideas and repeat his experiments. It seems a reasonable assumption that, even if Buchanan had never discovered psychometry, one of Reichenbach's followers would have done so.

In fact, it was a follower of Buchanan who opened up new and exciting vistas in the study of psychometry.

His name was William Denton, and he was an Englishman who had been born in Darlington in 1823, and became a popular lecturer on temperance after his conversion to Methodism at the age of 16. Seven years later he moved to the United States, and went to Cincinnatti, where, oddly enough, he seems to have failed to encounter Joseph Rodes Buchanan, professor at the newly founded Eclectic Institute. He nevertheless married a Cincinnatti girl, moved on to Dayton, Ohio, as a headmaster, and became interested in the latest ideas in geology. In fact, he embraced what was then the violently controversial idea that the earth had not been created a few thousand years ago, but many millions. It is recorded that this caused so much offence to orthodox Christians that on one of his lecture trips he was threatened with mob violence. But it was after he became Professor of

Geology at the University of Boston—in 1853—that he came upon Buchanan's idea, published in the *Journal of Man*. The second issue contained the remarkable passage about the past being entombed in the present. For a geologist, no idea could be more exciting:

'And why should not the world be filled with the monuments and unwritten records of its past history? . . . The geologist finds, in the different strata of the earth, in its curiously mingled and irregular structure, and in the fossil remains which it conceals in its bosom, the history of its various changes of surface, and of the antediluvian races of animals which have long been extinct. The huge saurian monsters, which he portrays from their fossil relics, rise before the eye as incredible chimeras. And over this fertile region, now occupied by prosperous States, he revives, by the magic power of science, the antediluvian seas and their strange inhabitants . . .'

Denton was carried away by Buchanan's daguerreotype theory. He also liked an experiment performed by G. H. Lewes, husband of the novelist George Eliot. Lewes laid a wafer on a surface of polished metal, and breathed on it. Then he allowed his breath to evaporate, removed the wafer, and breathed on the plate again. The image of the wafer appeared on the surface. It was still there months later. It even remained there when he carefully brushed the metal surface with a camelhair brush. Is it not conceivable, Denton reasoned, that nature is full of such daguerreotypes of past events?

His sister, Anne Cridge, seemed a suitable subject for experiment, since she was 'highly impressible'. Denton began by trying Buchanan's experiments with letters. Mrs Cridge revealed herself to be an excellent psychometrist: 'She saw and described the writings of letters he was examining, and their surroundings, telling at times even the colour of hair and eyes correctly.'

The next step was to try her with a geological specimen. Denton selected a piece of limestone which he had picked up near Quindaro, Kansas, on the Missouri River; it was full of tiny fossil shells. His sister was not told anything about the specimen, and it was wrapped in paper so she could not tell what it was. Her response was:

'It seems to me there is a deep hole here. Oh, what shells! small shells; so many. I see water; it looks like a river running along. What a high hill – almost perpendicular; it seems as if the water had cut it in two; it is not so high on the other side. The hill is covered with sand and gravel.'

This was an excellent beginning. Denton admitted that, as far as his memory served him, it was a very accurate description. 'This piece of rock had taken in the pictures of the turbid Missouri that swept past it, the hill that hung over it, and the country in general around it, and, to the eye of the psychometer, they became apparently as plainly visible as to a spectator on the spot'.

His wife, Elizabeth Denton, also proved to be a good psychometer. When he handed her a piece of quartz from Panama, she received an impression of a huge insect, with antennae nearly a foot long, resting its head against a quartz rock, and could see a snake coiled in the wiry grass. She remarked that the country seemed much warmer than North America, with tropical vegetation.

These experiments were encouraging. But the result of the next was spectacular. He handed his sister a fragment of volcanic lava from Kilauea, on Hawaii, wrapped in paper. Mrs Cridge had an impression of an ocean, with ships sailing on it, and could tell that it was an island. Then she saw 'an ocean of fire pouring over a precipice and boiling as it pours. I see it flow into the ocean, and the water boils intensely'. The vision was so real that it shattered her nerves, and the feeling of fear remained for the next hour. Denton knew that the piece of lava had, in fact, been ejected in the eruption of 1840, so the vision of ships was probably accurate.

At this point, Denton took a precaution which reveals that he was a genuine scientist, determined to rule out all possibility of auto-suggestion. He tried wrapping several specimens in separate sheets of paper, then mixing them up, so he had no idea which was which. Then he handed his wife one of them. She had a vision of a volcano, with molten lava flowing down its side. 'The specimen must be lava', said Mrs Denton, and she was right.

Denton's precaution seems to us merely common sense. But we have to bear in mind that, in 1853, telepathy was virtually unknown. The word itself was not even invented until 1882 (by

F.W.H. Myers, one of the founders of the Society for Psychical Research). Before that, most psychic faculties were bundled vaguely together under the general heading of 'clairvoyance', which included the ability to see ghosts, glimpse what was happening elsewhere, and foretell the future. Once the Society for Psychical Research began to investigate telepathy, it became clear that it is probably the commonest of psychic faculties. (Most married couples, for example, have had experiences of starting to say the same thing at the same time.) Professor Gilbert Murray, a determined rationalist, was so good at it that he treated it as a party game, leaving the room while the company thought up a subject from life or literature, then coming back in and telling them what they had decided upon. ('Jane Eyre at school standing on a stool and being called a liar by Mr Brocklehurst . . .') By 1949, telepathy was so widely accepted, even by scientists, that Sir Alister Hardy could say, in his presidential address to the zoological section of the British Association: 'I believe that no one who examines the evidence with an unbiased mind can reject it'—a statement that would have brought catcalls half a century earlier.

When we consider many of Buchanan's experiments, we often feel that the results could be explained by telepathy—particularly when the psychometer is his own wife. With Denton, this is ruled out from the early experiments, since he usually took the precaution of making sure that he himself had no idea what was wrapped in the paper.

Denton was understandably elated. 'From the first dawn of light upon this infant globe, when round its cradle the steamy curtains hung, to this moment, Nature has been busy photographing every moment'. It was—and is—a perfectly reasonable hypothesis. We now know that matter and energy are the same thing; matter is frozen energy. Energy from space—light, heat, cosmic rays—falls upon us in a continuous cosmic hail, knocking electrons from the surface of everything it strikes. Light falling on a sheet of metal 'evaporates' electrons as sunlight evaporates a sheet of water, producing the 'photo-electric effect', an electric current. So there can be no doubt that everything that happens in daylight *is* 'photographed' by the surrounding objects. But the 'film' is double- and treble- and multiple-exposed, so that even if it could be developed, it would be useless. In a science fiction novel, *Before the Dawn* (1934), the mathematician E. T. Bell invented a 'light decoder' that could sort out the various exposures and then 'play back' the resulting record of the ages like a film projector; since then, the invention of the computer has made the notion rather more plausible, since sorting out the exposures *would* be largely a matter of computer analysis. But the human brain is thousands of times more complex than any computer; so the assumption of Buchanan and Denton—that the mind has its own inbuilt decoder—is easier to accept today than it was in 1860.

Denton went to considerable lengths to rule out self-deception. For example, he would try the same specimen on the psychometer more than once, with an interval of weeks in-between, to see whether it produced the same impressions. From a fragment of bone obtained from a piece of limestone, Elizabeth Denton's first impression was:

'. . . a long, smooth beach . . . On that beach are quadrupeds of some kind. One is large, heavy, thick-skinned, dark coloured and thick necked; the flesh is not fibrous, but soft. Its head is broad, and horns rise up from its nose. I see another with a long neck and a head nearly as large as a sheep's, but in appearance like that of a snake, though it is a quadruped.'

This sounds like a plesiosaur, the species to which the fabled Loch Ness monster is supposed to belong. She was impressed by rocks covered with bright green moss.

Denton tried the same specimen on her a month later, making sure she had no idea of what it was (although this time, he took no precaution against telepathy.) Again she saw water, with water weeds that looked like moss; but this time she saw birdlike creatures with membranous wings in the shallow water. We know that pterodactyls fed on fish, so it seems conceivable they spent part of their time in the water, like seagulls.

On other occasions, Denton himself had no idea of what the psychometrist was examining; he would cover the table-top with various minerals and fossils, and the psychometrist would pick up one of them with closed eyes. When she described in detail a scene under the sea, the specimen proved to be a piece of Silurian coral. A tiny fragment of a mastodon's tooth, so small that it could not be recognized, immediately produced an impression of 'a perfect monster with heavy legs, unwieldy head, and very large body'. Various fragments of limestone produced magnificent and detailed descriptions of prehistoric landscapes. A small fragment of chamois horn produced a fine description of the Alps. A fossil from Cuba brought a description of a tropical island with some accurate geographical details. A piece of Indian pottery brought an immediate image of Red Indians. Fragments of meteorites—tried on several psychometrists—always brought visions of empty space, sometimes of the earth seen from a great height. A pebble from a glacier produced an immediate impression of being frozen in a great depth of ice. A fragment of rock from Table Rock, Niagara, brought an impression of looking down from a mountain into a 'deep hole' with something boiling up from it—the psychometrist thought it was a hot spring with steam, although she could hear the noise of a torrent, and see the Niagara River. Later in the experiment she recognized that 'the water makes that smoke; it looks like a rain-cloud or mist'. A fragment of stalactite brought a picture of 'pieces of rock hanging down; they look like icicles.'

When Denton tried his wife with a piece of hornstone brought from the Mount of Olives, the result was a description of a dry land with low rocky hills, 'so poor . . . they could not raise enough to eat', and horses, sheep and goats. She then went on to describe a large church, and a city with a wall and iron gates. Finally, by inference, she guessed she was looking at Jerusalem.

On a later occasion, Denton took the same fragment out of a box of mixed specimens without knowing what it was. Again, there followed a description of a walled city and a barren landscape, with the comment: 'I think the Bible might have been written here'. It was only when she had finished that Denton looked more closely at the rock and identified it as the hornstone he had used previously.

As the psychics became more skilled, they began to be able to distinguish different periods in the history of the specimens. One of these cases is among the most impressive Denton recorded. He handed his sister a fragment of mosaic pavement that had been dug up in 1760 and brought to England. It came from the villa of the Roman orator Cicero. Denton was hoping for a description of Cicero—or at least, of some ancient Romans. Instead, Mrs Cridge began by describing a prehistoric forest with a beast like a mastodon. Denton asked her to come forward to more modern times. Now she saw a country house standing in its own grounds, and an old man in knee-breeches and a swallow-tailed coat. This sounds like the house to which the fragment had been brought in 1760.

Denton decided to try it on his wife. She immediately sensed that her sister-in-law had already psychometrised it. Then she described a garden with a cascade which she felt to be landscaped ('there is human influence about this'). She went on to describe a sick-room scene in the house. All this was rather disappointing.

Some days later, Denton decided to try her again. This time she immediately saw a distinctly Roman scene, with a large building with pillars and steps leading up to it. In a room with uncomfortable furniture ('if furniture it can be called') the walls were hung with crimson velvet. She saw lines of helmeted soldiers, then a 'fleshy man with a broad face and blue eyes'. He wore a 'dress like a gown' (presumably a toga). 'He is majestic, yet has a good deal of geniality about him too. He regards himself as superior, and withdraws from others . . . It seems to me that he has something to do with those troops . . .'

Cicero *had* been a successful military commander at one point in his career; but he was tall and thin. Denton concluded that the man might have been Cicero, and ended his notes on the experiment '. . . at all events, we have a description in harmony with the time and people of the days of Cicero'.

By the time he came to republish the book—with an additional two volumes—in 1888, he had made an important discovery. The previous owner of Cicero's house had been the dictator Sulla, and his wife's description was altogether closer to what we know of Sulla (who died in 78 BC). He was one of the few Roman dictators who succeeded in dying in his bed. While some of his measures were ruthless and unpopular, he was known as a convivial man who was fond of his friends. His soldiers called him 'lucky Sulla'. Mrs Denton had apparently focused on Sulla rather than Cicero—an indication (like Mrs Cridge's 18th-century garden) that Denton's expectations had little or no influence on the psychometers. (In fact, most modern paragnosts would say that if they want to receive telepathic impressions, then they have to focus on the person whose mind they want to read; if they want psychometric impressions, they concentrate on the object.)

When Denton handed his wife a fragment of the Porcelain Tower, near Peking, he knew nothing whatever about it, except that it came from a place called the Porcelain Tower in China. His wife described a place like a temple, with massive walls and large urns; she saw a bell-shaped roof and a spire. After writing down her description, Denton checked in the *Iconographic Encyclopedia* to find out what the Porcelain Tower was used for (for all he knew, it was simply a monument like the leaning tower of Pisa). He discovered that it was a temple, with walls twelve feet thick.

If we can make the assumption that Denton's own knowledge of the objects had no telepathic influence on the psychometrist, then the experiments he describes in the first volume of *The Soul of Things* are stunningly impressive. Again and again they were able to pin down the place from which the object came. A piece of a limestone slab from Nineveh brought an impression of a vast temple; a Greek coin (kept unseen) brought a detailed description of the mint; a piece of curtain from the House of Representatives brought a large council chamber, and an impression of some members talking glibly and superficially; a piece of sandstone from Melrose Abbey in Scotland brought a description of an abbey with arched doorways, Gothic windows and an aisle. Three months later, Mrs Denton was handed the fragment a second time—with no knowledge that she had handled it before. Again she saw arches and a 'place of worship', but this time with some conference going on there. 'These people are ignorant and bigoted'. A check with an encyclopedia revealed that Melrose Abbey was 'usually involved in the rancorous events of border feud and international war'. ('Ignorant and bigoted' is an admirable description of the Scottish religious temperament of earlier centuries.) A piece of mosaic from a Roman bath brought a detailed description of a Roman bath, with an atmosphere of 'gaiety and voluptuousness'.

A piece of mosaic from Pompeii brought an interesting description of an ancient town with narrow streets, and a populace in the grip of war fever; Denton had hoped for some mention of the destruction of Pompeii. But a piece of volcanic rock from Pompeii brought far more satisfying results. It was the size of a small bean, and the psychometer was not allowed to see it. (Denton does not explain how he did this, but presumably it was wrapped in paper or cloth.) Mrs Denton saw coloured figures on a wall—frescoes—and observed that the building overlooked the sea. Out of the window, she could look towards the mountain-top, and see smoke and cinders rising up in a column. The black cloud of dust was spreading across the countryside. From a situation higher up the mountain she was able to observe the eruption. 'I feel the influence of human terror that I cannot describe.' The land below finally became a desert of cinders. Watching crowds fleeing from Pompeii (in fact, most of the population escaped before the final catastrophe) she is surprised that it resembles a modern town more than she had expected.

One interesting observation was that the volcano had also vomited water. In fact, Pompeii was engulfed by a kind of mud, not by molten lava. Bodies found encased in the hardened material were unscorched. A description of the eruption by Pliny the Younger describes a tree-like column of smoke rising from the volcano, then spreading out like branches—or a mushroom-cloud—which then descended and covered the town. Elizabeth Denton's description was startlingly close.

Almost a decade later, Denton returned to the subject of Pompeii. By now, his son Sherman was in his mid-teens; he had been practising psychometry since he was a child, and was in some ways more sensitive than his mother. The tests Denton conducted occupy more than fifty pages of his second volume, and they provide a remarkably rich and complex picture of life in Pompeii.

Sherman's first session—with a piece of plaster from the 'House of Sallust'—immediately brought one remarkable 'hit'. Over a doorway, Sherman 'saw' a painting of two winged children drawing a cart with another winged child riding in it. Denton later discovered an engraving of the painting in a book on Pompeii (which, he insists, neither he nor Sherman saw before the test), and he reproduces it in his text.

When Sherman spoke of wide streets, Denton was dubious; most streets in Pompeii were hardly six feet across. But he later discovered that the House of Sallust was not in the residential section, but on a square, in an area with wide streets. Sherman described a Pompeian boat with a prow like a swan's head and neck. Denton found engravings from nearby Herculaneum (also engulfed in the eruption) of the *cheniscus*, a birdlike head and neck attached to the prow of Roman vessels.

Sherman also comments: 'The labouring people seem to hate the rich. Where there is a number of them together, the rich pass them quickly, and seem to regard them as a man would a snake.' Denton makes no attempt to verify this statement. But from a modern book, *Pompeii and Herculaneum* (1960) by Marcel Brion, we learn that the walls of Pompeii contained such graffiti as 'This city is too rich' and 'I propose a share-out of the public wealth among the inhabitants'. The attitude of the rich must have added fuel to this feeling of social injustice; in the hall of the House of Vedius Siricus there was an inscription, *Salve Lucrum*—'Hail, Profit!' It also, comments Brion, meant 'Welcome to money', addressed as a welcome to other moneyed people who came to the house. The Pompeians, it becomes clear, took money-making very seriously indeed. In her earlier examination of a fragment from Pompeii, Mrs Denton had commented on the difference she sensed between the Pompeians and the ancient Egyptians: that for the Egyptians, religion was inherent in their way of life, while for the Pompeians, it was largely a matter of forms and observances. But the wealthy had statues of Mercury in their houses to bring luck to their business and ward off evil spirits that might harm it. 'Hail, profit!'

Another of Sherman's comments was that women seemed to play a prominent part in the life of Pompeii; Brion remarks that in Pompeii the women took a hand in business; even a rich woman advertised that she had shops to let.

Sherman's description of a theatrical performance makes it sound more like a circus with clowns and acrobats, and makes no mention of the kind of things a modern reader would expect—comedies by Plautus, Statius and Terence, Greek tragedies and so on. Denton remarks that his son's description of acrobats and comics sounds very modern. But Marcel Brion comments that the favourite form of dramatic entertainment at this time was the *atellanae*, popular farces that took their name from their town of origin, Atella; originally intended to relax the audience after performance of tragedies, they became so popular that they were performed on their own. Brion says of these performances: 'They might be compared to music-hall numbers of a rather low level, interspersed with dancing, clowning, obscenities, feats of skill and athletic exhibitions, the whole ending with a procession of nude girls.' Apart from the nude girls (which Denton would no doubt have censored out) this is a fairly accurate summary of Sherman Denton's lengthy description of a theatrical performance in Pompeii.

The descriptions of Pompeii are certainly the highlight of Denton's second volume; but there are other impressive things. By this time, Denton had become aware of the possibility of mind-reading, although he was inclined to discount it simply because he had noticed that his own expectations failed to influence the 'visions' of the psychometrist. But he devised one interesting experiment to show that the visions could be just as accurate when all possibility of mind-reading had been excluded. He had made the interesting discovery that the psychometer could look at a map, then close his eyes and experience a sensation of flying through the air until he came to the place he had seen. This faculty is known as 'travelling clairvoyance', and has been the subject of a great deal of modern research (for example, at Stanford University in the mid-1970s where, under laboratory conditions, the psychic Ingo Swann was able to demonstrate his ability to travel mentally to other places and describe accurately what was happening there). They chose at random the island of Socotra in the Gulf of Aden, and Mrs Denton was first asked to describe it. She stated that it was a rocky island, 'almost a rock in the sea', with one coast high and mountainous and the other—the inhabited coast—low. There seemed to be two types of people. Those inland, the natives, were poor, and 'there seems to be a wandering disposition about them'. Near the coast the people were 'yellowish' and engaged more in business. All this proved (from an encyclopedia article on Socotra) to be remarkably accurate. The geographical description is precise. The population consisted of two types—the original inhabitants, Bedouins, who lived inland and who were nomadic, and Arab traders and agriculturalists who lived near the coast.

By comparison, Sherman Denton's description sounds vague and inaccurate; he described it as a green island without mountains (in fact, the mountains are five thousand feet high), and continued with descriptions of natives who lived a hand-to-mouth existence. But the fact that Denton includes this relative failure is a testimony to his honesty.

These first two volumes of *The Soul of Things* are both impressive and exciting; with their long descriptions of past ages, they read almost like a novel. Denton was as convinced as Buchanan that psychometry was a normal human faculty, a 'telescope into the past' that could be developed by anyone who was willing to take the trouble. He gives the impression of being a rather better scientist than Buchanan, more anxious to exclude possible error, and to explain psychometry in terms of scientific theory. For example, he devotes a chapter to the psychological curiosity that is now known as 'eidetic imagery' or photographic memory—the ability some people (especially children) possess to look at some object, then to project an exact image of it onto a blank sheet of paper. Newton discovered that, during his optical experiments, the image of the sun (seen in a darkened glass) kept returning like a hallucination. It would vanish when he forgot about it; but he only had to call it to mind to make it appear in front of him. Denton discovered many other descriptions of the same phenomenon: not just of simple images like the sun, but of whole scenes. He quotes Professor Stevelly who, after watching bees swarming from hives, continued to have visual hallucinations of swarms of bees for days afterwards. A doctor named Ferriar described how, in the evening, he could conjure up in detail some scene he had looked at during the day—an old ruin, a fine house, a review of troops; he had only to go into a darkened room to see it as if in a coloured photograph. The geologist Hugh Miller had a similar ability. He wrote:

'There are, I suspect, provinces in the philosophy of mind into which the metaphysicians have not yet entered. Of that accessible storehouse, in which the memories of past events lie arranged and taped up, they appear to know a good deal; but of a mysterious cabinet of daguerreotype pictures, of which, though fast locked up on ordinary occasions, disease sometimes flings the door ajar, they seem to know nothing.'

More than a century later, Dr Wilder Penfield proved the truth of this observation when, during a brain operation, he touched the patient's temporal cortex with the electric probe, and the patient suddenly 'replayed' precise and lengthy memories of childhood, all as minutely detailed as if they were happening in the present.

It is difficult to see at first what connection Denton saw between these visual hallucinations and psychometry—after all, they seem to have little enough in common. But it slowly becomes clear that his wife and sister—and later his son—actually *saw* these visions of the past; if the cinema had been invented at the time, he might have compared it to a mental film show. These experiences of hallucination seemed to offer a clue to this strange faculty of psychometric vision. Particularly interesting is Newton's observation that he could make the image of the sun reappear before his eyes by *imagining* it. What is suggested here is that the image was so vividly imprinted on his brain that it could be 'projected' like a film by merely wanting to. This also seems to explain Stevelly's visions of the swarming bees and Ferriar's of old ruins of fine houses. The philosopher Berdyaev has a passage in which he describes his own hallucinatory vision of a woman called Mintslova—a disciple of Rudolph Steiner—whom he regarded as a pernicious influence:

I was lying in bed in my room half asleep; I could clearly see the room and the corner opposite me where an icon was hanging with a little burning oil lamp before it. I beheld the outline of Mintslova's face: its expression was quite horrifying—a face seemingly possessed of all the power of darkness. I gazed at her intently for a few seconds, and then, by an intense spiritual effort, forced the horrible vision to disappear.[1]

It is significant that Berdyaev was half asleep, so that what might have been merely a dream-image was projected as a hallucination.

The third volume of *The Soul of Things* makes us aware of the drawbacks of this ability. The frontispiece is a 'Map of

1. *Dream and Reality*, Chapter 7.

Jupiter', with a key underneath listing such items as 'Houses and city, seen 19 March 1870', 'Sugar loaf hills, seen 23 March 1870'. And the longest section in the book is a chapter called 'Astronomical Examinations', beginning with 'A boy's visit to Venus', 'Visit to a comet', and including accounts of Mars and Jupiter. Sherman Denton's observations on Venus begin promisingly with the comment that its mountains are higher than those on earth—which is true. But he then goes on to describe giant trees shaped like toadstools and full of sweet jelly, and an animal that was half-fish and half-muskrat. The 1962 Mariner space-probe revealed that the temperature on the surface of Venus is 900°F, hot enough to melt solder, and therefore too hot to support life. Sherman's visit to a comet is equally disappointing; he states that it is a planet that has become a kind of fireball. We are still not sure of where comets originate; but we know that they are of low density, and almost certainly very cold. Sherman's visit to the sun revealed that it is made of molten lava which is hardening in places into a crust. Modern astronomy has shown that the sun is a ball of gas. A visit to Mars revealed that it was much like earth, but peopled with men with four fingers, wide mouths, yellow hair and blue eyes. 'It seems warm, like summer weather.' (In fact, Mars would be very cold indeed, since it is more than 50,000,000 miles further from the sun than earth is.) Mrs Cridge and Mrs Denton also visited Mars, and described its religion, its art and its scientific inventions. Sherman and Mrs Cridge both described Jupiter, also peopled by blue-eyed blondes who can float in the air, and whose women all have plaits down to their waists. Modern space probes have revealed that Jupiter is basically a ball of freezing gas with a hot liquid core.

Volume three of *The Soul of Things* is undoubtedly an anti-climax, and no one could be blamed for being inclined to dismiss the whole work as an absurd piece of self-deception. But before we throw the baby out with the bath water, we might recollect the parallel case of Emanuel Swedenborg. That remarkable mystic devoted the first fifty-six years of his life to science and engineering; then he began having strange dreams, hallucinations and trances. In these visionary states, he believed he had visited heaven and hell, and his books contain detailed accounts of the 'afterworld', all of which his disciples—who were soon numbered in thousands—accepted as literal truth. A century before the rise of spiritualism, Swedenborg claimed to be able to converse with spirits of the dead. When the queen of Sweden asked him to give her greetings to her dead brother, the prince royal of Denmark, Swedenborg said he would. Soon after, he told her that her brother sent his greetings, and apologized for not answering her last letter. He would now do so through Swedenborg . . . As Swedenborg delivered the detailed message, the queen turned pale, and said, 'No one but God knows this secret'. On another occasion, in 1761, the widow of the Dutch ambassador told Swedenborg that she was having trouble with a silversmith who was demanding payment for a silver tea-service; a few days later, Swedenborg told her he had spoken to her husband, and that he *had* paid for the tea-service; the receipt would be found in a secret compartment in his bureau drawer. Swedenborg also mentioned some secret correspondence that would be found in the same drawer. Both the receipt and the correspondence were found where Swedenborg had said.

In July 1759, Swedenborg was able to tell guests at a party in Gothenburg that a great fire had broken out in Stockholm, 300 miles away. Two hours later he told one of the guests that the fire had been extinguished only three doors from his home. Two days later, a messenger arrived confirming these details.

So, understandably, Swedenborg's disciples believed him when he described the 'spirit realms', and his visits to other planets. Mercury, he said, had a moderate temperature, and its beings were more spiritual than human beings; the planet also had cattle that were a cross between cows and stags. Venus had two races living on opposite sides of the planet, one mild and humane, the other savage and violent—the latter being giants. Martians had faces that were half black and half white, and communicated by a kind of telepathy; they were also vegetarians. The inhabitants of Jupiter—whom Swedenborg claimed to know more intimately than those of any other planet—looked like human beings, but were far more gentle and humane, and naturally moral and virtuous. Those in warm regions went naked—except for a covering over the loins—and were astonished to be told that human beings could be sexually excited by another's nakedness.

The inhabitants of the moon had thunderous voices, which were produced by a kind of belching . . .

How can these contradictions be resolved? One answer is suggested by Dr Wilson Van Dusen in his book *Presence of Other Worlds*. Van Dusen argues that there is strong evidence that Swedenborg's visions were seen in 'hypnagogic states', the states in which we linger between sleep and waking. Swedenborg seems to confirm this when he writes: 'Once, when I awoke at daybreak, I saw . . . diversely shaped apparitions floating before my eyes . . .' Swedenborg's descriptions of various kinds of spirits—particularly the 'damned'—sound as if he is deliberately writing in parables; but the descriptions are as precise and detailed as those of a novelist. The most probable answer is that Swedenborg had developed a faculty very similar to that discussed by Denton in the chapter on Newton, Hugh Miller and others who experienced visual hallucinations. The severe mental crisis that changed him in his mid-fifties from a scientist to a visionary allowed the unconscious mind to erupt into consciousness; he could, in effect, dream with his eyes open.

But if the visions of planets—and probably of heaven and hell—were self-deception, then how do we explain the accuracy of the vision of the Stockholm fire, and the information about the secret drawer and the queen's letter? The answer is that, unfortunately, the possession of genuine 'clairvoyant' or mediumistic faculty is no guarantee of the truthfulness of other kinds of vision. In fact, the best clairvoyants and psychometrists have always been willing to admit that they can be confused by telepathic impressions from other people.

And so we must count the third volume of *The Soul of Things* a failure—but a most extraordinary failure which does little to obscure the achievement of the first two volumes. It is a pity that Mrs Denton and Mrs Cridge were unable to distinguish between genuine 'clairvoyance' and the products of their own imagination; But, to be fair, we should admit that they had no reason to.

Thomson Jay Hudson devotes some space to Denton and his geological experiments in *The Law of Psychic Phenomena*; (Denton was dead by that time—he had died in New Guinea in 1883, while on a world lecture tour.) Recalling what Hudson had to say about the hidden powers of the 'subjective mind', you might expect him to praise Denton as another explorer of the 'invisible palace'. Yet, oddly enough, he rejects Denton's 'telescope into the past' as self-deception. According to Hudson, everything Mrs Denton discovered could be explained by the telepathic powers of the subjective mind. She was simply able to read her husband's mind. But surely, Denton had gone to enormous trouble to make sure that even he did not know what was in the various brown paper parcels? Hudson dismisses this. The subjective mind possesses immense powers of observation and memory, and it would be child's play for the subjective mind to see through the elementary precautions taken by Denton . . .

This sounds plausible, until we look more closely into Denton's experiments. If the visions originated in his own mind, then why did his wife and sister—and later his son—often produce different pictures from different periods in the sample's history—as with the piece of mosaic from the villa of Cicero? Why did Mrs Denton describe a man who sounds like Sulla when Denton was expecting her to describe Cicero? And if, indeed, it was Sulla she described, and Denton had no idea that Sulla had lived in the villa, then telepathy would have been impossible.

Hudson could, of course, have countered these objections. If Denton's wife and sister selected different parts of the sample's history to describe, then they were merely selecting from the knowledge in Denton's mind. As to Denton not knowing that it was the dictator's villa, perhaps he *did* know, but had long ago forgotten that he had read it . . .

But the real objection to Hudson's arguments is that he is willing to credit the subjective mind with powers just as remarkable as psychometry—for example, healing a relative at a thousand miles. If the subjective mind can pick up vibrations from another mind, then why can it not pick up vibrations from a letter or a piece of mosaic? Hudson even credits the subjective mind with the power to foretell the future; he says that its deductive powers are so tremendous that it can calculate every possibility—like some gigantic computer—and select the likeliest one. He gives a great deal of space to the 'daemon' of Socrates—the inner voice that would give the philosopher good advice and warm him of impending danger; this, says Hudson, is simply the subjective mind making itself heard as a kind of voice inside the head. (A modern exponent of split-brain theory, Julian Jaynes, believes that the ancients heard 'voices' that came from the right cerebral hemisphere.) If the subjective mind possesses these remarkable powers, it seems contradictory to deny it the power of psychometry.

The explanation of Hudson's 'tough-minded' attitude is probably that he was unwilling to expose his newborn theory to ridicule by appearing too credulous. In fact, we can see in retrospect that many of his mistakes sprang out of being too sceptical. His chapter on crime and hypnosis provides two examples. He argues that no one could be made to commit a crime under hypnosis, because the prophetic powers of the subjective mind would make it aware that it might lead to disaster. In fact, many crimes have been committed under hypnosis—one of the best known examples being the Copenhagen case of 1951, when a man named Palle Hardrup robbed a bank and murdered the cashier under hypnotic suggestion. Hudson also remarks that committing suicide under hypnosis is as unlikely as committing a crime under hypnosis; in fact, this is precisely what did happen in the Sala case of 1929, when the hypnotist Sigwart Thurneman made a member of his criminal gang commit suicide by hypnotic suggestion.[1]

But these criticisms fail to obscure the remarkable nature of Hudson's achievement. *The Law of Psychic Phenomena* is one of the most important contributions to nineteenth-century thought, and deserves to be as well-known as *The Origin of Species* or *Das Kapital*. But, within a few years of the book's publication, Sigmund Freud's theory of the unconscious mind had become still more notorious. Freud also believed that the unconscious is far more powerful than the conscious mind; but Freud's unconscious is entirely negative, a kind of gigantic dustbin full of guilt, misery and repressions. Freud seemed even more sceptical and tough-minded than Hudson, and the result was that his more controversial theories won the day, and Hudson's were forgotten.

In fact, modern split-brain research has shown that Hudson's ideas have a sounder basis than Freud's. It is now a matter of

1. See *Antisocial or Criminal Acts and Hypnosis* by Paul J. Reiter; also my own *Written in Blood* (1990).

scientific fact that we have two 'selves' inside our heads, that one is intuitive and the other intellectual, and that genius, as Hudson said, is a close co-operation between the two. So it is important to look again at Hudson's contribution, and give careful thought to some of his insights. His most important recognition is that human beings possess mental powers of which they are unaware. He was right to emphasize the mystery of calculating prodigies; for their abilities seem to defy what we regard as the normal laws of the mind. They often appear out of the blue, in perfectly normal children, and later vanish just as abruptly. Archbishop Whately said that his own powers appeared at the age of six, when he knew nothing about figures except simple addition; suddenly, he could do tremendous calculations in his head. When he went to school three years later, 'the passion wore off', and he became a dunce at mathematics. The powers of such prodigies seem incredible. One 6-year-old boy, Benjamin Blyth, was out walking with his father when he asked what time he was born. His father told him four a.m. A few minutes later, the child stated the number of seconds he had lived. When they got home, his father worked it out on paper, and told Ben he was 172,800 seconds wrong. 'No', said the child, 'you have forgotten two leap years'.

Most calculating prodigies lose their powers in their teens, when life becomes more complex and difficult, and sexual changes in the body disturb the emotions. But the inference is that our brains have an extraordinary power that few of us ever bother to develop.

Where psychometry is concerned, the power of 'eidetic vision' is even more important, as Denton recognised. Modern research has revealed that between 8 and 20 per cent of all children may possess eidetic vision—the power to conjure up an image so powerfully that it looks like a film projection. One test involves the use of 'random dot stereograms'. Two sheets of paper contain apparently random patterns of ten thousand dots, but when these are superimposed, a picture emerges. Many children can look at one pattern, then move their eyes to the other sheet, and see the two patterns combining into a picture. This is obviously a right-brain function—it is the right brain that recognizes patterns and shapes—and again the inference is that we gradually lose it as the left brain becomes more powerful, to 'cope' with reality. But if this is correct, then all human beings possess a latent power to 'photograph' what they are looking at, and to project the photograph later in all its detail. As we have seen in the cases cited by Denton, this 'projection' is a deliberate act of will and imagination. But Hudson's artist friend was able to project purely imaginary scenes on his canvas. And this, again, would be perfectly natural. If we have the latent power to 'hold' mental photographs and keep them in some memory-file, then there is no reason why the imagination should not combine them, or simply invent its own mental photographs.

The psychologist C.G. Jung also recognized this power, which he called 'active imagination', and he believed that anyone could develop it with sufficient effort. Jung made the discovery accidentally. In 1913, after his break with Freud, Jung was experiencing severe mental problems that made him fear insanity. Sitting at his desk one day, he says, 'I let myself drop. Suddenly it was as though the ground literally gave way beneath my feet, and I plunged down into dark depths.' There followed a waking dream in which Jung found himself in an underground cave, guarded by a mummified dwarf, and saw the body of a blond youth with a wound in his head float past on a stream.

In his autobiography, *Memories, Dreams, Reflections*, Jung goes on to describe his deliberate development of techniques to enter this realm of 'waking dreams':

'In order to seize hold of the fantasies, I frequently imagined a steep descent. I even made several attempts to get to the very bottom. The first time I reached, as it were, a depth of about a thousand feet; the next time I found myself at the edge of a cosmic abyss. It was like a voyage to the moon, or a descent into empty space. First came the image of a crater, and I had a feeling that I was in the land of the dead. The atmosphere was that of the other world. Near the steep slope of a rock I caught sight of two figures, an old man with a white beard, and a beautiful young girl. I summoned up my courage and approached them as though they were real people, and listened attentively to what they told me . . .'

Here we can see clearly that Jung had entered a hypnagogic realm in which he remained wide-awake whilst at the same time encountering the strange creations of that 'other self' inside us. It is, admittedly, difficult for most of us to accept the notion of such an ability; but we should bear in mind that a dog would find it quite impossible to conceive the mental state of a child reading a book, with half his consciousness in the 'real world' and the other half in a world of fantasy. Jung's 'active imagination' is only a single step beyond this ability that every educated person possesses.

And now at last we are in a position to understand those detailed descriptions of 'other worlds' that we find in Swedenborg and Denton. A good psychometer possesses the power to 'read' objects in the way that a bloodhound can recognize scents. When this reading becomes second nature, it is accompanied by images—images that are sometimes so detailed and real that they amount to eidetic visions. When Mrs Denton described Cicero's villa, or when Sherman Denton described the theatre in ancient Pompeii, they were using active imagination as a tool to amplify their readings. But when they tried to 'psychometrize' Mars or Jupiter, there were no psychometric impressions to amplify, and the subjective mind—which, according to Van Dusen, is an incorrigible performer that hates to admit defeat—produced elaborate waking dreams.

This tendency of the unconscious to spin its own webs of fantasy certainly complicates the question of psychometry. But, unlike Swedenborg and Denton, we are at least aware of the problem; and this is already an important step toward solving it.

And what of those pioneers of the paranormal, Joseph Rodes Buchanan and William Denton? Sadly, it must be recorded that neither of them achieved the place in intellectual history that they undoubtedly deserve. Denton, the younger of the two, died in 1883, at the age of sixty, and was thereafter virtually forgotten. Buchanan fared slightly better. His *Manual of Psychometry* came out in 1885, and gained him new readers and followers. But by that time, his original 'nerve aura' theory of psychometry had been expanded to a point that most serious investigators found totally unacceptable.

The experiment that placed him beyond the limits of science was suggested by his interest in the new art of photography (for we are now retracing our steps to the 1850s). He tried handing photographs—suitably covered—to the psychometer, to see what impressions they produced. And with good psychometers like his wife he received convincing and accurate descriptions of the sitter. But this experiment ought *not* to have worked, since a photograph is mechanically produced, and therefore—unless its subject happened to have held it in his hands—should carry no personal 'vibrations'. Yet it *did* work. Buchanan concluded that 'there was not, in such cases, any emanation from the person described, and the picture was merely the presentation of an idea to be grasped *by the intuitive perception which is independent of vision*'. [My italics].

Clearly, this innocent-sounding statement either conceals a total breakdown of logic, or represents a revolutionary new theory of the nature of psychometry. According to Buchanan, it was a new theory. 'Hence', he declares, 'it became apparent that the object for psychometry was in such cases merely an index [he means an indication] leading the mind to the object represented, and need not be a picture, a relic, or anything associated in any way with the person or thing to be explored.'

If this 'intuitive perception which is independent of vision' could work on a photograph, it ought to work just as well on a mere name. Buchanan tried it 'I wrote the name of a friend and placed it in the hands of a good psychometer, who had no difficulty, notwithstanding her doubts of so novel a proceeding . . . in giving as good a description of Dr N. as if he had made the description from an autograph.'

Buchanan was carried away by wild enthusiasm. 'Psychometry', he declared, 'is the earthly IRRADIATION OF OMNISCIENCE and it will be known hereafter to penetrate all things.' And he went on to ask his sensitives to psychometrize the names of all kinds of famous people: Homer, Shakespeare, Bacon, Jesus, Socrates, Confucius, the Buddha and St Paul. A later volume called *Primitive Christianity* even contains a re-edited version of the Gospel of St John.

And if a psychometrist can gather information from the past, then why not from the future? By 1884, the whole world was talking about the Moslem revolt in the Sudan, led by a religious fanatic called the Mahdi. General Gordon had been sent to try to subdue him. Buchanan wrote the name 'Mahdi' on a sheet of paper, and asked a number of his students to try their powers on it. They produced impressions of a tropical country, a bloody war, men in Arab dress, and a leader of deep religious convictions—all of which might have been expected if they were unconsciously reading Buchanan's mind. What is rather more surprising is that many of their predictions for the future were accurate. Buchanan admired the Mahdi and disliked the British, so any predictions based on his subconscious hopes would involve victory for the Mahdi and defeat for the British. In fact, most of his students predicted that the Mahdi would ultimately be unsuccessful. When Buchanan asked 'Is he about to capture a city?' (meaning Khartoum) the reply was: 'He is preparing for an attack, but will be repulsed.' In fact, the Mahdi *did* attack Khartoum, and was repulsed. Later, Buchanan again asked his wife about the war, and she predicted another attack with terrible bloodshed; within two days, the Mahdi had stormed Khartoum and murdered all the defenders, including Gordon. She went on to prophesy that the war would not continue in the summer, and that the British would withdraw their troops; both things happened as she had said. The prediction that 'the war will be disastrous' for the Mahdi was also fulfilled; success made him fat and lazy; after the fall of Khartoum he withdrew into his harem for a prolonged debauch and died a few months later.

None of this surprised Buchanan; if, after all, psychometry was the 'irradiation of omniscience', the future should present no more problems than the past. Buchanan pointed out, reasonably, that there have been many well-authenticated cases of precognition— he devotes a whole appendix of his *Manual* to the remarkable story of the French author Jacques Cazotte who, at a dinner party just before the French Revolution, accurately foretold the fate of almost everyone sitting at the table: Chamfort would open his veins with a razor, Condorcet would take poison to avoid the guillotine, and a notorious atheist named La Harpe would become a Christian. La Harpe was so derisive that he went home and wrote it all down. But in due course, it all happened exactly as Cazotte had said—even to La Harpe becoming a monk. I shall discuss this more fully in Chapter 13.

As far as contemporary science was concerned, all this was enough to place Buchanan beyond the pale. Even the American Society for Psychical Research—formed in the same year that the *Manual* was published—found nothing of interest in Buchanan's latest theories. Yet it is worth remarking, in passing, that some of

Buchanan's own prophecies were surprisingly accurate. In 1859, he published in the *Louisville Journal* a prediction that America would experience six years of calamity; the Civil War lasted from 1861 to 1865. In 1885, he predicted a 'period of calamity thirty years hence'—twenty-nine years before the Great War. He also remarked that there would probably be an 'elemental convulsion' on the Pacific side of America, and that 'I would prefer not to reside in San Francisco at that time'. At the time Buchanan was writing, the only Californian earthquake in which there had been fatalities (40 dead) had occurred in 1868, and it involved six major cities. Buchanan had been dead six years when the San Francisco earthquake of 1906 destroyed 28,000 houses and killed 700 people.

He also had a prophecy concerning himself: that in the coming century he would be remembered as the 'herald of the coming illumination', and that a statue would be erected to him. This prophecy has not so far been fulfilled; but there is still time.

4.
The Coming of
the Spirits

THE ECLIPSE OF Buchanan, Denton and Hudson cannot be blamed entirely on Sigmund Freud. Equally decisive was the rise of the movement called Spiritualism, which swept across Europe and America in the 1850s, even reaching the most far-flung outposts of the Russian empire. This had its starting point in a series of extraordinary events that occurred in the home of the Fox family, in Hydesville, New York, which we shall examine in a moment. But long before anyone outside New York had heard of the Fox family, a book about 'spirits' was creating a sensation on the other side of the Atlantic. It was called *The Night Side of Nature*, and its authoress was an Edinburgh housewife named Catherine Crowe, who had already achieved a modest success with novels like *Susan Hopley* and *Lily Dawson*. *The Night Side of Nature*—subtitled 'Ghosts and Ghost Seers'—made her a celebrity, and went on to become one of the most influential books of the 19th century.

Regrettably, Mrs Crowe did not enjoy her success for long. In 1859, she produced a treatise called 'Spiritualism and the Age We Live In'—which, according to the *Dictionary of National Biography*, evinced 'a morbid and despondent turn of mind', and soon after this she went insane—a fate her contemporaries must have felt she had invited by her interest in such macabre subjects. She recovered, but wrote little between then and her death in 1876. *The Night Side of Nature* remained as popular as ever, and was still on sale on railway bookstalls (price two shillings) at the turn of the century.

The author of the piece in the *Dictionary of National Biography* was clearly not a believer in ghosts and ghost seers; for while he admits that the book is 'one of the best collections of supernatural stories in our language', he then attacks Mrs Crowe for being 'extremely credulous and uncritical'. The reproach is unfair; the book would not have become so influential if it had been merely a collection of ghost stories. What the Victorians liked about it was its air of sturdy commonsense, and its attempts to treat the phenomena with detachment. It would be more than thirty years before scientific investigators approached the supernatural in a spirit of systematic research. But Mrs Crowe did her best, citing letters and documents and offering names of witnesses and dates.

The book that inspired *The Night Side of Nature* was another nineteenth-century bestseller called *The Seeress of Prevorst*. It was written by Dr Justinus A.C. Kerner, a rich and eccentric doctor who was also a well-known poet and song-writer. In 1826, the 40-year-old Kerner was practising in Weinsberg, near Heilbronn, when he was consulted by the relatives of a woman called Friederike Hauffe, who was dying of a wasting disease. She had lost all her teeth and looked like a walking skeleton.

It seemed that marriage was responsible for her sad condition. Ever since childhood she had fallen into trances, seen visions, and conversed with invisible spirits. She could also accurately predict the future. When she was nineteen, she had married a cousin, and gone into depression; at twenty, her first child was born, and she began to develop hysterical symptoms. Every evening, she fell into a trance in which she saw spirits of the dead.

Kerner was at first inclined to be sceptical about her visions and spirits—he put them down to hysteria. Yet he found Friederike Hauffe a fascinating case for study. She claimed to be able to see into the human body, and certainly had a remarkably precise knowledge of the nervous system. She could read with her stomach—Kerner tested her by making her lie down with her eyes closed, and laid documents on her bare midriff; she read them perfectly. She could make geometrical drawings at great speed, even in the dark, and could draw perfect circles that looked as if they had been drawn by compasses. She claimed that her spirit often left her body and hovered above it.

Kerner tried ordinary medicines on her, but they had no effect. Friederike told him that if he placed her in a 'magnetic trance' the spirits would instruct him on how to treat her, but he was reluctant to accept this advice. Eventually, he decided that he might as well try the effects of mesmerism.

Friederike reacted well to 'magnetism', passing easily into a trance. But Kerner remained sceptical about the things she said in this condition. Then, one day, a remarkable experience changed his mind. Friederike declared that she was being haunted by an unpleasant man with a squint. From her description, Kerner recognised him as a man who had died a few years earlier. It seemed, according to Friederike, that the man was suffering from a guilty conscience. He had been involved in embezzlement and, after his death, another man had been blamed. Now he wanted to clear the man's name, for the sake of his widow. This could be done by means of a certain document, which would be found in a chest. The spirit 'showed' Friederike the room where the document was to be found, and a man who was working there. Her description was so good that Kerner was able to identify him as a certain Judge Heyd. In her 'vision', Friederike had seen Judge Heyd sitting in a certain place in this room, and the chest containing the document on the table. The document was apparently not in its proper numerical order, which is why it had not been found.

When Kerner told him about his patient's vision, Judge Heyd was astounded; he *had* been sitting in the position described on that particular day (Christmas Day), and the chest, contrary to regulations, had been left open on the table. When they searched, the document turned up where Friederike had said it would. The widow of the man who had been wrongly accused was able to obtain redress.

From now on, Kerner believed in Friederike's supernatural powers, and took whatever she said seriously. She told him that we are surrounded by spirits all the time, and that she was able to see them. These spirits often try to attract our attention in various ways: knocking, movement of objects, throwing of sand. And by way of convincing him, Friederike persuaded one of the spirits to make rapping noises, to make gravel and ash fall from the air, and to make a stool float up into the air. Kerner watched with amazement as the stool rose gently, then floated down again.

Friederike provided him with further proof of the accuracy of her visions when she succeeded in putting an end to a haunting. Kerner heard about a house where the ghost of an old man was frightening the inhabitants. He brought one of them, a woman, along to see Friederike; the seeress went into a trance and explained that the ghost was that of a man called Bellon, who was an 'earth-bound spirit' as a result of defrauding two orphans. Kerner made enquiries, but no one had ever heard of a man called Bellon. But since the ghost claimed that he had been Burgomeister, it seemed probable that some record existed. He claimed he had been Burgomeister in the year 1700, and had died at the age of 79 Armed with this information, Kerner asked the present mayor to check the legal documents; they soon found that in the year 1700, a man called Bellon *had* been Burgomeister and director of the local orphanage. He had died in 1740 at the age of 79. After 'confessing', the spirit took its departure.

While Friederike was in Kerner's house, there were constant poltergeist phenomena: knocks and raps, noises like the rattling of chains, gravel thrown through the window, and a knitting needle that flew through the air and landed in a glass of water. When Friederike was visited by a spirit one night her sister heard her say: 'Open it yourself', then saw a book on the table open itself. A poltergeist tugged her boots off her feet as she lay on the bed, and threw a lampshade across the room. In the Kerners' bedroom, a table was thrown across the room. The poltergeist threw a stool at a maidservant who went into Friederike's room while she lay asleep. It extinguished a night-light and made a candle glow.

Friederike also produced what would later be called 'spirit teachings', an amazingly complex system of philosophy in which man is described as consisting of body, soul and spirit, and of being surrounded by a nerve aura which carries on the vital processes. She spoke about various cycles in human existence—life cycles (or circles) and sun cycles, corresponding to various spiritual conditions. She also described a remarkable universal language from ancient times, said to be 'the language of the inner life'. (A mystical sect was founded to expound those doctrines after her death.)

All these mediumistic activities made Friederike more and more feeble, and she died in 1829 at the age of 28. Kerner's book *The Seeress of Prevorst* (the name of the Swabian village *where* she was born) created a sensation.

In the second half of the 19th century, as the scientific reaction against spiritualism increased, *The Seeress of Prevorst* ceased to be taken seriously by those engaged in psychical research, and by the 20th century it had been virtually forgotten. Writing about it in his *Modern Spiritualism* (1902), the sceptical Frank Podmore—who believed that all poltergeists are due to naughty children—dismisses most of the evidence as second-hand, while another eminent researcher, E.J. Dingwall (writing in *Abnormal Hypnotic Phenomena*) seems to feel that Kerner was stupid to take her claims seriously, and that if he had remained sceptical and treated her simply as a case of hysteria, she would have lived longer. But reading Kerner's own account, it is difficult to see how he would have remained sceptical without being downright dishonest or blind; on one occasion, he saw a cloudy figure hovering in front of her, and although it had vanished when he came back with a lamp, Friederike continued to stare at the spot as though listening to it.

In fact, we can see that the case of the seeress of Prevorst is a thoroughly typical case of poltergeist phenomena caused by a medium. In detail after detail, it sounds like any number of other cases of 'haunting'. If anyone killed Friederike Hauffe, it was the spirits themselves, who must have been using her energy to manifest themselves. No doubt the poltergeist phenomena were unspectacular because Friederike was weak from the moment Kerner set eyes on her. (In a case cited by the novelist William de Morgan, a maidservant who was able to cause rapping noises gradually lost her powers as she became weaker from tuberculosis.)

In another of his books, Kerner describes another remarkable case with some of the characteristics of poltergeist haunting. He was asked to treat a 'possessed' peasant girl in Orlach, near Stuttgart. For some reason which is not clear, she was persecuted by 'spirits' from the age of twenty, and there were the usual bangs and crashes, movements of furniture, and even outbreaks of fire. Then, after five months of this, she saw two ghosts, one of a nun dressed in white, the other of a monk dressed in black. The nun asserted that she had been smuggled into the monastery disguised as a cook, and had had two children by the black monk, both of whom he had killed at birth. He also murdered three monks during the four-year period she was with him; and, when he suspected she was about to betray him, he killed her too. The black monk also spoke to the possessed girl, saying that he was the son of a nobleman from nearby Geislingen, and that as the Superior at the monastery of Orlach, he had seduced a number of nuns and killed the children they bore. He also confessed to killing monks. The bodies, he said, he threw into a hole in a wall.

The white nun told the girl that her sufferings would cease only if her parents agreed to their cottage's demolition. By this time they were so desperate that they agreed. On March 5, 1833 the house was finally demolished. Most of the walls were made of mud, but one corner was constructed of limestone, obviously part of a far older building. When this was pulled down, they found underneath it an empty well containing a number of human bones, including those of children. The girl's possession ceased from the moment the wall collapsed.

The story sounds like a typical invention of a German romantic novelist; but Kerner devotes a whole book to it, describing it in the same detail as his investigation of Friederike Hauffe. In spite of this, modern investigators are inclined not to take it seriously. Yet readers who are impressed by the clarity and detail of Kerner's reporting may feel that this case of the possessed girl of Orlach is one of the most convincing arguments for the close connection between poltergeists and spirits of the dead.

Ten years after publication of *The Seeress of Prevorst*, another doctor—this time of philosophy—produced an equally remarkable account of a case of possession, this time benevolent. In *Die Schutzgeister (The Guardian Spirit*, 1839), Heinrich Werner identifies his 18-year-old subject only as 'R.O'. Like Friederike, she had been subject to all kinds of illnesses, then, at a certain point, found herself haunted by spirits. One day the girl fell into a trance; and from then on she was able to do so at will, and to supply Werner with all kinds of information obtained 'clairvoyantly'. She had a guardian spirit called Albert, who seems to have acted rather like the 'spirit guide' of later mediums. And the spirit who caused her so much trouble was—again—a wicked monk. One day, when the girl claimed that the wicked monk was present in the room, Werner was puzzled to hear an odd sound coming from a small table—like a cup rattling on a saucer. This occurred a number of times, becoming steadily louder (a typical characteristic of poltergeist noises); R.O. said that the monk was producing the noise, and was delighted at Werner's astonishment—which also sounds typical of a poltergeist.

One day, Werner was startled to hear a loud crash from an empty room; he rushed in to find that two large flowerpots, which had stood on the windowsill, had been hurled to the floor so violently that there was earth all over the room. The blind was closed and there was no breeze. One of the curtains had also been twisted around a birdcage. Later that day, Werner went to call on R.O., who went into a trance, and then told Werner that the black monk had been responsible for smashing the flowerpots (Werner had not mentioned this to her). Albert, apparently, had ejected him from the house.

Werner was greatly impressed by his patient's clairvoyant powers. She demonstrated these one day when she woke up from a trance and told him that she had seen herself driving in a green-lacquered chaise. Now Werner had, at the time, made some enquiries about a chaise that was for sale in a town some fifteen hours away, and he expected to get an answer in about a week. R.O. told him he would hear much sooner than that—in fact, the following afternoon; she also went on to describe the chaise, in some detail. The following afternoon, Werner received a message about the chaise, and discovered that the girl was right in every detail.

Her most dramatic piece of clairvoyance concerned her younger sister. One day, in a trance, she cried out 'Albert, help me! Emilie is falling down into the street.' Then, after a short period, she said: 'Thank God, help has already come!'

Asked what had happened, she explained that her little sister had been leaning out of a top-storey window, trying to grab a rope suspended from a winch above the window; she had been on the point of falling when her father had entered the room and pulled her back.

Werner contacted the father to ask if anything remarkable had happened on that particular day, and received a reply which Werner printed in his book; it said that the father had been sitting in his office when he had felt uneasy. He went home, and went upstairs, in time to find his daughter had leaned too far out of the window to catch the rope, and could not get back into the room; he grabbed her dress and hauled her back in. R.O. said that it was Albert, the guardian spirit, who had made her father feel uneasy.

The cases described by Justinus Kerner and Heinrich Werner excited widepread interest in Europe, and led to much serious discussion. Catherine Crowe read it and was deeply impressed. When her translation appeared in 1845, it aroused as much interest as it had in Germany. And it convinced Mrs Crowe of the reality of the supernatural.

So far, she had been the disciple of a famous Edinburgh doctor George Combe, Britain's most famous exponent of phrenology—the doctrine that a man's character can be read through the bumps on his skull—and Combe was a determined sceptic about ghosts and such matters. Kerner—and Friederike—made her a convert. It now came to her as a revelation that the 'scientific spirit' had gone too far. 'Because, in the 17th century, credulity outran reason and discretion, the 18th century, by a natural reaction, flung itself into an opposite extreme.' And the 19th century had carried this attitude to the point of absurdity; in fact, it had become a new kind of superstition, refusing to face facts that contradicted its dogmas.

Mrs Crowe was not particularly credulous. She set about unearthing her own facts, and found that they seemed to fit together into a logical pattern. Almost everything she wrote about would later be studied more systematically by parapsychologists, and carefully documented in scientific archives: dreaming of the future, death-bed visions, premonitions of disaster, 'phantasms' of the living and of the dead, poltergeists, spontaneous psychokinesis, even possession. She reproaches contemporary scientists for insisting that the supernatural can be explained in terms of hysteria or nervous derangement, and points out, quite fairly, that they 'arrange the facts to their theory, not their theory to the facts'. What is now needed, she says, is investigation. 'And by *investigation* I do not mean the hasty, captious, angry notice of an unwelcome fact . . . but the slow, modest, pains-taking examination that is content to wait upon nature, and humbly follow out her disclosures, however opposed to preconceived theories or mortifying to human pride.' Here she seems to be echoing a famous remark by Thomas Henry Huxley about the duty of the scientist: 'Sit down before fact as a little child, be prepared to give up every preconceived notion, follow humbly wherever and to whatever abysses nature leads, or you shall learn nothing.' It is interesting to discover that Huxley wrote this sentence in 1860, more than a decade after *The Night Side of Nature*, which was published in 1846; Huxley may, in fact, be echoing Mrs Crowe.

Her aim, she readily admits, is to see whether the evidence proves that some part of man can survive his death. The first step in this direction—and it was later followed by most of her eminent successors, such as Myers and Tyrrell—was to try to show that man possesses powers that cannot be explained by science. She devotes several chapters to dreams and presentiments of the future, and includes a number of experiences gathered from friends:

'Another friend lately dreamt, one Thursday night, that he saw an acquaintance of his thrown from his horse, and that he was lying on the ground with the blood streaming from his face, and was much cut. He mentioned his dream in the morning, and being an entire disbeliever in such phenomena, he was unable to account for the impression it made on his mind. This was so strong that, on Saturday, he could not forebear calling at his friend's house, who he was told was in bed, having been thrown from his horse on the previous day, and much injured about the face.'

If Mrs Crowe had lived to become a member of the Society for Physical Research, she would have gone to the trouble of getting signed statements from her friend, the man who had the accident, and the person he told about the dream the morning after. As a pioneer in the field, she obviously felt that this was unnecessary. Otherwise, it is difficult to fault her method.

Like every writer on the paranormal, she is particularly fascinated by out-of-the-body experiences, for she rightly regards these as potential proof that there is something in man that can exist outside the body. Again, she does her best to offer facts that could be checked:

'The late Mr John Holloway, of the Bank of England, brother to the engraver of that name, related of himself that being one night in bed with his wife and unable to sleep, he had fixed his eyes and thoughts with uncommon intensity on a beautiful star that was shining in at the window, when he suddenly found his spirit released from his body and soaring into that bright sphere. But, instantly seized with anxiety for the anguish of his wife, if she discovered his body apparently dead beside her, he returned and re-entered it with difficulty . . . He described that returning as returning to darkness; and that whilst the spirit was free, he was alternately in the light or in the dark, accordingly as his thoughts were with his wife or with the star. He said that he always avoided anything that could produce a repetition of this accident, the consequences of it being very distressing.'

Mrs Crowe's main problem was that, working mainly from hearsay, she had no simple way of distinguishing the authentic from the inauthentic. A typical example is a case she cites from Heinrich Jung-Stilling. Now Jung-Stilling was a serious investigator of the paranormal, a Professor of Economics, and a follower of the doctrines of Mesmer. He ought to have been a reliable authority. And the story he tells is in many ways a good case of what was later to be called a 'phantasm of the living'. In Philadelphia around the year 1740, says Jung-Stilling, a clairvoyant was approached by the wife of a sea captain, who was anxious because she had not heard from her husband for a long time. The clairvoyant asked her to excuse him, and went into another room. After a while, the woman became impatient, and went and peeped through a crack in the door; the clairvoyant was lying on a sofa, apparently asleep. When he came back, he told her that her husband was alive and well, but had been unable to write to her for various reasons, which he explained. At this moment, he said, the captain was in a coffee-house in London, and would soon be back home.

In due course, the captain returned, and confirmed the reasons that the clairvoyant had given for failing to write. And when he was introduced to the clairvoyant, the husband recognised him as a man he had seen in a London coffee-house on the eve of his departure for America. According to the captain, the man had spoken to him, asked him why he had not written to his wife, and then vanished into the crowd . . .

The clairvoyant's power of 'projecting' himself across the Atlantic brings to mind similar stories of Swedenborg bringing messages from the dead. His appearance in a London coffee-house has dozens of parallels in *Phantasms of the Living*, compiled in the 1880s by members of the Society for Psychical Research. What rings totally false here is the information that the captain spoke to him and explained why he had failed to write to his wife. There are hundreds of recorded cases of 'projection', but in very few (I can recall only one[1]) does the 'phantasm' actually talk to anybody. When we learn that these events supposedly took place in 1740—the year Jung-Stilling was born—it becomes clear that, even if basically true, the story had probably been 'improved' in the telling. Mrs Crowe had no way of knowing that the story failed to conform to the general pattern of 'phantasms of the living' because in her day there had not been enough research for the pattern to emerge.

In view of this difficulty, Mrs Crowe did remarkably well, and her book deserved its high reputation. Most of her conjectures would do credit to a modern investigator, and, in many ways, her 'credibility' was often far ahead of her time. She cites a story from another early researcher, Joseph Ennemoser:

1. In *Autobiography of a Yogi* by Parahansa Yogananda, the author describes how a visiting Yogi had told him that a friend was on his way. When the friend arrived, he told of how the Yogi had approached him in the street, and mentioned that Parahansa was waiting for him in his room. At the time this happened, the Yogi had been with Parahansa. From the point of view of a psychical investigator, the case is dubious because we have only the author's word for it.

'It appears that Van Helmont, having asserted that it was possible for a man to extinguish the life of a an animal by the eye alone (*oculis intentis*), Rousseau, the naturalist, repeated the experiment when in the East, and in this manner killed several toads; but on a subsequent occasion, whilst trying the same experiment at Lyons, the animal, on finding it could not escape, fixed its eyes immovably on him, so that he fell into a fainting fit, and was thought to be dead . . .'

This is the kind of tale that makes us smile sarcastically; we know that these stories of the hypnotic power of snakes and other creatures are old wives' tales. Yet we have already noted the recent investigations of Dr Ferenc András Völgyesi, who devoted many years to studying hypnosis in men and animals, and arrived at some interesting conclusions. He observed—and photographed—dozens of cases in which snakes 'fascinated' rabbits or rats and then ate them. He also observed many cases of 'battles of wills' between the snake and its potential victims—his book contains photographs of a giant anaconda 'fascinating' a rat, and a python immobilising a hare. Another shows a battle of wills between a bird, the *cucullus senegalensis*, and a rattlesnake. He states: 'The battle, which begins with a mutual fixing of the gaze, usually ends in victory for the bird.' Another photograph shows a toad winning a battle of wills with a cobra. Nor let us forget his description of the battle between two lizards; they confronted one another for about ten minutes, gazing intently at one another (as Mrs Crowe says, *oculis intentis*), then one slowly ate the other, which remained immobile. Van Helmont's tale about killing animals with the gaze may be an exaggeration, but it is based on an observed reality.

As we have seen, there is a great deal in the literature of hypnosis to support Mrs Crowe's view that it involves the deliberate use of some mental force. We may recall that in 1885 the French psychologist Pierre Janet observed the experiments of a doctor named Gibert, who could induce hypnosis in a patient called Leonie by merely thinking about her, and summon her from the other side of Le Havre by the same means. In the 1890s, Dr Paul Joire caused blindfolded and hypnotised patients to obey his mental commands, and the same kind of experiments were repeated in the 1920s by the Russian scientist L. L. Vasiliev, who described them in a book called *Experiments in Distant Influence*; it leaves no possible doubt that some kind of mental force *can* be exercised at a distance.

What fascinated Mrs Crowe was the clear implication that human powers are far greater than we realise. If people can leave their bodies and witness things that are going on elsewhere, if a hypnotised subject can describe things that are happening in the street, if a girl can turn into a human magnet, if a man can dream accurately about the future—then materialistic science must be somehow fundamentally mistaken about our human limitations. Mrs Crowe had translated *The Seeress of Prevorst*, and it was perfectly clear to her that unless Kerner was an out-and-out liar, then something *very* queer was going on. This was not the second-hand reporting of spooks and spectres, as in Jung-Stilling's *Pneumatology*; this was first-hand reporting by a man who had no reason to lie or deceive himself. Kerner described—and Mrs Crowe cites in *The Night Side of Nature*—how Friederike had awakened one night crying 'Oh, God!', and how a doctor who was sitting near the corpse of her father, many miles away, clearly heard the exclamation, and rushed into the room to see if the corpse had come to life. This was not a question of spirits; it was some curious power possessed by Friederike herself. And while such powers seem to be beyond the control of the individual who exercises them, Mrs Crowe could see that there is no earthly reason why this should always be so. That is why the hard-headed Victorians found her book so exciting. Their explorers were penetrating new continents, their railways were stretching to the ends of the earth, their industries were creating new wealth, their science was uncovering the secrets of the universe. And if Mrs Crowe was correct, a new science of the 'supernatural' would demonstrate that man himself was a far more extraordinary creature then he had ever suspected. Her book was not a morbid collection of tales-to-make-the-flesh-creep, but a work of buoyant optimism about human potentialities.

Unfortunately, a Victorian lady novelist was hardly the person to persuade scientists that they were ignoring an important subject. The Victorians had fought hard for their intellectual freedom. Witches were still being executed in the 1690s; as late as the 1750s, the Church forced the great naturalist Buffon to withdraw his statement that the earth was a fragment of the sun, and that fossils were the remains of primitive ancestors of present-day creatures. By 1800, intellectuals were utterly sick of the authority the Church had been exercising for centuries. They longed to see the downfall of these ecclesiastical bullies. So every time someone dared to challenge the intellectual authority of the Church, cheers echoed throughout Europe. In 1830, two years after *The Night Side of Nature* was published, the German theologian Ludwig Feuerbach produced a book, *Thoughts on Death and Immortality*, in which he dismissed the idea of a personal God, and jeered at the desire for immortality as selfish stupidity. Feuerbach was persecuted by the police and forced to give up his post at the university. Ten years later, Feuerbach published a far more radical book, *The Essence of Christianity*, which landed like a bombshell and frightened even the freethinkers; he declared that God and immortality were dangerous delusions, and that man has to learn to live in the present instead of wasting his time dreaming about a non-existent heaven. (The book had a deep influence on Karl Marx, who expressed its basic message in the phrase 'Religion is the opium of the people'.) In his novel *Green Heinrich*, the Swiss poet Gottfried Keller describes Feuerbach as 'a magician in the shape of a bird who sang God out of the hearts of thousands'. And the same book has a portrait of a schoolteacher who has lost his job because he is an atheist, but who travels around Germany exclaiming: 'Isn't it a joy to be alive?', and 'forever marvelling at the glory of being free from the encumbrance' of God.

This is why the scientists and philosophers were not willing to pay attention to the evidence for the 'supernatural'. They were too delighted to see the Church getting a black eye, and had no intention of letting religion sneak in again by the back door. So when Catherine Crowe began her book by admitting that she wanted to prove the reality of man's immortal soul, most of them read no further. Whether Mrs Crowe intended it or not, she was giving aid and comfort to the enemy.

In fact, in the year *The Night Side of Nature* was published, this particular enemy was preparing to mount a full-frontal assault . . .

With the wisdom of hindsight, we can see that the most interesting and significant pages of *The Night Side of Nature* are those that concern the haunting of a house owned by an industrialist named Joshua Proctor. Here Mrs Crowe presents the kind of carefully documented account that would be the aim of the later investigators of the Society for Psychical Research. This is the true stuff of psychical research. She prefaces the account with a letter from Joshua Proctor to herself, vouching for the accuracy of the details of the report that follows.

The haunted house was a millhouse; it had been built only forty years earlier, in 1800. The newly-built Newcastle and Shields railway passed overhead on a viaduct. In June 1840, news reached the outside world that the Proctor family—who were Quakers—had been disturbed by knocking noises, and had seen some unpleasant things. A surgeon named Edward Drury, who practised in Sunderland, heard about the haunting from a local farmer. Dr Drury was sceptical about such matters. Nevertheless, he had been fascinated by the account of a famous poltergeist haunting at Epworth, in the rectory of the Rev. Samuel Wesley, grandfather of the founder of Methodism (see Chapter 6). This spook, known as Old Jeffrey, had banged and groaned around the rectory for two months in 1716. There were sounds of heavy breathing, breaking glass, footsteps, and various unidentifiable noises. The Rev. Samuel noticed that the disturbances seemed in some way connected with his 19-year-old daughter Hetty, who trembled in her sleep before the sounds began. The scientist Joseph Priestley had investigated the case, and decided it was a hoax. Dr Drury was inclined to agree with him; so when he heard of the 'haunting' of Willington Mill, he wrote to its owner, Joshua Proctor, offering to 'unravel the mystery' (that is, expose the hoaxer). Mr Proctor replied politely, saying that he and his family were going away on a visit on the date Mr Drury had suggested; one of his employees was going to act as caretaker while they were away. Nevertheless, if Drury wanted to come and stay overnight, he was welcome.

Dr Drury decided to take a friend along for moral support. He also took a brace of pistols, intending to allow one of them to fall on the floor, as if by accident, to deter any practical joker. But when he arrived, he found that Joshua Proctor had returned—alone—from his holiday, and Mr Proctor was so obviously an honest man that Drury decided the 'accident' was unnecessary.

What happened to Edward Drury that night convinced him completely of the reality of the supernatural. It also gave him such a fright that he went partially deaf in one ear and suffered a temporary breakdown in health. He seems to have been too shattered to describe what he had seen immediately afterwards, but he promised to write Mr Proctor a letter with a full account. This letter was written on July 13, 1840, ten days after his night in the haunted millhouse.

He arrived with his friend, T. Hudson, and was made welcome by Mr Proctor, who showed him over the house. At eleven o'clock, Dr Drury and Mr Hudson settled down on the third-story landing outside the 'haunted room'. (Although he says he 'expected to account for any noises that he might hear in a philosophical manner', he presumably decided that discretion was the better part of valour.) About an hour later, they heard pattering noises, 'as if a number of people were pattering with their bare feet'. Then there was a knocking sound from the floorboards at their feet, as if someone was rapping with his knuckles. After this, they heard a 'hollow cough' from the haunted room, but seem to have decided not to investigate. Then they heard a rustling noise, as if someone was coming upstairs.

At a quarter to one, feeling cold, Dr Drury said he thought he would retire to bed; Mr Hudson said he intended to stay up until dawn. Drury looked at his watch, and noted the time. As he looked up, he saw a closet door open, and 'the figure of a female, attired in greyish garments, with the head inclining downwards, and one hand pressed upon the chest, as if in pain' walking towards him. Mr Hudson was fast asleep, but was awakened by Drury's 'awful yell'. Drury rushed at the figure, 'but instead of grasping it, I fell upon my friend, and I recollected nothing distinctly for nearly three hours afterwards. I have since learnt that I was carried down stairs in an agony of fear and terror.'

Mrs Crowe not only publishes the full correspondence between Dr Drury and Joshua Proctor, but an account by a local historian, another by the owner of a local journal, and descriptions by four other people who had seen the ghost. In fact, there seemed to be more than one; there was also a man in a surplice who glided across a second-floor room at a distance of a few feet from the floor. The local historian adds to his account the information that Mr Proctor has recently discovered an old book that states that similar hauntings had taken place in an older house that had been built on the same spot two hundred years before. Mrs Crowe ends her account by mentioning that Mr Proctor has now decided to leave the house, and turn it into 'small tenements' for his workpeople.

What makes this report so interesting is that the case resembles in so many respects the 'haunting' that would occur eight years later in Hydesville, New York, and that would launch the Spiritualism movement of the 19th century. In Willington, as in Hydesville, there was a mixture of 'poltergeist' phenomena and the more conventional type of haunting. If Dr Drury had shown the same kind of courage and curiosity shown later by Mrs Margaret Fox at Hydesville, it seems highly probable that the Spiritualist movement would have been launched ten years earlier in England.

The Hydesville affair began on March 31, 1848, in a wooden frame house inhabited by a Methodist farmer named James D. Fox, his wife Margaret, and their two daughters, Margaretta, aged 14, and Kate, aged 12. Hydesville is a small township not far from Rochester, New York. James Fox had moved into the house in the previous December. A previous tenant, Michael Weekman, had been disturbed by various loud knocks, for which he could find no cause.

The Fox family was also kept awake by various banging noises in the last days of March 1848; but since it was a windy month, they were not unduly disturbed. On Friday March 31, the family decided to retire early to make up for lost sleep. Mr Fox went round the house checking the shutters and sashes. The children observed that when he shook the sashes, to see how loose they were, banging noises seemed to reply like an echo.

The whole family slept in two beds in the same room. Just before the parents came to bed, the rapping noises started again. Kate said cheekily: 'Mr Splitfoot, do as I do', and began snapping her fingers. To the amazement of the girls, the raps imitated her. Margaret interrupted: 'Do as I do', and began to clap. Again, the sounds imitated her. Remembering that the next day would be April the first, the children decided that someone was playing a joke. In her account of what happened, Mrs Fox wrote:

'I then thought I could put a test that no one in the place could answer. I asked the noise to rap my different children's ages, successively. Instantly, each one of my children's ages was given correctly, pausing between them sufficiently long to individualise them until the seventh [child], at which a longer pause was made, and then three more emphatic little raps were given, corresponding to the age of the little one that died . . .'

Now rather frightened—this was evidently no joke—Mrs Fox asked if it was a human being who was making the raps; there was no reply. 'Is it a spirit? If it is, make two raps.' Two thunderous bangs followed, so loud that the house shook. She asked if it was an 'injured spirit', and again the bangs shook the house. Further questioning revealed that the knocker was a man who died at the age of 31, that he had been murdered in the house, and that he had a wife and five children. Mrs Fox asked if the spirit had any objection to her calling in the neighbours; the raps replied: 'No.'

The Foxes summoned in about fourteen neighbours. One of these was a man called William Duesler, who assured his own wife that the whole thing was ridiculous and that there could be nothing mysterious about the noises. When he got there, some of the neighbours were too nervous to go into the bedroom, but Duesler was not worried. He went and sat on the bed, and was astonished when Mrs Fox's questions were answered with a rapping noise that made the bed vibrate. (Later writers were to insist that the two children made all the noises by cracking their joints; but it is hard to see how the cracking of joints could make the house shake and cause a bed to vibrate.)

Duesler took up the questioning of the 'spirit'. By a code of knocks, he established that the entity was a man who had been murdered in the house, a pedlar named Charles B. Rosma, who had been attacked for the $500 he carried. The murder had taken place five years earlier, and had been committed by the man who was then the tenant of the house, a Mr Bell. A maid named

Lucretia Pulver later confirmed that a pedlar *had* spent the night in the house, and that she had been sent home; when she returned the next day, the pedlar had gone.

As news of these amazing occurrences spread throughout the community, hundreds of people came to the house. On Sunday, April 2, Duesler learned from the murdered man that his body had been buried in the cellar. This seemed to offer a method of verification, and James Fox and his neighbours took shovels to the cellar—which had an earth floor—and proceeded to dig. At a depth of three feet they encountered water, and abandoned the attempt. But in July, when the water had gone down, they dug again, and at a depth of five feet found a plank; underneath this, in quicklime, there was some human hair and a few bones.

Mr Bell, on being heard that he had been accused of murder by a ghost, indignantly denied it, and produced a testimonial to his good character from his new neighbours in Lyon, New York. The spirit had already prophesied that the murderer would never be brought to justice.

In his account of the case in *Modern Spiritualism*, the sceptical Frank Podmore comments: 'No corroborative evidence of the supposed murder, or even of the existence of the man supposed to have been murdered, was ever obtained.' This was written in 1902. Two years later, in November 1904, a wall in the cellar of the Fox house collapsed, revealing another wall behind it. Digging between the two walls uncovered a skeleton and a pedlar's tin box. It looked as if someone had dug up the body from its original grave and interred it next to the wall, then built another wall to confuse searchers.

In those days immediately after the first manifestations, a committee was set up to collect the statements of witnesses. Not all the investigators were convinced that the sounds had a supernatural origin; but no one suggested that the Fox family could be responsible. With the family all together in the same room, it was obviously impossible that either the parents or the children could be causing the bangs.

What everyone soon noticed was that nothing happened unless the children were in the house—particularly Kate. A committee of sceptical Rochester citizens came to the house to investigate; they agreed that Margaret was certainly not responsible. A second, a

124

third investigation produced the same result. The children were stripped and searched to see if they had some mechanical device for producing the sounds; there was nothing. They were made to stand on pillows with their ankles tied; still the raps occurred.

The children were separated; Kate was sent to stay with her elder sister Leah in Rochester, and Margaretta with her brother David in Auburn. The 'spirits' followed them both. Rapping noises were heard, and people felt themselves touched by invisible hands. In Leah's house, a lodger called Calvin Brown took a mildly satirical attitude towards the spirit, and it began to persecute him, throwing things at him. Mrs Fox's cap was pulled off and the comb pulled out of her hair. When members of the family knelt to pray, pins were jabbed into them. In brother David's boarding house, similar things were happening. It was clear that the murdered pedlar was not responsible for all this—he was back in the Hydesville house, making terrifying gurgling noises and sounds like a body being dragged across the floor. Mrs Fox's hair turned white. One spirit who communicated with Kate claimed to be a dead relative named Jacob Smith. Sister Leah Fish discovered that she could also communicate with the spirits, and began producing messages. One 16-year-old girl named Harriet Bebee, who visited the house in Auburn and witnessed the rapping noises, returned to her home miles away and found that the noises had followed her.

The Fox family moved to Rochester, but the manifestations continued. Sometimes the bangs were so loud that they could be heard miles away. Poltergeists had apparently taken over from the original 'injured spirit'. One day, a visitor named Isaac Post started asking the spirit questions, and was answered by a thunderous barrage of knocks. Then, by means of an alphabetical code, the 'spirit' spelled out a message: 'Dear friends, you must proclaim this truth to the world. This is the dawning of a new era; you must not try to conceal it any longer. God will protect you and good spirits will watch over you.' And now began a series of manifestations that were to become typical of 'Spiritualism'.[1] Tables moved and rapped with their legs;

1. When I speak of Spiritualism with a capital 'S', I refer to the 'religion' of that name; spiritualism with a small 's' denotes simply the belief in spirits or life after death.

musical instruments were played by unseen fingers, objects moved round the room. The 'spirits' intimated that they would prefer to manifest themselves in the dark—which confirmed the sceptics in their opinion. But other believers decided it was time to put the 'spirit''s injunction into operation and 'proclaim this truth to the world'. On November 14, 1849, the first Spiritualist meeting took place in the Corinthian hall in Rochester.

In his account of the haunting of Willington Mill, the local historian, M. A. Richardson, had remarked:

'Were we to draw an inference from the number of cases of reported visitations from the invisible world that have been made public of late, we might be led to imagine that the days of supernatural agency were about to recommence, and that ghosts and hobgoblins were about to resume their sway over the fears of mankind.'

For 1840, that was a remarkably perceptive observation. Whether it was merely due to improved communications and the increase in the number of newspapers, it *does* seem clear that there was an apparent increase in ghostly manifestations at about this period. In retrospect, it looks oddly as if the 'spirits' had decided that the time had come to make themselves noticed. Of course, there had been such manifestations for centuries—the Elizabethan astrologer Dr John Dee devoted a large book to an account of his communications with spirits through the agency of a 'scryer' (or, as they later came to be called, medium) called Edward Kelley. Cases like the Epworth poltergeist, the Stockwell poltergeist (described by Mrs Crowe), the Cock Lane ghost and the phantom drummer of Tedworth had aroused widespread excitement and been the subject of contemporary pamphlets. In 1847, a young American shoemaker named Andrew Jackson Davis was placed under hypnosis and wrote an extraordinary and erudite work called *The Principles of Nature* which subsequently became a literary sensation. In this remarkable book, Davis prophesies that 'the truth about spirits will ere long present itself in the form of a living demonstration, and the world will hail with delight the ushering in of that era when the interiors of men will be opened'. Within four years of its publication, Spiritualism had spread across America and was sweeping Europe.

For whatever reason, the Fox sisters began a Spiritualist explosion. People discovered that all they had to do was to sit in a darkened room, preferably with a 'medium' present—someone who had already established a communication with the spirits—and the manifestations would usually follow immediately. No apparatus was required, except possibly a few musical instruments. In the Rochester area, more than a hundred 'mediums' appeared in the year 1850. In Buffalo, New York, two brothers and a sister named Davenport attended a seance at which the Fox sisters produced their manifestations, and decided to try it themselves—in fact, inexplicable raps and bangs had sounded in their home in the year 1846, two years before the Hydesville manifestations. When Ira, William and Elizabeth Davenport sat in a darkened room, with their hands on a tabletop, the table began to move, raps were heard all over the room, and when Ira picked up a pencil his hand began to write automatically. A few nights later, with witnesses present, all three children were seen to levitate into the air. At their fifth 'seance', Ira was instructed—by means of raps—to fire a pistol in the corner of the room. As it exploded, it was taken from his hand, and by the light of the flash, a figure of a man was seen holding it. He vanished a moment later, and the pistol fell to the floor. The man introduced himself—through the code of raps—as John King; he was one of the first examples of a 'control' (or master of ceremonies), who acted as intermediary between the medium and the 'spirits'. 'John King' was soon taking over the brothers directly and speaking through their mouths. The Davenport brothers went on to become even more famous than the Fox sisters.

In Dover, Ohio, a well-to-do farmer named Jonathan Koons discovered his own talents as a medium by sitting in a dark room and going into a trance. The 'spirits' who spoke through him told him that all his eight children were gifted mediums. They instructed him to build a special house made of logs, sixteen feet by twelve, to be used exclusively for spiritualist activities. There were large numbers of musical instruments—drums, triangles, tambourines, a banjo, an accordion, a harp, a guitar, and so on. The room was dimly lighted by sheets of wet paper smeared with phosphorus. When the mediums—usually Koons and his 18-year-old son Nahum—were seated at a small table—with the audience on benches—Koons would play the violin, and the spirits would soon join in, producing the effect of a full orchestra. Witnesses also speak of a heavenly choir joining in. The racket was impressive, and could be heard a mile away. A voice would then deliver a homily, using a speaking trumpet, which floated in the air. A spirit hand floated round the room, touching people and shaking their hands. People came from all over the county to witness these marvels, and the spirits impressed everyone by producing information about strangers that none of the audience could have known.

This was, in fact, one of the most convincing things about the 'spirits'; they seemed to have access to all kinds of information. In Boston, the wife of a newspaper editor, Mrs W. R. Hayden, startled the wife of the English mathematician, Augustus de Morgan, by giving her detailed messages from dead friends about whom she could not possibly have known. The result was that Mrs de Morgan invited her to England, where she held seances under 'test conditions' in the de Morgans' home. She was loudly ridiculed by the English newspapers, who were convinced that this latest American craze must be based on fraud and deception (which the British were too sensible to swallow), but she convinced most of those who actually saw her. And respectable members of the British middle classes who tried 'table-turning' to while away the long evenings were amazed to discover that it actually worked. One journalist wrote a few years later: 'In those days you were invited to "Tea and Table Moving" as a new excitement, and made to revolve with the family like mad round articles of furniture.' Even Queen Victoria and Prince Albert tried it at Osborne, and the table moved so convincingly that the queen had no doubt whatever that no trickery was involved—she decided that the answer must lie in some form of electricity or magnetism.

The French were more than prepared to adopt this new form of entertainment, for half a century of controversy about Mesmer—who had taught that healing, clairvoyance and other such mysteries were due to a mysterious force called 'Animal Magnetism'—had accustomed them to strange phenomena; by 1851, table-turning had become the latest craze. And the spirits soon made a highly influential convert. He was a 50-year-old educationalist named Denizard-Hyppolyte-Leon Rivail, who was to become famous under the name Allan Kardec. Rivail had been a pupil of the celebrated educator Pestalozzi, and he had opened his own school at the age of 24. He had written popular books on arithmetic, grammar, spelling, how to calculate in your head, and educational reform, and given immensely successful courses of free lectures on astronomy, chemistry, physics and anatomy. He was also an enthusiastic student of phrenology and Animal Magnetism.

It was in May 1855 that Rivail attended a hypnotic session with a certain Madame Roger, who was placed in a trance by her 'magnetiser', M. Fortier, and was able to read minds and perform other puzzling feats. There Rivail met a certain Madame Plainemaison, who told him that even stranger phenomena were taking place regularly at her house in the rue Grange-Bateliere. Rivail agree to go, and was amazed by what he saw. The tables did more than merely 'turn'; they also jumped and ran about the room. The disciple of Mesmer felt that these phenomena challenged the powers of reason to which he had devoted his life, and he determined to try to get to the bottom of it. At Madame Plainemaison's, he met a man named Baudin, who told him that his two daughters practised automatic writing. The young ladies seem to have discovered their powers accidentally, in the course of entertaining their friends with table-turning; they were, says one commentator, 'of a worldly and frivolous disposition'. This did not deter the serious-minded Rivail, who proceeded to ask the table major philosophical questions. Asked if mankind would ever understand the first principles of the universe, it replied, 'No. There are things that cannot be understood by man in this world.' When Rivail asked if matter had always existed, the table replied (perhaps a trifle wearily), 'God only knows.'

It was obvious to Rivail that the entities who were communicating were genuine spirits, not the unconscious minds of the young ladies. (Even in those days, the concept of the unconscious was accepted.) In fact, the communicators identified themselves as 'spirits of genii', and said that some of them (but not all) had been the spirits of those who had been alive on earth.

With excitement, Rivail realised that this material had an impressive inner-consistency, and that the total pattern revealed a philosophical scheme that embraced the whole universe. Other friends who had been collecting 'automatic scripts'—including the playwright Sardou—handed over their own material to Rivail—more than fifty notebooks. And Rivail was told to bring all this material together into a book, which should be called *The Spirits' Book*. The spirits even gave Rivail the pseudonym under which he should publish the work: Allan Kardec; both of these names—according to the spirits—were names he had borne in previous incarnations.

The message of *The Spirits' Book* is easily summarised. Man is a fourfold being, made up of body, 'vital principle' (aura), intelligent soul and spiritual soul—the divisions we have already encountered in the *Seeress of Prevorst*. Spirits are intelligent beings, who constitute the 'population of the universe'. Man is a spirit enclosed in a physical body. The destiny of all spirits is to evolve towards perfection. There are three basic categories of spirit: the 'low spirits', who are trapped in materiality, the 'second degree spirits', whose moral nature has evolved to the point where they experience only a desire for good, and the 'perfect spirits', who have reached the peak of their evolution. The 'low spirits' range from evil spirits who are activated by malice to mere 'boisterous spirits' who enjoy getting into mischief. These latter are also known as poltergeists. After death, a spirit spends some time in the spirit world, and is then reincarnated on earth or some other world. The purpose of earthly life is to enable the spirit to evolve. To some extent, the spirit is able to choose the trials it will undergo in its next life. (This means that it is pointless to bemoan our lot, since we have chosen it ourselves.)

The Spirits' Book appeared in 1856, and created a sensation. Kardec became the founder-figure of the French spiritualist movement, and his works attained immense influence. But he died of a heart attack only thirteen years after the book was published, at the age of 65, and his influence was soon being widely questioned by the movement. Rivail was totally committed to the doctrine of reincarnation, the slow perfection of the spirit through a series of rebirths, which can be traced back to ancient India. But most of the 'spirits' who spoke through mediums at seances had nothing to say about reincarnation. So Rivail was inclined to be critical about trance mediums, while the trance mediums and their followers denounced Rivail as a dogmatic old man. After Rivail's death, his influence waned, and within a few years he was half-forgotten.

Now in Paris, in 1860, there was a particularly violent poltergeist in the Rue des Noyers; it smashed every window in the place, hurled all kinds of objects around the house (including many which the occupants had never seen before), and finally drove the unfortunate people out of the house. Rivail decided to try to find out what exactly had happened. His medium's 'control' (the spirit who acts as master of ceremonies) explained that the disturbances were the work of a mischievous spirit. And, at the request of the control (a spirit called Saint Louis), the poltergeist of the Rue des Noyers was summoned. He appeared to be in a bad temper, and asked irritably: 'Why do you call me? Do you want to have some stones thrown at you?' Rivail now asked the spirit: 'Was there anyone in the Rue des Noyers who helped you play tricks on the inmates?' Certainly, replied the spirit, it had had an excellent 'instrument'. It added, 'For I am merry and like to amuse myself sometimes.' Who was it? Rivail asked. 'A maidservant.'

'Was she unaware you were making use of her?'

'Oh yes, poor girl—she was the most frightened of them all.'

Rivail asked how the spirit managed to throw various objects about the place, and received the interesting answer: 'I helped myself through the electric nature of the girl, joined to my own . . . thus we were able to transport the objects between us.'

Rivail asked the spirit who it was. It replied that it had been dead about fifty years, and had been a rag-and-bone-man. People used to make fun of him because he drank too much, and this was why he decided to play tricks on the inhabitants of the Rue des Noyers. He indignantly denied that he had done these things out of malice; it was merely his way of amusing himself.

This spirit seemed to belong to a class described in *The Spirits' Book*: 'They are ignorant, mischievous, unreasonable, and addicted to mockery. They meddle with everything and reply to every question without paying attention to the truth.

So, according to Kardec, poltergeists are mischievous spirits who draw their energy from certain 'vulnerable' human beings.

In all but one respect, Kardec's 'spirit teaching' agreed basically with those of most other spiritualists since Swedenborg; but that one aspect, reincarnation, was to prove a source of severe contention within the French spiritualist movement. *The Spirits' Book* had already been anticipated by a work called *Arcanes de la vie future dévoilée—Secrets of the Future Life Unveiled*, by Alphonse Cahagnet, published in 1848 (and a second and third volume later). Cahagnet was a cabinet maker who had become fascinated by 'somnambulism' (hypnotism) in his mid-30s; he placed various subjects in a hypnotic trance—the most impressive being a woman called Adèle Maginot—and recorded what they told him of life after death. Adèle was so remarkable because her messages from the dead—and sometimes from living people who had disappeared—were so full of convincing evidence. Cahagnet started a journal called *The Spiritualist Magnetiser*, and this was later transformed into *The Spiritualist Revue*, edited by Z. Piérart. But Cahagnet, who was a follower of Swedenborg, did not believe in reincarnation. And the French spiritualist movement was soon split by a bitter war of words between the followers of Cahagnet and the followers of Kardec. Kardec was critical of trance mediums—like Adèle—because they had nothing to say about reincarnation, and Cahagnet and his followers regarded automatic writing with suspicion and disdain. But Kardec, who had heart problems, died in 1869, only thirteen years after *The Spirits' Book* was published, while Cahagnet lived and flourished until 1885, publishing many more influential books. So it was Kardec's version of spiritualism that gradually faded away as the movement became increasingly powerful. It was only in Brazil—a country whose witch-doctors frequently called on the spirits for magical aid—that Kardec's version of spiritualism took root, and where it still flourishes today as one of the country's major religions. We shall examine this at length in Chapter 9.

It may be as well, at this point, to pause and ask the question: What does it all mean? There is something about 'spiritualism' that is peculiarly irritating. It is one thing to accept that some people possess strange powers of clairvoyance, and quite another to swallow 'spirit teachings' that sound like the ramblings of an uninspired Sunday school teacher. It is not that the doctrines of Swedenborg or Kardec are in themselves unacceptable. The notion that man possesses a 'vital body', an astral body and an ego-body seems reasonable enough; some may even learn, through self-observation, to distinguish between the promptings of the 'low self' and the detached observations of some higher part of us that looks down ironically on our sufferings and humiliations. But when Kardec tells us that God created spirits, and then set them the task of evolving towards perfection, it sounds boringly abstract. *Why* did God bother to create spirits in the first place? Why did he not create them perfect in the first place? And surely spirits ought to have something better to do than to communicate with their living relatives through 'mediums' and deliver anti-climactic messages about the joys of the afterlife and the trivial problems of the living? If we compare the revelations of spiritualism with those of science or philosophy, or the visions of the great mystics, they seem oddly banal . . .

This explains why spiritualism aroused such instant hostility among scientists and philosophers. Spiritualism was like a volcanic explosion of belief; the scientists replied with a blast of scepticism that was like cold water. And the combination of boiling lava and cold water produced an enormous cloud of steam that obscured everything. It was not that most scientists disbelieved the evidence: they refused even to look at it. T. H. Huxley expressed the general feeling when he remarked: 'It may all be true, for anything that I know to the contrary, but really I cannot get up interest in the subject.'

Such an attitude can hardly be defended as scientific. For anyone who has an hour to spare, the evidence is seen to be overwhelming. There are hundreds—thousands—of descriptions of out-of-the-body experiences, of poltergeists, of 'apparitions of the dead', of accurate glimpses of the future. Any reasonable person ought to be prepared to come to terms with these, not to dismiss them with the comment: 'I really cannot get up any interest in the subject.'

Can we come to terms with them without making any commitment to life-after-death or the existence of 'spirits'? Just about. Consider, for example, the haunting of Willington Mill. One interesting point that emerged was that the male apparition walked across the room several feet above the ground, at the level of the window-sill. This suggests that it was walking on a floor that had now been demolished. And we know that the millhouse was built on the site of an older house. It looks as if the 'tape recording' theory (see p. 211) can explain this particular ghost. We also observe that the house was at the bottom of a valley, next to a stream, and therefore almost certainly damp. T. C. Lethbridge suggested that ghosts are 'recordings' on the electrical field of water, and are found most frequently in damp places . . .

We may also note the comment of the local historian that although the mill was built around 1800, no haunting was recorded from that time until the disturbances experienced by Mr Proctor's family—a family of young children. Later in the 19th century, investigators of poltergeist phenomena observed that children are usually present, and that one of them often seems to be the 'focus' of the disturbance—indeed, we may recall that the Rev. Samuel Wesley noticed that his daughter Hetty trembled in her sleep before 'Old Jeffrey' began banging around. Split-brain physiology has taught us that we have two people inside our heads. Perhaps 'Old Jeffrey' was some kind of manifestation of Hetty Wesley's unconscious mind or right brain?

Thomson Jay Hudson has some surprising things to say about Spiritualism in *The Law of Psychic Phenomena*. He admits that the things that happen in the seance room are undeniable, but he claims they are not produced by the spirits of the dead. What produces the phenomena is 'essentially a human intelligence, and neither rises above nor sinks below the ordinary intelligence of humanity'. And this is why spiritualism is so oddly boring and disappointing—because it is, as Nietzsche would say, 'human, all too human'. '. . . We have already seen what remarkable powers the subjective mind possesses in certain lines of intellectual activity, and with what limitations it is hedged about; and we find that the intellectual feats of mediums possess all the characteristics belonging to subjective intelligence—the same wonderful powers and the same limitations.'

It is a convincing theory, and surprisingly 'modern'; in all the years since *The Law of Psychic Phenomena* appeared, nothing more plausible or 'scientific' has been advanced. But does it really cover *all* the facts? Hudson's solution to the problem of spirits is that 'the subjective mind of the medium, being controlled by suggestion, believes itself to be the spirit of any deceased person whose name is suggested'. But this fails to explain cases—like Swedenborg's case of the 'secret drawer' mentioned in Chapter 3—where the medium was able to produce information that was only known to the dead person. It seems, on the whole, more straightforward to accept the possibility of life after death—or the spirit's independence of the body—as a working hypothesis.

The other major objection to spiritualism—that it somehow 'reduces' the spiritual to the material—was expressed by Dean Inge when he wrote: 'The moment we are asked to accept scientific evidence for spiritual truth, the alleged spiritual truth becomes neither spiritual nor true. It is degraded into an event in the phenomenal world.'[1] And, oddly enough, Rudolf Steiner agreed with him, remarking: 'The spiritualists are the greatest materialists of all.' This sounds baffling, in view of the fact that Steiner not only accepted the reality of life after death, but of reincarnation as well.

The explanation is important, and accounts for the general feeling of hostility that is so often aroused by Spiritualism. One of Steiner's basic doctrines was that 'the supersensible world appears to us in such a way that it resembles our perceptions of the sense world'.[2] So that he says of Swedenborg:

He was a man who, in the time of dawning natural science, had become accustomed only to recognise the sensible, the visible . . . Since he insisted on recognising as true only what he could calculate and perceive with his senses . . . he drew down the supersensible world into a lower sphere under the influence of his habits of natural science.'[3]

What Steiner is saying here is something that soon dawns on most readers of accounts of near-death experiences. Some find themselves walking towards a celestial city, some find themselves in flowery meadows, some find themselves drawn towards a heavenly gateway or a whirlpool of light. It looks as if everyone

1. *Outspoken Essays*, Vol. 1, p. 269, quoted by David Lorimer in *Survival?*, p. 160.
2. 'The History of Spiritism', lecture delivered in Berlin, May 30 1904.
3. *Ibid.*

is interpreting the experience in terms of their own familiar concepts. Steiner is suggesting that visionaries like Swedenborg, who have caught a glimpse of the 'supersensible world', are bound to interpret it according to their ingrained mental habits, and that this explains why the revelations of spiritualism often seem slightly ludicrous.

Oddly enough, Steiner thoroughly approved of Kardec, who obtained the material for his books from automatic writing. This clearly suggests that what Steiner disliked so much about Spiritualism was its literal-mindedness—the trumpets and accordions floating through the air, the tables dancing around the room, the spirits made of ectoplasm. His attitude could be compared to that of a Christian mystic who wishes to explain that heaven is *not* full of angels sitting around on clouds and playing harps.

At the same time, there is bound to be an element of unfairness in such an attitude. Many mediums who started off by producing automatic writing later became 'voice mediums', and some even 'materialisation mediums'. It is impossible to draw a sharp line between them. Steiner is not really criticising Spiritualism; he is criticising spiritualists. Once we have grasped this, one of the major problems disappears—or at least, is revealed as a misunderstanding.

It was a misunderstanding that caused a great deal of trouble and bitterness in the early days of Spiritualism. It was useless for investigators like Catherine Crowe and Allan Kardec to demand a fair hearing for the 'supernatural'; scientists and intellectuals felt they were being asked to swallow a farrago of childish nonsense. They pointed angrily at the Spiritualist churches that were springing up all over America, and asked how anybody could be serious about a religion started by two silly girls. Their scepticism seemed to be justified in April 1851, when a relative of the Fox family, a certain Mrs Norman Culver, announced in the *New York Herald* that Kate and Margaretta Fox had shown her how they made the rapping noises with their knees and toes. This may or may not have been true. The girls—and their mother—had become celebrities, and spent a great deal of time travelling around the East coast giving demonstrations. Fate had promoted them from the boredom of small-town life in upper New York State to the equivalent of stardom. If the spirits were occasionally unco-operative, it would have been surprising if they had not been tempted to do a little cheating. What seems perfectly clear is that the original phenomena—bangs that were strong enough to make the house vibrate—could not have been caused by cracking the joints of the knees. Neither could Kate and Margaretta have answered all the questions about the people in the room. The accusations of fraud were just one more excuse for refusing to look dispassionately at the evidence.

The real tragedy in all this was that the cloud of polemical steam obscured a great deal of serious research into the paranormal, including the work of Reichenbach, Buchanan, Denton and Hudson himself. We can see, in retrospect, that the sceptics and the scientists did not behave too badly; they were often narrow-minded and impatient, but they did their best to be fair. It was the spiritualists themselves who were largely to blame for all the hostility. They were too gullible, too prone to accept any banal nonsense as a message from 'the other side'. Hundreds of fake mediums took advantage of their credulity to practise barefaced impositions, and whenever one of them was caught in the act, scientists shook their heads wearily and made comparisons with the mediaeval witchcraft phenomenon. Most of them had become too blasé even to say 'I told you so'. Genuine mediums like the Davenport brothers did themselves no good by appearing in theatres and performing hair-raising feats of escapology that would have done credit to Houdini. They allowed themselves to be tied so tight that the ropes cut into their flesh and caused bruises; but after a brief period in a cabinet, they would step out with the ropes around their feet. Professor Benjamin Pierce, a member of an investigating committee, sat between them in the cabinet. As soon as the door was closed, a hand shot the bolt—both brothers were trussed up like mummies—and briefly felt the professor's face before going on to untie the brothers. Professor Loomis of the Georgetown Medical College admitted that the manifestations were produced by a force with which he was unacquainted. But this kind of testimony meant nothing compared to the fact that the brothers appeared on the same bill with conjurors and acrobats.

All this explains why so little was achieved by the most remarkable medium of the 19th century—perhaps of all time— Daniel Dunglas Home. Home retained his powers for more than a quarter of a century, with the exception of a period of one year when, as we shall see, the 'spirits' decided to punish him. He performed his astonishing feats in broad daylight. He caused heavy articles of furniture to float up to the ceiling; he himself floated out of one window and in at another; he washed his face in blazing coals; he could make himself several inches taller at will. He was tested dozens of times by committees of sceptics, and was never once caught out in anything that looked like fraud. Yet posterity remembers him chiefly as the man Dickens called 'that scoundrel Home', and about whom Robert Browning wrote a scurrilous poem called 'Mr Sludge the Medium'.

A typical Home seance is amusingly described by his biographer Jean Burton. It took place on an evening in January 1863, in the fashionable home of Madame Jauvin d'Attainville, and the guests included Princess Metternich and her husband, the Austrian ambassador. The guests—fifteen in all—sat at the table in the magnificent second empire drawing room, while Home sat in an armchair three or four yards away. When everyone was ready, he sat back in his chair, became paler, and went into a light trance. He asked 'Bryan, are you there?' (Bryan being his spirit guide). Sharp raps came from the table, the chandeliers began to swing, and a chair moved of its own accord across the room and stopped in front of the guests. At the same moment, Princess Metternich screamed, as she felt a powerful but invisible hand grip hers. Others also felt hands lightly touching them. (All this was in a room 'blazing with light'.) The tapestry tablecloth now rose into the air, and underneath it, something seemed to be moving, like a hand or a small animal, towards them. This was too much for the men, most of whom were sceptics; Prince Metternich dived under the cloth and tried to grab the 'creature'; there was nothing. One of the men pulled the cloth away, while others dived under the table to find the source of the raps; again, they were disappointed. As they scrambled out again, a hailstorm of raps sounded, as if in derision. The angry Prince Metternich was now convinced that they were coming from under the table, and scrambled underneath again. Raps sounded, and Metternich yelled indignantly: 'No jokes, please!' The company assured him that they were not responsible.

Apparently in a trance, Home pointed to a corsage of violets on the piano and asked that it should be brought over to them. The violets glided across the piano, floated unsteadily across the room, and fell into the princess's lap. Prince Metternich bounded forward and grabbed them, then proceeded to search for the thread that he was convinced must be attached; he found nothing.

In a faint voice, Home now demanded an accordion, a popular instrument of the period. When it came, the princess was asked to stand alone in the middle of the room with the instrument held high above her head. As she stood there, her arm in the air, an expression of astonishment crossed her face. There was a tug on the accordion, and it proceeded to play, moving in and out. What impressed everyone was that it was a fine performance, the playing so soft and melodious that it brought tears to the eyes of some of the audience. After that, anything would have been an anticlimax, so the seance finished. But, typically, the men began to speculate how it had been done; no one seemed to doubt that it had been some form of conjuring trick; others spoke of electro-biology and mass hypnosis. The princess had to admit that she had no sensation of being hypnotised . . .

Daniel Dunglas Home (he pronounced it Hume) was born near Edinburgh in March 1833—his mother was a highlander and had a reputation as a 'seer'. He was probably illegitimate—he liked to claim that his father was Lord Home. At the age of nine, he moved to America with an aunt, Mary Cook, and her husband. His mother and 'father', and seven brothers and sisters, were already there. Daniel suffered from tuberculosis, and was subject to fainting fits—a typical 'sick sensitive'. His closest friend was a boy called Edwin, and they went for long walks in the woods of Connecticut. They made a boyish pact—that whoever died first would show himself to the other. In 1846, when Daniel was thirteen, he told his aunt and uncle that he had just seen Edwin standing at the foot of his bed, and that the figure had made three circles in the air with his hand—which Daniel took to mean that he had died three days ago. It proved to be true.

There were no more supernatural experiences for another four years; then Home saw a vision of his mother, and knew she was dead. Soon after that, he was brushing his hair when he saw, in the glass, a chair moving across the room towards him. He was terrified and rushed out of the house. In bed, he was awakened by three loud bangs on the headboard. The next morning at breakfast, when his aunt was mildly teasing him about tiring himself out by attending too many prayer meetings (Home was a religious young man), raps sounded from all over the table, and his alarmed aunt cried: 'So you've brought the devil into my house, have you?' and threw a chair at him. The Baptist minister was called in to pray the devil away but had difficulty in making himself heard above the hail of knocks. Unaware that poltergeist phenomena are usually harmless, his aunt requested him to leave her house. So, at the age of seventeen, Home had to fend for himself.

But Home had such charm and gaiety that there were dozens of acquaintances who were delighted to offer him hospitality. And the spirits gave him their full support. He went easily into trance, and in that state talked fluently in French and Italian—neither of them languages in which he had become proficient. He could not have chosen a better time to launch himself on the world, with everyone in the United States talking about spirits. An evangelist named Dr George Bush—a professor of oriental languages—persuaded him that he ought to become a Swedenborgian and use his considerable preaching talent in the pulpit; Home agreed, then came back two days later to say that his dead mother had expressly forbidden it, telling him that he had a 'more extended' mission.

Looked after by the 'spirits', and by kindly acquaintances, Home wandered around through New England, always a welcome guest in the homes of the well-off middle classes; his pale good looks brought out the protectiveness in middle-aged ladies. In Springfield, Massachusetts, he stayed at the home of a wealthy citizen named Rufus Elmers, and agreed to be investigated by a delegation from Harvard, including the poet William Cullen Bryant. They, like many other 'delegations' after them, had no doubt about the genuineness of the phenomena. The table not only 'rapped' and floated off the floor, but stood on two legs like a circus horse while three members of the committee sat on it and tried to force it down again. The floor vibrated to shocks that were as powerful as cannon fire. All this took place in broad daylight, and members of the committee held Home's hands and feet while most of the phenomena were taking place. Their report, entitled 'The Modern Wonder', concluded: *'We know that we were not imposed upon nor deceived.'* Rufus Elmers was so impressed that he offered to adopt Home and make him his heir; Home declined with thanks.

In August 1852, sitting in a circle, Home floated up to the ceiling—a feat that became virtually his trademark. And his other phenomena continued to be almost as astonishing. Grand pianos would float across the room, bells would ring, cymbals clash, and there would be sounds of birdsong and assorted animal noises. One day, a table with a candle on it tilted at an angle, and the candle flame went on burning at the same angle, as if it was still resting on a horizontal surface. On another occasion, at the home of the Rev. S. B. Brittan, he went into a trance, and a voice announced: 'Hannah Brittan here.' Home began to wring his hands, and for the next half hour, talked in a wild, distracted way about the torments of hell. The Rev. Brittan was staggered, for he was certain that no one knew that the lady—a relative—had been a prey to religious mania, and had died insane, obsessed by visions of eternal punishment. (On a subsequent appearance, Hannah Brittan told them that her present life was calm, peaceful and beautiful and that the torments of hell had been a delusion of her distracted brain.)

Most women adored Home, who was attentive and thoughtful—he loved sending flowers on anniversaries. Men either liked him or loathed him. He had effeminate manners, and many suspected he was homosexual. (For some odd reason, a surprising number of mediums are.) He was undoubtedly rather vain about his pale good looks and silky, auburn hair. He loved expensive clothes. He was an outrageous snob, who took pleasure in being inaccessible. (He would only condescend to know people if introduced by a mutual acquaintance.) He would be mortally offended if anyone offered him money, and he resented being treated as a 'performer'; as far as he was concerned, he was the social equal of anyone he met, including kings. Yet he was becomingly modest about his achievement, insisting that he himself had nothing whatever to do with the phenomena. All he had to do was to relax and put himself in the right mood (and 'right' is probably here the operative word) and things simply happened.

By 1855, Home's consumptive cough had become so bad that his admirers decided he ought to move to a healthier climate. For some unaccountable reason, he chose England. Admirers paid his passage, and with a crowd waving frantically, he sailed from Boston in March; he was just twenty-two.

As usual, the spirits were looking after Home. In London, he moved into Cox's Hotel in Jermyn Street; the owner, William Cox, was a Spiritualist, and welcomed Home 'as a father would a son'. So Home got free lodgings and an introduction to the London society people who made regular use of the hotel. In no time at all he was calling on marchionesses and baronesses. He went to visit the novelist Lord Lytton, who made literary use of many of Home's seance phenomena—a luminous form that dissolved into a globe, a disembodied hand, loud bangs, fiery sparks—in his famous story 'The Haunted and the Haunters'. But Lytton declined to believe spirits were responsible: he thought the phenomena were due to Home's unconscious mind. He became a friend of the socialist Robert Owen, who was a convert to spiritualism, and who introduced him to his old friend Lord Henry Brougham, a Voltairean sceptic. Brougham and Sir David Brewster had a private session with Home at which the table rose into the air and a bell floated across the room. Brewster described these things in his diary and told them to friends, but later insisted that the table had only 'appeared' to rise, and that Home had probably moved the bell with some hidden apparatus. The resulting controversy brought Home much publicity, and provided the spiritualists with some excellent ammunition to use against scientific dogmatism, since Brewster's own diaries justify Home.

Elizabeth Barrett Browning called on Home, together with her husband Robert. Ghostly hands materialised, music sounded from the air, the table rapped loudly and invisible spirits caressed them. Mrs Browning was totally convinced; her husband— vigorous, sturdy, just over five feet tall—sat there scowling, and resolutely declined to accept the evidence of his eyes. Home became an unmentionable subject in the Browning household, and after his wife's death, Browning wrote the flagrantly unfair 'Mr Sludge the Medium'. He may have been prejudiced by an episode that took place at another Home seance, when a detached hand took up a garland of flowers and placed them on the poetess's brow; Browning was jealous of his wife. Home made things worse by telling people that Browning had tried to place himself in the trajectory of the wreath so it would alight on his brow . . .

By popular request of the English community, Home moved on to Florence. There the manifestations were stronger than ever. A grand piano floated up into the air and remained there while a countess played on it; a spirit conversed with a Polish princess in her own language; in a haunted convent, Home conversed with the spirit of a monk—also a murderer—and caused his skinny, yellow hands to materialise. When the novelist Nathaniel Hawthorne came to Florence three years later, people- were still talking about Home, and Hawthorne collected dozens of well-attested accounts of the phenomena. Hawthorne made the interesting and significant observation:

'These soberly attested incredibilities are so numerous that I forget nine tenths of them . . . they are absolutely proved to be sober facts by evidence that would satisfy us of any other alleged realities; and yet I cannot force my mind to interest itself in them.'

This is perhaps one of the most important comments ever made about Home or about spiritualism in general.

Unfortunately, Home's success began to go to his head. He was not a particularly strong character, and being treated as a messenger from the gods would have been enough to unbalance a far more independent nature. When he went to stay at the villa of a titled Englishwoman who was separated from her husband, former admirers were scandalised—English self-control produces a morbid fascination with sexual scandal—and he began to sense a new atmosphere of hostility. He was attacked on his way back to his hotel and slightly wounded—a sign that the spirits were becoming inefficient or lazy—and on February 10, 1856, the spirits told him that his recent conduct was not worthy of a representative of the other world, and that his powers were about to leave him for a year. A Polish count had invited him to Naples and Rome; Home felt obliged to admit to him that his powers had deserted him. But his luck held; the count insisted that it made no difference, and Home accompanied him to Naples. And in spite of the loss of his powers, he remained a social lion. They came back, as the spirits had prophesied, exactly one year to the day, on the stroke of midnight.

By now Home was in Paris, and had taken the precaution of insuring himself against the disapproval of the Church by becoming a Catholic. His father confessor—recommended by the Pope himself—was less than enthusiastic about the return of the spirits, whom he assumed to be demons—but there was little he could do about it. Neither would Home have wished it, for he was by now a favourite of the Emperor Napoleon III and the Empress Eugénie. His luck aroused widespread envy and hostility, but after the year of desertion by the spirits, he no longer allowed it to go to his head.

After a tour of northern Europe, he returned to Rome, where he met and wooed a beautiful 17-year-old Russian countess named Sacha; they went to St Petersburg (together with the novelist Dumas) and her relatives organised a spectacular wedding. Home was received by the Russian royal family as cordially as by Napoleon III. Unfortunately, Sacha caught his tuberculosis, and died not long after the birth of a son. At least her death was not a separation; Home was able to keep in constant touch with her.

In 1862 his luck again seemed to desert him. The police ordered him to leave Rome, declaring that he was a sorcerer (the spirits made things worse by rapping on the desk of the police chief). For the next four years he again became a wanderer. In 1866, he met an effusive and vulgar old lady with a working-class accent, Mrs Jane Lyon. who told him she wanted to adopt him as her son, and presented him with numerous large cheques. Home changed his name to Home-Lyon. But the two were far from soulmates, and the relationship soon began to deteriorate badly—he found her boringly affectionate and she found him cold. He had a breakdown, and fled to various watering places to take a cure. When he returned to London, he found that Mrs Lyon had transferred her allegiance to a female medium, and was brooding on how to recover her money. She wanted back about £30,000—only about half of what she had given him.

She accused him of extortion, and Home was arrested. At the trial in April 1868, she alleged that she had given him the money because he had brought her instructions to that effect from her dead husband; Home's case was that she had tried hard to seduce him after he became her 'son'. Mrs Lyon was undoubtedly—as Home declared—vengeful and untruthful, and many of her lies were exposed in court. But a 'spirit medium' stood no chance of getting an unprejudiced trial; the judge remarked that if everyone who gave money to a religious charity was allowed to ask for it back, the result would be chaos; however, since spiritualism was a fraud and a cheat he would make exception in the present case. Home was ordered to repay the money. The trial did Home immense damage, strengthening the impression already created by Browning's 'Mr Sludge', that he was a confidence trickster. But the notoriety had one advantage: a reading tour of England drew enormous audiences and helped to recoup his loss.

During his 'water cure' in Malvern, Home had met a young aristocrat, Lord Adare, and during the next year or two he spent much time with him. In 1870, Adare published *Experiences in Spiritualism with Mr D. D. Home*, perhaps one of the most extraordinary and impressive books about a medium ever written. Adare was an ordinary young Englishman, more interested in hunting, shooting and fishing than ghosts. It was Adare who saw Home float out of one upper-storey window and in at another. He also saw the materialisation of various spirits—including Sacha and the American actress Ada Mencken—and all the other phenomena that Home had been producing for the past twenty years. He saw Home stir up the fire until the coals were blazing, then pick them up in handfuls and rub his face in them—neither his face nor his hair was burnt. He also witnessed Home standing against a wall, where his height was carefully taken (five feet ten inches), after which Home elongated himself to six foot four.

In 1871, Home agreed to be investigated by the young scientist William (later Sir William) Crookes. The anti-spiritualists smiled with satisfaction; they had no doubt whatever that Crookes would finally demolish the conjuror's reputation. In the event, Crookes was totally convinced, and published a report to that effect—to the disgust of his fellow scientists, who decided that he had been duped. In the controversy that followed, Crookes exploded indignantly: 'I didn't say it was possible—I said it was true.'

In the following year, 1872, Home decided it was time to retire. A lawsuit about his wife's estate was decided in his favour, so he was a Russian landowner. He lived on for another fourteen years, to the age of 53, spending his time between Russia and the French Riviera. He was wasting away from consumption; but with a beautiful second wife, a comfortable income and hosts of admiring friends, his final years were far from unhappy.

The article on Home in *Encyclopedia Britannica* calls Home an 'unsolved enigma'. This is true, but not quite in the sense the writer intended. As far as Home was concerned, there was no enigma. He had simply inherited unusual psychic powers from his mother's side of the family (and he passed these on to his son Grisha). So the spirits were able to operate *through* him.

As we have seen, this answer failed to satisfy many people who witnessed his feats and accepted their genuineness. Lord Lytton thought that Home somehow caused the phenomena himself. Most modern researchers would probably agree with him, since most of them are unwilling to accept the spirit hypothesis. Yet one thing that becomes very clear to anyone who reads the accounts of Home's phenomena—as recorded by Lord Adare or Sir William Crookes—is that the spirits are not only the simplest explanation, but in many cases, the only explanation. A large percentage of the phenomena can only be explained if we assume the existence of disembodied intelligences. And at this point, it is necessary to acknowledge that, sooner or later, most investigators of the paranormal are finally driven to the conclusion that spirits almost certainly exist. They do this with the utmost reluctance. It would be far more convenient, and far more logically satisfying, if we could explain all the phenomena in terms of the unrecognised powers of the human mind. Total honesty forces the admission that this is impossible. And this is nowhere more obvious than in the case of Daniel Dunglas Home.

5.
Enter the Ghost Detectives

CASTING AN EYE over the history of spiritualism, it certainly looks as if the 'spirits' made a tremendous and concerted effort to convince the Victorians of their reality. If that is the case, it seems equally clear that they made a miscalculation. The leaders of Victorian public opinion—politicians, intellectuals, churchmen—remained indifferent. And most scientists were intensely hostile. In the decade after the 'Hydesville rappings', they made a determined attempt to destroy spiritualism by ridicule.

They were hardly to blame. If they had behaved in any other way, they would not have been Victorians. It was their very best qualities—their sense of excitement about the future, about the tremendous scientific and technical advances, and the possibilities of humanitarian social reforms—that made them turn their backs on the 'supernatural'. T. H. Huxley expressed this spirit in a burst of magnificent exasperation when someone tried to persuade him to attend a seance: 'If anybody could endow me with the faculty of listening to the chatter of old women and curates in the nearest cathedral town, I should decline the privilege, having better things to do.'

But when the less waspish investigators could be persuaded

to listen to the 'chatter of old women and curates', they often found it unexpectedly interesting. We have already encountered the schoolmaster Alfred Russel Wallace, who was a total sceptic and a disciple of Voltaire; when he went to listen to a lecture on mesmerism, he was sufficiently intrigued to try it out on his students. One boy proved to be an unusually good subject; seeming when placed in a trance to 'tune in' to Wallace's mind. Fifteen years later, Wallace became famous as the man who had, together with Charles Darwin, discovered evolution by natural selection—and who, moreover, had allowed Darwin to take priority. In 1865, Wallace attended a seance at the house of a sceptical friend, and witnessed a heavy table moving and vibrating—in broad daylight—while raps resounded from around the room. That convinced him. A year later, he met an enormous young lady named Agnes Nichols, and watched with incredulity as the elephantine girl floated up into the air. Agnes could also produce 'apports'—objects that fell from the air—and when Wallace asked if the spirits could produce a sunflower, a six-foot sunflower with a clod of earth round its roots fell on to the table. Agnes's spirits never did things by halves; on another occasion when someone requested flowers, what looked like the whole contents of a flower shop cascaded from the air. But their most spectacular feat occurred in Highbury on January 3, 1871, when Agnes herself (now married to a man called Guppy) became the 'apport'. She was seated at the dining-room table doing her accounts when she vanished as if the ground had swallowed her. Four miles away in Lambs Conduit Street, some ardent spiritualists were seated at a table with their eyes closed, begging the spirits to vouchsafe some small manifestation. There was an almighty crash that caused screams, and when someone struck a match, the mountainous Mrs Guppy was found lying on the table, still clutching her account book. But again, the spirits had miscalculated. The story of Mrs Guppy floating four miles certainly caused widespread hilarity, but it didn't bring thousands flocking to the Spiritualist churches.

Wallace had no doubt that Mrs Guppy could convince the sceptics, so he invited three of the most hostile—Professor W. B. Carpenter, Professor John Tyndall and G. H. Lewes, the husband of novelist George Eliot. Carpenter came, sat silently through a cannonade of raps, then went away without comment; he never came back. Neither did Tyndall, whose only comment was 'Show us something else'. Lewes simply refused to come, as did T. H. Huxley—this was the occasion when Huxley remarked that he simply could not 'get up an interest in the subject'.

Yet in spite of the refusal of scientists to believe their own eyes and ears, psychic phenomena remained a thorn in the flesh of Victorian intellectuals. After all, it was the business of science to explain mysteries, not ignore them. Some scientists—such as William Crookes, discoverer of the element thallium—developed a bad conscience about it, and decided to conduct their own investigations. When Crookes saw a concertina in a cage playing music of its own accord, while Daniel Dunglas Home held it up by one handle, he knew that he was dealing with unknown forces. His 'credulity' caused much head-shaking among his colleagues. And later, when he decided that a young lady called Florence Cook—whose guide, Katie King, materialised and walked round the room—was genuine, some of them whispered that Florence had become Crookes's mistress as the price of his co-operation.

The mathematician Charles Dodgson—who wrote *Alice in Wonderland*—was another who felt that the phenomena ought to be explained, not dismissed. He wrote to a friend in 1882:

'That trickery will *not* do as a complete explanation of all the phenomena . . . I am more than convinced. At the same time, I see no need as yet for believing that disembodied spirits have anything to do with it . . . All seems to point to the existence of a natural force, allied to electricity and nerve force by which brain can act on brain. I think we are close to the day when this shall be classified among the known natural forces . . .'

That was the ideal aim: to track down this unknown force and stick a label on it. This was the truly Victorian way of banishing this revival of witchcraft. The only problem was that the spirits often converted the sceptics who were trying to disprove their existence. There was, for example, the embarrassing case of the American Congressman Robert Dale Owen, son of the great social reformer Robert Owen. The latter had been a lifelong freethinker—until he encountered the American medium

Mrs Hayden. And then, at the age of 83, he declared himself a Spiritualist. His son, another freethinker and social reformer, was furious, and decided that the old man was senile. He was, at the time, American chargé d'affaires in Naples. In 1856, the Brazilian ambassador persuaded him to attend a seance in his apartment, and there Owen saw the table moving without human agency. It was, he decided, merely an 'electro-psychological phenomenon'. But he wanted to know how it worked. So he spent the next two years reading books on mesmerism and 'animal magnetism', and attending seances. He met Home, who had lost his powers at the time; but the stories of Home's powers made him feel that he should at least consider the possibility that spirits were responsible for the phenomena. As a result, he became convinced, and wrote a book called *Footfalls on the Boundary of Another World* that achieved the same popularity as Mrs Crowe's *Night Side of Nature*. *Footfalls* deserved its popularity; it was an exhaustive, carefully argued book, full of the latest discoveries in modern science, and of some highly convincing cases of clairvoyance, precognitions, poltergeists and 'phantasms of the living'. But it is doubtful that it convinced a single scientist.

What finally turned the tide in favour of spiritualism was not scientific evidence, but the deep Victorian craving for religious certainty. Nowadays the chief affliction of the intellectuals is *angst*, a kind of free-floating anxiety. In the Victorian age, it was Doubt with a capital 'D'. One of the great Victorian bestsellers was a novel called *Robert Ellesmere* by Mrs Humphry Ward, about a clergyman who experiences Doubts and feels obliged to resign his living. We find the idea slightly comic—Evelyn Waugh poked fun at it in *Decline and Fall*—but that is because we take doubt for granted. We can scarcely imagine what it was like to be born into the blissful certainty of a respectable Victorian household—certainty about salvation, about the inspiration of the Bible, about the truth of the Thirty-Nine Articles. Victorian children were brought up to believe that Adam was created in precisely 4004 BC, and that any kind of doubt on religious matters was as disgraceful as being a drunkard or a prostitute. So when Sir Charles Lyell's *Principles of Geology* (1830) argued that the earth was millions of years old, Victorians felt as shocked as if an active volcano had appeared in Trafalgar Square. It was from that point that they began to be undermined by Doubts.

One of these unhappy questioners was Professor Henry Sidgwick, of Trinity College, Cambridge. Doubt tormented him like a nagging tooth all his life. In 1869, at the age of 31, he even felt obliged to resign his fellowship at Trinity because he could no longer subscribe to the Thirty-Nine Articles of the Church of England. His fellow dons sympathised, and, the moment the religious tests were dropped, reappointed him. He went on to write a celebrated book on ethics that ended with the statement that all man's attempts to find a rational basis for human behaviour are foredoomed to failure.

Sidgwick's pupils regarded him as a kind of Socrates. There were many brilliant young men among them, including Arthur Balfour, a future Prime Minister, Edmund Gurney, heir to a Quaker fortune, and Frederick Myers, the son of a clergyman. Myers, another Fellow of Trinity, also felt obliged to resign because of Doubts.

One evening in December 1869, Myers paid his old master a visit, and they went for a walk under the stars. It was the year in which Sidgwick had resigned his fellowship, and inevitably, the subject of religion came up. Although neither of them could still call themselves Christians, neither of them could accept that the universe is a great machine and that human beings have been created by pure chance. It was Myers who asked, with a certain desperation, whether, since philosophy had failed to solve the riddle of the universe, there might be just a chance that the answer lay in the evidence for ghosts and spirits. Neither of them felt much optimism, but Sidgwick went on brooding about the idea—particularly when, in the following year, Crookes announced that he intended to investigate Daniel Dunglas Home. The attacks on Crookes outraged their sense of fair play, and in 1873 they formed a loose association for the investigation of spiritualism and the paranormal. Myers became a school inspector, which left him time to attend seances. But at first he found it discouraging work; he began to wonder whether there was something about him that made the spirits stay away. Then he had an experience that convinced him. He attended a seance with a medium named Charles Williams—at one of whose seances Mrs Guppy had landed on the table—and a hand materialised in the air. Myers held it in his own, and felt it grow smaller and smaller until it faded away, leaving nothing behind. That could not be trickery. Myers now began seeking actively for more evidence. Together with Edmund Gurney, Arthur Balfour, Sidgwick and Lord Rayleigh—the scientist who discovered the element argon—Myers became a dedicated 'psychical researcher'. They were joined by a remarkable clergyman, Stainton Moses, who was also an automatic-writing medium. His obvious genuineness reinforced Myers's conviction.

A new impetus came from an Irish professor of physics, William Barrett, who taught at the Royal College of Science in Dublin. Like Alfred Russel Wallace, Barrett had become interested in 'mesmerism', and when he was staying with a friend of County Westmeath, he persuaded some of the village children to subject themselves to hypnosis. Two proved to be excellent subjects, and with one of these Barrett observed what Wallace had experienced with his schoolboy two decades earlier, 'community of sensation'. When his friend placed his own hand over a lighted lamp, the girl snatched hers away as if afraid of burning. When he tasted sugar, she smiled; when he tasted salt, she frowned. She also proved to be able to read Barrett's mind. The sceptical Professor Carpenter had explained such phenomena by saying that people under hypnosis become abnormally sensitive, so they can recognise almost undetectable sounds or smells. But that would not explain how this girl could hold against her head a book containing a playing card, and describe the card exactly.

Barrett wrote a paper about the case, and sent it to the British Association in London. It would probably have been ignored, but it happened that Wallace was chairman of the committee that decided which papers to publish. He threw his weight behind Barrett, and although the committee eventually overruled him, Wallace made sure that Myers saw the paper.

By this time, Barrett had found another case that excited him—the family of a clergyman called Creery, who lived at Buxton, in Derbyshire. Creery's daughters were unusually good at playing a favourite party trick called the 'willing game', in which a person went out of the room while the others decided what he ought to do; when he came back, everyone had to try to 'will' him to do it. In Barrett's presence, Creery's four daughters demonstrated the 'willing game' again and again, with hardly a single failure.

Barrett met Myers and his fellow 'psychical investigators' in London, and suggested that they ought to form a society for investigating these mysteries. Myers and Gurney were dubious; they felt they were already doing their best. But Barrett's enthusiasm prevailed, and the result was the formation of the Society for Psychical Research (SPR), which met for the first time in February 1882. Its original members were the 'Cambridge group'—Myers, Gurney, Sidgwick (and his wife Eleanor), Balfour, Barrett, Rayleigh and Wallace. Soon they were joined by distinguished Victorians such as Tennyson, Gladstone, J. J. Thomson (discoverer of the electron), Mark Twain, William James, Lewis Carroll (Charles Dodgson), John Ruskin, Sir Oliver Lodge, and the painters Frederick Leighton and G. F. Watts.

The Society had no objection whatever to sceptics, for its aim was to bring the methods of science to bear on the 'psychic world', and try to prove or disprove it once and for all. One result was that Myers and Gurney accepted with pleasure the services of a sceptical post-office employee named Frank Podmore, whose original faith in spiritualism had been badly shaken in 1876 by the trial and subsequent flight of a 'slate-writing' medium named Henry Slade. (The anti-spiritualist Sir Ray Lankester had managed to grab the slate before the 'spirits' had had a chance to get to work, and found a message already on it. In spite of strong evidence in his favour, Slade was found guilty on the curious grounds that writing by spirits was a violation of the laws of nature, so he *had* to be a fraud.) The three-way collaboration produced the classic *Phantasms of the Living* (1886) which took four years to compile. The Society also produced a vast Census of Hallucinations, which showed that one person in every ten had experienced some kind of hallucination.

Now, at last, it should have been possible for the 'spirits' to win over the great majority of the British public. We have seen that mediums like Home, Mrs Hayden and Mrs Guppy had no problem convincing scientists once they were given a fair chance. In fact, the Society did some very impressive work, establishing the reality of apparitions, telepathy, clairvoyance and out-of-the-body experiences beyond all reasonable doubt. This early work culminated in Myers's masterpiece, *Human Personality and Its Survival of Bodily Death*.

But, astonishingly, all this did little or nothing to influence public opinion. The vast audience that had bought *The Night Side of Nature* and *Footfalls on the Boundary of Another World* could not be bothered to read huge works full of signed statements and detailed examinations of the evidence. And sceptics such as T. H. Huxley and Sir Ray Lankester felt there would be no point in reading them anyway, since anyone who could believe in such nonsense must be a gullible idiot.

Regrettably, there was another factor that prevented the public taking the SPR seriously. In its first two decades, a whole series of 'exposures' provided the sceptics with all the ammunition they could wish for; the result was that, by about 1902, the Society had become a kind of joke, rather like the Flat Earth Society.

One of the most damaging of the 'exposures' had taken place in 1880, two years before the Society was formed. The medium Florence Cook, with whom William Crookes had worked, was caught cheating by Sir George Sitwell—father of Edith, Osbert and Sacheverell. Florence was a 'materialisation medium'. She sat in a cabinet with drawn curtains in a dimly lighted room, and after a few minutes, a figure in white would emerge from the cabinet and talk to people in the audience. The 'spirit' called herself Marie, and claimed that she 'materialised' herself with substances taken from the medium's body. As she passed by Sitwell's chair, he grabbed her and held her tight until someone produced a light. Then it was found that 'Marie' was Florence Cook in her corset and petticoat; Florence's other clothes were found in the cabinet.

That looked conclusive, although spiritualists accepted Florence's explanation—that she was in a trance at the time and had no knowledge of what had happened. Sir William Crookes immediately came to her defence. He pointed out that in 1873 a man called Volckman had suddenly grabbed the 'spirit' as it walked around the room—in those days, a woman who called herself Katie King. One person present claimed that 'Katie's legs and feet had dissolved away and that she had escaped from Volckman's clutch with an upward movement like a seal'. The audience rushed to the cabinet and found Florence still there, dressed in black, her knots and seals intact. No trace of the white gown in which 'Katie' had been dressed was found in the cabinet.

Crookes also described how he had once been allowed to hold 'Katie' in his arms at a seance, and found her to be quite solid, like a normal woman. Naturally suspicious, he asked her if he could see Florence in her cabinet. 'Katie' agreed, and Crookes entered the cabinet and found Florence in a trance. As far as Crookes was concerned, that was conclusive. As far as the sceptics were concerned, it proved one of two things: either that Florence had an accomplice—perhaps her sister Katie, also a medium—or that Crookes was a liar.

After the Sitwell exposure, an authoress named Florence Marryat sat with Florence in the cabinet, tied to her with a rope; 'Marie' appeared as usual and walked out amongst the audience. But Florence's reputation had suffered badly, and she soon went into partial retirement.

Crookes *was* undoubtedly deceived by a personable general's daughter named Rosina Showers. He had no reason to suspect her, for she refused all payment for her seances, at which a figure dressed in white appeared. Crookes had devised a simple test to prevent Florence Cook from cheating; he had made her dip her hands in a coloured dye before the seance, then examined 'Katie King''s hands. 'Katie' passed the test without difficulty. But Rosina's 'apparition' had dyed hands. Crookes allowed himself to overlook this—after all, the 'spirit' drew its substance from the medium, and might have borrowed the dye too. But Rosina was unable to keep her secret to herself, and told the American medium Annie Fay that she had cheated. Mrs Fay immediately passed this on to Crookes, who demanded a private interview with Rosina. She confessed her deception, and promised never to do it again. Crookes, in turn, promised not to expose her. This promise was to cause him some embarrassment. Rosina's mother found out about the secret meeting, and put the worst possible construction on it. Having promised Rosina to keep silence, Crookes had to endure stoically while Mrs Showers spread scandal among her friends and accused him of being a Casanova who habitually seduced his mediums. It was already general gossip that he had slept with Florence Cook when he was 'investigating' her in his own house. Crookes finally decided that psychical research was more trouble than it was worth, and gave it up.

In 1888, there was a double scandal. The four Creery girls, whose 'will game' had so impressed Barrett—and caused him to found the SPR—were caught cheating. They had been constantly tested ever since Barrett discovered them, and had become thoroughly bored with it all. They admitted that they had devised various simple signals to aid their 'card guessing' games—an upward glance for hearts, down for diamonds, and so on. They insisted that they had only decided to cheat fairly recently, and Myers and Gurney believed them, having made quite sure that the girls could *not* cheat in their own earlier tests. But no one else believed them.

Then, worst of all, the two Fox girls whose manifestations had launched the Spiritualist movement publicly confessed that they were cheats. By 1888, both were in their fifties, both were widows, and both were drinking too much. People were no longer interested in spirit rappings. Sister Leah, on the other hand, was still doing rather well; she and her sisters were barely on speaking terms. It was Leah, in fact, who had launched the fashion for 'materialisations' when, at a seance with Robert Dale Owen in 1860, a veiled white figure had walked round the room. With a supporter like Owen, she could hardly fail. Her sisters, on the other hand, had been badly treated by life. Kate's children had been taken from her by the Society for the Prevention of Cruelty to Children as a result of her drunkenness. Margaretta had managed to smuggle them to England, to a guardian, but had been sorely tempted to commit suicide by jumping overboard on the return journey. Her strongest desire was to get her own back on her elder sister Leah. So when she arrived back in America, she took the opportunity of an interview with a reporter to declare that all the rappings had been a cheat. On October 21, 1888, she and Kate appeared on a platform at the New York Academy of Music, and Margaretta confessed that she had made the raps by means of a double joint in her big toe. She went on to demonstrate with a series of muffled raps. They were not in the least like the thunderous knockings that had shaken the bedroom of the Hydesville house, but the audience was willing to be convinced, and Margaretta and Kate were able to share $1,500 between them. The reporter Reuben Davenport, who had organised the confession, went on to write a book called *The Death Blow to Spiritualism*. Much of the $1,500 was spent on alcohol. In due course Margaretta wrote a recantation of the confession, which she handed to a wealthy spiritualist, who allowed her to live in an apartment he owned. Her alcoholism made her an impossible tenant and he had to evict her. She died in 1895 and was buried in a pauper's grave, followed soon afterwards by Kate. In retrospect, the most significant thing about her confession is that Kate sat silently beside her on stage. She neither confirmed the confession nor offered to demonstrate how *she* had been deceiving the public with raps for the past thirty years. The inference seems to be that she agreed to share the platform for the sake of the $750, but refused to go further than that.

Another embarrassment to organised psychical research was the remarkable Italian medium Eusapia Palladino. She was an illiterate peasant, of large proportions (like so many mediums), who had been discovered in Naples in 1872, when she was 18. She was the most powerful medium since Daniel Dunglas Home. Chairs retreated or moved towards her when she frowned or beckoned them, and hung suspended in the air. She herself could float up into the air and lie there as if on a couch. She had been investigated by the criminologist Cesare Lombroso, who had no doubt of her genuineness. But she was a highly unstable character, violent, impulsive and sly. When coming out of trances she would make openly sexual overtures to males who attracted her. And, what was worse, she cheated. The absurd thing was that her cheating was clumsy, and the least competent researcher had no difficulty in catching her at it. Eusapia herself claimed that this cheating was done by hostile spirits, which may or may not have been true (since she was often wide-awake when she did it). Yet her other phenomena were so impressive that there could be no question of cheating. The French astronomer Camille Flammarion found a better explanation of her cheating when he observed her over a period. After seances at which obviously genuine phenomena had occurred—such as musical instruments floating round the room when Eusapia was tied to her chair—he observed that she was violently ill, sometimes for as much as two days, vomiting up any food she tried to take.

If genuine phenomena produced this effect, it was no wonder she tried to get away with cheating . . . When Eusapia came to England in 1895, she was tested by the SPR at Cambridge, with the conjuror Maskelyne present. Her English hosts were far less indulgent towards her outrageous cheating than Lombroso had been, and issued a thoroughly unfavourable report. This should have convinced sceptics that the Society had no interest in protecting impostors. It only spread the impression that most mediums were such frauds that no sane person would waste time on them.

In 1888, the Society suffered another serious blow—the death of one of its most brilliant investigators, Edmund Gurney. In June, he went off to Brighton on some mysterious errand, and was found dead in his hotel bed the next morning with a bottle of chloroform beside him, and a sponge bag over his face. An inquest decided that he died accidentally when taking chloroform for a toothache, but there was gossip at the SPR that it was suicide. Gurney had been testing various Brighton youths for telepathy, and had been impressed. One of his 'telepaths' had to leave hastily for South Africa as a result of a divorce scandal, and twenty years later he published a confession, declaring that he had cheated consistently. It has been suggested that Gurney found out that he had been hoaxed for years, and that if he was honest about this, it would do even more damage to psychical research.[1] Whatever the truth, his death was a serious loss to the Society.

It was not the first time Gurney had been hoaxed. Just as he was putting the finishing touches to the second volume of *Phantasms of the Living* in 1886, he received a letter from a Portsmouth naval cadet named Sparks, who described how he had been hypnotising a fellow cadet named Cleave. One day when Cleave wondered what his girlfriend was doing in Wandsworth, Sparks hypnotised him and suggested that he should go to see her. When he came out of the trance, according to Sparks, Cleave said that he had gone into the room where the girl was sitting with her little brother; she had stared at him and looked pale as if she was going to faint . . . Two days later, Cleave received a letter from the girl

1. Trevor H. Hall, *The Strange Case of Edmund Gurney*, 1964.

asking whether anything had happened to him, because she had seen him in the room.

This case was too good to miss, so Gurney went to the trouble of getting confirmatory letters from Cleave (who was 18) and from the girlfriend, as well as from two other cadets who claim to have been present. He printed a full account in *Phantasms of the Living*. Ten years after his death, Myers and Podmore had to publish a note in the SPR *Proceedings* admitting that Cleave had now confessed to hoaxing Gurney. It was a lesson in not paying too much attention to 'witnessed' statements. Yet in another sense, the case vindicated the authors of *Phantasms*. The hoaxers had all been teenagers. The majority of people quoted in *Phantasms* are respectable middle-aged citizens, many of them clergymen, and most of them can have had no possible motive for hoaxing the SPR.

In 1898, Myers himself was involved in a minor scandal that brought discredit on the SPR. In the late 1880s, Myers had met an attractive girl named Ada Goodrich-Freer, who claimed to come from an upper-class Highland family and to be clairvoyant. Myers had a keen eye for a pretty girl, and he and the girl were soon convinced that they were soul mates. There is some evidence that they had a love affair. Myers persuaded her to try crystal-gazing, and he felt the results were impressive—she claimed to have located a lost key and a medical prescription, and obtained from the crystal an address she had accidentally destroyed. Myers wrote a paper about it which came out in the Society's journal (he called her simply 'Miss X'). The Society had no reason for doubting such a well-born and refined young lady—after all, why should she lie? What Myers did not know what that the upper-class Miss Goodrich-Freer was actually the daughter of an Uppingham vet, and her name was simply Freer. She was 30 when Myers met her, not a teenager, as she claimed. And she was a pathological liar. Her motivation has never been made clear, but it was probably simply a desire for attention.

The Society sent Miss Goodrich-Freer to the Highlands to investigate the whole subject of second sight; it emerged later that she simply borrowed a manuscript from a folklore-collecting priest and printed his material as her own. Sent to investigate a haunting in Surrey, she told the owners of the house that she had seen nothing, but told the SPR that she had seen a hooded female ghost as she dressed for dinner. That should have made them suspicious, but the attractive and well-mannered Miss Goodrich-Freer seemed above suspicion.

In 1897 she heard rumours that Ballechin House, in Scotland, was haunted, and persuaded a member of the SPR to rent it for her, for 'shooting and fishing'. Once there, she claimed to have witnessed all kinds of unearthly phenomena—thumps, bangs, ghostly screams, phantom footsteps, and elusive presences. There was a poltergeist that tore the clothes off the bed, and a ghostly nun, who was spotted by Miss Goodrich-Freer in a nearby glen. Oddly enough, guests who came to stay with Miss Goodrich-Freer never encountered the more terrifying phenomena, but they heard ominous bangs and footsteps. Back in London, she proceeded to write her *Alleged Haunting of Ballechin House*, but was incensed when one of her guests, a certain J. Callendar Ross, beat her past the post with an article in *The Times* entitled 'On the Trail of a Ghost'; its tone was sceptical, not to say satirical. A furious correspondence ensued in the columns of *The Times*, in the course of which it became clear that Miss Goodrich-Freer and the SPR had rented the house under false pretences. Its owner was naturally displeased at the damage to his rental prospects from all this sensational publicity. Myers, who had been a visitor to Ballechin House, naturally felt obliged to support Miss Goodrich-Freer. But when the wife of the owner denounced the SPR in *The Times*, he hastened to declare that he had long ago decided against publishing his own observations. Another guest who had been at Ballechin with him immediately contradicted him, saying that Myers had definitely expressed his intention of writing about the haunting. Miss Goodrich-Freer herself was enraged by what she felt to be Myers's unchivalrous desertion. And Mr Callendar Ross expressed the general feeling when he referred to 'the suspicion and disgust that close contact with the SPR tends to excite'. When Miss Goodrich-Freer published her book on Ballechin, there was still more bad feeling.

The scandal may well have brought on the illness that was to kill Myers in 1901. Miss Goodrich-Freer herself experienced a sudden coldness on the part of other SPR members, and, in his review of her book on Ballechin, Frank Podmore came very close to calling her a liar. There is evidence[1] that she was caught cheating at a table-rapping seance in 1901, and decided to leave England for Jerusalem, where she married a man who was sixteen years her junior—convincing him that she was two years younger than he was . . . She died in 1931 at the age of 74 but continued to lie to the end—her death certificate gives her age as 56.

These preposterous scandals—mediums in their underwear and ghosts with double-jointed big toes—had the unfortunate effect of suggesting that the SPR was a collection of bumbling crackpots. In fact, looking back after more than a century, we can see that its achievement during those first two decades was monumentally impressive. It had set out to answer the question: Can the paranormal be taken seriously, or is it a collection of old wives' tales and delusions? What undoubtedly surprised those pioneers was the sheer mass of evidence for the paranormal. It must have seemed incredible that one person in ten had experienced a hallucination, and that so many people had seen apparitions of dying relatives or had out-of-the-body experiences. Newspaper scandals about fake mediums may have impressed the public, but what impressed the SPR was that so many mediums were obviously genuine, and that so much evidence for life after death stood up to the strictest examination. When Callendar Ross spoke about the 'suspicion and disgust' excited by the SPR, he was expressing the feeling of most healthy-minded people towards a 'morbid' subject like psychical research. But morbid or not, it refused to go away. And the Society made it harder to ignore by accumulating a positive mountain of evidence. *Phantasms of the Living* may be one of the most boring books ever written, but its 2,000 pages of cases finally batter the mind into the recognition that this is something that has to be faced.

Since we have devoted so much space to scandals and exposures, it is only fair to look more closely at a cross-section of the kind of evidence that finally convinced those pioneers that they were dealing with reality.

On October 21, 1893, Prince Victor Duleep Singh, a son of a

1. John L. Campbell and Trevor Hall, *Strange Things*, 1968, p. 211.

maharajah, went to bed in a Berlin hotel, where he was staying together with Lord Carnarvon. Before switching off the light, he looked across the room at a framed picture that hung on the opposite wall. To his surprise, he saw the face of his father, looking at him with an intent expression. Thinking that the picture might resemble his father, he got out of bed to see; in fact, it showed a girl holding a rose and leaning on a balcony. Prince Victor described the experience to Lord Carnarvon the next morning. Later the same day, he received a telegram announcing that his father had died of a stroke the previous day. The prince had seen his father's face at the time when the maharajah was lying unconscious after the stroke, a few hours before he died.

On the night of October 16, 1902, the wife of a railway guard woke up about 3 a.m. for a drink of water. She was alone in bed, because her husband was on night duty, and the room was dimly lighted by a gas mantle. As she looked into the water, she saw a clear image of goods wagons smashing into one another, and observed which of them was most damaged. She was worried about her husband, in case he had had an accident. At nine the next morning he returned home, and she told him what she had seen. He told her that there *had* been an accident on the line that night, and it had happened just as she had seen.

The odd point about this case is that her husband had passed the scene of the accident twice: once at the time his wife had seen her 'vision' in the glass of water, and again four hours later, when his train was on its way back. But when he passed it for the first time, it was dark and he could not see what was happening. At 7 a.m. it was light, and he had then been able to see the scene clearly—as his wife had seen it in the water. Of course, her husband may have seen far more subconsciously than he was aware of seeing. But if this was telepathy, then he had managed to convey to his wife far more than he was aware of seeing.

The next case is perhaps one of the most famous ever recorded by the SPR. On July 9, 1904, the novelist Rider Haggard suffered such a bad nightmare that his wife shook him awake. In his dream, he had seen his daughter's black retriever dog, Bob, lying on its side among the undergrowth beside some water. Its head was at an unnatural angle, and it seemed to be trying to tell him that it was dying.

The next morning at breakfast Haggard told his daughter Angela about his dream. She was quite unworried because she had seen Bob the previous evening and he was safe and well. It was only later in the day that they learned that Bob was missing. Four days later, the dog's body was found floating in the nearby river. It had been struck by a train on the night Haggard had dreamed about it. He was able to work out the precise time the accident had taken place—a few hours before he had awakened from his nightmare.

On March 19, 1917, Mrs Dorothy Spearman was in her room in a hotel in Calcutta, feeding her baby son. Her little daughter was also in the room. She felt there was someone behind her, and looked round to see her half-brother, Eldred Bowyer-Bower, standing there; he was an officer in the Royal Flying Corps. He looked perfectly normal, and Mrs Spearman assumed he had been posted to India and come to see her. She told him that she would put the baby down, and then they could have a long talk. But when she had finished tucking in the baby, her half-brother had vanished. Her daughter did not appear to have seen anyone. She learned later that her half-brother had been shot down over the German lines at about the time she had seen him.

On December 7, 1918, Lieutenant J. J. Larkin, an RAF officer, was writing letters in the billet when he heard someone walking up the passage outside. Then the door opened, and his friend Lieutenant David McConnel shouted 'Hello boy!' Larkin turned and saw McConnel standing there, holding the doorknob in his hand. He said: 'Hello, back already?' and McConnel replied 'Yes, had a good trip'. He had been ferrying a plane to a nearby aerodrome. Then McConnel closed the door with a bang and clattered off.

When Larkin learned several hours later that McConnel had crashed that afternoon, he assumed that it must have been after he had seen him. In fact, McConnel had been killed at roughly the same time that Larkin saw him at the door.

The next case has also become famous, and is regarded as one of the strongest pieces of evidence for survival after death. In June 1925, James Chaffin of Davie County, North Carolina, dreamed that his father stood by his bedside, wearing an old black overcoat, and told him: 'You will find the will in my overcoat pocket.' The father, James L. Chaffin, had died four years earlier, leaving his farm to his third son Marshall, and nothing to his wife or other three sons. The will had not been contested, since there seemed no reason to do so.

The next morning, James Chaffin hurried to his mother and asked about his father's old black overcoat; she told him it had been given to his brother John. He found the coat at John's house and examined it carefully. Sewn into the lining of the inside pocket—which his father had indicated in the dream—he found a roll of paper stating: 'Read the 27th chapter of Genesis in my daddy's old Bible.'

Taking a neighbour as witness, James Chaffin went back to his mother's house, and unearthed the old Bible. In the 27th chapter of Genesis there was another will—made later than the one that left everything to Marshall—dividing the property between the wife and four sons. The first reaction of Marshall Chaffin was to contest the will, assuming it to be a forgery. But once he examined it, he had to admit that it was obviously genuine. Ten witnesses testified that it was in old Chaffin's handwriting. So the property was divided according to the wishes of the second will.

Like Marshall Chaffin, the reader's first reaction is to suspect skulduggery. But the Canadian member of the SPR who heard of the case hired a lawyer to investigate it, and the genuineness of the will was established beyond all doubt. The significance of the twenty-seventh chapter of Genesis is that it contains the story of how Jacob deceived his blind father Isaac into granting him the inheritance of his brother Esau. This thought had apparently come to old Chaffin not long before his death, and he made the new will. But instead of having it properly witnessed, he inserted it in the Bible, no doubt expecting it to be found after his death—together with its implied criticism of his son Marshall. Unfortunately, the Bible was decrepit, and it may have been that the Chaffin family was simply not religiously inclined; so after four years, it seems the old farmer had to draw attention to his change of heart . . .

Mrs Crowe's *Night Side of Nature* has a whole chapter devoted to similar cases, in which important messages are delivered by dreams or apparitions. She tells, for example, of a butcher who dreamed that he was going to be attacked and murdered on his way to market by two men dressed in blue. He decided to go to market with a neighbour, and, when he came to the place where the attack had taken place in his dream, saw the two men in blue waiting there . . . But all she tells us by way of detail is that the butcher's name was Bone and that he lived in Holytown. This can hardly be regarded as 'confirmatory detail'. The records of the SPR contain many equally melodramatic cases. But they took the trouble to get signed statements from all concerned, and the result is far more convincing. In a typical case of 1869, a couple, identified as 'Mr and Mrs P', were lying in bed in a dimly lighted room when 'Mrs P' saw a man dressed as a naval officer standing at the foot of the bed. Her husband was dozing, and she touched his shoulder and said: 'Willie, who is this?' Her husband roared indignantly: 'What on earth are you doing here, sir?' The naval officer said reproachfully: 'Willie!', and as 'Mr P' leapt out of bed, walked across the room, and disappeared into the wall. 'Mrs P' said he looked like a solid human being, and that as he passed a lamp on his way across the room, he threw a shadow.

Realising that they had seen a 'ghost', 'Mrs P' began to wonder if it foreboded some disaster to her brother, who was in the navy. When she mentioned this to her husband, he said: 'No, it was my father.' 'P''s father had been dead for some years.

After this visitation, 'Mr P' became seriously ill for several weeks. When he recovered, he told his wife that he had been in financial trouble for some time, and before seeing the apparition, he had decided to take the advice of a certain individual which, he now realised, would have ruined him and probably landed him in jail. He was convinced that the 'ghost' had come to warn him not to do it.

Intrinsically, this case is no more convincing that that of Mr Bone of Holytown. But the SPR obtained signed depositions from 'Mr and Mrs P', and from two friends to whom 'Mrs P' had told the story immediately after it had happened. It is still possible to dismiss it as a dream or a 'collective hallucination', or simply as a downright lie. But the signed statements make this seem at least unlikely.

An interesting point about the experience is 'Mrs P''s comment that the figure looked quite solid and normal—most 'ghosts' do—and that it cast a shadow. This obviously suggests that it was made of some kind of solid substance, like the 'materialisations' that appeared in the seance room.

A 'warning' of a different kind seems to have been involved in a case that came to be known as the 'red scratch' case. It involved a commercial traveller (identified as 'FG') who was in his hotel room in St Joseph, Missouri, in 1876, when he became aware of someone sitting at the table. It was his sister Annie, who had died of cholera nine years earlier. She looked exactly as she had when alive, except that she had a bright red scratch on her right cheek. As 'FG' sprang to his feet, his sister vanished.

He was so shaken that he took a train straight back to his parents' home in St Louis. When he told them about the scratch, his mother fainted. When she recovered, she told them that she had accidentally made the scratch on the face of the corpse. She had covered it up with powder, and never mentioned it to anyone.

A few weeks later, the mother died, 'happy in the belief that she would rejoin her favourite daughter'. Her son obviously took the view that the purpose of the apparition was to prepare her mother for her own death. This is another theme that runs fairly constantly through reports of apparitions and 'death-bed visions' collected by the SPR. Sir William Barrett was later to devote a book to them, and its opening case is typical of the kind of thoroughness the SPR brought to its investigations.

Barrett's wife was an obstetric surgeon in the Maternity Hospital at Clapton in North London. A woman she calls Mrs B was in labour and suffering from heart failure. As Lady Barrett was holding her hands, she said: 'It's getting dark.' Her mother and husband were sent for. Then 'Mrs B' looked at another part of the room and said: 'Oh, lovely.' 'What is lovely?' 'Lovely brightness—wonderful things.' Then she exclaimed: 'Why, it's father!' Her baby was brought in for her to see, and she asked: 'Do you think I ought to stay for the baby's sake?' She looked towards her 'father', and said: 'I can't stay.' When her husband had arrived, she looked across the room and said: 'Why, there's Vida!' Vida was her younger sister, who had died two weeks earlier. But her death had been kept from 'Mrs B', so as not to upset her. She died soon after. Lady Barrett, the matron and the husband and the mother all vouched that she seemed to remain conscious of the dead relatives up to the time of her death. With his usual thoroughness, Barrett obtained a letter verifying all this from the mother. It is the first of a number of cases cited by Barrett in which people on the point of death have 'seen' relatives whom they did not know to be dead. Barrett points out that there is no known case of a dying person 'seeing' someone who is still alive.

Sir Oliver Lodge, who was twice president of the SPR, was himself to supply one of the most convincing cases of 'communication with the dead'; it is recorded in his book *Raymond*.

On August 8, 1915, Sir Oliver Lodge received a message from a Boston medium, Leonore Piper, containing an obscure reference to a poem by the Roman poet Horace, about a tree being struck by lightning. Lodge interpreted this as a warning of some disaster. The message purported to come from Frederic Myers, who had been dead for fourteen years. A week later, Lodge heard that his youngest son Raymond had been killed in the Ypres campaign.

After this, a number of mediums relayed messages that purported to come from Raymond, but Lodge remained unconvinced— most of them were of the 'Having a lovely time' variety. But in the following month, Lodge's wife was taken by a friend to a seance with a remarkable medium, Mrs Osborne Leonard. Neither the medium nor Lady Lodge knew one another by sight, and they were not introduced. Nevertheless, Mrs Leonard announced that she had a message from 'Raymond', who stated that he had met many of his father's friends since death; asked to name one of them, Raymond replied 'Myers'.

Another 'message' from Raymond was relayed to Lady Lodge via a male medium called Vout Peters; in it, 'Raymond' spoke about a photograph showing himself in a group of people, and referring to a walking-stick. The Lodges knew nothing about such a photograph. Two months later, the mother of one of Raymond's fellow officers wrote to say that she had a group photograph including Raymond, and offering to send a copy. Before this arrived, Lodge himself visited Mrs Leonard, and when her 'control' 'Feda' announced Raymond's presence, he took the opportunity to ask about the photograph. Raymond explained that it had been taken outdoors, and mentioned that someone had wanted to lean on him. When the photograph arrived a few days later, it showed a group of officers outside a billet. Raymond, sitting in the front row, has a cane resting on his leg, and the officer sitting behind him is using Raymond's shoulder as an arm rest.

Lodge's book gives many more examples of evidence of Raymond's 'survival'; but, as he points out, this one is particularly convincing because it involves two mediums, both of whom spoke of the photograph before Lodge knew of its existence—thus ruling out any possibility of telepathy.

To conclude this chapter, here is a final example of a type of phenomenon so beloved of Mrs Crowe and other early writers on the 'supernatural': the full-scale haunting.

In February 1932, the grandchildren of a chimney-sweep named Samuel Bull refused to go to sleep, insisting that there was someone outside the door of the cottage. (They were sleeping in a downstairs room, recovering from influenza.) Their mother, Mary Edwards, looked outside the door, but there was no one there. Soon afterwards, she and the children saw the figure of Samuel Bull—who had been dead since the previous June—walk across the room, up the stairs, and through the door of the room in which he had died. (This was closed). They all screamed. This was the first of many appearances of the dead man at his cottage in Oxford Street, Ramsbury, Wiltshire. The 'ghost' was apparently aware of the presence of his family, for he twice placed his hand on the brow of his invalid wife Jane, and once spoke her name. Samuel Bull—who had died of cancer—looked quite solid, and could be seen so clearly that the children noticed the whiteness of his knuckles, which seemed to be protruding through the skin. They also noticed that the expression on his face was sad. After the first appearance, the family no longer felt alarmed—the children seemed 'awed' rather than frightened. They assumed that the ghost was looking sad because of the miserable conditions they were living in—the cottage was damp and some rooms were unfit for habitation. On the last two occasions on which he appeared, Samuel Bull no longer looked sad, and Mrs Edwards assumed that this was because the family was to be re-housed in a council-house.

The family was already on the move when the two investigators from the SPR arrived, but the local vicar had already interviewed the family and recorded their accounts of what took place. The investigators were understandably upset that they had not been told about the case earlier, but their conversations with witnesses, and the evidence of the vicar, left them in no doubt that the haunting was genuine.

This rag-bag of assorted visions and apparitions underlines the enormous variety of cases investigated by the SPR in the first century of its existence. None of them are, in themselves, more impressive than cases cited by Jung-Stilling or Catherine Crowe or Robert Dale Owen. But they are more convincing because honest investigators have obviously done their best to confirm that they are genuine. And anyone who is willing to spend a few hours browsing through volumes of the *Proceedings* of the SPR (or its American counterpart) is bound to end with a feeling that further scepticism is a waste of time. Even if half the cases proved to be fraudulent or misreported, the other half would still be overwhelming by reason of sheer volume. It is easy to understand the irritation of Professor James Hyslop when he wrote in *Life After Death*:

'I regard the existence of discarnate spirits as scientifically proved and I no longer refer to the sceptic as having any right to speak on the subject. Any man who does not accept the existence of discarnate spirits and the proof of it is either ignorant or a moral coward. I give him short shrift, and do not propose to argue with him on the supposition that he knows nothing about the subject.'

Where sceptics are concerned, he certainly has a point. Sir John Bland Sutton, a well-known surgeon, remarked: 'Death is the end of all. My experience is that all of those who have studied the subject scientifically and deeply have come to the same conclusion.' Such a statement simply lacks the ring of truth. There have been many basically sceptical investigators—Hyslop himself was notoriously 'tough-minded', and much disliked by fellow members of the SPR because he seemed an incorrigible 'doubting Thomas'—but in every single case where a sceptic has persisted in studying the facts, he has ended up more-or-less convinced of the reality of life after death. I say 'more or less' because a few investigators, such as Dr Gardner Murphy and Mrs Louisa Rhine, feel that most of the 'facts' can also be explained by what might be called 'super ESP'—mind-reading clairvoyance, and so on. Hyslop himself finally abandoned the 'super ESP' hypothesis through an experience that has become known as the 'red pyjamas case'. He received a communication from a medium in Ireland to the effect that a 'spirit' calling itself William James had asked him to pass on a message asking him if he remembered some red pyjamas. Now William James, who had died in 1910, had agreed with Hyslop that whichever of them died first should try to communicate with the other. But the message about red pyjamas meant nothing to Hyslop. Then suddenly he remembered. When he and James were young men, they went to Paris together, and discovered that their luggage had not yet arrived. Hyslop went out to buy some pyjamas, but could only find a bright red pair. For days James teased Hyslop about his poor taste in pyjamas. But Hyslop had long forgotten the incident. As far as he could see, there was no way of explaining the red pyjamas message except on the hypothesis that it was really William James who had passed it on.

Twenty-six years after Hyslop's death, he was quoted by the psychologist Carl Jung in a letter. Jung was discussing the question of the identity of 'spirits' who communicate through mediums:

'I once discussed the proof of identity for a long time with a friend of William James, Professor Hyslop, in New York. He admitted that, all things considered, all these metapsychic phenomena could be explained better by the hypothesis of spirits than by the qualities and peculiarities of the unconscious. And here, on the basis of my own experience, I am bound to concede he is right. In each individual case I must of necessity be sceptical, but in the long run I have to admit that the spirit hypothesis yields better results in practice than any other.'[1]

Yet it is significant that Jung never made this admission in any of his published work, where he continued to insist that the facts

1. *Collected Letters*, Vol. 1, p. 431.

about the paranormal could be explained in terms of the powers of the unconscious mind.[1]

As far as the present investigation is concerned, we shall proceed on Jung's assumption that the 'spirit hypothesis' fits the facts better than any other. The question of whether it is ultimately true must, for the time being, be left open.

1. This is discussed at length in my book on Jung, *The Lord of the Underworld* (1984).

6.
On the Trail of
the Poltergeist

ONE DAY IN March 1661, a magistrate named John Mompesson, who lived in Tedworth in Wiltshire, was visiting the small town of Ludgershall when he was startled by loud drumming noises that came from the street. He was told that the racket was being made by a vagrant named William Drury, who had been in town for a few days. Drury had been trying to persuade the local constables to give him public assistance, on the strength of a 'pass' signed by two eminent magistrates. The constable suspected that the pass was forged.

Mompesson ordered the drummer to be brought before him, and examined his papers; just as the bailiff had suspected, they were forged. Mompesson seems to have been an officious sort of man who enjoyed exercising his authority; he ordered the drummer—a middle-aged man—to be held until the next sitting of the local Bench, and meanwhile confiscated his drum. The man seems to have tried hard to persuade Mompesson to return the drum, but without success. As soon as Mompesson's back was turned, the constable seems to have allowed Drury to escape. But the drum stayed behind.

A few weeks later, the bailiff of Ludgershall sent the drum to

Mompesson's house in Tedworth. Mompesson was just on his way to London. When he came back he found the house in uproar. For three nights, there had been violent knockings and raps all over the house—both inside and out. That night, when the banging started, Mompesson leapt out of bed with a pistol and rushed to the room from which the sound was coming. It moved to another room. He tried to locate it, but it now seemed to be coming from outside. When he got back into bed, he was able to distinguish drumbeats among the rapping noises.

For the next two months, it was impossible to get to sleep until the middle of the night; the racket went on for at least two hours every night. It stopped briefly when Mrs Mompesson was in labour, and was silent for three weeks—an indication that the spirit was mischievous rather than malicious. Then the disturbances started up again, this time centring around Mompesson's children. The drumbeats would sound from around their beds, and the beds were often lifted up into the air. When the children were moved up into a loft, the drummer followed them. The servants even began to get used to it; one manservant saw a board move, and asked it to hand it to him; the board floated up to his hand, and a joking tug-of-war ensued for twenty minutes or so, until the master ordered them to stop. When the minister came to pray by the children, the spirit showed its disrespect by being noisier than usual, and leaving behind a disgusting sulphurous smell—presumably to imply it came from Hell. Scratching noises sounded like huge rats.

Things got worse. During the next two years lights were seen, doors slammed, unseen skirts rustled, and a Bible was burnt. The creature purred like a cat, panted like a dog, and made the coins in a man's pocket turn black. One day, Mompesson went into the stable and found his horse lying on its back with its hind hoof jammed into its mouth; it had to be pried out with a lever. The 'spirit' attacked the local blacksmith with a pair of pincers, snatched a sword from a guest, and grabbed a stick from a servant woman who was trying to bar its path. The Reverend Joseph Glanvil—who wrote about the case—came to investigate, and heard the strange noises from around the childrens' beds. When he went down to his horse, he found it sweating with terror, and the horse died soon afterwards.

The phantom drummer seems to have developed a voice; one morning, there was a bright light in the children's room and a voice kept shouting: 'A witch, a witch!'—at least a hundred times, according to Glanvil. Mompesson woke up one night to find himself looking at a vague shape with two great staring eyes, which slowly vanished. It also developed such unpleasant habits as emptying ashes and chamberpots into the childrens' beds.

In 1663, William Drury was arrested at Gloucester for stealing a pig. While he was in Gloucester jail, a Wiltshire man came to see him, and Drury asked what was happening in Wiltshire. When the man said 'Nothing,' Drury said: 'What, haven't you heard about the drumming in the house at Tedworth?' The man admitted that he had, whereupon Drury declared: 'I have plagued him, and he shall never be quiet until he has made me satisfaction for taking away my drum.' This, according to Glanvil, led to his being tried for a witch at Salisbury and sentenced to transportation. As soon as Drury was out of the country, peace descended on the Mompesson household. But the drummer somehow managed to escape and return to England—whereupon the disturbances began all over again. Mr Mompesson seems to have asked it—by means of raps—whether Drury was responsible, and it replied in the affirmative.

How the disturbances ended is not clear—presumably they faded away, like most poltergeists. Certainly they had ceased by the time Glanvil published his account twenty years later.

The 'ghost' that caused these disturbances in the Mompesson household belongs to the class of phenomena known as the 'poltergeist'. The word is German, and means 'noisy ghost'. It is the commonest type of spirit on record, and unless you are in the middle of an ocean or a desert, there is probably a poltergeist haunting going on within ten miles of the place where you are now reading this book . . .

What is a poltergeist? It is a 'spirit' that seems to specialise in mischievous tricks, such as making scratching or banging noises, and causing objects to fly through the air. It would not be quite accurate to say that they 'throw' things, for the objects often have a strange habit of changing direction abruptly in mid-air, as if they are being carried rather than thrown. Moreover, these objects have been known to go *through* walls, and to come out on the other side. It is as if the poltergeist can de-materialise things and then materialise them again—either that, or the world of the poltergeist possesses an extra dimension to our three normal dimensions of length, breadth and height, so it can somehow 'step over' obstacles like walls.

Glanvil wrote his book on strange occurrences—*Saducismus Triumphatus*—just before the dawning of the 18th century, the age of reason. Even in the 1660s, the magistrate Mompesson was widely suspected of somehow fabricating the story of the phantom drummer, and 'he suffered by it in his name, in his estate, in all his affairs . . .' A quarter of a century after its publication, Glanvil's book was regarded as an absurd relic of an age of credulity. The main reason was that the civilised world was finally—after four centuries—shaking off the belief in witchcraft. In England, there had been no mass trials of witches since the death of Matthew Hopkins, the 'witchfinder general', in 1646; in America, the witch hysteria came to an end after the Salem trials in 1692. The age of science had dawned; there was no room for books like *Saducismus Triumphatus* in the age of Newton and Leibniz.

One of the most remarkable cases of the early 18th century was investigated by the eminent scientist Joseph Priestley who, predictably, decided that the phenomena were caused by a hoaxer. It began at the rectory of Epworth, in Lincolnshire, inhabited by the family of the Reverend Samuel Wesley, grandfather of the founder of Methodism. On December 1, 1716, the Wesleys' maidservant was in the dining-room when she heard appalling groans, like someone dying. The family made a joke of it. But a few nights later, they were awakened by loud knocking sounds, which usually seemed to come from the garret or nursery. The only person who failed to hear them was the Reverend Wesley himself, and the family decided not to tell him in case he thought it was an omen of his death. When they finally told him, he refused to believe them; that night, as if to convince him, there were nine loud knocks by his bedside.

From then on, the house was in a constant state of disturbance, with footsteps in empty rooms and up and down the stairs—often more than one set of footsteps at a time—noises like smashing bottles, and a curious sound which was compared to the 'winding up of a jack' or someone planing wood. When Mrs Wesley heard knocking noises from the nursery, she tried repeating them, and the poltergeist then made the same knocks resound from the floorboards under her feet. When she looked under the bed, an animal like a badger ran out. A manservant who saw the animal sitting by the dining-room fire said it looked like a white rabbit.

The family were at first afraid that it portended someone's death, either that of the Reverend Samuel Wesley or of his elder son (of the same name). When nothing of the sort occurred, they decided that they were dealing with witchcraft—against which the Reverend Samuel had preached. Yet they also noticed that the disturbances seemed connected with the 19-year-old Hetty Wesley: she often trembled in her sleep before the sounds began.

After two months, the poltergeist went away, although it is said to have made occasional brief reappearances in later years. The family came to refer to it as 'Old Jeffrey'. And Mrs Wesley remained convinced that Old Jeffrey was the spirit of her brother, who worked for the East India Company, and who vanished without a trace. She could well have been right. In some respects, the poltergeist behaved like a ghost. Its activities always seemed to begin at a quarter to ten every night (few poltergeists keep to an exact timetable)—and the very first sounds heard were groans and heavy breathing, not the usual raps. Poltergeist disturbances usually—almost invariably—occur in a certain sequence. The earliest stage is usually some kind of scratching noise like rats; then raps and bangs, then flying stones or other small objects, then larger objects, then other forms of physical mischief—moving furniture, blankets pulled off beds. If voices occur, they usually occur after this stage—as we shall see in the case of the Bell Witch. It is almost unknown for phenomena to occur in a different order. So in that respect, the Wesley case is unusual, starting with what is usually one of the later developments. The chief objection to Mrs Wesley's theory is that if the spirit of her dead brother was behind the disturbances, then why did he not try to communicate—for example, when the Reverend Samuel tried to get him to answer questions by means of raps?

One of the more obvious features of the Epworth case is that there were none of the usual physical phenomena—falling stones, dancing furniture. The explanation, presumably, is that there was not enough energy available for the poltergeist to do anything more spectacular than make noises. This is also true of the most notorious poltergeist of the 18th century, the 'Cock Lane ghost'. This began with knocking noises in the house of Richard Parsons, clerk of St Sepulchre's church in Smithfield, London, in November 1759. One night, a woman named Fanny Lynes, who was lodging in the house, asked 10-year-old Elizabeth Parsons, the eldest daughter, to sleep with her while her common-law husband was away on business. All went well for a few nights; then the two were kept awake one night by scratching and rapping noises from behind the wainscot. When they told Richard Parsons about it, he said it was probably the cobbler next door.

Soon afterwards, Fanny became ill with smallpox; she was six months pregnant, and her 'husband' was understandably anxious. He and Fanny were unmarried only because she was his deceased wife's sister. William Kent had married Elizabeth Lynes two years earlier, but she had died in childbirth; now it looked rather as if the story was repeating itself. He moved Fanny into a house nearby, where, on February 2, 1760, she died of smallpox.

Meanwhile, the rappings in Richard Parsons' house were continuing; Parsons actually called in a carpenter to take down the wainscotting, but nothing was found. Meanwhile, the knockings got louder, and the story of the 'haunted house' spread throughout the neighbourhood. They seemed to be associated with Elizabeth; they came from behind her bed, and when they were about to begin, she would begin to tremble and shiver—like Hetty Wesley in the Epworth case. Later that year, Elizabeth began to suffer from convulsions.

Like so many victims of poltergeist phenomena, Richard Parsons decided to call in a friend, the Reverend John Moore, assistant preacher at St Sepulchre's. And the Reverend Moore proceeded to communicate with the 'spirit', asking it to answer his questions in the usual manner—one rap for yes, two for no. (They added a scratching noise to indicate it was displeased.)

By this means the spirit told its upsetting story. It was, it declared, the ghost of Fanny Lynes, returned from the dead to denounce her late 'husband', William Kent, for killing her by poison. He had, it seemed, administered red arsenic in her 'purl', a mixture of herbs and beer.

Richard Parsons was not entirely displeased to hear this story, for he was nursing a grudge against his late tenant. William Kent was a fairly rich man, having been a successful innkeeper in Norfolk, and he had lent Parsons £20, on the understanding that Parsons should repay it at a pound a month. Parsons, who seems to have been a drunkard, had failed to repay anything, possibly because he had discovered that Kent and Fanny were not married, and hoped to blackmail Kent into forgetting the loan. Kent had put the matter into the hands of his attorney.

If Parsons had been less anxious to believe the worst of his ex-tenant, he might have suspected the ghost of untruthfulness. To begin with, the knocking had begun while Fanny Lynes was still alive. And a publican named Franzen swore that he had seen a spirit in white one evening in December 1759, when Fanny had just moved from the Cock Lane house. Parsons apparently found it easier to believe that the earlier knockings had been caused by Kent's first wife Elizabeth—who was presumably also trying to denounce him for murder.

Throughout 1761, the house in Cock Lane acquired an increasing reputation for its ghosts, and the tale about Kent's supposed murders gained wide currency in the area. Kent himself heard nothing about it until January 1762, when he saw an item in the *Public Ledger* about a man who had brought a young lady from Norfolk and poisoned her in London. A few days later, another item about the Cock Lane ghost and its revelations led Kent to go along to see the Reverend John Moore. Moore, a respectable and well-liked man, could only advise Kent to attend a seance in Elizabeth's bedroom, and see for himself. Kent did this, taking with him the doctor and apothecary who had attended Fanny in her last illness. The small bedroom was crowded, and Elizabeth and her younger sister lay side by side in the bed. At first the 'ghost' declined to manifest itself; but when the room had been emptied, Moore succeeded in persuading it, and they all trooped back. Now Kent listened with something like panic as he heard Moore asking the spirit if it was Kent's wife—one knock—if it had been murdered by him—one knock—and if anyone else was concerned in the murder plot—two knocks. Kent shouted indignantly, 'Thou art a lying spirit!'

Now, suddenly, the ghost was famous all over London, and

Cock Lane was crowded with carriages. In February, a clergyman named Aldrich persuaded Parsons to allow his daughter to come to his vicarage in Clerkenwell to be tested. An investigating committee, including the famous Dr Johnson, was present. Inevitably, the ghost declined to manifest itself. Nor would the ghost rap on the coffin of Fanny Lynes in the vault of the church. Dr Johnson concluded it was a fraud. And this was the opinion of most of London.

On the day following this fiasco, Elizabeth was staying at the house of a comb-maker in Cow Lane when the bell of Newgate Prison began to toll—a sign that someone was to be hanged. The comb-maker asked the ghost whether someone was about to be hanged and whether it was a man or woman; the ghost answered both questions correctly. Later that day, a loose curtain began to spin on its rod—the only physical manifestation in the case.

The following day, as Elizabeth lay asleep, her father heard whispering noises; he carried a candle over to her bed, but she seemed to be asleep. The whispering continued, although the child's lips were plainly closed. In fact, the poltergeist seemed to be increasing in strength. Two nights later, the noises were so violent that their host asked them to leave. (Presumably she was sleeping away from home to avoid crowds.) Elizabeth and her father moved to the house of a Mr Missiter, near Covent Garden, and the manifestations continued, even when a maid lay in bed beside Elizabeth and held her hands and feet.

By now, the unfortunate Kent was determined to prove his innocence through the law; so the burden of proof now lay on Parsons and his daughter. Elizabeth was told that unless the ghost made itself heard that night, her father and mother would be thrown into prison. Naturally, she made sure something happened. The servants peered through a crack in the door, and saw her take a piece of board and hide it in the bed. Later, when there were people in the room, the knocking noises sounded from the bed. In fact, the listeners noticed that the knocks were coming from the bed and not, as usual, from around the room. The bed was searched and the board found. And the next day, the newspapers published the story of the 'fraud'.

On February 25, 1762, there appeared a pamphlet entitled: *The Mystery Revealed; Containing a Series of Transactions and*

Authentic Testimonials respecting the supposed Cock Lane Ghost, which have been concealed from the Public—the author was probably Johnson's friend Oliver Goldsmith. A satirical play called *The Drummer or the Haunted House* was presented at Covent Garden. And William Kent began legal proceedings against Richard Parsons. In July 1762, Mr and Mrs Parsons, and a woman called Mary Frazer—who had often acted as 'questioner' to the ghost—appeared before magistrates in the Guildhall. Parsons was charged with trying to take away the life of William Kent by charging him with murder. The judges remained unconvinced by the evidence of neighbours who had heard raps resounding from all over the room, and who were certain that Elizabeth could not have made them. And finally, Parsons was sentenced to two years in prison, and to stand three times in the pillory; his wife was sentenced to one year, and Mary Frazer to six months. The Reverend Moore and one of his associates had to pay out £588 in damages to Kent. There was universal sympathy for Parsons, and when he stood in the pillory, the mob took up a collection for him—an unusual gesture for a period when malefactors were often badly injured in the pillory. (Later in the year a man convicted of sodomy was stoned to death in the same pillory.)

For more than two centuries, the Cock Lane ghost became a synonym for an imposture. When Andrew Lang wrote about it in 1894, he began his chapter: 'If one phantom is more discredited than another, it is the Cock Lane ghost.' Yet for anyone studying the case today, this view seems absurd. Nothing could be more obvious than that the Cock Lane ghost was a poltergeist like the hundreds of others that have been recorded down the ages. Unfortunately, it is now too late for us to discover certain essential facts that might help to explain it. For example, what kind of a girl *was* Elizabeth Parsons? She was rather younger than most poltergeist-children, but she may well have been sexually mature for her age. If her father was something of a drunkard and a spendthrift—as the records indicate—then it seems fairly certain that the Parsons household was not a happy one. The father of Christine Beauchamp—Morton Prince's famous case of multiple personality—was a similar type of person, and his daughter had severe psychological problems as a consequence. We know that

Christine Beauchamp became fixated on her father's closest friend William Jones, and transferred to him all her adoration. It is conceivable that Elizabeth Parsons felt the same about William Kent. In which case, sleeping in his bed while he was away must have aroused morbid emotions—especially if she was aware that Kent and Fanny were 'living in sin'. The convulsions that began a year after the disturbances certainly suggest she was passing through a period of emotional upheaval. But since we know so little about Elizabeth, all these things must remain a matter for speculation.

Only one thing seems fairly certain: that the spirit itself was neither that of Elizabeth Kent nor of Fanny Lynes; it was the usual mischievous poltergeist, bent on creating as much havoc and confusion as possible. It seems to confirm Chesterton's remark that the only definite thing that can be said about such spirits is that they teli lies.

The Epworth poltergeist and the Cock Lane ghost confined themselves to rappings (although the Cock Lane ghost seemed to be attempting more ambitious phenomena towards the end). A poltergeist that haunted a farm in Stockwell, London, in 1772 showed altogether less restraint. It began by throwing rows of plates off the kitchen shelf and smashing them. When the owner of the house, Mrs Golding, fainted, the doctor bled her; the blood had only just congealed when it leapt out of the basin, and the basin smashed in pieces. When Mrs Golding offered some of the assembled guests a drink of wine or rum, these bottles also shattered. Joints of ham leapt off their hooks on the ceiling and fell to the floor. The racket was so tremendous that they were afraid the house would fall down, and the children were sent off to the barn. The maid, Ann Robinson, went with them, and as soon as she was out of the house, the disturbances stopped. The moment she returned, they started again. The coal scuttle overturned, candlesticks flew through the air, a nine-gallon cask of beer was turned upside down, and a bucket of cold water 'boiled like a pot'—as in the Amherst case of a century later. Mrs Golding decided to sack the maid, and the uproar promptly ceased.

This case attracted little attention at the time—if Dr Johnson heard of it, he no doubt dismissed it as another fraud. Catherine

Crowe unearthed it a century later for her book *The Night Side of Nature*. And in her chapter on the poltergeist, she makes some sensible and pertinent suggestions. She discusses the case of a French girl called Angélique Cottin, who was weaving silk gloves on January 15, 1846, when the loom began to jerk violently. The other girls were terrified, and retreated to the far end of the room; then, one by one, they went back to examine the loom, which had a heavy oak frame. As soon as Angélique approached, it began to dance again.

From this time on, Angélique developed the power of giving people violent electric shocks—she was, in fact, a 'human electric eel'. Objects laid on her apron flew off violently, and the power was strong enough to raise a heavy tub with a man sitting on it. Oddly enough, metals were not affected, indicating that this form of 'electricity' was not the usual kind. When Angélique was tired, the current would diminish. It also diminished when she was on a carpet, but was most powerful when she was on bare earth—another indication that the force seems to come from the earth, and is probably connected with the force that convulses some dowsers. She had to sleep on a stone covered with a cork mat. The phenomena continued for four months, and were widely studied by men of science; then they ceased.

Mrs Crowe makes the reasonable suggestion that poltergeist phenomena may be electrical in nature, and cites a number of other cases, including a Mlle. Emmerich, sister of the professor of theology at Strasbourg, who became a human electric battery after receiving a severe fright, the nature of which is not specified. (We have already noticed that many mediums seem to develop their powers after accidents.) The interesting thing about Mlle. Emmerich was that she could give people shocks even when they were not touching her. She gave her brother a shock when he was several rooms away; when he rushed to her bedroom, she laughed and said: 'Ah, you felt it, did you?'

Mrs Crowe adds the interesting remark: 'Many somnambulistic persons [she means persons under hypnosis] are capable of giving an electric shock; and I have met with one person, not somnambulistic, who informs me that he has frequently been able to do it by an effort of will.'

Clearly, if someone *was* able to produce electric currents at will, he or she might be in a position to cause poltergeist phenomena—perhaps even at a distance, like Mlle. Emmerich; in that case, we might have some kind of explanation for the magical powers of the drummer of Tedworth. But although the theory is attractive, it could only explain the least spectacular abilities of the poltergeist—like causing raps and smashing plates. How, for example, could it account for the extraordinary case that has become known as the Bell Witch, in which a poltergeist mistreated its victim until he died?

This case, as the paranormal investigator Nandor Fodor pointed out, took place at an interesting time when Americans had ceased to believe in witchcraft, and had not yet discovered Spiritualism. As a result, there was no proper investigation. It is fortunate that the records that have survived are so detailed.

In 1817, a farmer named John Bell lived with his family in Robertson County, Tennessee, with his wife Lucy and nine children. One of these, Betsy, was a girl of twelve.

At first, the disturbances were so slight that no one paid much attention. There were knocking and scraping noises, and sounds like rats gnawing inside the walls. As usual, nothing could be found to account for these sounds. They seemed to be mostly the kind of noises that might be made by animals, and so did not cause a great deal of excitement. An invisible dog seemed to be clawing at the floor, an invisible bird flapped against the ceiling, then two chained dogs sounded as if they were having a fight. When lamps were lit and people got out of bed to search, the noises stopped—poltergeists seem to have an odd dislike of being observed. Then the entity started pulling the clothes off beds, and making various 'human' noises—choking and gulping sounds followed by a gasping noise as if someone was being strangled. Next, stones were thrown and chairs turned upside down. Slowly, the poltergeist began to get into its stride. The girl Betsy—Elizabeth—seemed to be the focus; things only happened when she was around.

When the disturbances had been going on for roughly a year, the household was in permanent chaos. They seldom got a good night's sleep; the house often shook with the noises. The thing seemed to be able to be in several places at once—one night,

Richard Williams Bell was awakened by something pulling his hair so hard that he thought the top of his head would come off; as he yelled with pain, Betsy, on the floor above, also began to scream as something pulled her hair.

Like the Fox family thirty years later, the Bells decided to ask the advice of neighbours. A friend named James Johnson came to the house. When the 'ghost' made a sound like sucking air in through the teeth, he told it to be quiet, and it obeyed him. But poltergeists dislike being given orders (they seem to react best to a friendly approach), and this one redoubled its persecution of Betsy; there would be a sharp slapping noise and her cheek would go red from a blow, or her hair would be grabbed by an invisible hand and pulled. At least, Johnson had discovered that the entity understood English; so he advised Bell to invite in more neighbours. At this stage, he still seems to have entertained the obviously absurd idea that the children might be responsible. They tried sending Elizabeth to stay with a neighbour; the disturbances in the Bell household stopped, but Elizabeth continued to be persecuted with blows and scratches.

Poltergeist phenomena always work their way up from small effects to larger ones—from scratches or raps to flying stones and furniture; it never happens the other way around. The 'Bell Witch' seemed to take pleasure in developing new ways of upsetting everybody. Strange lights flitted about the yard after dark. As the children came home from school, stones and chunks of wood were thrown at them. These were usually thrown from a particular thicket, and (as usual in such cases) never hurt anyone; if the children threw them back, they were promptly thrown again. But visitors to the house received stinging slaps—as did the children if they tried to resist when the covers were dragged off their beds.

The next stage was a whistling sound, which gradually changed to a voice. Poltergeist voices do not sound at all like ordinary human voices; at least, not to begin with. It seems as if the entity is having to master a strange medium, to form sounds into words. (Even the rapping noises are probably 'manufactured' sounds, not genuine raps made by hard objects.) Most talking ghosts and poltergeists begin in a guttural voice that sounds as if it is made up from grunts or groans; the Bell witch made gasping, whispering noises more like an asthmatic cough. Gradually, the voice developed until it was a low but audible whisper. It made such remarks as 'I can't stand the smell of a nigger'. And Betsy undoubtedly provided the energy for these demonstrations; she became fatigued and miserable, short of breath, and subject to fainting spells. Whenever she was unconscious, the voice ceased, which led some neighbours to suspect that she was a ventriloquist. But, as Nandor Fodor has pointed out, it sounds much more as if she slipped into mediumistic trance. At the same time, John Bell himself began to suffer. His tongue swelled, and his jaw felt stiff as if someone had pushed a stick inside his mouth, pushing on both sides of the jaw. It gradually became worse, until he was often unable to eat for a day at a time. The 'witch' also seemed to direct more and more of its malice towards 'old Jack Bell', declaring that he would be tormented for the rest of his life.

Meanwhile, the voice had graduated from a whisper to a normal voice; it used to repeat bits of the sermons of various local parsons. Then it began using bad language—again, a common characteristic of 'talking ghosts'. In fact, 'it' talked in several voices. One of its earliest utterances in a normal voice was: 'I am a spirit who was once very happy, but have been disturbed and am now unhappy.' And it stated that it would torment John Bell and kill him in the end. It identified itself as an Indian whose bones had been scattered, then as a witch called Old Kate Batts. Then four more voices made their appearance—the 'family' of the witch; they identified themselves as Blackdog, Mathematics, Cypocryphy and Jerusalem. Blackdog had a harsh, masculine voice, Jerusalem a boy's voice, while the other two sounded 'delicate and feminine'. They apparently indulged in debauches, talking drunkenly and filling the house with the smell of whisky.

As much as the witch detested John Bell, it seemed to have gentler feelings for the rest of the family, especially for John Bell's wife Lucy. When she fell ill the witch lamented 'Luce, poor Luce' and showered hazel nuts on her. At Betsy's birthday party, it called 'I have a surprise for you', and materialised a basket of fruit, including oranges and bananas, which it claimed to have brought from the West Indies.

A local 'witch-doctor' offered to cure Betsy with some revolting medicine which would make her vomit; when she duly retched, her vomit was found to be full of brass pins and needles. Meanwhile the witch screamed with laughter and said that if Betsy could be made to vomit again, she would have enough pins and needles to set up a shop.

One day in winter, as the children were sitting on a sledge, the witch called 'Hold tight', and hauled the sledge at great speed round the house three times.

It was also able to spit; it had a particular aversion to a negro slave girl called Anky, and one day covered her head with a foam like white spittle.

It also showed a tendency to interfere in the personal lives of the family. In due course, Betsy became engaged to a youth called Joshua Gardner. As soon as the witch found out, she began to whisper: 'Please, Betsy Bell, don't have Joshua Gardner.' Betsy finally gave in, and returned Joshua's ring.

Meanwhile, the persecution of John Bell became steadily worse. His sufferings sound like the torments of the possessed nuns and priests of Loudun; but they were of a more physical nature. When he was ill in bed, the witch cursed and raved, using foul language. When he went outside, it followed him and jerked off his shoes. Then he was struck in the face so hard that he was stunned and had to sit down on a log. His face began to jerk and contort—another of the witch's favourite methods of tormenting him—then his body convulsed. His shoes kept flying off, and every time his son Richard put them on they flew off again. The witch shrieked with laughter and sang derisive songs (many poltergeists have shown themselves to be musical, although their taste seldom rises above popular songs). Finally, the attacks ceased, and the unfortunate man sat there stunned, with the tears rolling down his cheeks. The witch had been tormenting him for more than three years. When they got him back indoors, he took to his bed. On December 19, 1820, he was found to be in a deep stupor. In the medicine cupboard, his son John found a dark bottle one-third full of a smoky-looking liquid. The witch began to exult: 'It's useless for you to try to relieve old Jack—I've got him this time.' Asked about the medicine, the witch replied: 'I put it there, and gave old Jack a dose last night while he was asleep, which fixed him.' When the doctor arrived, they tested the 'medicine' by dipping a straw into it and allowing a drop to fall on the cat's tongue; the cat jumped and whirled around, then died. John Bell himself died the next day, while the witch filled the house with shrieks of triumph, and sang, 'Row me up some brandy, O'.

As Fodor points out, there is something very odd about this death. The witch had often revealed strength enough to strangle Bell, or kill him by hitting him with some object; yet she never made any such attempt—only, as it were, drove him to despair, then administered some powerful drug when he was probably dying anyway. In most poltergeist cases we may feel that the entity is not particularly malicious, and that this explains the lack of injury—bullying children often threaten their victims with physical damage, and may even seem to be on the point of carrying out their threat; but there is an abyss of difference between the threat—or, perhaps, lashing out with a stick and missing by a hair's breadth—and actually causing bodily harm. Yet the Bell Witch seems to have been more malicious than most. It leads to the speculation that these entities may not be 'allowed' to do actual harm; they are allowed to torment, but not to damage. This, admittedly, explains nothing; but it is certainly an observation that has struck everyone who has studied the poltergeist.

After the death of John Bell, the witch seemed to lose interest. It apparently refused to help John Jnr to speak to his dead father, declaring that the dead could not be brought back; but on one occasion, it told John to go to the window, on a snowy day, then made footprints appear in the snow, which it claimed to be identifical with those made by his father's boots—John did not bother to test this claim.

In 1821, four years after the disturbances began (an unusually long period), the family was sitting at supper one evening when there was a tremendous noise in the chimney—as if a cannon-ball had rolled down it and out into the room. It burst into a ball of smoke. The witch's voice called: 'I am going, and will be gone for seven years—goodbye to all.' And the disturbances ceased.

Seven years later, only Lucy Bell and two of her sons remained in the homestead; the rest, including Betsy, had married or left. Once again, the manifestations started from the beginning, with scratching noises, then the covers being pulled off the bed. But the family ignored all this, and after two weeks, the manifestations ceased. John Jnr claimed that the witch paid him two visits in his new home, and promised to return to one of his descendants in hundred and seven years; but 1935 passed without any direct descendant of the Bell family being 'haunted'.

The case of the Bell Witch was fully documented in a book written in 1846 by Richard Bell, who had been seven when the witch first appeared, and was later the subject of a full length book by M.V. Ingram (1894). Nandor Fodor, who has written extensively on the poltergeist, discusses it fully in his book *The Poltergeist Down the Centuries*. As well as being a student of the paranormal, Fodor was also a Freudian psychiatrist, and he takes the view that the poltergeist is sexual in origin. Undoubtedly, he is partly correct—the poltergeist seems to be at its best when it can draw on the energies of a girl (or, less often, a boy) who has just reached puberty. But Fodor goes further than this, and suggests that the explanation of the Bell Witch lies in an incestuous attack made on Betsy by her father. This caused Betsy to hate her father, and her repressed hatred expressed itself in the form of 'recurrent spontaneous psychokinesis'. He also believes that John Bell felt a deep guilt about the supposed attack, and cites an occasion when Bell went to dinner with neighbours named Dearden, yet said nothing all evening, seeming depressed and confused; the next day he rode over specially to explain, saying that his tongue had been affected as if his mouth had become filled with fungus. This, says Fodor, probably represents 'self-aggression'.

But this theory hardly stands up to examination. As we have seen, poltergeists often take a delight in embarrassing people by revealing their most intimate secrets in public—in the Bell Witch case, it hastened the break-up of Betsy and Joshua by embarrassing them with personal revelations. So it is hard to see why it should have failed to state publicly that John Bell had committed—or tried to commit—incest with Betsy. Even if it *had* said so, we would be justified in treating the accusation with caution: poltergeists are not noted for truthfulness. The fact that it failed to say so weighs heavily against the incest theory. As to the notion that Betsy's unconscious aggressions caused the disturbances this fails to explain why Betsy herself was—at first—treated so badly. It also fails to explain how the witch managed to return when Betsy had left home and was married.

Rather more interesting are Fodor's speculations about the nature of the poltergeist. He thinks that its denial of communication with the dead proves that it was not the spirit of a dead person. He is inclined to feel that the witch was 'a fragment of a living personality that has broken free in some mysterious way of some of the three-dimensional limitations of the mind of the main personality'. In other words, poltergeists are explainable as fragments of the 'split personality'. But this leaves us exactly where we were before—in complete ignorance of how the split personality performs its paranormal feats.

The truth is that this explanation—about the unconscious mind—sounded far more convincing in the 1930s than it does today, when Freud is no longer regarded as infallible. Moreover, it simply fails to fit the facts of the 'haunting'. On the other hand, Kardec's views fit them like a glove. According to *The Spirits' Book*, only a small proportion of the spirits involved in poltergeist cases are those of dead people—there are many other kinds. Besides, it seems clear that in the Bell Witch case, there was not one spirit, but several. So Kardec's explanation would be that the haunting in the Bell household was the work of a group of rowdy and mischievous spirits or 'elementals' of no particular intelligence—the other-worldly equivalent of a cageful of monkeys. A house with nine children, many of them teenagers, would provide plenty of the energy poltergeists find necessary to perform their antics. We must suppose that the Bell household was not a particularly happy one—this deduction arises from the fact that there is no record of a poltergeist haunting taking place in a happy family. No doubt John Bell was a typical 19th century patriarch, dictatorial and bad-tempered; and on a farmstead in a remote rural area, there was no doubt plenty of reason for tension and frustration in the family.

As to why the witch disliked John Bell so much, the reason may lie in an event that took place very early in the case. Before the first scratching noises were heard, John Bell saw one day a strange, dog-like creature sitting between two corn rows, and shot at it. The 'witch' stated on a number of occasions that she could assume the shape of an animal. Poltergeists dislike aggression against themselves, and if the strange animal *was* the witch, then it had a cause for feeling resentment about John Bell. Apart from that, he was the head of the household, the 'tyrant'. If the witch was capable of showing generosity and affection towards various members of the family—Lucy, Betsy, young John—then she (they?) would also dislike the bullying paterfamilias. This is, admittedly, speculation; but it fits better than Fodor's Freudian guesses.

Thirty years after the Bell Witch, there occurred in Stratford, Connecticut, a case that has seems to demonstrate beyond all doubt the inadequacies of Fodor's Freudian theories.

The Stratford minister, the Rev. Eliakim Phelps, had married a widow with four children. He was interested in clairvoyance, and attempted to treat illnesses by means of mesmerism. He was understandably excited by the news of the strange events at the home of the Fox family in 1849. And in March 1850, when he entertained a visitor from New York, the two of them arranged some kind of amateur seance, which was not particularly successful, although they managed to obtain a few raps.

A few days later, on Sunday March 10, the family returned from church to find the front door wide open and the place in disorder. Their first assumption was that they had been burgled; but inspection showed that nothing had been taken, and a gold watch left on a table was untouched. That afternoon, the family went off to church again, but this time the Reverend Phelps stayed behind to keep watch. He may well have dozed; at all events, nothing disturbed him. But when the family returned from church, the place again showed signs of an intruder. Furniture was scattered, and in the main bedroom, a nightgown and chemise had been laid out on the bed, with the arms folded across the breast, and a pair of stockings placed to make it look like a corpse laid out for burial. In another room, clothing and cushions had been used to make various dummies, which were arranged in a tableau, 'in attitudes of extreme devotion, some with their foreheads nearly touching the floor', and with open

Bibles in front of them. Clearly, the poltergeist had a sense of ironic humour.

From then on, the Phelps poltergeist practised its skill as a designer of tableaux. The astonishing thing was that these were done so quickly. One observer, a Dr Webster, remarked that it would have taken half a dozen women several hours to construct the 'dummies' that the poltergeist made within minutes. One figure was so life-like that when the 3-year-old boy went into the room, he thought his mother was kneeling in prayer, and that she whispered 'Be still . . .'

That it *was* a poltergeist became clear the following day, when objects began to fly through the air. A bucket flew downstairs, an umbrella leapt through the air, and spoons, bits of tin and keys were thrown around. A candlestick jumped off the mantelpiece, then beat the floor violently until it broke. There were loud pounding noises as if someone was trying to demolish the house with an axe, and loud screams.

The poltergeist probably derived its strength from the fact that it had two 'focuses' in the house—Harry, aged 12, and Anna, who was 16. Harry was persecuted by the 'spirit'. When he went for a drive in the carriage with his stepfather, twenty stones were flung into the carriage. On one occasion he was snatched up into the air so that his head nearly struck the ceiling; he was thrown into a cistern of water, and tied up and suspended from a tree. In front of a visiting clergyman, the legs of his trousers were violently torn open from the bottom to above the knee.

After this, the poltergeist started to break glass; it smashed seventy-one window panes and various glass articles. Another of its favourite tricks was to write on sheets of paper; when the Reverend Phelps turned his back on his writing table, he heard the scratching of the pen, and found written on the paper: 'Very nice paper and nice ink for the devil.' (Typically, poltergeists seem to object to being watched while they do things like this; they wait until no one is looking.)

Phelps tried communicating with the 'spirit' by means of raps, and found that it would answer his questions. There seemed to be more than one spirit present; but the author of most of the mischief seemed to be a French clerk, who had handled a settlement for Mrs Phelps, and who had since died; he now claimed to be in hell because he had cheated Mrs Phelps. Her husband investigated this claim, and found that there *had* been a minor fraud; but it had hardly been as serious as the 'spirit' seemed to believe. On another occasion the raps told Phelps to put his hand under the table; when he did this his hand was grasped by another hand, warm and human.

The well-known psychic Andrew Jackson Davis visited the Phelps home, and put forward a theory very similar to that of Mrs Crowe. He said that the phenomena were caused by 'magnetism' and by 'electricity', the magnetism attracting objects towards the boy and girl, the electricity causing them to fly in the opposite direction. But Davis—the author of the bestselling work of 'spirit dictation' called *The Principles of Nature*—also agreed that there were spirits present—he claimed to have seen five of them.

The poltergeist—or poltergeists—became increasingly destructive. Pieces of paper burst into flame, although always where they could be seen; sometimes, the ashes of burnt papers were found in drawers. All kinds of objects were smashed—Phelps estimated that the poltergeist had done about two hundred dollars' worth of damage. And the poltergeist also attacked the eldest girl, Anna. A reporter was sitting with the mother and daughter when the girl shouted that someone had pinched her; they rolled up her sleeve and found a severe fresh pinch mark on her arm. On another occasion, there was a loud smacking noise, and a red mark appeared on her face.

In October 1851, more than a year after the disturbances began, the mother and children went off to Pennsylvania and stayed there until the following spring. The poltergeist did not follow them, and when they returned to Stratford, nothing more happened.

What seems very clear is that the poltergeist haunting would never have taken place if the Rev. Phelps had not made the mistake of dabbling in an amateur seance. Presumably this attracted the attention of some juvenile delinquents of the spirit world, who discovered that there were two excellent mediums in the house, and proceeded to make use of their energies. When Mrs Phelps took the children away, the poltergeist was starved of energy and went away. Here it seems obvious that the 'Freudian' explanation is both unnecessary and irrelevant.

The Phelps case has been described as 'one of the most amazing poltergeist dramas of which we have record'.[1] In fact, most students of the paranormal would agree that this distinction should go to the case that has become known as 'the Amherst mystery', which took place in Nova Scotia in 1878.

A shoe worker named Daniel Teed lived in a two-storey house with his wife and two sons, his wife's two unmarried sisters, Jane and Esther Cox, who were aged 22 and 18, his wife's brother William, and his own brother, John. (The house must have been grossly overcrowded.) All were Methodists. Jane, the elder sister, was pretty; Esther was short and rather stout. Nevertheless, Esther had a boyfriend, a local factory worker named Bob MacNeal.

In late August, Daniel Teed complained that someone had been milking the cow; Esther was a suspect as she was unusually fond of milk. Esther was suffering from nervous tensions, and ran up from the cellar one night screaming that a rat had run over her leg. Her troubles were probably sexual in origin, as seems to be revealed by a dream she had at the time: hundreds of black bulls with bright blue eyes and blood dripping from their mouths tried to break into the house, while Esther frantically locked the doors . . .

The following evening, Esther and Bob MacNeal went out for a drive. Bob, who had a bad reputation locally, tried to persuade Esther to go into the woods with him, but she refused. He pulled out a gun and ordered her to get down from the buggy; he looked as if he might fire when the sound of an approaching vehicle distracted him. He leapt on to the buggy, drove back at a dangerous speed, let Esther off, then left Amherst for good. Esther cried herself to sleep, and for the next few days had red eyes.

On September 4, a damp, misty evening, Jane heard Esther sobbing in bed. Then Esther screamed that there was a mouse in bed with her. They searched, but no mouse was found. The following night, both heard a rustling noise, and made a search. It

1. Fr. Herbert Thurston, S.J. *Ghosts and Poltergeists*, 1953.

seemed to be coming from a cardboard box containing patchwork, so Jane stood it in the middle of the room, expecting a mouse to run out. Instead the box jumped into the air and fell over. She stood it up, and it jumped again.

Daniel Teed came in to see what the noise was about, pushed the box under the bed, and told them to go to sleep.

The next night, Esther went to bed early. Soon after the light went out, she leapt out of bed shouting: 'Jane, I'm dying.' Jane lit the lamp and saw that Esther's face was bright red, and her hair was standing on end. Daniel Teed came in, together with the other two men. Esther got back into bed, but began to scream. Her body appeared to be swelling like a balloon. Suddenly, there was a loud report like a clap of thunder. The men rushed out to search the house, but found nothing. When they came back, Esther was back to normal and fast asleep.

Two days later, as Esther was getting into bed, she began to feel ill again. All the bedclothes flew off the bed, and landed in the far corner of the room. Jane fainted. Esther began to swell again. The men rushed in, and someone replaced the bedclothes; they promptly flew off again, and a pillow hit John Teed on the head; he left the house never to return. Again, there were some loud explosions. Esther stopped swelling, and fell asleep.

The following day, a doctor came to see Esther. As she lay in bed, the pillow under her head inflated, as if filled up with air, then collapsed, then re-inflated itself. Raps sounded around the room. The bedclothes flew off. There was a scratching noise above Esther's bed and, as they all watched, they saw writing appearing on the wall. It said: 'Esther, you are mine to kill.' A lump of plaster detached itself from elsewhere on the wall and flew across the room to the doctor's feet. Then rappings and bangs continued for the next two hours, while Esther lay, terrified, on her bed.

The following day, Esther complained of an 'electric' feeling running through her body. The doctor gave her morphine; instantly, there was a series of bangs and crashes that seemed to go up to the roof.

These disturbances continued for another three weeks. Then, one night, Esther fell into a trance, became rigid, and told the story of what had happened with Bob MacNeal. When she recovered consciousness, she admitted it was true. When Jane said that Bob must be responsible for Esther's problems, loud knocks suggested that the 'spirit' agreed completely. Jane remarked that it seemed to understand what she said, whereupon there were three distinct raps. The doctor tried asking the 'spirit' simple questions, with one rap for no, two for 'no answer', three for yes. But the doctor's attempts to get it to explain itself were a total failure.

Esther became a subject of controversy; the house was permanently full of people. When a minister called to see her, a bucket of cold water on the kitchen table began to bubble as if it was boiling.

In December, Esther developed a severe sore throat which turned to diphtheria. While she was ill, the manifestations ceased. Then she went away to convalesce. When she returned, the manifestations started immediately. Esther said she heard a voice telling her that the house was going to be set on fire. As she told the others about this, a lighted match fell from the air on to the bed, and the sheets caught fire. Jane quickly put it out. More lighted matches fell around the room, most of them going out immediately. The rapping noises started later, and when the family asked the 'spirit' whether the house would be set alight, it replied that it would not be. At that moment there was smoke from under Esther's bed; they found that a dress had somehow transferred itself from the bedroom door, and had been set on fire.

Three days later, Mrs Teed smelled smoke coming from the cellar. They found a barrel of wood shavings burning vigorously and had some trouble putting it out.

The villagers were alarmed about this; if the Teeds' house caught fire, half the village would probably be burned down. They suggested that Esther ought to be sent away. A neighbour named John White offered to take her in if she would do some housework. For two weeks, all went well; then a scrubbing brush flew out of Esther's hand, went up to the ceiling, and came down and hit her on the head.

White owned a restaurant, and Esther went to work there. An oven door refused to stay closed, and jumped off its hinges. Metal objects began flying at Esther as if she were a magnet, and a boy's clasp-knife made her back bleed. When iron spikes were laid in her lap, they quickly became too hot to touch.

All this seemed to support the suspicion that Esther was somehow 'electrified'. They tried making her wear a special pair of shoes with glass soles; but these gave her headaches and made her nose bleed.

When furniture began to move around the restaurant, John White decided it was time for Esther to go home. Again, she left Amherst for a few months; first to stay with a man and his wife in New Brunswick, then to a farm three miles from Amherst. She told various visitors about the 'voices' that spoke to her—voices which claimed to be the spirits that were causing the mischief. One of these spirits, 'Bob Nickle', threatened her with fire and stabbing.

In June, 1879, a stage magician named Walter Hubbell moved into the Teeds' cottage as a paying guest; he had heard about the 'haunting' and thought it might make the subject of a book. Within a few minutes of arriving, he had no doubt that this was no fraud. His umbrella sailed through the air, then a carving knife landed at his feet, then his bag was 'thrown', then a chair shot across the room and hit his own so hard that he nearly fell on the floor. From then on, the chairs in every room he entered performed a dance. Esther told him he was unpopular with the spirits. Undeterred, Hubbell tried asking them questions by means of raps, and the spirits were able to tell him the number engraved on his watch, and the dates of coins in his pockets. Later, Hubbell lay down on the settee and closed his eyes; Esther came into the room, and Hubbell cautiously peeped at her, perhaps hoping that she would give herself away as a cheat. Instead, he saw a large glass paperweight float up across the room and rebound off the arm of the settee.

During the next few days the poltergeist put on a special show for Hubbell. Objects floated around, strange noises were heard—like sawing wood and drumming on a washboard—and Esther was attacked by 'six spirits' who stuck no fewer than thirty pins in her. Small fires broke out—on one day there were forty-five of them—and the sound of a trumpet echoed through the house; they later found a small silver trumpet which no one had ever seen before. When Esther went to the local minister to pray, 'Bob Nickle' attacked her viciously on her return, cutting her head open with a bone and stabbing her in the face with a fork.

Hubbell thought he saw a way of making money. He hired a hall and persuaded Esther to put on a 'show' for the people of Amherst. Inevitably, the spirits declined to operate, and the audience demanded their money back.

Tired of the non-stop disturbances, Daniel Teed sent Esther off to stay with some obliging friends; Hubbell, who now had enough material for his book, went to St John to write it. It appeared in due course and went through several editions.

During Esther's stay with her friends, the spirits let her alone. She then took a job on a farm owned by people called Davidson. Her friends found that various articles were missing, and these were located in the Davidsons' barn. Esther was suspected of theft, but before the case could be investigated the barn caught fire and burned to the ground. Esther was accused of arson, and was sentenced to four months in jail. After this, the manifestations came suddenly to an end.

This abrupt termination of the 'haunting' seems to favour the view that Esther's own unconscious mind was responsible. This is, in fact, the view I favoured when I described the case briefly in a book called *Mysteries*. Esther was sexually frustrated, and if Bob MacNeal had adopted a more gentlemanly way of seducing her, there would have been no 'Great Amherst Mystery' (the title of Hubbell's book). Esther was a classic case of 'the divided self': a part of her longing to give herself to her lover, while the inhibitions induced by her background and training made this impossible. So when she rejected his advances, and he vanished into the night, her unconscious mind said, in effect: 'Now see what you've done, stupid!', and set out to punish her. As to the effects themselves, many of them fit the hypothesis I have suggested: that the 'energy' comes from the earth. When Esther wore shoes with glass soles, the manifestations stopped but she developed headaches and nosebleeds. Her sensation of electric currents is also highly suggestive. There have been dozens of well-authenticated cases of 'human electric batteries'. Again, nearly all concern girls or boys at the age of puberty. Caroline Clare of Bondon, Ontario, began to lose weight at the age of seventeen (in 1877), then developed such powerful electric currents that people who touched her received severe shocks; pieces of metal stuck to her as if she were a magnet. Jennie Morgan of Sedalia, Missouri, became an electric battery at fourteen; when she touched metal objects, sparks flew. Frank McKinistry, also of Missouri, would develop an electric charge during the night and slowly lose it during the day. When highly charged, his feet would stiek to the ground so that he had difficulty in walking—which sounds again as if the electricity comes from the earth. (Good dowsers receive a 'tingling' sensation when they touch standing stones.) The Amherst minister, the Reverend Edwin Clay, was convinced that the secret of Esther's manifestations was electricity, and even delivered a lecture to that effect.

But how did Esther's unconscious mind know the number of Hubbell's watch and the dates of coins in his pocket—which no doubt he did not know himself? How did her mind scratch 'Esther, you are mine to kill' on the wall above her head? How did it blow a trumpet all over the house? The truth is that the unconscious mind theory needs to be stretched so much that it loses the chief virtue of a good theory—simplicity.

But perhaps the strongest argument against the unconscious mind theory is simply that Esther's torment went on for so long. To actually read the case in detail is to feel that no one could get so angry with herself that she would continue relentlessly for more than a year. We may say, 'Oh, I could kick myself,' when we do something stupid; but no one has ever *done* it.

The fraud hypothesis also fails to stand up to close examination. If Hubbell's book was the main piece of evidence, then we might well feel suspicious, since he went to Amherst with the hope of writing it, and eventually made a great deal of money from no fewer than ten editions. But there are accounts in the *Amherst Gazette* that confirm everything Hubbell says. Moreover, in 1907, more than a quarter of a century after the events, the researcher Hereward Carrington went to Amherst and took various depositions from people who had witnessed the manifestations. By this time, Esther was unhappily married, and had turned into a sullen middle-aged woman, who agreed to talk to Carrington only on the payment of $100; Carrington felt that such testimony would be valueless. But there could be no doubt that most of the people involved believed that the manifestations were genuine, including the farmer, Davidson, whose barn had been destroyed—he said that he had often watched Esther as she came downstairs and had noticed that she seemed to fly or float. (In the Middle Ages, levitation used to be one of the criteria for demoniacal possession.)

But this question of demoniacal possession must be left until a later chapter.

7.
The Scientist Investigates

THE NEXT MAJOR STEP forward in the history of poltergeist investigation was taken by an unlikely figure, Professor Cesare Lombroso. He was an unlikely investigator because he was known throughout Europe as a hard-line sceptic and materialist. And this, in turn, was due to the fact that he had been born—in 1835—in Verona, which was then a part of the Austro-Hungarian empire, which was Roman Catholic. And since Lombroso was a Jewish Italian, he naturally hated the Austrians and their religion. His distaste was increased by several years under Jesuit schoolmasters—he felt they were trying to thrust him back into the Middle Ages. When he discovered science, he took to it like a duck to water—the simile is painfully hackneyed, but in this case gives an accurate sense of his enthusiasm. By the time Lombroso was 30, Garibaldi had freed Italy from the stranglehold of Austria—and Roman Catholicism—and Lombroso could proclaim his materialism without danger of finding himself in jail. Lombroso himself had played a small part in freeing Italy by serving in the army as a surgeon.

When he became a Professor of Psychiatry at Pavia, and the director of a lunatic asylum in Pesaro, he set out to try and prove that insanity is a purely physical illness—he had to believe this, of course, since (as a good materialist) he did not believe that the mind exists. He spent years studying the brains of madmen and carefully staining their nerve fibres, in an attempt to track down the 'germ' of insanity—without success. Then he learned that the German physiologist Verchow had discovered certain 'atavistic' features about the skulls of criminals—that is, that they have a touch of the cave-man about them. This was the clue he had been looking for. He proceeded to make a careful study of the inmates in the local prison, and at the age of 41, announced to the world his discovery that the criminal is a throwback to our cave-man ancestors, a kind of human ape. In other words, a man born with these tendencies can no more help committing crimes than a born cripple can help limping. The book *Criminal Man* (*L'Uomo Delinquente*) made him famous throughout Europe. Naturally, it gave violent offence to the Catholic Church, which has always felt that wickedness is a matter of choice; but it also upset psychologists, who liked to feel that man possesses at least an atom of free-will.

Yet in spite of his reputation for aggressive materialism, Lombroso was too good a scientist not to be willing to study new facts. And in 1882, he encountered a case that baffled him. A teenage girl had apparently developed some rather peculiar powers—although it sounded too silly to be taken seriously. According to her parents, she could see through her ear and smell through her chin. When Lombroso went to see her, he expected to find some absurd deception.

She was a tall, thin girl of 14, and the trouble had begun when she started to menstruate. She began sleep-walking, and developed hysterical blindness. Yet she was still able to see through the tip of her nose, and through her left ear. Lombroso tried binding her eyes with a bandage, then took a letter out of his pocket and held it a few inches away from her nose; she read it as if her eyes were uncovered. To make sure she was not peeping under the bandages, Lombroso held another page near her left ear; again, she read it aloud without difficulty. And even without the bandage, she would not have been able to read a letter held at the side of her head.

Next he tried holding a bottle of strong smelling salts under her nose; it did not make the slightest impression. But when it was held under her chin, she winced and gasped. He tried substances with only the slightest trace of odour—substances he could not smell if he held them two inches away from his own nose. When they were under her chin, she could identify every one of them.

If he still had any doubts, they vanished during the next few weeks when her sense of smell suddenly transferred itself to the back of her foot. If disagreeable smells were brought close to her heel, she writhed in agony; pleasant ones made her sigh with delight.

This was not all. The girl also developed the power of prediction. She was able to predict weeks ahead precisely when she would have fits, and exactly how they could be cured. Lombroso, naturally, did not accept this as genuine prediction, since she might have been inducing the fits—consciously or otherwise—to make her predictions come true. But she then began to predict things that would happen to other members of the family; and these came about just as she had foretold.

In medical journals, Lombroso found many similar cases. One girl who developed hysterical symptoms at puberty could accurately distinguish colours with her hands. An 11-year-old girl who suffered a back wound was able to hear through her elbow. Another pubescent girl could read a book with her stomach when her eyes were bandaged. Another hysterical woman developed X-ray eyes, and said she could see worms in her intestines—she actually counted them and said there were thirty-three; in due course she excreted precisely this number of worms. A young man suffering from hysteria could read people's minds, and reproduce drawings and words written on a sheet of paper when his eyes were tightly bandaged.

Lombroso may have been a determined materialist; but he was willing to study the facts. And the facts led him into stranger and stranger regions of speculation. To begin with, he developed a simple and ingenious theory of the human faculties, pointing out that seeing, hearing, smelling and feeling all take place through the nerves, and that if one of these faculties becomes paralysed, there is no scientific reason why another should not take over. When he attended a seance with the famous 'medium' Eusapia

Palladino, and saw a table floating up into the air, he simply extended his theory, and argued that there is no reason why 'psychological force' should not change into 'motor force'. But when he began to study other cases of prediction and 'second sight', he had to admit that it became increasingly difficult to keep the explanations within the bounds of materialistic science. There was the case of a woman who refused to stay in a theatre because she suddenly had a conviction that her father was dying; she got home and found a telegram to that effect. A doctor who suffered from hysterical symptoms foresaw the great fire of 1894 at the Como Exposition, and persuaded his family to sell their shares in a fire insurance company which had to meet the claims; when the fire occurred, his family were glad they took his advice. A woman whose daughter was playing near a railway line heard a voice telling her the child was in danger; she fetched her indoors half an hour before a train jumped the rails and ploughed through the spot where her daughter had been playing.

Slowly, and with painful reluctance, the sceptical scientist was converted to the view that the world was a far more complex place than his theories allowed. His colleagues were outraged. His biographer and translator, Hans Kurella, came to the conclusion that this was all a painful aberration due to the decay of his faculties—an argument difficult to sustain, since Lombroso was only 47 when he became interested in these matters, and he lived for more than a quarter of a century longer. Kurella can only bring himself to mention 'Lombroso's Spiritualistic Researches' in a short afterword to his biography, and his comments are scathing. Talking about Eusapia Palladino, whose seances he had attended, he agreed that she was indeed a 'miracle'—'a miracle of adroitness, false bonhomie, well-simulated candour, naivety and artistic command of all the symptoms of hysterico-epilepsy'. Which may well be true, but still does not explain how she was able to make a table rise up into the air when Lombroso and other scientists were holding her hands and feet.

Lombroso struggled manfully to stay within the bounds of science; he devised all kinds of ingenious instruments for testing mediums during seances. But, little by little, he found himself sucked into that ambiguous, twilit world of the 'paranormal'. Having studied mediums in civilised society, he turned his attention to tribal witch-doctors and shamans, and found that they could produce the same phenomena. But they always insisted that they did this with the help of the 'spirit world'—the world of the dead. And the more he looked into this, the more convincing it began to appear. And so, finally, he turned his attention to the topic that every good scientist dismisses as an old wives' tale: haunted houses. Here again, personal experience soon convinced him of their reality.

His most celebrated case concerned a wine shop in the Via Bava in Turin. In November 1900, he heard interesting rumours about how a destructive ghost was making life very difficult for the family of the proprietor, a Signor Fumero. Bottles smashed, tables and chairs danced about, kitchen utensils flew across the room. So Lombroso went along to the wine shop, and asked the proprietor if there was any truth in the stories. Indeed there was, said Fumero, but the disturbances had now stopped. Professor Lombroso had visited the house, and the ghost had now gone away. 'You interest me extremely,' replied Lombroso. 'Allow me to introduce myself.' And he presented his card. Fumero looked deeply embarrassed, and admitted that the story about Lombroso was an invention, intended to discourage the curious. For it seemed that the Italian police had been called in, and that they had witnessed the strange disturbances and told Signor Fumero that, unless this stopped at once, he would find himself in serious trouble. So Fumero had invented this story of how the famous Professor Lombroso had visited the house, and the ghost had taken his departure.

In fact, the proprietor admitted, the ghost was as active as ever; and if the professor would care to see with his own eyes, he only had to step down to the cellar.

Down below the house was a deep wine-cellar, approached by a flight of stairs and a long passageway. The proprietor led the way. The cellar was in complete darkness; but as they entered there was a noise of smashing glass, and some bottles struck Lombroso's foot. A lighted candle revealed rows of shelves with bottles of wine. And as Lombroso stood there, three empty bottles began to spin across the floor, and shattered against the leg of a table that stood in the middle of the cellar. On the floor, below the shelves, were the remains of broken bottles and wine. Lombroso took the candle over to the shelves, and examined them closely to see if there could be invisible wires to cause the movement. There were none; but as he looked, half a dozen bottles gently rose from the shelves, as if someone had lifted them, and exploded on the floor. Finally, as they left the cellar and closed the door behind them, they heard the smashing of another bottle.

The cellar was not the only place in the house where these things occurred. Chairs and plates flew around the kitchen. In the servants' room, a brass grinding machine flew across the room so violently that it was flattened out of shape; Lombroso examined it with amazement. The force to flatten it must have been considerable; if it had struck someone's head, it would surely have killed him. The odd thing was that the ghost seemed to do no one any harm. On one occasion, as the proprietor was bending down in the cellar, a large bottle of wine had burst beside his head; if it had struck him it would have done him a severe injury. Moreover, the 'entity' seemed to have the power to make bottles 'explode' without dropping them. They would hear a distinct cracking sound; then a bottle would fly into splinters.

Now Lombroso knew enough about hauntings to know that this was not an ordinary ghost. The ordinary ghost stays around in a house for many years, perhaps for centuries, and manifests itself to many people. But this bottle-smashing ghost was of the kind that the Germans call a poltergeist—or noisy spirit. Such 'hauntings' usually last only a short period—seldom more than six months—and they often seem to be associated with a 'medium'—that is, with some particular person who 'causes' them, in exactly the same way that Eusapia Palladino caused a table to rise into the air.

In this case, Lombroso suspected the wife of Signor Fumero, a skinny little woman of 50, who seemed to him to be distinctly neurotic. She admitted that ever since infancy she had been subject to neuralgia, nervous tremors and hallucinations; she had also had an operation to remove her ovaries. Ever since the case of the girl who could see with her ear, Lombroso had noticed that these people with peculiar 'powers' seemed to be nervously unstable. He therefore advised Signor Fumero to try sending his wife for a holiday. She went back to her native town for three days, and during that period, the wine shop was blessedly quiet—although Signora Fumero suffered from hallucinations while she was away, believing she could see people who were invisible to everyone else.

It looked as if Lombroso had stumbled on the correct solution. But it was not so simple. On Signora Fumero's return, all the disturbances began again; so, to make doubly sure, Lombroso again suggested that she should go home for a few days. The poor woman was understandably irritated at being banished from her home on account of the spirits; and before she left, she cursed them vigorously. That apparently annoyed them, for this time the disturbances went on while she was away. On the day she left, a pair of her shoes came floating out of her bedroom and down the stairs, and landed at the feet of some customers who were drinking in the bar. The following day the shoes vanished completely, to reappear under the bed a week later. Worse still, plates and bottles in the kitchen exploded or fell on the floor. But Signor Fumero noticed an interesting fact. It was only the plates and bottles *that had been touched by his wife* that smashed. If another woman set the table—preferably in another place—nothing happened. It was almost as if the objects she had touched had picked up some form of *energy* from her . . .

So his wife came back from her home town, and the disturbances continued as before. A bottle of soda water rose up gently in the bar, floated across the room as if someone were carrying it, and smashed on the floor.

It seemed, then, that Signora Fumero was not to blame; at least, not entirely. So who was? There were only three other suspects. Signor Fumero could be dismissed—he was a 'brave old soldier', and not at all the hysterical type. There was a head waiter, who seemed to be an ordinary, typical Italian. But there was also a young waiter—a lad of thirteen, unusually tall . . . Lombroso may have recalled that the girl who could see through her ear was also unusually tall, and that she had grown about six inches in a year immediately before her problems began. This boy had also reached puberty.

Accordingly, he was dismissed. And the 'haunting' of number 6 Via Bava immediately ceased.

As a scientist, Lombroso's problem was to find an explanation that would cover the facts. At a fairly early stage, he was convinced that they were facts, and not delusions. He wrote to a friend in 1891:

'I am ashamed and sorrowful that with so much obstinacy I have contested the possibility of the so-called spiritualistic facts. I say the *facts*, for I am inclined to reject the spiritualistic *theory*; but the facts exist, and as regards facts I glory in saying that I am their slave.'

By 'spiritualistic theory' he meant belief in life after death. At this stage he was inclined to believe that he was dealing with some kind of purely mental force.

Lombroso's study of hypnotism had convinced him of the reality of thought transference (or telepathy), and he went on to make the startling suggestion that *thought itself* could make objects fly through the air.

'I see nothing inadmissible in the supposition that in hysterical and hypnotised persons the stimulation of certain centres, which become powerful owing to the paralysing of all the others, and thus give rise to a transposition and transmission of psychical forces, may also result in a transformation into luminous or motor force.'

He compared it to the action of a magnet in deflecting a compass needle. But ten years later he had come to recognise that this theory failed to cover 'the facts'. It might be stretched to cover the case of the wine-shop poltergeist, if the young waiter was an 'unconscious' medium, and was using his 'magnetic powers' without realising it. But by that time, Lombroso had also studied many cases of haunted houses. And he concluded that there are basically two types: those like the Via Bava, in which there is a 'medium' (and which usually last only a few weeks or months), and the more traditional haunting, which may last for centuries. Lombroso apparently never had a chance to study this second type directly, but he went about collecting evidence from witnesses he judged reliable. When he heard about Glenlee, a haunted house in Scotland, he asked a friend named Professor Scott Elliott to investigate. Elliott went to see a girl who had lived in the house, and sent Lombroso the following story: Glenlee was owned by a family called Maxwell, and was supposed to be haunted by the ghost of a lady who had poisoned her husband. A visitor named Mrs Stamford Raffles was lying in bed beside her husband when she saw—in the firelight—a cloud of mist, which gradually turned into the shape of an old woman. The room became icy-cold. The old woman seemed to be looking at the clock on the mantelpiece. Another visitor, Mrs Robert Gladstone, had the same experience—but during the day, with the sun shining: the same cloud of mist, the same old woman looking at the clock.

Since the stories cited by Lombroso are second-hand, and lacking in the kind of precise detail that is to be found in that of the wine shop, let me offer here a case of haunting that provides a better comparison. It is to be found in *Lord Halifax's Ghost Book*.

In the 1890s, the Reverend Sabine Baring-Gould published in the *Cornhill Magazine* a 'true ghost story' about a house in Lille. A Mrs Pennyman, who had been involved in the case, wrote a long letter in which she corrected the inaccuracies of Baring-Gould's account. Her own is as follows:

In 1865, when she was a girl, Mrs Pennyman's family had gone to France so that the children could learn French; and they rented a house in Lille, where they had a number of introductions. The rent of the house—in the Place du Lion d'Or—struck them as remarkably low. When they went to the bank to cash a letter of credit, they found out why. The place was reputed to have a *revenant*—a ghost. In fact, the girl and her mother *had* been awakened by footsteps overhead, but had assumed it was a servant moving about. After the visit to the bank, they enquired who was sleeping overhead, and were told that it was an empty garret.

Their maid soon heard the story of the *revenant* from the French servants. A young man who was heir to the house had disappeared under mysterious circumstances. The story had it that he had been confined in an iron cage in the attic by his uncle, who later killed him. The uncle sold the house, but it had never been occupied for long because of the ghost.

The family went to look in the garret, and found that there *was* a cage. It was eight feet high and four feet square, and was attached to the wall. Inside there was an iron collar on a rusty chain.

Ten days later, the maidservant asked if she could change rooms. She and another maid slept in a room between the main stairs and the back staircase, and which therefore had two doors. They had seen a tall, thin man walking through the room, and had buried their faces under the bedclothes. The mother told the maids to move into another bedroom.

Soon after this, the girl and her brother went upstairs to fetch something from their mother's room, and saw 'a thin figure in a powdering gown and wearing hair down the back' going up the stairs in front of them. They thought it was a servant called Hannah, and called after her, 'You can't frighten us.' But when they got back to their mother, she told them that Hannah had gone to bed with a headache; they checked and found her fast asleep. When they described the figure, the maids said that it was the one which they had seen.

Another brother came from university to stay. He was awakened by a noise, and looked out of the door to see a man on the stairs. He assumed his mother had sent a servant to see if he had put out his candle, and was angry about it. His mother told him she had not sent anyone.

By now, the family had found themselves another house. Some English friends named Atkyns called a few days before they left, and were interested to hear about the ghost. Mrs Atkyns volunteered to sleep in the room with her dog. The next morning, Mrs Atkyns looked tired and distraught. She had also seen the man wandering through the bedroom. The dog seems to have refused to attack it.

Just before they left the house, the girl herself saw the ghost. By this time they were so accustomed to the footsteps that they ignored them; but they kept a candle burning in their room. She woke up to see a tall, thin figure in a long gown, its arm resting on a chest of drawers. She could clearly see the face, which was that of a young man with a melancholy expression. When she looked again, he had disappeared. The bedroom door was locked.

This was the story as told by Mrs Pennyman. Lord Halifax sent it to the Reverend Baring-Gould, who later sent him a letter he received from a reader of his account in the *Cornhill Magazine*. From this letter, it appeared that the haunted house had been transformed into a hotel in the 1880s. The reader—a lady—described how she and two friends had stayed at the Hotel du Lion d'Or in May 1887, and it is clear that one of the bedrooms they were given was the room in which the two servant girls had seen the ghost. The lady herself slept in the next room, and settled down after dinner to write letters. The hotel was very quiet—they were apparently the only guests—but towards midnight she heard footsteps on the landing outside the door. Then one of the ladies in the next bedroom—which was connected to her own—tapped on the door and asked if she was all right; she had been awakened by footsteps walking up and down. The two ladies unlocked the door and peered out on to the landing; but there was no one there, and no sound either. So they went back to bed. As she fell asleep, the lady continued to hear the slow, dragging steps which seemed to come from outside her door. They left Lille the next morning, and she thought no more about the experience until she read Baring-Gould's account in the *Cornhill* and realised that she had probably heard the ghost of the Place du Lion d'Or.

Stories of this type inevitably raise suspicions in the mind of the scientific investigator; they sound just a little too dramatic to be true—the young man confined in an iron cage, and so on. Yet since the foundation of the Society for Psychical Research in 1882, thousands of well-authenticated cases have been recorded. Sir Ernest Bennett's *Apparitions and Haunted Houses*, for example, contains more than a hundred carefully documented cases, and many of these have the same suspiciously dramatic air that suggests an active imagination. Case five will serve as an illustration: a General Barter of County Cork describes seeing the ghost of a certain Lieutenant B in India—riding on a pony in the moonlight, complete with two Hindu servants. When the general said: 'Hello, what the devil do you want?' the ghost came to a halt and looked down at him; and the general noticed that he now had a beard, and that his face was fatter than when he knew him some years before. Another officer who had known Lieutenant B immediately before his death, later verified that he had grown a beard and become stout, and that the pony he was riding had been purchased at Peshawur (where he died of some sickness) and killed through reckless riding.

It certainly sounds a highly unlikely story. Yet it is confirmed (in writing) by an officer to whom the general told it immediately afterwards, by the general's wife, and by a major. The wife also states that they heard a horse galloping at breakneck speed around their house at night on several occasions, and adds that the house was built by Lieutenant B. Finally, Bennett himself confirmed with the war office that Lieutenant B had died at Peshawur in January 1854. So although only General Barter saw the ghost, the evidence for the truth of his story seems strong. Other ghosts cited by Bennett were witnessed by many people—for example, the ghost of a chimney sweep who died of cancer, and who returned to his cottage every night for two months, until the whole family (including five children) began to take it for granted.

It is worth noting that nearly all ghosts mentioned in the records of the Society for Psychical Research look like ordinary, solid human beings; so it seems probable that most people have at some time seen a ghost without realising it. The late T.C. Lethbridge has described in his book *Ghost and Ghoul* how, when he was about to leave a friend's room at Cambridge in 1922, he saw a man in a top-hat come into the room—he presumed it was a college porter who had to give a message. The next day he asked his friend what the porter wanted, and the friend flatly denied that anyone had come into the room as Lethbridge went out. It then struck Lethbridge that the man had been wearing hunting kit. If he had not happened to mention it to his friend, he would never have known that he had seen a ghost.

Now Lombroso, who died in 1909, gradually abandoned his scepticism, and came to accept the 'spiritualistic hypothesis'—that ghosts are, quite simply, spirits of the dead, and that the same probably applies to poltergeists, even though these can only manifest themselves when there is a 'medium' present. The title of his book about his researches—which was published posthumously—was *After Death—What?*—a question that would have struck him as regrettably sensational twenty years earlier. In other words, Lombroso made no clear distinction between poltergeists and 'apparitions'. But even in 1909, this assumption would have been widely questioned. One of the most obvious things that emerged from the thousands of cases recorded by the SPR was that the majority of ghosts do not seem to notice the onlookers. (In this respect, General Barter's case was an exception.) In fact, they behave exactly as if they are a kind of film projection. They wander across a room looking anxious—like the ghost of the Lion d'Or—as if re-enacting some event from the past. This led a number of eminent investigators—among them Sir Oliver Lodge—to suggest that *some* ghosts, at any rate, may be no more than a kind of 'recording'. In *Man and the Universe*, Lodge writes:

Occasionally a person appears able to respond to stimuli embedded . . . among psycho-physical surroundings in a manner at present ill-understood and almost incredible:—*as if strong emotions could be unconsciously recorded in matter* [my italics], so that the deposit shall thereafter affect a sufficiently sensitive organism and cause similar emotions to reproduce themselves in his sub-consciousness, in a manner analogous to the customary conscious interpretation of photographic or phonographic records, and indeed of pictures or music and artistic embodiment generally.

'Take, for example, a haunted house . . . wherein some one room is the scene of a ghostly representation of some long past tragedy. On a psychometric hypothesis the original tragedy has been literally *photographed* on its material surroundings, nay, even on the ether itself, by reason of the intensity of emotion felt by those who enacted it; and thenceforth in certain persons an hallucinatory effect is experienced corresponding to such an impression. It is this theory that is made to account for the feeling one has on entering certain rooms, that there is an alien presence therein, though it is invisible and inaudible to mortal sense . . .'

But why should this 'hallucinatory effect' be produced on only certain persons? Why not everybody? The answer lies in those words 'psychometric hypothesis'. Lodge is talking about the theory of Buchanan and Denton we examined in Chapter 3. And of course, only certain persons can hold an object in their hands and 'see' its history. In the same way, according to Lodge, only certain persons can see the 'tape recording' known as a ghost.

Half a century after Lodge, T.C. Lethbridge—who was Keeper of Anglo-Saxon Antiquities at Cambridge—stumbled on the 'psychometric' theory as a result of his own observations. When he saw the 'ghost' of the man in a hunting kit, he was at first inclined to wonder whether it had been purely a mental picture, perhaps 'picked up' from somebody else's mind. Perhaps the huntsman had been a former occupant of the rooms, and was sitting in his armchair at home sipping a whisky as he thought about the good old days at Cambridge; and perhaps somehow the image had got itself transferred into Lethbridge's mind . . .

He was also intrigued by a much later experience. A woman who lived close to his home in Devon—reputed to be a witch—had died under mysterious circumstances suggesting murder. Lethbridge and his wife had both noticed a curiously 'nasty' feeling around her cottage just after her death. Moreover, he could step in and out of it, as if it ended quite sharply. Could this, he wondered, be some kind of field, analogous to a magnetic field? He was an excellent dowser—or water diviner—and his experience led him to speculate that certain places can 'record' strong emotions, and that people who can dowse are more likely to 'pick up' these recordings than people who can't. In other words, a dowser is more likely to see a ghost than most people.

Lethbridge developed his theory about ghosts in a number of books written in the last ten years of his life (he died in 1972).[1] It is a natural and logical extension of Buchanan's 'psychometry' and of Lodge's theory about 'recordings'. But Lethbridge has also placed it on a more scientific basis by suggesting that what does the 'recording' is some kind of magnetic field associated with water. The principle sounds very much like that of a tape recorder, where a magnetic field 'imprints' the sounds on an iron-oxide tape. In Lethbridge's theory, the magnetic field of water records emotions and prints them on its surroundings—in the case of the 'old witch', on the walls of her damp cottage.

All this helps to explain why Lombroso's theory about haunted houses struck many contemporary researchers as 'unscientific'. The 'psychometric hypothesis' seems to explain the majority of hauntings. For example, the ghost of the young man in the Place du Lion d'Or gave no sign of being aware of the presence of the various people who saw him, and that is what you would expect if a ghost is some kind of 'film' or recording of a long-past event.

1. Lethbridge's theories will be further discussed in Chapter 14.

As to the poltergeist, the 'mischievous spirit' theory found little acceptance among investigators even in the earliest days of psychical research. The reason was simply that a scientific investigator prefers natural explanations. And where poltergeists were concerned, there were a number of plausible ones. Eusapia Palladino could cause tables to rise into the air. The famous Victorian medium Daniel Dunglas Home frequently caused heavy objects of furniture to float right up to the ceiling, while he himself floated out of third-storey windows and came back by the window on the other side of the room. Home and Palladino claimed that their powers came from spirits; but they might have been deceiving themselves. One of the first thing that struck the early scientific investigators of poltergeists is that there usually seemed to be a disturbed adolescent in the house—usually a girl. Lombroso himself had noticed how often teenage girls seemed to be involved in his paranormal cases—like the girl who could see with her ear. And his original 'nervous force' theory struck most investigators as far more plausible than his later belief in mischievous spirits.

This younger generation of investigators had another reason for dismissing the spirit theory. By 1909, Freud had made most psychologists aware that the unconscious mind is a far more powerful force than Lombroso had recognised. Lombroso has a section on the unconscious in *After Death—What?* and it reveals that he thought of it as little more than another name for absent-mindedness or poetic inspiration. Freud had made people aware that the unconscious is a kind of ocean, full of dangerous currents and strange monsters. Moreover, Freud emphasised that the most powerful of these unconscious forces is the sex drive. Could it be coincidence that most poltergeist cases involve adolescents at the age of puberty?

This, of course, still fails to explain how the unconscious mind of a disturbed adolescent can make bottles fly through the air. But again, science had some plausible theories. In Basle, a university student named Carl Jung was intrigued by a female cousin who began to go into trances at the age of puberty, and spoke with strange voices. And at about the time this started, the dining-room table suddenly split apart with a loud report. There was also a sudden explosion from a sideboard, and when they looked inside, they found that a bread knife had shattered into several pieces. Jung suspected that his cousin's 'illness' was responsible for these events, and he coined the term 'exteriorisation phenomenon' to explain them—meaning more-or-less what Lombroso meant by 'nerve force'. Jung had no doubt that it was caused by the unconscious mind, and a personal experience confirmed him in this view. One day he was arguing with Freud about 'exteriorisation' and Freud was highly sceptical. Jung's rising irritation caused a burning sensation in his chest 'as if my diaphragm was becoming red hot!' Suddenly, there was a loud explosion in the bookcase. 'There,' said Jung, '*that* was an exteriorisation phenomenon.' 'Bosh,' said Freud, to which Jung replied: 'It is not bosh, and to prove it, there will be another explosion in a moment.' And a second explosion occurred. Jung had no doubt that he had somehow caused the explosions by getting angry.

Most modern investigators of poltergeist phenomena would agree with Jung. One of the rare exceptions was the late Harry Price, who wrote in *Poltergeist Over England*: 'My own view is that they are invisible, intangible, malicious and noisy entities . . .' He adds: 'Poltergeists are able, by laws yet unknown to our physicists, to extract energy from living persons, often from the young, and usually from girl adolescents, especially if they suffer from some mental disorder.' Unfortunately, Price's reputation has declined steadily since his death in 1948, with accusations of lying, cheating, publicity-seeking and fraud; so most psychical researchers would dismiss his views on poltergeists as a deliberate attempt at sensationalism. Besides, Price himself admitted that poltergeists seem to be connected with sexual energies; and he described how the husband of the Austrian medium Frieda Weisl told him that, during their early married life, ornaments jumped off the mantelshelf when she had a sexual orgasm. This certainly sounds like Jung's 'exteriorisation phenomenon'.

We may say, then, that the modern consensus of opinion is that a poltergeist is a person, not a spirit. The view is summed up by Richard Cavendish[1]:

1. *Encyclopedia of the Unexplained*, p. 197.

'Because poltergeist incidents usually occur in close proximity to a living person, parapsychologists tend to regard them as instances of psychokinesis or PK. Since poltergeist incidents are recurrent and arise unexpectedly and spontaneously, they are commonly referred to as instances of 'recurrent spontaneous psychokinesis' or RSPK. They appear to be unconscious cases of PK since the person who seems to bring them about is usually unaware of his involvement. Some persons remain convinced that RSPK phenomena are due to the agency of an incorporeal entity, such as the spirit of a deceased person or a 'demon' which has attached itself to some living person and which causes the incidents by PK. However, since there is no evidence for such spirits apart from the phenomena themselves, most parapsychologists are of the opinion that poltergeist phenomena are examples of unconscious PK exercised by the person around whom they occur.'

'Psychokinesis' means, of course, 'mind over matter'. And it has been widely accepted by investigators since the mid-1930s, when Dr J.B. Rhine, of Duke University, conducted a series of experiments with a gambler who claimed that he could influence the fall of the dice by concentrating on them. Rhine's experiments showed that the gambler was correct; he could, to some extent, influence the dice to make it turn up sixes. Since then, there have been thousands of similar experiments, and the evidence for PK is regarded as overwhelming.

Yet it has to be admitted that even its 'star performers'—Nina Kulagina, Felicia Parise, Ingo Swann, Uri Geller—cannot make objects fly around the room as poltergeists seem to be able to. The Russian Kulagina first came to the attention of scientists when she was in hospital after a nervous breakdown; her doctors were fascinated to see that she could reach into her sewing basket and take out any colour of thread she wanted without looking at it. They tested her and found that she could, beyond all doubt, 'see' colours with her fingertips. Her healing powers were also remarkable—for example, she could make wounds heal up in a very short time simply by holding her hand above them. But it was when they tested her for PK that they discovered her outstanding abilities. She could sit at a table, stare at a small object—like a matchbox or a wineglass—and make it move without touching it.

She told investigators that when her concentration 'worked', she felt a sharp pain in her spine, and her eyesight blurred. Her blood pressure would rise abruptly.

Nina Kulagina's most spectacular feat was to make an apple fall off a table. Ingo Swann, an American, is able to deflect compass needles by PK. Felicia Parise, who was inspired to try 'mind over matter' after seeing a film about Kulagina, can move small objects like matchsticks and pieces of paper. Uri Geller, the world's best-known 'psychic', can bend spoons by gently rubbing them with his finger, and snap metal rings by simply holding his hand above them.

Now Geller has, in fact, produced certain 'poltergeist effects'. In 1976, I spent some time with Geller in Barcelona, interviewing him for a book I subsequently wrote about him. A number of objects fell out of the air when I was with him, and these seemed to be typical examples of 'teleportation'. Another friend, Jesse Lasky, has described to me how, when Uri was having dinner at their flat, there was a pinging noise like a bullet, and a silver button flew across the kitchen; it had come out of the bedroom drawer of Jesse's wife, Pat. Geller was standing by the refrigerator with a bottle of milk in one hand and a tin of Coca Cola in the other when it happened. Another odd feature of this incident is that the button—if it came from the bedroom drawer—must have somehow travelled through three walls to reach the kitchen. 'Interpenetration of matter' is another curious feature in many poltergeist cases.

But then, Geller was not trying to make this happen. As I discovered when getting to know him, odd events seem to happen when he is around. On the morning I went to meet him, at an office in the West End of London, he asked me, 'Do you have any connection with Spain?' I said that I didn't. A moment before I walked into the office, a Spanish coin had risen out of the ashtray on the desk, and floated across to the other side of the room, where Geller and a public relations officer were standing. I subsequently came to know the P.R.O well enough to accept her word that this really took place. When Geller left the Laskys' flat in central London, he buzzed them from the intercom at the front door and explained with embarrassment that he had damaged the door. A wrought-iron dragon which decorated the centre of the door had been twisted—fortunately they were able to force it back without breaking it. Geller explained that he is never sure when such things will happen, or even whether the razor with which he shaves is likely to buckle in his hand.

In short, it seems that even the most talented practitioners of psychokinesis cannot produce real 'poltergeist effect' *at will*. But then, of course, we already know that there is another interesting possibility: that the effects *may* be produced by 'Stan', that person in the other side of the brain. If there is another person living in the right hemisphere of your brain, is it not possible that he is the one who is responsible for 'spontaneous psychokinesis'?

But even if we are willing to entertain this hypothesis, it still leaves us with the question: how does the right brain *do* it? In fact, is there any evidence whatsoever that the right brain possesses paranormal powers?

And the answer to this is a qualified yes. We can begin with one of the simplest and best authenticated of all 'paranormal powers', water divining. The water diviner, or dowser, holds a forked hazel twig (or even a forked rod made from two strips out of a whalebone corset, tied at the end) in both hands, so there is a certain tension—a certain 'springiness'—on the rod. And when he walks over an underground stream or spring, the rod twists either upwards or downwards in their hands.

In fact, dowsers can dowse for almost anything, from oil and minerals to a coin hidden under the carpet. It seems that they merely have to decide what they're looking for, and the unconscious mind—or the 'other self'—does the rest.

I have described elsewhere[1] how I discovered, to my own astonishment, that I could dowse. I was visiting a circle of standing stones called the Merry Maidens, in Cornwall—a circle that probably dates back to the same period as Stonehenge. When I held the rod—made of two strips of plastic tied at the end—so as to give it a certain tension, it responded powerfully when I approached the stones. It would twist upwards as I came close to the stone, and then dip again as I stepped back or walked past it. What surprised me was that I felt nothing—no tingling in the hands, no sense of expectancy. It seemed to happen as

1. In *Mysteries*, p. 116.

automatically as the response of a voltmeter in an electric circuit. Since then I have shown dozens of people how to dowse. It is my own experience that nine out of ten people can dowse, and that all young children can do it. Some adults have to 'tune in'—to learn to allow the mind and muscles to relax—but this can usually be done in a few minutes.

Scientific tests have shown that what happens in dowsing is that the muscles convulse—or tighten—of their own accord. And if the dowser holds a pendulum—made of a wooden bob on a short length of string—then the pendulum goes into a circular swing over standing stones or underground water—once again, through some unconscious action of the muscles.

Another experiment performed by Roger Sperry throws an interesting light on dowsing. He tried flashing green or red lights at random into the 'blind' eye of split-brain patients (into the left visual field, connected to the right cerebral hemisphere). The patients were then asked what colour had just been seen. Naturally, they had no idea, and the guesses showed a random score. But if they were allowed a second guess, they would always get it right. They might say: 'Red—oh no, green . . .' The right side of the brain had overheard the wrong guess, and communicated by *causing the patient's muscles to twitch*. It was the equivalent of a kick under the table.

Unable to communicate in any other way, the right brain did it by contracting the muscles.

It seems, therefore, a reasonable guess that this is also what happens in dowsing. The right brain knows there is water down there, or some peculiar magnetic force in the standing stones; it communicates this knowledge by causing the muscles to tense, which makes the rod jerk upwards.

Most 'psychics' observe that deliberate effort inhibits their powers. One psychic, Lois Bourne, has written:

'One of the greatest barriers to mediumship is the intellect, and the most serious problem I had to learn in my early psychic career was the suspension of my intellect. If, during the practice of extra-sensory perception, I allowed logic to prevail, and permitted myself to rationalise the impressions I received, and the things I said, I would be hopelessly lost within a conflict. It is necessary that I totally by-pass my conscious mind . . .'

Similarly, Felicia Parise found that she was at first totally unable to cause 'PK effects', no matter how hard she tried. But one day, when she had received an emotional shock—the news that her grandmother was dying—she reached out for a small plastic bottle and it moved away from her hand. From then on, she had the 'trick' of causing PK.

All this underlines something that should be quite clear in any case: that, in a sense, we are *all* 'split-brain patients'. The logical self interferes with the natural operations of the right brain. This is why the artist has to wait for 'inspiration'—for the left brain to relax and allow the right to take over. Mozart was an example of an artist who was born with an unusual harmony between the two halves of his brain, and he commented once that tunes were always 'walking into his head'—meaning into his left brain. In most of us, a certain self-mistrust, a tendency to ask questions, sits like a bad-tempered door-keeper between the two halves of the brain. When we become subject to increasing tension and worry, this has the effect of increasing the door-keeper's mistrustfulness. He thinks he is performing a useful service in keeping out the impulses from the 'other half'. In fact, he is simply isolating the left-brain self and making it more tense and miserable. Nervous breakdown is due to the increasingly desperate attempts of this door-keeper to cope with problems in what he considers to be the right way, and which is, in fact, the worst possible way.

What Lois Bourne has said about suspending the rational intellect seems to apply to most forms of 'extra-sensory perception' and paranormal abilities. Most people have had the experience of reaching out to pick up the telephone and *knowing* who is on the other end. Everyone has had the experience of thinking about someone they haven't heard from in years, and receiving a letter from them the same day. 'Extra-sensory perception' (ESP) seems to operate when we are relaxed, and thinking about something else.

All this, then, *seems* to offer a basis for an explanation of the poltergeist. It is true that human powers of psychokinesis seem rather feeble—it would be far more convincing if we could point to some medium or psychic who could cause objects to fly around the room at will. But then, perhaps the explanation is that the 'door-keeper' inhibits the natural powers of the right brain. Even good 'mediums' cannot put themselves into a 'sensitive' state at will; some of them need to go into a trance; others need to be in the right frame of mind. Trance mediums who try to 'work normally' (i.e. when wide-awake) often find it exhausting and frustrating, because the 'censor' keeps getting in the way. So if the poltergeist *is* some peculiar power or force residing in the right brain, perhaps this explains why it cannot be called upon at will, even by gifted psychics such as Uri Geller.

Dowsing also provides us with a possible explanation of the origin of that force. In some dowsers, the presence of underground water produces such a powerful effect that they go into violent convulsions. One of the most famous of French dowsers, Barthelemy Bléton, discovered his powers accidentally at the age of 7; he was taking his father's meal out to the fields when he sat down on a certain spot, and felt sick and faint. Digging at this spot revealed a powerful underground stream. Again, an old lady who is a member of the British Society of Dowsers described at a conference a few years ago how she could pick up a large branch from the ground, and it would swing around in her hand like a pointer until it indicated water.

If the dowsing rod is responding to some magnetic force, either in water or standing stones, it seems possible that this same force, channelled through the right brain, could provide the energy for poltergeist effects.

It looks, then, as if the modern psychical investigator is in a far better position than his predecessor of a century ago when it comes to constructing theories about the paranormal. The recognition of the 'two people' inside our heads may be the most important step ever taken in this direction.

Having said this, it is necessary to admit that most of the mystery remains unexplained. Lodge's 'psychometric hypothesis' and Lethbridge's theory of 'ghouls' may provide an explanation for the majority of ghosts—but what about all those cases in which the witnesses insist that the ghost behaved as if it saw them? Again, it would certainly be convenient if we could explain the poltergeist in terms of 'unconscious psychokinesis'. But why has no psychic been able to duplicate poltergeist effects? It is not really an answer to say that they have not learned to switch the power on and off. Many psychics can switch other powers on and off—telepathy, psychokinesis, second sight. So why not poltergeist effects?

These awkward questions remind us that there are others we have failed to answer. In the case of Lombroso's bottle-smashing poltergeist in the Via Bava, why did it stop smashing bottles when the wife went away for the first time? If Lombroso is correct, and the poltergeist was a 'spirit' that drew its energy from people, then we have our explanation. The spirit needed energy from both the wife and the young waiter to smash bottles and crockery. When the wife went away for the first time, it lost half its energy supply and decided to take a rest. But the second time she went away, she cursed it, and it made a special effort to be disagreeable. In order to do this, it had to make use of the 'vestigial energy' she had left on dishes and other objects she had touched. When the young waiter was eventually dismissed, the wife alone could not provide sufficient energy for its needs and it went elsewhere . . .

Modern psychical research has a way of ignoring such questions. It prefers straightforward distinctions. If there is a 'medium' present (or, as we now say, a 'focus'), then it is a poltergeist; if not, then it is a ghost.

But even this pleasantly simple distinction proves to be less useful than it looks. The 'spirits' themselves seem to dislike being type-cast, and often decline to stick to their proper role. A case that starts as an ordinary haunting may develop into a poltergeist haunting, and vice versa. And then, just to confuse the issue, the spirits occasionally identify themselves as devils and demons, and manifest themselves in the highly disturbing form known as 'possession'. This subject is so complex that it deserves a chapter to itself.

8.
Ghost Hunters

BY THE TIME Lombroso died, in 1909, psychical research was marking time. Spiritualism continued to flourish; but as scientific investigation, it had come to a halt. The reason can be seen by anyone who reads Owen's *Footfalls on the Boundary of Another World* and then turns to Lombroso's *After Death—What?* The books were published fifty years apart; yet they might both have been written at exactly the same time. Lombroso offers some 'scientific evidence', by way of a few experiments in telepathy; otherwise, he presents just the same kind of evidence that Robert Dale Owen had presented. There was plenty of evidence for ghosts, for poltergeists, for telepathy, for precognition, for 'out of the body experiences', and a dozen other varieties of 'paranormal' experience. But the evidence seemed to lead nowhere. One remarkable case had even proved life after death, to the satisfaction of most open-minded enquirers. This was the celebrated 'cross-correspondences'. By 1904, three of the chief founders of the SPR—Henry Sidgwick, Frederick Myers and Edmund Gurney— were dead, and it seemed logical to hope that if they were still alive in another world, they would try to communicate through mediums. In the previous year, a psychic named Mrs Holland, the sister of Rudyard Kipling, began receiving written messages— through automatic writing—that seemed far more intelligent and thoughtful than the majority of such scripts. And in 1904, another psychic, Mrs Verrall—the wife of a Cambridge don—also received some messages, one of which included the words 'Record the bits, and when fitted they will make the whole'.

And it slowly became clear that the 'senders' claimed to be the spirits of Sidgwick, Myers and Gurney, and that what they were attempting was a 'proof' of such complexity that there could be no possibility of fraud. In effect, they seemed to be using a large number of mediums—others included Mrs Flemming, Mrs Forbes, and the famous American medium Mrs Piper—to produce a complex jigsaw puzzle or conundrum, giving each woman only part of the puzzle, so that there could be no possible doubt that there was no collusion between them. Unfortunately, the conundrums were so complex that it would take a short book even to give a simple outline. A typical one is as follows:

In 1906, Mrs Flemming produced a script containing the words Dawn, Evening and Morning, a reference to bay leaves, and the name Laurence. Six weeks later, Mrs Verrall wrote out a message mentioning 'laurel' and a library. Mrs Piper came out of a trance speaking of laurel, 'nigger', and a phrase that sounded like 'more head'. Mrs Flemming produced more scripts referring to Night and Day, Evening and Morning, and also a reference to Alexander's tomb with laurel leaves. And eventually, all these clues pointed to the tomb of the Medicis in the Church of San Lorenzo in Florence. It had been designed by Michelangelo, and contained his sculpture of Night and Day, Evening and Morning. Lorenzo de Medici's emblem was the laurel, and near the tombs is the Laurentian Library. Alexander (or Alessandro) de Medici was half negro; after his murder, his body was hidden in the tomb of Giuliano. 'More head' was actually 'Moor head'—the head of a negro. This conundrum was solved only four years after the first 'clue', and there could be no question of telepathy between the mediums, since they did not understand what it was all about. Altogether, the case of the cross-correspondences is one of the most impressive—perhaps the most impressive—in the history of psychical research. It is true that the various 'clues' are so complicated that few people have ever taken the trouble to study the case. Yet the sheer complexity of the code at least indicates that it originated on a far higher level of intelligence than most spirit messages. In addition to which, it effectively disposes of the objection that spirits never have anything interesting to say.

If the 'spirits' of Myers, Gurney and Sidgwick failed to convince the world of the reality of the afterlife, a far more skilful and flamboyant publicist was now preparing to launch himself into the project.

Harry Price, ghost-hunter extraordinary, claimed that he was born in Shrewsbury, son of a wealthy paper manufacturer. A brilliant critical biography by Trevor Hall, *The Search for Harry Price*, reveals that he was, in fact, the son of an unsuccessful grocer, and that he was born in London in 1881. From then until he was about 40, he seems to have supported himself by a variety of jobs, including commercial travelling, manufacturing patent medicines, journalism and giving gramophone concerts. What *is* certain is that his lifelong interest in stage magic began at the age of 8, when he saw an itinerant magician and patent medicine salesman, the Great Sequah, giving a public performance. Price began collecting books on magic, and became an expert magician. It may have been the interest in magic that led him to join the Society for Psychical Research in 1920—the SPR was then, as now, much concerned with trying to detect fraud in mediums. E.J. Dingwall, who was then Research Officer for the Society, asked Price if he would care to come with him to Munich, to attend some seances of a remarkable German medium, Willi Schneider—one of two brothers. The man who arranged the seances was the German investigator, Baron von Schrenk-Notzing, a friend of Lombroso's, and the author of a sensationally successful book called *Materialisation Phenomena*, which had aroused wide-spread scepticism in Germany when it appeared in 1914. Schrenk-Notzing himself was something of a flamboyant publicist, and Trevor Hall suggests that Harry Price took his example to heart, and decided that this was the way to achieve the fame he craved. (He admitted frankly that he had always wanted to get his name in *Who's Who*.)

The Schneider brothers, Willi and Rudi, the most psychic members of a psychic family, were born at Braunau-am-Inn and, according to one friend of the family, the phenomena began after they had spent an evening playing with a ouija board. Willi had then—in 1916—reached the age of puberty and the family was disturbed by loud knocking noises. Then objects began moving around, and Willi saw a ghost in the sitting room. Neighbours became so alarmed about the racket that the family were on the point of vacating the flat. By means of the ouija board, they tried questioning the 'spirit', which identified itself as a girl named Olga Lindtner, who claimed to be a reincarnation of the notorious Lola Montez. In due course, Willi went into a trance, and Olga spoke through him. In spite of doubts later raised by Harry Price—after he had quarrelled with the brothers—there can be no doubt that the phenomena were genuine. The novelist Thomas Mann attended one seance, and has recorded how, as he pressed Willi's knees tightly between his own, and two other people held his hands, a handkerchief floated into the air, a bell began to ring and then floated into the air, a music box played, and the keys of a typewriter were struck. Mann was convinced that deception was impossible.

Harry Price and E.J. Dingwall witnessed similar occurrences, and also saw a white hand which materialised in front of them; they had no doubt whatever of the genuineness of the phenomena, and said as much at a lecture to the SPR. But by way of keeping his options open, Price helped to edit and publish a book called *Revelations of a Spirit Medium*, in which a fake medium described the tricks of the trade.

In 1923, Price got into conversation with a young nurse on a train; her name was Stella Cranshawe. He was fascinated to hear that mild poltergeist phenomena occurred around her—a feeling like a breeze, movement of small objects, rapping noises, and flashes of light. By this time, Price knew enough about psychical research to realise that the girl was probably, without knowing it, a medium. He persuaded her to allow herself to be investigated. And at the first seance, a heavy table levitated and moved across the room on two legs, raps sounded, lights flashed, and the temperature in the room dropped considerably. (At later sittings it became very low indeed.) At another seance, the table hit Harry Price under the chin, then three of its legs snapped off, the top broke into two pieces, then the whole table crumbled into matchwood. Stella herself found all these phenomena rather boring and, after she married in 1928, refused to take any part in further experiments. It is possible, in any case, that her powers would have vanished with marriage; many investigators have noted that there is a connection between sexual frustration and 'poltergeist effects', and that such effects cease when the 'focus' leads a normal sex life. (She may also have felt that seances were bad for her health—they often leave the medium exhausted.)

In 1926, Price came upon one of the most remarkable poltergeist cases of all time. In February 1925, a 13-year-old Rumanian peasant girl called Eleonora Zugun went to visit her grandmother at the village of Buhai, and on the way found some money by the roadside, which she spent on sweets. Her grandmother, who was 105 years old, and had a reputation as a witch, told Eleonora that the money had been left by the devil, and that she would now be possessed by the devil. The next day, stones rained down on the house, smashing windows, and small objects near Eleonora rose up in the air. Eleonora was quickly sent home to Talpa, and the phenomena continued there. A jug full of water rose slowly in the air and floated several feet. A trunk rocked up and down. A porridge bowl hit a visitor on the head and made a nasty wound. Eleonora was sent to a nearby monastery, then shut in a lunatic asylum. A psychical researcher managed to get her removed and taken back to the monastery. There he witnessed all kinds of things flying through the air. The 'spirit' also began slapping the girl. Then a countess with an interest in psychical research—Zoë Wassilko-Serecki—heard about Eleonora, went to see her, and brought her back with her to Vienna. Eleonora was delighted with her new life in the countess's flat, and began training as a hairdresser. And the poltergeist phenomena continued—indicating, perhaps, that a poltergeist does not need a psychologically 'disturbed' teenager for its manifestations. The countess observed what most other researchers into poltergeist activity have noted: that the poltergeist seems to dislike anyone actually seeing it move objects; the countess noted that various small items would fall from the air without being seen to move from their original place. The poltergeist—or *dracu* (demon), as Eleonora called it—communicated by automatic writing, and even spoke a few sentences in a 'breathy and toneless voice'.

But what it had to say indicated that its level of intelligence was extremely low.

The *dracu* also punched and slapped Eleonora, threw her out of bed, pulled her hair, filled her shoes with water (the poltergeist seems to be able to create water, as we shall see), and stole her favourite possessions. In March 1926, it began scratching and biting her, as well as sticking needles into her. The bite marks were often damp with saliva.

Price came to Vienna at the end of April 1926, and was soon convinced that this was a genuine poltergeist. He took her back to London, where she was subjected to laboratory tests. The movement of objects was less violent than in Vienna, but the bites and scratches continued to appear. One day, when she was tying up a parcel in front of several witnesses, she gave a gasp, and teeth marks appeared on her wrist, then scratches appeared on her forearm, cheeks and forehead.

Back in Vienna, the movement of objects ceased, but the scratches and bites continued, now often accompanied by quantities of an unpleasant spittle. Subjected to chemical analysis, this was found to be swarming with micro-organisms (whereas Eleonora's own saliva was relatively free from them). When she went to Berlin to be studied by Schrenk-Notzing, a researcher named Hans Rosenbusch accused her of cheating—with the co-operation of the countess; but this seems to be typical of the extreme scepticism of certain investigators. Finally, in 1927, the 'spirit' got tired of tormenting her, and went away. She moved to Czernowitz, in Rumania, and ran a successful hairdressing business.

The countess was convinced that Eleonora herself—or rather, her unconscious mind—was responsible for the attacks: she believed that Eleonora had powerfully developed sexual urges, and that these were fixated on her father (it sounds as if she had been impressed by Freud); so the 'attacks' were a form of self-punishment. Harry Price was inclined to agree, likening the bites to the 'stigmata' that appear on the hands of saints and religious fanatics. Yet as we read the account of Eleanor's sufferings at the hands of the *dracu* (there is an excellent account in Alan Gauld's *Poltergeists*), these explanations seem more and more preposterous. A girl does not go on scratching and biting herself for two years because she feels guilty about her sexual desires, particularly if she finds herself transformed, like Cinderella, into the protégée of a wealthy countess. Then what exactly happened?

Clearly, the grandmother was in some way responsible for 'triggering' the attacks. Eleonora had reached the age—13—at which such things happen; she was not particularly happy in her present surroundings in Talpa, so there was an underlying sense of frustration. Peasants are superstitious, and when her grandmother told her that from now on she would belong to the devil and never get rid of him, the effect must have been traumatic. Eleanora's energies began to 'leak'. And some delinquent entity saw its chance, and made use of them. It may or may not be relevant that her grandmother had a reputation as a witch. If magic—and presumably witchcraft—makes use of 'spirits', as Guy Playfair suggests, then her grandmother's house may have been the worst possible place for a frustrated adolescent like Eleonora. (This matter of witchcraft is a subject to which we shall return in Chapter 10.)

As to Harry Price, he continued his triumphant career as the chief Public Relations Officer of the spirit world. He investigated fire-walking and the Indian rope trick, organised seances, was photographed in 'haunted beds' (with 'Professor' Joad), and staged an experiment on the summit of the Brocken to try to change a goat into a young man. (This was a failure.) Price loved publicity, and lost no opportunity to be photographed by journalists. He was delighted that so many correspondents seemed to think that his name was Sir Harry Price. Yet he also made the general public conscious of psychical research in a way it had never been before. Because Price emphasised that he was a sceptic and a scientist, not a Spiritualist, people took him more seriously than they did a 'believer' like Conan Doyle or Sir Oliver Lodge. When he announced in 1933 that he now felt that Rudi Schneider might be a fake, and produced a photograph that seemed to show him cheating during a seance, people felt that he was showing unflinching honesty. (In fact, the photograph was later shown to be a fake; Price's motive was almost certainly a desire to get his own back on Rudi for, as he saw it, 'deserting' him for another investigator, Lord Charles Hope, whose findings Price denounced.)

Yet in spite of his craving for publicity and his desire to get into *Who's Who*, Price did much important and valuable work during these years. In a sense, his motivation is irrelevant; he was a genuine enthusiast for psychical research. The majority of his investigations were not spectacular: just the plodding, day-to-day work of a patient researcher, sitting with mediums, psychometrists, healers, miracle workers. And, if anything, Price was inclined to be over-critical. In Norway, he visited the home of Judge Ludwig Dahl, and had a sitting with the judge's daughter Ingeborg, whose 'controls' were her two dead brothers. While not regarding her as a downright fake, Price was unimpressed. Yet one of the dead brothers prophesied that their father would die on August 8, 1934, seven years later, and this was precisely the day on which he did die from a stroke during a swim.

A case which certainly deserves mention in any account of Price's career is the curious affair of the talking mongoose of Cashen's Gap. It was far from being one of Price's successes; yet it remains an intriguing mystery.

In 1932, Price heard about a farmer called Irving, at Cashen's Gap on the Isle of Man, who had made friends with a mongoose that could speak several languages. It could also read minds and sing hymns. Price could not find time to go to the Isle of Man, but a friend of his, a Captain M.H. Macdonald, offered to go.

It seemed that the Irving family—who (significantly) had a 13-year-old daughter named Voirrey—had been disturbed by noises from behind the panels of the house: barking, spitting and blowing noises. The farmer lay in wait with a gun, without success, and tried putting down poison; the creature eluded him. So the farmer tried communicating with it, making various animal noises; to his astonishment, it seemed to be able to imitate them. Voirrey tried nursery rhymes, and it began to repeat these. Finally, it showed itself—a small, bushy-tailed creature that claimed to be a mongoose. They called it Gef. And Gef told them he was from India. Mr Irving seldom saw Gef, except in glimpses, as he ran along a beam, but Voirrey and Mrs Irving often saw him face to face.

Macdonald arrived at the farm on February 26, 1932, and saw nothing. When he left to go to his hotel a shrill voice screamed: 'Go away! Who is that man?' The farmer said this was Gef. The next day, as Macdonald was having tea with the Irvings, a large needle bounced off the teapot; and Irving remarked that Gef was always throwing things. Later, he heard the shrill voice upstairs talking with Voirrey and Mrs Irving; when he called to ask if the mongoose would come down, the voice screamed: 'No, I don't like you.' He tried sneaking upstairs, but the mongoose heard a stair creak, and shrieked: 'He's coming!' And from then on, Macdonald saw and heard no more of Gef.

According to Irving, who kept a diary, Gef talked in a language he claimed to be Russian, sang in Spanish and recited a poem in Welsh. He killed rabbits for them—by strangling them—and left them outside. He claimed to have made visits to the nearest town, and told the Irvings what various people had been doing; Irving checked and found he was correct. He was able to tell Irving what was happening ten miles away without leaving the farm. And when he was asked if he was a spirit, Gef replied: 'I am an earth-bound spirit.'

In March 1935, Gef told Irving that he had plucked some hairs from his tail and left them on the mantelpiece; these were forwarded to Price, who had them examined. They proved to be dog hairs—probably from the collie dog on the farm.

When Harry Price was mentioned, Gef said he didn't like him because he 'had his doubting cap on'. And when Price finally visited Cashen's Gap, the visit was a waste of time. Gef only came back to the farm after Price had left. And this, virtually, was the end of the story—although Macdonald paid a second visit to the farm and again heard the mongoose talking in its shrill voice.

It is possible, of course, that the Irvings were hoaxers. But they struck the investigators as honest. And it is difficult to see why, if they wanted attention, they should invent anything as bizarre as a talking mongoose. Why should Irving have invited Price to stay if he was simply a hoaxer?

What seems rather more probable is that Gef was a poltergeist— an 'earth-bound spirit', as he himself claimed. Voirrey was a lonely girl who had just reached puberty. The disturbances started like most poltergeist disturbances, with noises in the woodwork, scratchings and other sounds. Later small objects flew through the air, and Gef was assumed to have 'thrown' them. But he also seemed to be able to cause 'action at a distance': when a saucepan of water turned over on the stove and soaked Irving's shoes, he assumed this was Gef. The clairvoyance also sounds like a poltergeist, and the knowledge of other people's affairs. And it seems odd that the rabbits were strangled—not a mongoose's normal method of killing. In fact, the Gef case seems to belong on the borderland between the straightforward poltergeist and the elemental or hobgoblin. (In the mid-19th century, as Robert Dale Owen points out, the word poltergeist was usually translated hobgoblin.)

Trevor Hall is of the opinion that the poltergeist case which Price claimed to be his first experience of 'ghost hunting' was pure invention, and he could be right—Price says that it took place when he was 15 at a village which he calls Parton Magna; but since the rest of the details concern his wealthy relatives and his return to a public school, we are probably safe in assuming it never took place. But with Price, one can never be sure. In *Confessions of a Ghost Hunter* (1936), he has a chapter called 'The Strange Exploits of a London Poltergeist', in which he states that he is forced to disguise the names and the location because it occurred so recently. But the case which he goes on to describe is thoroughly well authenticated, and is, in fact, one of the most remarkable of this century.

It actually took place in No. 8 Eland Road, Battersea, and began on November 29, 1927, when lumps of coal, chunks of washing soda, and copper coins began to rain down on the conservatory roof. The house was occupied by an 86-year-old invalid, Henry Robinson, his son Frederick (27), his three daughters, and a grandson of 14, Peter. When some of the falling objects smashed the glass, they sent for the police. As the constable stood in the back-garden, a lump of coal knocked off his helmet. He rushed to the garden wall and pulled himself up—but there was no one around.

The Robinsons' washerwoman was terrified when she went into the wash-house and found the place full of smoke, and a pile of red-hot cinders on the floor; she gave notice.

Then the poltergeist began to get into its stride—and it was an exceptionally destructive spirit. Ornaments smashed against walls, articles of furniture overturned, windows were broken. When they moved the old man out of his bedroom, a huge chest of drawers toppled over; a few minutes later the hall stand began to move, and broke in two when Frederick tried to hold it.

In January, an out-of-work journalist named Jane Cunningham was passing the house when she heard an almighty crash. A young man in shirtsleeves ran out. Jane grabbed her notebook and went in to investigate. This time, the poltergeist had smashed the whole conservatory just as if it had placed a bomb in it—all over the garden there was glass, lumps of coal and washing soda—and pennies. Her report on the occurrence led to widespread press interest in the case.

Price went to see the house, and the poltergeist threw a gas-lighter past him; otherwise, nothing much happened. Soon afterwards, Frederick had a mental breakdown and had to be sent into hospital. Chairs marched down the hallway in single file. When Mrs Perkins—the mother of the boy Peter—tried to lay the table, chairs kept scattering all the crockery.

Price assumed that Peter was the 'focus' and suggested he should be sent away; he went to stay with relatives in the country. But the poltergeist remained. Objects continued to be thrown around. The old man had to be removed to hospital, and one of the daughters fell ill. The police could only advise the family to vacate the house for the time being, which they did, staying with friends.

A medium held a seance in the house, and began to shiver. But she was unsuccessful in identifying the 'spirit'. Price paid another visit, with a newspaperman, and more objects were thrown—although not when anyone was watching. Finally, Frederick Robinson came home from the mental home where he had been confined, and quickly moved the whole family elsewhere. This was virtually the end of the story.

Yet there was a postscript. Price had heard that small slips of paper with writing on them had fluttered from the air. Frederick, sick of the whole business, declined to comment. But many years later, in 1941, he broke silence in the Spiritualist newspaper *Two Worlds*, stating that slips of paper *had* fallen from the air, and that some of them contained writing made by tiny pinholes. (The Seeress of Prevorst also produced sheets of paper with geometrical drawings made by the same method.) One of these messages read: 'I am having a bad time here. I cannot rest. I was born during the reign of William the Conqueror.' It was signed 'Tom Blood'. Other messages were signed 'Jessie Blood'.

The Battersea poltergeist seems to be in every way typical of the species. Whether or not it was genuinely an earthbound spirit from the days of William the Conqueror must remain in doubt; poltergeists are not necessarily truthful. (But, as the Rocha case (see p. 282) shows, the dead have no sense of passing time.) The chief mystery of the case is where it obtained the energy to continue the 'haunting' after the boy Peter left—for it seems reasonable to assume he was the 'focus'. The answer may be provided by Price's observation that at the back of the house there was a mental home. Price actually suggested that some ex-servicemen patients in this home might have thrown lumps of coal (but this is probably an example of his desire to be regarded as a hard-headed sceptic). The mentally disturbed are often the 'focuses' of poltergeist activity, so it seems possible that the 'spirit' found a convenient reservoir of surplus energy just over the garden wall.

The case with which Price's name has become most widely associated is, of course, that of Borley Rectory. And in spite of the 'debunking' that has taken place since Price's death in 1948, it remains one of the most interesting hauntings of the 20th century. After Price's death, a whole volume of the *Proceedings of the Society for Psychical Research* was devoted to *The Haunting of Borley Rectory*, 'A Critical Survey of the Evidence', by Dingwall, Trevor Hall and Kate Goldney. They allege that Price probably produced some of the 'poltergeist' phenomena himself by tossing pebbles—which, from our knowledge of Price, must be admitted as possible. Their overall conclusion is that there are so many doubts that it would probably be simplest to regard the haunting of Borley as a fairy story. But this is to ignore the fact that stories of hauntings were common long before Price came on the scene, and have continued since he left it. Anyone who feels that the SPR survey proves that Price was a liar should read the long account of Borley in Peter Underwood's *Gazetteer of British Ghosts*, with Underwood's own first-hand reports from interviews with witnesses.

Borley Rectory was built in 1863 on the site of Borley Manor House, which in turn seems to have been built on the site of a

Benedictine abbey. It was built by the Reverend H.D.E. Bull. It is difficult to pin down the earliest known 'sightings', but it is clear that, during Henry Bull's tenancy, a number of people saw the apparition of a nun. Henry Bull himself knew of the legend that a nun and a Benedictine monk had tried to elope, been caught, and had both been killed, the nun being bricked up alive. Bull's daughter Ethel confirmed in a letter to Trevor Hall in 1953 that she had awakened to find a strange man standing beside her bed, and had felt someone sitting down on the bed on several occasions; she also told Peter Underwood how, on July 28, 1900, she and her two sisters all saw a nun-like figure gliding along 'Nun's Walk', apparently telling her beads. The other sister, Elsie, saw the nun, who looked quite solid, and went to ask her what she wanted; the nun vanished.

After the Reverend Henry Bull's death, his son, the Reverend Harry Bull, took over the rectory. He was interested in psychical research, and claimed that he saw many ghosts. His daughter told Price that he had seen a legendary phantom coach (in which the lovers were supposed to have fled) and that, one day in the garden, the retriever had howled with terror, looking towards some legs visible under a fruit tree. Bull, thinking this was a poacher, followed the legs as they walked towards a postern gate; at which point he realised that the 'poacher' was somehow incomplete. The legs disappeared through the gate without opening it.

Harry Bull died in 1927, and the rectory was empty until 1928, when the Reverend Guy Smith and his wife moved in. One stormy night, there was a furious ringing of the doorbell; when Smith arrived there, he found no one. It happened again later—a peal so prolonged that Smith was able to get to the door before it stopped; again, there was no one. After that, all the keys of all the rooms fell out of the locks overnight; later, they vanished. Then they began hearing slippered footsteps. Stones were thrown—small pebbles. Lights were switched on. One day, Mrs Smith thought she saw a horse-drawn coach in the drive. Mr Smith thought he heard someone whisper, 'Don't, Carlos, don't', as he was walking into the chapel. The Smiths decided to contact the *Daily Mirror*, who asked Harry Price if he would be willing to go along with an investigator. They told Price their story, and gave him every facility to investigate. But within nine months, they had had enough of the place—perhaps because its plumbing left much to be desired—and moved to Norfolk. According to the SPR report, the Smiths only called the *Daily Mirror* because they were concerned about all the stories that the house was haunted, and wanted to reassure their parishioners by getting the place a clean bill of health. This story sounds, on the face of it, absurd. Moreover, there exists a letter from Mr Smith to Harry Price stating: 'Borley is undoubtedly haunted.' (It is true that Mrs Smith wrote a letter to the *Church Times* in 1929 saying she did not believe the house to be haunted, but this seems to have been a belated attempt to stem the flood of sensational publicity that followed the *Daily Mirror* story.)

In October 1930, the rectory was taken over by the Reverend L.A. Foyster, and his much younger wife Marianne. Foyster, oddly enough, had lived near Amherst at the time of the Esther Cox case, and the SPR survey makes much of this coincidence; however, it seems doubtful that the vicar would attempt to fake disturbances on the model of his earlier experience. Certainly, the Foyster incumbency saw the most spectacular exhibitions of the Borley poltergeist. Foyster kept a diary of the disturbances. Bells were rung, bricks thrown, footsteps heard and water out of a jug poured over the couple when in bed. Foyster was even awakened by a violent blow on the head from his own hairbrush. They saw a number of apparitions, including the nun and a clergyman who was identified as the Reverend Henry Bull, the builder of the rectory. Writing appeared on the walls, asking for a mass to be said, and asking for 'Light'.

There is much independent confirmation of all these events. A Justice of the Peace named Guy L'Estrange visited Borley at the invitation of the Foysters, and wrote a lengthy account of it. As soon as he arrived, he saw a dim figure near the porch, which vanished as soon as he approached. Mrs Foyster had a bruise on her forehead—something 'like a man's fist' had struck her the previous evening. The Foysters were telling L'Estrange about mysterious fires that kept breaking out in locked rooms when there was a loud crash in the hall they found it littered with broken crockery. Then bottles began flying about. L'Estrange notes that they seemed to appear suddenly in mid-air. The bottles were coming from a locked storage shed outside. All the bells began to ring, making a deafening clamour—but all the bell wires had been cut. L'Estrange shouted: 'If some invisible person is present, please stop ringing for a moment.' Instantly, the bells stopped—stopped dead, as if each clapper had been grabbed by an unseen hand. Later, sitting alone in front of the fire, L'Estrange heard footsteps behind him; he turned, but the room was empty. The footsteps had come from a part of the wall where there had once been a door. In bed, L'Estrange felt the room become icy cold, and saw a kind of shape materialising from a patch of luminosity; he walked towards it, and had a feeling of something trying to push him back. He spoke to it, and it slowly vanished. He was luckier than another visitor who thought that the ghostly figure was someone playing a joke, and tried to grab it; he was given a hard blow in the eye.

The rector and others tried praying in the chapel, taking with them a relic of the Curé of Ars, and then went around the house making signs of the cross. Finally, they all spent the night in the Blue Room, where Henry Bull (and others) had died; they asked that the entity should stop troubling the inmates of the house; a black shadow began to form against the wall, then dissolved. But after this, temporary peace descended on Borley Rectory.

In 1935, the Foysters decided they had had enough, and moved. Price rented the rectory in 1937, and arranged for a team of investigators to go in. But the major phenomena were over. Even so, the chief investigator, Sidney Glanville, a retired engineer, became completely convinced of the reality of the haunting.

In March 1938, the team were experimenting with a planchette, which wrote the message that Borley would be destroyed by fire. This happened in February 1939, when the house mysteriously burned down. Yet the phenomena continued; a Cambridge team investigating the ruins heard footsteps, saw patches of light, and recorded sudden sharp drops in temperature.

In August 1943, Price decided to try digging in the cellars at Borley—which he had been advised to do by a planchette message which claimed to come from 'Glanvil'—the same Glanvil who wrote the account of the Tedworth drummer. They found a cream jug, which had also been referred to by the planchette, and some fragments of a human skull. The jawbone showed signs of a deep-seated abscess—Peter Underwood speculates that this is why the phantom nun always looked miserable.

The SPR survey on Borley, which appeared eight years after Price's death, had the effect of seriously undermining his credit. Trevor Hall's *Search for Harry Price* (1978) completed the work of destroying his reputation. yet although this leaves no doubt that Price lied about his origins—perhaps romanced would be a better word—and hungered for fame, it produces no evidence that Price was not exactly what he always claimed to be: an enthusiastic scientific investigator of paranormal phenomena. To assume that, because Price wanted to be thought a 'gentleman', he was also dishonest as a paranormal researcher, is surely poor psychology. Price was one of those ambitious men who crave an outlet for their energies. He was 40 years old before he found the opportunity he was looking for—a long time for a man of Price's impatient temperament. It came when Dingwall invited him to Munich to study the Schneider brothers. From then on, Price had discovered his vocation; at last, he had found the outlet he needed for his explosive energy and romanticism. And when a man as energetic and romantic as Harry Price finally finds what he is looking for, he does not risk spoiling everything with a little cheap skulduggery. It only takes one scandal to destroy a scientist's reputation. But to put it this way is to imply that Price disciplined his natural dishonesty solely to maintain his reputation, and this is to miss the real point: that once a man has found his vocation, he pours into it all that is best about himself. Bernard Shaw has left an interesting description of the socialist Edward Aveling, who was Eleanor Marx's common-law husband; he was an inveterate seducer, and a borrower who never paid his debts, yet where socialism was concerned, he was fiercely sincere. Everything we know about Price reveals that, where psychical research was concerned, he was totally dedicated—although not above grabbing publicity wherever he could find it.

In short, it would be of no advantage to him to pretend the Borley phenomena were genuine when they were not. His reputation was based on his scepticism as much as on his support of the reality of psychic phenomena. Possibly—like most of us—he was capable of stretching a fact when it appealed to his romanticism. But in the case of Borley, there was no need to stretch facts. The haunting of Borley does not rest on Price's evidence alone; there are dozens of other witnesses, such as Guy L'Estrange—or Dom Richard Whitehouse, cited by Underwood, who witnessed just as many incredible occurrences: flying objects, ringing of bells, writing on walls, outbreaks of fire, materialisation of bottles.

And is there evidence that Price *did* stretch the facts? The SPR survey cites as an example of his dishonesty the episode of the pair of legs that Harry Bull saw walking through the postern gate. Price says, admittedly, that when the man energed from behind the fruit trees, he was headless. But the report then goes on to cite Price's original notes, which read: 'Rev. Harry Bull saw coach, Juvenal, retriever, terrified and growled. Saw man's legs rest hid by fruit trees, thought poacher, followed with Juvenal, gate shut, but saw legs disappear through gate.' Clearly, what Bull saw disappearing through the gate was not a complete man, or Price would not refer only to the legs. It sounds as if the upper half of his body was missing—in which case, headless is a fair description.

What seems clear from all accounts of the case is that the 'ground' itself is haunted, and continues to be so. Borley is a 'place of power', the kind of place that *would* be chosen for a monastery, and that probably held some pagan site of worship long before that (See Chapter 15). In the Rectory's early days, Harry Bull himself—son of the Reverend Henry Bull—was probably the unconscious focus or medium; Paul Tabori says that he was probably psychic. This is borne out by the fact that young Bull saw so many of the 'ghosts', including the coach and the nun. It is important to realise that not all people can see ghosts. The 'ghost hunter' Andrew Green describes, in *Our Haunted Kingdom*, a visit that he and other members of the Ealing Psychical Research Society paid to Borley in 1951:

'One of the Society members grabbed my arm and, although obviously terrified, proceeded to describe a phantom that he could see some thirty feet in front of him, standing at the end of the 'Nun's Walk'. It was of a Woman in a long white gown, and moved slowly towards the end of the neglected garden . . .

the witness was perspiring profusely with fear and, later with annoyance that I had failed to see the ghost.'

Green had only *heard* the rustle of trees and bushes, as if something was walking through the undergrowth. We may assume, then, that if Green had been a tenant of Borley before its destruction, he would probably have seen no ghosts. Bull *was*, it seems, enough of a 'medium' to see the ghosts. And Marianne Foyster was a far more powerful medium who changed the character of the haunting into poltergeist activity. (Most of the messages scrawled on walls were addressed to her.) The reason that the subsequent investigation of Borley (during Price's tenancy) was so unsuccessful was that there was no medium present to provide the energy.

Asked about the 'ley system' of the Borley area, the ley expert Stephen Jenkins replied as follows: 'Norfolk and Suffolk are a spider-web of alignments, many of which are linked to curious manifestations. Borley church stands at a node where four lines cross, one going from Asher church to Sproughton church . . .' After giving further details of the ley system, he goes on:

'My wife photographed me as I was standing with my back to the south wall of Borley churchyard, at ten o'clock on the morning of Saturday the 1st of September, 1979. Recently, this was borrowed for a magazine article, and the editor kindly sent me an enlargement. No less than three people, not one of them known to the others, have on separate occasions noted in the enlargement some odd—and not very prepossessing—faces among the trees close to the church. The same identifications have been made without possibility of collusion.

'More dramatic than unexpected faces in a photograph, which can always be explained away as 'simulacra', or something wrong with the emulsion, is an incident of Sunday the 28th of August, 1977, on the road north of Belchamp Walter Hall. The time was precisely 12.52 pm, and we were driving south west along the minor road which marks the north end of the Hall grounds, when on the road in front, in the act of turning left into the hedge (I mean our left, across the path of the car), *instantaneously* appeared four men in black—I thought them hooded and cloaked—carrying a black, old-fashioned coffin, ornately trimmed with silver. The impression made on both of us was one of absolute *physical* presence, of complete material reality. Thelma and I at once agreed to make separate notes without comparing impressions. We did so, and the descriptions tallied exactly, except that she noted the near left bearer turn his face towards her. I did not see this as I was abruptly braking at the time.

'What I had seen as a hood, she described as a soft tall hat, with a kind of scarf falling to the left shoulder, thrown across the cloaked body to the right. The face was that of a skull . . .

'The next day we returned to the precise spot at exactly the same time and took a picture. It is a Kodak colour slide. In the hedge near the gap where the 'funeral party' vanished (there is a path there leading to Belchamp Walter churchyard) is a short figure, apparently cloaked, its face lowered with a skull-like dome to the head. A year later I returned searching the area where it had apparently stood. There was nothing, no post or stump that might have provided such an image, nor was there the slightest sign of the ground having been disturbed by the removal of anything that might have been rooted in it. The image is simply there on the film—we saw nothing wrong with the eye.

'That minor road alongside the north edge of the Belchamp Walter Estate precisely coincides with a line passing through the node in the water west of Heaven Wood. That node itself linked with the node at Borley.'

He adds a postscript: 'I hazard a guess that the dress of the coffin-bearer is that of the late 14th century. There seems to be no local legend of a phantom funeral.'

If Price invented the ghosts of Borley, he must have been in collusion with a remarkable number of people.

'I did not like [Harry Price] because he was a difficult man to like. He was intensely selfish, jealous, and intent on his own glory at all costs, but these weaknesses of his character do not detract from his investigation as an honest investigator and ruthless exposer of frauds. This was the shining feature of his life.'

These words were written by another man who deserves to be remembered as one of the prominent ghost-hunters of the 20th century. Unlike Price, Nandor Fodor seems to have had no great compulsion to achieve personal glory; the result is that, since his death in 1964, his name has been largely forgotten, and most of his books are out of print. Yet at least one of his books—his account of the Thornton Heath poltergeist case—deserves the status of a classic.

Fodor was born in Hungary in 1895, studied law, then became a journalist, and visited America. In 1926, he interviewed two remarkable men: Hereward Carrington, the psychical researcher, and Sandor Ferenczi, one of Freud's most prominent disciples. Fodor became simultaneously fascinated by psychoanalysis and psychical research and, in due course, became himself a psychoanalyst. Predictably, therefore, his analysis of poltergeist cases is dominated by the conviction that they have a sexual origin. But since—as we have seen—there is a large element of truth in this view, Fodor's psychoanalytical beliefs distorted his outlook rather less than is often the case with Freudians.

Fodor attended his first seance at the house of a well-known American medium, Arthur Ford, in October 1927, and what he heard there left him in no doubt that the dead can communicate. In the semi-darkness, a trumpet sailed up into the air, then a voice began to speak. Various relatives of people who were present then came and (apparently) talked through the medium. Fodor then asked if the 'control' could bring someone who spoke Hungarian. It was, perhaps, an unreasonable request, but an excellent test for the medium. And after a few moments, a voice spoke from the air saying: 'Fodor, journalist', using the German pronunciation of the word—just as Fodor's father did. Then the entity proceeded to speak to Fodor in Hungarian. The voice identified itself as Fodor's father, and mentioned various relatives; it named his oldest brother by his pet name. The 'spirit' was having great difficulty communicating—because, explained the control, it was the first time he had tried to speak. The control helped out by telling Fodor that his father died on January 16. The 'spirit' ended by saying 'Isten áldjon meg. Édes fiam'—'God bless you, my dear son'. After this, another

Hungarian came through—the deceased brother of Fodor's wife, who was present. It mentioned that 'poor Uncle Vilmos' was ill and would go blind. And, in due course, this is exactly what happened to Uncle Vilmos.

It emerged later that the medium—a man called Cartheuser—*could* speak Hungarian. Yet this scarcely helps to explain his knowledge of Fodor's father, and the prophecy about Uncle Vilmos. Cartheuser also had a speech impediment, due to a hare-lip; the voices had no such impediment.

Fodor came to England to work for Lord Northcliffe—owner of the *Daily Mail*—and, in his spare time, compiled an *Encyclopedia of Psychic Science*, which is still one of the best available (a new edition combines it with a similar work by Lewis Spence). After publishing the book, in 1934, Fodor had first-hand experience of the ambiguous nature of 'psychic phenomena'. He heard of a remarkable Hungarian medium called Lajos Pap, a carpenter, whose speciality was causing 'apports' of live birds, animals and beetles to appear at seances. In June 1933, Fodor attended such a seance in Budapest. Pap was undressed and searched, then dressed again in a robe of luminous cloth, so that his movements in the dark could be clearly seen. Two men held Pap's wrists during the seance, although he could move his hands with their hands on him. In an hour-long seance, Pap groped into the air and produced thirty live beetles, many of them an inch long. He also produced a cactus plant with soil on the roots and a rose bush. On other occasions, Pap had produced birds, caterpillars, dragonflies, snakes and a live goldfish. His 'control', the Rabbi Isaac (who claimed to have lived six hundred years earlier in Galicia) had a sense of humour. At one seance, a toy pistol arrived, and a number of explosive caps were fired; the Rabbi claimed to have shot dead twenty-one crickets and, after the seance, dead crickets were found in the room.

On another occasion, nine lumps of dirty snow arrived during the seance, and proved to be mixed with horse manure and straw. The temperature in the room was 72 degrees Fahrenheit, so it would have been difficult to keep the snow unmelted for long if it had been concealed under the medium's robe.

Fodor arranged for Lajos Pap to be brought to London. At a seance there a dead snake, more than two feet long, appeared.

Fodor was impressed; but he nevertheless insisted that Pap should have an X-ray examination to find out whether he could have anything secreted in his body. To Fodor's surprise and dismay, Pap proved to be wearing a belt of linen and whalebone under his robe. He said it was a kind of rupture truss, because he had a dropped kidney; but Fodor decided regretfully that this was where the dead snake had been hidden, and that it had been worked out through the neck of the robe. Accordingly, in his subsequent report, 'The Lajos Pap Experiments', Fodor concluded that Pap's psychic powers should be regarded as 'not proven'. Yet he adds:

'Nor would I be willing to declare him a fraud and nothing but a fraud. Too long has psychical research been the victim of the fatal delusion that a medium is either genuine or fraudulent. It is a minimal assumption that mediumship means a dissociation of personality. There was plenty of evidence that Lajos Pap was suffering from such a dissociation.'

In fact, Pap is still regarded as a non-fraudulent medium, and accounts of his seances at which live birds and insects appeared seem to indicate that his powers *were* remarkable.

Fodor had been appointed Research Officer of the International Institute for Psychical Research. In November 1936, he was asked to investigate a case of poltergeist haunting at Aldborough Manor in Yorkshire. The bells for summoning servants had rung almost non-stop for five days, doors had opened and closed of their own accord, and two maids had seen a ghost above an ancient cradle. Lady Lawson-Tancred, who lived in the house, was afraid she would have to move out if the haunting continued. But when Fodor arrived, it was already over. One of the two maids had had a nervous breakdown and left. The bells had rung during the night she left and the following morning, then stopped. To Fodor, therefore, it was clear that the maid was the 'focus' of the disturbance. Her nervous breakdown was probably caused by the 'drain' upon her energies caused by the poltergeist. The other maid, a very pretty girl, also had a strange power over animals; birds would settle on her shoulders, and mice run into her hands. Lady Lawson-Tancred thought that she might also be connected with the disturbances, and dismissed her. (Fodor seems to have explained to her the difference between a poltergeist and a real 'haunting', where the house itself seems to concentrate the negative forces, as at Borley.) After this, Aldborough Manor became peaceful.

The same solution was found in the case of a Chelsea poltergeist that disturbed a house with its knockings. Fodor went to the house, in Elm Park Gardens, and heard the rappings himself—he said they were like hammer blows. Fodor looked around for the focus, and soon found it: a 17-year-old servant girl named Florrie. He engaged her in conversation, and she told him that this was not her first experience of mysterious knockings—the same thing had happened at home four years before, when she was 13. The children were all sent away, and when they returned, the knocking had stopped. Clearly, Florrie was quite unaware that she had been the 'cause' of the knockings.

Fodor told the house's owner, Dr Aidan Redmond, that Florrie was probably the unconscious medium. That night, the raps were like machine-gun fire. Dr Redmond regretfully sacked Florrie. And silence descended on the house.

In July 1936, Fodor investigated a case in which the distinction between ghost and poltergeist becomes blurred; this was at Ash Manor, in Sussex, and he disguises the family under the name of Keel. It is among the most remarkable ghost stories ever recorded.

The house was bought by the family in June 1934; when they said they could not pay the price demanded, the owner dropped his demand so surprisingly that the Keels decided there must be something wrong with the place, probably the sanitation. But the wife soon began to get extremely unpleasant feelings in a bedroom that had been used for servants. (The previous owner said they had run away.)

The first manifestations were stamping noises from the attic. But this room had no floorboards—only the bare joists. In November 1934 Mr Keel was awakened by three violent bangs on his door. He went to his wife's room down the corridor—she had also heard them. This happened at 3 a.m. The next night, there were two thumps on the door at the same time, and the following night, one loud thump. Keel went away on business for a few days, and when he returned, decided to stay awake until 3 a.m. to see if anything happened. Nothing did, and he fell asleep. Then a violent bang woke him up. Although the room was dark, he could see quite clearly a small, oldish man dressed in a green smock, with muddy breeches and a handkerchief round his neck. He looked so solid and normal that Keel was convinced this was an intruder and, when he got no reply, jumped out of bed and tried to grab him. His hand went through him, and Keel fainted. When he came to, he ran to his wife's bedroom, babbling incoherently, and his wife rushed out to get some brandy. Outside her husband's room she saw the feet and leggings of a man, then looked up and saw the same little old man. She was also able to see him quite clearly in the dark, although he did not seem to be shining. She observed that he was wearing a pudding basin hat, that his face was very red, 'the eyes malevolent and horrid', and that his mouth was dribbling. She also asked him who he was and what he wanted. When he made no reply, she tried to hit him. Her fist went through him, and she hurt her knuckles on the doorpost. Her husband was in a faint in her room at the time, so he had not had an opportunity to describe the man he saw; it was only later that they realised both had seen the same ghost.

After this, they continued to see the little old man in green several times a week. They also heard footsteps and knocking. The old man usually walked across Keel's bedroom, appearing from the chimney on the landing, and vanished into a cupboard which had once been a priest hole. After a while, the family ceased to be afraid of him. The wife discovered that she could make him vanish by extending a finger and trying to touch him. The third time she saw him, the old man raised his head, and Mrs Keel could see that his throat was cut and his windpipe was sticking out. One day she heard heavy footsteps approaching along the corridor, and thought it was her husband. Her bedroom door—which was locked—flew open and invisible footsteps crashed across the room (although the floor was carpeted), then the footsteps went upwards towards the ceiling, as if they were mounting a staircase. A trapdoor in the ceiling flew open, and the footsteps continued in the attic—again, sounding as if they were on floorboards, although these had been removed. A dog in the room was terrified. Mrs Keel's 16-year-old daughter Pat was sleeping in her mother's room, and witnessed the whole episode. The man who sold them the house told them that there *had* been a staircase in the room, which he had had removed to replace it with the fireplace.

Two psychical investigators who were called in declared that the house had been built on the site of a Druid stone circle, and that this explained why it was haunted. The ghost, they said, was a man called Henry Knowles, who had cut his throat in 1819 when a milkmaid had jilted him.

As the Research Officer for the International Institute, Fodor was called in to investigate; he had with him Mrs Maude ffoulkes, who also published the story of the manor house in her book *True Ghost Stories* later that year (thus providing independent corroboration of the story). An amateur photographer had succeeded in taking a picture of a dim shape on the haunted landing, so Fodor took his own photographic equipment.

Fodor now had enough experience of hauntings to look for unhappiness in the house. The daughter, Pat, struck him as nervous and very jealous of any attention given to her mother, and admitted to suffering from temper tantrums. On the first night, nothing happened. The next time, Fodor slept in the 'haunted room', but, apart from awful nightmares, had nothing to record. He decided to ask the help of the famous American medium, Eileen Garrett, who happened to be in England. In late July Mrs Garrett came to the house and immediately had strong psychic impressions. The ghost, she said, was a man who had been imprisoned nearby. There had been a king's palace nearby, and the man had been tortured. He had something to do with a king called Edward. Her further observations suggested that the 'ghost' she saw was not the same old man, for she described him as sharp-featured, with blond hair, and said he had taken part in a rebellion against his half-brother, the king. (In fact, there were two royal castles in the area, Farnham and Guildford.)

Mrs Garrett went into a trance, and was taken over by her trance personality, Uvani, an Arabian. Uvani made the interesting comment that hauntings take place only when there is someone in a 'bad emotional state' who can revivify old unhappy memories. There were bad emotional states in this house, said Uvani. 'Life cannot die,' said Uvani, 'you can explode its dynamism, but you cannot dissipate its energy. If you suffered where life suffered, the essence that once filled the frame will take from you something to dramatise and live again.' About five hundred yards to the west of this house, said Uvani, there had been a jail in the early part of the 15th century, and many unfortunate men and women had died there. 'There are dozens of unhappy souls about.' (The early 15th century was the period of the battle of Agincourt, Joan of Arc, and many revolts and rebellions. The plot against Edward the Fourth—by his brother the Duke of Clarence—was in 1470.)

'According to this', says Fodor[1], 'our ghost was a spectral automaton, living on life borrowed from human wrecks—a fascinating conception which was very different from ordinary spiritualistic conceptions and very damning for the owners of the house.'

Uvani then said that he would allow the ghost to take possession of Mrs Garrett's body. The medium grew stiff and her breathing became laboured. She seemed to be trying to speak, but was unable. The 'spirit' pointed to its lips, tapped them as if to signal it was dumb, then felt its throat gingerly. He beckoned to Fodor, then seized his hand in such a powerful grip that Fodor howled with pain. Although another person present tried to help him free his hand, it was impossible. Fodor's hand went numb, and was useless for days after the seance.

The 'man' threw himself on his knees in front of Fodor, seemed to be pleading, and clicked his tongue as if trying to speak. Then it called 'Eleison, eleison'—pleading for mercy in the words of the mass. Aware that the ghost was taking him for its gaoler, Fodor tried to reassure it, and said they were trying to help him. Finally, the man seemed reassured, and sat down. He began to speak in an odd, mediaeval English (unfortunately, tape recorders did not exist in those days—it would have been fascinating to have an authentic example of the English of Chaucer's period), and spoke about the Earl of Huntingdon, calling him ungrateful. It asked Fodor to help him find his wife, then raged about the Duke of Buckingham, (perhaps the one who led a rebellion against Richard III in the late 15th century). It seemed that the Duke of Buckingham had offered the man 'broad acres and ducats' in exchange for his wife, then betrayed him. The spirit identified

1. *The Haunted Mind*, Chapter 8.

itself as Charles Edward Henley, son of Lord Henley. On a sheet of paper, it wrote its name, then 'Lord Huntingdon', and the word 'Esse', which was the mediaeval name for the village near the manor house. It made the curious statement that Buckingham, the friend of his childhood, had 'forced her eyes', 'her' being his wife Dorothy. He added: 'Malgré her father lies buried in Esse', and went on: 'You being friend, you proved yourself a brother, do not leave me, but help me to attain my vengeance.'

Remembering that, according to the teachings of Spiritualism, it is remorse or desire for vengeance that often keeps spirits bound to earth, Fodor and another sitter, a Dr Lindsay, tried hard to persuade the spirit to abandon its hatred. Finally, it seemed to agree, then cried out, 'Hold me, hold me, I cannot stay, I am slipping . . .' Then it was gone, and Mrs Garrett woke up.

During this seance, the Keels had been present. Mrs Keel peered closely at the medium's face while 'Henley' was speaking through her, and was horrified to see that it now looked like the old man she had seen.

But *had* the ghost been laid? Apparently not. Some time later, Keel rang Fodor to tell him that the old man was back again, standing in the doorway and trying to speak.

Dr Lindsay, who had been present at the seance, had also had a remarkable experience. At the College of Psychic Science, he had been involved in a seance with another medium when the ghost of 'Henley' came through. He complained that Fodor had promised to stand by him, but that when he had come back the following night, there was no one there. The old man said he had seen his son, for whom he had been searching, but not his wife.

They had another session with Mrs Garrett that afternoon. Again, the ghost came through, and made more pleas for help, as well as saying a little more about his background. He was not particularly informative; but the control, Uvani, had some interesting things to say. He asserted that the Keels had been 'using' the ghost to 'embarrass' each other. What was being suggested was that the ghost-laying ceremony *would* have worked if the Keels had not wanted to cling on to the ghost as a device for somehow 'getting at' one another.

Following this hint, Fodor talked to Mrs Keel. She then admitted that Uvani was right about the unhappiness in the household. Her husband was homosexual, so their sex lives left much to be desired. And the daughter was jealous of her mother—Fodor hints that it was a classic Oedipus complex. Mrs Keel was keeping up her spirits with drugs.

Soon after this, the case began to reach a kind of climax. Mr Keel himself was becoming 'possessed' by the spirit, talking in his sleep and saying things about 'Henley' and his life. Fodor sent him a transcription of the things Uvani had said about the desire of the Keels' to 'hold on' to the ghost; as a result, Keel rang him to admit he felt it was true.

This confession had the effect that Fodor's 'ghost-laying ceremony' had failed to achieve: the ghost of Ash Manor disappeared and did not return.

This is undoubtedly one of the most interesting cases of haunting on record, for a number of reasons. First, the corroboration is impressive: the story was also written up by Maude ffoulkes and published in 1936.[1] And the participation of Eileen Garrett rules out any suggestion that Fodor might simply have invented the whole story—a suggestion that *has* been made about one of Harry Price's most impressive cases, 'Rosalie'.[2] Second, the behaviour of the ghost seems to show that the 'tape recording' theory of Lethbridge and Sir Oliver Lodge does *not* cover all hauntings: 'Henley' was clearly more than a 'recording'. And third, it demonstrates very clearly that there is no clear dividing line between a ghost and a poltergeist. This case started with bangings and rappings, and then developed into a haunting. And, if we can accept Uvani's statements as any kind of evidence, it also suggests that there are such things as 'earth-bound' spirits, probably in dismaying abundance. The other implications—about the nature of such spirits—must be left until later.

If Fodor had possessed Price's flair for publicity, the 'Henley' case might have made him as famous as Borley made Price. But he made no attempt to publicise it. Neither did he attempt to make capital out of a visit to study the talking mongoose of Cashen's Gap (except for a single chapter in a book), although his investigation was rather more painstaking—if hardly more

1. It is also described in *Unbidden Guests* by William O. Stevens, 1945.
2. See *The Occult*, Part 3, Chapter 2.

successful—than Price's. (Fodor concluded that the mongoose was probably genuine, but denied that it was a poltergeist on the dubious grounds that poltergeists are always invisible; we have seen that 'elementals' are rather less easy to classify than this implies.) In fact, Fodor's only flash of notoriety occurred almost accidentally as a result of a libel action he brought against *Psychic News*. He was asked whether it was true that he wanted to take a medium, Mrs Fielding, to the Tower of London to steal the Crown Jewels by psychic means, and he admitted that this was true, and that he had been willing to go to prison if the experiment had been successful. However, it had been forbidden by the other members of the International Institute. From then on, Fodor was known as the man who wanted to 'spirit away' the Crown Jewels.

Mrs Fielding was, in fact, the 'focus' of the most interesting and complex poltergeist case he ever investigated. Mrs Fielding (Fodor calls her Mrs Forbes in his book *On the Trail of the Poltergeist*) was a 35 year-old London housewife, living at Thornton Heath, an attractive woman with a 17-year-old son. The disturbances began on Friday February 19, 1938, as the Fieldings were in bed, and on the point of sleep. A glass shattered on the floor, and when they put on the light, another glass flew past their heads. They put off the light, and the eiderdown flew up in their faces. They tried to switch on the light again, but the bulb had been removed. A pot of face cream was thrown at their son when he came in to see what was happening. The next day, cups, saucers and ornaments flew through the air. They notified the *Sunday Pictorial*, and two reporters came. The poltergeist obliged with an impressive display. A cup and saucer in Mrs Fielding's hand shattered and cut her badly, a huge piece of coal struck the wall with such force that it left a big hole, an egg cup shattered in the hand of one reporter, and Mrs Fielding was thrown out of her chair by some force. As Mr Fielding went upstairs, a vase flew through the air and struck him with a crash—yet although he looked dazed, his head was not bruised. Within three days of the coming of the poltergeist, it had broken thirty-six tumblers, twenty-four wine glasses, fifteen egg-cups and a long list of other articles.

When Fodor arrived a few days later, the poltergeist did not disappoint. Fodor records twenty-nine poltergeist incidents during that first visit. Again and again, he had his eyes on Mrs Fielding when things happened—glasses flew off tables, a saucer smashed against the wall, glasses were snatched from her hands and broke on the floor. It was soon clear that Mrs Fielding, and not her 17-year-old son, was the focus and 'cause' of the disturbances. One glass flew out of her hand and split in mid-air with a loud ping, as if it had been hit by a hammer.

Fodor asked Mrs Fielding to come to the headquarters of the Institute, Walton House, for tests. She was dressed in a one-piece garment after being searched (a precaution he may have learned from the Lajos Pap case) and they went into the seance room. While Mrs Fielding was standing in full view, with three witnesses around her, there was a clatter, and a brass-bound hair brush appeared on the floor. It was warm, as 'apports' usually are (the theory being that they are 'dematerialised' and then re-materialised). Mrs Fielding identified it as her own, and said she had left it in her bedroom at home. The poltergeist then obliged with several more apports, and also made saucers fly out of Mrs Fielding's hands and split with a ping in mid-air. Strong men found that they could not break them in their hands.

The idea of stealing the Crown Jewels probably came to Fodor when he and Mrs Fielding went into a gift shop and she decided against buying a small elephant; as they were getting into the car, a box in Mrs Fielding's hand rattled, and they found the elephant in it; they had committed 'psychic shop-lifting'.

At a later 'sitting', Mrs Fielding produced some impressive results. On one occasion she sat with her hands tightly clenched while someone held them. The person holding them felt one hand convulse 'as if something was being born', and when Mrs Fielding opened her hand, there was a tortoiseshell cross in it.

She also began to experience 'psychic projections', finding herself in other places in her trance states. In the seance room, in a semi-trance, she projected herself back to her home. They telephoned her husband, who said she was there, and even handed her the telephone; at that moment, they were cut off. Mrs Fielding's 'double' handed her husband a recipe that she had written in the seance room; he read it back to them over the telephone, and it was identical with the one they had in front of them. He also handed the 'double' a compass, which then reappeared in the seance room, ten miles away. The 'double' had walked out of the front door with the compass.

A full account of Mrs Fielding's phenomena would occupy a whole chapter. She produced some ancient artifacts like Roman lamps and pottery labelled 'Carthage', white mice and a bird, and a spray of violet perfume around her body (as well as violets which fell from the air). Under increasing strain, she started to show signs of breakdown. She began going hysterically blind, burn marks appeared on her neck, and she claimed she was being clawed by an invisible tiger (producing an unpleasant 'zoo' odour). When her husband said jokingly that he would like an elephant, there was a crash and an elephant's tooth appeared in the hall. She also had a phantom pregnancy.

At a seance, a spirit that claimed to be her grandfather declared that he was responsible for the apports. Asked to prove its identity by bringing something of its own, it materialised a silver matchbox—which Mrs Fielding said had belonged to her grandfather—in her clasped hands.

And at this point, the story took a bewildering turn. Mrs Fielding apparently began cheating. Fodor saw her producing a 'breeze' during a seance by blowing on the back of someone's neck. Fodor became convinced that she was producing small 'apports' from under her clothes, and an X-ray photograph showed a brooch hidden beneath her left breast. Later, she produced this brooch as an apport. When being undressed, a small square of linen fell from between her legs, stained with vaginal secretion; it looked as if she was also using her vagina to hide apports.

Two days after this, she claimed to have been attacked by a vampire. There were two small puncture marks on her neck, and she looked listless and pale.

One of the oddest incidents occurred when Fodor was walking with her into the Institute. With no attempt at concealment, she opened her handbag, took something out, and threw a stone over her shoulder. When Fodor asked her about this, she indignantly denied it.

In his account of the case in *The Haunted Mind*, Fodor makes the statement: 'This discovery . . . eliminated any remaining suspicion that a spirit or psychic force was still at work.' But the 'still' implies that he felt there had been genuine psychic forces at work at an earlier stage. Reading his full account of the case, this seems self-evident. It would have been impossible for Mrs Fielding to have faked the poltergeist occurrences in her home, and later in the Institute.

Fodor's own analysis is as follows:

As a child, Mrs Fielding was both accident- and illness-prone. At the age of 6, recovering from tonsillitis, she thought that a muscular black arm tried to strangle her in bed; it vanished when her mother ran in. She was bitten by a mad dog, and attacked (and scarred) by a parrot. She lived in a house with a reputation for being haunted, and Fodor states as a fact that neither the windows nor mirrors ever needed cleaning—they were cleaned by invisible hands during the night.

At 16, she had 'visions' of a ghost; a cupboard in her room opened and a man stepped out, then vanished. Subsequently she saw him several times. On one occasion he left a piece of paper with sooty scrawls on it beside her, but her mother burned it. A bicycle accident at this time led to a kidney abscess, which later necessitated many operations. At 17 she made a runaway marriage, had her first baby at 18, her second at 21. (This died of meningitis.) At 20 she contracted anthrax poisoning, and tried to stab her husband with a carving knife. She ran into the street in her nightdress screaming 'Murder, fire', and recovered after having twenty-eight teeth extracted.

At 24 she had a vision of her father, trying to pull her away from her husband. He made the sign of the cross over her left breast. When she woke from her trance, this was bleeding. At hospital they discovered she had a breast cancer, and the breast was amputated. At 26, she had an attack of hysterical blindness which lasted for six weeks and, at 27, was in an accident on a steamer which was smashed against Margate pier. At 28 she aborted twins after being terrified when she found a dead rat in among her washing. At 30 she had a kidney operation, and, at 32, pleurisy. Altogether, it can be seen, Mrs Fielding was a thoroughly unlucky woman.

Fodor then proceeds to interpret the evidence from the Freudian point of view. He is convinced that the basic truth is that Mrs Fielding was attacked and raped, probably in a churchyard, by a man in round glasses, before she was 5 years old. Everything else, he thinks, springs from this trauma. On two occasions, when lying awake at night, she felt a shape like a man—but as cold as a corpse—get into bed with her; then it 'behaved like a man' (i.e. had sexual intercourse). One day, on her way to the Institute, Mrs Fielding was attacked by a man on the train. Fodor does not doubt that she was attacked—she arrived in an upset condition—but thinks that the man's round glasses may have aroused in her a mixture of loathing and desire which was wrongly interpreted by the man as an invitation. Fodor goes on to suggest that her husband became somehow identified in her mind with her attacker, so that the poltergeist attacks were due to her unconscious aggressions against him.

There are times when Fodor's Freudian interpretations verge on the comic. For example, he is convinced that her apports are a cipher 'in which her tragic life story is hidden'. On one evening, the apports were: elephant's tooth, tiger claw, Carthage pottery, a tropical nutshell and a piece of coral. These, says Fodor, symbolise the hugeness of the man who assaulted her (an elephant), his savagery and beastliness, his scaliness (the nutshell), while the pottery symbolises the breaking of her hymen; the coral stands for music from the church nearby. (Organ music always made Mrs Fielding cry, and Fodor surmises that the coral was organ-pipe coral.)

There is, of course, one basic objection to the whole theory: Mrs Fielding did not tell Fodor she had been raped, and apparently had no such memory. Fodor naturally thinks it was suppressed. But do memories of that type become so suppressed that they vanish completely? It seems highly unlikely.

Fodor was never able to bring the case to a satisfactory conclusion. When he began explaining his rape theories to the Institute for Psychical Research, they objected so strongly that he felt obliged to drop the case. At least it enabled him to believe that Mrs Fielding was getting closer and closer to remembering her rape experience, and would one day have confirmed all his theories. It will be recalled that, in the case of the Bell Witch, Fodor believed that Betsy had been sexually attacked by her father, and that this produced the poltergeist, 'tearing loose part of the mental system and letting it float free like a disembodied entity'. As a good Freudian, he felt bound to seek a sexual explanation in the Thornton Heath case. Yet, like so many of the 'primal scenes' that Freud believed caused lifelong illness, the one posited by Fodor is completely unverifiable.

It would be a pity to leave this case without at least an attempt at an alternative explanation. And the simplest and most obvious is that Mrs Fielding was a born medium. Her many illnesses turned her into what 19th century investigators liked to call a 'sick sensitive'. Her vision of the black arm that tried to strangle her in bed may not have been a dream or hallucination, as Fodor thinks. If she lived in a haunted house, then it seems likely that spirit entities drew energy from her, increasing her tendency to illness. And later in life, she actually developed into a medium. During the investigation, she often went into trances, and a 'control' called Bremba spoke through her. Sitting near a pub—and a church—in Coulsdon, she had a vision of an evil, leering face, which she continued to see for ten minutes. 'Bremba' later stated at a seance that the man she saw had belonged to the church, and had been hanged for interfering with small children. 'She was probably sitting on the spot where one of the outrages took place.' When Mrs Fielding came out of her trance, she could not speak or even whisper, then, as they all watched, strangulation marks appeared on her throat. When she could speak she said: 'I feel as if I am being pulled up'—as if she was suffering from the man's hanging. Later, when she was telling friends about it, the noose marks again appeared on her throat. Fodor uses this as a support for his theory about the early rape; but it could, in fact, be ordinary mediumship. Bremba could have been telling the truth about the man hanged for sexual offences against children.

Then why did Mrs Fielding begin to cheat? There are two possible explanations. One is that she was enjoying her new position as a subject of investigation. She was a bored housewife, and, as Fodor says, the phenomena meant 'a new interest, a new life for her'. This could be true; but *if* Mrs Fielding was developing genuine powers as a medium, then she had no need to cheat in order to keep them. It sounds as if they had been latent since childhood; all she had to do was to allow them to develop.

The other explanation is that she was unconscious that she was cheating—which would explain the stone thrown in front of Fodor, with no attempt at concealment, and her subsequent denial. In a case cited by William Roll, a man being investigated was seen, through a one-way mirror, to throw an object—yet a lie detector test supported his denial that he had done it. We have seen that there is considerable evidence that poltergeists can enter the mind and influence people—mediums more than others.

To anyone who reads straight through Fodor's *On the Trail of the Poltergeist*, it seems obvious that the 'spirit entity' theory fits better than most. Both the Fieldings had been ill for some time before the first outbreak. So Mrs Fielding may have been in a suitably 'low' condition to enable the entity to begin using her energy. From then on, it used her continually, and accordingly she began to suffer from nervous exhaustion. Yet her attitude towards all this must have been ambiguous, for it brought new interest into her life; this could have enabled the entity—or entities—to manipulate her to cheat. And why should they? Because, for some reason, poltergeists seem to delight in producing bewilderment and confusion.

The one point that emerges above all others is that Mrs Fielding was not just the focus of the poltergeist disturbances: she was a *medium*, and soon began to develop her ability, with apports, travelling clairvoyance, projection of the 'double', and so on. In short, Mrs Fielding was a potential Daniel Dunglas Home or Eusapia Palladino. And this, it seems probable, is true for all the people who became 'focuses' for poltergeist phenomena. With her illnesses, her early marriage, even the loss of her teeth, Mrs Fielding calls to mind another medium, the 'Seeress of Prevorst', whose history we have looked at in an earlier chapter. Nandor Fodor, like Justinus Kerner, was a medical man. Yet it cannot be said that his study of Mrs Fielding is as penetrating or a suggestive as Kerner's study of Friederike Hauffe. To read *On the Trail of the Poltergeist* after *The Seeress of Prevorst* is a depressing experience. It is to realise that a century of psychical research has brought very few advances—that, on the contrary, an unimaginative and over-cautious approach to the phenomena has only made them less comprehensible than ever.

9.
The Spirit Mafia

CONSIDERING THAT poltergeists have been recorded for more than a thousand years, and that eminent scientists have been studying them for about a century, it seems a little surprising that they are still regarded as an insoluble mystery. In the past two decades, there have been three major scientific studies of the poltergeist: Dr A.R.G.Owen's *Can We Explain the Poltergeist?*, William Roll's *The Poltergeist*, and *Poltergeists* by Alan Gauld and Tony Cornell. All three raise the question of whether poltergeists could be spirits of the dead or other types of disembodied entity; all three decide that this is unlikely, and that therefore poltergeists are probably some kind of manifestation of the unconcious mind: that is, of 'spontaneous psychokinesis'. Owen points out that a large number of children in poltergeist cases have mental problems; Roll notes that most objects tends to move counter-clockwise, and suggests that there is some kind of whirlpool or psychic vortex that drags them into motion. But no one explains why poltergeist effects are so much more powerful than the kind of psychokinesis that has been studied in the laboratory.

There is, admittedly, one case that seems to be an exception to this rule. In the early 1970s, members of the Toronto Society for Psychical Research, under the direction of A.R.G. Owen, decided to try to manufacture a ghost. For this purpose, they invented the case history of a man called Philip, a contemporary of Oliver Cromwell, who had an affair with a beautiful gypsy girl. When Philip's wife found out, she had the girl accused of witchcraft and burned at the stake; Philip committed suicide.

Having elaborated this story and created a suitable background—an ancient manor house—they set about trying to conjure up the spirit of Philip. For several months, there were no results. Then one evening, as they were relaxing and singing songs, there was a rap on the table. They used the usual code (one rap for yes, two for no), to question the 'spirit', which claimed to be Philip and repeated the story they had invented for him. At later seances, Philip made the table dance all around the room, and even made it levitate in front of TV cameras.

Owen's group rightly regarded this 'creation' of a ghost as something of a triumph, making the natural assumption that Philip was a product of their unconscious minds. But this assumption is questionable. What they did, in effect, was to hold a series of seances until they got results. Philip *may* have been a manifestation of their collective unconscious minds. Or he may have been another of those bored and untruthful 'spirits' we have already encountered, joining in the game for want of anything better to do. The Philip case cannot be regarded as a proof or disproof of the psychokinesis theory.

The trouble is that when scientists start looking for patterns, they are inclined to see what they are expecting to see. If they are good scientists, they finally notice the facts that contradict their theories, and modify the theories. But this sometimes takes a very long time; sometimes, it never happens at all.

On the whole, the scientist is better off if he collects his facts by accident, little by little, so he can study them before he tries to fit them into a jigsaw puzzle. This is how the late Tom Lethbridge came to arrive at his theories about other dimensions of reality. It is also how Guy Lyon Playfair came to develop his own theories about the nature of the poltergeist.

In 1961, Guy Playfair had been down from Cambridge for two years—he had graduated in modern languages—and was finding life in England difficult and rather boring. And when he saw an advertisement in the personal column of *The Times* saying that teachers were wanted for Rio de Janeiro at £1,000 a year, he applied immediately. He signed a two-year contract, and at the end of the two years decided to stay on in Rio as a freelance journalist. He was reasonably successful, working as a correspondent for *Time* and *The Economist*, then as a writer in the information section of the US Agency for International Development. When Nixon cut the foreign budget in 1971, Guy Playfair was offered a golden handshake, and took it; as a result he was able to move into a comfortable house with a good view of the harbour.

One of his neighbours was an American film actor called Larry Carr, and it was through him that Playfair became involved in the world of Brazilian Spiritism. One day, Carr asked him casually if he would like to go and watch a healer. Just as casually—having nothing better to do—Playfair accepted. They drove out to a Spiritist centre in an area full of warehouses and run-down bars—'the kind of street you end up in if you get lost on the way to an airport'. The healer, a man named Edivaldo, was late, having had to drive five hundred miles from his home town; he was a school-teacher who, with his spectacles and neat moustache, looked more like a bank clerk, or possibly a bank manager. When Playfair's group entered the consulting room, Edivaldo would prod the area that was giving the trouble, write something on a prescription pad, and pass on to the next. When Playfair's turn came, Edivaldo's hand went straight to the spot on his stomach which had been giving him trouble; pills were prescribed, and Playfair was told to come back later for 'a little operation'. A few months later, he went back for his operation. When he went into the room, an old man was lying on the bed, and Edivaldo was bending over him. The old man's stomach had been ripped open, exposing the entrails. Playfair admits that he did not observe as well as he might because he found it all too bewildering. 'He was sloshing around in blood—it was a pretty gruesome sight.' He looked away for a moment, and when he looked back again, the man's stomach was 'all neat and tidy', and was being covered with bandage. The man got up, and was helped out by his wife. One of the helpers told Playfair to lie down on the bed. He unbuttoned his shirt. Edivaldo came over and ran his hand over his stomach, then his hands seemed to find what they were looking for and he pressed. Playfair felt a distinct plop and the hands entered his skin and went into his stomach.

'My stomach immediately felt wet all over, as if I were bleeding to death. I could feel a sort of tickling inside, but no pain at all.' He seemed to smell ether. Then it was all over and he was told he could get up and go home. He felt curiously stiff as if his middle had been anaesthetised, unable to bend. (This so intrigued him that he later tried to reproduce the same effect—with the aid of a friendly doctor who gave him twenty jabs of local anaesthetic: 'It wasn't the same thing at all.') When he got home, he had to take off his shoes by kicking each one off with the other foot. On his stomach there was a jagged red line where Edivaldo had pressed his thumbs, and two bright red dots nearby.

Later, after a second operation, two more red dots appeared. And Playfair's stomach complaint, though not permanently cured, was considerably eased.

Some time later, Playfair interviewed Edivaldo, and heard the remarkable story of how he had become a healer. One evening in 1962 he had been called in to sit with a neighbour who had gone temporarily insane. He became unconscious, and during this period he smashed up the room. But when he recovered consciousness, the woman was cured. Soon after that, he visited a woman who had become rigid after childbirth. He suddenly became rigid himself, and the woman's rigidity disappeared. It was clear that he was somehow 'taking on' the illness of other people. A psychiatrist told him he was probably a medium, and advised that he should go to a Spiritist centre. The first evening he did this, he again went into a trance. When he came to, he was being driven home, and was told that he had performed several operations. Apparently he was 'taken over' by various spirits who had been surgeons while alive—a Dr Calazans, a Frenchman called Pierre, a Londoner called Johnson, and a German called Dr Fritz, who also worked through the famous psychic surgeon Arigó.

For another year, Playfair continued to spend a great deal of time at Edivaldo's surgeries, and watched innumerable operations—on one occasion, Edivaldo (or rather, the 'spirit' who was controlling him) took Playfair's hand and thrust it into the open stomach. By this time, he was convinced he had discovered the subject he wanted to write about. He began to attend Spiritist sessions (Spiritism is Brazil's version of Spiritualism, and is based on the teachings of Kardec). When he encountered Hernani Andrade, founder of the IBPP—Brazilian Institute for Psycho Biophysical Research—he decided to move from Rio de Janeiro to São Paulo, a move that struck his friends as eccentric, since it is the equivalent of moving from, let us say, the Cornish Riviera to the industrial Midlands, or from Florida to Detroit. But Andrade offered Guy Playfair full and unrestricted access to his files, as well as the insights of forty years of Spiritism. As a consequence, Playfair's interest came to extend from psychic healing to poltergeists, reincarnation, black magic and life-after-death.

In São Paulo, he began by investigating more psychic surgeons. Then he heard of a case of poltergeist haunting, and offered to help the IBPP look into it.

At the time he heard about it, in 1973, the case had been going on for about six years. The family consisted of a Portuguese mother, who had been married to a Lithuanian immigrant, and was now divorced. She had a son and daughter, both adults. There had been the usual bangs and crashes, clothing and bedding had caught fire, or had been soaked with water; and as a result of these disturbances, the family had already moved house three times. There also seemed to be some evidence of black magic involved; photographs of a girl with thread stitched through it had been found in the house. The troubles had begun after the son of the family had married a girl called Nora.

It was to their house that Guy Playfair went in October 1973, taking his tape recorder with him. He sat up into the early hours of the morning, reading Frank Podmore—one of the early psychic investigators—on the subject of poltergeists. Podmore came to the conclusion that they are invariably fakes—an example of the kind of stupidity to which members of the SPR occasionally seem to be subject—and at this stage, Playfair thought he might well be correct. Finally, just as he was on the point of dozing off to sleep, he was awakened by a series of bangs that shook the house. The poltergeist had arrived. Playfair was struck by the timing—that it began as he was drifting off to sleep; the same thing had happened to Suzuko Hashizume, the investigator who had spent the previous night in the house. Playfair subsequently came to suspect that poltergeists have an uncanny sense of timing which suggest that they are able to foretell the exact moment when the investigator will be looking the other way.

There was something odd about the bangs. They caused nothing to vibrate, as such bangs normally do, and they seemed to echo longer than they should. Kardec has noted in *The Medium's Book*:

Spirit sounds are usually of a peculiar character; they have an intensity and a character of their own, and, notwithstanding their great variety, can hardly be mistaken, so that they are not easily confused with common noises, such as the creaking of wood, the crackling of a fire, or the ticking of a clock; spirit raps are clear and sharp, sometimes soft and light . . .'

In fact, a researcher, Dr J.L. Whitton, subjected tape-recording of 'spirit raps' to laboratory analysis, and found that they are quite different in character from normal raps. Shown on a graph, an ordinary sound has a distinctive curve, rising and falling like the slopes of a mountain; spirit raps begin and end abruptly, like cliffs. In fact, they seem to be 'manufactured' noises, as if the poltergeist had a BBC sound laboratory at its disposal and had to concoct the noises electronically.

The other odd thing about these loud bangs was that they did not disturb the four dogs, which had barked themselves frantic when Guy Playfair arrived; either they failed to hear them or accepted them as perfectly normal.

These bangs were followed by more, at intervals. Later, Playfair tried to make similar bangs by thumping the end of a broom handle on the floor; it was impossible to make them as loud.

The following night, when Playfair was asleep in the downstairs room, a footstool bounced down the stairs, then a bedroom drawer full of clothes was hurled out of a window into the yard. A pillow shot out from under Nora's head and flew across the room. Again and again, Playfair noted the poltergeist's sense of timing—how things seemed to happen precisely as people were falling asleep or waking up. Bumps happened mainly at night. Outbreaks of fire could happen at any time—on one occasion, a wardrobe full of clothes caught fire, and would have burned the house down if it had not been caught in time.

At this point, the IBPP called in their poltergeist-clearance team of mediums, who went into the house, sat in the kitchen, and asked their spirit guides to persuade the poltergeist to move. After this, there was silence for two weeks; then minor disturbances began again. This time, the family decided to call in a *candomblé* specialist—*candomblé* being one of the largest of Brazil's many African-influenced cults. This man brought with him a team of helpers. He told the family that this struck him as a particularly nasty case of black magic. Rites were performed and incense burned. And at the end of it all, the poltergeist finally left the family in peace. (At least, it had not reappeared by the time Playfair wrote his book about two years later.)

Now the notion of a poltergeist being associated with black magic is one that European investigators will find bizarre and outlandish. But in Brazil, it is taken for granted. Hernani Andrade is quoted as saying:

In every case of person-directed poltergeist activity where I have been able to study the family background, there has been evidence that somebody in the house could be the target of revenge from a spirit. It may be a former lover who committed suicide, a jealous relation, a spiteful neighbour, or even a member of the same family bearing some trivial grudge. Any Brazilian is well aware that this country is full of backyard *terreiros* of *quimbanda* (black magic centres) where people use spirit forces for evil purposes.

'You can use a knife to cut bread or to cut a man's throat, and so it is with the hidden powers of man; they can be turned to good or bad ends, though they remain the same powers. To produce a successful poltergeist, all you need is a group of bad spirits prepared to do your work for you, for a suitable reward, and a susceptible victim who is insufficiently developed spiritually to be able to resist. Black magic is a really serious social problem in Brazil, and we must find reliable ways of getting rid of it.'

Playfair goes on to cite another case in a town near São Paulo, in which the poltergeist made a number of attempts to burn the baby. One day, the baby disappeared, and the mother heard stifled cries coming from a laundry basket. She rushed to it and found the baby buried inside dirty clothes, in the process of stifling to death. The poltergeist also smashed furniture and wrecked the roof by pounding on it; when the family finally left the house, it looked as if it had been hit by a bomb. All this is, of course, no proof that poltergeists can be called up by magic, but it indicates that they can, on occasion, behave with something like demonic malevolence.

In his book *The Indefinite Boundary*, Playfair devotes a chapter called 'The Psi Underworld' to this problem of magic and malevolence. He cites the disturbing case of 11-year-old Maria José Ferreira, who, in December 1965, became the centre of violent poltergeist activity. Pieces of brick began to fall inside the house, in Jabuticabal, near São Paulo, and an attempt at exorcism made things much worse. (Poltergeists, as we have seen, seem contemptuous of attempts to exorcise them.) A neighbour who knew about Kardec took the child into his house; things got worse, with bombardments of stones and eggs. One large stone descended from the ceiling and split into two; when someone picked up the two pieces, they snapped together as if they were magnetically attracted to each other. (We have already seen that poltergeists seem to have an affinity with electricity; it is interesting to speculate whether the force that caused the stones to snap together was an example of 'ley power' or what has been called 'Telluric force'.)

For a while, the poltergeist seemed to be in an amiable mood; Maria could ask for a flower or piece of candy, and it would instantly drop at her feet. Then, quite suddenly, the poltergeist began to attack her, biting her and slapping her on the face or bottom. It tried to suffocate her while she was asleep by placing cups or glasses over her mouth and nostrils. Then it began to set her clothes on fire.

When Maria was taken to a Spiritist centre, the hope of 'curing' her disappeared. A spirit came and spoke through the medium, saying: 'She was a witch. A lot of people suffered, and I died because of her. Now we are making her suffer too . . .' Spirits, of course, are not invariably truthful, and this one may have been inventing the tale that Maria had been a witch in a previous existence. (Kardec, it must be remembered, taught reincarnation as an integral part of Spiritism.) Special prayers and appeals to the spirits failed to stop the attacks on the girl. And, when she was 13, she took a dose of ant killer in a soft drink and was dead when they found her. It would be interesting to know whether Maria took the poison deliberately, or whether the poltergeist placed it there, as the 'Bell Witch' dosed John Bell's medicine.

All this makes it rather difficult to follow William Roll's reasoning in this central paragraph from his book on poltergeists:

'I do not know of any evidence for the existence of the poltergeist as an incorporeal entity other than the disturbances themselves, and these can be explained more simply as PK effects from a flesh-and-blood entity who is at their center. This is not to say that we should close our minds to the possibility that some cases of RSPK might be due to incorporeal entities. But there is no reason to postulate such an entity when the incidents occur around a living person. It is easier to suppose that the central person is himself the source of the PK energy.'

The source, possibly. But the whole *cause* of the phenomena? It is true that in some cases—perhaps the majority—we can interpret the disturbances as an unconscious attempt by the 'focus' to draw attention to his or her problems, as an unsuccessful suicide attempt does. Esther Cox's manifestations ceased after she was put in prison. But if Maria's unconscious aggressions were causing her clothes to catch on fire and bite marks to appear all over her body, surely the despair that finally drove her to suicide would have reached through to the rebellious part of her mind and persuaded it to stop? It simply fails to make sense to believe that Maria's own unconscious aggressions drove her to kill herself.

The point is underlined by one of the most remarkable cases described by Guy Playfair, that of a girl who inadvertently incurred a 'black magic curse'. He calls her Marcia F and mentions that she had a master's degree in psychology. In May 1973, when Marcia was 28, she went for a family outing to the Atlantic coast near São Paulo. As they walked along the beach, Marcia noticed something lying in the sand—a plaster statue of a woman about six inches high, with much of the paint worn off by the sea. She took it back home to her apartment, which she shared with another girl—in spite of her aunt's warning that it might bring bad luck to take a statue of the sea goddess Yemanjá, which had obviously been placed there as an offering in return for some favour. But Marcia was a good Catholic as well as a psychology graduate, and thought that the talk of bad luck was nonsense. She placed it on her mantelpiece.

Some days later she was violently ill with food poisoning after eating chocolate. Then she began to lose weight and feel run down. Her vitality was draining away. She began to spit blood, and X-rays showed a patch on her lung. Yet a few weeks later the patch had disappeared—it would normally have taken at least a year. After a holiday at home with her parents, Marcia returned to her flat. The pressure cooker blew up and she suffered second degree burns on her arms and face. Then the oven exploded, shooting out a sheet of flame toward Marcia; an engineer found the incident unexplainable. A few days later, a friend told her that at the moment when her pressure cooker had exploded, Marcia's photograph had jumped from the wall in her parents' home.

When a friend warned her again about the statue of Yemanjá, Marcia again dismissed the idea as preposterous.

Now she began to experience suicidal impulses. Crossing the road at a traffic light, she suddenly felt a powerful desire to fling herself under the oncoming cars. Opening the window of her apartment (which was on the fifteenth floor) she seemed to hear a voice inside her urging her to throw herself out.

And at this point, the first unmistakable suggestion of witchcraft entered the case. Her bedroom seemed to be full of presences. Then they entered her bed, and she felt herself being touched all over. And one night, she felt the presence of a male body, which moved on top of her; she felt a penis entering her, and lay there while the entity had sexual intercourse. This went on happening for several nights, until Marcia, wondering if she was going insane, went again to stay with her parents. There, by chance, they were visited by a Spiritist, to whom Marcia told her story. He advised her to go to the local *umbanda* centre—*umbanda* is the most popular Afro-Brazilian cult. She also took along the statue, at the insistence of her flatmate. The director of the centre listened to her story, and told her that her problem was undoubtedly a case of a black magic *trabalho* (work or job) being directed at her because of her removal of the statue. It was only then that Marcia looked more closely at the statue—which had only patches of paint left on it—and realised suddenly that each remaining patch corresponded to a part of her own body that had been damaged: the burn marks on her arms, neck and face matched exactly the paint on the statue, and the patch on the back was just above the 'patch' that had been found in her lung. The statue still had paint on its blue eyes, which was ominous. She took the advice of the director, and returned the statue to the spot on the beach where she had found it. Immediately, the run of bad luck ceased.

Playfair personally investigated the case of Marcia, and was not surprised when she told him that, as a result of her experience, her scepticism about 'bad luck' and *trabalho* had given way to a more pragmatic attitude.

Playfair's observations received strong support from those of another investigator, his friend David St Clair, who has described his experiences of Brazil in a book called *Drum and Candle*. He speaks of walking down Copacabana Avenue with some friends on his first night in Rio, and noticing on the pavement a circle of burning candles around a clay statue of the devil. When he reached out to touch it, one of his friends pulled him back, saying: 'It's *despacho*—an offering to a spirit.'

'But you surely don't believe that stuff?' said St Clair. 'You're all college graduates.' His friends admitted that they did not believe in it—but nevertheless would not allow him to touch the statue.

After that, St Clair saw many such offerings. He saw offerings of cooked chicken, and the starving beggars who stared at them, then quietly went away. He even saw a dog sniff at such an offering, then back away.

St Clair has many stories about *candomblé* and Spiritism. But the final chapter of the book describes his own experience of a *trabalho*. He had been living in Rio de Janeiro for eight years, and had a comfortable apartment with a fine view. He also had an attractive maid named Edna, a pretty, brown-coloured girl. She was, he assures the reader, a maid and nothing more. Her life had been hard: deserted by the father, her family had been brought up in a shack in a slum. She was obviously delighted with the comfort and security of her job with St Clair. She joined a folk-dance group and, after a television appearance, became something of a local celebrity. And one day, St Clair told her that he had decided it was time for him to leave Brazil. Edna was now doing so well that he had no doubt she would easily find another job; he told her he would give her 6 months' wages.

Then things began to go wrong. A book he had written failed to make any headway; his typist made a mess of it, then fell ill so that it sat in her desk for weeks. A New York publisher rejected it. An inheritance he was expecting failed to materialise. His plans for moving to Greece had to be shelved. A love affair went disastrously wrong, and a friend he asked for a loan refused it. He even fell ill with malaria.

One day, he met a psychic friend in the Avenida Copacabana; she took one look at him and said: 'Someone has put the evil eye on you. All your paths have been closed.' A few days later, another friend wrote to say he had been to an *umbanda* session, and a spirit had warned him that one of his friends was in grave danger due to a curse, all his paths had been closed.

An actor friend—who was also a Spiritist—immediately divined that it was Edna who had put the curse on him. St Clair thought this absurd. To begin with, Edna was a Catholic, and had often expressed her disapproval of Spiritism and *umbanda*. But his actor friend told him he had attended a Spiritist session where he had been assured that David St Clair's apartment was cursed. But how could Edna do that, St Clair wanted to know. All she had to do, his friend replied, was to go to a *quimbanda*—black magic—session and take some item of his clothing, which could be used in a ritual to put a curse on him. And now his friend mentioned it, St Clair recalled that his socks *had* been disappearing recently. Edna had claimed the wind was blowing them off the line.

St Clair told Edna he believed himself to be cursed; she pooh-poohed the idea. But he told her he wanted her to take him to an *umbanda* session. After much protest, she allowed herself to be forced into it.

That Saturday evening, Edna took him to a long, white house in a remote area outside Rio. On the walls were paintings of the devil, Exú. Towards midnight, drums started up, and the negroes sitting on the floor began to chant. A ritual dance began. Then the *umbanda* priestess came in like a whirlwind—a huge negress dressed in layers of lace and a white silk turban. She danced, and the other women began to jerk as if possessed. The priestess went out, and when she came in again, was dressed in red, the colour of Exú/Satan. She took a swig of alcohol, then lit a cigar. After more dancing, she noticed St Clair, and offered him a drink from a bottle whose neck was covered with her saliva. Then she spat a mouthful of the alcohol into his face. After more chanting, a medium was asked who had put the curse on him. She replied: 'The person who brought him here tonight! She wants you to marry her. Either that, or to buy her a house and a piece of land . . .' The priestess ordered Edna to leave. Then she said: 'Now we will get rid of the curse.' There was more ritual drumming and dancing, then the priestess said: 'Now you are free. The curse has been lifted, and it will now come down doubly hard upon the person who placed it on you.' When he protested, he was told it was too late—it had already been done.

Three days later, St Clair received a telegram from a magazine, asking for a story; he had suggested it to them months before but they had turned it down. Now, unexpectedly, they changed their minds, and sent him money. A week later, the inheritance came through. The book was accepted. And ten days later he received a letter asking if his broken love affair could be restarted where it had left off. Then Edna became ill. A stomach-growth was diagnosed, and she had to have an operation, for which St Clair paid. But her health continued to decline. She went to see an *umbanda* priest, who told her that the curse she had put on St Clair had rebounded on her, and that she would suffer as long as she stayed near him. She admitted trying to get him to marry her by black magic. She declined his offer to buy her a house or an apartment, and walked out of his life.

In *The Indefinite Boundary*, Playfair goes on to discuss black magic. It seems, he says, to be based on an exchange of favours between incarnate and discarnate—man and spirit:

'Incarnate man wants a favour done; he wants a better job, to marry a certain girl, to win the state lottery, to stop somebody from running after his daughter . . . Discarnate spirits, for their part, want to enjoy the pleasures of the flesh once more; a good square meal, a drink of the best *cachaça* rum, a fine cigar, and perhaps even sexual relations with an incarnate being.

'The spirit has the upper hand in all this. He calls the shots. He wants his meal left in a certain place at a certain time, and the rum and the cigar had better be of good quality. Incarnate man is ready to oblige, and it is remarkable how many members of Brazil's poorest classes, who are about as poor as anyone can be, will somehow manage to lay out a magnificent banquet for a spirit who has agreed to work some magic for them . . .

'Who are these spirits? Orthodox Kardecists and *Umbandistas* see them as inferior discarnates living in a low astral plane, who are close to the physical world, not having evolved since physical death . . . In *Umbanda* they are known as *exús*, spirits who seem to have no morals at all, and are equally prepared to work for or against people. Like Mafia gunmen, they do what the boss says without asking questions.'

He adds the interesting comment:

'The *exú* reminds us of the traditional spirits of the four elements: the gnomes of earth, the mermaids of water, the sylphs of air, and the salamanders of fire. These creatures are traditionally thought of as part human and part 'elemental', integral forces of nature that can act upon human beings subject to certain conditions. There is an enormous number of *exús*, each with his own speciality. To catch one and persuade him to work for you, it is necessary to bribe him outright with food, drink and general flattery. An *exú* is a vain and temperamental entity, and despite his total lack of morals he is very fussy about observing the rituals properly.'

All this sounds so much like the poltergeist that it is tempting to feel that we have finally pinned down his true nature and character.

Studying the background of the 'Nora' case—already described—Playfair found strong evidence that the poltergeist had been unleashed on the family by black magic. In 1968 an 'offering' of bottles, candles and cigars had appeared in their garden, indicating that someone was working a *trabalho* against the family. Playfair lists the suspects. A former boyfriend of Iracy, the daughter, had committed suicide; then there was an elderly aunt who had died abandoned by the rest of the family, and may have borne a grudge. Then Iracy had had a love affair with a man who was (unknown to her) already married; the man's wife could have organised the *trabalho*. Or it could possibly have been some former disgruntled lover of Nora, the girl who married the son of the family; photographs of Nora's husband were frequently disfigured, and they found many notes claiming that she was having an affair with another man.

Playfair mentions that, at the time he was investigating the 'Nora' case, Andrade was studying one in the town of Osasco where there was definite evidence that a poltergeist was caused by black magic. Two neighbouring families were having a lengthy dispute about boundaries, and one of the families ordered a curse against the other. The result was that the other family was haunted by a poltergeist that caused stones to fall on the roof, loud rapping noises, and spontaneous fires. One original feature of this case was that when the family went to ladle a meal out of a saucepan—which had been covered with a lid—they found that the food had been spoiled by a large cigar.

Candomblé—one of the bigger Afro-Brazilian cults—seems to have originated among freed negro slaves in the 1830s, and it has the same origin as voodoo, which began in Haiti when the first slaves arrived early in the 17th century. This, in turn, originated in Africa as ju-ju. Europeans are naturally inclined to dismiss this as the outcome of ignorance and stupidity; but few who have had direct experience of it maintain that sceptical attitude.

On the evening of September 9, 1977, Guy Playfair attended a lecture on poltergeists at the Society for Psychical Research, and found himself sitting next to a man named Maurice Grosse. After the lecture, Grosse announced that he was in the middle of a case, and would be glad of some help. No one volunteered. A few days later, Playfair heard a broadcast on BBC Radio 4 in which

Maurice Grosse described some of the amazing things that were happening in the house of the Harper family down at Enfield. Reluctantly—because he had just finished a book and was looking forward to a holiday—Playfair decided to offer some help.

The Enfield poltergeist had put in its first appearance on the evening of August 30, 1977. There were four children in the house: Rose, 13, Janet, 11, Pete, 10 and Jimmy, 7; their mother was separated from her husband. Pete and Janet shared a bedroom. That evening, just after Pete and Janet had gone to bed, their beds began to shake in an odd way. They called their mother, but the shaking had stopped. She assumed they were 'larking about' and told them to get to sleep. The next evening, the children heard a shuffling noise, like a chair moving. Mrs Harper came in and asked them to be quiet. The room all seemed to be perfectly normal. But when she switched off the light, she also heard the shuffling noise. It sounded like someone shuffling across the room in slippers. Then there were four loud, clear knocks. And when Mrs Harper put the light on again, she saw the heavy chest of drawers moving on its own. It slid a distance of about eighteen inches across the floor. She pushed it back. It slid back again. She tried to push it back, but it wouldn't budge—it was as if someone was standing on the other side, preventing it from moving. Mrs Harper began to shake with fear. 'All right, downstairs everybody . . .'

She went next door and asked the help of their neighbours. Vic Nottingham and his son went back to the Harpers' house, and searched it from top to bottom. Then the knocking started. Vic Nottingham rushed outside, to see if it was some practical joker on the other side of the wall. There was no one there.

They sent for the police. When the lights were switched off, the knocking started. Then, in the light from the kitchen, everyone saw a chair that was wobbling into motion. It slid towards the kitchen for three or four feet.

The police could do nothing about ghosts, so they left. And the Harper family slept in the living-room.

The next day, all was quiet until evening. Then the poltergeist began throwing things. Marbles and Lego bricks came zinging through the air as if shot from a catapult. When someone picked up one of the marbles, it was found to be burning hot.

Wondering what to do, Mrs Harper allowed her neighbour to phone the *Daily Mirror*. A reporter and photographer arrived, but saw nothing. They decided to go in the early hours of the morning. As soon as they were outside, the Lego bombardment began again. Mrs Harper rushed out and told them. As the photographer came in, his camera raised, a Lego brick flew across the room and hit him over the right eye. It caused quite a bruise—one of the few examples of a poltergeist actually hurting someone. Yet the photograph showed no Lego brick flying towards him—it must have been just beyond the range of the camera. It was later to occur to Guy Playfair that the poltergeist seemed to go to great trouble not to be *seen* doing things.

The *Daily Mirror* contacted the Society for Psychical Research, and the SPR contacted Maurice Grosse, a recent member who was looking for a case to investigate. A few days later, Guy Playfair made his way down to the house in Enfield. It was the beginning of a two-year involvement.

Playfair was inclined to suspect Janet, an extremely lively little girl. He asked Mrs Harper to keep a special watch on her, adding: 'Even if Janet is playing tricks, it may not be her fault.' For he had come across a curious discovery made by earlier researchers like Nandor Fodor and William Roll: that the 'focus' of a poltergeist case may throw things—in the ordinary way—without being aware of it. The implication seems to be that a poltergeist can get *inside* someone and 'make them do things'.

While Playfair and a *Mirror* photographer waited in the dark in Janet's bedroom, a marble landed with a bang on the floor. The odd thing was it did not roll, as a marble normally would. It stayed put. Playfair tried hard to duplicate this, but found it impossible; unless dropped from very close to the floor, a marble will roll, particularly on smooth linoleum.

When the photographer tried taking a test picture, all three flash-guns on all three cameras failed to work. When he examined the guns, he found that they had all been drained of power—although he had charged them a few minutes before trying to take the photograph.

Playfair tried tying the leg of Janet's bedside chair to the leg of her bed. He used wire. Within minutes, the chair had fallen over; the wire had been snapped. He bound it with several twists of wire. Not long after, the chair fell over again—the wire had snapped once more. A big armchair tipped over, then the bed shot across the room. A book flew off the shelf, hit the door, proceeded on at right angles, and landed upright on the floor; it was called *Fun and Games for Children*. As they looked at one of the pillows on a bed, an indentation appeared on it, as if an invisible head was resting there. The head seemed to be a small one, which led Mrs Harper to voice her suspicion that this was the ghost of a 4-year-old girl who had been suffocated by her father in a nearby house; some of the furniture from the house has found its way into the Harper home, and Mrs Harper had already thrown it out, suspecting it might be the cause of the trouble. Clearly, she was mistaken.

There came a point when Guy Playfair began to feel that the 'entity' wanted to communicate—it kept up its knocking on one occasion for two hours and a half. A medium named Annie Shaw came to the house with her husband George. Annie went into a trance, then suddenly screamed, 'Go away', and began to cackle. When her husband spoke to her, she spat at him. She moaned: 'Gozer, Gozer, help me. Elvie, come here.' George spoke firmly to the 'entity' that had taken over her body, advising it to go away and leave the Harper family alone. When Annie returned to normal, she stated that the haunting centred around Janet, and that there were several entities behind it, including an old woman. George added: 'This Gozer is a nasty piece of work, a sort of Black Magic chap. The other one, Elvie, is an elemental.' Annie explained that the auric field around Janet and her mother was 'leaking', and that when this happens, poltergeists can use the energy for their manifestations. The Shaws 'cleaned' their auras by a well-known technique—moving their hands from head to foot around the contours of the body, about six inches away. The trouble, said the Shaws, was due to the negative atmosphere in the house—and Mrs Harper admitted that she *did* feel bitter about her ex-husband, and had been keeping the feeling bottled up for years. One way of preventing a poltergeist from manifesting itself, said Annie Shaw, was to learn to control one's energies, so they stop 'leaking'.

For a few weeks after this healing session, the manifestations almost ceased. Then, in late October, they started up again—furniture flung around, beds shaking, blankets ripped off beds—Playfair and Grosse recorded about four hundred incidents in a brief space. Pools of water also began to appear on the kitchen floor—pools with very distinct outlines, as if made by pouring water from a jug immediately on to the lino. One puddle was shaped like a human figure.

The entity began doing things that could have caused serious damage. One evening, an iron grille from the bottom of a fireplace sailed across the room and landed on Jimmy's pillow—a little closer, and it could have killed him. The next evening, the heavy gas fire was ripped out of the wall—it had been cemented into the brickwork. (Poltergeists can display frightening strength; in *The Flying Cow* Playfair records a poltergeist that lifted a Jeep forty yards through the air.)

On the advice of the veteran researcher E.J. Dingwall, Playfair tried communicating with the 'entity'. When it rapped, he rapped back. When he asked it to use the usual code—one rap for yes, two for no—there followed a volley of loud raps. Playfair asked: 'Don't you realise *you are dead?*' which seemed to infuriate it. Crashes came from a bedroom, and when they rushed up, the room was in chaos, with objects scattered all over. Evidently 'Gozer' was not anxious to make polite conversation.

Maurice Grosse was more successful a few weeks later. 'Did you die in this house?' The rap-code indicated 'Yes'. 'Will you go away?' A loud thud said 'No'. The entity indicated that it had lived in the house for a long time—more than thirty years. It had left fifty-three years ago. When the raps seemed to become nonsensical, Grosse asked: 'Are you having a game with me?' A cardboard box containing cushions flew across the room and struck Grosse on the forehead. Guy Playfair, who was outside the door with his tape recorder (the poltergeist had taken a dislike to him), recorded all this on tape; the box made an odd swishing noise. Yet no one actually saw the box flying across the room. It was as if it had vanished from its old position, and rematerialised as it struck Maurice Grosse on the head.

Like most poltergeists, this one was getting into its stride as it became more skilled. The children began to see shadowy figures, and 7-year-old Jimmy was terrified when he looked towards the wall, and saw a disembodied face—an old man's face with big white teeth—staring at him. In front of Grosse and several other witnesses, it threw Janet off her chair, across the room, a distance of eight feet. As Rose, the eldest girl, went upstairs, the ghost literally pulled her leg—the investigators found her standing on one leg, the other stretched out behind her, unable to move. She was only able to walk when Grosse twisted her sideways.

They decided to ask the ghost to write out a message, and left a pencil and paper. A few minutes later, they found that someone had written: 'I *will stay in this house. Do not show this to anyone else or I will retaliate.*' Another message read: '*Can I have a tea bag.*' Mrs Harper placed one on the table and, a few moments later, a second tea bag appeared beside it.

When Mrs Harper's husband came to call to pay his maintenance money, he expressed disbelief in all this, and Mrs Harper showed him the message—forgetting that it had ordered her not to. She said out loud: 'I'm sorry, I forgot.' Another piece of paper appeared on the table: '*A misunderstanding. Don't do it again.*'

A few days after this, the Society for Psychical Research sent a team of investigators to look at the place. They had evidently decided that the poltergeist activity was all due to the girls. Balloons full of water were placed under the beds for some reason; and, when they burst, water dripped through the ceiling. When the team had left, Grosse and Playfair—who had been present—had some irritable things to say about the SPR's obsession with fraud.

By now it was very clear that Janet was the poltergeist's main target. She was often thrown out of bed seven or eight times before she succeeded in getting to sleep. When she fell asleep, she twitched and moaned; Playfair began to feel increasingly that she was 'possessed'. He recalled the case of Maria Ferreira, the South American girl who had been driven to suicide by a poltergeist, and felt some misgiving. On one occasion, with a photographer in the bedroom, Janet was hurled out of bed—the event was photographed—and then, as the photographer and Maurice Grosse tried to hold her, she went into convulsions, screamed hysterically, and bit Grosse. When finally put back into bed, she fell asleep. Later, there was a crash, and they found her lying on top of the radio set, still fast asleep.

The following night, Janet had more convulsions, and wandered around, talking aloud, 'Where's Gober. He'll kill you.'

Two of Playfair's friends from Brazil, who happened to be in London, called at the Enfield house, and succeeded in bringing Janet out of one of her trance-like states. Their view was that Janet was a powerful medium and ought to be trained to use her powers. One of the two Brazilian mediums wrote on a sheet of paper: 'I see this child, Janet, in the Middle Ages, a cruel and wanton woman who caused suffering to families of yeomen—some of these seem to have now to get even with the family.' Soon after this, Janet began producing drawings, in a state of semi-trance; one of them showed a woman with blood pouring out of her throat, with the name 'Watson' written underneath. Other drawings continued this theme of blood, knives and death. When Playfair asked Mrs Harper if she knew of a Watson, she replied that it was the name of the previous tenants of the house. Mrs Watson had died of a tumour of the throat.

Playfair asked Janet if she could bend a spoon like Uri Geller. He glanced away for a moment, as Mrs Harper spoke to him; when he looked back, the spoon was bent in the middle—it was lying in the centre of the table. Janet said she had experienced a sudden feeling of headache as the spoon bent.

In December 1977, the poltergeist began making noises—whistling and barking sounds. Maurice Grosse decided to try asking it to speak. 'Call out my name, Maurice Grosse.' He went out of the room, and a strange voice said: '*Maurice . . . O . . .*' Grosse asked it to say its own name. '*Joe Watson.*' When Guy Playfair asked: 'Do you know you are dead?' the voice said angrily: '*Shut up!*' And to further requests that it go away, it replied: '*Fuck off.*' Joe seemed to be incapable of polite conversation. When another researcher, Anita Gregory, asked it questions, she was told to bugger off.

The investigators wondered whether Janet could be simulating this voice, although it seemed unlikely; it was a masculine growl, and had an odd quality, as if electronically produced. (I have one of Guy Playfair's tape recordings of the voice, and it reminds me strongly of a record I have of an electronic brain singing 'Daisy, Daisy'.) The voice would not speak if the investigators were in the room. But their attempts were rewarded with long sentences.

The voice now identified itself as Bill, and said it had a dog called Gober the Ghost. Asked why it kept shaking Janet's bed it replied: '*I was sleeping here.*' 'Then why do you keep on shaking it?' '*Get Janet out.*' Rose asked: 'Why do you use bad language?' '*Fuck off you,*' replied Bill. And when Janet asked why it played games with them it replied: '*I like annoying you.*' 'Where do you come from?' '*From the graveyard.*' It even named the graveyard—Durant's Park, which is in the area.

At Guy Playfair's suggestion, Rose asked why it didn't go away. '*I don't believe in that.*' 'Why? What's so different about being up there?' asked Rose, and received the wistful reply: '*I'm not a heaven man.*' It went on to say in a jerky manner: '*I am Bill Haylock and I come from Durant's Park and I am 72 years old and I have come here to see my family but they are not here now.*'

On the tape, the words come out one by one, as if the speaker is so breathless that he can only get out one at a time. (The voice is so obviously that of an old man that the notion of Janet producing it by ventriloquism is absurd.) Rose's next question is interrupted by a furious outburst: '*You fucking old bitch, shut up. I want some jazz music. Now go and get me some, else I'll go barmy.*'

Maurice Grosse's son Richard paid a visit to the house and succeeded in holding a lengthy conversation with the voice. When he asked it what it had done with thirty pence that had vanished it said it had hidden the money in the radio—which is where it was found. Asked how he had died, 'Bill' replied that he went blind and had a haemorrhage—he fell asleep and died in a chair downstairs.

Richard Grosse found that if he looked at Janet's face while the voice was speaking, it would stop. If he *thought* of looking round, the voice would also stop, as if reading his mind.

Another researcher named David Robertson had no difficulty getting the voice to talk, although the main thing it wanted to discuss was girls' periods. Then the ghost was asked to levitate Janet, and then draw a line round the light on the ceiling. Robertson withdrew outside, and heard Janet being bounced up and down on the bed. Suddenly there was a gasp and silence. He tried to open the door and found that it was jammed tight. When it opened again, Janet was on the bed and there was a red line around the light. Janet claimed that she had floated through the wall, into the bedroom of the next house—belonging to Peggy Nottingham (who was with David Robertson at the time). She described it as 'all white'—a fairly accurate description of the light wallpaper. Peggy asked her to try doing it again, and went next door to see what happened. Janet was not there. But on the floor, there was the book *Fun and Games for Children*, which had been on the mantelpiece in Janet's bedroom a few minutes earlier.

Robertson handed a red plastic cushion to Janet and said: 'See what you can do with that.' '*All right, David boy,*' said the invisible entity—which seemed to like Robertson—'*I'll make it disappear.*' Robertson went out of the room, and there was a cry from Janet. When he went back, the cushion had vanished; the window was tightly shut. But a neighbour who was passing the house at that moment suddenly saw a red cushion appear on the roof. Another neighbour later testified that she had also seen the cushion as she walked past. And, looking at Janet's bedroom window, she had seen books and cushions striking the window, and Janet rising into the air—in a horizontal position—and descending again, as if being bounced on a trampoline. 'She was definitely lying horizontal, coming up and down.' Guy Playfair tried bouncing on Janet's bed, and found that no matter how hard he bounced, it was impossible to get up into the air.

Playfair was struck by Janet's comment that when she had floated through the wall into Peggy's bedroom, it was 'all white' and there were no colours. He arrived at the conclusion that what had happened was that Janet had had an 'out of the body' experience—other astral travellers have observed the lack of colour during 'OOBs'. But this fails to explain how the book also passed through the wall.

Was there, Playfair asked himself at this point, any more the poltergeist could do to demonstrate its versatility? In fact, it went on to produce a whole variety of new phenomena. It became rather more violent with Janet, making an attempt to suffocate her with the curtains, and making a knife follow her around in the air. (The voice claimed that this was the doing of another entity called Tommy.) It produced a biscuit out of nowhere and stuck it into Janet's mouth. It put butter and cheese on a piece of bread. (When Guy Playfair tried to touch it the voice rasped, 'Leave it alone.') It smeared ordure around the place. It began causing fires in closed drawers—fires which, fortunately, extinguished themselves. It produced some appalling stinks, like rotten cabbages. After a visit from the psychic Matthew Manning, it began scrawling obscene messages on the kitchen walls. When the two pet goldfish died, the 'voice' claimed it had electrocuted them by accident (which, if true, seems to confirm that poltergeists use some form of electrical energy).

A medium called Gerry Sherrick told the Harpers that they had all been together in a previous existence, and that the girls had dabbled in witchcraft. He also told them he felt that a nasty old woman was connected with the 'haunting', and that she had lived near Spitalfields market. Had there been any smells like rotten vegetables? After this, he went into a trance, and an old woman's voice announced: 'I come here when I like . . . I'm not bleedin' dead, and I'm not going to go away.' Sherrick performed 'psychic healing' on the family—to heal the 'leaks' that were causing the trouble. After his visit, the Enfield house became quiet for several weeks, as it had after the two previous visits by mediums.

The case was beginning to turn into something more like a normal haunting. Mrs Harper saw an apparition of a pair of legs in blue trousers going upstairs, and also saw a child. The children continued to see old men. A neighbour who was looking after the house when the Harpers went to the seaside saw a man in his shirtsleeves sitting at the table. Another neighbour knocked on the front door, and through the window saw Maurice Grosse in the hall, then watched him go upstairs. When finally admitted, she discovered that Maurice Grosse had been in the upper part of the house for the past half hour or so. The poltergeist was 'imitating' him.

In mid-1978, Janet went into the Maudsley Hospital for observation and testing. Playfair expected the disturbances in Enfield to cease while she was away; in fact, they continued, although on a smaller scale. And Janet claimed that a number of small poltergeist incidents happened to her while in hospital. But Janet's spell in the Maudsley—which made her healthier and stronger—was the beginning of the end of the Enfield case.

The haunting seems to have been brought to an end by a Dutch clairvoyant named Dono Gmelig-Meyling, who was brought to the house by a Dutch journalist who wanted to study the case. The day before their first visit had been eventful—overturned furniture, knocks, footsteps, sounds of breathing, and excrement smeared on the floor. Dono spent some time in the house, then returned to his hotel. There, he later told Playfair, he went on an 'astral trip', and met a 24-year-old girl who was somehow involved with the case. This was an interesting new departure. Later, Dono met Maurice Grosse, and again had a strong sense that he was somehow connected with the haunting—and not purely as an investigator. When Grosse mentioned that his own daughter had been killed in a motor-cycle accident two years before—she would have been 24 if still alive—Dono said: 'Well that's it. It's your daughter . . .' There was no suggestion that she was responsible for any of the poltergeist activity, only that she was somehow connected. In the final chapter of his account of the Enfield case, *This House is Haunted*, Playfair tries to draw together his speculations about the disturbances. His suggestion is that Maurice Grosse's daughter—whose name was also Janet—was involved indirectly. It was she who had drawn her father's attention to the case. Janet had died after a motor-cycle crash in 1976, and Grosse had been impressed by a series of odd events and coincidences. A birthday card she had sent to her brother just before the accident showed someone with her head swathed in bandages, and an inscription about falling on it. Janet had died of head injuries. Grosse found himself wondering if Janet was somehow still alive, and thought that a suitable sign would be some rain—there had been a drought for months. The next morning, the kitchen roof below Janet's bedroom window was wet, although everywhere else was dry. It had been because of Janet's death that Grosse had thought about engaging in active psychical research, and his first case had been the Enfield haunting.

Playfair speculates that it was Janet who had somehow put it into the neighbour's head to ring the *Daily Mirror*, and who put it into the journalist's head to ring the SPR. So her father became involved in investigating a case that centred around another Janet. (Kardec claims that spirits often influence our thoughts.)

As to how the poltergeist haunting came about in the first place, Playfair's speculation is as follows:

'When Mr and Mrs Harper were divorced, an atmosphere of tension built up among the children and their mother, just at the time when the two girls were approaching physical maturity. They were a very energetic pair to start with, both of them school sports champions, but even they could not use up the tremendous energy they were generating. So a number of entities came in and helped themselves to it.'

As to the identity of the 'entities': 'It looks as if we had half the local graveyard at one time or another.' These included Joe Watson, husband of the woman who had died of a cancer of the throat, and Bill Haylock, later identified as a former local resident. There could well have been a dozen entities altogether, and they were able to take energy from practically everyone in the house. (Mrs Harper experienced premonitory headaches before things happened, and while Janet was in hospital, the youngest boy, Jimmy, began having trances.) The Dutch clairvoyant Dono Gmelig-Meyling stated confidently that he would be able to put an end to the haunting (by some kind of intervention 'on the astral plane'), and it is a fact that his visits marked the end of the Enfield case.

And *why* did so many entities invade the Harper residence? The answer, Playfair believes, may be provided by Kardec, who states that many dead people are quite unaware that they are dead. In *The Flying Cow* he cites the interesting Ruytemberg Rocha case in support of this view. In November 1961, a spiritist group in São Paulo found themselves listening to a voice—coming through the medium—which identified itself as Ruytemberg Rocha, a pupil in the second year of the Officers' School of the São Paulo State Police. The voice gave details of its family and date of birth, and added that it was wounded by shrapnel in the revolution in 1932. When Dr Carvalho—in charge of the session—said that this was now 1961, the spirit was astonished, and said that that was impossible. Carvalho assured him that he was dead, and that they would do all they could to help him.

It was an excellent case for verification, since the spirit had given so many details about himself and his family. A little research revealed that it all checked out—the family, the officer school, the battle in which he had died. One minor discrepancy was that Rocha had been killed by a bullet through the head, while the spirit spoke only about a shrapnel wound in the chest. But a bullet in the brain *could* have stimulated the chest area, giving him the impression that this was where he was wounded. According to Kardec, the state of confusion happens mostly in cases of sudden death, and may last for anything from hours to years. In the Enfield case, we have seen how angry the 'entity' became when Playfair declared that it was dead, and how the quarrelsome old woman asserted 'I'm *not* bleedin' dead.'

Yet, as usual in poltergeist cases, it is practically impossible to get at the truth. The spirits themselves seldom seem to have any interest in the truth. In the present case, there are intriguing hints about a man called Gozer or Gober who practised black magic, and about the involvement of Janet and Rose in witchcraft in a previous existence. There was a former resident of the house called Joe Watson, who did die in the house much as described by Janet's bass voice and whose wife did die of throat cancer, and there was a former neighbour called Bill Haylock. All of which adds at least a semblance of logic and reason to one of the best-authenticated poltergeist cases on record.

Perhaps the last word should go to a medium—and police commissioner—called Dr Rafael Ranieri, quoted by Playfair in *The Flying Cow*:

'A medium is an open door to the invisible world. What comes through that door depends to a large extent upon the personality of the medium, and it is quite wrong to suppose that the spirit world consists entirely of angelic beings devoted to our welfare. There are plenty of evil spirits around, also others who seem to have nothing better to do than fool about and amuse themselves at our expense by such elementary . . . parlour tricks as lifting up tables and throwing things around the room. This would seem to be the level of spirit most often to be found at some of the widely publicised seances, and those who find spirit communications trivial, as many are, should blame the mediums, not the spirits.'

If Janet and other members of the Harper family *are* unconscious mediums, perhaps it is hardly surprising that the entities who make use of their energies should belong to a fairly low level of the spirit hierarchy.

10.
The Power of the Witch

THE MOST UNEXPECTED bestseller of 1926 was a book called *The History of Witchcraft and Demonology* by the Rev. Montague Summers. Issued by Routledge and Kegan Paul as part of their *History of Civilisation*, it was an obviously serious work, full of Latin quotations, lengthy footnotes, and a comprehensive bibliography. What startled the reviewers was that the author clearly believed every word he wrote about the 'enormous wickedness' of witches, warlocks and devil worshippers. H. G. Wells was so incensed by the book that he launched a vituperative attack on it in the *Sunday Express*. *The Times*, equally disapproving, contented itself with the comment that 'the more Mr Summers gives proof of general ability, of scholarship and of wide reading, the more the suspicion deepens that a mystification is in progress and that he is amusing himself at our expense'.

Was it a legpull? Or a cynical attempt to achieve a *succès de scandale*? Apparently neither. The Reverend Montague Summers was a respectable Catholic scholar, editor of several Restoration dramatists, and founder of a theatrical society called the Phoenix, which revived Restoration plays on the London stage. It is true that his name was not to be found in the clergy lists of either the

Roman Catholic Church or the Church of England; but this was not—as rumour had it—because he was an unfrocked priest; in fact he had been ordained a Deacon of the Church of England in 1908, a year before he became a Roman Catholic convert. It is also true that he allowed people to suppose that he was a Roman Catholic priest, and used to say Mass in his own private oratory, in spite of the fact that he had been rejected as a Candidate for the priesthood by his superiors. The gusto with which he recounts sexual details of the satanic rites—even though most of them are decently clothed in Latin—may suggest why his superiors had found him unsuitable. In spite of these foibles, Summers was a genuine scholar. And the views he expressed were the views held by the Roman Catholic Church in his own day—as they still are.

What is the truth about witchcraft?

Between 1275 and 1692, thousands of men and women were tortured and burnt to death in Europe, accused of worshipping the Devil, and having intercourse with spirits and demons.

The first known victim was a 60-year-old woman called Angéle de la Barthe, who was accused of having had sexual intercourse with a demon, and given birth to a monster. This creature had to be fed on the flesh of dead babies, so—according to the accusation—Angéle either murdered children, or dug up their corpses from graveyards. Tried before the Inquisitor Hugues de Baniols at Toulouse, she was sentenced to be burned to death.

It is natural for us to feel outrage at such appalling inhumanity, and to conclude that the evidence against Angéle amounted to the grossest superstition. Yet the last chapter suggests another possibility. If the *umbanda* magicians of Brazil are capable of 'using' spirits to cause mischief—even to wreck houses—how can we be certain that at least a few of the witches of the Middle Ages were not guilty as charged?

Before we attempt to answer that question, let us look briefly at the history of the 'witchcraft craze'.

The first thing we have to understand is that witches are as old as history, and that they were not sinister old ladies who dabbled in black magic, but priestesses whose business was to aid the hunters of the tribe in their search for game, and later, to ensure a good harvest. (We call male witches *shamans*.) They were servants of the moon goddess, known in Egypt as Isis, in Greece as

Selene, and in Rome as Diana. Early witches were beautiful enchantresses, like Homer's Circe, who turned men into swine, or Theocritus's Samaetha, who performs a magical ceremony to bring back her faithless lover. It was only in later years that the image of the witch changed to the horrible old crone who digs up corpses or raises the spirits of the dead—like the Witch of Endor in the Bible. On the whole, witches were regarded as useful—if rather frightening—members of society.

Then why does the Bible say: 'Thou shalt not suffer a witch to live'? Because as the old Nature religion disappeared, to be replaced by religions like Judaism and Christianity, the witch was regarded with increasing dislike and suspicion. She was a remnant of mankind's dark past, and everyone wanted to forget her.

It was another Christian invention, the Devil, that made the witch an object of superstitious terror. The Satan of the Old Testament—like the Book of Job—was *a* satan, the Hebrew word meaning an adversary or obstructor—in other words, a kind of demon, but not *the* Prince of Darkness. The Christian Devil can be traced back to St Paul, who invented the idea that Jesus had died to save man from the sin of Adam (a claim Jesus himself never made), and that Adam fell because Eve was tempted by the Devil in the form of a serpent. (There is no suggestion in the Old Testament that the serpent was anything but an ordinary snake.)

In the hands of the early Church Fathers, Christianity became a grim religion, obsessed by sin and evil—and, of course, by the Devil. When the Emperor Constantine made Christianity the official religion of the Roman Empire in 313 AD, Christians immediately began to torture and burn one another—the aim being to stamp out 'heresy'. But as the Church became increasingly successful, it also became—inevitably—increasingly corrupt. Reformers who felt the Church was growing too fat and self-indulgent now became the Enemy, servants of the Devil. The Cathars, for example, (the name means 'pure ones') wanted to respiritualise Christianity. The Church of Rome declared a crusade against them in 1208, and thousands of Cathars were slaughtered in France, particularly in the area of Toulouse (where 20,000 were burned or put to the sword). The few survivors withdrew to remote mountain villages, where they continued to practise their religion. They were known under various names (Albigenses, Waldenses, Bogomils), but as far as the Church was concerned, they were all Devil-worshippers. They became known as 'witches'. And Angéle de la Barthe, whom we have met, was accused of being one of them. She was tried—and burned—for heresy, not for witchcraft.

A century after the slaughter of the Cathars, witchcraft—or rather, black magic—was again used as an excuse to commit murder on a massive scale. The victims this time were an order of knights called the Knight Templars. They had been founded in the Holy Land after the First Crusade—in 1118—to protect Christian pilgrims trying to get to Jerusalem, and they became immensely rich. By 1303 they had been driven out of the Holy Land, and took refuge in Cyprus, but large numbers lived in France. King Philip IV of France—known as the Fair—often borrowed money from them, and dreamed of laying his hands on their wealth. The excuse he chose was to accuse them of Devil-worship and homosexuality. At daybreak on October 13, 1307, the authorities swooped on Templars all over France and arrested them. At their trial, the judges were told that in order to become a Templar, a man had to become a sodomite, and kiss the mouth, navel and anus of his sponsor; they also had to swear allegiance to the demon Baphomet. Under horrible tortures, many confessed. In 1310, 54 were burned to death—all refusing to confess. Jacques de Molay, the Grand Master of the order, was one who confessed, and was sentenced to life imprisonment; but when exposed in public to repeat his confession to the populace, he declared that he had been made to confess under torture, and that the order was innocent. He was burned alive on a slow fire. His last words were to summon the king and pope to meet him before God's throne within a year; in fact, both died within that time.

The persecution of witches started off slowly. It was more than a century after the death of Angéle de la Barthe that a woman was first tried as a witch—that is, for black magic rather than heresy. Her name was Jehanne de Brigue, and the interesting thing about the case is that she probably *was* a witch. In 1390, she was accused in Paris by a man called Jehane de Ruilly, who had become convinced that he had been 'hexed' (or bewitched) by his ex-mistress Gilete, who had borne him two children. Her spells had brought him close to death, but Jehanne de Brigue had saved him by making a waxen figure of Gilete and suckling two toads, (i.e. placing their open mouths over her nipples.) It is not clear why Ruilly decided to accuse her of witchcraft when she had saved his life. Jehanne at first denied being a witch, but, after three months in prison, admitted that she had learned witchcraft from her aunt, and that she performed her sorceries with the aid of a demon named Haussibut.

She was sentenced to death, but given a temporary reprieve because she was pregnant. She decided to appeal to the Parlement of Paris, but this proved to be a mistake, for the Parlement suggested she should be put to the torture. Hereupon, Jehanne confessed that the whole affair had been inspired by Ruilly's wife Macette, to get revenge on him for beating her; Jehanne had concocted a 'philtre' to poison him, and also made a waxen image.

Macette was arrested and tortured until she confessed; then both women were burned to death.

Our natural inclination is to believe that they were victims of mediaeval superstition. And indeed, there is no real evidence against Macette. But Jeanne had already been jailed in Meaux as a witch before her arrest in Paris. There seems little doubt that she *believed* she was a witch, and *believed* that she performed her magic with the aid of a demon.

The first 'epidemic' of witchcraft took place seventy years later in Arras, in northern France, and soon came to an end because common-sense prevailed—a weak-minded woman named Deniselle Grenoieres was burned alive, together with four accomplices she had named under torture; but the Archbishop of Rheims declared that the whole thing was a delusion, and the Parlement of Paris ordered the release of more suspects in 1460. But this tendency to regard witchcraft as a delusion worried Pope Innocent, and in 1484 he issued a papal bull denouncing witchcraft.

But the witchcraft persecutions that led to so much misery during the next two centuries were actually caused by an invention that would later cause the Church endless trouble: printing (invented by Gutenberg around 1440). For in 1486 there appeared a work that was directly inspired by the witch-obsessed pope, the *Malleus Maleficarum*, or Hammer of Witches, by Jacob Sprenger and Heinrich Kramer. Its description of the sexual antics of witches undoubtedly explain its wide popularity—it described how witches have intercourse with demons (or incubi), and how male witches enjoy female demons, or succubi, but it was the invention of printing that turned it into a bestseller in many languages. As far as the Church was concerned, printing was a dubious blessing, since it enabled people to read the Bible for themselves—and so undermined the authority of the priests—and enabled Martin Luther's denunciations of Rome (posted on the church door in Wittenberg in 1517) to be read all over Europe . . .

Even so, the persecutions got off to a slow start. In Toulouse (the old centre of the Cathar heresy) 40 witches were burned in 1557. Six years later, England passed a witchcraft bill under Queen Elizabeth. And in 1566, and again in 1582 and 1587, there were witchcraft trials at Chelmsford, in Essex, the first two of which resulted in two hangings, and the third in four.

But by that time in Germany, the great witchcraft craze was well under way. In Treves, five women were burned as witches in 1572, but this was only a prelude to the trials that began in 1582. By then, the harvest had been poor for several years, and witches were blamed. (Such troubles often seem to cause witch persecutions: a hundred years later, Massachusetts was having all kinds of political problems when the Salem 'witch scare' helped to release the sense of oppression and helplessness.) Between 1587 and 1594, 306 persons were accused of being witches, and they involved another 6,000 people in their confessions as accomplices. In his *History of Treves* Johan Linden, canon of the cathedral, notes: 'Scarcely any of those who were accused escaped punishment'. Dietrich Flade, Vice-Governor of Treves and Rector of the university, objected that many of the trials were illegal, and was himself accused as a witch and burned.

Franz Buirmann was a German equivalent of the English 'witch-finder' Matthew Hopkins; but there were many like him, and his career has survived only because Hermann Löher, a humanitarian court official who was forced to flee to Holland, wrote about his personal knowledge of Buirmann in a book published many years later. Löher lived at Rheinbach, near Bonn, a quiet village that had little crime. Buirmann, described as a 'shrewd man of low birth', had been appointed itinerant judge and witch-hunter by the Archbishop of Cologne; he was able to claim the property of those he condemned as witches, and, as a consequence, became affluent. In 1631 and 1636 he paid two visits to Rheinbach and two nearby villages, and burned 150 people out of 300 households. In further persecutions at Siegburg later the same year, Buirmann even had the executioner burned as a witch.

The German witch persecutions occurred mainly in towns that remained Catholic (like Treves). Other such areas were Strasbourg, Breslau, Fulda, Würzburg and Bamberg. Würzburg and Bamberg were ruled by cousins, one of whom burned 900 people, the other 600. In Bamberg, the witch burning began around 1609, under Bishop von Aschhausen, who in thirteen years burned 300 witches. In another series of trials between 1626 and 1630, 400 people were burned. When the Vice-Chancellor tried stopping the trials, he was accused as a witch and executed with his wife and daughter. (The Prince-Archbishop ignored an order from the Emperor ordering their release.) But the Bamberg trials stopped as abruptly as they had started, in 1630, partly because of the invasion of Leipzig by the Swedish King Gustavus, which gave the instigators of the trials other things to think about, partly because of the continued opposition of the Emperor.

In Würzburg in 1629, the Chancellor described in a letter how he had seen many children executed for intercourse with the devil—their ages ranging from three to fifteen. He adds that it is 'beyond doubt that in a place called the Fraw Rengberg the Devil in person with 8,000 of his followers held an assembly and celebrated a black mass'. In 1629 there were 29 executions totalling 157 persons, many of them children. The Prince-Bishop even had his sole heir, a youth, beheaded as a witch. After this execution, the Prince-Bishop seems to have experienced a change of heart, and instituted commemorative services for the victims. Here, as in Bamberg, the Inquisitors and witch-finders were Jesuits. Prince-Bishop Philip Adolf, the man responsible for all these deaths, is described by one historian as 'otherwise noble and pious'.

Yet there were waves of revulsion and resistance to all the torture and murder. In 1663, a magistrate and 'witch-finder' named Geiss, who had been torturing and burning the citizens of Lindheim for two years, turned his attention to a wealthy miller named Johann Schüler. (Here, as in so many other cases, the basic motive was undoubtedly financial.) Schüler's wife had borne a stillborn child the previous year, and Geiss forced the midwife to 'confess' that they had murdered the child and used the body for witchcraft. The child's body was exhumed and found to be intact (the midwife alleged it had been cut up), and the midwife and six people she had implicated were burned. Not long after, Geiss persuaded another suspected witch—through torture—to implicate Frau Schüler, who was arrested: an old scar was declared to be a 'devil mark'. Schüler hastened to Würzburg to try to persuade the Dean of the Cathedral to help, but in his absence, Frau Schüler was tortured into confession. On his return, Schüler was thrown into the 'witch's tower' and then tortured into confessing. However, as soon as the torture stopped, he recanted. He was tortured again; again he confessed and recanted. Geiss was preparing to torture him a third time when angry townspeople rioted, and Schüler and other suspected witches managed to escape. They succeeded in getting to Speyer, the seat of the Supreme Court, where the sight of their tortured and scarred bodies—particularly the women—aroused indignation. But in Schüler's absence, and in spite of popular anger, Geiss burnt Frau Schüler alive. The townspeople rose up in force, and Geiss and his men had to flee. The Dean of Würzburg suggested to Baron Oynhausen—responsible for Geiss's appointment—that he ought to assuage the popular fury by censuring Geiss, and Oynhausen dismissed him, to Geiss's indignation—he insisted that he had only been doing his duty.

The Protestant states executed less witches, and ceased the witchcraft persecutions earlier than Catholic states; in Prussia, King Frederick William put a stop to witch trials in 1714. The last execution for witchcraft in Germany took place in 1775.

Why were the witch trials so widespread in Germany—more than in any other country? Rossell Hope Robbins, the highly sceptical author of *An Encyclopedia of Witchcraft and Demonology*, comments: 'Germany was the land of torture . . .' and cites a case in Tettwang, near Constance, in 1608, when a father died in prison from torture, his wife was hoisted in the strappado 11 times (a device for dislocating the shoulders), and their 29-year-old daughter was also hoisted 11 times with a 50 pound weight attached to her legs. The torturer allowed her to recover for ten weeks before subjecting her to more torture—not out of mercy, but because he was afraid she would die under it.

The case of Buirmann and Geiss makes it obvious that many of the 'witch-finders' were sexual sadists, for whom the persecutions were an opportunity to give free rein to their impulses. (Criminologists have noted that Germany has a higher percentage of mass murders and sadistic murders than any other country—although in the past few decades America is beginning to catch up.) The rise of Protestantism in Germany also seems to explain a great deal (although some cities that persecuted witches—like Leipzig—were Protestant) as the Catholic Church struggled to regain its authority through a reign of terror.

Again, our horror at the appalling cruelty tends to blind us to the important question of whether any of the thousands of witches who were burned were genuine practitioners of magic—in the sense of the *umbanda* magicians described in the last chapter. But a case that occurred in North Berwick, in Scotland, in the 1590s raises that question all over again.

What happened was this. A young maidservant named Gilly Duncan was able to cure various ailments by some form of faith healing. In 1590 her master David Seaton, deputy bailiff of Tranent, near Edinburgh, tortured her with a rope around her neck to make her 'confess' to intercourse with the devil, which eventually she did. She was handed over to the authorities, and soon confessed that her accomplices—about 70 in number—included many highly respectable citizens of Edinburgh, amongst them one Agnes Sampson, an elderly gentlewoman of good education. Under prolonged torture, Agnes Sampson finally confessed—although not until her inquisitors found on her a 'devil's mark' in the area of her vagina. John Fian, a schoolmaster from Saltpans, and two other women, Euphemia Maclean and Barbara Napier, 'reputed for as civil, honest women as any that dwelled within the city of Edinburgh', were also accused. Agnes Sampson now gave a full account of her attempts to bewitch the king—James VI of Scotland (later James I of England)—who, understandably, took an active interest in the proceedings. Fian confessed under torture, but later managed to escape; when recaptured, he recanted his confession, and the most appalling tortures failed to make him change his mind. He was strangled and burned. Euphemia Maclean was burned without being first strangled—probably because she was a Catholic—but Barbara Napier managed to get her sentence delayed on the grounds that she was pregnant, and finally escaped.

Certainly, this sounds like a case of horrifying injustice. James the First, who wrote a famous *Dæmonologie*, later decided that most witchcraft was superstition, and persecution of witches almost ceased towards the end of his reign.

Fuller examination of the case raises doubts about their innocence. John Fian had been secretary to the Earl of Bothwell, a man with a reputation for dabbling in black magic, and who had every reason for wanting to kill the king, since he himself was heir to the throne. James was himself sceptical about the confession of Agnes Sampson until—according to the chronicle *Newes from Scotland*—she took him aside and whispered in his ear certain words that had passed between him and his bride, Anne of Denmark, on their wedding night. No one but the king and his bride knew what they were. Naturally, James was convinced.

Agnes Sampson also confessed that she and the others had raised a storm to attempt to drown the King on his way back from Denmark—and indeed, the king *had* almost been drowned in a tremendous storm. She described how she had tied a toad by its back legs, collected the venom that dripped from it in an oyster-shell, and kept it until some occasion when she could get hold of some of the king's soiled linen, which would enable her to bewitch him to death, making him feel 'as if he had been lying upon sharp thorns and ends of needles . . .' The method is reminiscent of the one still used by African witch-doctors.

Fian himself seems to have declared that the devil appeared to him in his cell on the night after his original confession. Since he had already confessed, he was not under the threat of torture, which again leads to the suspicion that he may not have been as innocent as Robbins assumes.

Montague Summers is, of course, convinced that the witches were guilty as charged. He writes: 'The most celebrated occasion when witches raised a storm was that which played so important a part in the trial of Dr Fian and his coven, 1590–91, when the witches, in order to drown King James and Queen Anne on their voyage from Denmark, 'took a cat and christened it,' and after they had bound a dismembered corpse to the animal 'in the night following the said cat was convayed into the middest of the sea by all these witches, sayling in their riddles or cives . . . this donne, then did arise such a tempest in the sea, as a greater hath not bene seene'.' It all sounds preposterous enough, particularly 'sailing in sieves'; but if African witch-doctors can cause rain—or (see p. 304)—then Summers could well be basically correct. There is at least a fifty per cent possibility that Fian was involved in a real witchcraft plot to kill the king; and if witchcraft sometimes works, then we cannot rule out the possibility that Agnes Sampson and her associates really caused the storm which almost wrecked the king's ship.

And what of this statement of Fian that the Devil appeared to him? This would seem to brand the confession an invention wrung from him by fear of further torture. Yet again, we should not assume that this is the only possible explanation. As we have seen, in his book about magic and witchcraft in Brazil *The Flying Cow*, Guy Playfair advances the theory that he himself has come to accept through the study of many cases that 'black magic' involves the conjuring of 'low grade' entities or spirits. And this is, of course, consistent with the view of magic held by witch-doctors and *shamans*. If we are willing to admit, as a possibility, that magic involves non-human entities, then Fian may have believed that he saw—or heard—the Devil on the night after his confession. We may reject Summers' view that the Devil actually exists as the adversary of God—after all, most of what we call evil can be regarded as stupidity or the outcome of frustration—but there is a certain amount of evidence in psychical research for 'mischievous' entities (who, in many cases, seem to be half-witted). 'Evil' spirits may be exhibiting the same kind of stupidity and malevolence as evil human beings.

The same disturbing questions are raised by the extraordinary case of Isobel Gowdie and the Auldearne witches, which took place in Scotland in 1662.

Isobel Gowdie was an attractive, red-headed girl who married a farmer of Lochloy, near Auldearne in Morayshire. She was childless and her husband is said to have been a stupid and boorish man. In April 1662, she startled and shocked the elders of the local kirk when she announced that she had been a practising witch for the past fifteen years, had attended Sabbats, had sexual intercourse with the Devil and even killed people by witchcraft. She was tried at Auldearne, near Inverness, in the summer of 1662, together with others she had mentioned in her confession. Astonishingly enough, some of these confirmed what she said in detail.

According to Isobel—who made four confessions between April and her trial—she encountered the Devil, a man dressed in grey, when she was travelling between two farms, and she seems to have promised herself to him and agreed to meet him at the church in Auldearne. She did so, and the Devil stood in the pulpit with a black book in his hand, and made her renounce Jesus. A woman called Margaret Brodie held her while the Devil sucked blood from her shoulder, making a Devil's mark, and baptised her. She described the Devil as a big, black, hairy man, who came to her a few days later and copulated with her. He would copulate freely with all the female witches, who thoroughly enjoyed it. (Another of the accused, Janet Breadhead, described how the women sat on either side of the Devil at a meeting, and next, how the Devil copulated with all of them—which, unless he was phenomenally potent, seems to dispose of Margaret Murray's belief that he was a man dressed in a goat skin.) Sometimes the Devil changed himself to an animal—such as a deer or bull—before he copulated. It was Isobel who first used the word 'coven' of a group of witches, and declared that the number was 13. She said that each member had a spirit to wait upon her, (or him—there seem to have been male members). They had a Grand Meeting four times a year.

The confessions become wilder and stranger. She flew to Sabbats on a little horse. The witches could change themselves into any shape they wished, such as a cat, a hare, a crow. They would blast people's harvests and kill their children—Janet Breadhead says they made clay images of children, which were continually watered and baked until the child died; in this way, she says, they killed two children of the local laird, who was himself later bewitched to death. Isobel Gowdie says she killed several people using arrows given to her by the Devil. She also described a visit to fairyland, when the Downie Hill opened, and they were all generously fed by the Queen of Faery, who was clothed in white linen. Afterwards they went shooting with the Devil; Isobel shot a woman, and the others brought down a ploughman.

It is a pity that no trial records have been found, so we have no idea of whether the witches were all sentenced to be burned—most commentators feel reasonably certain that they were, and, given the verdicts in similar trials at the time, this seems highly likely.

The mystery remains. The whole thing could not have been Isobel's fantasy, or the others would not have confirmed what she said (no mention of torture is made). And so we seem to be left with only two possibilities: either that Isobel and her fellow witches were insane, or that the various 'demons' were as genuine as the 'spirits' conjured up by modern *umbanda* magicians.

By the second half of the 17th century, the witchcraft craze was coming to an end. In Germany, this was largely due to the influence of Protestantism, and its reaction against the kind of 'popish' hysteria that had fuelled the great persecutions of the previous century. In England and America, ordinary common-sense finally prevailed.

The career of Matthew Hopkins had the effect of virtually ending the witchcraft persecution in England. Even the Rev. Montague Summers admits that his insincerity 'made his name stink in men's nostrils', and described him as 'the foulest of foul parasites, an obscene bird of prey . . .'

The career of Hopkins snowballed from his first denunciation of a witch in 1644. Hopkins was a not-particularly-successful lawyer, son of a clergyman, who moved to the small village of Manningtree in Essex because he was unable to make a living in Ipswich. It was during the Civil War, East Anglia was on Cromwell's side, but tensions were considerable. In March 1644, Hopkins became convinced that there were witches who lived in Manningtree, and that they held meetings close to his house. He may possibly have been correct—country areas are full of witches. Hopkins decided that an old woman named Elizabeth Clarke was involved, and denounced her. She was arrested and stripped, to be searched for devil's marks. They discovered, apparently, something like a supernumerary teat. After being deprived of sleep for days, she confessed to suckling her familiars with it—a spaniel, a rabbit, a greyhound and a polecat. The witch fever spread through the village, and five other women were arrested. Four of these confessed readily to possessing familiars. Thirty-two women were eventually thrown into jail, where four of them died. Twenty-eight stood trial in a special court at Chelmsford. Hopkins now had four assistants to help him in routing out witches, and no doubt this taste of power convinced him that he had discovered the road to fame and success. But it seems fairly certain that he was willing to perjure himself freely from the beginning—he asserted in court that he had seen Elizabeth Clarke's familiars, and his assistants backed him up. Nineteen women were hanged, on charges ranging from entertaining evil spirits to bewitching people to death. Five of these were reprieved, and the remaining eight were thrown back into jail for further investigations.

Before the Chelmsford trial was finished, Hopkins found himself greatly in demand. In times of war and public misfortune, distractions are welcomed. Hopkins moved around Essex, finding more witches, and accepting payment for his trouble; at Aldeburgh he was paid £6 for finding a witch, and at Stowmarket the local authorities paid him £23. In the days when a working wage was sixpence a day, these were large sums. During his year as witchfinder, Hopkins and his assistants made about £1,000, according to Summers. In Bury St Edmunds, he played his part in having 200 people arrested; 68 of whom were hanged. He moved around Suffolk and Norfolk, finding witches in every place that invited him, and in a few that he selected for himself.

In April 1646, a Huntingdon clergyman named Gaule attacked Hopkins from the pulpit and published a pamphlet about his methods of 'torture'. Torture of witches was still forbidden by law in England, but Hopkins used other methods—'pricking' for Devil's marks (areas the Devil had touched were supposed to be insensitive to pain), 'swimming'—which meant that the bound victim was tossed into a pond, and if she floated, she was innocent—and depriving of sleep for days on end, a method still used in 'brain-washing'. The pamphlet was widely read, and it turned the tide against Hopkins. One historian of witchcraft relates that Hopkins was seized by an angry crowd and made to endure the water ordeal. He was, in any case, a sick man.

He retired to Manningtree, and died there later that year of tuberculosis.

Robbins estimates that Hopkins was responsible for several hundred hangings (witches in England were never burnt, although the North Berwick witches in Scotland were burned for having plotted against the king's person). And with his downfall, mass witch trials ceased in England. In America, the most famous was still to come. The explosion of superstition and violence that occurred in Salem, Massachusetts, in 1692, is still one of the most puzzling episodes in American history. For most writers on the case—including Arthur Miller, who dramatised it in *The Crucible*—there is no mystery: a few bored and naughty children became obsessed by the voodoo tales of a black servant, and decided to pretend they were bewitched. Egged on by the local minister, a man of paranoid tendencies, they accused various people of witchcraft. The whole thing snowballed until over 200 people were accused, 22 of whom were executed or died in prison. Then, as suddenly as it began, the hysteria faded away. And the Salem witchcraft trials virtually ended the 'witchcraft craze' in America as the downfall of Matthew Hopkins ended it in England.

The case may not be as simple as it looks. Even Rossell Hope Robbins admits 'motives are very elusive'. Clearly, these children were not really 'bewitched'. But they behaved in some ways like the 'possessed' nuns of Loudun or Aix-en-Provence, or like some teenagers who are the 'focus' of poltergeist occurrences.

The Revd. Samuel Parris was not a popular man, for he seems to have been an unpleasant character, mean and bad-tempered. He had brought with him from Barbados a number of black servants, including a woman called Tituba, and her husband, 'John Indian'. During the long winter evenings, Tituba talked to the children about witches and spirits. His daughter Elizabeth, aged 9, her cousin Abigail Williams, aged 11, and a friend called Ann Putnam, 12, soon began behaving very oddly, having convulsions, screaming and talking disconnected nonsense. A doctor called in to 'cure' Elizabeth said he thought she was bewitched. Other ministers were consulted, and decided that the Devil was involved. Questioned—and beaten—by Parris, Tituba agreed that the Devil had inspired her to 'work mischief' against the children, and named a pipe-smoking beggar woman named

Sarah Good as an accomplice. The children also mentioned Sarah Good as well as a bedridden old woman, Sarah Osborne. When a magistrate named Hathorne asked the girls about their convulsions, they began to moan with pain, and declared that the 'spirit' (or spectre) of Sarah Good was biting and pinching them. Sarah Good and Sarah Osborne both denied in court that they knew anything about witchcraft, but Tituba admitted it all with a certain relish; she went on expanding her confessions for three days. Tituba declared that Sarah Good and Sarah Osborne had been present at a witches' Sabbat, and added that there were two more local women whom she did not know. This caused widespread gossip and speculation. 12-year-old Ann Putnam put an end to this by declaring that one of the witches was a woman called Martha Cory—who had laughed unbelievingly when the girls threw their convulsions—and that the other was a saintly old lady named Rebecca Nurse. A farmer named Proctor—another sceptic—was also accused.

The whole area was now in the grip of a witchcraft scare; people were afraid to go out after dark because witches were supposed to be able to turn themselves into animals or night-birds—a remnant of legends of werewolves and vampires. Eight more local children became 'afflicted' and screamed out the names of 'witches' who were tormenting them. A woman named Bridget Bishop—who had a reputation for being 'fast'—was tried and executed in June 1692. Sarah Osborne died in prison, but Sarah Good was tried and executed, together with four others, in July. A minister named George Burroughs was denounced, and he was also tried and executed.

The more hysteria increased, the more the girls—now eleven of them—seemed to be tormented by devils. By September, the death toll had increased to 20, and one unfortunate man—Giles Corey—was literally pressed to death under enormous weights in an effort to force him to confess. He refused (although it would have saved his life) because his goods would have been forfeit to the state, and he had no intention of dying a pauper. His wife was hanged as a witch.

The various girls were called to neighbouring towns to identify witches, and it looked as if the trials and executions would spread to Andover and Boston. The Andover magistrate declined to sign more than 40 warrants and had to flee with his wife to escape being tried as a witch. Then the girls began to overreach themselves. They named the wife of the governor, Sir William Phips, as a witch, and the president of Harvard College; the magistrates told them sternly that they were mistaken, and this was the beginning of the end of the persecutions. When Governor Phips returned from fighting Indians on the Canadian border, he dismissed the court and released many of the accused. In further trials, 'spectral evidence'—the notion that the disembodied spirits of witches could torment their victims—was disallowed, and only three people out of 52 were condemned. Phips reprieved them, released all others from prison, and the Salem craze ended abruptly about a year after it began. One of the girls, Ann Putnam, later confessed that she had been 'deluded by Satan' when she accused Rebecca Nurse and others. The Reverend Parris, now attacked and denounced, left Salem with his family. Abigail Williams, according to legend, became a prostitute.

Even Montague Summers agrees that the Salem trials were the result of hysteria and the 'diseased imaginings of neurotic children'. But he was convinced that there *is* positive evidence of involvement in witchcraft in a few of the cases. It seems probable that George Burroughs, Bridget Bishop and Martha Carrier were members of a coven—although they had nothing to do with 'bewitching' the children.

And what about the children? All writers on the affair assume that they were mischievous, 'prankish', and that the whole thing snowballed out of a harmless game. But what was this game? The answer, fairly certainly, is some form of 'magic'. Tituba was familiar with voodoo and obeah. And the essence of voodoo rituals—as David St Clair emphasises in *Drum and Candle* and Guy Playfair in *The Flying Cow*—is the evocation of 'low grade' spirits to do the bidding of the magician. The three children, bored with the long winter in the dreary New England village, undoubtedly 'tried out' what Tituba had taught them. Their intentions were harmless enough—rather like a modern child playing with a ouija board or automatic writing. But two of them at least were at the dangerous age when children become the focus of poltergeist phenomena—Ann Putnam was twelve and looked older. We do not know very much about 'possession', and the usual theory is that it is pure hysteria; but again, anyone who takes the trouble to read T.K. Oesterreich's classic *Possession: Demoniacal and Other*, or Martin Ebon's anthology *Exorcism: Fact not Fiction* will see that there is a very thin dividing line between 'possession' and being a focus of poltergeist activity. This is a matter to which we shall return in the next chapter.

The storm that ended the witchcraft craze in France emphasises once again that witchcraft can have a genuinely sinister face.

In 1673, during the reign of Louis XIV, two priests informed the police in Paris that a number of penitents had asked absolution for murdering their spouses. No names were mentioned, because of the secrecy of the confessional, but it alerted the Chief of Police, Nicholas de la Reynie. What was happening, it seemed, was that a ring of fortune-tellers and 'sorcerers' were supplying 'succession powders'—a euphemism for poisons—to wealthy men and women who preferred lovers to matrimonial entanglements.

De la Reynie could only keep his ear to the ground. It took him four years to fit together the clues that led him to the recognition that there was an international 'poisons ring'—much as there are now drugs rings—headed by men of influence. A remark of a fortune-teller, Marie Bosse, about being ready to retire when she had arranged three more poisonings, provided the lead he had been waiting for. A disguised policewoman consulted Marie Bosse on how she could get rid of her husband, and made an arrest when she was sold poison. Many poisons were found in Marie Bosse's house. She and her husband and two sons were arrested; also, another fortune-teller known as La Vigoreux, who shared a communal bed with the family.

Interrogations began to reveal the names of their customers, and the revelation shocked the King. It seemed that half the aristocracy were trying to poison one another, and that two ladies had even approached another fortune-teller for means of getting rid of one of his own mistresses Louise de la Vallière.

But this was not simply a matter of murder or attempted murder. The customers were also convinced that the fortune-tellers could produce charms and magic potions to secure the affections of their admirers, and apparently had no objection if the Devil was involved.

Stern and decisive action was called for—after all, the king might be the next victim . . . He created a special commission, a kind of Star Chamber, which sat in a room draped in black curtains and lit with candles—hence the *Chambre Ardente*—the lighted (or burning) chamber.

What made it so frightening was that the methods of poisoning were so subtle. A Madame de Poulaillon, who wanted to kill her aged husband so she could marry her young lover, had been impregnating his shirts with arsenic, which would cause symptoms similar to those of syphilis; she would then rub the sores with a 'healing ointment' that would kill him in ten weeks—and there would be no suspicion.

The chief defendants were Marie Bosse, La Vigoreux, an abortionist known as La Lepère, and a well known fortune-teller called Catherine Deshayes, known as La Voisin. La Vigoreux and Marie Bosse were quickly condemned—on May 6, 1678—to be burnt alive and one son, François Bosse, hanged. La Voisin was horribly tortured, and, when she refused to confess to poisoning, burnt alive in an iron chair—Mme de Sevigné described in a letter how the old woman cursed violently and threw off the straw half a dozen times, until the flames became too strong and she disappeared in them.

All this was kept secret; one reason being that the king's mistress Mme. de Montespan was deeply involved. And more investigation revealed that various priests had performed Black Masses and even sacrificed babies to the Devil. A hunchback, the Abbé Guibourg used as an altar the naked body of a woman, placing the chalice on her belly; Mme. de Montespan had often served as the altar. A baby would then be sacrificed by having its throat cut, and the body thrown into an oven. La Voisin confessed at her trial that she had disposed of 2,500 babies like this. On another occasion, Mme. des Oillets came to make a charm for the king, accompanied by a man. The priest said that sperm from both was necessary, but since Mme. des Oillets was menstruating, he accepted a few drops of menstrual blood from her, while the man masturbated into the chalice.

Many other priests proved to be involved, and it became clear that an alarming number of churchmen had no objections to dealings with the Devil. One had consecrated a stone altar in a brothel, another strangled a baby after baptising it with oil reserved for Extreme Unction, another copulated with the girl who was serving as an altar in full view of his audience; another fortune teller described how she had sacrificed her own new-born baby at a Black Mass.

By 1680, it had struck the king that a full-scale scandal could lead to unforeseen results, since so many nobles were involved. He decided to suspend the Chambre Ardente. No noblemen—or women—were sentenced, but de la Reynie continued to arrest and torture fortune-tellers. 104 people were sentenced: 36 to death, others to slavery in the galleys or banishment. The chief result of the case was that fortune-tellers were banned by law, and witchcraft was declared to be a superstition. After that, people accused of witchcraft were sent to a madhouse, the Salpêtrière. In fact, a man was executed in Bordeaux in 1718 for causing a man to become impotent and his wife barren; but then, working 'fancied acts of magic' was still a hanging offence.

Louis attempted to suppress all the evidence for the affair in 1709 by ordering all papers to be destroyed; but the official transcripts were overlooked.

It seems incredible that, at the time Isaac Newton was writing the *Principia*, priests and 'witches' should be sacrificing babies at Black Masses. If we take the rational view of witchcraft—as a mediaeval superstition—it is virtually impossible to understand what they thought they were doing. Was it all, perhaps, a kind of escapism, a desire to indulge in 'wickedness' for the sake of excitement, like some of the modern witchcraft covens? The French aristocracy was decadent, but surely not decadent enough to indulge in the 17th century equivalent of 'snuff movies'? The truth is obviously simpler: that Marie Bosse, Catherine Deshayes and La Voisin had learned witchcraft from their aunts or grandmothers—like Jehanne de Brigue—and were simply practising a traditional craft that had been handed down for centuries. And the aristocrats who patronised them did so because they knew that their 'magic' often worked. The witches themselves were sure it worked.

That view offends modern common-sense. It offended *my* common-sense at the time I wrote *The Occult*. Yet in retrospect, I can see that I was not being quite entirely logical. For as early as 1964, in a book called *Rasputin and the Fall of the Romanovs*, I had cited a number of cases that seemed to show that African witchcraft really works. The travel writer Negley Farson, whom I knew well during the last ten years of his life, told me that on several occasions he had seen a Liberian witch-doctor conjure rain out of a clear sky. And a neighbour, Martin Delany, who had been the Managing Director of a large company in Nigeria, and himself possessed slight thaumaturgical gifts, had described to me how the local witch-doctor had promised that the heavy rain which had been falling for days would stop for two hours to allow a garden party to take place; the rain had stopped a few minutes before the party was due to start, and begun again a minute after it finished. The stoppage was confined to an area of approximately 10,000 sq. yds.

This, of course, could have been some natural ability akin to 'psychokinesis'—I have a book called *The Power of the Mind* by Rolf Alexander which has four photographs claiming to show how a large cloud was disintegrated by psychokinesis in eight minutes at Orillia, Ontario, on September 12, 1954. But the same explanation cannot be applied to another strange event described by Martin Delany, which I quote from his own account:

'Having just returned from leave in Europe, I was informed by my European sawmill manager that an extraordinary incident had taken place in the sawmill a few days prior to my return. A hen, from a nearby compound, had flown straight into the large Brenta band-saw and was instantly cut to pieces by the blade of the saw, which revolves at about 10,000 revolutions per minute. The Nigerian mill-workers were very perturbed by this—they knew now that the 'Iron God' was angry and seeking blood and, unless blood was offered by the witch doctor to appease the 'God', then he would demand other victims. They therefore requested that the band-saw should be stopped until the necessary sacrifice had been made by the witch doctor.

'I refused their request for two reasons, firstly because an urgent export order for lumber had to be completed, and secondly because the sacrifice involved decapitating a puppy dog and sprinkling the blood over the machine, and this I was most reluctant to permit. In fact, I hoped that the whole thing was an isolated incident soon to be forgotten. Two days afterwards another hen flew into the band-saw. This caused consternation among the Nigerian workers, who again approached me, but I again refused. Four days after this incident the European manager was asked by the Nigerian foreman in my presence if he would come to the band-saw to adjust the saw-guides as the saw-blade was not cutting evenly; this adjustment was usually done by the manager. We watched as the very rigid drill, essential when adjustments or repairs were made to the band-saw, was carried out. The electricity was cut off at the mains and the starter switches were put in the 'Off' position. Then, and only then, was anyone permitted to commence work on the band-saw. I watched with interest, pleased to note that the drill had been faithfully carried out, and turned to leave the mill when suddenly, to my horror, I heard the first sounds which indicated that the saw had commenced to turn. Rushing to the band-saw I discovered that the manager's hand had been badly cut by the saw-blade which had revolved possibly six or seven times. By now, the Nigerian staff were in a state of extreme fear, so I decided to close the mill for the rest of the day and sent for two European experts, one an electrician, the other a sawmiller. They examined the machine, the starter motors, the mains switches, checking in every possible way, only to state that everything was in perfect order and that it was utterly impossible for the band-saw to start up when the mains and starter motor switches were off. I confess that I was badly shaken by this last incident, but still refused to have the witch doctor in because of a natural repugnance to the particular form of sacrifice. I suggested finding blood for the sacrifice from a dead hen or the local meat market, but to this the witch doctor would not agree. The men were persuaded to return to work only by an offer of additional money and the assurance that the machine, etcetera, were in perfect order, having been checked by the European experts. There was a lull for about two weeks and everyone concerned was beginning to relax when with horrifying and brutal suddenness the 'Iron God' struck. The band-saw had just commenced to saw through a log, the 7-inch wide saw-blade was turning at maximum revolutions when without warning and for no known reason the saw-blade started to peel in a thin strip commencing at the rear. Within a second or so a tangled mass of peeled saw-blade burst out and struck the operator in the chest and face, inflicting serious wounds; in fact, he died before he could be carried out to the waiting estate car. Operators are never protected (i.e. caged in with protective mesh) with this type of saw as normally there is no need, the saws having adequate guards. A Mr Stenner of Stenners Ltd. of Tiverton said some time later that never before in his many years of manufacturing band-saws had he heard of such a thing occurring. So I finally gave way to the demands of the workmen, who would not have worked in the sawmill at any price until the witch doctor had made the sacrifice to the 'Iron God'. The band-saw stopped operating two years ago, but during the eight years from the date of the operator's death it functioned without hitch. The death of the operator was duly recorded in police records. It is interesting to note that when the United Africa Company opened their very large sawmill, costing several million pounds, at Sapele in Eastern Nigeria, the witch doctor was called in to make the appropriate sacrifice to the 'Iron God'.'

Martin Delany was not of the opinion that the witch doctor himself had caused these accidents by some form of 'psycho-kinesis'—he described him as an amiable old gentleman. He believed that if the occurrences were not simply accidents, then they were caused by the fear of the natives somehow acting upon the saw—a form of negative psycho-kinesis.

It seems clear that witchcraft is still a living force in Africa and that it has been witnessed by many balanced and level-headed western observers. In a book called *Ju-ju in My Life*, James H. Neal, former Chief Investigations Officer for the Government of Ghana, tells some baffling stories. His first acquaintance with African witchcraft occurred when he visited a port being built at Tema and was told that a certain small tree had defied all efforts to move it. The most powerful bulldozers failed to tear it out of the ground. The African foreman explained that the tree was a Fetich—that it was inhabited by a spirit, and that the only way to move it was to ask the spirit to leave it for another tree. Finally, the Fetich Priest was called; he asked for three sheep, three bottles of gin, and a hundred pounds if he succeeded in moving the tree. The blood of the sheep was sprinkled round the base of the tree, then the gin; then the priest went into a semi-trance, and begged the spirit of the tree to vacate it for a better tree, on the grounds that the port would afford employment for many blacks. After various rituals, the priest announced that the spirit had agreed to leave. To Neal's astonishment, a small team of men then had no difficulty in pulling the tree out of the ground with a rope . . .

This story is interesting because it makes clear the place of 'spirits'—often nature spirits—in witchcraft. This aspect, I am inclined to believe, is more important than anyone has given it credit for. It emerges again clearly in an episode in Laurens Van Der Post's book *The Lost World of the Kalahari*, in which he describes how a guide offered to take him to a mysterious region called the Slippery Hills—the one condition being that there must be no killing of animals. Van Der Post forgot to tell the advance party, who shot a warthog; from then on, everything went wrong. The camera and tape recorder jammed continually, although they had given no trouble before, and the camera swivel failed. They were attacked by bees. Their guide warned them that the spirits were angry; when he tried to pray, some invisible force pulled him over backwards. Finally, he threaded a needle, placed it in his hand, then went into a semi-trance, staring at it. He began to speak to invisible presences, and told Van Der Post that the spirits would have killed him if they had not known that his intentions—in visiting the Slippery Hills—were pure. Van Der Post suggested that he wrote a letter of apology, which they all signed, and buried in a bottle at the foot of a sacred rock painting; from that moment, the 'jinx' went away. The guide remarked later that the spirits were now far less powerful than they used to be—once they would have killed on sight anyone who had approached so unceremoniously.

The notion of elemental spirits—inhabiting trees or hills—strikes the western mind as totally preposterous. Yet it was not always so. In Ireland—even in Cornwall, where I live—there is still a great deal of belief in fairies and nature spirits in remote country areas. In the 1920s, a psychic named Geoffrey Hodson specialised in describing elementals and nature spirits, and his book about them—entitled, rather off-puttingly, *Fairies at Work and Play* was taken seriously by many people involved in psychical research. (Hodson himself was a Theosophist.) Here is a typical description of what he calls a 'nature deva', encountered in June 1922 when climbing in the Lake District:

'After a scramble of several hundred feet up a rocky glen we turned out to one side, on to the open fell where it faces a high crag. Immediately on reaching the open we became aware, with startling suddenness, of the presence of a great nature-deva, who appeared to be partly within the hillside.

'My first impression was of a huge, brilliant crimson bat-like thing, which fixed a pair of burning eyes upon me.

'The form was not concentrated into the true human shape, but was somehow spread out like a bat with a human face and eyes, and with wings outstretched on the mountain-side. As soon as it felt itself to be observed it flashed into its proper shape, as if to confront us, fixed its piercing eyes upon us, and then sank into the hillside and disappeared. When first seen its aura must have covered several hundred feet of space . . .'

We find such notions absurd; but they would be accepted by most primitive peoples. From the Eskimos to the Ainus of Northern Japan, from the Orochon of Siberia to the Indians of Tierra del Fuego, the *shaman* is the intermediary between this world and the world of spirits. A man became a *shaman* through painful ordeals, both physical and spiritual. An Eskimo *shaman* told the Danish explorer Rasmussen: 'I could see and hear in a totally different way. I had gained my enlightenment, the *shaman's* light of brain and body, and this in such a manner that it was not only I who could see through the darkness of life, but the same bright light also shone out from me, imperceptible to human beings, but visible to all spirits of earth and sky and sea, and these now came to me as my helping spirits.' The idea of being able to see the world of the spirits 'of earth and sky and sea' can be found in all shamanistic religions.

This curious oneness with nature enables the *shaman* or witch-doctor to exert his power over animals. In *The Occult* I have quoted that amazing passage from Sir Arthur Grimble's book *Pattern of Islands*, describing how a 'porpoise caller' withdrew into his hut for several hours, where he went into a trance; in this trance, apparently, his spirit went out to sea and summoned the porpoises. Finally, he rushed out of the hut calling 'They come, they come'. And to Grimble's astonishment, they *did* come. The villagers waded into the sea and stood breast deep and hundreds of porpoises swam slowly into the beach, apparently in a state of hypnosis, allowing themselves to be beaten to death.

Ross Salmon, a British explorer who spent much of the 1960s and 70s in search of the 'lost world of the Incas', has described in a book called *My Quest For El Dorado* a ceremony among the Callaway Indians of northern Bolivia which reveals this same intimacy between man and nature. A girl named Wakchu had been accused of being unfaithful to her husband during his absence, and the village elders decided that she would be 'tried' by the condor, the sacred bird of the village, which was believed to embody the spirit of a famous hero. Ross Salmon was given permission to film the whole ceremony. He described, in a television interview accompanying his film, his incredulity at the idea that the priests could summon a condor—a shy bird, which he had never seen at close quarters. Wakchu was tied to a pole at the top of the cliff, wearing only a loincloth, and the three priests began a ceremony to call the condor, supported by a chorus of women. For half an hour, nothing happened, and Salmon became convinced it was a waste of time. Then, to his amazement, an enormous condor flew overhead, together with two females. It landed near Wakchu, strutted around for a while, then ran towards her and pointed its beak at her throat. The villagers murmured 'Guilty'. One of the camera crew threw a stone at the bird, which flew off. Wakchu committed suicide a few days later by throwing herself from a cliff. She evidently accepted the judgement of the condor.[1]

Another account of life among South American Indians conveys this same sense of intimacy with nature. *Wizard of the Upper Amazon* by F. Bruce Lamb tells the story of Manuel Córdova-Rios, who was kidnapped by the Amahuaca Indians of the Amazon, and who lived among them for many years. Much of their 'magic' was involved with hunting, and apparently worked. Rios witnessed a method of luring pigs. It was important for the hunters to kill the sow who led a band of pigs. Then her head was buried in a hole, facing the opposite direction from which the hunters were travelling. The hole was filled in while the hunters

1. Salmon's version in the book differs in some particulars from his account on Westward Television; I have preferred the television version, which Salmon claims embodies his considered opinion.

sang chants to the spirits of the forest. If this was done correctly, the pigs would continue to pass over this spot at regular intervals, in the circuit of their territory.

It also seems that the Amahuaca Indians are capable of group telepathy as well as of this kind of direct contact with nature. Clearly, their modes of perception are more 'right-brain' than ours. But since we now know that our left-brain perception has been developed by the pressures of civilisation, and that the being who lives in the right is virtually a stranger, there is less reason for dismissing these stories of primitive empathy with nature as old wives' tales.

It now becomes possible to understand the ceremonies performed by our Cro-Magnon ancestors before setting out on hunting expeditions, and those cave paintings of *shamans* performing ritual dances and wearing the skins of animals. The purpose is not simply to locate the herd of animals to be hunted the next day (*shamans* should be regarded as mediums rather than magicians), but to somehow *lure* it to a place where the hunters can find it, as Grimble's porpoise-caller lured the porpoises.

Recent research has demonstrated fairly convincingly that circles of standing stones like Stonehenge and Avebury were intended as solar and lunar calendars. The discoveries of 'ley hunters' like John Michell seem to suggest that there were also temples for the performance of fertility rituals. But I remain convinced that if we are to understand the real purpose of the standing stones, we have to put ourselves into the state of mind of the Callawayas or Amahuacas, and understand that the ancient priests were probably *shamans* who went into a trance and *conversed* with nature spirits, asking them to guarantee the abundance of the harvest.

Once we begin to understand this, we can also understand the origins of 'witchcraft'. A *shaman* who has the power to converse with 'spirits' to ask them to bless his tribe may also make use of them to revenge himself on an enemy. In *The Occult*, I have described the theory advanced by anthropologist Ivar Lissner about why our ancestors suddenly ceased to make images of human beings. They reasoned that if 'magic' could be used to destroy a reindeer or bear, it could also be used to destroy another human being. So the making of images became taboo—or something carried out in secret by 'black' magicians—those who would later be called 'followers of the left hand path'. (It is significant that our ancestors equated the left with the sinister—sinister in Latin means left—while right was synonymous with goodness; they were clearly aware that the two aspects of the human mind are separate, but had no means of knowing that the right half of the brain governs the left half of the body and vice versa.)

Neal's *Ju-ju in My Life* describes his own gradual conversion to belief in the malevolent power of witch-doctors—in this case, through unpleasant personal experience. When, as chief investigations officer for the Government of Ghana, Neal caused the arrest of a man who had been extorting bribes, he found that he was the target for a ju-ju attack. It began with the disappearance of small personal items of clothing—as in the case of David St Clair. One day he found the seat of his car scattered with a black powder; his chauffeur carefully brushed it off, and urinated in it to destroy its power. Then, one night, Neal became feverish, and experienced pains from head to foot. He felt he was going to die. Suddenly, he found himself outside his body, looking down at himself on the bed. He passed through the bedroom wall, and seemed to be travelling at great speed, when suddenly he seemed to receive a message that it was not yet his time to die; he passed back into his room, and into his body. After this he spent three weeks in hospital suffering from an illness that the doctors were unable to diagnose. An African police inspector told him he was being subjected to a ju-ju attack. More black powder was scattered in his car. One night, lying in bed, he felt invisible creatures with long snouts attacking his solar plexus and draining his vitality. A witch-doctor who was called in described in detail two men who were responsible for the attacks—giving an accurate description of two men involved in the bribery case. Finally, after a ceremony performed by a Muslim holy man—who surrounded the house with a wall of protection—Neal slowly recovered. The white doctor who tended him agreed that he had been victim of a ju-ju attack.

He also describes how, not long after the 'exorcism' ritual, his servant killed a cobra outside his bungalow. As they were exulting about the death of the snake, Neal noticed another snake—this time a small grey one—slithering towards them. When he drew the servant's attention to it, the man went pale. This, the man said, was a 'bad snake'—meaning a snake created artificially by witch-doctors; a man bitten by such a snake has no chance of recovery. Neal was understandably sceptical. Then he saw the snake—which was still slithering at a great speed towards them—come to a halt as if against an invisible wall. It had encountered the 'wall of protection' put there by the holy man. With a single stroke, the servant chopped off its head with a cutlass. No blood came out. Soon after this, Neal began to itch all over. Two perfectly healthy trees just beyond the 'wall of protection' split down the middle with a loud crash. Consultation with another skilled sorcerer elicited the information that both Neal and his servant were victims of a new ju-ju attack, but that because of the 'protection', Neal could not be seriously harmed; the itch was the worst the magician could do.

This kind of witchcraft can be found in primitive societies all over the world. In a book called *Mitsinari*, a Catholic priest, Father André Dupreyat, describes his years in Papua, New Guinea. When he clashed with local sorcerers, he was also placed under a 'snake curse'. One day, walking towards a village, he was surprised to see a silvery-coloured snake wriggling towards him. The villagers all scattered. Knowing it would have to lower its head to come closer, Dupreyat waited until it was no longer in a position to strike, and killed it with his stick. The next day, when he was lying in a hut, a snake lowered itself from the roof-beam and dropped on to his chest. He lay perfectly still until it slid down to the floor, when he was able to kill it with a stick. A few days later, as he lay in a hammock, a native warned him that two black snakes had writhed up the support of the hammock, and were close enough to bite him. They cautiously handed him a knife and told him when to strike; he succeeded in killing both snakes.

Dupreyat also has a remarkable account of a local sorcerer named Isidoro who was able to turn himself into a cassowary (a kind of ostrich). One evening as they all sat talking of Isidoro, they heard the distinctive sound of a cassowary running, and Isidoro came into the hut. He talked with them for a while, then said he would be staying in a house in the village overnight, and went out. They again heard the sound of a cassowary running. Dupreyat checked, and found that Isidoro was not in the house where he had claimed he would be staying. The next day, he visited Isidoro's village—five hours away on the other side of the mountain. There he was greeted by Isidoro. Villagers assured him that Isidoro had spent the early part of the previous evening in the communal hut, then gone away at seven o'clock. By nine o'clock he had been with Dupreyat, a five-hour journey away on the other side of the mountain. And at dawn, he had been observed in his own village again. Yet in the dark, it was at least an eight-hour journey away.

James Neal's own experiences of witchcraft in Ghana ended disastrously. Leaving his home in a hurry, on a morning when he intended to go to the Accra races—to capture a race-course gang—he left behind a protecting amulet that had been given him by the holy man. From an almost empty grandstand he watched the men being arrested by his own officers. Then, walking down from the grandstand, with no one within twenty yards of him, he was pushed violently, and fell. The multiple fractures he sustained kept him in hospital for months; and when he recovered, his broken bones prevented him from continuing his police work and he was forced to resign. The holy man, who came to see him in hospital, told him that he had been pushed by an 'astral entity'. Neal insists that, as he was pushed, he twisted round to see who was responsible, and that there was no one there.

It was while writing about cases like these that I came to recognise that it was illogical to accept evidence about witchcraft in Africa, and reject the same kind of evidence about witchcraft in Europe. It is possible that the Chelmsford witches, the North Berwick witches, the Auldearne witches, were innocent victims of a barbarous superstition. It is equally possible that, like the *umbanda* magicians of Brazil, they had learned to make use of the 'spirit world' for their own purposes. Montague Summers was not being as absurd as he sounded when he declared that modern spiritualism is a revival of mediaeval witchcraft.

It was in the 1880s, at the time when the Society for Psychical Research was trying to place the study of the paranormal on a scientific footing, that modern scholarship turned its attention to witchcraft. An American scholar named Charles Leland became fascinated by the English Gypsies—as George Borrow had been half a century earlier—and became president of the Gypsy Lore Society. In 1886 he went to Florence, continuing his studies of Gypsy magic and lore, and encountered an Italian witch named Maddalena, who told fortunes and sold amulets. He employed Maddalena to gather what traditions she could about the origins of Italian witchcraft, which was known as *la vecchia religione*, the old religion. She finally provided him with a handwritten manuscript called *Aradia*, or the Gospel of the Witches. This tells the story of how the goddess Diana had an incestuous affair with her brother Lucifer, and gave birth to Aradia (or Herodias); it was Aradia who eventually came down to earth and taught men and women the secrets of magic. This, according to the Gospel of the Witches, was because the Church and the aristocracy were treating the poor with such cruelty that Diana felt they needed to be provided with some means of self-defence. That is to say, witchcraft was originally a movement of *social protest*, like the Peasants' Revolt. In his *Witchcraft, Magic and Alchemy* (1931), Grillot de Givry hits upon the same idea: '. . . it is perfectly logical that certain men . . . having seen that God possessed his rich and honoured Church on earth . . . should have asked themselves—above all, if they believed that they had a right to complain of God, Who had condemned them to a wretched state of life and denied them worldly goods—why Satan . . . should not have his Church also . . . why they themselves should not be priests of this demon, who would, perhaps, give them what God did not deign to give . . .'

There is every reason to believe that *Aradia* is a genuine document, for there could be no possible reason to forge such a work. It would hardly attract the attention of anyone but a folk-lorist—and, in fact, it went out of print almost immediately. It provides one of the most powerful pieces of evidence that witchcraft was a survival of a pagan cult of the moon and earth goddess—a fertility cult.

During the First World War, an English archaeologist named Margaret Murray was living in Glastonbury when she decided to study the history of witchcraft. Without, apparently, studying *Aradia* (at least, she never mentions it), Margaret Murray reached the conclusion that witchcraft was a survival of a pagan fertility cult. It was her view that the image of the Devil—as a horned man with a tail—originated in the hunting rituals of our

Cro-Magnon ancestors in which the *shaman* wore the skin of the animal about to be hunted. When man became a farmer rather than a hunter, he directed his magic towards the earth with the object of ensuring a good harvest. These innocent pagan festivals continued down the ages. The Church attempted to stamp them out, partly because they were a pagan survival, partly because of their strong sexual undertones—but in many country areas the 'old religion' was simply blended with the new; dances around a maypole replaced the pagan fertility ceremony with its ritual phallus.

In recent years, Margaret Murray's theory—which was once accepted by most respectable scholars—has been violently attacked, on the grounds that she censored the evidence about witchcraft cults and sabbats to support her theories. And there can be no doubt that her later book *The Divine King in England* (which appeared when she was 94) is wildly eccentric, with its theory that many English kings were members of the 'old religion'. Yet no one who looks impartially at the evidence can doubt that witchcraft was closely bound up with the cult of Diana, and that many of its ceremonies were pagan survivals. In his book *The Roots of Witchcraft*, Michael Harrison mentions that after the Second World War, Professor Geoffrey Webb was given the task of surveying damaged churches, and discovered that many altars of churches built before the Black Death contained stone phalluses. (Scholars have long been puzzled by carvings on many ancient churches showing a crouching woman holding open the lips of her vagina—they are known as Sheila-na-gigs.) Harrison also mentions an event documented in the Bishop's Register of Exeter in the 14th century, which states that the monks of Frithelstock Priory in Devon were caught by the Bishop worshipping a statue of 'the unchaste Diana' in the woods, and made them destroy it. Why 'unchaste' Diana, when she is usually known as the 'queen and huntress, chaste and fair'? Because the Bishop recognised the ceremony for what it was—a fertility ritual.

Amusingly enough, Montague Summers is enraged by the theory of Margaret Murray, and denounces it as imaginative moonshine. He is determined to promote his own view that the witches were genuine heretics, inspired by the devil, and that the church was right to 'stamp out the infection lest the whole of society be corrupted and damned'. As we have seen, there is a great deal to be said for his opinions—even though he takes them to the point of absurdity. He is almost certainly in the right when he attacks Margaret Murray's view that Joan of Arc and Gilles de Rais were priests of the Dianic cult who were sacrificed for their faith.

All of which only demonstrates that the subject of witchcraft is far more complicated than at first appears. The truth seems to be roughly this: the 'old religion' survived from the days of our Cro-Magnon ancestors, and in late Neolithic times led to the construction of stone 'temples' like Avebury, Stonehenge and Carnac. This religion involved the invocation of earth spirits and deities—like Van Der Post's 'spirits of the Slippery Hills'. It managed to co-exist quietly with Christianity in Europe— although the authors of the Canon Episcopi knew about it nearly a thousand years before John XXII made it a crime. Almost certainly, it had nothing to do with the rise of Catharism, whose roots are in Manichaeism and Gnosticism. But the persecution of the Cathars drew the attention of the Church to the Old Religion, with dire results. In fact, one of the first results of the persecution of witches was probably to cause them to band together and take their stand against the doctrines of Christianity. So, to some extent, the church created the heresy it was so determined to destroy. If we can believe *Aradia*, they did worship the devil—or Lucifer, the sun god—as well as his sister Diana. And many of them probably practised ancient forms of magic passed down from palaeolithic times. It was not the Church that stamped out witchcraft—it was Newton and Leibniz and Dalton.

1951 was a watershed in the history of witchcraft, for it was in that year that the Witchcraft Act was finally repealed in Britain. In the view of the British Parliament, the act was obsolete. Legislators believed that there were no witches in Britain, and probably never had been.

One man who strongly disagreed with this point of view was Gerald Gardner. He was the author of a book called *High Magic's Aid*, which described in detail various rituals used by medieval witches. In 1954, three years after the repeal of the Witchcraft Act, Gardner published a book called *Witchcraft Today* in which he made it fairly clear that he was himself a practising witch. He declared that there were still dozens of *covens*—groups of witches—in England, practising the rites he had described in his earlier book.

Witchcraft Today is a fascinating but irritating book. In her introduction to it Margaret Murray says that 'Dr Gardner has shown in his book how much of the so-called "witchcraft" is descended from ancient rituals, and has nothing to do with spell-casting and other evil practices.' In fact Gardner shows nothing of the kind. What he does is to develop and popularise the views put forward thirty years earlier by Margaret Murray herself. As we have seen, Dr Murray maintained that witchcraft, or the 'Dianic Cult' as she called it, is an ancient pagan religion, older by far than Christianity. She traced the cult back to prehistoric worship of the fertile Great Mother, the oldest of all ancient gods, and of the Horned God, a primitive symbol of power. Taking up this theme, Gardner declared that witchcraft was the religion of the first inhabitants of Britain. He suggested that these ancient Britons were pygmies or 'little people', and were the origin of the legends of fairies, elves, and dwarfs. Under successive waves of invaders these Little People were driven into hiding, taking with them their old religion. When the rest of Britain became Christianised they continued to hold their strange, orgiastic ceremonies in remote places. The superstitious peasants were afraid of them, but noblemen and their ladies often joined in.

These incredible assertions, along with the implication that modern witches practised sexual orgies, aroused the interest of the British press. At the age of 70, Gardner suddenly found himself famous. Popular Sunday newspapers sought him out and printed his descriptions of witches' meetings called Sabbaths or Sabbats—complete with naked witches and ritual floggings. Gardner himself turned out to be the kind of man who makes good copy for sensational journalists. He was born in Lancashire in 1884, the son of a wealthy timber merchant. His father was a noted eccentric who used to remove all his clothes and sit on them whenever it rained. Gardner developed a taste for voyeurism and for being spanked, during boyhood travels in the Middle East with a buxom Irish nurse. Later, nudity and ritual flagellation were to feature prominently in his writings about witchcraft. He lived in the East until 1936, developing a taste for weapons, particularly knives. His first book was a study of the Malayan *kris*, a dagger with a wavy blade. Then he returned to England and became a student and practitioner of magic. According to his own account, his introduction to witchcraft occurred in 1946 when he was living in the New Forest in southern England. There he met a witch called Old Dorothy—allegedly an aristocrat—who taught him about the cult of witchcraft, and convinced him that it was the survival of an ancient pagan religion.

The truth of this account has since been widely questioned. Some of Gardner's 'age-old' rituals have been criticized as the products of his own imagination—both by sceptics unsympathetic to witchcraft and by witches unsympathetic to Gardner. He was not, apparently, a particularly truthful man. In various reference books he described himself as a Ph.D. and a D.Litt. Elsewhere he admitted that he had never attended a university. A professor at Leeds University has told how Gardner read a paper on Manx fishing craft to an International Congress on Maritime Folklore, conveying the impression that it was based on his own research. In fact, the paper had been lifted almost entirely from an article that had appeared in the Proceedings of the Isle of Man Natural History Society. In spite of his critics, however, Gardner drew hundreds of new recruits to the cult of witchcraft, and when he died at the age of 80, British newspapers ran headlines on the death of the 'King of the Witches'. Whatever his standing as a scholar, Gardner had become recognized as the leading figure in the witchcraft revival. Since his death witchcraft covens have sprung up all over Britain and the United States, and there are now estimated to be between 10,000 and 20,000 active witches in the United States alone.

Under the influence of Margaret Murray and Gerald Gardner, witchcraft today is dominated by the so-called white witches who claim to be on the side of good. Sybil Leek, one of America's leading living witches, was formerly head of an English coven centred in the New Forest. In an interview with London's *Daily Express* in 1964 she declared, 'I am a white witch and come from a long line of white witches, who exist only to do good.'

The white witches of the 20th century stand outside the

European-American witch tradition with its emphasis on Devil-worship. Modern white witches claim, like Gardner, to be the inheritors of an ancient religious tradition, and not a cult of evil. They point to the derivation of the word 'witch' from the Anglo-Saxon *wicca* meaning 'the wise one,' and use the word Wicca as a name for their cult. The white witches, like their black opposites, use many of the techniques of sorcery and engage in activities that resemble many of the quasi-religious ceremonies of traditional witches. Their worship, however, is directed toward the Earth Mother and the Horned God, and they emphatically deny that there is any link between the Horned God and the Devil. According to Gardner, the two-faced Horned God worshipped by the followers of Wicca is not Satan, but a fertility god usually known by the Roman name of Dianus or Janus. He represents the cycle of the seasons and the crops, and the rites performed in his honour are designed to ensure the continued fruitfulness of the earth. He has also been related to the famous prehistoric painting in the Trois Frères Caves in the French Pyrenees, which appears to depict a dancer in the skin of an animal with great branching antlers. Gardner suggests that the horns on the god led to the confusion with Satan in the minds of Christians, and that some witches may have encouraged this confusion to keep their enemies at a distance.

In the later years of his life, Gardner settled in Castletown on the Isle of Man, where he founded a witchcraft museum. After his death the museum was taken over by Monique Wilson, a Scottish witch who is known as 'the Lady Olwen', and her husband Campbell, a former bomber pilot. Monique Wilson also assumed the title of 'Queen of the Witches'. In a recent interview with the British journalist Colin Cross she explained: 'It is a title conferred by three or more witch covens. It is supposed to be an honour but really it means that I carry the can when anything goes wrong. I adjudicate on disputes that arise in covens under my jurisdiction. Of course there are many covens which are entirely independent. I used to be the only Witch Queen but a few years ago we crowned one for America, where witchcraft is growing very rapidly.'

Monique Wilson estimated that there were about 2,500 witches in Britain. Others have put the figure much higher, at between 5000 and 10,000. 'A coven consists of a minimum of two members and a maximum of 13; when it reaches the limit, it subdivides,' Mrs. Wilson explained. 'A female witch is always initiated by a man, and a male one by a woman.'

Witches are usually naked for their rituals, but the Wilsons denied that the witchcraft movement is really a cover for sex. 'I daresay there are one or two so-called covens which operate for sexual reasons,' said Campbell Wilson. 'Anyone can read a book and start his own coven with his own rules. But in real witchcraft sex is only a very small part of the whole.'

The Wilsons went on to say that there are a few black witches—those who use their power to do people harm—but in their view such witches were rare. However, sufficient evidence exists to suggest that these darker powers of witchcraft—the power to cast damaging spells and lay curses—are no mere superstition, and that they are still being practised today.

In the encyclopedia *Man, Myth and Magic*, the photographer Serge Kordiev described how he and his wife became members of a coven. After he had written an article in a Sunday newspaper describing his interest in the occult, he received a telephone call from a man who asked whether he would be interested in joining a witch cult. He said yes. By appointment the Kordievs were picked up in an expensive car and driven to a large old house. After being given drinks at a bar they were told to strip and put on small black satin aprons. They were then taken into a large room with a black floor and red carpets hanging on the walls. Half a dozen hooded figures stood in front of an altar. A naked man, his body gleaming with oil, appeared before the altar. Two black-robed girls stood on either side of him. The Kordievs were ordered to kneel, to swear perpetual homage to Satan, and to sign their oaths in blood. They were then given magical names, and the naked man placed his hand on their genitals, causing 'a curious tingling sensation'.

After several more meetings the Kordievs began to have second thoughts about the cult. On one occasion a young girl was accused of betraying the group's secrets. She was made to serve as a human altar while a Black Mass was said over her, after which she was ravished by the Master. When the Kordievs discovered that they still had to go through a 'confirmation ceremony' which involved sexual intercourse with the Master and with a High Priestess, they decided to leave the group. Almost immediately their troubles began. One day they returned home late at night to discover an enormous toad sitting on the front doorstep. On another occasion they heard sounds of maniacal laughter and smashing glass coming from Kordiev's studio. When they investigated they found that the studio had been wrecked. But the doors were still locked, and the windows had apparently been smashed from *inside*, with all the glass scattered outside on the lawn. There followed many months of bad luck.

In his book *Experiences of a Present Day Exorcist*, the Reverend Donald Omand gives his opinion that a great deal of 'black magic' is the result of a kind of hostile thought-pressure. He is firmly convinced, for example, that when a worker in a factory is 'sent to Conventry' (an English term for ignoring a co-worker as punishment) the hostile thought waves from the others may cause actual physical and psychological damage—quite apart from any effects that could be ascribed to the power of suggestion. Readers of Ira Levin's novel *Rosemary's Baby* will remember the episode in which a circle of black witches cause someone's death by 'ill wishing'. It could well be that 'ill wishing' and the Reverend Donald Omand's 'hostile thought-pressure' are one and the same phenomenon.

Witchcraft and black magic have achieved an even greater popularity in the United States today than in Britain. The white witches of the United States closely resemble their British counterparts, however, and their activities are largely based on the rituals revived or devised by Gerald Gardner. The two leading white witches of the United States, Sybil Leek and Raymond Buckland, are both of British origin. Sybil Leek claims to trace her witch ancestry back to the 12th century. After her arrival in the United States in 1964, she rapidly became a popular radio and television personality. She now lives in Houston, Texas, where she organizes classes in the occult, broadcasts a nightly radio show, and runs a restaurant called 'Sybil Leek's Cauldron'.

Compared with Sybil Leek, Raymond Buckland has a far more reserved approach to his craft, but he has probably done more than any other American witch to give modern witchcraft a serious image. The High Priest of a New York coven, Buckland edits a monthly magazine on witchcraft called *Beyond*, and has founded his own witchcraft museum on Bay Shore, Long Island.

A one-time disciple of Gerald Gardner, Buckland is scornful of those who claim to be 'King' or 'Queen' of the witches, declaring that the witchcraft movement is far too scattered for such a title to have any meaning. Nevertheless, there have been many attempts to unite the witches of the United States, including the New York-based Witches International Craft Association. This organization is a kind of 'Witches' Liberation Movement'.

American witchcraft also has its darker side with an upsurge of interest in the practice of black magic and Satanism. Most of the black magic groups are located in California, and the rise of such evil cults has been linked with the increased use of hallucinogenic drugs such as mescalin and LSD.

America's most notorious black witch is an ex-circus ring-master and police photographer, Anton Szandor La Vey. On April 30, 1966 La Vey initiated the 'First Church of Satan' on California Street in San Francisco (April 30 is Walpurgis Night, the great feast of the witches' year). La Vey and his followers openly practice black magic, putting evil curses on their opponents, performing weddings, funerals, and baptisms in the name of Lord Satan, and preaching 'indulgence instead of abstinence'. The Church of Satan is dedicated to the worship of the Devil and the glorification of carnal pleasures—a far cry from the assurances of Sybil Leek and the Wilsons.

La Vey, known variously as the 'High Priest of Hell' and the 'Black Pope of America', goes out of his way to look satanic by wearing a pointed black beard, Fu Manchu moustache, and shaven head. He is the author of a work called *The Satanic Bible*, which contains invocations to Satan in a language called 'Enochian' and La Vey's own system of 'satanic morality'. States La Vey, 'Blessed are the strong, for they shall possess the earth. Cursed are the feeble, for they shall be blotted out!'

La Vey's church is expanding, but there are many students of the occult who claim that no one can handle black magic without risk. An event that took place in 1967 seems to support this view. On the evening of June 29 a middle-aged man suddenly collapsed on the floor of his San Francisco apartment. He and his family were all members of La Vey's church. As his wife and son knelt beside him, trying to revive him, they heard a woman's voice coming from his lips, saying, 'I don't want to die.'

The mother and son immediately recognized the voice as that of actress Jayne Mansfield, a fellow member of La Vey's congregation. Later they learned that the actress had died in a road accident earlier that very evening. She had been driving with her attorney on a narrow road near San Francisco when a truck hurtled from under a narrow bridge, and crashed into their car. Jayne Mansfield was decapitated, and her attorney, Sam Brody, was also killed.

Newspaper reporters soon unearthed a story of violent conflict between Brody, who was Jayne Mansfield's lover as well as her attorney, and La Vey. It arose because Jayne Mansfield's film studio was grooming her as a successor to Marilyn Monroe, and rumours of her membership of the Church of Satan were bad publicity. Brody threatened to start a newspaper campaign that would drive La Vey out of San Francisco, and La Vey retaliated by pronouncing a solemn ritual curse on Brody. He told Brody that he would see him dead within a year, and shortly before Jayne Mansfield's death he warned her not to share Brody's car. 'She was the victim of her own frivolity,' said La Vey dispassionately after the crash; but there were members of California's occult underground who declared openly that La Vey's curse had got out of hand, killing the disciple as well as the unbeliever.

In Britain, it has also become clear that the modern witchcraft cult has its negative side, as cases involving 'black magic' and ritual child abuse have made national headlines. Just before midnight on July 10, 1971, two police officers on the island of Jersey, in the English Channel, set off in pursuit of a car that had shot through a red light at high speed. After a chase they caught up with the driver when he abandoned his car in the middle of a field. More police arrived and helped subdue the furiously struggling man. As they bundled him into a police car, one of them noticed something strange about his clothes. Two rows of sharp nails protruded from the shoulders of his jacket. He had another row of nails on his lapels, and wore bands studded with nails on his wrist. At the police station the man was searched. In his pockets police found a wig, a rubber face mask, and a length of pajama cord. It seemed that they had finally caught the 'Jersey rapist'—a man who had been terrorising the island for more than a decade.

The attacks had begun in 1957 when three women had been assaulted by a man with a knife. In April 1958, a man threw a rope around the neck of a girl, dragged her into a field, and raped her. In October 1958, a girl was dragged from a cottage and raped. For over a year attacks ceased. Then in January 1960, they took a more alarming turn. A 10-year-old girl woke up to find a man in her bedroom. He warned her that if she cried out he would shoot both her parents. The man was wearing a rubber mask. He sexually assaulted the girl in her own bed and left by the window, driving off in her father's car. One month later the rapist assaulted a 12-year-old boy. For the next eleven years repeated attacks made Jersey an island of terror. In many cases the masked rapist carried a child out into the garden, committed the assault, and took his victim back to the bedroom.

When the police in 1971 captured the man with a mask and a pajama cord in his pocket, they had little doubt that he was the rapist. His name was Edward John Louis Paisnel, and he was in his early 50s.

Questioned about the peculiar attire he was wearing when he was found, Paisnel told the police that he was on his way to some sort of 'orgy'. He implied that this gathering was connected with black magic, and explained that all the participants were unknown to one another, because they wore masks.

When the police visited Paisnel's home, they discovered that he slept apart from his wife in his own room. In this room they found an alcove containing what appeared to be a small altar. On the altar stood a china toad and a small chalice. Suspended above these objects was a dagger on a length of cord.

In the same room the police found a cupboard that swung away from the wall on hinges. Behind it was a small room containing a blue track suit and a fawn raincoat with nail-studded lapels. Earlier descriptions of the Jersey rapist had mentioned a blue track suit and fawn raincoat.

Nevertheless, Paisnel continued to protest his innocence. He insisted that he was a member of a black magic group and had no connection with the rapes. Then came the break. The car Paisnel had been driving before his arrest proved to have been stolen. In the glove compartment the police discovered a crucifix made of palm fronds—apparently the property of the car's owner. The detective in charge of the case threw it on the table in front of Paisnel and asked: 'Is this yours?'

Paisnel's face went red. His eyes bulged. Then he began to laugh. 'No, it's not mine.' Then after a pause: 'My master would laugh very long and very loud at this.'

The detective had no need to ask him the name of his 'master'. In Paisnel's room the police had found various books on witchcraft and black magic. Paisnel was speaking of the Devil.

The police made one more interesting find. Among Paisnel's books was a biography of the 15th-century child-murderer, Gilles de Rais—the man on whom the story of Bluebeard was based. Gilles de Rais had been one of the richest noblemen in Europe, and had fought bravely at the side of Joan of Arc against the English. His extravagance forced him to mortgage many of his estates, and finally he began to practise black magic, hoping that with the aid of the Devil he could discover the secret of turning lead into gold. Some of these black magic rituals require the 'blood of innocent virgins', and this may explain how Gilles came to acquire his taste for killing children. When Gilles was arrested—for assaulting a priest in the course of a quarrel—his mansion was searched, and the dismembered remains of more than fifty children were found in a locked tower. Gilles admitted that he had murdered the children after committing sadistic attacks on them. He was burned at the stake in October 1440.

It gradually became clear to the police that Paisnel was obsessed by Gilles de Rais. It even seems likely that he believed himself to be a reincarnation of Gilles. No other members of the 'black magic group' were ever discovered. Presumably they existed only in Paisnel's imagination. Charged with seven sexual assaults, Paisnel was found guilty and sentenced to thirty years' imprisonment.

It seems certain that Paisnel was no armchair student of the occult. He practised black magic, and he believed that he had sold his soul to the Devil. He worshipped his 'master' before an altar, and he probably offered up prayers before he set off in search of victims.

The logical view of all this is that he was simply a 'sex maniac' who indulged in devil-worship as a kind of imaginative exercise that enabled him to ignore his conscience. (A 'devotee' always has that advantage over an unbeliever.) But this chapter should at least have raised some doubts about the logical view. The truth is that our scientific rationalism has blinded us to the truth behind witchcraft. And in order to grasp that truth, we have to begin by recognising that *all* primitive people take the reality of the 'spirit world' for granted. We also have to recognise that circumstantial reports of ghosts can be counted in their thousands, that they date back as far as recorded history, and that to try to dismiss all this as superstition is mere silliness. We may reject the Christian notion of the Devil as an embodiment of evil (because surely evil is merely another name for stupidity?), just as we reject the Manichaean notion that matter itself is evil, while still recognising that the evidence for the existence of 'spirits' is very powerful indeed. And the history of spiritualism, like the history of witchcraft, demonstrates that it is not difficult for human beings to establish contact with 'spirits', and that some do so easily and naturally.

So it would probably be a mistake to dismiss Paisnel's devil-worship as sheer self-delusion. The more likely truth is that he was a man whose fantasies had opened him to certain dark forces, and who had become a willing tool of those forces in exchange for the satisfaction of sexual cravings—in short, that he had done what a mediaeval theologian would call 'sold his soul to the Devil'.

It is also interesting to note that his charmed life of immunity came to an end when he stole a car containing a Christian crucifix . . .

11.
Possession: Illusion or Reality?

ACCORDING TO Allan Kardec's *Spirits' Book*, people who die suddenly, or are unprepared for death by reason of wasted lives, are often unaware that they are dead, and become homeless wanderers on the earth, attracted by human beings of like mind, and sharing their lives and experiences. They are able, to some extent, to influence these like-minded people and to make them do their will through suggestion. Some 'low spirits' are activated by malice; others are merely mischievous, and can use energy drawn from human beings to cause physical disturbances—these are known as poltergeists. When Kardec asked: 'Do spirits influence our thoughts and actions?', the answer was: 'Their influence upon [human beings] is greater than you suppose, for it is very often they who direct both.' Asked about possession, the 'spirit' explained that spirits cannot actually take over another person's body, since that belongs to its owner; but a spirit can assimilate itself to a person who has the same defects and qualities as himself, and may dominate such a person. In short, such spirits could be described as 'mind parasites'. (According to Kardec's view, when people indulge in sexual fantasy, they may be providing a kind of pornographic film-show for some homeless spirit, which will then try to influence them to providing more of the same kind of entertainment by putting sexual thoughts into their heads.)

The classic modern book on the subject—*Possession, Demoniacal and Other* (1921)—is by a Tübingen professor, T.K. Oesterreich, and it takes, as one might expect of a respectable academic, a totally sceptical view: Oesterreich dismisses the 'spirit' explanation, insisting that possession is always a case of hysteria or mental illness. He will not even accept the hypothesis of multiple personality, since he cannot believe that the human personality can 'split'.

One of his most impressive pieces of evidence for the hysteria theory is a lengthy account of the famous case of 'Achille', described by the psychiatrist Pierre Janet. Achille, a moderately successful businessman, came from a peasant background, and married early. In the winter of 1890, when he was 33, Achille returned from a business trip in a depressed condition, then suddenly went dumb. One day, he sent for his wife and child, embraced them despairingly, then went into a cataleptic state for two days. When he woke up he was suffering from delusions; he seemed to think he was in Hell, and that demons were burning him and cutting him in pieces. The room, he said, was full of imps, and he was possessed by a devil. After a number of suicide attempts, he was sent to the Salpêtrière Hospital in Paris, under the care of the famous physician Charcot. The latter placed Janet in charge of the case.

Janet watched with interest as Achille displayed all the signs of demoniacal possession, as described in the Middle Ages: in a deep voice he cursed God, then in a shrill voice protested that the Devil had forced him to do it.

At first all Janet's efforts to communicate were a failure; Achille refused to listen to him and resisted all attempts to hypnotise him. Janet saw a possible solution when he observed that Achille was extremely 'absent-minded'—he compares him to someone searching for an umbrella which he holds in his hand. While Achille was raving, Janet quietly inserted a pencil in his hand, then tried ordering him, in a whisper, to make writing movements. The pencil wrote: 'I won't.' 'Who are you?' asked Janet, and the pencil wrote: 'The Devil.' 'I shan't believe you,' Janet replied, 'unless you can give me proof. Can you make Achille raise his left arm without knowing it?' 'Of course . . .'—and Achille raised his arm. 'Why are you doing that?' Janet asked Achille in his normal voice, and Achille looked at his raised arm with astonishment.

The demon went on to demonstrate his powers by making Achille dance, stick out his tongue and kiss a piece of paper. Finally, Janet asked him if he could put Achille into a deep sleep. Moments later, Achille was in a trance. And now Janet was able to question him about the cause of his illness, and quickly learned that Achille had been unfaithful to his wife while away on his business trip, and that deep and intense guilt had caused the depression and other symptoms. Now he was able to induce hallucinations, Janet made Achille believe that his wife was in the room, and had forgiven him for his infidelity. (It is not quite clear from Janet's account whether the wife actually came to the hospital.) After this, Achille's psychological problems soon cleared up.

This is certainly a remarkable case. Yet as a refutation of the 'spirit' view, it is obviously open to one serious objection. If Kardec is correct, it is obvious that people suffering from nervous traumas or states of intense guilt and misery are more likely to become 'obsessed' by spirits than normal healthy persons. Kardec would point out that Achille may have been genuinely 'obsessed' by a mischievous spirit, and that as soon as Janet had made him feel that he was forgiven, the spirit was 'driven out'.

The same view of 'possession' was expressed by Carl Wickland, a Los Angeles doctor: in his book *Thirty Years Among the Dead*, he argues that a great deal of mental illness is caused by a kind of mental invasion by 'homeless spirits'.

Wickland, born in Leiden (Sweden) in 1861, had emigrated to Chicago, where he gained his medical degree; he became a member of the National Association for the Advancement of Science, and a medical adviser to the Los Angeles branch of the National Psychological Institute. It seems likely that he decided to burn his boats and publish his book because, at 63, he was on the verge of retirement anyway, and ridicule would make no difference.

It all began, he explained, with a patient whom he calls Mrs Bl-, who began to practise automatic writing, and who soon began to have fits of derangement in which she used vile language and claimed she was an actress; she had to be committed to an asylum. Another woman, 'an artist and lady of refinement', became convinced that she was a damned soul and knelt in the mud to pray at the top of her voice. Another woman, who owned a millinery shop, posed in her window in her nightclothes, declaring that she was Napoleon, and had to be removed by the police.

Now at this time—in the mid-1890s—the main theory of mental illness was that it could be explained in purely physical terms; many a head physician in a mental home was appointed because he had a working knowledge of brain anatomy. Freud himself was an early convert to this theory (known as organicism), his professor, Dr Theodore Meynert, being one of his chief advocates—he later turned his back on Freud when the latter returned from Paris espousing a new 'psychological' explanation of neurosis based on the idea of the unconscious mind. In America, the favourite theory of mental illness was that it was due to poisons in the system due to such causes as infected tonsils or decayed teeth. But Wickland was intrigued by the case of a youth called Frank James who, after a fall from a motor-cycle at the age of ten, changed from an affectionate, obedient boy to a juvenile delinquent who spent many terms in reformatories and jails. Declared hopelessly insane, he succeeded in escaping from the criminal asylum, and during his recapture was hit on the head with a club. On awakening, he had once again reverted to his earlier personality—gentle and good-natured.

This convinced Wickland of the inadequacy of the 'toxaemia' theory. And while he was still a medical student, the accident of marrying a woman who proved to be an excellent 'medium' soon provided him with evidence of an alternative theory. One day, Wickland was dissecting a leg in the medical school, and, on his return home, was alarmed when his wife Anna seemed to be about to faint. He placed his hand on her shoulder, and was startled when she drew herself up and said threateningly: 'What do you mean by cutting me?' After a few questions, it became clear that he was speaking to the spirit of the owner of the leg he had been dissecting. Wickland guided Anna to a chair, and the spirit objected that he had no right to touch him. When Wickland replied that he was touching his wife, it retorted: 'What are you talking about? I am no woman—I'm a man.' Eventually, Wickland reasoned it into recognising that it was dead, and that dissecting its old body would do it no harm. When it asked for a chew of tobacco or a pipe, Wickland had to explain that his wife was a non-smoker. (The next day he observed that the teeth of the corpse were heavily stained with tobacco.) More detailed explanation finally convinced the man that he was dead, and he left.

This showed Wickland that a 'ghost' may believe that it is still alive—particularly if death came unexpectedly. He also encountered a case that seemed to demonstrate that spirits did not need to manifest themselves through a 'medium'. When he was alone one day, dissecting a female corpse, he thought he heard a distant voice shout: 'Don't murder me!' A newspaper on the floor made a rustling noise, as if it was being crushed. Some days later, at a seance, a spirit who gave her name as Minnie Morgan claimed that it was she had shouted 'Don't murder me!' and crushed the newspaper. Minnie also had to be convinced that she was no longer alive.

At seances, entities who spoke through his wife later explained to Wickland that such 'homeless spirits'—those who are unaware that they are dead—are attracted by the warmth of the 'human aura'—a kind of energy-sphere which is supposed to surround the human body—and, under certain circumstances, may attach themselves to its owner as a kind of mental parasite. In effect, such spirits are in a state of sleep, in which dreams and reality are confused, and—as in sleep—the dreamer is unaware that he is dreaming.

In her introduction to a new edition of Oesterreich's *Possession*, the paranormal investigator Anita Gregory has some harsh words to say about Wickland and his *Thirty Years Among the Dead*. She points out that there is a basic sameness about all his cases—he always has to convince a spirit that it is dead—and his account of how the spirits of Madame Blavatsky and Mary Baker Eddy expressed contrition for their false doctrines is almost laughable. Yet anyone who then turns to Wickland's book will have to admit that these objections are less important than they sound. For the central issue is of Wickland's honesty. Unless we decide to take the view that he was a liar and self-deceiver on a practically unimaginable scale—which seems unlikely—then it seems clear that his evidence is in total agreement with Kardec's views on possession. Even Anita Gregory has to admit that Oesterreich's rationalism is often crude and unconvincing, and that he deals with subtleties by ignoring them.

Perhaps the most obvious example of Oesterreich's failure to allow facts to speak for themselves is in his account of one of the most famous of all cases of 'possession', that of 'the Watseka wonder', a girl called Lurancy Vennum. In July 1877, 13-year-old Lurancy, of Watseka, Illinois, had a fit, after which she became prone to trances. In these trances she became a medium, and a number of disagreeable personalities manifested themselves through her. On February 11, 1878, placed under hypnosis by a local doctor, Lurancy stated that there was a spirit in the room called Mary Roff, and a Mrs Roff who was also present exclaimed: 'That's my daughter'. Mary had died at the age of 18, twelve years earlier. Lurancy then stated that Mary was going to be allowed to take over her body for the next three months.

The next day, Lurancy claimed to be Mary Roff. She asked to be taken back to the Roffs' home, and on the way there recognised their previous home, in which they had lived while she was alive, and which was unknown to Lurancy. She also recognised Mary Roff's sister, who was standing at the window. And during the next few weeks, 'Mary' showed a precise and detailed knowledge of the Roff household and of Mary's past, recognising old acquaintances and toys and recalling long-forgotten incidents. On May 21, the day she had declared she had to leave, she took a tearful farewell of her family, and on the way home 'became' Lurancy again. The case was investigated by Richard Hodgson, one of the most sceptical members of the Society for Psychical Research, who was convinced of its genuineness.

Readers of Hodgson's account of the 'Watseka wonder' will find it very hard to find loopholes; Mary provided such detailed proof of her knowledge of her early years, and of the family background—recognising unhesitatingly anyone Mary had known—that the notion of trickery or delusion becomes untenable; it is perhaps the single most convincing case of 'possession' in the history of psychical research. But Oesterreich merely quotes William James's summary of the case—from *Principles of Psychology*—making no attempt to analyse it, and passing on quickly to other matters—in spite of the fact that James himself had spoken of 'the plausibility of the spiritualistic interpretation of the phenomenon'. And Anita Gregory concludes her own introduction by admitting that she is unable to declare that all the people in Oesterreich's book are frauds, dupes, lunatics and psychopaths, and ends: 'So I shall conclude . . . that the phenomena described by Oesterreich are very much in need of an explanation.'

Oesterreich's *pièce de résistance* is a long account of the famous case of the 'Devils of Loudun', which, in 1952, was made the subject of a full-length study by Aldous Huxley. In 1633, Urbain Grandier, the parish priest of the small French town of Loudun, was charged with bewitching the nuns in a local convent and causing them to be possessed by demons, so that they screamed blasphemies and obscenities, and writhed about on the floor displaying their private parts. Grandier had become notorious for his immoralities—he had impregnated two of his penitents and seduced many others—and had made many enemies. Inquisitors claimed to find 'devil's marks' on his body, and in a trial that was a travesty of justice, he was found guilty and sentenced to be burned alive. Even under torture, and later at the stake, Grandier maintained his innocence. His death made no difference, and the nuns continued to be possessed by 'demons' for many years after.

Oesterreich, like Aldous Huxley, takes the view that all this could be explained simply in terms of hysteria, (a view I must admit that I shared at the time I wrote *The Occult*) while another authority, Rossell Hope Robbins, goes even further in his *Encyclopedia of Witchcraft and Demonology*, and attributes the manifestations to outright imposture. But a careful reading of Huxley's own book makes either of these explanations seem implausible. It is easy to see how sex-starved nuns could deceive themselves into believing that they were possessed by devils—the Mother Superior of the convent, Soeur Jeanne des Anges, admits in her autobiography that she made no real attempt to combat the possession because she enjoyed the sexual stirrings aroused in her by the demons. But it is far more difficult to understand what then happened to the exorcists themselves. Fr. Lactance, who had superintended the torture, became 'possessed' and died insane within a month; five years later, Fr. Tranquille died of exhaustion after months of battling against the 'invaders' of his psyche, and was amazed to witness his body writhing on the ground and hear himself uttering blasphemies which he was powerless to prevent. Fr. Lucas, another of Grandier's persecutors, met the same fate. The 'witch pricker', Dr Mannouri, also died in delirium. Fr. Jean-Joseph Surin, a genuinely saintly man, who was called to Loudun to try and exorcise the nuns after Grandier's execution, himself fell victim to the 'devils', and became periodically insane for twenty-five years. It is difficult to believe that ordinary hysteria could produce such results. Surin described in a letter how the 'alien spirit' was united to his own, 'constituting a second me, as though I had two souls . . .' Considering these facts, the sceptical Anita Gregory admits that 'one is probably not justified in assuming that . . . the Loudun pandemonium [was] necessarily nothing but collective delusion.' And bearing in mind Kardec's comment that 'a spirit does not enter into a body as you enter into a house . . . he assimilates himself to a [person] who has the same defects and the same qualities as himself', the hypothesis that the Loudun 'pandemonium' was caused by Wickland's earth-bound spirits seems, on the whole, more plausible than religious hysteria.

It is difficult to draw a clear dividing line between 'possession' and poltergeist manifestations. The most widely held current view, as we have seen, is that they are a form of 'spontaneous psychokinesis' (mind over matter) caused by the unconscious mind of an emotionally disturbed adolescent, but this theory fails to explain how the unconscious mind can cause heavy objects to fly through the air—in laboratory experiments, 'psychics' have so far failed to move any object larger than a compass needle. According to Kardec's 'informants', poltergeists are earthbound spirits who are, under certain conditions, able to draw energy from the living, and to make use of negative energies 'exuded' by the emotionally disturbed and the sexually frustrated.

The Loudun case seems to provide support for this view. Soeur Jeanne's autobiography makes it clear that her own sexual frustrations alone could have provided a host of 'entities' with the necessary energy. And by the time a dozen or so nuns were writhing on the floor and making suggestions that caused even decadent aristocrats to blush, the convent must have been awash with sexual energy. Most cases of possession in nunneries seem to involve the same feverish sexuality. Two decades before the

Loudun case, 14-year-old Madeleine de Demandolx de la Palud was seduced by her confessor, Fr. Louis Gaufridi, twenty years her senior; the liaison was broken up, and she was sent to a nunnery at Aix-en-Provence. Two years later, Madeleine began to see devils, and smashed a crucifix. Her hysteria soon spread to the other nuns; Madeleine accused Gaufridi not only of seducing her, but of introducing her to various diabolic practices. Gaufridi was asked to try and exorcise the demons, and, when he failed, was put in prison.

At his trial, Madeleine declared that her allegations were all imaginings, after which she began to move her hips back and forth in a 'lascivious manner'. The judge chose to disbelieve her disclaimer, and Gaufridi was tortured until he 'confessed', then was burned at the stake.

It is important to realise that fornication among the clergy was a commonplace in the 17th century, and that seduction of nuns by their confessors was far from rare. In 1625, an orphan named Madeleine Bavent was seduced by a Franciscan priest, appropriately called Bonnetemps. In the following year she entered a convent at Louviers run by Fr. Pierre David, who secretly belonged to the Illuminati—a sect who believed that the Holy Spirit could do no harm, and that therefore sex was perfectly acceptable among priests. Fr. David apparently insisted that Madeleine should strip to the waist as he administered communion; other nuns, she later claimed, strolled around naked. She claimed that she and Fr David never engaged in actual intercourse—only mutual masturbation—and that when Fr. David died in 1628, his successor Fr. Mathurin Picard continued to caress her genitals during confession.

It was after Fr. Picard's death in 1642 (when Madeleine was 35) that the nuns began to manifest the usual signs of possession, writhing on the ground, contorting their bodies, and making howling noises like animals, as they alleged they were being ravished by demons. Fourteen of the 52 nuns exhibited these symptoms, and all put the blame on Madeleine.

Madeleine then told the full story of Fr. David, Fr. Picard, and the latter's assistant Fr. Boulle. She claimed that Fr. Picard and Fr. Boulle had indulged in various 'magical' acts involving communion wafers and menstrual blood, and eventually in 'sabbats', in which a Black Mass was recited. The priests had draped their erections with consecrated wafers with a hole cut in the middle and 'thus arrayed gave themselves to the women present'—Madeleine being favoured five or six times.

Madeleine was accused of being a witch and discharged from the order; the corpse of Fr. Picard was dug up, excommunicated, and tossed on to a refuse heap. This led the priest's brother to create a scandal, and the result was a trial that ended with Fr. Boulle being tortured and burned alive, together with another priest called Duval. Madeleine, confined in a convent and brutally treated, made several suicide attempts, and finally died at the age of 40. The Louviers nuns were all dispersed to other convents.

Madeleine's descriptions of sabbats and Black Masses sound like pure invention. But, as we saw in the previous chapter, the notorious Chambre Ardente (Lighted Chamber) affair, half a century later, revealed that many priests took part in such practices. It is difficult for us to understand why the Church was involved in this wave of demonology—the likeliest explanation is that 17th century rationalism was undermining its authority, and that the protest against this authority took the form of licentiousness and black magic. Whatever the explanation, the Chambre Ardente transcripts leave no doubt but that it really happened.

Another investigator who came to believe that 'possession' was due to spirits was Max Freedom Long, an American schoolmaster who arrived in Hawaii in 1917, at the age of 27, and began to make a study of its native 'magicians', the Kahunas or 'keepers of the secret.'[1] According to the Huna religion, Long discovered, man has three 'selves', the 'low self', the 'middle self' and the 'high self'. The low self is basically emotional, and corresponds roughly to Freud's unconscious mind. The middle self is our ordinary, everyday consciousness. The high self might be called the superconscious mind, and can foresee the future. After death, the three selves may become separated, and it is the low self that sometimes becomes a poltergeist. The middle self may become a 'ghost'. In his book *The Secret Science Behind Miracles*, Long also discusses the phenomenon of multiple personality, and expresses

1. See article on 'The Curse of the Pharaohs' in my *Encyclopedia of Unsolved Mysteries*, volume one.

the view that this is often due to 'possession', either by a low self or a middle self, or a combination of the two. He describes the case of a Californian girl with two personalities, which took over the body for years at a time, and how, when doctors tried to amalgamate the two under hypnosis, a third personality appeared, who told them that the girl should be left as she was, with two spirits sharing the body. This third personality Long believes to be the 'high self'.

Two more eminent American investigators came to accept the possibility of 'possession'. The philosopher William James was converted from his early scepticism to a belief in 'spirits' through the mediumship of Mrs Leonore Piper, whose 'control', Phinuit, was able to tell him all kinds of things that he could not possibly know by normal means. James was to agree that if a medium can be 'possessed' by a spirit, then it is possible that other people might be. James's close friend Professor James Hyslop was another sceptic who was 'converted' by Mrs Piper. But he had a more practical reason for becoming convinced of the reality of 'possession'. When Hyslop was president of the American Society for Psychical Research in 1907, he was visited by a goldsmith named Frederick Thompson, who was convinced that he had become 'possessed' by the spirit of a painter, Robert Swain Gifford, whom he had met on a few occasions. After Gifford's death, Thompson had begun to hear Gifford's voice urging him to draw and paint—something he had never done before. Although he had no artistic training, Thompson began to paint in Gifford's style. What convinced Hyslop was that Thompson painted pictures of places that he had never been to, but which Gifford *had*. Some of these proved to be identical to Gifford's final sketches—which Thompson had never seen—and when Hyslop visited the New England swamps and coastal regions he recognised them as the subject of these sketches.

Hyslop consulted a neurologist, Dr Titus Bull, about Thompson. And Bull himself was to to conclude that many cases of mental illness really involved 'possession'. In one case, the patient—who had suffered a head injury—claimed that he had been 'taken over' by the spirit of a painter named Josef Selleny, who had been a friend of the Emperor Maximilian, and who was 'forcing' him to paint. (Wickland claimed that such accidents as head injuries would provide opportunity for alien 'entities' to invade.) Lengthy researches by Bull's assistant Helen Lambert—a wealthy woman with time to spare—finally uncovered the existence of a real Josef Selleny (the encyclopedias mistakenly spelt it Joseph, but the patient spelt it correctly), who had, indeed, been a friend of the Emperor Maximilian. A medium who worked with Dr Bull was able to reveal that the patient was being possessed by several 'entities', one of whom seized possession of her body and grabbed Bull by the throat. Eventually, the various entities were dislodged or persuaded to go away. Mrs Lambert's account, later published in her book *A General Survey of Psychic Phenomena*, sounds remarkably like many cases described by Carl Wickland. The few available cases make it clear that Bull's name deserves a distinguished place in the annals of psychical research.

Dr Adam Crabtree, a psychiatrist who lives and works in Toronto, began to give serious consideration to the idea of possession as a result of treating patients who claimed to hear 'voices' inside their heads.

Now such cases are not particularly rare, and 'hearing voices' is certainly not a sign of madness. Dr Julian Jaynes, a Princeton psychologist, began to make a study of auditory hallucinations after experiencing one himself—he was lying on a couch when he heard a voice speaking from the air above his head. Naturally concerned about his sanity, Jaynes discovered, to his relief, that about ten per cent of people have had hallucinations of some sort, and that about a third of these take the form of 'phantom voices'. One perfectly normal young housewife told him that she held long conversations with her dead grandmother every morning when she made the beds.

Jaynes, of course, takes it for granted that such experiences *are* hallucinations, and for a long time Adam Crabtree shared that belief. Then he encountered a case that raised some basic doubts. It concerned a young woman named Sarah Worthington, who was the patient of a female colleague of Crabtree's called Jenny. After a treatment that had been initially successful, Sarah Worthington had suddenly plunged into moods of depression in which she was tempted to commit suicide.

The three of them met in Crabtree's office, and he began to probe her difficulties. One of his questions was whether she had ever heard voices inside her head, and she admitted that she had. Crabtree asked her to lie down and relax, and to do her best to try to recall these inner conversations. Almost immediately, the girl's body tensed, and she exclaimed: 'Oh, the heat! I'm hot!' And as she went on speaking, both psychiatrists observed the change in her voice. Sarah lacked confidence; this new personality had the voice of someone who was used to exercising authority. When they asked the woman what she wanted to do, she replied: 'Help Sarah.' It was a clear indication that this was *not* Sarah. They asked the woman her name, and she replied: 'Sarah Jackson.' She identified herself as Sarah's grandmother. Crabtree explained that he and Jenny were also trying to help Sarah, and asked the 'grandmother' if she would be willing to help; she replied yes. This ended the first session.

At the next session, the grandmother soon came back. She was still talking about a fire, and at one point she asked: 'Where is Jason?' Jason, it transpired, was her son, and the fire she was referring to had taken place in 1910. Sarah Jackson had rushed home as soon as she heard that there was a fire in her street—her seven-year-old son had been left in the house alone. The whole neighbourhood was ablaze. In fact, Jason had been moved to safety by neighbours, but it took Sarah Jackson another hour to discover this, and in the meantime she had rushed around the streets in a frenzy, stifling in the heat. The experience had imprinted itself deep in her consciousness.

According to the grandmother, she had 'taken possession' of Sarah Worthington when her granddaughter was playing the piano—both of them loved music. And it soon became clear that, in spite of her avowed intention of helping her granddaughter, it was Sarah Jackson herself who was in need of help. She was tormented by guilt feelings about her own life—particularly about how badly she had treated her daughter Elizabeth, Sarah's mother. Elizabeth had developed into an unhappy, neurotic girl, who had in turn treated her own daughter badly. And Sarah's relations with her mother were a strange duplicate of Elizabeth's relations with *her* mother. Both mothers had greatly preferred their son to their daughter, and had taught the daughter that men were everything and women nothing. The grandmother had become fully aware of all this by the time she died, which is why she now felt that she had to help her granddaughter. Instead of helping, she had made things worse; Sarah was frightened and confused by the voice inside her, and was becoming desperate.

Now grandmother Jackson was 'out in the open', things became much easier. She was able to give the psychiatrists invaluable information about Sarah's family background. And although Sarah was at first astonished to realise that her grandmother was speaking through her, she gradually learned to accept it, and began to achieve deeper insight into her problems. At the end of two months she was cured. The grandmother remained a 'possessing presence', but now Sarah understood it she was no longer afraid; in fact, it gave her a sense of comfort to feel that her grandmother was a vaguely beneficent presence in the background of her life.

The reader's reaction to this story is probably much the same as my own, when I first read it in the typescript of Adam Crabtree's *Multiple Man*: that there must be some purely psychological explanation. Sarah had known her grandmother as a child; perhaps she had heard the story about the fire from her own lips. Perhaps she recognised how similar her mother's problems had been to her own. And her unconscious mind had 're-told' her the story as a rationalisation of her own sufferings . . . But the more I read of Crabtree's book (which his publishers had sent to me, asking if I would write an introduction) the more I saw that such explanations are unacceptable. He goes on to recount another eight cases from his practice, each one involving some type of 'possession'. And after the third or fourth case, the unconscious mind explanation had begun to wear very thin. A social worker named Susan was unable to sustain any normal relationship with a male, and recognised, correctly, that this was due to some deep resentment towards her father. Crabtree was able to speak to her father—who had died in a car crash—just as he spoke to Sarah's grandmother, and he learned that he had been sexually obsessed with his daughter. Until she was 16, he had crept into her bedroom after she was asleep and had fondled her genitals. On some unconscious level, she was aware of what was happening. She recognised his desire for her, and treated him with contempt, behaving provocatively and exercising her new-found sexual power to make him squirm. The contempt spread into her relations with boyfriends and caused problems. When her father died in the car crash, he was drawn to his daughter as a 'place of refuge', and she was vulnerable to him because of the sexual interference. Once 'inside' her, he was in a condition of 'foggy sleep', unaware of his identity or his present position. Crabtree patiently explained to Susan's father that he was actually dead, and that he ought to leave his daughter alone. And one day, he simply failed to appear at the therapeutic session; Susan experienced a sense of relief and freedom.

I found one case particularly fascinating and intriguing; it concerned a university professor called Art, whose first marriage had been unsuccessful, and who was about to embark on a second. He was beginning to experience a deep reluctance to go through with the marriage, and he associated this with 'inner storms' in which a censorious voice criticised him and various people he knew. He was vaguely aware that the voice sounded like his mother—who was living in Detroit—and he had arrived at the commonsense explanation that the voice was some negative aspect of himself, and that he had somehow incorporated elements of his mother, who had always been intensely possessive towards him.

Crabtree followed his usual procedure, placing Art in a state of deep relaxation, and then opening a dialogue with the mother, who was called Veronica. Veronica was perfectly willing to talk at length about her relation to her son, and about why she disapproved of so many of his friends. 'Veronica came across as blatantly, almost naively, self-centred . . .' She explained that she simply wanted to make her son recognise that many people he trusted—including his future wife—were stupid and scheming and not worthy of his respect.

Crabtree asked her if she thought all this interference could be good for her son, or even good for herself, and she finally admitted that the answer was probably no. In Detroit she was living a drab and boring life, and Crabtree pointed out that if she paid more attention to her own affairs and less to her son's, things might improve.

During the therapy, Art's mother discovered that she had a cancerous growth, and had to have an operation. The 'Veronica' who spoke through Art's mouth agreed that this might be because she was robbing herself of vitality by 'possessing' her son. And at this point, Art's 'inner voice' began to fade, until he finally ceased to hear it. But there was a remarkable change in his mother in Detroit. She had been experiencing a slow deterioration, and emotional withdrawal from life. Now, suddenly, her vitality began to return; she started going out and making new friends. 'She seemed to have gained the proverbial new lease on life.'

Crabtree insists that his own attitude towards such cases is not that of a believer in the paranormal; he claims to be merely an observer, a phenomenologist, who simply treats each case 'as if' it were possession. And clearly, there is nothing contradictory in such an attitude; Susan and Sarah and Art *could* have been manufacturing the voices themselves; the unconscious mind is capable of far more remarkable feats. Still, the fact remains that most readers will feel that, taken all together, these cases make an overwhelming impression of being something more than unconscious self-deception.

I turned back to Julian Jaynes to see what he had to say about 'disembodied voices'. He outlines his theory in a remarkable work called *The Origin of Consciousness in the Breakdown of the Bicameral Mind*, published in 1976 ('bicameral' means simply having two compartments.) Jaynes advances the extraordinary theory that our remote ancestors heard 'voices' all the time, the reason being that—according to Jaynes—early man lacked all self-awareness in our modern sense of the word. Jaynes believes that our cave-man ancestors could not look inside themselves and say: 'Now let me think . . .', because they had no 'inner me'. Their eyes were like a car's headlamps, directed permanently towards the outside world. So if one of these men was ordered to go and build a dam down the river, he would find it extremely difficult to remember why he was ambling along the river bank. But his sense of purpose would be refreshed by a voice—the voice of his chief—which seemed to come from the air above his head, and which would repeat his instructions.

And where would such voices come from? According to Jaynes, from the right side of the brain—the hemisphere which, as we have seen, houses the 'other self', Hudson's 'subjective mind'. If that is correct, it certainly offers a plausible explanation for the voice of Sarah's grandmother and Susan's father and Art's mother—in fact, in the latter case, it sounds far more convincing than the notion that a living woman in Detroit could somehow 'get inside' her son's head in distant Toronto.

It is when Jaynes goes on to discuss the voices heard by mental patients that certain doubts begin to arise. He points out that most of the cases that have been studied involve schizophrenics, and says: 'They converse, threaten, curse, criticise, consult, often in short sentences. They admonish, console, mock, command, or sometimes simply announce everything that's happening. They yell, whine, sneer, and vary from the slightest whisper to a thunderous shout. Often the voices take on some special peculiarity, such as speaking very slowly, scanning, rhyming, or in rhythms, or even foreign languages. There may be one particular voice, more often a few voices, and occasionally many . . .'

The voices described by Crabtree do not sound in the least like this bewildering babble; they apparently conversed like any normal person. And the same applies to the housewife who held long conversations with her grandmother as she was making the beds. There is no reason, of course, why 'phantom voices' should not sound like those of a normal person; but it seems to be a fact that most of them don't.

This is confirmed by a study made by another clinical psychologist, Dr Wilson Van Dusen, formerly of the Mendocino State Hospital in California. Van Dusen spent sixteen years observing the effect of hallucinations, and he describes his findings in a chapter called 'The Presence of Spirits in Madness' in his book *The Presence of Other Worlds*. His conclusions are, perhaps, even more startling than those of Julian Jaynes.

Van Dusen explains that most patients who are hallucinating prefer to keep their experiences to themselves, since they know it will be taken as a proof that they are mad. However, one unusually co-operative patient asked him if he would mind talking directly with her hallucinations, and he did. Naturally, the hallucination could not answer Van Dusen direct: he had to ask the patient to give an account of what he could hear and see. But there was nothing to stop Van Dusen addressing the hallucination directly. 'In this way I could hold long dialogues with a patient's hallucinations and record both my questions and their answers.'

And, like Adam Crabtree, he insists: 'My method was that of phenomenology. My only purpose was to describe the patient's experiences as accurately as possible. The reader may notice that I treat the hallucinations as realities—that is what they are to the patient.'

One consistent finding, says Van Dusen, was that the patients felt as if they had contact with another world or order of beings. 'Most thought these other persons were living. All objected to the term "hallucination".'

'For most individuals the hallucinations came on quite suddenly. One woman was working in the garden when an unseen man addressed her. Another man described sudden loud noises and voices he heard when riding in a bus. Most were frightened, and adjusted with difficulty to this new experience. All the patients described voices as having the quality of a real voice, sometimes louder, sometimes softer, than normal voices. The experience they described was quite unlike thoughts or fantasies; when things are seen they appear fully real. For instance, a patient described being awakened one night by air force officers calling him to the service of his country. He got up and was dressing when he noticed their insignia wasn't quite right, then their faces altered. With this he knew they were of the Other Order and struck one hard in the face. He hit the wall and injured his hand. He could not distinguish them from reality until he noticed the insignia . . .

'Most patients soon realise that they are having experiences that others do not share, and for this reason learn to keep quiet about them. Many suffer insults, threats and attacks for years from voices with no one around them aware of it.'

Perhaps Van Dusen's most significant finding is that he learned that his patients seemed to experience two distinct kinds of 'voices'; he speaks of these as the 'higher order' and the 'lower order':

'Lower order voices are similar to drunken bums at a bar who like to tease and torment just for the fun of it. They suggest lewd acts and then scold the patient for considering them. They find a weak point of conscience, and work on it interminably.

For instance, one man heard voices teasing him for three years over a ten cent debt he had already paid. They call the patient every conceivable name, suggest every lewd act, steal memories or ideas right out of consciousness, threaten death, and work on the patient's credibility in every way. For instance, they brag that they will produce some disaster on the morrow and then claim credit for one in the daily paper. They suggest foolish acts, such as raise your right hand in the air and stay that way, and tease if he does it and threaten him if he doesn't.'

In fact, it seems clear that these 'lower order' hallucinations behave exactly like bored children with nothing better to do.

'The vocabulary and range of ideas of the lower order is limited, but they have a persistent will to destroy. They invade every nook and cranny of privacy, work on every weakness and belief, claim awesome powers, make promises, and then undermine the patient's will . . .'

'A few ideas can be repeated endlessly. One voice just said 'hey' for months while the patient tried to figure out whether 'hey' or 'hay' was meant. Even when I was supposedly speaking to an engineer . . . the engineer was unable to do any more arithmetic than simple sums . . . The lower order voices seem incapable of sequential reasoning. Though they often claim to be in some distant city, they cannot report more than the patient hears, sees or remembers. They seem imprisoned in the lowest level of the patient's mind . . .'

The 'lower order', then, are basically tormenters. But about one fifth of the hallucinations seem to be of a higher order, and they, on the other hand, seem concerned with helping the patient. The 'higher order' is much more likely to be symbolic, religious, supportive, genuinely instructive; it can communicate directly with the inner feelings of the patient. It is similar to Jung's archetypes, whereas the 'lower order' is like Freud's id. Van Dusen mentions a case of a gaspipe fitter who experienced a 'higher-order' hallucination of a lovely woman who entertained him while showing him thousands of symbols: '. . . his female vision showed a knowledge of religion and myth far beyond the patient's comprehension.' After Van Dusen had been holding a dialogue with this 'higher-order' hallucination, the gaspipe fitter asked for just one clue to what they had been talking about.

Van Dusen reports that he has been told by these 'higher-order' beings 'that the purpose of the lower order is to illuminate all of the person's weaknesses'. And the purpose—or one of the purposes—of the 'higher order' seems to be to protect people against the 'lower order':

'This contrast may be illustrated by the experiences of one man. He had heard the lower order arguing for a long while about how they would murder him. He also had a light come to him at night, like the sun. He knew it was a different order because the light respected his freedom and would withdraw if it frightened him. In contrast, the lower order worked against his will, and would attack if it could sense fear in him. This rarer higher order seldom speaks, whereas the lower order can talk endlessly.'

While the 'lower order' 'is consistently nonreligious and anti-religious', jeering angrily at the least mention of religion, the 'higher order' 'appeared strangely gifted, sensitive, wise and religious'.

Van Dusen made one extremely striking observation about the hallucinations. Although he was able to observe a very large number of them over the years, he soon realised that 'after 20 patients, there wasn't much to be learned' because the hallucinations were all so similar. This in itself seems baffling. After all, one would expect to find as many different types of hallucination as there are people. For example, one might expect vets to have hallucinations that claim to be talking animals, engineers to be tormented by talking machines, gardeners to be haunted by talking plants or trees, librarians by talking books, dentists by talking sets of false teeth. Nothing of the sort. The 'lower-order' hallucinations were all strikingly similar; so were those of the 'higher order'. This either implies some basic similarity in the part of our minds that create hallucinations, or something far stranger . . .

Van Dusen is inclined to believe in something far stranger. Through his interest in 'hypnagogic phenomena'—the odd dreams and visions we sometimes experience on the edge of sleep—Van Dusen seems to have turned to the writings of Emanuel Swedenborg, whose *Journal of Dreams* is full of fascinating raw material for the psychiatrist.

Swedenborg described at some length what it was like to be 'possessed' by spirits, and Van Dusen was struck by the extraordinary similarity between Swedenborg's accounts and the hallucinations described by patients in the Mendocino State Hospital. Swedenborg says that spirits and angels can converse with man directly by entering 'by an internal way into his organ of hearing, thus affecting it from within'. Swedenborg goes on: 'To speak with spirits at this day is rarely granted because it is dangerous . . .', which clearly seems to imply that there was some past age in which men could converse more directly with 'spirits'. The explanation Swedenborg gives is that spirits do not normally know 'they are with man', because there is a kind of barrier between these entities and man's own consciousness. If spirits get through this barrier—or are allowed through because a man has dabbled in 'the occult'—they are likely to become a nuisance. 'Evil spirits are such that they regard man with deadly hatred, and desire nothing more than to destroy him, both body and soul.' Swedenborg also mentions that the barrier between spirits and human consciousness may be broken by people who 'indulge much in fantasies, so as to remove themselves from the delights proper to the natural man'. This, says Van Dusen, is a pretty good description of what we now call schizophrenia. (We should note that schizophrenia does *not* mean 'split personality'—as the modern misconception has it—but simply a withdrawal from reality.)

'All of Swedenborg's observations on the effect of evil spirits entering man's consciousness conform to my findings,' says Van Dusen. And he mentions passages in Swedenborg in which the characteristics of the 'lower order' are described: their determination to destroy a man, their ability to cause anxiety or pain, their desire to destroy conscience, their hatred of religion, their tendency to bully, threaten, deceive and lie, and their curious skill at mimicry. All these characteristics of the 'lower order', as experienced by mental patients, are specifically described in the writings of Swedenborg. Van Dusen was particularly struck by their hatred of religion. 'If voices are merely the patient's unconscious coming forth, I would have no reason to expect them to be particularly for or against religion. Yet the lower order can be counted on to give its most scurrilous comments to any suggestion of religion.' Swedenborg also notes the obsession of the 'lower order' with filth and obscenity, another point noted by Van Dusen.

Van Dusen also observed that although the lower order claim to be individuals, they seldom reveal any trace of real personal identity. Swedenborg explains that the personal memory is taken from them at death, so they are forced to rely on the memory and abilities of the person they are 'possessing'. Another striking similarity between Swedenborg's spirits and the 'lower order' is the attempt to possess some organ or part of the patient's body. 'Several worked on one patient's ear, and he seemed to grow deafer. One voice worked for two years to capture a patient's eye, which went visibly out of alignment.' They often set out to possess the genitals. 'One female patient described her sexual relations with her male spirit as both more pleasurable and more inward than normal intercourse.'

There is an equally striking correspondence between the 'higher order' described by mental patients and the entities Swedenborg calls 'angels'. The angels are kind, helpful and wise. The reason that they are so sparing of words is that man's 'interior mind' does not think in words, but in 'universals which comprise many particulars'—that is to say, in intuitive insights. They are, in short, a right-brain function. Or, to put it another way, 'angels' communicate through the right cerebral hemisphere, and prefer symbols—we may recollect Van Dusen's gaspipe fitter who was shown hundreds of universal symbols in an hour by his 'higher order' mentor. Swedenborg also notes that 'higher order' spirits can see the lower ones, but not vice versa—which again corresponded to Van Dusen's own experience.

Van Dusen was inclined to wonder why 'higher-order' hallucinations are so much rarer than those of the 'lower order' (approximately one fifth as many). Swedenborg suggests an answer. Angels, he says, possess the very interior of man, and their 'influx is tacit'. So they are simply less apparent than the hostile spirits, who make sure their presence is recognised. What are we to make of all this? Both Crabtree and Van Dusen insist that they try to function solely as observers, implying that the reader can choose which explanation he prefers—spirits or the unconscious mind. But we have seen that Van Dusen is inclined to wonder why, if the 'lower order' is merely the patient's unconscious, they should show such consistent hostility to religion. And how can we explain the following story from Crabtree's book? An acquaintance of Crabtree's called Pat was invited by a girlfriend to spend a weekend at her grandparents' farm. The grandparents turned out to be dabblers in the occult, and parts of the house, such as the attic, gave Pat peculiar feelings of uneasiness. Later, the grandparents suggested that Pat should try automatic writing, which she did with some misgivings. The moment she took the pen in her hand and relaxed, she slipped into a drugged, trance-like state, and experienced a numbness in her hand and arm. She seemed to see a woman who appeared behind her; the woman had a doll-like face, and wore a long mauve gown. Pat felt as though her energies were being usurped by this woman, and suddenly her hand wrote: 'Elizabeth Barrett Browning here.' (Her hosts had earlier mentioned Elizabeth Barrett Browning.) There followed a long message which included the information that Mrs Browning and Robert were having difficulty getting used to their 'new surroundings'. Slowly, the energy seemed to diminish until the writing stopped. But Pat felt oddly dissociated for the rest of the day.

Later that evening a second session was held. This time several different 'entities' used Pat's hand to write, and the messages were of a 'coarse nature'. At a third session, 'Mrs Browning' answered the question 'Where do you live now?' 'Everywhere . . . nowhere. We are you and you are us.' After that she seemed to become very cagey.

Then the handwriting changed to that of Pat's deceased brother Tom, and there was a message of love and comfort. But when Pat said how moved she felt, her girlfriend snapped: 'That wasn't Tom. They'll pretend to be anyone.' Evidently she knew a great deal about 'lower-order' entities.

Later, one of the grandparents remarked that some entity no longer seemed to be in the house; it had left because it was attracted to Pat's aura. Pat was disturbed at the thought that she had been used as a kind of sponge to soak up some dubious force.

Back home again, Pat began to hear 'Elizabeth' 's voice inside her head, and she felt oddly detached from reality. 'Elizabeth' tried to persuade her to do more automatic writing, but she felt that if she did this, she would only be consolidating the 'spirit's' hold. 'We need you', said 'Elizabeth'. 'If you refuse to speak to us we shall live in your room, in your walls.'

Pat's girlfriend had told her that if she ignored the entity, it would soon go away. She found that it was not as easy as that. She tried reading a trashy novel and ignoring the voice, but a sensation that someone was pressing her face against her own made it hard to concentrate. In bed she tossed and turned so violently that she had to remake the bed several times. But she felt that her 'starvation' technique was the right one. After a few days, her ability to concentrate began to return; slowly, little by little, the influence of the entities (for she felt there was more than one) began to diminish. Finally, she had the impression that she could actually see the woman in the mauve dress receding, turning first into a mauve mass, then into a 'low grade vibration'.

Pat may have been very suggestible, and her unconscious mind may have created the woman in mauve, but it must be admitted that this explanation seems less convincing than the alternative—that Pat had willingly opened herself to one of the 'lower order', and had to extricate herself as best she could. Descriptions of this type of possession are familiar in 'occult' literature. The American researcher Alan Vaughan describes how he himself became 'possessed' for a time. He had bought himself a ouija board, to amuse a friend who was convalescing. Soon he was receiving all kinds of messages, some of which seemed to convey information that was not available to Vaughan's own unconscious mind—for example, when the radio announced the death of the newspaper columnist Dorothy Kilgallen, from a heart attack, they asked the board if this was true; it replied that she had actually died of poison. Ten days later, this proved to be true. (It was suspected—and still is—that she died because she knew too much about the John F. Kennedy assassination.) Then, to his alarm, Vaughan found that a spirit who called itself 'Nada' ('nothing'—recalling 'Elizabeth' 's answer to the question about where she lived) had 'got inside his head'. 'I could hear her voice repeating the same phrases over and over again'—in the typical manner of the 'lower order'. When asked about this, the board replied: 'Awful consequences—possession.'

A friend who understood such matters undertook to help Vaughan, and another 'spirit' took possession of his hand and made him write a message: 'Each of us has a spirit while living. Do not meddle with the spirits of the dead.' Then the spirit seemed to cause an uprising of energy in Vaughan's body which pushed both 'Nada' and the helpful entity out of the top of Vaughan's head:

'I felt a tremendous sense of elation and physical wellbeing . . . My mind began to race in some extended dimension that knew no confines of time or space. For the first time, I began to sense what was going on in other people's minds, and, to my astonishment, I began to sense the future through some kind of extended awareness . . .'[1]

Here again, we can see that Vaughan's account seems to tally closely with what Swedenborg had to say about angels and spirits. 'Nada' repeated the same phrases over and over again, as the 'lower order' always do. She identified herself as the wife of a Nantucket sea captain, and Vaughan remarks that she seemed to resent the fact that he was alive and she was dead. The entity that helped to push 'Nada' out of Vaughan's head sounds very much like one of Swedenborg's angels.

But could not both entities have been a product of Vaughan's 'right brain', as Julian Jaynes suggests? This is conceivable; yet again, there *does* seem to be a distinction between the manifestations of the right brain, and 'lower order' entities. The right brain is the intuitive self—the aspect of us that provides insight and 'inspiration'—such as the tunes that 'walked into' Mozart's head. It has better things to do than repeat the same stupid phrase over and over again.

The distinction can be seen clearly in a case I have described elsewhere,[2] that of Brad Absetz, an American teacher living in Finland, who accidentally stumbled upon the trick of establishing contact with his 'other self'. After the death of their child from cancer, Brad Absetz's wife retreated into a state of schizophrenia.

1. Alan Vaughan: *Patterns of Prophecy*, 1973, p. 4.
2. *Access to Inner Worlds: The Story of Brad Absetz*, 1983.

For hours at a time, she would lie on the bed, her eyes closed, struggling with guilt and depression. Brad would lie there beside her, waiting for her to emerge from these sessions of gloomy introspection so he could comfort and encourage her. He lay totally alert, waiting for the slightest movement that would indicate that she was returning to normal awareness. Yet clearly, a man who lies on a bed for hours at a time will drift into a state of relaxation. One day, as he lay there in this combined state of relaxation and alertness, he experienced a curious sense of inner freedom, of release from the body, almost as if floating clear of the bed. Then he noticed an impulse in the muscles of his arm, as if it wanted to move. Brad mentally gave his arm 'permission to move', and it floated up into the air. Soon both arms were making spontaneous movements, while he looked on as a bystander.

In the dining hall, where buffet meals were served, his hands showed a disposition to select food for themselves; for several weeks, he allowed them to select the food they preferred—it was seldom what he would have chosen himself—and noticed that he began to lose weight, and to feel fitter than ever before. His 'hand' later used crayons and paints to create an extraordinary series of paintings, and to make metal sculptures. It also began to write poems in free-verse form, and these poems were remarkable for a certain clarity and purity of language.

What had happened is that the right-brain self had begun to express itself; we might say that in the parliament of his mind, the member for the unconscious had worked up the courage to start making speeches. Psychologists refer to the right brain as the 'non-dominant hemisphere'; in most of us, it behaves like a suppressed housewife who never dares to utter her own opinion. Brad's hours of quiescence had taught her to overcome her shyness.

One day when he took up a pencil to allow his hand to write, the handwriting was quite different from his own. A woman named herself and briefly introduced herself. Brad's immediate reaction was a powerful sense of rejection. He pushed the paper away, and said forcefully: 'I will not be a mouthpiece for anyone but myself.' The 'communicator' went away and did not return. Here we seem to have a clear distinction between the 'voice' of the right brain and some external communicator or spirit.

In short, whether we accept it or not, it seems there is a *prima facie* case for the existence of disembodied entities that can, under certain circumstances, 'get inside the heads' of human beings. When this happens 'by invitation'—that is, when the human being goes into a trance and allows himself—or herself—to be used by the entity, it is known as mediumship. When it happens involuntarily, as in the case of Alan Vaughan, it is known as possession.

The case that first drew Adam Crabtree's attention to the phenomenon dated from the last decade of the 19th century, and had been described in a pamphlet called *Begone Satan*, by the Rev. Carl Vogel. In 1896, a 14-year-old Wisconsin girl named Anna Ecklund began to be troubled by a desire to commit what she considered 'unspeakable sexual acts', and by an inability to enter Catholic churches, complicated by a desire to attack holy objects. Her problems were ignored for sixteen years, then Reisinger, a Capuchin monk from the nearby community of St Anthony at Marathon, performed an exorcism which brought relief. But it was only temporary. In 1928—when Anna was 46—he decided to try again, this time at the convent of Earling, Iowa. The results of the 23-day exorcism were spectacular, and many of the nuns were so exhausted by the appalling goings-on that they had to be transferred to another convent.

Before the exorcism began, a number of the strongest nuns held Anna down on the bed. But as soon as Reisinger began to speak, Anna's body shot up into the air and landed high up on the wall, apparently holding on 'with catlike grip'. She was dragged down to the bed again, and as soon as Reisinger began again, began to howl and screech so loudly that people in the street ran to the convent to find out what was happening. Then various 'demons' spoke through the girl in different voices, although her mouth did not move. Her face became twisted, and her whole body contorted into extraordinary positions. Her head swelled and became bright red. She also vomited large quantities of 'foul matter'.

She also displayed another common phenomenon of possession: speaking in languages of which she had no conscious knowledge; when the exorcist spoke in German or Latin, she would reply in the same language. When food was sprinkled surreptitiously with holy water, she knew it instantly.

A 'demon' who identified himself as Beelzebub told the exorcist that he and his cohorts had been invited to enter the girl by her father, who had been infuriated by her rejection of his attempts at incest. The exorcist succeeded in 'summoning' the father, who confirmed this story. His common-law wife also spoke through Anna's mouth, and admitted to killing four of her babies (she was probably referring to abortions). During all this time, Anna herself was 'unconscious', so in fact the spirits were speaking through her as through a medium.

During the course of the exorcism, the pastor was involved in a strange car accident. And on the twenty-third day, Anna's body shot erect off the bed so that only her heels remained in contact. Then she collapsed on her knees, and a terrible voice repeated the names of the departing spirits, until it seemed to die away in the distance. As a kind of parting shot, the room filled with an appalling stench. At this point, Anna opened her eyes and smiled.

Crabtree interviewed the monk who had translated Vogel's pamphlet into English, and who was able to confirm the details. So when he encountered the case of Sarah Worthington, he found it easier to accept that he was dealing with a case of 'possession'.

In fact, Crabtree insists that he merely accepts possession as a working hypothesis—a hypothesis that happens, in fact, to work. He is saying, in effect, that his cases might really involve some strange, complex activity of the unconscious—like 'multiple personality'—but that by treating it as possession, he can cure his patients.

But Ralph Allison, another psychiatrist whose work interested Crabtree, had been forced to go a step further. In 1972, Allison was treating a mousy little woman called Janette, who experienced impulses to kill her husband and children. When another psychiatrist expressed the view that Janette was a case of dual personality, Allison asked her to relax deeply (in effect, into a semi-hypnotic state) and asked to speak to the 'other person'. Immediately, a harsh, grating voice that identified itself as 'Lydia' remarked: 'God, it's good to be rid of that piss-ass Janette'. Like

Gibert's patient Leonie in Le Havre, Janette clearly had a hostile alter-ego.

Allison came to the interesting and perceptive conclusion that Janette was simply too passive, and that if she became a more active person, Lydia would gradually vanish. And now—as in the Leonie case—a third and altogether more balanced personality also emerged (identifying heself as Karen). Allison came to refer to such personalities as the 'inner self-helper'. And with Karen's help—and Janette's efforts to be a less passive person—Allison was able to effect a cure. In this case, he was undoubtedly dealing with a case of multiple personality.

In this case, the basic hypothesis of multiple personality covered the facts—that a traumatic childhood had caused the 'prime personality' to withdraw from the problems of life, like an ostrich burying its head in the sand. But Allison's next patient, a girl called Carrie, forced him to take the 'possession' hypothesis seriously. Carrie was another 'multiple' with a history of childhood traumas, including a gang rape. Even without hypnosis, an alter-ego called Wanda emerged and talked to Allison. But it seemed clear that Wanda was not responsible for the suicidal impulses. When told that a 'psychic' claimed that Carrie was possessed by the spirit of a drug addict who had died of an overdose in New York in 1968, Allison decided to 'give the concept of spirit possession a try'. Under deep hypnosis, Carrie agreed that the drug-addict was influencing her life, and Allison's makeshift 'exorcism'—using a swinging crystal ball on a chain—apparently succeeded. Then Allison tried 'exorcising' Wanda, and was again apparently successful. Unfortunately, the treatment still failed to dislodge two other personalities, and Carrie eventually committed suicide.

Yet Allison continued to reject the notion of 'spirit possession' until he encountered a girl called Elise, who revealed several personalities under hypnosis. Most of these were able to describe their history—what trauma had caused them to be 'born'. But one of them claimed to be a man called Dennis, who explained that he had entered Elise's body when she was experimenting with black magic as a teenager, and that he enjoyed remaining there because he liked having sex with another of Elise's personalities, a girl called Shannon. The sex was not, as might be supposed, a bodiless intercourse between two 'spirits': when Shannon took over Elise's body, and had sex with a man, Dennis would enter the man's body. And although Elise and Shannon shared the same body, Dennis was not interested in sex with Elise, only with Shannon. Eventually, with the help of another 'inner self-helper', Elise was cured. It was this case that finally convinced Allison that multiple personality may sometimes be a case of spirit possession.

It was William Blatty's book *The Exorcist*—and the film based on it—that caused a flood of popular books and articles on exorcism. The case took place in a Washington suburb, Mount Rainier, in 1949.

13-year-old Douglass Deen was the 'focus' of the occurrences, which began with a scratching noise in the walls. A rat extermination company was able to find no sign of rats or mice. The sounds occurred only when Douglass was near by. Then more usual poltergeist phenomena began to occur: dishes flew through the air, fruit was hurled against the wall. A picture floated off the wall, hovered in the air, then went back to its old position. After this, Douglass's bed began to shake and quiver when he was in it.

The family asked the local minister, the Reverend M. Winston, for help, and on February 17, 1949 Douglass spent the night in his home. The two retired to a room with twin beds. Douglass's bed soon began to vibrate, and there were scratching noises in the walls. Winston asked Douglass to sleep in an armchair. The chair slid over to the wall, then slowly tilted until it threw the boy on the floor. The minister improvised a bed on the floor; as soon as Douglass was in it, the bed slid across the room.

As these events continued, the boy was taken to two hospitals— Georgetown and St Louis University, both Jesuit institutions. All attempts to treat him medically and psychiatrically were unsuccessful. Finally, a Jesuit priest undertook the exorcism. He fasted for two and a half months on bread and water, and repeated the ritual of exorcism no fewer than thirty times. The 'spirit' showed its objection to these rituals—or perhaps its contempt—by sending the boy into convulsions, making him scream obscenities and blasphemies in a shrill voice, and sometimes making him reply to the exorcism in Latin—a language he had never studied. Finally, in May 1949, the phenomena ceased; the thirtieth exorcism was apparently successful. But then, as we have seen, most poltergeist phenomena last only a month or so; it may have gone away of its own accord.

Here, then, we have a case of poltergeist disturbances that turned into 'demoniacal possession', with all the phenomena that occurred in the Loudun case. The 'psychological' explanation would be that Douglass Deen's 'other self' began by producing poltergeist disturbances, then took up the game of demonic possession suggested by the Jesuit fathers. (His ability to speak Latin is not as surprising as it sounds; he must have heard a great deal of Latin during his life—at mass—and may have picked it up unconsciously.) But Kardec's explanation about a mischievous spirit fits equally well. If Kardec is correct, then the physical changes that occur during puberty cause a 'leakage' of a certain type of energy that can be used by a poltergeist; this energy is probably some form of nerve-force. When the physical adjustments of puberty have been made, the leak stops, and the poltergeist can no longer manifest itself.

Why did a poltergeist invade the Deen family home? In the film of *The Exorcist*, a reason is provided: the daughter of the house plays with a ouija board. There is no evidence that this happened in the Deen case, but it is certainly consistent with what we know about poltergeists—we may recall the Phelps case (Chapter 6), which started when the Rev. Phelps began trying to contact 'spirits'.

All this sounds thoroughly alarming, and may worry people of nervous disposition. But a number of points should be borne in mind. Spirits, according to Swedenborg, have no power to actually 'invade' the body—or mind—of a normal person. If they manage to do so because they are more-or-less invited—as in the case of Crabtree's patient Pat, who became hostess to 'Elizabeth Barrett Browning'—the sitting tenant is at a basic advantage, as a householder is encountering a squatter. Pat's determined refusal to encourage her 'squatter' finally had the desired effect, and 'Elizabeth' went away.

The conclusion is straightforward. The fact that 'possession' can actually occur is no more alarming than the fact that black holes exist. It merely indicates that the universe is a stranger and more complex place than our great-grandparents assumed. But then, even our great-grandparents knew that it is better to be acquainted with facts than to be ignorant of them.

Postscript: A Note on Reincarnation.

The case of Lurancy Vennum and Mary Roff, cited at the beginning of this chapter, raises another important question. The account is consistent with the teaching of Allen Kardec who—as we have seen—asserts the reality of reincarnation in *The Spirits' Book*. It is also consistent with Kardec's view that the body is merely a vehicle which, like any other vehicle, might be used by more than one driver.

Reincarnation, the notion that we return to earth many times, is a part of the religious belief of Hindus and Buddhists. Some of the most convincing accounts of reincarnation come from India.

In the early 1930s the case of a girl called Shanti Devi excited worldwide attention. Kumari Shanti Devi was born in Delhi on October 12, 1926, and, when she was 4, she began to talk about a town called Muttra, a hundred miles away. She claimed that she had lived there in a yellow house, and that her husband had been a man called Kedar Nath Chaubey. The principal of the local school was so intrigued by all this that he examined Shanti, and asked where her husband lived; Shanti gave him an address. The principal wrote to Kedar Nath, and to his astonishment received a reply verifying that he was a widower, whose wife—a girl called Ludgi—had died ten years earlier. He confirmed in detail many things that Shanti had related.

However, a hundred miles was a long way to travel, so Kedar Nath wrote to a cousin in Delhi and asked him to call on Shanti Devi's family.

The cousin, Kanji Mal, arrived at the door, and was instantly recognized by Shanti. He went away totally convinced. The result was that Kedar Nath hurried to Delhi. Shanti, wildly excited, flung herself into his arms. She then answered in detail all kinds of questions about her life with him. All Kedar's doubts vanished. This was undoubtedly his former wife. But what on earth could he *do* about it? He could hardly take a 10-year-old girl back to his home . . . So, sad and perplexed, he returned to Muttra. A few days later, Shanti was taken to Muttra by her parents, together with three scientific investigators. And from the moment she arrived, no one had the slightest doubt that she was genuine. Among the crowd on the station platform she recognized an elderly man as her brother-in-law. Then, in a carriage, she directed ⁺he driver, and showed an intimate knowledge of the town—also pointing out a number of houses that had been built since she died. She directed the carriage to the house in which she had lived with Kedar, then to another house into which they had moved later. She led them to an old well, which had now been filled in, and showed the spot in one of the rooms where she had buried a hundred rupees in the earth floor. The men dug, and found only an empty jewel-box—at which point Kedar Nath admitted with embarrassment that he had found the box and spent the money. Later, Shanti recognized her former parents and her brother in the crowd. All this was placed on record, and caused such a stir that it was reported in newspapers all over the world.

Cases like that of Shanti Devi—and there were many others—were studied by Professor Hemendra Banerjee of Rajasthan University. And in America Dr Ian Stevenson of the University of Virginia began an exhaustive scientific study of such cases, his first results being published in 1966 under the cautious title of *Twenty Cases Suggestive of Reincarnation*. His cases come from India, Ceylon (now Sri Lanka), Brazil and Alaska, and all are full of documented evidence. A single one will give a sample of his astonishing material.

In 1954 a 3-year-old boy called Jasbir Lal Jat died of smallpox. Before he could be buried the next day, the corpse stirred and revived. It was some weeks before the child could speak, but when he did his parents were astonished that his personality had changed completely. He announced that he was the son of a Brahmin family (a higher caste than his 'present' family) who lived in the village of Vehedi, and he refused to eat food unless it was cooked by a Brahmin. He said that he had been poisoned by some doctored sweets, and had fallen off a cart, smashed his skull and died. Jasbir's family were, understandably, sceptical, assuming that his illness had affected his mind. But they began to reconsider in 1957 when a Brahmin lady from Vehedi came to Jasbir's village, and he instantly recognized her as his aunt. Jasbir was taken back to Vehedi and, like Shanti Devi, led the party round the village, showing a detailed knowledge of its lay-out, and recognized members of his family. His name, in his previous existence, had been Sobha Ram. The accusation about the poisoned sweets was never satisfactorily cleared up—Sobha Ram was said to have died of smallpox—but Dr Stevenson's detailed account leaves no doubt that Jasbir knew too much about Vehedi and the life of Sobha Ram for any deception to have taken place.

The oddest point about this case, of course, is that Jasbir was already three and a half when he 'died', and was taken over by the 'spirit' of Sobha Ram—*who died at the same time*. The logical explanation, therefore, would seem to be that Jasbir really died, and that the spirit of Sobha Ram grabbed the body before 'brain death' occurred and fought his way back to life. This raises some fascinating questions about the whole relation between spirit and matter, life and death . . .

Stevenson points out that most of the really convincing cases of reincarnation take place in cultures that already accept reincarnation as a fact. This, as we have already seen, is not always so. In 1910 a 5-year-old girl named Alexandrina Samona died in Palermo, Sicily, and her mother was wild with grief. Soon after, she had a dream in which her dead child assured her that she would return in the form of a baby. Later that year Adela Samona gave birth to twins, one of whom was the double of Alexandrina, and who was therefore given her name. (The other was a totally different personality.) When the new Alexandrina was ten, her mother took her on an outing to the town of Monreale, where Alexandrina had never been before. Yet the child insisted that she *had*. She described various things she had seen in the town, and said that she had been there with her mother and a woman with 'horns' on her forehead—whereupon Signora Samona recalled that a few months before the death of the first Alexandrina they *had* been to Monreale, accompanied by a neighbour who had unsightly cysts on her forehead. Other details recalled by Alexandrina also proved correct. This case gave rise to widespread interest, and was reported together with lengthy depositions of everyone concerned, leaving little doubt about the basic accuracy of the facts.

In recent years there has been a steadily increasing interest in reincarnation, dating from 1956 when a book entitled *The Search for Bridey Murphy* became a best-seller. A hypnotist named Morey Bernstein placed a Colorado housewife, Virginia Tighe, in a trance, and asked her questions about the period before she was born (a technique known as 'regression'). Mrs Tighe declared that in the 19th century she had been an Irish girl named Bridey Murphy, who lived in Cork—she gave extremely detailed information about her life there. The case caused a sensation, which collapsed abruptly when an American newspaper ran an 'exposé', declaring that Mrs Tighe had had an Irish aunt who told her endless stories about Ireland, and that as a child she had lived opposite a woman called Bridey Corkell, with whose son she was in love. . . . Yet on closer investigation it is impossible to dismiss the Bridey Murphy case as unconscious self-deception. To begin with, the newspaper that did the exposé was the one that had failed to gain the serial rights on Bernstein's book, which had gone to a rival. It emerged that Virginia had never met her 'Irish aunt' until she was eighteen, and that she was certainly never in love with Mrs Corkell's son—who turned out to be the editor of the Sunday edition of the newspaper that denounced her. But the general public are not interested in such fine points as these; as far as they were concerned, Bridey Murphy had been proved to be a fake.

Other hypnotists, like Arnall Bloxham (an Englishman) and Joe Keeton, began to try the techniques of 'regression', and produced astonishing information that seemed to prove that patients *could* recall their 'past lives'. One of Bloxham's subjects gave an impressive account of being a naval gunner at the time of Nelson; while another, a housewife, recalled many past lives, including one of being a Jewess involved in an anti-semitic pogrom in York. Her knowledge of ancient history proved to be astonishingly detailed (as Jeffrey Iverson has recounted in his book *More Lives than One?*). A professor identified the church she had described—in the crypt of which the hunted Jews took refuge—as St Mary's, the only problem being that St Mary's had no crypt. A few months later, workmen renovating the church discovered the crypt.

Now book after book appeared with powerful evidence for reincarnation. In *The Cathars and Reincarnation*, Dr Arthur Guirdham described a patient called 'Mrs Smith' who had dreams and visions of being alive in 13th-century France, as a member of a persecuted sect called the Cathars, who were finally exterminated by the Inquisition. Guirdham had himself been interested in the Cathars because he had also had strange dreams about them. Now, stimulated by Mrs Smith's detailed 'dream knowledge' of the period, he investigated Catharism with the aid of French scholars, and found that she was correct again and again; when she and scholars disagreed, it was usually she who turned out to be correct. In *Second Time Round* Edward Ryall described in detail memories of a previous existence as a West-Country farmer who lived during the reign of Charles II and took part in the battle of Sedgemoor. In *Lives to Remember*, Peter Underwood and Leonard Wilder described hypnotic experiments with a housewife, Peggy Bailey, and detailed memories of three of her previous lives.

Yet obviously the problem here is one of how far we can accept the evidence of people who have become convinced that reincarnation is a reality. To many sceptics Arthur Guirdham's case is undermined by his admission that he was also a Cathar in a previous existence, and—by a strange coincidence—the lover of the previous Mrs Smith. The reader of A. J. Stewart's *Died 1513, Born 1929* is bound to experience a certain incredulity to learn that, in her previous existence, Miss Stewart was James II of Scotland.

In 1981 the sceptics found a formidable champion in Ian Wilson, whose book *Mind Out of Time?* is a devastating analysis of some of the cases of reincarnation. I myself am quoted approvingly because of an experiment I conducted on BBC television in which a housewife was made to hallucinate as an evil clergyman by means of post-hypnotic suggestion. Wilson goes on to show how easily our unconscious minds can deceive us, citing many cases in which people have convinced themselves that long-buried memories of some book they once read are actually memories of past lives. He points out, for example, that the man who thought he had been a gunner in one of Nelson's ships had read C. S. Forester's Hornblower novels as a child and could easily have picked up his 'facts' from them. His final considered assessment is that most cases of reincarnation are actually examples of the strange psychological illness known as 'multiple personality'.

Wilson's scepticism is salutary and bracing. But the book suffers from the defect of most attempts to 'explode' a particular belief: it seems to ignore some of the most convincing evidence. Anyone who is interested in reincarnation immediately turns to the index to see what he makes of the Lurancy Vennum case—and discovers that, for some odd reason, he does not even mention it. Discussing Stevenson's cases, he objects that so many involve young children, and points out that children often fantasise about being somebody else. But he only has one brief and indirect reference to the astonishing case of Jasbir Lal Jat, and prefers to pick holes and find minor errors in less well-documented cases.

And then Wilson seriously undermines his own arguments by citing one of the most remarkable cases of recent years—that of the Pollock twins. In May 1975 two sisters—Joanna and Jacqueline Pollock, aged 11 and 6—were killed by a car that mounted the pavement. In October 1958 Mrs Pollock had female twins, who were called Jennifer and Gillian. Jennifer had a scar on her forehead in exactly the place her dead sister Jacqueline had had one. When the twins were only four months old, the family moved away from Hexham to Whitley Bay. But when the twins were taken back three years later, they behaved as if they had known it all their lives, recognizing the school, the playground and the old house where their sisters had lived. When Mrs Pollock decided to open a locked cupboard in which she had kept the dead children's toys, the twins immediately recognised them item by item, naming all the dolls. One day Mrs Pollock was shocked to find them playing a game in which one twin cradled the other's head saying, 'The blood's coming out of your eyes. That's where the car hit you.' But the Pollocks had been careful never to tell their children anything about how their sisters had died.

So although Mr Wilson points out that the evidence is by no means watertight—because John Pollock himself believes in reincarnation—he leaves most readers with the impression

364

that it is quite strong enough for any reasonable person. And when, at the end of his discussion of the Bridey Murphy case, he admits reluctantly: '. . . when the dubious and the downright spurious has been discarded, there remain signs of some not yet understood phenomenon at work,' most readers will be inclined to wonder why he considers himself a sceptic.

12.
Magicians and Wonder Workers

IT WOULD BE A mistake to think of the magician as the male form of the witch. (In fact, the word 'witch' can apply to both men and women.) But in the long occult tradition, the magician is distinguished from the witch by his desire to achieve *intellectual* mastery over the principles of nature. Magicians like Paracelsus and Cornelius Agrippa regarded themselves as scientists rather than as sorcerers—as becomes clear from Lynn Thorndike's vast *History of Magic and Experimental Science*, in which there is no attempt to distinguish one from the other.

But what also becomes very clear from the history of magic is that most of the 'great magicians' were driven by another motive: the desire for personal fame and power. And, more often than not, this has been their downfall.

In primitive tribal societies, the magician was indistinguishable from the witch. We have seen—in the chapter on witches—how modern tribal *shamans*—like those described in F. Bruce Lamb's *Wizard of the Upper Amazon*—are actually able to lure animals into the area where hunters are waiting for them. And there seems no reason to doubt that the *shamans* depicted by our Cro-magnon ancestors in their cave paintings were able to do the same thing.

Slowly, over the course of many thousands of years, the tribal shaman evolved into the modern sorcerer. That is, he ceased to be what is called a white witch—a benevolent and helpful worker of magic—and became more interested in obtaining power for himself. We can see this transformation beginning in the Old Testament prophets such as Moses, Joshua, Elijah, and Daniel. It is true that they are men of God, and that their power apparently comes from God. But it is significant how often they are engaged in magical contests in which they demonstrate their power at the expense of competing magicians. Aaron throws down his rod in front of the Pharaoh and it turns into a snake. The rival Egyptian magicians do the same thing and their rods also become snakes. But Aaron's snake eats up all the other snakes. Elijah challenges four hundred and fifty priests of Baal to a test of magic in which they are to call on their god to light the fire under a sacrificial bullock. Their god fails them. Elijah, with great dramatic flair, tells his people to drench his bullock and firewood with water three times. Then he calls upon Jehovah. The God of the Jews sends down a fire that consumes the bullock, the wood, and the water. After this, Elijah orders the people to kill all the priests of Baal. The will to power swaggers through the whole story.

The desire to dominate, to assert themselves, to humiliate or destroy those who oppose them is something that can be observed again and again in the lives of the great magicians. Moreover, the magical contest—the battle with a rival—is a standard feature of the lives of the magicians. In the 1st century AD the Greek magician Apollonius of Tyana engaged in a contest with a rival named Euphrates. Simon Magus, the magician of Samaria referred to in the Acts of the Apostles, was supposed to have been challenged by St. Peter. The legend is that Simon conjured up huge black hounds that rushed at Peter.

The apostle held out a loaf of holy bread, and the hounds vanished into thin air. In one version of the legend, Simon then rose into the air, hovered for a moment, and flew through a window. Peter fell to his knees and prayed, whereupon Simon plummeted to the ground. He died from his injuries in this fall.

There can be no doubt that many such stories are pure invention. Others, however, are too detailed—and too widely reported—to be wholly invented. The interesting question is:

What genuine powers did men such as Simon Magus possess? The account of him given in the Acts of the Apostles is, understandably, belittling. Describing himself as 'some great one,' Simon angered St. Peter by offering him money in exchange for the gift of the Holy Spirit. Christian documents are inclined to regard Simon as a charlatan. He claimed to be able to make himself invisible, change himself into an animal, and walk unharmed through fire. The Christians said that all this was achieved by bewitching the senses of the onlookers. Modern writers have taken this to mean that he used some form of hypnosis. For example, legend says that when Simon went to Rome, Nero ordered him to be decapitated by one of his officers. Simon, however, bewitched the officer into decapitating a ram instead. When he reappeared with his head still on his shoulders, Nero was so impressed by his powers that he made Simon his court magician.

But was Simon's means of control over the officer ordinary hypnosis or was it the kind of Psi power exercised by Wolf Messing (see p. 54) when he induced the bank clerk to hand over ten thousand roubles. The latter is altogether more likely, because hypnosis usually takes the co-operation of the person about to be hypnotised. It is unlikely that Simon was able to make himself invisible or turn himself into an animal. But he certainly seemed to have command of the power of thought pressure, just as some people are born with a green thumb.

At this point, it is time to raise the question of how such a power could work. Let us look more closely at some of the recorded examples.

The poet W. B. Yeats was a member of the order of the *Golden Dawn*, one of the first and best known occult societies of late 19th century England. In his autobiography Yeats describes an incident that occurred on a walk taken by one of the other Golden Dawn members and MacGregor Mathers, one of the order's founders. 'Look at those sheep,' said Mathers. 'I am going to imagine myself a ram.' The sheep immediately began to run after him.

Mathers could also use his strange powers on people, just as the Swedish playwright August Strindberg believed he himself could. Once when Strindberg was eating alone in a restaurant, he recognised two friends among some drunk people at another table. To his dismay, one of them began to approach him. Strindberg fixed his eyes on the man. At this, the friend looked bewildered and returned to his table apparently convinced that Strindberg was a stranger.

Strindberg once attempted to practise black magic, and he believed that his later suffering and bad luck was a result of this dabbling with evil forces. It was when he was separated from his second wife. He wanted desperately to bring about a reconciliation, and had to think of a way of seeing her. He decided to use his telepathic powers to make his daughter just sick enough to require a visit from him. Using a photograph of the girl, he tried to bring about her illness. When the two children of his first marriage got sick a short time later, he felt that he was responsible, and that his use of the evil eye had misfired. Strindberg dates his misfortunes from then on.

A mixture of hypnosis and telepathy was used in a series of experiments conducted by the Soviet scientist Leonid Vasiliev in the 1920s and 1930s. The aim of the experiments was to discover not only whether telepathic communication was possible but also if it could be proved. In one test, Vasiliev used a hypnotist and a hypnotic subject who, the hypnotist claimed, could be made to fall asleep by telepathic suggestion. The hypnotist was placed in one room, and the subject in another. Only Vasiliev and his assistants knew precisely when the hypnotist made the mental suggestion. In repeated tests, they established that the subject fell asleep within one and a half minutes of the suggestion. Later, they discovered that distance made no difference. A subject in the Crimean city of Sebastopol fell asleep at a telepathic suggestion made in Leningrad, more than one thousand miles away. Vasiliev wondered whether telepathic communication might depend upon some kind of electromagnetic radiation, and tried sealing the hypnotist up in a lead chamber. It made no difference whatever, proving that the waves involved in telepathy have nothing in common with radio waves.

After Simon Magus, the most famous magician in European history is Faust, also known as Dr Faustus. The Faust legend has maintained its potency for almost five centuries, and has inspired at least three great works of literature—Christopher Marlowe's *Dr Faustus* (1604), Goethe's *Faust* (1808 and 1832), and Thomas Mann's *Doctor Faustus* (1947)—as well as many musical works. From all these, the picture that emerges of Faust is of a brilliant, proud, restless man who longs to share the secrets of the gods. But these characteristics have evolved over the centuries, and as we go backward in time we come closer to the truth about the person who called himself Faust. Thomas Mann's Faust is a great musician; Goethe's Faust is a restless scholar, chafing against the frustration of being merely human; Marlowe's Faustus is a scholar who has been led into temptation by the lust for power. The book on which all these were based is Johann Spies' *Historia von D. Johann Faustus*, which appeared in Berlin in 1587. Its hero is little more than a magical confidence trickster. Significantly, his chief gift is hypnosis—although, of course, the author does not use that word.

In a typical episode in the Spies' book, Faust goes to a Jew and offers to leave behind his arm or leg as security for a loan. The Jew accepts, and Faust appears to saw off his leg. Embarrassed and disgusted by this, the Jew later throws the leg into a river—whereupon Faust appears and demands his leg back. The Jew is forced to pay him heavy compensation. In another anecdote, Faust asks a wagoner with a load of hay how much hay he will allow him to eat for a few pence. The wagoner says jokingly: 'As much as you like.' When Faust has eaten half the wagonload, the wagoner repents his generosity and offers Faust a gold piece on condition he leaves the rest undevoured. When he reaches home the wagoner discovers that his load is intact, 'for the delusion which the doctor had raised was vanished'.

Even the Faust of this original book is described as 'a scholar and a gentleman.' He is said to have been the son of honest German peasants, born near Weimar in 1491, but brought up by a well-to-do uncle in Wittenberg. This uncle sent him to university. Faust's 'strong powers of mind' soon distinguish him, and his friends urge him to enter the Church. But Faust has greater ambitions. He begins to dabble in sorcery. He studies Chaldean, Greek, and Arabic. He takes his degree of Doctor of Divinity, and also a medical degree. In due course, he becomes a famous doctor. It is intellectual brilliance that is his downfall, 'the boldness of his profane enquiries'—a quality that later generations would consider a virtue, and for which even Spies has a sneaking admiration. Faust wishes to become a great magician, and this is why he invokes the Devil. Having entered into his pact with the Devil, Faust is corrupted by the Prince of Darkness, who proceeds to fill him with greed and lust for power.

At this point, it is worth quoting the *Historia* on a subject that has some bearing on the lives of magicians. 'It used to be an old saying that the magician, charm he ever so wisely for a year together, was never a sixpence richer for all his efforts.' This belief that unusual powers cannot be used for financial gain is fundamental and persistent. And there seems to be some truth in it. None of the great magicians from Simon Magus to MacGregor Mathers has died rich, and most of them have died paupers. The few who have succeeded in living comfortably—Emmanuel Swedenborg and Gurdjieff, for example—made their money in other ways than magic.

When we pass from the Faust legends to the obscure original, as described by some of his contemporaries, we encounter exactly the sort of person that this investigation has led us to expect: a coarse, vulgar, boastful man, with some natural talent and an overmastering desire for fame. We don't know if he was named Georg Sabellicus or Johannes, but he was often called Faustus Junior. The first we hear of him is in 1507 when, through the good offices of a nobleman, he obtained a post as a teacher in a boys' school in Kreuznach near Frankfurt. Apparently he was a homosexual, for he proceeded to seduce some of his pupils, 'indulging in the most dastardly kind of lewdness'. When found out, he fled. In 1509, Johannes Faust was given a degree in theology in Heidelberg, some forty miles from Kreuznach. In 1513, the canon of St. Mary's church in Gotha in what is now East Germany, recorded that he had heard Georg Faust, known as 'the demigod of Heidelberg', boasting and talking nonsense in an inn in nearby Erfurt.

The alchemist Trithemius recalls a meeting with Faustus Junior as early as 1507, and dismisses him as a fool, a boaster, and a charlatan. In the few other references we have he is casting horoscopes, making prophecies, or being driven from town to town by his unsavoury reputation as a sodomite and *necromancer* (one who foretells the future by communicating with the dead). From Johann Wier, an acquaintance of Faust who wrote about him, we learn that Faust was wont to boast about 'his friend the Devil'—which may have been nothing more than a typical piece of bombast. A story of Faust's malicious humour recorded by Wier describes how Faust, when a prisoner in the castle of Baron Hermann of Batenburg, offered to show the nobleman's chaplain how to remove his beard without a razor, in exchange for a bottle of wine. The chaplain was to rub his beard with the 'magic formula', arsenic. The gullible chaplain did this. His beard fell out, just as Faust had prophesied—but it took most of the chaplain's skin with it. Wier also tells us that Faust was a drunken wanderer who spent much of his time in low taverns, impressing the locals with conjuring tricks. Other contemporary chroniclers describe him as a liar and a 'low juggler'.

We do not know when Faust died—it was probably in the 1540s—but we do know how his legendary fame began. A Swiss Protestant clergyman, Johanne Gast, once dined with Faust, and was unfavourably impressed by him—perhaps because of Faust's hints at his pact with the Devil. At all events Gast later spoke of Faust in one of his sermons, declaring that he had been strangled by the Devil, and that his corpse had persisted in lying on its face, although it had been turned on its back five times. This story had the right touch of horror to appeal to the imaginations of his congregation. Soon other stories grew up. One told how the Devil had twisted Faust's head around completely so that it looked down his back. Another recounted how, toward the end of his life, Faust began to hope that he might escape the Devil's clutches—but the trembling of the house at night warned him that the end was near.

The 16th century was an age of religious persecution, a time when a man could be executed on the mere suspicion that he did not believe in the Trinity. The very idea of a man selling his soul to the Devil was enough to make Faust's contemporaries turn pale. Little wonder, then, that Spies' *Historia* became one of the most popular works of its time. Phillip Melancthon, a follower of Luther, also preached about Faust. He gilded the lily somewhat with a story that Faust had defeated and eaten a rival magician in Vienna. Luther also has two slighting references to Faust in his *Table Talk*, from which it is clear that he regarded Faust as a common charlatan rather a demonic wonder worker. The only powers that some of Faust's educated contemporaries were willing to grant him were the gifts of casting accurate horoscopes and of foretelling the future. In 1535, for instance, Faust correctly predicted that the Bishop of Munster would recapture the city, and in 1540 he foretold the defeat of the European armies in Venezuela.

Legend has made Faust the most famous figure in the history of necromancy. But when we peer through the legendary mist, what do we find? Most of the more sensational stories about the man as told by people who knew him, tell of feats that have been more or less duplicated by other men of strange powers down the ages. It is difficult to decide whether this helps to support or to discredit Faust's credentials as a magician. When we try to sift fact from legend, it becomes clear that Faust knew something about hypnosis. It may be that he also knew how to conjure poltergeists. The priest Gast claimed that when Faust was angered by the poor hospitality offered to him by some monks, he sent a poltergeist to trouble them. Apparently the rattling spirit created such a furore that the monks had to abandon their monastery. Accounts made it plain that Faust was stupid, boastful, and malicious. The same is true of many men of strange powers. As we shall see, Faust's restless egoism, his desire to impress, his need to bend nature to his will are characteristic of many of the best-known magicians from Simon Magus onward. Magicians are not comfortable people to know.

Faust was not the most celebrated magician of his age. He had two remarkable contemporaries, Cornelius Agrippa and Paracelsus, whose fame greatly and deservedly surpassed his own, and who were undoubtedly white magicians. Agrippa and Paracelsus were both students of that strange mystical system of knowledge called the Cabala, whose purpose is to show the fallen man his way back to Paradise and the godhead. The two works that contain the essence of cabalistic teaching—the *Sefer Yetsirah*, Book of Creation, and the *Zohar*, Book of Splendor—are of such profound importance in the history of magic that we must say a few words about them here.

The Book of Creation dates from the 2nd century AD. The Book of Splendor appeared in an Aramaic manuscript written by a student named Moses de Léon in the late 13th century. It is, however, a tradition that the teachings of both books date from the beginning of human history, when angéls taught Adam the secret of how to recover his lost bliss. Cabalists think of man as a being who is tied up and enveloped in a complicated straitjacket—like Houdini before one of his celebrated escapes— and whose problem is to discover how to untie all the knots. Most men do not even realise that they are tied up. The cabalist not only knows it: he knows also that man's highest state is total freedom.

According to the Cabala, when Adam sinned he fell from a state of union with God. He fell down through 10 lower states of consciousness into a state of amnesia, in which he totally forgot his divine origin, his true identity. Man's task, therefore, is to clamber back until he once more attains his highest state. The journey is long and hard. It is not simply a matter of climbing, like Jack clambering up the beanstalk, because the 'beanstalk' passes through 10 different 'realms'. But even that image is too simple: the beanstalk does not pass straight upward, like a fireman's pole, but wanders from side to side.

The image of the beanstalk is apt because the Cabala is essentially the study of a sacred tree—the Tree of Life. At the top of the tree is God the Creator, who is called Kether (the crown). The nine other branches of the tree are wisdom, beauty, power, understanding, love, endurance, majesty, foundation, and kingdom. These are known collectively as the Sefiroth— emanations, or potencies, and it is they that constitute the realms through which the beanstalk passes. There is a further complication. The traditional picture of the Tree of Life looks rather like a diagram of a chemical molecule, in which the atoms are connected to each other by lines. These lines correspond to the 22 paths of the Cabala that connect the realms.

The Tree of Life no longer grows on earth. How, then, does the aspirant set about climbing it? There are three main ways. First, one may explore the realms on the astral plane. Another way to explore the realms of the Cabala is through inner vision—that is, by achieving a semi-trancelike or visionary state in which the realms appear before the inner eye. A third way is the obvious one: study of the Cabala itself. It is, however, perhaps the most difficult way of all, because its revelations of man's consciousness and destiny are not spoken of directly, but lie hidden in an enormously complex system of symbols.

The realms of the Sefiroth, however, are not themselves symbols. According to the Cabala, they are real worlds. For instance, if the wandering astral body finds itself in a realm containing doves and spotted leopards, a land bursting with an almost overwhelming glory of life, it is almost certainly in the realm of Netshah, or Venus—symbol of endurance and victory.

The doctrines of the Cabala were probably far above the head of a charlatan such as Faust. But Cornelius Agrippa and Paracelsus were not charlatans. They regarded themselves as scientists and philosophers, and they were far more intelligent than Faust. Yet both of them were flawed by the defects we have come to realize are characteristic of so many magicians: a craving to be admired, and a crude will to power. When these ambitions are frustrated, even men of genuine powers will often misuse their powers like a charlatan.

Like Faust, Cornelius Agrippa became the subject of many remarkable legends. What was the truth behind such incredible tales? Cornelius Agrippa—whose real name was Heinrich Cornelis —was born in Cologne in 1486. His parents were sufficiently well-off to send him to the recently founded university of Cologne, where he proved to be a brilliant scholar. It was an exciting time for young intellectuals. Gutenberg had invented the printing press some 50 years before Agrippa was born, and the printed book had created the same kind of revolution as radio and television were to do five centuries later. Agrippa read everything he could lay his hands on. One day he discovered the Cabala, and it at once appealed to something deep within him. A magician was made.

At the age of 20 Agrippa became a court secretary to the Holy Roman Emperor, and a distinguished career seemed assured for him. But Agrippa was a divided man. Part of him, as we have said, craved celebrity and power; but he loathed the world of diplomacy and courtly intrigue by which such success could be achieved. By now he was also obsessed by the ultimate other world of the Cabala.

At about this time, he attended the University of Paris where he studied mysticism and philosophy. There he met a Spaniard named Gerona, who had recently been forced to flee from his estate in Catalonia after a peasants' revolt. Agrippa offered to help him, sensing that if their mission succeeded, Gerona's gratitude might enable Agrippa to settle in Spain and devote his life to study of the Cabala. They went to Catalonia, and Agrippa devised a brilliant plan that enabled them to capture a stronghold from the rebels. But they were later besieged, Agrippa was forced to flee, and Gerona was captured and probably murdered. The episode was typical of the bad luck that was to pursue Agrippa for the rest of his life.

He returned to his job as court secretary, but he felt so frustrated that he left after a few months and began wandering around Europe. Within a year or two he had acquired a reputation as a black magician, and it was to cause him a great deal of trouble. In 1509 he taught in Dôle, France under the patronage of Queen Margaret of Austria. The local monks became jealous of this patronage, however, and plotted against him. When one of them preached against him in the presence of the queen, Agrippa decided it was time to move on. In 1515 he was knighted on a battlefield in Italy, and became Cornelius Agrippa von Nettesheim—a name taken from that of a small village near Cologne.

He was granted a pension by King Francis I of France, but this was revoked when Agrippa refused to cast horoscopes for the king's mother. Agrippa was later made official historian by Queen Margaret, but was unwise enough to publish a work in which he attempted to demonstrate that all knowledge is useless. This so enraged his academic colleagues that he lost his job. Soon he was imprisoned for debt. Agrippa certainly lacked tact, for after this he again made the mistake of speaking his mind about Queen Margaret, for which he was thrown into prison and tortured. His health broken, he died in 1535 at the age of 49. Legend says that, as he lay on his deathbed, he cursed his wasted life and the black arts that had seduced him. Whereupon his black dog rushed out of the house and threw itself into a river—clearly proving thereby that it was a demon in disguise.

These biographical snippets, however richly spiced with legends, hardly add up to a man of strange powers. The certainty that Agrippa was indeed a magician, however, lies in the three volumes of his treatise *The Occult Philosophy*, which is regarded as one of the great magical texts. The book makes it clear that Agrippa knew all about thought pressure. Magic, he insists, is a faculty that springs from the power of the mind and imagination. There are mysterious relations between the human body and the universe, and between the earth on which we live and higher spiritual worlds. Thus, he argued, a stone can teach us about the nature of the stars. Agrippa believed that all nature is bound together by a kind of vast spider's web. Most human beings never learn to use their innate magical powers because they believe that they are cut off from the rest of nature. The magician, on the contrary, knows that his thought, if properly directed, can set the web vibrating and cause effects in far distant places.

Agrippa wrote his extraordinary masterwork when he was only 23 years old. It shows that, even at this early age, his study of the Cabala had given him some profound insights. Because he was always in danger of being burned as a black magician, he was careful to insist in his book that his knowledge is of a kind that any serious student can acquire from study of the great philosophers and mystics. But he also admits that he has successfully practised divination and foretelling the future. For example, he describes two methods by which he claims to have detected the identity of thieves. One method is to pivot a sieve on forceps held between the index fingers of two students. The sieve will begin to swing like a pendulum when the name of the guilty person is mentioned. Similarly, if the sieve is pivoted so that it can be made to spin, it will stop spinning when the thief's name is spoken.

Agrippa insists that the success of these and other magical techniques are due to spirits—similar, presumably, to the spirits that help fakirs to perform their wonders. The overwhelming impression that emerges from the book is that Agrippa was a sensitive—born with the gifts of precognition, telepathy, and the ability to influence events by using the power of his mind. His belief that mind is more powerful than matter runs like a thread through the book. *The Occult Philosophy* is the work of a young man—full of vitality and brilliance—and of a dreamer who peered into a world that few of us have the gift to see.

The case of Paracelsus is even more tantalising than that of Agrippa. His writings prove him to have been a more remarkable man—a great scientist as well as a magician. But, again, seeking the truth about him is like groping about in a fog, so obscured is his life with myth and legend.

He was born as Theophrastus Bombastus von Hohenheim in 1493, the son of an impoverished Swiss nobleman who had become a doctor. He studied medicine in Basel and completed his education at universities in Italy and Germany. His gifts as a physician were immediately apparent, and a series of remarkable cures soon earned him a formidable reputation. In 1524, when he was only 29 years old, he was appointed professor of medicine at Basel University. In nine years he had become one of the great names in medicine in Europe.

It was at this point that his career, so rich in both achievement and promise, was undermined by the same kind of character defects that brought ruin to Agrippa, and that seem to be hallmarks of so many magicians. He was vainglorious. He chose the pseudonym 'Paracelsus' because it implied that he was greater than Celsus, the famous physician of ancient Rome. He was a heavy drinker, and was prey to sudden violent tempers. One of his first acts as professor at Basel University was to order his students to hold a public burning of the books of Avicenna, Galen, and other famous doctors of the past. This enraged his colleagues, who condemned him as an exhibitionist and a charlatan. When they plotted against him, Paracelsus compounded his unpopularity by calling them names—like many paranoid people he had a powerful gift for invective. For a while his reputation held his enemies at bay and when he cured the publisher Frobenius of an infected leg that other doctors had decided to amputate, it seemed that he had become invulnerable to attack. Soon after this, however, a patient declined to pay his bill and Paracelsus took him to court. Owing to the plots of his enemies, he lost the case, whereupon he rained such violent abuse on the heads of the judges that a warrant was issued for his arrest. He was forced to flee Basel—and his long soul-destroying downfall had begun.

For the remainder of his life Paracelsus wandered all over Europe as an itinerant doctor, writing book after book of which few were published in his lifetime, and pouring scorn and invective on his enemies. Fourteen years of wandering and disappointment wore him out. In 1541, when he was 48 years old, he was invited by the Prince Palatine to settle at his seat in Salzburg. At last he might have found contentment in a quiet life of study. But he continued to drink too much, and six months later he rolled down a hill in a drunken stupor, and died of his injuries.

Then, ironically, his books began to be published, and they spread his fame over Europe once more. They have a range and boldness of imagination that is reminiscent of Leonardo da Vinci's notebooks. Paracelsus immediately became a kind of patron saint of occultism—a position he maintains even today, with his writings being studied by a new generation of occultists.

As with Agrippa, it is difficult to discover four centuries later what genuine powers lay behind the many legends of Paracelsus's magical prowess. One thing is clear: most of the stories concern remarkable cures, and this suggests that he was primarily gifted with seemingly magical powers of healing. For example, we are told that he cured an innkeeper's daughter who since birth had been paralysed from the waist down. The medicine he gave her was probably saltpetre in teaspoonfuls of wine. This would obviously have had no effect, but it seems that the hypnotic force of his personality and his natural healing power brought about a cure. We are also again confronted by the paradox of the split personality: a man who was bad-tempered, thin-skinned, and boastful, yet who could be taken over by some strange power that rose from his subconscious depths and made him a great healer.

So we reach the odd conclusion that the contemporaries of Agrippa and Paracelsus were probably right when they called them charlatans—but that, at the same time, both men possessed genuine powers. It would be another four centuries before the great Swiss psychologist Carl Jung attempted to explain these powers scientifically in terms of that vast reservoir of energy known as the subconscious mind.

In the 16th century it was still dangerous for a man of knowledge to gain a reputation as a wizard or sorcerer. The witch hunting craze was spreading across Europe, and many people were being burned for being in league with the Devil. This no doubt explains why we know so little of the lives of the alchemists who followed in the footsteps of Agrippa and Paracelsus. That remarkable 16th century French physician and prophet Nostradamus took care to hide his visions in verse of such obscurity that even nowadays we cannot be certain what most of them mean.

Dr John Dee, the most highly regarded magician of Shakespeare's time, is almost unique among magicians in that he possessed practically no occult powers. Perhaps this is why he managed to avoid the usual magician's destiny of spectacular success and tragic downfall.

He was born in 1527, the son of a minor official in the court of King Henry VIII. From childhood on he was an avid reader, and when he went to Cambridge University at the age of 15, he allowed himself only four hours' sleep a night. After Cambridge he went to the University of Louvain in Belgium, where Agrippa had also studied. When Dee read Agrippa's *Occult Philosophy*, he knew that he had stumbled on his life's work—the pursuit of magical knowledge. At the age of 23 he gave a series of free lectures on geometry in Rheims, France, and was so popular that he was offered a professorship. But he preferred to return to England to pursue his occult studies.

When Elizabeth I came to the throne in 1558, she asked Dee to cast a suitable date for her coronation. Dee did so, and from this time on he enjoyed royal protection. Even so, as one suspected of magical practices, he still had to behave with extreme caution. Moreover, Queen Elizabeth was notoriously stingy: her patronage did nothing to improve Dee's finances, and he remained poor all his life. Dee married a lady-in-waiting who bore him eight children. He lived quietly and studied astrology, crystal-gazing, and alchemy.

The aim of crystal-gazing is to induce a semi-trancelike state in which the subconscious mind projects future events as images in the crystal. Dee was too much of an intellectual to be good at this. He realized that what he needed was a working partner with natural occult faculties, especially in scrying. In 1582 he met Edward Kelley, a young Irishman who claimed to have second sight. Kelley was undoubtedly a crook—he had had both his ears cut off for forgery—but it seems equally certain that he did possess second sight, and that he was also a medium. Dee's wife took an immediate dislike to the Irishman, but when Kelley went into a trance and began to get in touch with spirits, Dee was so delighted that he overruled his wife's objections.

How did Dee and Kelley go about summoning the spirits? One famous print shows them in a graveyard practicing necromancy. From what we know of the pious Dee, however, it seems unlikely that he went in for this sort of thing. We can learn more from his *Spiritual Diaries*. It is clear that he went into training before endeavouring to summon the spirits. He abstained for three days from sexual intercourse, overeating, and the consumption of alcohol, and he took care to shave his beard and cut his nails. Then began a two-week period of magical invocations in Latin and Hebrew beginning at dawn and continuing until noon, then beginning again at sunset and continuing until midnight. Kelley, meanwhile, gazed intently into the crystal ball. At the end of fourteen days, Kelley would begin to see angels and demons in the crystal. Later, these spirits would walk about the room. Dee, however, does not seem to have seen the spirits, but he recorded lengthy dialogues he had with them.

One's instant response to this is the conviction that Kelley made Dee believe that nonexistent spirits had manifested themselves. The trouble with this view is that the conversations, which came via the mouth of Kelley, were often so crammed with abstruse magical lore that it is almost inconceivable that the illiterate Irishman could have made them up as he went along. Dee, of course, was familiar with the lore, and certain of the demons quoted chunks of Agrippa's *Occult Philosophy*. This makes it possible that Dee transmitted them telepathically to Kelley. The likeliest explanation, however, is that Kelley was a natural medium.

Count Adalbert Laski, a servant of Henry III of France, was so impressed by these seances of Dee and Kelley that he invited them to visit the king of Germany. Dee and his family, and Kelley and his wife spent four years travelling around Europe as guests of various kings and noblemen, and their performances were sensationally successful.

Kelley was a difficult man, given to sudden tantrums and to fits of boredom and depression; but in spite of their ups and downs, he and Dee continued to work together for many years. They finally separated while they were still on their travels in Europe. Kelley achieved some success on his own as an alchemist and scryer, but eventually he died in prison. Dee returned to England in 1589 and lived for another nineteen years, hoping in vain that the spirits would lead him to a crock of gold. Today his reputation among occultists is secure, for he was the first magician on record to make use of spirit communication. He was two hundred years before his time; but in spite of his lack of worldly success, he remains one of the great names in the history of magic.

The tide turned in the 17th and 18th centuries—the age of scientists such as Newton, Huygens, and Harvey—and the seeker after forbidden knowledge once again became respectable, at least in Protestant countries. Sir Isaac Newton—one of the greatest names in science and philosophy—spent as much time in his alchemical laboratory as at his telescope.

The career of Anton Mesmer—which was described in Chapter 2—illustrates the difficulty of distinguishing between the scientist, and the magician. Mesmer regarded himself as a scientist, but his belief in the 'vital forces' of the universe classifies him among the mystics and magicians. Mesmer has an important place in the history of magic for another reason: that unlike some of his great predecessors, it is difficult to draw a line between where the scientist ended and the charlatan began. And this, as we shall see, is a problem that continues to plague the history of magic into the second half of the 20th century.

Nowhere is this more apparent than in the case of the man whose name has become synonymous with seduction: Jacques Casanova, the adventurer and confidence trickster who flourished in the second half of the 18th century. Not only was Casanova an accomplished faith-healer (he cured an ailing Venetian senator by means of suggestion), but he was also remarkably successful at fortune-telling by means of cards and other oracles. Indeed, the accuracy of his predictions sometimes alarmed Casanova himself. For instance, he told one girl that she would go to Paris and become the King's mistress—and that is exactly what happened. Casanova believed that he somehow conjured up real spirits when he was muttering his bogus incantations. What seems more likely is that he possessed the same occult faculty as Paracelsus or Faust to some degree.

Casanova met, and immediately disliked, another charlatan who acquired a reputation as a great magician: the man who called himself the 'Count of Saint-Germain'. When Saint-Germain arrived in Vienna in the mid-1740s he seemed to be about 30 years old—a man of powerful and dominant personality, with the typical magician's streak of boastfulness and desire to astonish. In Vienna he was befriended by members of the nobility, and was brought to Paris by the Marshal de Belle-Isle. By 1758 he had become a close friend of Louis XV and his mistress Madame de Pompadour.

Part of Saint-Germain's attraction was his reputation as a man of mystery. No one seemed to have any idea of where or when he was born. But his knowledge of history seemed to be enormous, and occasionally he said things that suggested he knew far more about certain events in the remote past than any mere student possibly could know. In short, he implied that he had actually witnessed them in person. He would learnedly discourse on the priesthood of Egypt in a way that suggested he had studied in ancient Thebes or Heliopolis. Another puzzle was that he was never seen to eat, although it is now known that he had a special diet. He explained that he lived on some elixir of which only he knew the formula. He was a student of alchemy, and claimed to have discovered the secret of the Philosopher's Stone. What is certain is that he had learned a great deal about metallurgy and chemistry.

Saint-Germain continues to fascinate students of occultism. Many of them believe he is alive today—possibly in Tibet. The unromantic truth is that he died in his mid-70s in 1784, suffering from rheumatism and morbid depression. Accounts of people who met him indicate that, far from being a man of mystery and an enigma, he struck many intelligent people as a fool, charlatan, boaster, and swindler.

If Saint-Germain seems to have been fundamentally a confidence man, the same cannot be said of his famous contemporary Count Alessandro di Cagliostro. That he was a fraud there can be little doubt, but that he also possessed highly developed occult faculties is fairly certain. His enemies said that Cagliostro's real name was Giuseppe Balsamo, and that he had been a confidence trickster in his native Italy. As a schoolboy he was exuberant and ungovernable, and ran away from seminary school several times. In his teens he became a wanderer, like many talented and penniless young men, and lived by his wits. But he was also an avid student of alchemy, astrology, and ritual magic, and he soon had a wide, if not very coherent, knowledge of occultism.

At the age of 26 in 1769 Cagliostro fell in love with Lorenza, the beautiful 14-year-old daughter of a coppersmith. They married, and for many years she was his partner in adventure and fraud, her beauty being one of their greatest assets. When Casanova met them in the south of France the year after their marriage, as they were returning from a pilgrimage to Santiago de Compostella in Spain, they appeared to be people of means, travelling in style and distributing alms to the poor. In Paris, the couple came under the protection of a nobleman, who then seduced Lorenza and tried to make her leave her husband. Cagliostro had her thrown into jail, but later reunited with her and took her to England.

In London he joined the Freemasons. Soon, however, he founded his own masonic order, infusing its ceremonies with occult rituals purportedly based on ancient Egyptian practices that Cagliostro claimed he had discovered in an Egyptian manuscript on a bookstall. Cagliostro was undoubtedly convinced that his Egyptian masonry was the product of divine inspiration. It was certainly the turning-point in his fortunes. From London he journeyed to Venice, Berlin, Nuremberg, and Leipzig. In each city, he visited the masonic lodge, made speeches on his Egyptian rite, and initiated members. His argument seems to have been that the Egyptian rite was as different from, and as superior to, established freemasonry as New Testament Christianity is from Old Testament Judaism. He was fêted and admired, and became a rich man.

Cagliostro came to Strasbourg in 1780, and soon became the most talked about man in town. Although he was wealthy, he lived modestly in a room above a tobacco shop. His cures became legendary. He was often able to heal the sick simply by the laying on of hands. On one occasion he successfully delivered a baby after midwives had given up the mother for dead.

It was in Strasbourg that he met the man who was to bring about his downfall: Cardinal de Rohan. He was a churchman who longed for royal favour, but who unfortunately was disliked by Queen Marie Antoinette. Cagliostro deeply impressed Rohan, who spoke of his luminous and hypnotic eyes with almost religious fervor.

The cardinal's downfall occured in 1785 in the famous Affair of the Diamond Necklace. A pretty swindler who called herself the Countess de la Motte Valois became Rohan's mistress, and persuaded him that the queen wanted him to secretly buy a diamond necklace worth $300,000. In fact, the queen knew nothing of it, and the money raised by the cardinal went straight into the countess's pocket. When the jewellers finally approached the queen for a long overdue instalment on the money, the whole affair came to light. The countess was tried and publicly flogged. Rohan and Cagliostro were also tried and, although they were acquitted, the scandal damaged both of them irreparably. In addition, the months that Cagliostro spent in jail before trial broke his nerve—and his luck.

Cagliostro went to London after leaving prison. There he accurately predicted the nature and date of the French Revolution and of the fall of the Bastille. Then he travelled around Europe, often hounded by the police. Finally, he made the extraordinary error of going to Rome to propagate his Egyptian freemasonry under the nose of the Pope. He was arrested and thrown into the papal prison in the Castel Sant'Angelo, and was later transferred to the even worse prison of San Leo. Eight years after his arrest in 1787, French soldiers captured San Leo prison and searched for Cagliostro, intending to treat him as a revolutionary hero. In fact, he had been dead for several years—though exactly when and how he died is still unknown.

Of all the great charlatan-magicians, Cagliostro is the most tragic. One of his enemies said that he possessed 'a demonic power that paralyzes the will'. But in retrospect he seems less a demon than a fallen angel.

In 1801 there appeared in London a work called *The Magus, or Celestial Intelligencer* by Francis Barrett. It was supposed to be 'a complete system of occult philosophy'. Nowadays it is not highly regarded by students and adepts of the magic arts, because many of the rituals it details are garbled and inaccurate. Nevertheless, it was an important work for it was almost the first attempt at a serious description of magical practices since Agrippa's *Occult Philosophy* nearly three centuries earlier. After Agrippa's time, fear of persecution had driven the magicians underground for two hundred years.

The Age of Reason, as thinkers and writers of mid-18th century Europe called their period, had made magic superfluous—or at least unfashionable. But the tide soon turned again. For the popular imagination, at least, reason was not enough. All over western Europe novels such as Horace Walpole's *The Castle of Otranto* began to appear, in which high adventure and crimes of passion were mixed with supernatural events. Of course, most readers did not really believe in the supernatural trappings of such stories—but their enormous popularity shows that ghosts, magic, and the paranormal continued to fascinate. At the end of *The Magus*, Barrett printed an advertisement asking for students to help him found a 'magic circle', and an active group was established at Cambridge.

Nine years after publication of *The Magus*, there was born in Paris a remarkable man who, more than any other, was responsible for the great magical revival that swept across Europe in the 19th century: Alphonse-Louis Constant, better known as Eliphas Lévi. The son of a poor shoemaker, Lévi was a dreamy, sickly, highly intelligent and imaginative child with powerful religious inclinations. At the age of 12 in 1822, he decided he was destined for the Church. He had a craving to belong to some spiritual order, some great organization, that would enable him to devote his life to the truths of the spirit. His teacher at the seminary of Saint Nicholas du Chardonnet was Abbot Frere-Colonna, a remarkable idealist who believed that man was slowly ascending toward God, and that a great age of the Holy Spirit was at hand. The abbot had studied Mesmer's doctrines, and believed that they were inspired by the Devil. He devoted some time to denouncing them in class, but succeeded only in awakening young Lévi's interest in such forbidden matters. When the abbot was dismissed through the intrigues of jealous colleagues, Lévi's disillusion with the Church began.

Lévi still hungered for a faith, however. He became a sub-deacon, and one of his chief tasks was teaching catechism to the young girls. One day a poor woman begged him to prepare her daughter for first communion, and Lévi's initial feelings of protectiveness developed into a wild infatuation for the girl. Nothing came of it, but the experience convinced him that he was not intended for the priesthood. When he turned away from his vocation, his mother committed suicide.

After fourteen years in a seminary, Lévi found the world a hard place to adjust to. He still wanted to be a believer, and dreamed of Frere-Colonna's spiritual rebirth of mankind. So, although he began to write for radical newspapers—and spent time in prison on sedition charges as a result—his search for a faith continued. He discovered the writings of Swedenborg, and then the Cabala with its doctrine that man can overcome original sin and rise toward the godhead. Honoré de Balzac's mystical novel *Louis Lambert* was also a vital influence. Lévi studied that strange fortune-telling deck of cards known as the Tarot, and linked its 22 cards of the Major Arcana with the 22 paths of the Cabala. Lévi came to certain important conclusions about magic. The first was that the will is a far greater power than we realize, and that magic is learning how to use this power. The second was that all space is permeated with a medium that Lévi called astral light, which can take the impression of thoughts and feelings, and is the medium through which thoughts are conveyed in telepathy. Third, he believed deeply in the microcosm-macrocosm doctrine enshrined in Hermes Trismegistus's inscription, 'As above, so below.'

Lévi was in his 40s when his *Dogma and Ritual of High Magic* was published in 1856, and it established a reputation that was consolidated four years later by his *History of Magic*. In the first book he describes one of the most curious incidents of his life. On a visit to London, he records, he was asked to try to raise the spirit of the ancient Greek magician Apollonius of Tyana. After a month of preparation and fasting, Lévi spent twelve hours in ritual incantations. At last, the shade of Apollonius appeared in a gray shroud, and telepathically answered questions Lévi put to it about the future of two of his acquaintances. It prophesied the death of both. Lévi's description of the invocation has considerable dramatic quality:

'I kindled two fires with the requisite prepared substances, and began reading the invocations of the "Ritual" in a voice at first low, but rising by degrees. The smoke spread, the flame caused the objects on which it fell to waver, then it went out, the smoke still floating white and slow about the marble altar. I seemed to feel a quaking of the earth, my ears tingled, my heart beat quickly. I heaped more twigs and perfumes on the chafing dishes, and as the flames again burst up, I beheld distinctly, before the altar, the figure of a man of more than normal size, which dissolved and vanished away. I re-commenced the evocations, and placed myself within a circle which I had drawn previously between the tripod and the altar. Thereupon the mirror which was behind the altar seemed to brighten in its depth, and a wan form was outlined therein, which increased and seemed to approach by degrees. Three times, and with closed eyes, I invoked Apollonius. When I again looked forth there was a man in front of me, wrapped from head to foot in a species of shroud, which seemed more gray than white. He was lean, melancholy, and beardless, and did not altogether correspond to my preconceived notion of Apollonius. I experienced an abnormally cold sensation, and when I endeavoured to question the phantom I could not articulate a syllable. I therefore placed my hand upon the sign of the pentagram, and pointed the sword at the figure, commanding it mentally to obey and not alarm me, in virtue of the said sign. The form thereupon became vague, and suddenly disappeared. I directed it to return, and presently felt, as it were, a breath close by me; something touched my hand which was holding the sword, and the arm became immediately benumbed as far as the elbow. I divined that the sword displeased the spirit, and I therefore placed it point downward, close by me, within the circle. The human figure reappeared immediately, but I experienced such an intense weakness in all my limbs, and a swooning sensation came so quickly over me, that I made two steps to sit down, whereupon I fell into profound lethargy, accompanied by dreams, of which I had only a confused recollection when I came to myself. For several subsequent days, the arm remained benumbed and painful.'

In spite of these setbacks, Lévi persisted and, according to his own account, was able to consult the spirit on two more occasions on some fine points of cabalism.

Lévi was a widely respected magician for the remainder of his life, and attracted many disciples. That he had occult powers—or that his disciples were convinced he had—is certain. A disciple to whom Lévi had given a prayer to recite before he fell asleep found that the words of the prayer were glowing in the dark, and that Lévi's spirit was standing by his bed. It seems likely that Lévi possessed the power of projecting his astral body.

His books strike the modern reader as wildly imaginative and confused, but they exerted an immense influence on a whole generation of students of the occult. His death in 1875 was mourned by hundreds of occultists in France, Germany, and England, who regarded him as the great master.

In 1831, when Lévi was still studying for the priesthood, there was born in Russia a woman who was to exert an even greater influence than he on 19th-century occultism: Elena Hahn, later Petrovna, but known as Madame Blavatsky. Born into an aristocratic family, she married at 16, left her husband soon after, and began to travel around the world. She was an explosive, charming, delightful personality. For a while she worked as a bareback rider in a circus, and dabbled in many odd interests. She had undoubted mediumistic powers, and throughout her life odd manifestations were apt to occur in her presence: inexplicable rappings, ringing of bells, and movements of objects. In fact, it seems that she had the power of raising poltergeists. After living carelessly until she was just past 40, and then wondering how to make a living, she decided to turn her occult abilities to account and become a medium.

On going to the United States she met Colonel Olcott, a lawyer and journalist who became her lifelong admirer and tireless publicist. She told Olcott that she was in touch with a certain spiritual Brotherhood of Luxor, presumably priests of ancient Egypt, and he believed her—as he believed everything else she told him. Together they formed the Theosophical Society, a movement for the study of ancient wisdom. For three years it flourished in America. In 1879, as interest seemed to wane, they decided to move to India, which Madame Blavatsky regarded as the fountainhead of spiritual wisdom.

In Bombay, Theosophy was an immediate success. The charismatic personality of Madame Blavatsky fascinated the

Hindus even more than it had fascinated the Americans. She claimed that the Secret Masters in Tibet, a group of spiritual initiates, had imparted their wisdom to her. When disciples asked her questions about these matters, paper notes fell from the air. The notes contained detailed replies to the questions and were signed 'Koot Hoomi'. These notes later became famous as the Mahatma Letters. Koot Hoomi, a semi-divine Master, was even seen by some devotees one moonlight night.

In 1884 the bombshell came. A housekeeper with whom Madame Blavatsky had quarrelled told a Western journalist that most of the magical effects were merely tricks. The Mahatma Letters were simply dropped through a crack in the ceiling of the room in which the disciples had gathered, and the seven-foot-tall Koot Hoomi was actually a model carried around on someone's shoulders. Examination of a cabinet in which many manifestations had occurred revealed a secret panel. The Society for Psychical Research, which had been investigating her powers, issued a sceptical report.

It might seem that the Blavatsky reputation was irretrievable. Not a bit of it. Madame Blavatsky set sail for London—and soon the Theosophical Society was flourishing again, although it never achieved anything like its earlier success. Once again, accounts of Madame Blavatsky's magical powers began to circulate among occultists. The poet W. B. Yeats, a serious and long-term student of the occult—reported that when he visited Madame Blavatsky, her cuckoo clock made hooting noises at him. A. P. Sinnett, who later became her faithful disciple, complained when he visited her that he had attempted to raise spirits at seances, but could not even get rapping sounds. 'Oh, raps are the easiest thing to get,' she replied—and raps immediately sounded from all parts of the room.

When Madame Blavatsky died in 1891, six years after the fiasco that drove her out of India, she left behind a host of disciples who firmly believed in the existence of Koot Hoomi and the Tibetan Masters. She also left behind two huge books, *Isis Unveiled* and *The Secret Doctrine*, in which she explains that the earth is destined to evolve through seven 'root races', of which we are the fifth. Much of these enormous, bewildering books is taken up with descriptions of the root races.

In retrospect, it seems fairly certain that Madame Blavatsky was a genuine medium of unusual powers. It is more certain that, when her somewhat erratic powers were feeble, she helped them out with trickery—a temptation to which dozens of bona fide mediums and magicians have succumbed. She was in short both a charlatan and a genuine magician, and her hypnotically powerful personality made her one of the most remarkable women of the 19th century.

The next major step in the history of magic was the founding of the Hermetic Order of the Golden Dawn. One day in 1885 a middle-aged clergyman named Woodford was passing an idle hour at a secondhand bookstall on Farringdon Street in London. Among the dusty volumes he came upon a bound, handwritten manuscript that was obviously in cipher. Woodford was a student of the occult, and he recognised certain symbols of the Cabala in the text. He bought the manuscript but, after several unsuccessful attempts to decode it, put it aside. Two years later, in the summer of 1887, he sent the manuscript to a friend, Dr William Wynn Westcott, a coroner who was interested in occultism and freemasonry. Westcott was familiar with the first major work on ciphers, the *Steganographia* by the 15th-century alchemist Abbot Johann Trithemius, and it did not take him long to conclude that the mysterious pages were actually written in Trithemius's code. When deciphered they proved to be five magical rituals for introducing newcomers into a secret society, together with notes on various cabalistic matters.

Concealed among the pages Westcott found a letter in German, which stated that anyone interested in these rituals should contact a certain Fräulein Sprengel at an address in Stuttgart. Westcott lost no time in writing to her. Fräulein Sprengel replied, divulging that she was a member of a German magical order. A correspondence about magic ensued, and eventually Fräulein Sprengel gave Westcott permission to found an English branch of the order, and to use the rituals to initiate members. Accordingly, in 1888, Westcott founded a society called The Isis-Urania Temple of the Golden Dawn. (Its pretentious title perhaps reflects the influence of Madame Blavatsky, who had arrived in London from India a few months previously.) Two other students of the occult were co-founders: William Woodman, a retired doctor who had studied the Cabala in Hebrew, and Samuel Liddell Mathers, an eccentric scholar of aristocratic leanings. Before long the Golden Dawn had branches in Edinburgh, Weston-super-Mare, and Bradford, and an enthusiastic following of displaced intellectuals and cranks. Its members included the beautiful actress Florence Farr, the poet W. B. Yeats, and the young and as yet unknown Aleister Crowley.

This, at any rate, is the story of the founding of the Golden Dawn as put about by Westcott and Mathers. In recent years Ellic Howe, the historian of magic, has looked into the matter closely, and has concluded that Fräulein Sprengel never existed. The cipher manuscript was probably genuine, but it came from a collection of occultist Fred Hockley, who died in 1885, and not from a bookstall in Farringdon Street. Westcott, probably with the connivance of Mathers, forged various letters in German purporting to come from Fräulein Sprengel. His aim evidently was to give the society a certain authority rooted in ancient practices. Mathers was later to denounce the Sprengel letters as forgeries, although he must have known about them from the beginning. Westcott seems to have been a Jekyll and Hyde character. Indeed, his split personality was so marked that he wrote in two completely different styles of handwriting. As for Mathers, who was to change his name to MacGregor Mathers and pose as a Scottish aristocrat, he was one of those curious figures who seem to occur so often in the history of magic—a kind of confidence trickster whose aim was not so much to swindle as to gain respect, admiration, and power.

Does all this mean, then, that the Order of the Golden Dawn was nothing more than a combination of chicanery and wishful thinking? By no means. Its members did, beyond question, pursue serious and genuine studies of the magical arts. At this point, then, we must have a closer look at the whole subject of magic and those who practice it.

First of all, we have to admit that common-sense insists that magic is bound to be nonsense. How could some semi-religious ceremony have the slightest influence on the real world? Clergymen in church may pray for rain, or prosperity, or victory in battle, but they do not expect their prayers to produce a definite effect; they merely hope that God will pay attention. So why should some magic ceremony, not even addressed to God, have the power to influence actual events?

This is, I repeat, the commonsense view, the so-called scientific approach. But every day, thousands of events occur that science refuses to recognise because they appear to flout scientific laws. Dowsing, telepathy, precognition of future events, and spectres of the living are only a few examples. Perhaps we cannot really blame scientists for declining to pay too much attention to these things. The aim of science is to describe the universe in terms of natural laws, especially laws that forge unbreakable links between cause and effect—between an occurrence and the forces that make it happen. It is the apparent absence of such a link in magical events that makes scientists sceptical of them. The occultist responds to such scepticism by claiming that scientists refuse, or are unable, to spread their net of inquiry wide enough to encompass strange events. What is beyond dispute is that such events do occur.

When we try to take account of occult events, and to devise some kind of theory that helps to account for them, we discover an interesting thing. Such a theory has already existed for thousands of years. It does not matter whether we call it magic, occultism, shamanism, the Hermetic tradition as based on the works of Hermes Trismegistus. It all amounts to the same thing. Its basic assertion is that there is a far more intimate connection between man and nature than we are inclined to believe. The world is full of unseen forces, and of laws of whose nature we have no inkling. Perhaps there is some strange medium that stretches throughout space—such as Eliphas Lévi's astral light—that transmits these forces as the air transmits sound waves.

How do we make contact with such forces? The answer seems to be that you have to want to with an intense inner compulsion. In his autobiography, the painter Oscar Kokoschka tells of how his mother, who was having tea with his aunt one day in Prague, Czechoslovakia, suddenly leaped to her feet and announced that she must rush home because her youngest son was bleeding. The aunt tried to persuade her that her idea was nonsense, but his mother hurried home—and found that her son had cut his leg with a hatchet while trying to chop down a tree. He would certainly have bled to death if she had arrived any later. This story—and hundred of others like it equally well attested—indicates that strange powers come into operation where our deepest desires or needs are involved. As we go through our everyday lives, we do not need to exercise much will power; but occasionally, something stirs us to some really deep effort. It is this kind of effort that is likely to produce magical effects. The 20th-century poet Robert Graves has remarked that many young men use a form of unconscious 'sorcery' to seduce young women. This is another word for thought pressure.

We could say, then, that organizations such as the Hermetic Order of the Golden Dawn set out to experiment with will power, and to explore the possibilities of reaching deep subconscious levels of the will. Perhaps their magic was a hit-and-miss affair that worked only occasionally; but at least they were trying to learn about the possibilities of the true will.

The magic practiced by the members of the Golden Dawn was based on a number of simple principles. To begin with, they believed that certain basic symbols or ideas have a deep meaning for all human beings. On one occasion, Mathers handed Florence Farr a piece of cardboard with a geometrical symbol on it, and told her to close her eyes and place it against her forehead. She immediately saw in her mind's eye a cliff top above the sea, with gulls shrieking. Mathers had shown her the water symbol from the Cabala. There is a close connection between such symbols and the theory of archetypes of the psychologist Carl Jung, who believed that certain symbols are able to strike a chord in the unconscious mind of every human being.

The Golden Dawn taught its students to try to train their imagination, which is the trigger of the will, and gain control over it. One of their exercises was to control likes and dislikes until they could like something they normally hated, and hate something they usually liked. Another exercise was to attempt to see the world through other people's eyes rather than their own—in other words, to completely change their normal point of view. Many modern psychologists would agree that such exercises are valuable and healthy. They are, in fact, similar to exercises practised in yoga and other meditation disciplines.

The Golden Dawn also made a genuine attempt to draw together all that was best in the ancient magical traditions: Hermeticism, Cabalism, Enochian magic (based on the Apocryphal *Book of Enoch*, which tells of the fall of the Angels and their magic practices), and such magic textbooks as *The Key of Solomon*, *The Magic of Abrahemelin the Mage*, and the *Grimoire of Pope Honorius*.

On the face of it, the Golden Dawn should have been a wholly beneficial and healthy influence. Unfortunately, too many of its leading figures were driven by the craving that has been the downfall of so many magicians: the will to power, not only over themselves but also over everyone else. Gerald Yorke, a friend of Aleister Crowley, concluded that the story of the Golden Dawn showed that 'the majority of those who attempt to tread the occult path of power become the victims of their creative imagination, inflate their egos, and fall'. There was a great deal of infighting for the leadership of the Golden Dawn. Dr Westcott saw himself as the leader, but MacGregor Mathers felt the position should rightly be his. Mathers claimed to be in direct touch with the Secret Chiefs, semi-divine spirits, who dictated new rituals to him through his wife as a medium. Then there was A. E. Waite, a learned American historian of magic. His interests, however, were more mystical than magical, and he was not a very inspiring person. Finally, there was Aleister Crowley, a remarkable and demonic magician whose career brought ruin to many others as well as himself.

Crowley was the son of a wealthy and puritanical brewer. He was born in Leamington near Stratford-upon-Avon in 1875. His birthplace gave him opportunity to remark with typical bombast and arrogance: 'It is a strange coincidence that one small county [Leamington and Stratford are in Warwickshire] should have given England her two greatest poets—for one must not forget Shakespeare.' It sounds like a joke, but in fact Crowley was convinced that he was a great poet. However, though his verse shows considerable talent, he lacked the discipline and sense of language to be even a good poet.

Crowley was a spoiled child who developed an intense dislike of the Plymouth Brethren, the strict religious sect to which his father belonged. He was also obsessed by sex. His first of numerous seductions occurred with a young servant when he was 14 years old. At university he wrote a great deal of poetry, which he published at his own expense. He also developed an incurable desire that lasted all his life to shock respectable people. In his late teens he discovered Mathers' translation of a book called *The Kabbalah Unveiled*, as well as a work by A. E. Waite on ceremonial magic. He quickly established contact with the Golden Dawn.

By the time Crowley entered the Golden Dawn in 1898, the struggle for its control had already been going on for some time. In 1891 Mathers had returned from France to announce that he had met three of the Secret Chiefs in Paris, and had had various magical secrets imparted to him. Dr Woodman died that year and for the next six years there was a certain amount of tension within the movement. Dr Westcott resigned from the Order—apparently having been told by his superiors on the London Council that magic was not a suitable occupation for a respectable public official. Mathers spent a great deal of time in Paris working on magical manuscripts at the Bibliothèque Nationale, so the struggle for leadership of the movement continued.

In August 1899 Crowley rented a house in Boleskine, Scotland on the shores of Loch Ness, conferred on himself the title 'Laird of Boleskine', donned a kilt; and proceeded to practise the magic of Abrahamelin the Mage—a system which, he claimed, he had learned about in the writings of John Dee.

In December 1899, convinced that it was time he moved up to a higher grade in the Golden Dawn, Crowley went to London to demand initiation. This was refused through the efforts of Yeats and various other senior members, who regarded him as an overgrown juvenile delinquent. Crowley therefore went to Paris and persuaded Mathers to perform the necessary rituals. He also took the opportunity to stir up trouble, convincing Mathers that he had a revolt on his hands. Mathers sent him back to London with instructions to break into the Golden Dawn headquarters, and to put new locks on all the doors. Yeats, Florence Farr, and the other London initiates were enraged.

The legal wrangle that ensued in 1901 broke up the original Golden Dawn thirteen years after it had been founded. One group of members, under the leadership of A. E. Waite, managed to continue for another four years, still calling themselves the Golden Dawn. Another group, including Yeats, Florence Farr, and the novelist Arthur Machen, was led until 1905 by Dr R. W. Felkin, who then founded a magical society called the Stella Matutina, or Morning Star. Finally, in the 1920s, a talented young medium and occultist who called herself Dion Fortune founded the Society of the Inner Light, based on Golden Dawn rituals obtained from Mrs Mathers—Mathers himself having died in the influenza epidemic of 1918.

The same year of the legal problems the Golden Dawn had received another blow in the form of a sudden spate of unwelcome publicity. It happened when a couple of confidence tricksters who called themselves Mr and Mrs Horos were accused of raping a 16-year-old girl. Mrs Horos had learned that it was supposed to have been Fräulein Sprengel who had given the Golden Dawn its charter. She went to Paris and introduced herself to Mathers as Fräulein Sprengel. Oddly enough, Mathers was taken in—which could argue that he was not at that time aware that Fräulein Sprengel had been invented by Westcott. Mathers soon became suspicious of the couple, whereupon Mrs Horos and her husband stole some of the rituals of the Golden Dawn and fled to London. There they launched into a career of confidence trickery based on a mixture of spurious occultism, extortion, and sex. When charged with their crimes they claimed to be leaders of the Golden Dawn. As a consequence, many of the most intimate secrets of the order were made public and sensationalised by the press. The publicity, combined with the power struggles within it, sealed the fate of the Golden Dawn.

Crowley had decided to get away before the Horos scandal broke. Late in 1900 he had gone to Mexico, where he studied the Cabala, practiced yoga, and—according to his own account—finally became a true magician. When he returned to Paris in 1902 he tried to persuade Mathers to take up yoga. Mathers declined, and their relation became several degrees colder. Eventually it turned into hatred, with Mathers and Crowley pronouncing magical curses on one another. Crowley claimed that his curses were actually responsible for the death of Mathers.

Back in England, Crowley married Rose Kelly, and they travelled to Ceylon and Egypt. They called themselves the

Prince and Princess Chioa Khan. In Cairo, Crowley performed various rituals with the intention of invoking the Egyptian god Horus. On April 8, 1904, he received instructions from his wife, who had taken to uttering strange messages while in a trance-like state, to go into a room he had furnished as a temple. Suddenly he heard a disembodied voice ordering him to write. What Crowley wrote was an odd document called *The Book of the Law*, which became the cornerstone of his later teaching. He claimed that it was dictated by Aiwass, one of the Secret Chiefs. Its basic teaching was expressed in the phrase: 'Do what you will.'

In 1905 Crowley went to the Himalayas to attempt the climb of Kanchenjunga, third highest mountain in the world. During the climb he quarrelled with the rest of the team and, when they were buried in an avalanche, made no attempt to help them. Several were killed. He deserted his wife and baby in India where the baby died of typhoid. Rose later became an alcoholic, and died insane. In a magazine called *The Equinox* Crowley began to publish the secret rituals of the Golden Dawn. Mathers took him to court for this, but lost his case.

In 1912 Crowley received a communication from another magical organization, the Order of the Temple of the Orient, reproaching him for publishing its secrets. Puzzled by the accusation, Crowley went to see Theodor Reuss, one of the O.T.O.'s leaders. It appeared that the secret in question was something called sex magic. It arose from the system of yoga known as Tantra, which attempts to use the power of sexual energy to fuel the drive toward higher consciousness. The O.T.O. had, it seems, developed its own form of Tantric techniques. Crowley was fascinated, and promptly availed himself of Reuss's permission to set up an English branch of the O.T.O. Magical ritual performed by Crowley often involved sex magic—with his disciple Victor Neuberg it was an act of sodomy. Sex magic remained one of Crowley's central enthusiasms for the rest of his life—though addiction to heroin and cocaine lessened his sex drive in later years.

In the United States during World War I Crowley had an endless series of mistresses, each of whom he liked to call the 'Scarlet Woman'. He undoubtedly had an exceptional sexual appetite, but it must also be said that he genuinely believed that sex magic heightened his self-awareness, and enabled him to tap increasing profound levels of consciousness. At all events during this period Crowley steadily developed a kind of hypnotic power that it is as difficult to account for as it is to describe. William Seabrook, an American writer on the occult, witnessed the use of this power one day when he and Crowley were walking on Fifth Avenue in New York City. Crowley began to follow a complete stranger who was walking along the sidewalk. Crowley followed a few yards behind, keeping in perfect step with him. Suddenly, Crowley allowed his knees to buckle, and dropped momentarily to the ground. At exactly the same moment, the man he was following collapsed in precisely the same manner.

By the early 1920s Crowley, who was suffering from asthma, was almost permanently in debt. A legacy of $12,000 enabled him to move to a small farmhouse in Cefalu, Italy. He called it the Abbey of Thelema, which means 'Do what you will', began to practise magic, and invited disciples to join him. He provided apparently limitless quantities of drugs for anyone who wished to use them, and attractive women devotees were expected to help Crowley practise his sex magic. Even with the legacy, however, the money problem remained pressing. Crowley wrote a novel called *Diary of a Drug Fiend* and started his *Confessions*, which he called his hagiography (the biography of a saint). He announced that the earth had now passed beyond Christianity and had entered the new epoch of Crowleyanity. But when one of his disciples died after sacrificing a cat and drinking its blood, the resulting newspaper scandal drove Crowley out of Sicily.

The British press denounced him as 'the wickedest man in the world' and, although he loved the publicity, he soon discovered that his notoriety made publishers shy away from his books. He deserted his disciples, one of whom committed suicide, and married again. His second wife, like the first, became insane. Hoping to make money, he sued the English sculptress Nina Hamnett for calling him a black magician. But when witnesses described Crowley's magic, the judge stopped the case, declaring he had never heard such 'dreadful, horrible, blasphemous, and abominable stuff'.

By the outbreak of World War II Crowley had added alcoholism to his drug-addiction even though his daily intake of heroin at the time would have killed a dozen ordinary men. Every now and again he found rich disciples to support him until, inevitably, they lost patience with him. He retired to a rooming house near Hastings in southern England, and died there in December 1947 at the age of 72. John Symonds, a writer who had met him in his last years, later wrote his biography—a hilarious but often disturbing book. Other friends, notably Richard Cammell and Israel Regardie, wrote more sober and admiring accounts of his career. But it was not until the magical revival that began in the mid-1960s that Crowley's reputation began to rise again. Nowadays more than a dozen of his books are in print, and a new generation ardently practises the magic rituals described in them. The Beast has finally achieved the fame he craved. Nonetheless, and fortunately, the great age of Crowleyanity seems as far away as ever.

Occult powers seem to be a matter of national temperament. Second sight and telepathy come naturally to the Irish. The Germans seem to produce more gifted astrologers than other nations. The Dutch have produced two of the most gifted clairvoyants of this century: Croiset and Hurkos. Russia tends to produce mages—men or women who impress by their spiritual authority; no other nation has a spiritual equivalent of Tolstoy and Dostoevsky or even of Rozanov, Merezhkovsky, Soloviev, Fedorov, Berdyaev, Shestov. Certainly no other nation has come near to producing anyone like Madame Blavatsky, Grigory Rasputin or George Gurdjieff. Each is completely unique.

Grigory Rasputin's body was taken from the frozen river Neva, in Petrograd, on January 1, 1917. He had been murdered three days before, and was one of the most notorious figures in Russia. Now that he was dead, he would become a legend all over the world—a symbol of evil, cunning, and lust. If ever you see a magazine story entitled 'Rasputin, the Mad Monk', you can be sure it will be full of lurid details of how Rasputin spent his days in drunken carousing, his nights in sexual debauchery; how he deceived the czar and czarina into thinking he was a miracle worker; how he was the evil genius who brought about the Russian Revolution and the downfall of the Romanov dynasty. It is all untrue. Yet it makes such a good story that there is little chance that Rasputin will ever receive justice. The truth about him is that he really was a miracle worker and a man of strange powers. He was certainly no saint—very few magicians are—and tales of his heavy drinking and sexual prowess are undoubtedly based on fact. But he was no diabolical schemer.

Rasputin was born in the village of Pokrovskoe in 1870. His father was a fairly well-to-do peasant. As a young man, Rasputin had a reputation for wildness until he visited a monastery and spent four months there in prayer and meditation. For the remainder of his life, he was obsessed by religion. He married at 19 and became a prosperous carter. Then the call came again; he left his family and took to the road as a kind of wandering monk. When eventually he returned, he was a changed man, exuding an extraordinarily powerful magnetism. The young people of his village were fascinated by him. He converted one room in his house into a church, and it was always full. The local priest became envious of his following, however, and Rasputin was forced to leave home again.

Rasputin had always possessed the gift of second sight. One day during his childhood this gift had revealed to him the identity of a peasant who had stolen a horse and hidden it in a barn. Now, on his second round of travels, he also began to develop extraordinary healing powers. He would kneel by the beds of the sick and pray; then he would lay hands on them, and cure many of them. When he came to what is now Leningrad, probably late in 1903, he already had a reputation as a wonder worker. Soon he was accepted in aristocratic society in spite of his rough peasant manners.

It was in 1907 that he suddenly became the power behind the throne. Three years before, Czarina Alexandra had given birth to a longed-for heir to the throne, Prince Alexei. But it was soon apparent that Alexei had inherited haemophilia, a disease that prevents the blood from clotting, and from which a victim may bleed to death even with a small cut. At the age of 3, the prince fell and bruised himself so severely that an internal hemorrhage developed. He lay in a fever for days, and doctors despaired of his life. Then the czarina recalled the man of God she had met two years earlier, and sent for Rasputin. As soon as he came in he said calmly: 'Do not worry the child. He will be all right.' He laid his hand on the boy's forehead, sat down on the edge of the bed, and began to talk to him in a quiet voice. Then he knelt and prayed. In a few minutes the boy was in a deep and peaceful sleep, and the crisis was over.

Henceforward the czarina felt a powerful emotional dependence on Rasputin—a dependence nourished by the thinly veiled hostility with which Alexandra, a German, was treated at court. Rasputin's homely strength brought her a feeling of security. The czar also began to confide in Rasputin, who became a man of influence at court. Nicholas II was a poor ruler, not so much cruel as weak, and too indecisive to stem the rising tide of social discontent. His opponents began to believe that Rasputin was responsible for some of the czar's reactionary policies, and a host of powerful enemies began to gather. On several occasions the czar had to give way to the pressure and order Rasputin to leave the city. On one such occasion, the young prince fell and hurt himself again. For several days he tossed in agony, until he seemed too weak to survive. The czarina dispatched a telegram to Rasputin, and he telegraphed back: 'The illness is not as dangerous as it seems.' From the moment it was received, the prince began to recover.

World War I brought political revolution and military catastrophe to Russia. Its outbreak was marked by a strange coincidence: Rasputin was stabbed by a madwoman at precisely the same moment as the Archduke Franz Ferdinand was shot at Sarajevo. Rasputin hated war, and might have been able to dissuade the czar from leading Russia into the conflict. But he was in bed recovering from his stab wound when the moment of decision came.

Rasputin's end was planned by conspirators in the last days of 1916. He was lured to a cellar by Prince Felix Yussupov, a man he trusted. After feeding him poisoned cakes, Yussupov shot him in the back; then Rasputin was beaten with an iron bar. Such was his immense vitality that he was still alive when the murderers dropped him through the hole in the ice into the Neva. Among his papers was found a strange testament addressed to the czar. It stated that he had a strong feeling he would die by violence before January 1, 1917, and that if he were killed by peasants, the czar would reign for many years to come; but, if he were killed by aristocrats—as he was—then 'none of your children or relations will remain alive for more than two years'. He was right. The czar and his family were all murdered in July 1918—an amazing example, among many, of Rasputin's gift of precognition.

Rasputin—in fact as well as in legend—was one of the most remarkable men in Russia. Also remarkable was his compatriot and near contemporary Georgei Gurdjieff, who greatly influenced 20th-century occultism. Gurdjieff differs from most other men of strange powers in one important respect: he was not primarily a mage or wonder worker, but a philosopher obsessed by the problems of human futility. Why are human beings so weak? Why is human consciousness so narrow? Why do we spend our lives in a state of dullness resembling sleep? Above all, by what practical methods can we break through to the great 'source of power, meaning, and purpose' buried deep within ourselves? It was to questions like these that Gurdjieff addressed his life and work.

Gurdjieff was born in America in 1873. His parents were Greek, but he was Russian by nationality. From an early age he was intrigued by magic. One of the young men in his village could predict the future with astonishing accuracy after sitting between two lighted candles and going into a trance. At about this time Gurdjieff also witnessed a demonstration of the power of suggestion. He saw a boy who belonged to one of the many obscure local religious sects trapped in the middle of a magic circle drawn on the ground by some children of the village. He was psychologically incapable of stepping beyond the perimeter of the circle.

While still in his teens, Gurdjieff set out on what became twenty years of travel in Asia, Africa, and Europe in search of the secret wisdom that, he was convinced, was somewhere to be found. He learned the techniques of yoga and other forms of meditation in Tibetan monasteries and in Arab mosques; he studied hypnosis; he spent months with dervishes and with fakirs. In 1912, he returned to Russia, ready to teach some of the mysteries he had learned. Among the close circle of people who joined his group in Moscow was Peter Ouspensky, a young occultist and philosopher who was to become his most distinguished student.

On the outbreak of the Russian Revolution in 1917, Gurdjieff left Moscow for his family home, then in the Caucasus. There he founded his Institute for the Harmonious Development of Man, and was soon joined by Ouspensky and others of his disciples. However, political conditions became too harsh in the Caucasus and, after attempting to settle in Istanbul and in Germany, Gurdjieff re-established the Institute at the Prieuré near Paris in 1922.

Gurdjieff's system of teaching was based on the idea that, under normal circumstances, man is asleep, and that he is enslaved by a robot that controls not only his automatic functions but also much of his intellectual and emotional life. Gurfjieff's aim was to teach man how to outflank the robot by taking control of the vital reserves that exist in all of us, but that most people can tap only in times of crisis. We can all remember occasions in our lives when, faced with exceptionally difficult and perhaps dangerous situations, we have been forced—if only briefly—to excel ourselves physically or mentally. At the moment of success we feel marvellously alive. We are aware of a feeling of freedom—and rightly so, for the greatest freedom consists in our capacity to control and direct our own most deep-seated powers. We say, with quite literal truth, 'I didn't know I had it in me!'

Gurdjieff's method was to force his pupils constantly to extend their mental and physical limits. They lived almost monastic lives at the Prieuré, working from dawn to dusk and performing exercises designed to bring the mind, emotions, and body into harmony and under control. The aim was to achieve a state that Gurdjieff called 'self-remembering'—a state in which a person is not only intensely aware of his surroundings but also aware of himself observing and participating in them: a marriage of total inner and outer awareness. If you want to test how difficult this is, try a simple exercise. Close your eyes and direct your attention inward until you are aware only of your inner self. Now open your eyes and and direct your attention toward the outside world. Now try to direct your attention to both at once—your inner self and the outside world. You will find that you can only do it for a few seconds at a time; then you 'forget', and become aware only of either your inner self or the outside world. In certain moments of great excitement or intensity, however, you realise that you can maintain a state of self-remembering for much longer.

Undoubtedly, Gurdjieff's mastery of these disciplines gave him remarkable Psi powers—the way he could revitalise an exhausted follower by some inexplicable transmission of energy is only one example. He was also able to establish telepathic links with his followers. Ouspensky has recalled how, when they were in Finland, he began to hear Gurdjieff's voice inside his chest, and was able to carry on conversations with Gurdjieff who was in another part of the house. At the Prieuré Gurdjieff's pupils would give displays of telepathy for visitors, transmitting the names or shapes of various hidden objects from the audience to the stage. Gurdjieff obviously had profound psychic gifts. One day he told his pupils that a newcomer, who was out of the room, was susceptible to a certain chord of music. When the person came in he struck the chord on the piano, and she immediately underwent a kind of hysterical fit.

There are many stories of Gurdjieff's fund-raising skills that demonstrate not only his special psychological insight but also his sense of humour. Before one of his parties to raise money in New York, Gurdjieff asked Fritz Peters to teach him all the most obscene four-letter words he knew. When a large number of respectable and rich New Yorkers arrived, Gurdjieff began to talk to them about his ideas, gradually introducing more and more talk of sex. Finally his conversation consisted almost entirely of four-letter words. His guests relaxed, and then began to flirt with one another. Eventually, all inhibitions gone, they proceeded to behave with total abandon. Suddenly Gurdjieff stood up in the centre of the room, thunderously demanded their attention, and then pointed out that he had revealed to them something about themselves that they had never suspected. Surely, he asked, that was worth a large contribution to his institute? At the end of the evening, he was some thousands of dollars richer.

During his lifetime Gurdjieff did not publish any books on the techniques of his teaching, and his pupils were bound to secrecy on the subject. Since his death in Paris in 1949, however, many of his works have been published, and there has been a flood of memoirs by disciples and admirers. Gurdjieff was in almost every respect the antithesis of Aleister Crowley. Whereas Crowley craved publicity, Gurdjieff shunned it. Crowley was forgotten for two decades after his death; Gurdjieff, on the contrary, has become steadily better known, and his influence continues to grow. One of the main reasons for this is that there was so little of the charlatan about him. He is no cult figure with hordes of gullible disciples. What he has to teach makes an appeal to the intelligence, and can be fully understood only by those who are prepared to make a serious effort.

Nevertheless, Gurdjieff undoubtedly understood all the tricks of thought pressure. One of the most typical stories of him is told by the writer and traveler Rom Landau. One day, Landau was sitting in a restaurant with an attractive lady novelist. She was facing away from Gurdjieff, who was sitting on the other side of the restaurant. Suddenly she turned as if she had been struck, and her eyes met Gurdjieff's. Then, blushing, she turned away. Later she admitted to Landau that Gurdjieff had somehow 'struck her through her sexual center', including a powerful sexual response as if with an intimate caress.

Like Rasputin, Gurdjieff was no saint in his personal relations with women. Unlike Rasputin, however, he knew how to direct and control his extraordinary powers. His disciples regard him as one of the greatest men of the 20th century, and it is not necessary to be a disciple of Gurdjieff's to think that they may be right.

Among the most remarkable—and at present underestimated —magicians of the 20th century is the brilliantly talented writer who called herself Dion Fortune.

Little is known of her childhood, as her biographer, Alan Richardson, admits.[1] Born in Llandudno on December 6, 1890, the only child of a lawyer, and of a mother who became an ardent Christian Scientist, Violet Mary Firth seems to have been an introverted child who began to have 'visions' at the age of 4. (She later came to believe they were of past lives.) She was also sensitive to psychic phenomena from early childhood. Another well-known psychic, Phoebe Payne, has described how as a child she always saw pretty 'auras' surrounding flowers, and was surprised to discover later that they were invisible to most people. Violet Firth found that she was able to sense people's

1. *Priestess, The Life and Magic of Dion Fortune*, Aquarian Press 1987.

hidden thoughts and feelings. From the beginning, she 'walked in two worlds', and later developed into a good medium.

At the age of 20 in 1911 she became a teacher in a private school. The principal was a highly domineering woman—a power-hungry bully who had studied the occult in India. After several fierce arguments with the principal, Dion Fortune decided to quit her job. A colleague advised her to leave without telling the principal, saying that if she did not, she would never get away. Against this advice she told her superior. The principal said she was welcome to leave if she first admitted that she was incompetent and had no self-confidence. Dion Fortune indignantly denied the charges. The principal then fixed her with her eyes and repeated the statement hundreds of times for four hours.

Eventually some deep instinct warned Dion Fortune to pretend to give way, and to beg her principal's pardon. The older woman then relented and let her go. But the damage was done: Dion Fortune was a physical and mental wreck for the next three years. After more than a year of the illness, she later wrote, 'my body was like an electric battery that has been completely discharged'. A psychologist's diagnosis would probably be that the principal had used a kind of hypnotic power to deflate her self-esteem, to make her feel helpless and accident-prone. The effect was to drain her vital reserves, as Gurdjieff would have put it, so that the slightest effort exhausted her. She came to the conclusion that the woman had damaged her with a 'psychic attack', causing her astral body to leak vital energy. She plunged deep into the study of occultism as an antidote. Perhaps the most interesting part of her account of this experience is her statement that the principal had used not merely hypnotism but also telepathic suggestion—in other words, thought pressure.

It seems to have been this encounter that decided her to become a student of psychoanalysis, which was just then arousing much hostile attention amongst the British medical fraternity. In *Psychic Self Defense*, her story of the battle with the domineering principal, she states briefly: 'I took up the subject and became a student, and eventually a lecturer, at a clinic that was founded in London.' This was the Medico-Psychological Clinic in Brunswick Square. She goes on to explain that she soon noticed that some patients left her psychologically drained, and that when one of the nurses told her that some patients seemed to 'take it out' of the electrical machines, and could absorb high voltages without turning a hair, she began to wonder whether she was not dealing with some vital force that was quite distinct from Freud's libido. She became convinced that some people are 'psychic vampires'—a conclusion in accordance with the principles of 'occultism'.

When she discovered that the Theosophical Society had founded a club not far from the clinic in Brunswick Square, she joined it—not, as she explains, because she was interested in Theosophy, but because it was a convenient place to get a cheap meal. As a Freudian, she was contemptuous of the doctrines of the Theosophists; but when one day she decided to attend a meditation class—'in a spirit of mischief'—she was startled to observe in front of her eyes a clear image of a garden with blue plants. When the leader of the group announced that she was trying to transfer the image of delphiniums, she realised that some kind of thought-transference had taken place. Feeling that thought-reading would be an admirable gift for a psychoanalyst, she became a regular member of the meditation class. And as she recognised the reality of thought-transference, she also began to feel increasingly dissatisfied with the narrow materialism of the Freudians. With typical honesty, she decided to give up psychoanalysis and join the Land Army, which she felt to be a more useful job in war time. She was placed in charge of a laboratory where research was being conducted into food. Her job involved hours of waiting while bacteria brewed in an incubator. And in the long hours of silence, her vision turned inward. The result, she explains, was the sudden opening of 'astral sight', 'which gave me one of the frights of my life'. With a sense of being helplessly swept into something she failed to understand, she hurried along to the library of the Theosophical Society in Tavistock Square, and borrowed Annie Besant's book *The Ancient Wisdom*. Suddenly, she was converted to a belief in the Masters (although she always maintained that Madame Blavatsky was stretching the truth when she insisted that she had seen them in the flesh). For the next ten days she seemed to live in a strange, twilit world (which she would later identify as the 'astral plane' of the Cabala). On the tenth night she had a dream of tremendous vividness, in which she stood in the presence of the Master Jesus, and other Masters. In her dream, she was accepted as a pupil. When she woke up, she was convinced of the reality of her experience. A second Master she later identified as the Comte de St Germain.

Now her problem was to understand what was happening to her. She read R.M. Bucke's classic *Cosmic Consciousness*, and Madame Blavatsky's *Isis Unveiled*. She also met an Irishman named Theodore William Moriarty, a Freemason and occultist who became her teacher in magic. (She later fictionalised him as her 'psychic detective' Doctor Taverner.) Soon she had become a member of a group of female disciples who studied with him at a house in Bishops Stortford and another in Eversley, near Wokingham. More extraordinary psychic events took place there, which she describes in *Psychic Self Defense*. It seems, though, that Violet Firth was not much liked by her fellow disciples, who regarded her as 'pushing'.

While she was still a member of the Moriarty group, she renewed acquaintance with a lady named Maiya Curtis-Webb, whom she had known since childhood. She was a 'walking encyclopedia of occultism', and it was she who introduced Violet Firth to J.W. Brodie-Innes of the Golden Dawn. The result was that, in 1919, Violet Firth was initiated into the London Temple of the Golden Dawn, where she was given the magical name 'Deo, non Fortune', which she later transmuted into Dion Fortune.

It was at the London Temple that she met Moina Mathers, the widow of MacGregor Mathers, who was still running a remnant of the Golden Dawn. Mrs Mathers at first liked the attractive younger woman, and even agreed when Dion Fortune proposed forming a group of occultists more open to the general public—an idea directly opposed to the secrecy of the original Order. However, after Dion Fortune had written a number of books and articles on occultism, Mrs Mathers began to feel threatened by the energy and talent of the newcomer. It seems probable that Mrs Mathers hoped to turn the Golden Dawn into a source of income. In any case, Mrs Mathers ordered her to stop publicising the secrets of the Order. According to Dion Fortune, when she ignored the other woman's wishes, Mrs Mathers launched a black-magic attack on her. The opening salvo seems to have been a plague of black cats: dozens of them invaded Dion Fortune's house, and two of her friends were bothered by the odour of cats in their respective offices several miles away. Then one morning Dion Fortune saw a giant cat walking down the stairs toward her. As she stared, terrified, it vanished—and she realized that someone was using a kind of telepathic hypnotism on her. An hour later, the street outside her home was filled with dozens of howling black cats.

Dion Fortune's major struggle occurred when she made an astral journey. Her description of this is interesting because it gives us some insight into what magicians actually do when they visit the astral plane. A number of her followers formed a circle around her as she lay down and went into a light trance. 'In the language of psychology,' she wrote, 'it is autohypnosis by means of a symbol.' (Bear in mind that the Golden Dawn believed certain symbols are universal archetypes from the racial unconscious. Each of these symbols has a precise meaning, and will therefore elicit a particular response.) 'The trained initiate, therefore, does not wander on the astral plane like an uneasy ghost, but comes and goes by well-known corridors.' In other words, it is essentially a voyage into inner space, which the occultist believes to have a geography as precise as the world we live in, and to be common territory, like the world outside us, in which separate individuals may sometimes meet.

As soon as she had entered this inner space, Dion Fortune became aware of Mrs Mathers in her magical robes, barring her path. Mrs Mathers was of a higher grade in magic than Dion Fortune and, therefore, theoretically, stronger. 'There ensued a battle of wills in which I experienced the sensation of being whirled through the air and falling from a great height, and found myself back in my body.' When she emerged from her trance, her followers were in disarray: she had somersaulted across the room, bowling them over, and was lying in a corner. Realising that if she were to continue as a magician she had to return to the fight, she ordered the group to reform the circle. After invoking the Secret Chiefs, she went into a trance. 'This time, there was a short sharp struggle, and I was through. I had the Vision of the Inner Chiefs and returned. The fight was over. I have never had any trouble since.' That night when she undressed to go to bed,

Dion Fortune found that her back was scratched—as if clawed by a huge cat.

Of course this story could be pure invention. Yet, in one important respect, that is not the question at issue. We have no way of determining whether the story is objectively true—whether Dion Fortune actually journeyed the corridors of the astral plane. The question is whether the account has its own kind of integrity, and whether the experience was different in kind from an ordinary nightmare. Dion Fortune, like other magicians, certainly took the concept of the magical attack very seriously. She described in one of her books how one of her followers, Netta Fornario, was killed by an 'astral attack'. Miss Fornario had gone to the Holy Isle of Iona in western Scotland to practice astral travel. One day she seemed panic-stricken and told her landlady that she was being attacked telepathically—her silver jewellery had all turned black overnight. The next day her body was found some miles away, dressed only in a magical robe. The soles of her feet were lacerated as if she had run over sharp stones. She had died of a heart attack, and Dion Fortune was convinced that Mrs Mathers was responsible.

It was inevitable that Mrs Mathers and Dion Fortune would go their separate ways. In 1924, Dion Fortune founded the Community (later, Fraternity) of the Inner Light; originally conceived as a part of the Golden Dawn, it assumed its own identity, four years later, with Dion Fortune as its 'Warden'. Her inner Master was now Melchizedec, 'Lord of Flame and also of Mind', and after initiation her pupils became High Priests of the Order of Melchizedec. Other Masters were Thomas Erskine, a Lord Chancellor at the time of Dr Johnson, Sir Thomas More, and—oddly enough—Socrates. She came to believe that Socrates was responsible for much of her magical *magnum opus*, *The Cosmic Doctrine*.

In the year of *The Cosmic Doctrine*, 1927, she married a handsome and charming Welshman, Thomas Penry Evans, who was a doctor and two years her junior—she called him Merl, after Merlin. In 1930, she leased a house called The Belfry in West Halkin Street, near Belgrave Square. She ran her 'magical school' at a house in Glastonbury, Chalice Orchard (later bought by the Arthurian scholar Geoffrey Ashe), and gave lectures at

3 Queensborough Terrace in London. During the next twelve years she wrote her novels *The Winged Bull* (1935), *The Goat-Foot God* (1936), *The Sea Priestess* (1938)—regarded as her masterpiece—and *Moon Magic* (1939.) They have been described as the finest novels about magic ever written, and there is no doubt that they are works of extraordinary fascination—certainly among the best fiction ever written by an 'occultist'.

She also tells us a great deal in the novels about the gradual break-up of her marriage. There seem to have been many reasons—her lack of interest in physical sexuality, her increasing bulk (it seems to be a characteristic of mediums that they put on weight), her autocratic temperament. In 1938, her husband went to Barcelona to help the Republican government with the nutritional problems of children; on his return, he met a younger woman, and asked his wife for a divorce, which she granted.

During the war years, her life became increasingly dark. One of her leading disciples, Charles Seymour, defected—she regarded him as a great magician. Grandiose schemes for a national occult movement came to nothing. She became convinced that a black magician who was a member of Hitler's entourage was launching a magical assault on her, and her health declined.

In 1945, using the name 'Mrs Matthews,' she asked for an appointment with a Jungian psychiatrist, Dr Laurence Bendit. (Dion Fortune had become a 'Jungian', having long ago abandoned Freud.) She told him she felt she was approaching a crisis in her life, and wanted analysis. Bendit was struck by her keen intelligence. She described a number of dreams full of mythological images, but all, he noted, with an underlying tone of darkness. One day, as they were talking about the Cabala, Dr Bendit mentioned that the only book he had read on it was Dion Fortune's *The Mystical Qabalah*, and went on to make some criticism of her interpretation of Tiphereth. His patient then told him: 'I am Dion Fortune.' (The book Dr Bendit mentioned is generally acknowledged to be her most important contribution to the theory of ritual magic.)

Mrs Bendit had seen Dion Fortune passing through the waiting room, and had asked the identity of 'that strange woman'. When her husband asked why she wanted to know, Mrs Bendit remarked: 'I couldn't help noticing she was just a burned-out shell.'

At Christmas, as she made another appointment, Dr Bendit had a sudden intuitive certainty that she would not keep it. And when he sent her cheque to his bank in the New Year, it was returned stamped 'Drawer deceased'. What had seemed a general malaise had suddenly flared into acute leukaemia.

It seems appropriate that Dion Fortune should be the last 'great magician' of the 20th century. More than any other, she has left a personal record of herself in her works, and these are unique in that they reveal the inner life of an 'adept' in such intimate detail. They make it clear that the destiny of a magician is at the same time one of the most fascinating and one of the most difficult in the world.

13.
The Mystery of Time

IT WAS THE LATE 'Professor' Joad who, in his *Guide to Modern Thought*, used the phrase 'the undoubted queerness of time'. The case he refers to was recorded by two maiden ladies, Charlotte Moberly and Eleanor Jourdain, successive principals of an Oxford college, in their book *An Adventure*, published in 1911. On August 10, 1901, the two ladies visited the Trianon park at Versailles and were surprised to encounter a number of people in 18th century dress. Two 'gardeners' gave them directions, and a man who hurried past them warned them not to take a certain path. They passed a woman in old-fashioned dress who was drawing, but only Miss Moberly saw her. Both ladies felt oddly depressed and experienced a dream-like sensation. They went into the Petit Trianon, followed a wedding party at a distance, then went back to their hotel for tea. A week later, when Miss Moberly was describing the visit in a letter, the two ladies compared notes and decided that there had been something odd about the afternoon. Miss Jourdain wrote her own detailed account. The following January, she returned alone to Versailles on a cold, rainy afternoon. Again she experienced 'the old eerie feeling'; 'it was as if I had crossed a line and was suddenly in a circle of influence'. She saw two labourers in bright tunics and hoods loading a cart; when she looked back a second later, they had vanished, although she could see a long way in all directions. She heard the rustling of silk dresses around her and heard voices, but she saw no one.

When the two ladies returned to the gardens three years later, they found everything totally changed. The trees had vanished; so had a rustic bridge, a ravine, a cascade and a 'kiosk'. Convinced now that they had seen the place as it was in the reign of Marie Antoinette and Louis XVI, they studied books on the period and concluded that they had actually seen historical personages of the period just before the Revolution, and that the woman seen by Charlotte Moberly could well have been Marie Antoinette. After publication of their book in 1911, three people who had lived in a house overlooking the park at Versailles told them that they had experienced the same kind of thing so often that they had ceased to pay any attention to it.

In 1938, a member of the Society for Psychical Research, J. E. Sturge-Whiting, strongly criticised the account of the two ladies. He had examined the grounds and concluded that they had simply followed paths that still exist on the first occasion and failed to locate them on their second visit. In 1965, Philippe Jullian published a biography of Count Robert de Montesquiou (the dandy on whom Proust based Baron de Charlus), which described how Montesquiou took a house near Versailles in the early 1890s and often spent whole days in the park. His friend Mme de Greffulhe organised a fancy-dress party in the Dairy. And this, remarks Jullian in an aside, could easily explain the 'adventure' of the two English ladies. 'Perhaps . . . the "ghosts" . . . were, quite simply, Mme Greffulhe, dressed as a shepherdess, rehearsing an entertainment with some friends . . .'

The explanation sounds plausible, and together with Sturge-Whiting's theory of the paths, it so convinced Dame Joan Evans, the literary executor of the two ladies, that she decided to allow *An Adventure* to go out of print. Yet on closer examination, the two theories still leave nine-tenths of the incidents unexplained. Sturge-Whiting fails to explain away the topographical problem. Charlotte Moberly says quite clearly about her 1904 visit:

'From this point [the guard house] everything was changed . . . We came directly to the gardener's house, which was quite different in appearance from the cottage described by Miss Jourdain in 1901 . . . Beyond the gardener's house was a parterre with flower beds and a smooth lawn of many years' careful tendance. It did not seem to be the place where we had met the garden officials. We spent a long time looking for the old paths. Not only was there no trace of them, but the distances were contracted . . . The kiosk was gone; so was the ravine and the little cascade which had fallen from a height above our heads, and the little bridge over the ravine . . .'

And so on for several more detailed pages. Which suggests that either the ladies were exaggerating, or Sturge-Whiting must be wrong.

Philippe Jullian apparently failed to check the date of the Versailles adventure. Montesquiou moved to Versailles in the early 1890s and moved again—to Neuilly—in 1894, so the fancy-dress party took place at least seven years too early for the English ladies to have seen a rehearsal.

Finally, Joan Evans makes no attempt to explain what happened on Miss Jourdain's 1902 visit, when she saw the disappearing carters. On this occasion, Miss Jourdain again saw the 'old' Versailles, as on her first visit. During the next two years, she returned many times and must have become fairly familiar with the geography of the park; on all these occasions she found the place completely changed and 'modernised'.

And so on the Versailles adventure remains one of the most baffling and incongruous incidents in the history of modern psychical research.

Joad concludes: 'While admitting that the hypothesis of the present existence of the past is beset with difficulties of a metaphysical character . . . I think that it indicates the most fruitful basis for the investigation of these intriguing experiences.' What exactly did he mean by 'the present existence of the past'? He never bothered to explain. But the phrase seems to suggest a notion that is not too difficult to grasp: that the past is somehow alive and still among us, like the voice of Caruso preserved on gramophone records.

In fact, as we have seen, Joseph Rodes Buchanan, and his disciple William Denton, meant roughly the same thing by 'psychometry' (Chapter 3), and Denton even coined the phrase 'telescope into the past'. But then, psychometry is not literally the ability to see into the past—any more than a gramophone stylus is a time machine that can transport you back into the life of Caruso. If the faculty exists—and there is much convincing evidence that it does—then it could be explained simply as a very highly developed ability to 'read' the history of objects, rather as Sherlock Holmes was able to tell Watson the history of his alcoholic brother from the evidence of his watch. And this, I suspect, is not precisely what Joad meant by the 'undoubted queerness of time'. For, in the section before his account of the 'adventure' of Miss Moberly and Miss Jourdain, he discusses J.W. Dunne's book *An Experiment with Time*; and Dunne's book is an account of how he had certain clear and detailed dreams of the *future*. If Dunne's book is to be believed—and, again, he had a reputation for integrity—then he dreamed of such events as the great Martinique earthquake some weeks before it happened. And this is utterly unexplainable on any 'scientific' theory of time, no matter how abstract and complex: the scientists' view of time dictates that the future cannot affect the past. I may be able to explain certain personal premonitions—say, the death of a relative—in logical terms (i.e., I knew he was ill and suffered from a bad heart), but to dream of a volcanic explosion on an island you know nothing about is obviously an event of a different order.

There, then, is the problem. The files of the Society for Psychical Research and the College of Psychic Studies are full of convincing cases or premonitions of the future and curious visions of the past. The two examples that follow both concern the same man: Air-Marshal Sir Victor Goddard.

In 1935, when he was a Wing Commander, Goddard was sent to visit a disused First World War airfield at Drem, near Edinburgh. It proved to be in a state of dilapidation, with disintegrating hangars and cracked tarmac. Cattle grazed on the old airfield. Later that day Goddard took off in his Hawker Hart biplane from Turnhouse, Edinburgh, to head for home. But he soon encountered thick cloud and heavy rain, and as he tried to descend below the cloud ceiling the plane spun for a few moments out of control. He managed to straighten out close to the ground—so close that he almost hit a woman who was running with a pram. Ahead of him was the Firth of Forth, and Goddard decided to head for Drem airfield to get his bearings.

It was still raining heavily as he crossed the airfield boundary. Then an odd thing happened: he suddenly found himself in bright sunlight. And Drem airfield was no longer an overgrown field, but a neat, orderly place, with four yellow planes parked in front of open hangar doors and mechanics in blue overalls walking around. Both these things surprised Goddard, for in those days all RAF planes were painted with aluminium and mechanics wore khaki overalls. Moreover the mechanics did not even glance up as the plane roared a few feet overhead: Goddard had the feeling that they did not see him. He also had the feeling of 'something ethereal about the sunlight'.

When he landed he told his immediate superior about his 'hallucination', and was advised to lay off the whisky. So Goddard said nothing about his 'vision' in his official report. It was not until four years later, when war broke out, that he received an even greater shock. Next time he saw Drem it had been transformed into the airfield of his vision. The 'trainers' were now painted yellow and the mechanics wore blue overalls. A monoplane he had failed to recognise four years earlier he now identified as a Miles Magister.

Recordings from the past are a reality, as every film and gramophone record demonstrates. But a recording from the future sounds preposterous. Even if we assume it was a hallucination, and not a 'time-slip' into the future, it remains just as impossible.

The second episode concerns a glimpse of the more immediate future.

In 1946 Sir Victor Goddard was attending a party given in his honour in Shanghai. He was talking to some friends when he overheard someone behind him announcing that he—Goddard—was dead. He turned round and found himself looking into the face of a British naval commander, Captain Gerald Gladstone. Gladstone immediately recognised him, and looked appalled. 'I'm terribly sorry! I do apologize!' 'But what made you think I was dead?' 'I dreamt it.'

Gladstone went on to describe his dream. He had seen the crash of a transport passenger plane, perhaps a Dakota, on a rocky coast: it had been driven down by a terrible snowstorm. In addition to its RAF crew the plane also carried three civilians, two men and a women: they had emerged from the plane, but Air Marshal Goddard had not. Gladstone had awakened with a strong conviction that Goddard was dead, and throughout that day he expected to hear the news.

Goddard was not too worried: he *was* due to fly to Tokyo in a Dakota, but there would be no civilians on board. He and Gladstone spent a pleasant half hour or so discussing Dunne's theory of time. But during dinner there were alarming developments. A *Daily Telegraph* journalist asked if he could beg a lift to Japan. Then the Consul General told Goddard that he had received orders to return to Tokyo immediately and asked if he could travel too; he also asked if they could find room for a female secretary. With deep misgivings, Goddard agreed. And when the plane took off from Shanghai, he personally had no doubt whatever that he was about to die.

The Dakota was caught in heavy cloud over mountains— another detail Captain Gladstone had 'seen'—then ran into a fierce snowstorm. Finally the pilot was forced to crash-land on the rocky coastline of an island off the shore of Japan. But Gladstone proved to be mistaken about Goddard's death: everyone on board survived.

Such incidents flatly contradict everything that human beings know—intuitively—about time. The one thing that is absolutely certain about our world is that everything that is born ends eventually by dying, and that, in between these two events, it gets steadily older. Time is irreversible. With the aid of a tape recorder, I can replay the voice of someone who is dead; but, if I happen to feel guilty about the way I have treated him, there is absolutely no way in which I can go back in time and 'unhappen' what has happened. We all know this. It is not only a fundamental part of our experience; it seems to be a law of the Universe.

Now when, in 1895, H.G. Wells wrote his science-fiction story *The Time Machine* he introduced his readers to an exciting and fascinating new hypothesis. Time, says Wells's Time Traveller, is nothing more than a fourth dimension of space. Consider photographs of a man at the ages of 8, 15, 17, 23, and so on. These are basically three-dimensional representations of a four-dimensional being, rather as you might take slices or cross-sections of a length of soft clay. What this implies is that each cross-section is in some way false or, at least, misleading—exactly as those flat Egyptian portraits of solid human beings are misleading. Seen from the perspective of the fourth dimension, a man is a single chunk of matter stretching from one point in time to another, not a three-dimensional chunk of matter *moving* from one moment to the next.

One of the Time Traveller's companions objects that we cannot move about in time; whereupon he makes an interesting reply: 'You are wrong to say that we cannot move about in Time. For instance, if I am recalling an incident very vividly I go back to the instant of its occurrence: I become absent-minded, as you say. I jump back for a moment. Of course, we have no means of staying back for any length of Time, any more than a savage or animal has of staying six feet above the ground. But a civilized man is better off than the savage in this respect. He can go up against gravitation in a balloon, and why should he not hope that ultimately he may even be able to stop or accelerate his drift along the Time-Dimension, or even turn about and travel the other way . . .?'

The Traveller, of course, claims to have invented a machine for doing precisely this. But the interesting point of the above explanation is that it suggests a quite different method of time travel. Wells says that when we recall an event vividly, we move back into the past for a moment; but we have no capacity to stay there. Time, he says, in another paragraph, is essentially *mental* travel from the cradle to the grave. What Wells is suggesting is that time travel is a mental faculty we already possess, but to a very slight extent.

Wells himself apparently forgot that important suggestion, thrown off casually in the opening chapter of *The Time Machine*. And the remainder of his story—with its mechanical flight through time—raises the kind of paradoxical questions that have become a commonplace of science fiction ever since. For example, as he moves into the future, he sees his housekeeper come into the room and move across it with the speed of a bullet: for now he is moving more swiftly through time, her action happens in a shorter space of time. If he had been going backwards in time, he would have seen her move across the room backwards, her actions reversed. But then, would he not also have seen *himself*, as he was a few minutes before, or the day or month before? In fact, what was to prevent him halting the Time Machine and going to shake hands with his 'self' of yesterday? Or why should he not go forward to his self of tomorrow and ask him what horse won the Grand National? He could even ask his self of tomorrow and his self of yesterday to climb into the Time Machine and accompany him back to today for dinner . . .

And already we see the emergence of the paradox. What right has the Time Traveller to regard his own time as *the* present, and his own 'self' as *the* Time Traveller? Wells sidesteps this question by sending the Traveller backwards or forwards in time *beyond* his own life span. So if he went back to 1812 to meet Napoleon or 1066 to meet King Harold, it would *sound* perfectly logical, if unbelievable. But if the Time Traveller consists of millions of 'selves', one for every split second of his life, then the same goes for every other person and object in the Universe. The trouble with this is that every one of these multiple beings would have its own past and future, since each is a separate individual. (For example, if the Time Traveller invited his selves of yesterday and tomorrow for dinner, each would proceed to travel into the future separately as three separate beings.) You end up with an absurd vision of a multiple-multiple Universe in which everyone is fragmented into an infinite number of selves . . .

It is, of course, mere fiction, so we can forgive its shortcomings. But then, the actual experience of time travel is *not* mere fiction. I suggested, for example, that the Time Traveller of today might pay a call on his self of tomorrow to enquire the winner of the Grand National; he could then go back to his own time and place a large bet on it . . . But such events have, in fact, occurred. In 1976 I made a television programme for BBC2 about John Godley, Lord Kilbracken, who, as an Oxford undergraduate, dreamed winners of horse races, and made several useful sums of money through his curious ability. Peter Fairley, the science correspondent of Independent Television, had a similar experience. In a BBC broadcast, he told how, as he was driving to work one day in 1965, he heard a request on the car radio for a Mrs Blakeney; he had just driven through the village of Blakeney, and a few minutes later, heard a reference to another—totally unconnected—Blakeney. At the office he heard the name again, this time a horse running in the Derby. He backed it and it won. From then on, he explained, he could pick winners merely by looking down a list of horses; the winner would 'leap off the page' at him. He said that as soon as he began to think about it and worry about it, the faculty vanished . . .

Now this is altogether closer to Wells's suggestion of Time Travel as a purely mental faculty. And it is certainly far more convincing than the version involving time machines.

Let us, then, agree that the usual notion of time travel, derived from Wells, is absurd and self-contradictory. In *that* sense, the past is the past and the future is the future, and we can never hope to explore either with the aid of a Time Machine. For in this sense, time does not exist; it is a semantic misunderstanding. I tried to explain the reason for this in a passage of my book *The Occult*. Suppose people were born on moving trains and stayed on them until they died. They might invent a word to describe the everyday sensation of scenery flowing past the window, a word like 'zyme'. When the train stops in stations they would say that zyme has halted; if the train reverses, they would say zyme is flowing backwards. But if someone spoke of zyme as an entity, they would obviously be committing a logical error; it consists of *many* things—a railway carriage, scenery, motion and so on. The same goes for time. It is basically a *process* which involves physical objects. If you think of a completely 'empty' Universe, or a completely static Universe, it would obviously have no time. *This* is why Wells's time machine is an absurdity.

If Peter Fairley could really predict which horse would win a race, then there is clearly something wrong with our human notion of time; for the idea that the future has already taken place—which it must have done if you are to 'know' it—is self-contradictory, a paradox. But then, our minds are a paradox in precisely the same sense. You and I apparently exist in a solid, three-dimensional Universe: we are physical objects. Then where, precisely, is my mind? Inside my head? 'Realist' philosophers have tried hard to explain mind in physical terms—the brain and the nervous system—but they end with a static model, rather like a computer. And a computer needs to be *worked* by somebody. When I struggle with an intellectual or emotional problem, I am aware of an element that I call 'me' trying to get the best out of the computer. This being can look on quite detachedly while 'I' am flooded with a powerful emotion. It applies the accelerator or brake to my moods and feelings. It seems to exist in a dimension apart from this physical world we live in.

To me, these considerations suggest that these two paradoxical concepts—time and the mind—are closely connected. Our bodies exist in the realm of one-way time, but our minds do not. As Wells points out, when I become absent-minded, my mind goes 'elsewhere'. But on the whole, these visits to other times and places are far less vivid than our everyday lives. Yet this is not so much a limitation of our minds as of the 'computer' they use, the brain.

For example, there is an important experience of the philosopher J.B. Bennett described in his autobiography *Witness*. Bennett tells how, when he was staying at the Gurdjieff Institute at Fontainebleau, he woke up one morning feeling exceptionally weak from dysentery, but nevertheless forced himself to get up. Later that morning he took part in some Gurdjieff exercises— incredibly difficult and complex physical movements. One by one, the other disciples dropped out; but, in spite of extreme fatigue and discomfort, Bennett forced himself to go on. Then, quite suddenly, 'I was filled with an influx of an immense power. My body seemed to have turned into light.' All fatigue vanished. When he went outside, he decided to test this power by digging at a rate he could not ordinarily maintain for more than a few minutes; he was able to continue for half an hour without fatigue. He walked out into the forest, and decided to try to test his control over his emotions. He willed himself to feel astonishment. 'Instantly, I was overwhelmed with amazement, not only at my own state, but at everything I looked at or thought of.' The thought of 'fear' fill him with immense dread; the thought of 'joy' filled him with rapture; the thought of 'love' flooded him with a tremendous tenderness and compassion. Finally, bewildered by this new ability to feel anything he liked, he willed it to go away, and it instantly vanished.

Now what is involved here is obviously what William James calls 'vital reserves'. James points out that we can feel exhausted, push ourselves *beyond* the exhaustion, and suddenly feel full of energy again. It is the phenomenon of 'second wind'. It seems that we possess vast energy reserves that we fail to make use of. But a sudden emergency will bring them into operation. Bennett's tremendous effort not to drop out of the Gurdjieff exercises somehow pushed him into a heightened state of 'second wind', and brought a completely new level of control over his 'computer'. It is a pity that he did not try the experiment of recalling some event from his past; I suspect that he would have been able to 'replay' it in the most accurate detail.

In fact, as Dr Wilder Penfield discovered, our brains contain the stored 'memory tapes' of everything we have ever seen or felt, and these tapes can be 'replayed' by stimulating the temporal cortex of the brain with an electric probe. If we could achieve Bennett's state of 'second wind', the electric probe would be unnecessary; all the memory tapes of the brain would become instantly accessible to us . . .

But that, you will object, is still not time travel; it is merely playing back a recording. True. But, if Joseph Rodes Buchanan and William Denton were correct about 'psychometry', then the brain also has the power to play back the history of any object it chooses to scan—for example, a five billion-year-old meteorite. Buchanan's 'sensitives' could hold a sealed letter and describe not only its contents but also the state of mind of the person who had written it. And this, you may point out, is still not time travel. True. But it is something very like it. And I would remind you that we have already agreed that time travel, in Wells's sense, is an absurdity. You cannot literally go back 'before' the Battle of Hastings, because the Battle of Hastings has already happened, and it cannot be unhappened. Yet, if Buchanan and Denton are correct, then it should be possible for a 'sensitive' to literally relive a day in the life of a soldier who fought at the battle of Hastings. And Dunne's experiment with time seems to suggest that it might be possible to do the same for the future, and 'relive' a day that has not yet taken place. And this, I think, *would* qualify as time travel.

What I am now suggesting is a view of the human mind that has been forcing itself upon me for many years. My starting-point, in books like *The Outsider* and *Religion and the Rebel*, was the experiences of certain poets and mystics. The romantic poets of the 19th century seemed to differ from their predecessors in one important respect: they seemed to have an altogether greater capacity for sustaining *imaginative intensity*. We live our lives confined by space and time and the trivial necessities of everyday life; consciousness is basically a device for perceiving what goes on around us. Poets and mystics seem to be able to use it for a quite different purpose—to build up a kind of internal world whose intensity rivals that of the physical reality that surrounds us. When I came—almost by accident—to turn my attention to the realm of the 'occult' or paranormal, it struck me that the 'psychic' is only another type of poet: a person for whom the physical world is only one aspect of reality.

Now this view seems to me, on reflection, logical and reasonable enough. Consciousness is tied to the physical world for a simple reason: if it weren't, we would have been extinct long ago. As H.G. Wells pointed out, all animals are 'up against it' from the moment they are born. In the Victorian age, children began work at six in the morning and finished at eight in the evening. Life is still brutal and hard for well over a half of the human race. *I* am lucky that I can sit at my desk, in a comfortable room, and address my mind to this interesting problem of the nature of time; you are lucky that you can sit down and read it. If you and I had to work a fourteen-hour day in a factory we would long for a little leisure to relax and allow the mind to wing its way through the worlds of imagination.

Because of this harsh physical necessity, consciousness has accustomed itself to sticking to the material world: which means, in effect, that it has never had a chance to explore its own capacities—or rather, the capacities of that extraordinary computer called the brain. But here we come to one of the strangest parts of the story. For some odd reason, the capacity of this computer is far greater than it needs to be—at least, in terms of Darwinian evolution. For example, it is quite clear that we never make use of that vast library of 'memory tapes' that Wilder Penfield discovered; we don't *need* to make use of them for everyday survival. Then why are they there? Why has evolution dictated that the brain should remember every tiny event and idea of our lives? Again, I have always been fascinated by the capacity of calculating prodigies—usually young children of ordinary intelligence—who can multiply or divide immense sums in their heads. Equally extraordinary is the class known as 'idiot savants'—children whose IQ may be on the moron level, yet who, in one particular field, have some incredible mental gift—one, for example, could reel off the name of every musical film ever made and every actor who played every part. Moreover, some of these idiot savants have highly developed 'psychic' powers; for example, one boy declined a lift home with his teacher because, he said, his mother would be meeting him out of school. In fact, his mother *did* arrive to meet him; but she had decided to do so only half an hour before, when another trip took her close to the school . . .

And this example brings me to the starting-point of my book *The Occult*: the observation that 'psychic powers' often seem to involve a breakdown—or at least, loss of efficiency—in our normal mental powers. For example, a Dutch house painter named Peter van der Hurk fell off his ladder and fractured his skull; when he woke up in hospital, he discovered that he 'knew' all kinds of things about his fellow patients, about their past and even their future. This strange capacity has remained with him and, under the name of Peter Hurkos, he has made a considerable reputation as a 'clairvoyant' and psychometrist, often helping the police to solve murder cases. But, in the days immediately following his accident, he found life difficult because his new psychic powers made it impossible for him to concentrate on ordinary, everyday jobs; he might have starved if someone had not suggested using his powers to make a living as a stage 'magician'. When I read this story in Hurkos' autobiography I found myself thinking of all those romantic poets and artists who had died in poverty because they found it impossible to concentrate on the dreary necessities of material existence. There is obviously a close analogy.

All this seems to suggest that our brains possess extraordinary powers that most of us never have reason to use. The problem of survival demands that we are tied down to the everyday world; if this were not so, we might all be calculating prodigies and psychics, and probably literary and artistic geniuses into the bargain.

But to phrase it this way suggests that it is a question of either/or: either we get rid of such unusual faculties or we lose our ability to survive. But is the choice really as harsh as that? I am inclined to doubt it. Life for most of us is safer and more secure than at any other time in history. Modern man is far less likely to be knocked down by a car than his ancestors were to be eaten by wild beasts or killed by their fellow men. (Even as recently as the age of Dr Johnson, remote country houses were often besieged by gangs of ruffians who killed those who resisted and carried off everything of value.) Most of us have hours of leisure every week in which we might explore the possibilities of human consciousness. No, the real problem is a force of habit so deeply ingrained that it would be better to refer to it as hypnosis. If you force a chicken's beak against the floor, then draw a chalk line straight in front of it, the chicken will be unable to raise its head when you let it go; for some odd reason it focuses attention on the chalk line, and becomes hypnotized by it. We all suffer from a similar tendency; the moment we relax, habit induces a state similar to hypnosis, in which the attention becomes fixed on the external world. Sartre wrote about the café proprietor in *Nausea*: 'When his café empties, his head empties too.' But it is not confined to the illiterate or unintelligent. There is a story told of the famous mathematician Hilbert. Before a dinner party, his wife sent him upstairs to change his tie; when, after an hour, he had still not reappeared, she went to see what had happened; he was in bed fast asleep. He explained that as soon as he had removed his tie, he had automatically taken off the rest of his clothes, put on his pyjamas and climbed into bed.

This is the problem of human consciousness: habits that bundle us into bed and off to sleep when there are far more interesting things to be done. Chesterton asked why the world is so full of bright children and dud grown-ups. The reason is that our most interesting potentialities fail to survive adolescence; we slip into a habit of using only a fraction of our powers.

When habit is broken, anything can happen. In a book called *Mysteries* (1978) I have cited the case of a lady named Jane O'Neill who, when driving to London airport, witnessed a serious accident and helped to free badly injured people from a wrecked coach. The shock was so severe that she had to take several weeks off from work. She began to experience strange waking visions, some of which were oddly accurate: for example, she 'saw' a close friend chained in the galleys; told about this, her friend replied that her ancestors were Huguenots and many *had* found themselves in the galleys. One day in Fotheringhay Church, Jane O'Neill was impressed by a picture behind the altar. She later mentioned this to the friend who had accompanied her, and her friend said that *she* had not seen any picture. Miss O'Neill was so puzzled that she rang the lady who cleaned the church and asked her about it; the lady replied that there was no such picture. Later, the two women revisited the church; to Jane O'Neill's surprise, the inside was quite different from what she had seen before—it was much smaller—and the picture was not there. She asked an expert on East Anglian churches, who put her in touch with a historian who knew the history of Fotheringhay. He was able to tell her that the church she had 'seen' had been the church as it was more than four centuries ago; it had been rebuilt in 1553 . . .

Jane O'Neill's experience is, in its way, as well authenticated as that of Miss Moberly and Miss Jourdain. In one sense, it is more convincing; I heard of it by accident, through a friend, and wrote to Miss O'Neill, who was kind enough to send me a full account, together with the exchange of letters with the historian which established that she had 'seen' the earlier church. Miss O'Neill had made no attempt to publish her interesting story, so cannot be accused of attention-seeking.

But how can we reconcile a story as extraordinary as this with our everyday experience of the real world? Most scientists have a short and convenient method of dealing with such anomalies; they dismiss them as lies, distortions or mistakes. Whether intellectually justified or not (on grounds of 'the laws of probability'), this is bound to strike anyone interested in such matters as pure mental laziness. If an answer is to be found, I believe that its starting-point must be the notion that the powers of the human mind are far less limited than we naturally assume. This was a conclusion I had reached many years before I became interested in the paranormal; so that, for example, in *Religion and the Rebel* (1957), I had suggested that our everyday consciousness is as limited as the middle few notes of a piano keyboard, and that its possible range is as wide as the whole keyboard. In states of great happiness or relief, or when involved in some absorbing adventure, we receive a clear intuition that the world is an infinitely richer and more complex place than ordinary consciousness permits us to perceive. And, moreover, that the mind is perfectly capable of taking a wider grip on that breadth and complexity . . .

Hurkos's accident, like Jane O'Neill's, shook his mind out of its usual narrow rut, and made him aware that 'everyday consciousness' is basically unreliable in its report about the actuality that surrounds us. But then, is not such narrowness preferable to the state of confused inefficiency that accompanied his powers of 'second sight'? Was Jane O'Neill's glimpse of Fotheringhay in the 16th century (or earlier) *worth* the mental shock of the coach accident? These questions raise serious doubts about the desirability of such powers. But then, we are assuming that it is possible to investigate the unknown powers of the mind only by destroying our everyday sense of reality. And this, fortunately, is untrue.

We may recall the story told by Alan Vaughan in his book *Patterns of Prophecy*, cited in Chapter 11 (p. 350), in which he became 'possessed' by the wife of a Nantucket sea captain, and how he was 'exorcised' by an occultist, who caused an entity called 'Z' to drive out the sea captain's wife through the top of Vaughan's head:

'I began to feel an energy rising up within my body and entering my brain. It pushed out both "Nada" and "Z". My friends noted that my face, which had been white and pinched, suddenly flooded with colour. I felt a tremendous sense of elation and physical wellbeing. The energy grew stronger and seemed to extend beyond my body. My mind seemed to race in some extended dimension that knew no confines of time or space. For the first time, I began to sense what was going on in other people's minds and—to my astonishment—I began to sense the future through some kind of extended awareness. My first act in this strange but exciting state was to throw the Ouija down an incinerator chute . . .'

It was this experience that led Vaughan to study the whole question of prophetic glimpses of the future. He had *seen* this 'extended dimension that knew no confines of time or space', and decided that it deserved to be investigated. The poet Robert Graves described a similar experience in a story called 'The Abominable Mr Gunn' (which, he told me, was autobiographical): 'One fine summer evening as I sat alone on the roller behind the cricket pavilion, with nothing in my head, I received a celestial illumination: it occurred to me that I knew everything. I remember letting my mind range rapidly over all its familiar subjects of knowledge; only to find that this was no foolish fancy. I did know everything. To be plain: though conscious of having come less than a third of the way along the path of formal education . . . I nevertheless held the key of truth in my hand, and could use it to open any lock of any door. Mine was no religious or philosophical theory, but a simple method of looking sideways at disorderly facts so as to make perfect sense of them.'

The 'secret', Graves says, was still there when he woke up the next morning; but, when he tried writing it down, it vanished.

It is true that Graves fails to explain just what he meant by the 'secret', except to say that it was 'a sudden infantile awareness of the power of intuition, the supra-logic that cuts out all routine processes of thought and leaps straight from problem to answer'. But he offers a further clue in citing the case of another boy in the school who was able to solve a highly complicated arithmetical problem merely by looking at it. The form master—'Mr Gunn'—accused the boy of looking at the answer at the end of the book; the boy replied that he *had* checked with the answer—later—and that its last two figures were wrong—they should be 35, not 53. The unsympathetic and obtuse Mr Gunn sent the boy to the headmaster for a caning, declining to believe that he could simply have 'seen' the answer . . .

So it seems that Graves is speaking of a power related to that of mathematical prodigies, the ability of the mind to *see* the answer to a problem in a single flash. And how, precisely, does such an ability work? Is it some form of lightning calculation, that is, a process of ordinary reason in which everything is speeded up, as in the famous Trachtenberg speed system of mathematics? Apparently not. We know this from the case of Zerah Colburn, the Canadian calculating prodigy, who was asked whether a certain immense number was a prime (i.e. could not be divided by any other number), and who replied instantly: No, it can be divided by 641. Now there is no mathematical method of determining whether a certain number is a prime—except the painful method of trial and error, dividing it by every smaller number and deciding that none of them works (shortcuts exist: if it can't be divided by 3 it can't be divided by 6, 9, 12, 15 . . .). Obviously, Colburn 'saw' the answer, as Graves's fellow pupil F.F. Smilley did—from 'above', as it were: a kind of bird's eye view. And Graves' 'secret' was, presumably, some similar method of grasping the answer to any problem by instantaneous intuition . . .

We have seen in Chapter 2 that man is a double being, with two selves who live one in each half of the brain. The being you call 'you'—your ego—resides in the left cerebral hemisphere. A few inches away, in the right hemisphere, there is another 'you'; but it is dumb.

When I work out a sum on paper, I am using my left hemisphere—with a certain amount of occasional assistance from the right, by way of sudden insights. And this, on the whole, seems to be the way the human brain works: the left is the 'front man', the ego that deals with the world; and the right has to express itself *via* the left. And, on the whole, the right has a fairly hard time of it; for the left is always in a hurry, always working out problems, and it tends to treat the right with impatience. This is why civilized Man seems to possess so little intuition.

It seems probable that calculating prodigies have not yet fallen victim to this bullying dominance of the left. The 'shades of the prison house' have not yet begun to close. They *see* the answer to a problem, and pass it on instantaneously, unimpeded by the usual red tape of the bureaucrat who lives in the left brain.

For this, I must stress, is the real problem of civilized Man. We have evolved to our present level through the use of language and concepts. We use these so constantly that we 'identify' with the left half of the brain. This does no real harm, for in a sense the 'personality' *is* the linguistic part of us. The trouble arises from the *attitude* of the ego to the non-ego who lives in the right cerebral hemisphere. We tend to treat it as an idiot, as a kind of inarticulate and not-very-bright younger brother who is always being ignored and told to shut up. If we took the trouble to listen to it, we might learn a great deal. Occasionally, it may become so alarmed at our carefully calculated stupidities that it takes the law into its own hands and interferes. Here I can cite a personal example. The hill that leads up from Pentewan to Mevagissey is long, and has several abrupt curves. One day, I was driving up this hill with the sun in my eyes, almost completely blinded. At a certain point I reasoned that I must be approaching a bend, and tried to turn the steering-wheel. *My hands ignored me*: they kept the wheel steady. My right brain knew I had not yet reached the bend, and simply cancelled my order to turn the steering-wheel.

Even this last sentence illustrates our basic mistake. I say '*my* hands', '*my* right brain', as if they were both my property, like my clothes. But the being who calls himself 'I' is a usurper. It is his brother, who lives next door, who is the rightful heir to the throne. I say this because the left, for all its naïve egoism, cannot live without the intuitions and insights of the right—there are many creatures in the world who live perfectly well without language or ideas. But the ideal state is one of close co-operation between the two halves, with the left treating the right as a wise counsellor and trusted adviser, not as the village idiot.

Significantly, the left brain has a strong sense of time; the right has absolutely none. It strolls along at its own pace, with its hands in its pockets. This does not mean that the right lacks the ability to calculate time—on the contrary, when you tell yourself that you must wake up at six o'clock precisely and you open your eyes on the stroke of six, this is the work of the right. But it declines to take time too seriously. And it is right to feel sceptical. The left is stupidly obsessed by time. An anecdote told by William Seabrook of Aleister Crowley illustrates the point. When Crowley was on the island of Sicily, a film star named Jane Wolfe came to pay him a visit; she was in a state of permanent nervous tension. Crowley told her that she must begin her cure with a month of meditation on the cliff top. The idea dismayed her, but she agreed. She lived in a lean-to shelter and a boy brought up water, bread and grapes every day at dusk. For the first few days she was bored and irritable. By the 19th day she felt nothing but boredom. Then, quite suddenly, she passed into a state of deep calm and peace, with no desire to move. What had happened was simply that her over-dominant left brain—accustomed to the Hollywood rat race—had gradually realised that it could stop running; then the right took over, with its sense of timelessness and serenity.

What is being suggested is that *time is an invention of the left brain*. Time, as such, does not exist in nature. Nature knows only what Whitehead calls 'process'—things happening. What human beings call time is a psychological concept; moreover, it is a left-brain concept.

Now the left brain, as we know, sees things in rigid categories, and nature does not operate within such categories. Consider Zeno's paradox of the arrow. At any moment it is either where it is or where it isn't. It *can't* be where it isn't; but if it is where it *is*, then it can't be moving. The paradox of Achilles and the tortoise depends on the same kind of logic. But the arrow *does* move; Achilles *does* overtake the tortoise, although it is 'logically' impossible. According to the left brain, there is no logical way of deciding whether a large number is a prime except by trial and error, but Zerah Colburn's right brain solved it instantly; and, in the same way, Peter Fairley's right brain knew in advance which horses would win at the races. (Significantly, Fairley had suffered temporary blindness just before he developed this ability; it seems probably that the shock was responsible for 'short-circuiting' the usual left-brain processes.)

This chapter is, of course, written in language, and it makes use of concepts; consequently its aim is, to some extent, self-defeating. How can I convey in words the notion that time itself is merely a concept? The above examples can at least take us in the right direction. For most people have known what it is to suddenly 'know' the answer to a problem without thinking it out. Everyone has had the experience of trying hard to remember something, and then having it stroll into his brain when he was no longer trying—almost as if another person had knocked on the door of the left brain and said: 'Is this what you were looking for?'

Which brings me to the most important step in this argument: that everyone has experienced the most basic 'right-brain'insight, the curious ability that in *The Occult* I labelled 'Faculty X'. This is simply that odd ability to suddenly grasp the *reality* of some other time or other place. I have elsewhere cited the example of the experience that led Arnold Toynbee to begin his *Study of History*. Toynbee was sitting at the summit of the citadel of Mistrà, in Sparta, looking at the ruins that had been left by the wild highlanders who had overwhelmed it in 1821, when he was suddenly struck by the *reality* of what had happened—as if the highlanders were, at that very minute, pouring over the horizon and overwhelming the city. He goes on to describe half a dozen more occasions when the 'historical imagination' has suddenly 'brought the past to life' and made it real, and ends by describing a semi-mystical experience that occurred as he was passing Victoria Station, London, during World War I, when he found himself 'in communion, not just with this or that episode in History, but with all that had been, and was, and was to come'.

Chesterton once said: 'We say thank you when someone passes us the salt, but we don't *mean* it. We say the Earth is round, but we don't mean it, even though it's true.' We mean something only when we feel it intensely, here and now. And this is what happens in flashes of Faculty X: the mind suddenly conjures up the *reality* of some other time and place, as Proust's hero suddenly became aware of the reality of his childhood as he tasted the cake dipped in herb tea.

Faculty X is another name for insight, the sudden flash of understanding, of direct knowledge. And it enables us to see precisely how the left and right co-operate. At school, I may learn some mathematical formula, like those for doing long division or extracting square roots; but I use it mechanically. If one day I forget the formula, and have to work it out for myself, I achieve insight into the reasons that lie behind it. But I can quite easily forget this insight, and go back to a mechanical use of the formula. The left brain deals with surfaces, with forms; the right brain deals with insights, with what lies beneath the surface. The left brain is a labour-saving device, an energy-saving device—exactly like using some simple mnemonic to remember the colours of the spectrum or the black notes on the piano. It is when you are full of energy—perhaps on a spring morning—that the right brain produces that odd glowing sense of reality. When you are very tired, the left brain takes over. Constant mental fatigue can produce the state Sartre calls 'nausea', in which the left brain scans the world but lacks all insight into its meaning—the right has gone off duty: reality seems crude and meaningless.

But here is the most difficult part of the argument to grasp. It is the right brain which presents us with 'reality'. The left presents us only with *immediacy*, what happens to be here and now. The left 'scans' the world; the right adds meaning and value. And your eyes, which are now scanning these words, are actually *telling you lies*. For they are presenting an essentially unreal world to you as the only reality. 'This is real,' I say, knocking on the table with my knuckles; but my knuckles are only scanners, like my eyes.

If, as you read these lines, you can penetrate to the meaning I am trying to convey, you will do it by a mental *leap*, from left to right. And if you can make that leap, you will also be able to grasp how Peter Fairley could know the winners of a race that had not yet taken place, or how Zerah Colburn could 'know' that 4,294,967,297 is divisible by 641. Somehow, the right 'thinks' vertically, by taking a kind of upward leap and simply looking down on the answer. You will object that this still doesn't explain how it could 'look down on' the future, but this is because you are still thinking in left-brain terms. How would you, in fact, go about predicting some future event, assuming that someone made it worth your while to do so? You would ploddingly try to assemble thousands of present 'trends', and try to work them out according to the law of probabilities. And because there are so many billions of possibilities, we say the future is unpredictable. The right brain appears to know better . . .

Let me try to summarize the argument so far. We have begun by dismissing 'time' in the Wellsian sense, the kind of time in which you could travel with the aid of a time machine. Like 'zyme', this time is a logical error. What really happens out there is 'process', and it would be absurd to speak of travelling in process. Time is actually a clock ticking inside the head—and, what is more, in only one side of the head. Our senses, which are built to 'scan' the world, chop up process into seconds and minutes. They force us to see the world in these rigid terms of spatial and temporal location. Kant was quite right when he said that we see the world through 'categories'. Think of the Kantian categories as a weird pair of prismatic spectacles you wear on your nose, spectacles which turn everything you see into the strangest angles and corners. *This* is space and time, as our brains grasp it.

All this, of course, fails to answer a basic question: how future time—that is, process which has not yet taken place—can be predictable. The only scientific explanation is the one we have considered, the statistical assessment of 'trends'. But it seems fairly clear that Peter Fairley was unable to spot winners by this method, for he knew nothing about racing, let alone about the complex possibilities presented by all the horses in the race. Anyway, experiment has shown that this cannot be the explanation. The well-known psychical investigator S. G. Soal performed a series of experiments in telepathy with a man named Basil Shackleton, and both were disappointed that the results seemed to be negative. Then a careful look at the results revealed an interesting thing: Shackleton was guessing the *next* ESP card that would be chosen. This was confirmed by substituting cards with animal pictures—zebras, giraffes, and so on. Now there could be no possible doubt. If Soal uncovered a card of a zebra, and Shackleton (sitting in the next room) named it as a giraffe, it was almost certain that the *next* card Soal turned over would be a giraffe. Other experimenters—like J. B. Rhine and Charles Tart—have produced similar results.

So it looks as if we are faced with a basic fact: that, whether it is impossible or not, precognition actually takes place—precise and detailed precognition of the future—which suggests clearly that the 'Kantian' theory is basically correct: there is something *wrong* with what our senses—and left brain—tell us about the world.

I could easily spend the remainder of this chapter raising questions about precisely how our senses could be mistaken. Such an approach would be interesting; but I doubt whether it would be very conclusive. Besides, much of my time would be taken up in summarising Edmund Husserl's book *The Phenomenology of Internal Time Consciousness*; and those who are interested would do better to read it for themselves. Instead, let us, for the sake of argument, assume that this part of the case is proved—that there is something wrong with our left-brain conception of time—and look more closely into the other half of the equation: the curious power that, under certain circumstances, seems to enable us to foresee the future.

In a fascinating and lucid book, *The Case Against Jones*, John Vyvyan cites two interesting cases, one of precognition, one of retrocognition.

The first concerns a priest named Canon Guarnier, who dreamed with exceptional clarity of an Italian landscape—a mountain road, a white house, a woman knitting with her daughter looking on, three men dressed in aprons and pointed hats sitting at a table, a sleeping dog, three sheep in a field . . . The scene was detailed and vivid. Three years later, on his way to Rome, Guarnier's carriage stopped to change horses, and he found himself looking at the identical scene, accurate in every detail. 'Nothing is changed; the people are exactly those I saw, as I saw them, doing the same things in the same attitudes, with the same gestures . . .'

The other case concerns the novelist George Gissing, who fell into a fever at Crotone in southern Italy. After a nightmare, he fell into a 'visionary state', in which he saw a series of pictures of Roman history. These are described in considerable detail—too long to quote here. But Gissing himself had no doubt that he had somehow witnessed real scenes of history, not simply imaginative pictures. 'If the picture corresponded to nothing real, tell me who can, by what power I reconstructed, to the last perfection of intimacy, a world known to me only in ruined fragments.'

This, of course, is no proof that it was not imagination. What strikes me in reading Gissing's account—for example, of seeing Hannibal's slaughter of two thousand mercenaries on the seashore by Crotone—is its similarity to Toynbee's 'visions' of the past. Wells's account of Gissing's death—in the *Experiment in Autobiography*—makes it clear that Gissing saw these visions again on his deathbed. Like John Vyvyan, I am certainly inclined to disbelieve that it was mere hallucination. His insistence on the clarity of the scene recalls Guarnier's dream, and the experiences of Jane O'Neill and of Misses Moberly and Jourdain.

I formulated the theory of Faculty X in my book *The Occult* (1971). But four years before this, I had made use of the concept in fiction, in a novel called *The Philosopher's Stone*, which is centrally concerned with this notion of 'mental time travel'. In this novel I suggested that the pre-frontal lobes of the brain (I didn't then know about the rôles of the right and left brains) are somehow connected with 'poetic' experience: Wordsworth's feeling as a child that meadow, grove and stream were 'apparelled in celestial light'. No one seems certain of the precise purpose of the pre-frontal lobes, but we know that, when an adult's pre-frontal lobes are damaged, it seems to make little difference to his functioning, except that he becomes coarser. In children, on the other hand, pre-frontal damage causes an obvious drop in intelligence: that is, children *use* the pre-frontal lobes. Could this explain why children experience the 'glory and the freshness of a dream', while adults live in an altogether drearier world—that adults have ceased to use this 'visionary' function of the pre-frontal lobes?

In *The Philosopher's Stone* I posit a brain operation that is able to restore the 'glory and the freshness' to the pre-frontal lobes. Whoever has this operation experiences a kind of revelation. The world becomes alive and exciting and infinitely fascinating, a place of constant 'magic'.

The underlying assumption here is that the rational intellect—the left brain—is to blame for the dullness of everyday consciousness, with its accompanying sense of triviality and futility. The dullness and rationality are *necessary* if we are to deal with the complexities of adult life; but we somehow *forget* the reality that lies behind our systems of abstraction. And since our vitality is fed by the sense of reality—and purpose—this forgetfulness causes a gradual withering-away of some essential faculty, just as blindness would cause a gradual forgetfulness of the reality of colour. The pre-frontal operation remedies this forgetfulness, generating a sudden enormous sense of the purpose of human existence.

One of the central scenes of the novel occurs when the hero is seated in a Stratford garden, basking in the peace and serenity, and enjoying the sense of timelessness that Jane Wolfe experienced after a month of meditation in Sicily. He finds himself wondering idly what this garden would have looked like in the age of Shakespeare—then suddenly realises that he *knows* the answer; that he possesses a faculty that can tell him exactly what he wants to know. In writing this scene, it struck me as quite obvious that if one could retreat into a deep enough state of serenity, all such questions would become answerable. Yet I was fully aware that 'insight' can deal only with questions of a logical nature, not with those involving particularities or facts (e.g., no amount of insight could normally tell me the name of Cleopatra's great-grandmother: I have to turn to the history books).

When I thought about this question, it seemed to me that the answer lay in something we know intuitively about states of deep serenity. And this 'something' is probably the notion I have already discussed in connection with Buchanan and psychometry: the feeling that the world contains an infinitude of information, and that we possess, although we seldom use, the senses to make use of it. *If* psychometry works—and there is an impressive body of experimental evidence that it does—it must be because objects somehow record everything that has ever happened to them. But we have already noted that our brains also record everything that has ever happened to us. At this point we should observe that, no matter how much information we have access to, we can make use of it only by cross-checking it with information inside us (e.g. faced with a broken-down car, a man who knew nothing about cars would be helpless, even if he had a massive handbook on cars; before he can make use of it, he needs to have certain basic information about cars *inside* his brain). But with an infinitude of information outside us, and something like an infinitude inside us, we possess the basic necessities for answering almost any question.

I am still by no means certain that this 'paradigm' is the answer. How, for example, can it explain something that happened to a musician friend of mine, Mark Bredin, as he was travelling back late one night by taxi along the Bayswater Road? Suddenly, he felt certain that, at the next traffic light—Queensway—a taxi would jump the lights and hit them, side-on. But it seemed absurd to tap the driver on the shoulder and say 'Excuse me, but . . .' So he said nothing. At the next traffic light, a taxi ignored a red light, and hit them sideways-on . . . Could it have been some kind of extrasensory perception that told him of the approach of the taxi along Queensway at a certain speed, and that the impatient driver would arrive just as the light was turning red?

All that *does* seem clear is that Bredin was tired and very relaxed but that, after a concert, his senses were still alert. The great roaring machine of everyday awareness, with all its irrelevant information, had been switched off and he could become aware of normally-unperceived items of knowledge.

It was after writing *The Occult*, and while I was working on my book *Mysteries*, that I became aware that the problem was probably complicated by another factor. My discovery that I could use a dowsing-rod, and that it reacted powerfully in the area of ancient standing stones, made me clearly aware of this 'other' me, the non-ego, who lives in the right hemisphere. I also became increasingly interested in the work of that remarkable man, the late Tom Lethbridge, a retired Cambridge don who studied the use of the pendulum in dowsing for various materials. After exhaustive experiments, Lethbridge concluded that the pendulum responds, *at various lengths*, to every known substance in our world i.e. that in the hands of a good dowser a fourteen-inch pendulum will go into strong gyrations over sand, while a twenty-five-inch pendulum will detect aluminium. But, having established this to his own satisfaction, Lethbridge was astonished to discover that the pendulum would respond equally definitely to feelings and ideas i.e. that a ten-inch pendulum would respond to the thought of light or youth, while a twenty-nine-inch pendulum would respond to danger or yellow. This seemed to connect with another baffling phenomenon, which I myself have witnessed: map dowsing. It sounds preposterous, but some dowsers are able to locate whatever they are looking for over a map as well as over the actual area of ground. 'Professor' Joad, a confirmed sceptic, described in a Brains Trust programme how he had seen a map dowser accurately trace all the streams on a map from which they had been removed. I have seen a map dowser, Bill Lewis, accurately trace the course of an underground waterpipe on a sketch map drawn by my wife.

And at this point I became fascinated by another equally strange phenomenon, that of 'multiple personality'. There are dozens of recorded cases of patients who slip in and out of a series of totally different personalities. One of the most widely publicised was described in the book *The Three Faces of Eve*. In *Mysteries* I have described in detail the equally strange cases of Christine Beauchamp and Doris Fischer. In her book *Sybil* Flora Schreiber has described the case of a girl who had 16 different personalities. Such cases actually look like old-fashioned accounts of 'demonic possession'. The resident personality, so to speak, is suddenly expelled from the body, and a stranger takes over. When the 'resident personality' comes back, he (or she) has no memory of what has taken place in the meantime.

What interested me about such cases is that the various personalities seem to have a definite pecking order or hierarchy, with the most powerful at the top, the next most powerful next to the top, and so on. (The 'resident personality' is usually about halfway down the ladder.) Moreover, the 'top' personality knows all about all those underneath; the next one down knows about all those underneath, but *not* about the one above. And so it goes on, with the bottom-most personality knowing only about himself/herself.

I made another interesting observation. In many cases, the 'top' personality is a more mature and balanced individual *than the patient has ever had the opportunity to become.* For example, Jung's cousin, who was such a case, was a teenager; yet her 'top' personality was a mature woman at least ten years older.

In 1973, my own experience of 'panic attacks', brought on by overwork and stress, suggested a further insight: that we are basically *all* multiple personalities, although, in well-balanced human beings, the others never actually unseat the resident personality. In my panic attacks, I found that I could gain a measure of control by calling upon what seemed to be a higher level of my own being, a kind of 'higher me'. This led me to wonder how many 'higher me's' there are. *And* whether the solution of some of these mysteries of paranormal powers—like precognition—may not lie in this higher level of 'myself'. In short, whether, as Aldous Huxley once suggested, the mind possesses a superconscious attic as well as a subconscious basement—a superconscious mind of which we are unaware, as we are unaware of the subconscious. My own picture of the 'ladder of selves' seemed to suggest that the attic has several storeys.

Lethbridge had begun to formulate a similar theory to explain the accuracy of his pendulum: that there is a part of the mind that knows the answer to these questions, but which can communicate only indirectly. This, of course, sounds more like the right cerebral hemisphere than the 'superconscious mind'. But then, the right cerebral hemisphere might well be the 'seat' of the superconscious mind, if such a thing exists.

Of course, we are all aware that we develop into a series of different people over the course of a lifetime. But we say this is 'only a manner of speaking'. Is it, though? Some people experience a total personality change when they get behind the wheel of a car; they feel as if a more reckless and impatient 'self' has taken over their body. A person involved in lovemaking for the first time may find that he/she is 'taken over' by another self, with its own biological purposes, and that he/she suddenly becomes oddly self-confident and purposeful. A mother holding her first baby is startled to feel a kind of archetypal mother inside herself taking over her responses and her mind . . .

This leads me to speculate that we may all begin life as a whole series of selves, encapsulated like those Japanese paper flowers, waiting for the right moment to unfold. Someone who never loses their virginity, a woman who never becomes a mother, never allows that particular self to enter the world of the living. Yet a priest who becomes a saint may allow still higher 'selves' to unfold, while the rest of us remain trapped in a routine of getting and spending. A Queen Elizabeth or Florence Nightingale may develop areas of her being which remain unconscious in the satisfied housewife.

All this seems to provide a possible explanation for Alan Vaughan's experience, when 'Z' drove the Nantucket 'spirit' out of his head. He obviously felt an immense and boundless relief, an explosion of sheer delight. Could this have lifted him, as it were, to a higher rung on the 'ladder of selves'? For one thing is perfectly clear: the 'lower' we feel, the more we are subject to time. At the beginning of a railway journey, I may feel so concentrated and absorbed that I can simply look out of the window, and experience all kinds of interesting insights and sensations. Later on, I feel less absorbed, but can nevertheless find pleasure in a book. If the journey is far too long, and the train breaks down, and I get cold and hungry, all my concentration vanishes, and time now drags itself slowly, 'like a wounded snake'. The less absorbed I become, the slower time passes. It seems, therefore, reasonable to assume that if I could reach some entirely new level of delight and concentration, time would virtually disappear. In such a state, I might well know what was passing in other people's minds, and know the future. At all events, it seems clear that psychological time is closely related to our control over our own inner states. It seems likely that someone who had achieved a perfect level of collaboration between the right and left hemispheres, instead of the present mutual misunderstanding and confusion, would be able to slow time down or speed it up at will. Therefore, whatever we know or do not know about time, one thing seems certain: that increased understanding of our own latent powers will bring increased insight into the nature of time.

It could also bring insight into the oddest of all mysteries connected with time: the problem of synchronicity.

The word was coined by the psychologist C. G. Jung to describe what he called 'meaningful coincidence'. As an example, he offers the amusing case of M. Fortgibu, as recounted by the French scientist Camille Flammarion, in his book *The Unknown*. This is Flammarion's own account:

'Emile Deschamps, a distinguished poet, somewhat overlooked in these days, one of the authors of the libretto of the 'Huguenots', tells of a curious series of fortuitous coincidences as follows:

'In his childhood, being at a boarding-school at Orleans, he chanced to find himself on a certain day at table with a M. de Fortgibu, an *émigré* recently returned from England, who made him taste a plum-pudding, a dish almost unknown at that time in France.

'The remembrance of that feast had by degrees faded from his memory, when, ten years later, passing by a restaurant on the Boulevard Poissonière, he perceived inside it a plum-pudding of most excellent appearance.

'He went in and asked for a slice of it, but was informed that the whole had been ordered by another customer. 'M. de Fortgibu,' cried the *dame du comptoir*, seeing that Deschamps looked disappointed, 'would you have the goodness to share your plum-pudding with this gentleman?'

'Deschamps had some difficulty in recognizing M. de Fortgibu in an elderly man, with powdered hair, dressed in a colonel's uniform, who was taking his dinner at one of the tables.

'The officer said it would give him pleasure to offer part of his pudding to the gentleman.

'Long years had passed since Deschamps had even thought of plum-pudding, or of M. de Fortgibu.

'One day he was invited to a dinner where there was to be a real English plum-pudding. He accepted the invitation, but told the lady of the house, as a joke, that he knew M. de Fortgibu would be of the party, and he caused much amusement by giving the reason.

'The day came, and he went to the house. Ten guests occupied the ten places at table, and a magnificent plum-pudding was served. They were beginning to laugh at Deschamps about his M. de Fortgibu, when the door opened and a servant announced:

'"M. de Fortgibu."

'An old man entered, walking feebly, with the help of a servant. He went slowly round the table, as if looking for somebody, and he seemed greatly disconcerted. Was it a vision? or was it a joke?

'It was the time of the Carnival, and Deschamps was sure it was a trick. But as the old man approached him he was forced to recognize M. de Fortgibu in person.

'"My hair stood up on my head," he said. "Don Juan, in the *chef d'œuvre* of Mozart, was not more terrified by his guest of stone."

'All was soon explained. M. de Fortgibu had been asked to dinner by a friend who lived in the same house, but had mistaken the door of his apartment.

'There is really in this story a series of coincidences which confounds us, and we can understand the exclamation of the author when the remembrance of a thing so extraordinary occurred to him: "Three times in my life have I eaten plum-pudding, and three times have I seen M. de Fortgibu! A fourth time I should feel capable of anything . . . or capable of nothing!"'

This last comment recalls Richard Church's feeling, described in Chapter 1, when he realised that the blows of the wood-chopper's axe were not synchronising with its sound: the sudden exultant feeling that time is somehow a cheat, and that man is far more *free* than he realises – a recognition that allowed Church to float off the ground and fly. The word 'synchronicity' was coined by Jung in connection with the *I Ching*, the Chinese *Book of Changes*, which the Chinese consult as an 'oracle'. The method of 'consulting' the *I Ching* consists of throwing down three coins at random half a dozen times and noting whether there are more heads or tails. Two or three tails gives a line with a break in the middle, as in the diagram below; three heads gives an unbroken line. The six lines, placed on top of one another, form a 'hexagram':

The above hexagram is number 58, 'The Joyous—Lake', with a 'Judgement': 'The Joyous, Success—Perseverance is favourable.' But from the logical point of view it is obviously impossible to explain how throwing down coins at random can provide an answer—even if the question has been very clearly and precisely formulated in the mind before the coins are thrown.

If, against all reason, it actually works, then we must conclude that there is some 'hidden mechanism' that causes it to work. Such a mechanism could only involve a connection between the mind and the external world, so that the one could influence the other. One obvious possibility is 'extra-sensory perception' (ESP). Dame Rebecca West has described how she was in the London Library, trying to check up on an episode in one of the Nuremberg war crimes trials, and how she discovered, to her annoyance, that the trials were not arranged in alphabetical order. After an hour of fruitless searching, she addressed a librarian who was approaching her and started to complain, reaching out as she did so to illustrate her point by showing him a typical volume. The one she picked opened at the page she had been looking for.

This certainly sounds like some form of ESP, some unconscious knowledge of where the passage was located. But what about the chance that caused the librarian to be standing in front of the book at the right moment? We have here such a complex situation that it is difficult to think of an answer in terms of some 'passive' faculty like ESP.

Another story concerning Rebecca West underlines this point. Again in the London Library, she was waiting for a copy of Gounod's Memoirs to arrive. She was approached by an American who recognised her, and who asked if it was true that she possessed some lithographs by the artist Delpeche. They were still talking about Delpeche when the Memoirs arrived; she opened it casually, and found herself looking at the name Delpeche—a passage in which Gounod described how Delpeche had been kind to his mother. The assistant was already on his way to collect the Memoirs when the artist approached her, so again we have a complex situation that cannot be explained in terms of ESP. We are forced to fall back on 'coincidence'.

But some synchronicities seem so preposterous that this explanation seems increasingly hollow. The best example I can give is a personal one. When writing an article about synchronicity (for *An Encyclopedia of Unsolved Mysteries*), I began to experience a series of absurd synchronicities, the oddest of which was as follows. I was describing an experience of the 'Ufologist' Jacques Vallee, who became interested in a Los Angeles religious cult known as the Order of Melchizedec—Melchizedek being one of the obscurer Biblical prophets. (We have already encountered him in connection with Dion Fortune.) Vallee had searched for information about the prophet, but without much success. In the midst of this search, he took a taxi to Los Angeles airport, and asked his lady taxi driver for a receipt. She gave him a receipt signed 'M. Melchizedec'. He thought this an amusing coincidence, which suggested that there were more Melchizedecs around than he had assumed. But when he checked the Los Angeles telephone directory—a vast compilation in several volumes—he found only one Melchizedec—his taxi driver.

Vallee said it was as if he had stuck a notice on some universal notice board: 'Wanted—Melchizedecs', and some earnest guardian angel had asked: 'How about this?' 'No, no, that's no good—that's a taxi driver . . .'

Vallee points out that there are two ways in which a librarian can store information. One is in alphabetical order. But a simpler system would be to place each book on the nearest shelf as it arrived, and have some straightforward method of retrieving it—like a 'beeper' on the spine of every book, which would respond to a radio signal by making a noise to signal its position. Vallee is suggesting that this may be how the universe is constructed—on a system known as a 'random data base'—and that it could explain apparent 'synchronicities'.

After I had finished writing this passage, I broke off my day's work to take my dogs for a walk. As I was leaving my work room, I noticed on the camp-bed a book that had obviously fallen off the shelf, and which I did not recognise. It was called *You Are Sentenced to Life*, by a Dr W. D. Chesney, and I had obviously bought it many years before in California and sent it for binding. But I had never actually read it. When I came back from my walk, I glanced through the book—and discovered, at the very end, a page headed ORDER OF MELCHIZEDEC. It was a letter to the author from the founder of the Order, Grace Hooper Pettipher.

I had cited Vallee's story about Melchizedec as one of the most proposterous synchronicities I know. Finding yet another reference to the Order within an hour or so of writing about it—I have about 30,000 books in my house—obviously involved a coincidence that would be beyond numerical calculation. It was as if the 'guardian angel' had said: 'You think that's preposterous?—well how about this?'

It was shortly after this that, reading some text about Hermes Trismegistus, the legendary founder of magic, and his famous formula 'As above, so below' (which is supposed to express the essence of magic), I felt for the first time that I understood the inner meaning of the saying. It is generally taken to refer to the magical system of 'correspondences', the idea that earthly things have a heavenly connection. (For example, the days of the weeks are named after gods, and a magician who wished to perform a ceremony to ensure wealth would choose Sunday as the best day, since the sun is associated with gold . . .) What suddenly struck me is that we are all accustomed to the fact that the environment can act upon the mind—so that a dull day can make us depressed, and so on. But the fundamental tenet of 'occultism' (and the basic assertion of this book) is that the mind possesses *hidden powers* that can influence the external world. This seems to happen by a process of 'induction', not unlike that involved in a simple electrical transformer. If, for example, I wish to use my British electric razor when I am in America, I have to buy a transformer which will 'step-up' American voltage (120) to British voltage (240.) If I want to use an American razor in England, I have to reverse the same transformer (which merely involves connecting it up back-to-front) to step-down 240 volts to 120.

Like most people, I have often observed that when I am in an optimistic and purposeful state, things tend to 'go right'. When I am tired and depressed, they go wrong—as if I have wired up my 'mind transformer' the wrong way round, so it causes 'lower' vibrations in the external world. Optimism, on the other hand, seems to induce more powerful vibrations in the external world, and these in turn induce 'serendipity'—a term coined by Horace Walpole, meaning 'the faculty of making happy and unexpected discoveries by chance'.

Religion has always taught that the gods have power over matter, but man is its slave: if this interpretation is correct, 'As above, so below' means that man has the same potential power to control matter as the gods.

This is obviously the essence of Richard Church's insight when the sound of the hatchet and its impact on the tree became 'de-synchronised' (see page 9): 'I had found that time and space are not absolute. Their power was *not* law . . .' This is obviously the beginning of a *totally different* attitude towards reality, an attitude that contradicts our 'normal' basic assumptions.

Let me attempt to express this more clearly. Life on earth has always had a difficult struggle to maintain itself. And man, one of the youngest of life forms, has had to fight against every kind of obstacle. What is so remarkable is that, unlike his fellow animals, he has learned to use his *mind* as his most important tool in the struggle for existence. This has carried him into an extraordinary realm of imagination and ideas. Our domestic animals live in the physical world; but our children already inhabit a strange electronic world of video-recorders and computers that would be beyond the grasp of any dog or cat. Man has become a creature of two worlds, with one foot on the solid earth and one foot in the world of the mind.

But because he is one of the youngest of all earth's creatures (only a few viruses are younger), he is extremely unsure of himself. With very few exceptions, each individual feels himself to be surrounded by a vast, hostile world that makes him feel like a pygmy. Above all, this huge and complex world makes him feel *passive*, a 'creature of circumstance'. Some primitive creature from another planet might well assume man sees himself as a god, but he would be mistaken. We feel that we have very little influence over our complicated lives. Moreover, as soon as we feel tired or worried, we feel even more 'trapped', and our estimate of ourselves sinks almost to zero.

This is absurd. If we can make the imaginative effort of placing ourselves behind the eyes of one of our cave-man ancestors of the late Pleistocene era, we can imagine his amazement if he could catch a glimpse of the ziggurats of the Sumerians, the pyramids of Egypt, the temples of Greece, the aqueducts of the Romans; and if he could see our modern skyscrapers and space probes, he would regard us as a race of supermen. And in a sense he would be right. It is we who fail to grasp the magnitude of our own achievement. We remain subject to a crippling kind of modesty, a neurosis of self-belittlement. Because of our inability to achieve a certain detachment from our own lives—to see them as it were, from a bird's eye view rather than a worm's eye view—we remain gloomily self-critical, convinced that all our technical and intellectual achievements are a kind of vanity or a prelude to catastrophe.

Yet in the past century or so, we have, in fact, begun to develop a kind of 'bird's eye view', a certain capacity to soar above the trivia of our everyday lives into the realm of imagination and intellectual detachment. It is this capacity that promises that man will finally begin to grasp the magnitude of his own achievement, and to live on a far higher level of zest and vitality.

One thing seems clear: that the various 'hidden powers' we have spoken of in the course of this book are called into operation when we are in moods of optimism and relaxation. And, what is more, they *induce* a feeling of optimism and relaxation, as we can see in the case of Richard Church; in other words, there is a 'feedback' effect. All this suggests that there is a close connection between optimism, the 'bird's eye view', and the development of these 'hidden powers'. It also suggests that the most important step in this direction is the ability to grasp what is at issue in the puzzling phenomenon of synchronicity.

Alan Vaughan's vision of the future reminds us that there have always been men and women who possessed this curious ability; they are known as 'prophets'. One of the chief problems about the great prophets of the past—Nostradamus, Paracelsus, Mother Shipton, the Brahan Seer—is that their prophecies are so frequently ambiguous. The 'magician' Paracelsus published in 1530 (eleven years before his death) a number of obscure prophecies, including one of wars, riots, slaughters and conflagrations in the North countries, warning the inhabitants of Brabant, Flanders and Zealand to beware. At the time Paracelsus wrote, the Low Countries were peaceful and prosperous; fourteen years after his death, they passed from the Emperor Charles V to his son Philip of Spain, who attempted to impose Catholicism with the aid of the Inquisition, bringing about one of the most appalling reigns of terror in history. As a prophecy, then, it is impressive, but it could be no more than a fortunate guess—after all, in a world full of warlike princes, nothing is more likely than slaughters, riots and conflagrations.

Michel Nostradamus, who died a quarter of a century after Paracelsus, is the most controversial of all 'prophets'. In 1555, he published the first edition of his 'quatrains', four-line stanzas arranged in centuries (lots of 100—a dozen in all, although several are incomplete.) Most of these are incredibly obscure, and, since they are all mixed up together, it is difficult to guess what period they are supposed to apply to. What, for example, can one make of this:

> *Milan, Ferrare, Turin et Aquilleye,*
> *Capne, Brundis, vexez par gent Celtique,*
> *Par le Lyon et phalange aquilee,*
> *Quand Rome aura le chef vieux Britannique.*
>
> (5:99)

Literally translated, this seems to mean: 'Milan, Ferrara, Turin and Aquila, Capua, Brindisi vexed by a Celtic (i.e. French) gentleman, by the lion and eagle phalanx, when Rome has the old British chief.'

It seems to be utter nonsense. But one of its interpreters, Stewart Robb, finds hidden meaning there. The French army used the eagle as an emblem for the first time under Napoleon, so presumably he is the 'French gent' referred to. Napoleon also taught his army to form into Macedonian 'phalanxes'. Napoleon liked to think of himself as 'the lion', and even thought of adopting it as his emblem. So it would seem that the stanza refers to Napoleon's Italian campaigns (1796-7). But who is the 'old British chief' whom Rome will have? Well, apparently the Brother of Bonnie Prince Charlie was living in Rome at the time, and the Jacobites liked to refer to him as Henry IX of Great Britain, since his brother was now dead . . .

An interesting interpretation which is by no means unconvincing. But is the Brother of Bonnie Prince Charlie really so important that he deserves a mention in the same breath as Napoleon's Italian campaigns? If Napoleon had met him, or if he had played some part in the campaign, it would be very convincing; as it is, we must feel that the case for Napoleon is unproven.

Having said which, it must be admitted that there are some very convincing quatrains. There is one which runs:

Du nuit viendra par le foret de Reines
Deux pars, valtorte, Herne la pierre blanche,
Le moin noir en gris dedans Varenne,
Eleu Cap. cause tempeste, feu, sang, tranche.

By night will come through the forest of Reines
Two partners, by a tortuous valley, Herne the
    white stone,
The black monk in grey into Varenne:
Elected capet, cause tempest, fire,
    blood and slicing.

Varennes only appears once in French history, and this was when king Louis XVI fled there with Marie Antoinette from the French Revolution. They went via the forest of Reins, and lost their way, having chosen a bad route ('tortuous valley'). The king wore a grey suit, and he was, in fact, an elected king (capet), the first France had had. And his flight and subsequent arrest at Varennes led to the Terror, which ended with them losing their heads (the word 'tranche' almost sounds like the fall of the guillotine).

This is an impressive number of 'hits'. But we have still failed to explain 'Herne the white stone', and the black monk. The king was of monkish temperament and had been impotent, so it *could* refer to this; one commentator says that Herne is an anagram of reine—queen, and that Marie Antoinette always dressed in white.

Other 'hits' concern Henry of France, the French Revolution, and the massacre at Nantes. But literally hundreds of other stanzas remain totally obscure, like the following:

Weak warships will be united together
False enemies, the strongest one on the ramparts,
The weak attacked, Bratislava trembles,
Lübeck and Misnen will hold the barbarous part.

The only word that leaps out of all this is Bratislava, the capital of Czechoslovakia, and since two German place-names are also mentioned, a modern interpretation will obviously start out from the assumption that this is about Hitler's annexation of Czechoslovakia in 1939, and possibly his invasion of North Africa in 1941 ('the barbarous part'). The German navy was not strong in 1939. Jean Charles de Fontbrune explains in his edition of Nostradamus that the 'false enemies' are the Hungarians whose threat led Czechoslovakia to proclaim independence; the 'strongest one on the ramparts' is presumably Hitler, but what he is doing on the ramparts is not clear (Fontbrune suggests keeping watch). Czechoslovakia has no sea coast, so it is hard to see why Bratislava is trembling at the German navy, or why Lübeck, which is 15 kilometres inland from the Baltic, should be mentioned. (Misnen *is* on the North Sea.) Altogether, it requires something of an act of faith to believe that Nostradamus was really prophesying the events of 1939 and 1941.

This should bring comfort to those who recall Nostradamus's most famous prophecy:

L'an mille neuf cens nonante neuf sept mois
Du ciel viendra un grand Roi deffrayeur.
Rescusciter le grand Roi d'Angolmois
Avant que Mars regner par bonheur.

This declares that in July 1999, the 'great king of terror' will come from the sky. The great king of the Mongols, Genghis Khan, will be resuscitated (Angolmois is supposed to be an anagram of Mongolais), before which Mars (war?) will reign happily. But the Millennium was regarded with superstitious terror in the Middle Ages (and even today, the word is synonymous with breathtaking events, either agreeable or appalling). Mother Shipton, another remarkable prophet who lived in Yorkshire at the time of Nostradamus declared confidently that

> The world to an end shall come
> In eighteen hundred and eighty one.

Mother Shipton also prophesied 'carriages without horses', thought that would fly around the world 'in the twinkling of an eye', iron ships that would float on water, and men flying in the air—a remarkable record of success. She even prophesied that Cardinal Wolsey would see York but fail to reach it, and was correct—he saw it from the top of a castle tower, but was then recalled to London, and died on the way. But it also seems clear that her powers of prophecy lost their accuracy as they reached into the distant future.

Another prophet who predicted horseless carriages—but this time drawn by chariots of fire (i.e railway engines)—was known as the Brahan Seer, and he lived a century after Nostradamus. Coinneach Odhar (or Kenneth Mackenzie) was born in Uig, on the Island of Lewis (in the Hebrides) around 1600. News of his powers of 'second sight' reached his feudal overlord, Kenneth Cabarfeidh Mackenzie—Lord Mackenzie of Kintail—who lived in Brahan Castle—and he released the seer from his job as a farm labourer and allowed him to live rent-free in a sod-roofed cottage. The seer attributed his powers to a 'divining stone' with a hole in it, through which he used to look to see the future. It was his powers of short-term prophecy that impressed Lord Mackenzie, as when he predicted that a Lochalsh woman would weep over the grave of a Frenchman in Lochalsh graveyard. It seemed unlikely, since there were few Frenchmen in Scotland; but, within a few months, Mackenzie heard of a Lochalsh woman who spent much of her time weeping beside the grave of her French husband, a footman, who had died after the seer's prediction. When an elderly man, Duncan Macrae, asked the seer how he would end his days, there was general incredulity when Odhar said he would die by the sword, since there had been peace for some time. In 1654, General Monck led Cromwellian troops to Kintail, and when he met Macrae, asked him some question which Macrae failed to understand. Macrae put his hand on his sword, and was promptly cut down.

In 1630, the seer was passing over a patch of moorland when he predicted that it would be 'stained with the best blood of the Highlands: 116 years later, it was the site of the battle of Culloden. Perhaps his 'longest shot' was a prophecy that a woman called Annabella Mackenzie would live in the village of Baile Mhuilinn, and that she would die of measles. This prophecy took more than two centuries to be fulfilled; then an old lady of that name *did* die of measles in Baile Mhuilinn—at the age of 95.

There are two stories about the end of the seer. One states that his lord's wife asked him what her husband was doing—Mackenzie was at that time in Paris—and Odhar was injudicious enough to tell her that he saw him kneeling at the feet of a fair lady. The Countess then ordered him to be burned in a tar barrel. The more likely story states that when the local gentry were gathered at Brahan Castle, the seer remarked (in Gaelic) that he saw more in the children of footmen and grooms than in the children of gentlemen. Apparently this remark was interpreted as meaning that the aristocratic guests had actually been fathered by footmen and grooms. The Countess sentenced him to be burned; Lord Mackenzie arrived home too late to save him, although he rode like the wind to try to prevent the execution. Before his death, the seer made predictions about the Mackenzie (Seaforth) family, including the statement that the last of the line would be deaf and dumb, that four sons would precede him to the tomb (one of them dying by water), and that his 'white hooded' daughter would kill her sister. In fact, the last Lord Mackenzie was born in 1754, and scarlet fever impaired his hearing at the age of 12; in later life his speech also became affected. His four sons all predeceased him (one being drowned). His daughter Mary married Admiral Samuel Hood, and when her husband died, her widows weeds included a white hood; she was driving a carriage with ponies when the animals bolted and the carriage overturned, killing her sister.

Perhaps the best-authenticated stories of accurate prediction of the future concerns the French essayist and occultist Jacques Cazotte, best known for his novel *Le Diable Amoureux*, in which the Devil takes the form of an attractive girl who wins the love of a Spaniard who made the mistake of invoking him. Early in 1788, Cazotte (who was then 69) attended a dinner given by the Duchesse de Grammont, at which Jean de la Harpe, a well-known atheist, was present, and he wrote down at some length an account of a prophecy made by Cazotte. After dinner, the talk turned to the possibility of revolution, which was obviously in the air, and which most of them (being liberals) welcomed. Cazotte suddenly declared that he could tell them that they would see the revolution very soon. The philosopher Condorcet asked for more information, and was told that he would die, lying on the floor of a prison cell, of poison that he had taken to cheat the executioner. The dramatist Chamfort, he said, would cut his own veins, but would die some months later. The astronomer Bailly would die at the hands of the mob. The duchess herself would be taken to the scaffold with her hands tied behind her, as would 'even greater ladies'. The atheist de la Harpe was told he would become a Christian. An M. Vicq-d'Azir would die on the scaffold, as would M. de Nicolai.

All these prophecies proved to be accurate. De la Harpe himself became a monk, and his account of the evening was found after his death in 1803. A scholar named Walter Borman went into the whole matter in the early 20th century and found abundant evidence for Cazotte's prophecy in journals and letters of the time. (Harpe's own 'account' could, of course, have been a forgery; it was published as part of a new edition of *Le Diable Amoureux* in 1871, edited by Gerard de Nerval.) Moreover, the Baroness d'Oberkirch described in her autobiography (1852) how a group of people in her salon discussed Cazotte's prophecy before it was fulfilled, and how a medium who had been brought along by the Marquis de Puységur (the discoverer of hypnotism) had then made some even more astonishing prophecies about people who were present, all of which proved accurate. Oddly enough, Cazotte failed to foretell his own death on the guillotine in 1792; but it is generally accepted that 'prophets' are unable to foretell their own future.

The whole subject of precognition raises a fundamental question: of whether, in some sense, the future has already taken place—in other words, whether our lives are totally predetermined. In a book called *Beyond the Occult*, I suggested that the answer to that question is: probably yes.

'As I now look out of the window I can see the wind blowing washing on the line and also swaying the syringa bush. To me, the next movement of the bush or the clothes seems purely a matter of chance; in fact, they are just as predetermined as the movements of the stars—as the weathermen could tell you. What *is* true is that human beings introduce an element of genuine chance into the picture; my wife may decide to water the garden instead of hanging out the washing. But the bushes, although alive, can introduce little chance into the picture. Moreover, even free will can be described in terms of statistics. The sociologist Durkheim was surprised to discover that it is possible to predict the suicide rate with considerable precision. This seems to imply that, with sufficiently detailed knowledge, we could predict exactly who will kill himself next year.'

The mathematician Laplace took a similar view. He wrote a classic book on the movements of the heavenly bodies, and remarked that if a human being had sufficient knowledge of the present state of every particle of matter in the universe, he could go on to predict the whole future of the universe.

Understandably, we find such a notion disturbing, for it seems to suggest that we are merely cogs in a gigantic machine. I go on to suggest that this negative attitude is absurd, because we accept *spatial* 'predetermination' every day without concern—on the contrary, I would be very worried if I didn't know whether the next bus would take me to Piccadilly or Pontefract. What is more, I realise that spatial predetermination makes no difference to my free will; I can *choose* whether to go north, south, east or west.

Yet there is a paradox in all this. In *Man and Time*, J. B. Priestley quotes a case from Dr Louisa Rhine. A young mother had a dream in which she was camping with some friends on the bank of a creek. She took her baby with her to the edge of the water, intending to wash some clothes. Then she remembered that she had left the soap in the tent, and went back to fetch it. When she returned, the baby was lying face down in the creek, and when she pulled him out, she discovered he was dead.

In fact, that summer she went camping with some friends, and they set up their tents on the bank of a creek. She was just about to do some washing when she remembered that she had forgotten the soap. At that point she remembered her dream. So instead of leaving the baby behind, she tucked him under her arm and took him back with her to the tent.

If we assume that her dream was a genuine premonition, then it saved her from disaster, and changed her future.

Brian Inglis quotes another interesting example in his book *The Power of Dreams*. A girl woke up in bed one morning, and, before she opened her eyes, had a strong impression that she was in the bed of a male colleague. He was not a man in whom she had taken any particular interest, and, in fact, he had a girlfriend and she was in love with someone else. When she opened her eyes, the feeling vanished.

That evening, at some official university function, she and the male colleague got bored, and slipped out to a nearby pub. Eventually they ended up in a 'necking situation' in a car, and he pressed her to return home with him. She was about to agree when she recollected her odd 'dream' of that morning, and changed her mind. It struck her later that she might have averted disaster: in those days of inadequate contraception, she might have ended up pregnant, faced with a shotgun wedding or single parentage and the loss of her job. She concluded that the 'dream' had been intended as a warning.

Many other stories could be cited to make the same point: that premonitions *can* change the future. One man (cited in Arthur Osborn's *The Future is Now*) had a premonition that a car would come round a corner on the wrong side of the road; in fact, as he approached the corner later in the day he recalled his premonition and pulled over to the other side of the road. Seconds later, the car came round the corner at high speed.

The conclusion would seem to be that the future is *not* predetermined as far as human beings are concerned—at least, not rigidly predetermined. We *can* affect it with our decisions.

At the time I was writing *Beyond the Occult* I was unaware of the discoveries of 'Chaos Theory', developed by scientists and mathematicians like Benoit Mandelbrot, Mitchell Feigenbaum, Kenneth Wilson and Edward Lorenz. Chaos theory flatly contradicts Laplace. Edward Lorenz was responsible for the original discovery in 1961, after devising a computer programme that would simulate the weather for some months ahead. In re-running a part of the programme, he decided to save space by cutting down some decimals from six figures to three, assuming that the difference of one part in a thousand was unimportant. In fact, this tiny difference caused an increasing change in the weather pattern of the future. He summarised his discovery by saying that an event as small as a butterfly flapping its wings in Siberia could alter the long-term weather pattern. This means, in practice, that no matter how sophisticated our computers, the weather pattern cannot be accurately forecast for more than a day or so ahead. Beyond that, it begins to diverge more and more widely from the forecast.

Benoit Mandelbrot cast this discovery in mathematical form (to which he gave the name of 'fractals'.) He began by considering the question of how long is a coastline. It sounds simple enough —you merely have to trace the outline of a map with a small measuring device involving a wheel. But a map is a simplification of reality. A larger, more accurate map would give a larger figure, since it would trace all kinds of small details not included in the smaller map. In fact, every small part of the coastline would have its own extra details, and these details in turn would have *their* own details and so on until you had reduced the coastline to the atomic scale, and it would be impossible to get more detailed.

But if a rough coastline is generated by a computer, this 'atomic' limit is never reached. Imagine a giant magnifying glass, capable of infinite magnification, getting closer and closer to a coastline generated by a computer programme. The coastline would go on getting more detailed *forever*. And the million-millionth magnification would still look oddly similar to the first.

It is, in effect, like a decimal that can go on forever without repeating itself.

Mandelbrot's fractals also apply to the weather; its possibilities for variation are infinite. And so, scientifically speaking, chaos theory disproves the notion that everything that happens is predetermined. The picture of the universe I suggested in *Beyond the Occult* is something like a giant clock, proceeding inevitably along its predestined course. Human beings can introduce small variations, but on such a minute scale that they are as important as tiny floating grains of dust in Big Ben. According to chaos theory, these grains of dust, like the butterfly's wings, can cause virtually infinite changes. If chaos theory is correct, the future is infinitely *un*determined.

And yet, just as the whole idea of precognition contradicts our commonsense view of reality—that what has not yet happened cannot be known—so the actuality of precognition contradicts chaos theory. Ten days before the *Titanic* was due to sail, in April 1912, a man named J. Connon Middleton dreamed twice of a sinking ocean liner. Since he was due to sail on the *Titanic*, he was understandably worried, and greatly relieved when the conference he was due to attend was cancelled. A marine engineer named Colin MacDonald also had premonitions of disaster and declined to sign on the *Titanic*; the man who accepted the job was drowned when the *Titanic* sank on April 14, 1912.

Chaos theory states that it would be impossible to predict the weather ten days in advance. So even if we suppose some 'super-ESP' that could gain access to the relevant information—about icebergs in the Atlantic, the strength of the *Titanic*'s hull, etc—it would still be impossible to have an accurate premonition of the disaster.

In fact, a novel called *The Wreck of the Titan*, published in 1898, fourteen years before the disaster, predicts the catastrophe with uncanny accuracy: the *Titan*, like the *Titanic*, was on her maiden voyage from Southampton. It was 70,000 tons; the *Titanic* was 66,000. Both were triple-screw vessels capable of 25 knots. The *Titan* had 24 lifeboats, the *Titanic* 20. Its author, Morgan Robertson, was a 'semi-automatic' writer, who felt that some other writer took over when he wrote. If *The Wreck of the*

Titan was not a genuine piece of precognition, then it was a highly convincing example of synchronicity.

In short, it seems that we are as far as ever from some 'scientific' explanation of the time mystery. All that seems obvious is that there is some sense in which our perceptions are independent of time, and that human beings therefore possess more freedom than they realise.

14.
Vampires, Werewolves and Elementals

IN A BOOK CALLED *The Paranormal*, the psychologist Stan Gooch has described how, at the age of 26, he attended a seance in Coventry with a friend, and spontaneously fell into a trance condition. 'And then suddenly it seemed to me that a great wind was rushing through the room. In my ears was the deafening sound of roaring waters . . . As I felt myself swept away I became unconscious.' When he woke up, he learned that several 'spirits' had spoken through him. Gooch had discovered that he was a 'medium'.

It was during this period—Gooch reveals in a later book called *Creatures from Inner Space*—that he had his first experience of a 'psychic invasion'. He was lying in bed one Saturday morning with his eyes closed when he felt a movement on the pillow beside his head, as if someone had gently pressed a hand against it. The movement continued for some time; but when he opened his eyes, he was alone.

Twenty years later, lying half awake in the early morning, he became aware that someone else was in bed with him. He felt that it was a composite of various girls he had known. 'On this first occasion my conscious interest in the situation got the better of me, and the succubus gradually faded away. On subsequent occasions, however, the presence of the entity was maintained, until finally we actually made love.' He notes that, 'From some points of view the sex is actually more satisfying than that with a real woman, because in the paranormal encounter archetypal elements are both involved and invoked.'

Oddly enough, Gooch does not believe that his succubus (or female demon) was real; he thinks such entities are creations of the human mind. He cites cases of hypnotised subjects who have been able to see and touch hallucinations suggested by the hypnotist, and a book called *The Story of Ruth*, by Dr Morton Schatzman, describing how a girl whose father had tried to rape her as a child began to have hallucinations of her father and believe that he was in the room with her. He seems to believe that his succubus was a similar hallucination. Yet this view seems to be contradicted by other cases he cites in the book.

The first of these concerns a policeman, Martin Pryer, who had always been 'psychic'. At one point he decided to try practising the control of hypnagogic imagery—the imagery we experience on the verge of sleep—and soon began to have alarming experiences. On one occasion, some strange entity began to cling to his back like a limpet, and held on until he staggered across the room and switched on the light. On another occasion, he thought that a former girlfriend was outside the window, and when he asked what she was doing, she replied: 'You sent for me.' Then some female entity seemed to seize him from behind, clinging on to his back; he sensed that it wanted him to make love to her 'in a crude and violent manner.' After some minutes it faded away.

Gooch goes on to describe the experiences of an actress friend called Sandy, who was also 'psychic'. One night, she woke up and felt that the spotlight in the corner of her ceiling had changed into an eye that was watching her. Then she felt an entity—she felt it was male—lying on top of her and trying to make love to her. 'One part of her was quite willing for the lovemaking to proceed, but another part of her knew that she wanted it to stop.' The entity became heavier and another force seemed to be dragging her down through the mattress. She made an effort to imagine that she was pulling herself up through the mattress, and the pressure suddenly vanished. But when she went into the bathroom, she discovered that her mouth was rimmed with dark streaks, and when she opened it, proved to be full of dried blood. There was no sign of a nosebleed or any other injury that could account for the blood.

We have already encountered Guy Playfair's case of 'Marcia', the Brazilian schoolteacher who had experiences with an 'incubus' after picking up a statue of the sea goddess Yemanjá on the beach (Chapter 9, page 265). Such cases make it difficult to accept Gooch's view that these entities are some kind of hypnotic hallucination. He seems to have arrived at that conclusion because his 'succubus' was a blend of previous girlfriends. But on the 'earthbound spirit' hypothesis put forward by Carl Wickland (Chapter 11), it seems more likely that the entity put these ideas into his mind—that is, into his imagination. He says: 'In short, this entity, though possessing physical and even psychological attributes familiar to me, was none the less essentially its own independent self.' And he agrees that the 'archetypal elements' were, to some extent, 'invoked'—that is, that he himself was conjuring them up. Sandy was able to free herself from the 'psychic invasion' by *imagining* that she was pulling herself back up through the mattress, indicating that the entity was controlling her imagination, not her body.

We also note that these 'psychic invasions' occurred when all three subjects—Gooch, Martin Pryer and Sandy—were either asleep or hovering between sleep and waking, and therefore in a trance condition akin to mediumship.

The 'succubus' (or incubus) was, as the Rev. Montague Summers states in his book *The Vampire*, an early version of that mythical creature the vampire or blood-drinker. And the various accounts of possession we have considered seem to lead naturally to the question: was the vampire real, or is it—as most sensible people assume—just a myth?

The vampire as depicted in stories like Bram Stoker's *Dracula* (1897) is a kind of walking corpse that drinks blood. Stoker based his character on a real historical personage: Vlad Tepes (the Impaler), King of Wallachia (1456–77) was, as his nickname implies, a man of sadistic temperament whose greatest pleasure was to impale his 'enemies' (which meant anyone against whom he had a grudge) on pointed stakes; the stake—driven into the ground—was inserted into the anus (or, in the case of women, the vagina), and the victim was allowed to slowly impale himself under his own weight—Vlad often had the point blunted to make the agony last longer. In his own time he was known as Dracula, which means son of a dragon (or of the devil). It is estimated that Dracula had about 100,000 people impaled during the course of his lifetime. When he conquered Brasov, in Transylvania, he had all its inhabitants impaled on poles, then gave a feast among the corpses. When one nobleman held his nose at the stench, Vlad sent for a specially long pole and had him impaled. When he was a prisoner in Hungary, Vlad was kept supplied with birds, rats and toads, which he impaled on small stakes. A brave and fearless warrior, he was finally killed in battle—or possibly assassinated by his own soldiers—and his head sent to Constantinople. Four hundred and twenty years later, in 1897, he was immortalised by Bram Stoker as the sinister Count Dracula, no longer a sadistic maniac, but a drinker of blood . . .[1]

But how did the legend of the blood-drinking vampire begin? The story first reached Europe soon after 1718, when Charles VI, Emperor of Austria, drove the Turks out of Eastern Europe, which they had dominated for the past four centuries, marching in and out of Transylvania, Wallachia and Hungary and even conquering Constantinople (1453). Don John of Austria defeated them at the great sea battle of Lepanto (1571), but it was their failure to capture Vienna after a siege in 1683 that caused the break-up of the Ottoman empire. During the earlier stages of this war between Europe and Turkey, Vlad the Impaler struck blow after blow against the Turks, until they killed and beheaded him in 1477. When the Turks were finally defeated, two hundred and forty-one years later, their conquerors were intrigued to hear strange stories about dead people who could cause death to the living. Such stories had been known to travellers in Greece down the centuries. There the vampire was known as the *vrykolakas*, and on January 1, 1701, a French botanist named Pitton de Tornefort had visited the island of Mykonos and been present at a gruesome scene of dissection. An unnamed peasant, of sullen and

1. For a longer account of Vlad the Impaler, see *The Mammoth Book of True Crime 2*.

quarrelsome disposition, was murdered in the fields by persons unknown. Two days after burial, his ghost was reported to be wandering around at night, overturning furniture and 'playing a thousand roguish tricks'. Ten days after his burial, a mass was said to 'drive out the demon' that was believed to be in the corpse, after which the body was disinterred, and the local butcher given the task of tearing out the heart. His knowledge of anatomy seemed to be defective, and he tore open the stomach and rummaged around in the intestines, causing such a vile stench that incense had to be burned. In the smoke-filled church, people began shouting 'Vrykolakas' and alleging that some of the smoke poured out of the corpse itself.

Even after the heart had been burned on the seashore, the ghost continued to cause havoc, until the villagers finally burnt the corpse on a pyre.

De Tornefort takes a highly superior attitude about all this, convinced that it is simply mass hysteria. 'I have never viewed anything so pitiable as the state of this island. Everyone's head was turned; the wisest people were stricken like the others.' Although the year is only 1701, de Tornefort's attitude is that of a typical French rationalist of the 18th century.

Attitudes began to change after 1718, as the highly circumstantial accounts of vampires began to reach western Europe—just how precise and circumstantial is illustrated by the following report, known as *Visum et Repertum* (Seen and Discovered), which dates from 1732, and was witnessed by no less than five Austrian officers:

'After it had been reported in the village of Medvegia (near Belgrade) that so-called vampires had killed some people by sucking their blood, I was, by high decree of a local Honorable Supreme Command, sent there to investigate the matter thoroughly, along with officers detailed for that purpose and two subordinate medical officers, and therefore carried out and heard the present enquiry in the company of the Captain of the Stallath company of haiduks, Hadnack Gorschiz, the standard-bearer and the oldest haiduk of the village. (They reported), unanimously, as follows. About five years ago, a local haiduk called Arnod Paole broke his neck in a fall from a hay wagon. This man had, during his lifetime, often described how, near Gossova in

Turkish Serbia, he had been troubled by a vampire, wherefore he had eaten from the earth of the vampire's grave and had smeared himself with the vampire's blood, in order to be free of the vexation he had suffered. In twenty or thirty days after his death, some people complained that they were being bothered by this same Arnod Paole; and in fact, four people were killed by him. In order to end this evil, they dug up Arnod Paole forty days after his death—this on the advice of their Hadnack, who had been present at such events before; and they found that he was quite complete and undecayed, and that fresh blood had flowed from his eyes, nose, mouth and ears; that the shirt, the covering and the coffin were completely blood; that the old nails on his hands and feet, along with the skin, had fallen off, and that new ones had grown. And since they saw from this that he was a true vampire, they drove a stake through his heart—according to their custom—whereupon he gave an audible groan and bled copiously. Thereupon they burned the body to ashes the same day and threw these into the grave. These same people also say that all those who have been tormented and killed by vampires must themselves become vampires. Therefore they disinterred the above-mentioned four people in the same way. Then they also add that this same Arnod Paole attacked not only people but cattle, and sucked out their blood. And since some people ate the flesh of such cattle, it would appear that (this is the reason that) some vampires are again present here, inasmuch as in a period of three months, seventeen young and old people died, among them some who, with no previous illness, died in two or at most three days. In addition, the haiduk Jovitsa reports that his stepdaughter, by name Stanacka, lay down to sleep fifteen days ago, fresh and healthy, but that at midnight she started up out of her sleep with a terrible cry, fearful and trembling, and complained that she had been throttled by the son of a haiduk by the name of Milloe (who had died nine weeks earlier), whereupon she had experienced a great pain in the chest, and become worse hour by hour, until finally she died on the third day.

'At this, we went the same afternoon to the graveyard, along with the aforementioned oldest haiduks of the village, in order to cause the suspicious graves to be opened, and to examine the bodies in them. Whereby, after all of them had been (exhumed and) dissected, the following was found:

'1. A woman by the name of Stana, 20 years old, who had died in childbirth two months ago, after a three days illness, and who had herself said before her death that she had painted herself with the blood of a vampire—wherefore both she and the child, which had died soon after birth and through careless burial had been half eaten by dogs—must also become vampires. She was quite complete and undecayed. After the opening of the body there was found in the *cavitate pectoris* a quantity of fresh extravascular blood. The vessels of the *arteriae*, like the *ventriculis cordis*, were not, as is usual, filled with coagulated blood; and the whole viscera—that is, the lung, liver, stomach, spleen and intestines—were quite fresh, as they would be in a healthy person. The uterus was however quite enlarged and very inflamed externally, for the placenta and lochia had remained in place, wherefore the same was in complete putrefaction. The skin on her hands and feet, along with the old nails, fell away on their own, but on the other hand completely new nails were evident, along with a fresh and vivid skin.

'2. There was a woman by the name of Militsa, 60 years old, who had died after a three month sickness and had been buried ninety or so days earlier. In the chest much liquid blood was found, and the other viscera were—like those mentioned above—in good condition. During her dissection, all the haiduks who were standing around marvelled greatly at her plumpness and perfect body, uniformly stating that they had known the woman well from her youth, and that she had throughout her life been very lean and dried up; they emphasised that she had come to such surprising plumpness in the grave. They also said that it was she who had started the vampires this time, because she had been eating of the flesh of those sheep who had been killed by previous vampires.

'3. There was an eight-day old child which had lain in the grave for ninety days, and which was also in a condition of vampirism.

'4. The son of a haiduk, 16 years old, named Milloe, was dug up, having lain in the earth for nine weeks, after he had died from a three day illness, and was found to be like the other vampires.

[This is obviously the vampire who had attacked the stepdaughter of the haiduk Jovitsa.]

'Joachim, also the son of a haiduk, 17 years old, had died after a three day illness. He had been buried eight weeks and four days and, on being dissected, was found in similar condition.

'6. A woman by the name of Ruscha who had died after a ten day illness and been buried six weeks earlier, in whom there was much fresh blood, not only in the chest but also *in fundo ventriculi*. The same showed itself in her child, which was eighteen days old, and had died five weeks earlier.

'7. No less did a girl of 10 years of age, who had died two months previously, find herself in the above-mentioned condition, quite complete and undecayed, and had much fresh blood in her chest . . .

'8. They caused the wife of the Hadnack to be dug up, along with her child. She had died seven weeks earlier, her child—who was eight weeks old—twenty one days previously, and it was found that mother and child were completely decomposed, although earth and grave were like those of the vampires lying nearby.

'9. A servant of the local corporal of the haiduks, by the name of Rhade, 23 years old, died after a three month illness, and after being buried five weeks, was found completely decomposed.

'10. The wife of the local standard bearer, along with her child, were also completely decomposed.

'11. With Stanche, a haiduk, 60 years old, who had died six weeks previously, I noticed a profuse liquid blood, like the others, in the chest and stomach. The entire body was in the above mentioned condition of vampirism.

'12. Milloe, a haiduk, 25 years old, who had lain for six weeks in the earth, was also found in a condition of vampirism.

'13. Stanoicka, (earlier called Stanacka), the wife of a haiduk, 23 years old, died after a three day illness, and had been buried eighteen days earlier. In the dissection I found that her countenance was quite red and of a vivid colour; as was mentioned above, she had been throttled at midnight, by Milloe, the son of a haiduk, and there was also to be seen, on the right side under the ear, a bloodshot blue mark (i.e. a bruise) the length of a finger (demonstrating that she had been throttled). As she was being taken out of the grave, a quantity of fresh blood flowed from her nose. With the dissection I found—as so often mentioned already—a regular fragrant fresh bleeding, not only in the chest cavity, but also in the heart ventricle. All the viscera were found in a completely good and healthy condition. The skin of the entire body, along with the nails on the hands and feet, were as though completely fresh.

'After the examination had taken place, the heads of the vampires were cut off by the local gypsies, and then burned along with the bodies, after which the ashes were thrown into the river Morava. The decomposed bodies, however, were laid back in their own graves. Which I attest along with those assistant medical officers provided for me. *Actum ut supra*:

'L.S. (Signed) Johannes Fluchinger, Regimental Medical Officer of the Foot Regiment of the Honorable B. Furstenbusch.

'L.S. J.H. Sigel, Medical Officer of the Honorable Morall Regiment.

'L.S. Johann Friedrich Baumgarten, Medical Officer of the Foot Regiment of the Honorable B. Furstenbusch.

'The undersigned attest herewith that all which the Regiment Medical officer of the Honorable Furstenbusch had observed in the matter of vampires—along with both medical officers who signed with him—is in every way truthful, and has been undertaken, observed and examined in our own presence. In confirmation thereof is our signature in our own hand, of our own making, Belgrade, January 26, 1732.

'L.S. Buttener, Lieutenant Colonel of the Honorable Alexandrian Regiment.

'L.S. J.H. von Lindenfels, Officer of the Honorable Alexandrian Regiment.'

The first thing we note in this account is that the 'vampires' were obviously not able to get up and walk out of their graves, since they were sealed in their coffins. It was clearly their spirits that caused the trouble. And the girl Stanacka was not attacked in the manner we associate with Dracula—by the vampire's fangs—but was apparently throttled. Moreover, we note in the case of the *vrykolakas* reported by the French botanist Tornefort that the vampire wandered around the town 'playing a thousand roguish tricks'. This sounds more like a poltergeist than the traditional vampire.

Another vampire described in a lengthy official report of 1725, Peter Plogojowitz, also seems to have come to his victims 'in their sleep, laid himself upon them, and throttled them'. But someone who is throttled dies immediately. In vampire reports we have people who lived on—like Stanacka—for days. It sounds as if the vampire is *draining their vitality*, not their blood. This would, of course, produce a feeling of suffocation, or throttling. In other words, the vampire seems to be a demonic entity that *possesses* the victim, as in so many of the cases we encountered in Chapter 11, causing them to die of exhaustion, like Father Tranquille in the Loudun case.

The details of the blood in the chest of the exhumed vampire seems puzzling, until we note that the blood is found in the breast cavity (*cavitate pectoris*) of the woman called Stana, while the lungs are mentioned separately in the same sentence. If she had been *drinking* blood, it would be in the stomach, not the breast cavity. The blood found in the chest is presumably the vampire's own, and is merely a proof that the creature is 'undead'.

Now, in fact, reports of 'lamias', or predatory ghosts, date back to ancient Greece—Keats's poem *Lamia* tells a traditional story about one, which he borrows from a biography of the magician Apollonius of Tyana by Philostratus.

There are even earlier accounts of the walking dead. The French expert on vampires, Jean Marigny, remarks:

'Well, before the 18th century, the epoch when the word "vampire" first appeared, people believed in Europe that the dead were able to rise from their graves to suck the blood of the living. The oldest chronicles in Latin mention manifestations of this type, and their authors, instead of employing the word "vampire" (which did not yet exist) utilised a term just as explicit, the word "sanguisugae" (Latin for leech, bloodsucker). The oldest of these chronicles date from the 12th and 13th centuries, and, contrary to what one might expect, are not set in remote parts of Europe, but in England and Scotland.'[1]

1. 'La Tradition Legendaire du Vampire en Europe', in 'Les Cahiers du G.E.R.F' (Groupe d'Etudes et de Recherche sur La Fantastique', Grenoble University of Languages and Letters, 1987.)

He goes on to cite four cases described by the 12th century chronicler William of Newburgh, author of *Historia Rerum Anglicarum*. These are too long to cite here (although they can be found in full in Montague Summers' *The Vampire in Europe*). The first, 'Of the extraordinary happening when a dead man wandered abroad out of his grave', describes a case in Buckinghamshire, recounted to the chronicler by the local archdeacon. It describes how a man returned from the grave the night after his burial, and attacked his wife. When this happened again the following night, the wife asked various neighbours to spend the night with her, and their shouts drove the ghost away. Then the ghost began to create a general disturbance in the town, attacking animals and alarming people. That he *was* a ghost, and not a physical body, is proved by the comment that some people could see him while others could not (although they 'perceptibly felt his horrible presence'). The archdeacon consulted the bishop, Hugh of Lincoln, who—on the advice of various learned men—suggested that the body should be dug up and burnt to ashes. Then he decided this would be 'undesirable', and instead wrote out a charter of absolution. When the tomb was opened, the body proved to be 'uncorrupt', just as on the day it was buried. The absolution was placed on his chest and the grave closed again; after that, the ghost ceased to wander abroad.

One of William of Newburgh's other accounts sounds slightly more like the traditional vampire in that the ghost—of a wealthy man who had died at Berwick on Tweed—had an odour of decomposition which affected the air and caused plague. The body was exhumed (it is not recorded whether it was undecayed) and burned.

Stories like these have the touches of absurdity that might be expected from an eccesiastical chronicler of that period; yet their similarity to the other chronicles cited suggests that they have some common basis. The same applies to another work, *De Nugis Curialium* by Walter Map (1193), also cited at length by Summers.

All these cases took place long before Western Europe heard tales of vampires from former Turkish dominions, and in only one of them is there is any suggestion of blood-drinking. But in most ways, the revenants behave very much like Peter Plogojowitz and the vampires of Medvegia. They haunt the living, climb into bed with people when they are asleep, and then throttle them, leaving them drained of energy. And when the bodies are disinterred, they are found to be undecayed. It seems very clear that there is no basic difference between the vampires of 1732 and the revenants of the 12th century. And when we look more closely into the accounts of the vampires, we discover that they are energy-suckers rather than blood suckers. Peter Plogojowitz has fresh blood on his mouth, but it is merely a matter of hearsay that he sucked the blood of his victims—the account mentions only throttling. Otherwise, these earlier revenants behave very much like the paranormal phenomenon known as the poltergeist.

Two 16th century cases also bear a close resemblance to the later vampire legends. One is known as known as the Shoemaker of Breslau, and is to be found in Henry's More's *Antidote Against Atheism* of 1653. This describes how, on September 21, 1591, a well-to-do shoemaker of Breslau, in Silesia—one account gives his name as Weinrichius—cut his throat with a knife, and soon after died from the wound. Since suicide was regarded as a mortal sin, his wife tried to conceal it, and announced that her husband had died of a stroke. An old woman was taken into the secret, and she washed the body and bound up the throat so skilfully that the wound was invisible. A priest who came to comfort the widow was taken to view the corpse, and noticed nothing suspicious. The shoemaker was buried on the following day, September 22, 1591.

Perhaps because of this unseemly haste, and the refusal of the wife to allow neighbours to view the body, a rumour sprang up that the shoemaker had committed suicide. After this, his ghost began to be seen in the town. Soon it was climbing into bed with people and squeezing them so hard that it left the marks of its fingers on their flesh. This finally became such a nuisance that in the year following the burial, on April 18, 1592, the council ordered the grave to be opened. The body was complete and undamaged by decay, but 'blown up like a drum'. On his feet the skin had peeled away, and another had grown, 'much purer and stronger than the first.' He had a 'mole like a rose' on his big toe—which was interpreted as a witch's mark—and there was no smell of decay, except in the shroud itself. Even the wound in the throat was undecayed. The corpse was laid under a gallows, but the ghost continued to appear. By May 7, it had grown 'much fuller of flesh'. Finally, the council ordered that the corpse should be beheaded and dismembered. When the body was opened up, the heart was found to be 'as good as that of a freshly slaughtered calf'. Finally, the body was burnt on a huge bonfire of wood and pitch, and the ashes thrown into the river. After this, the ghost ceased to appear.

Paul Barber, citing the case in *Vampires, Burial and Death*, agrees that 'much in this story is implausible', but points out that so many details—notably the description of the body—are so precise as to leave no doubt 'that we are dealing with real events'.

But what are these 'real events'? Before we comment further, let us consider another well known case from the same year, 1592, (which is, of course, more than a century earlier than the famous vampire outbreak in eastern Europe). This is also to be found in More, and concerns an alderman of Pentsch (or Pentach) in Silesia named Johannes Cuntze (whose name More latinises to Cuntius). On his way to dinner with the mayor, Cuntze tried to examine a loose shoe of a mettlesome horse, and received a kick, presumably on the head. The blow seems to have unsettled his reason; he complained that he was a great sinner, and that his body was burning. He also refused to see a priest. This gave rise to all kinds of rumours about him, including that he had made a pact with the devil.

As Cuntze was dying, with his son beside the bed, the casement opened and a black cat jumped into the room and leapt on to Cuntze's face, scratching him badly; he died soon after. At his funeral on February 8, 1592, 'a great tempest arose', which continued to rage as he was buried beside the altar of the local church.

Before he was buried, there were stories that his ghost had appeared and attempted to rape a woman. After the burial, the ghost began to behave like a mischievous hobgoblin, throwing things about, opening doors, and causing banging noises so that 'the whole house shaked again'—on the morning after these events, animal footprints or hoofmarks were found outside in the snow. His widow had the maid sleeping in her bed; the ghost of Cuntze appeared and demanded to be allowed to take his proper place beside his wife. And the parson of the parish (who is mentioned as the chronicler of these events) dreamed that Cuntze was 'squeezing' him, and woke up feeling utterly exhausted. The spirit was also able to cause a nauseating stench to fill the room.

The conclusion is much as in the story of the shoemaker of Breslau. Cuntze was finally disinterred on July 20, five months after his burial, and was found to be undecayed, and when a vein in the leg was opened, the blood that ran out was 'as fresh as the living'. After having been transported to the bonfire with some difficulty—his body had apparently become as heavy as a stone—he was dismembered (the blood was found to be quite fresh) and burnt to ashes.

So the earlier vampire stories are very clearly about poltergeists, not blood-drinkers. And the Greek and eastern European cases bear a strong resemblance to stories of 'demonic possession', like so many reported in Chapter 11.

If we can once concede the possibility of 'psychic invasion', as well as the possibility of 'spirits', then the notion of vampires suddenly seems less absurd. In *The Magus of Strovolos*, an American academic, Kyriacos C. Markides, has described his friendship with a modern Cypriot mystic and 'magus', Spyros Sathi, known as Daskalos, who lives in Nicosia. Daskalos takes the actual reality of spirits for granted. It also becomes clear that Daskalos takes 'possession' for granted, and Markides tells a number of stories, in some of which he was personally involved.

There are, Daskalos, claims, three kinds of possession: by ill-disposed human spirits, by demonic entities, and by elementals (the latter being human thoughts and desires which have taken on a life of their own). And he goes on to describe a case of spirit possession of the first type: Daskalos was approached by the parents of a girl who claimed that she was being haunted by the spirit of her dead fiancé. Although they had lived together, she had refused to allow him to possess her until they were married. He died of tuberculosis, haunted by unfulfilled cravings. 'Each night before she would go to bed he would semi-hypnotise her and induce her to keep the window of her room open. He would then enter inside a bat and would come to her. The bat would wedge itself on her neck and draw blood and etheric (energy).' The local priest told Daskalos how to deal with it. He must wait in the next room, and when he heard the bat entering, should go in and quickly shut the window; then, since the bat would attack him, he must stun it with a broom. Then he must wrap the bat in a towel and burn it in a brasier (stove). Daskalos did this, and as the bat burned, the girl screamed and groaned. Then she calmed down and asked: 'Why were you trying to burn me?' The 'haunting' ceased thereafter.

Daskalos told another story that has elements of vampirism. On a journey in southern Greece he had encountered another girl who was being haunted by a former lover. A shepherd who had been in love with her had died in a motor accident. Five years later, when looking for some goats, the girl saw the shepherd—whose name was Loizo—and he followed her, finally making her feel very sleepy so she felt obliged to sit down. He then 'hypnotised' her, and caused her to experience intense sexual pleasure. When she reported the incident, she was medically examined and found to be a virgin. But three days later the shepherd came to her bed and made love to her. Medical examination revealed she was no longer a virgin. Daskalos noticed two reddish spots on her neck. 'He kisses me there, but his kisses are strange. They are like sucking, and I like them.'

Daskalos claimed that, two days later, he saw the shepherd coming into the house and greeted him. Loizo explained that he had wanted the girl for many years, and had never had sexual relations with a woman—only with animals like donkeys and goats. Now he was possessing her, he had no intention of letting her go. He refused to believe it when Daskalos told him he was dead. Daskalos warned him that if he persisted in possessing the girl, he would remain 'in a narcotised state like a vampire'. His arguments finally convinced the shepherd, who agreed to go away.

The doctor who examined the girl believed that she had torn the hymen with her own fingers; Daskalos seems to accept this, but believes that Loizo made her do this.

These two cases, taken in conjunction with the others we have considered, offer some interesting clues about the nature of the vampire. According to Daskalos, the 'earthbound spirit' of the dead fiancé was able to enter an ordinary bat and then to suck her blood. This was an expression of his sexual desire, his desire to possess her. There had been many cases in the history of sex crime of so-called 'vampirism'. In the early 1870s, an Italian youth named Vincent Verzeni murdered three women and attempted to strangle several more. Verzeni was possessed by a powerful desire to throttle women (and even birds and animals). After throttling a 14-year-old girl named Johanna Motta, he disembowelled her and drank her blood. Verzeni admitted that it gave him keen pleasure to sniff women's clothing, and 'it satisfied me to seize women by the neck and suck their blood'. So it is easy to imagine that the earth-bound fiancé mentioned by Daskalos should enjoy drinking the girl's blood. But we can also see that his desire to 'possess' her was also satisfied in another way—by somehow controlling her imagination. As the bat was burning, the girl cried out, 'Why are you trying to burn me?'.

Again, in the case of Loizo, we can see that the shepherd had entered the girl's body and taken possession of her imagination, enough to cause her to tear her own hymen with her fingers. This implies—as we would expect—that the lovemaking was not on the physical level, since Loizo possessed no body.

All this has an interesting implications. The act of lovemaking seems to involve a paradox, since it is an attempt at inter-penetration by two bodies, an attempt which is doomed to failure by their separateness. Plato expresses the paradox in an amusing myth. Human beings were originally spherical beings who possessed the characteristics of both sexes. Because their sheer vitality made them a challenge to the gods, Zeus decided that they had to be enfeebled. So he sliced them all down the centre, 'as you and I might slice an apple', and turned their faces back to front. And now the separated parts spent their lives in a desperate search for their other half, and they ceased to constitute a challenge to the gods.

It is also clear that, in its crudest form, the male sexual urge is basically a desire for 'possession', and that the act of physical penetration is an act of aggression. (Most writers on *Dracula* have noted that it is basically a rape fantasy.). As a man holds a woman in his arms, he experiences a desire to absorb her, to blend with her, and the actual penetration is only a token union. So we might say that a 'vampire' like Loizo is able to achieve what every lover dreams about: a possession that involves total interpenetration.

The notion of vampirism that begins to emerge from all this is simple and (provided one can accept the notion of 'earthbound spirits') plausible. Daskalos told Markides that those who commit suicide may become trapped in the 'etheric of the gross material world', unable to move to the higher psychic planes. A suicide dies in 'a state of despair and confusion', and 'may vibrate too close to the material world, which will not allow him to find rest'. He becomes a 'hungry ghost', wandering in and out of the minds of human beings like a man wandering through a deserted city. Yet he is incapable of influencing his involuntary host, or of making his presence felt, unless the host also happens to be on the same 'wavelength' and to share the same desires.

Vampirism, then, involves the notion—which we have already encountered in Wickland's *Thirty years Among the Dead*—that 'earthbound spirits' are attracted by the vitality of the human aura, and may do their best to share it. A book called *Hungry Ghosts*, by the journalist Joe Fisher, makes this point with great force. Fisher had written a book about reincarnation, in the course of which he had become convinced of its reality. One day, after being interviewed on radio in Toronto (where he lives), he received a phone call from a woman who explained that she had accidentally become a mouthpiece of 'discarnate entities'. She was being hypnotised in an attempt to cure her of leukaemia, and various 'spirit guides' had begun speaking through her mouth. (Myers points out that a 'spirit' can only enter a body when the usual 'tenant' is absent, a point to note when considering that early accounts of vampires involve attack *during sleep*.)

The first time Fisher went to her house, a 'spirit' named Russell spoke through her mouth with a reassuring Yorkshire accent, and told him that he had a female 'guide', a Greek girl named Filipa, who had been his mistress in a previous existence three centuries earlier. This struck Fisher as plausible, since he had always felt some affinity with Greece. He began attending the seances regularly, and devoting some time every morning to relaxing and trying to contact Filipa. Eventually he succeeded; buzzing noises in his ears would be succeeded by a feeling of bliss and communication. Filipa was a sensual little creature who liked to be hugged, and Fisher implies that, in some sense, they became lovers. It broke up his current love affair; his live-in girlfriend felt she was no match for a ghost.

Other people at the seances were told about their 'guides'

or guardian angels. One guide was an ex-RAF pilot named Ernest Scott, another an amusing cockney named Harry Maddox. Fisher's disillusionment began when, on a trip back to England, he decided to try and verify Ernest Scott's war stories—with no doubt whatever that they would prove genuine. The airfield was certainly genuine; so was the squadron Ernest claimed to have belonged to; the descriptions of wartime raids were accurate; so were the descriptions of the squadron's moves from airfield to airfield. But there had been no Ernest Scott in the squadron, and a long search in the Public Record Office failed to throw up his name. Fisher went back to Canada in a bitter mood and accused Ernest of lying. Ernest strenuously denied it. Anyway, he said, he was due to reincarnate in another body, so had to leave . . . The 'guide' Russell later told Fisher that Ernest had been reborn in England, and gave the name of the parents and date of birth. Oddly enough, when Fisher checked on this it proved to be accurate. He even contacted the parents, who were intrigued, but decided they had no wish to get more deeply involved.

With Russell's approval, Fisher tried to track down the farm in Yorkshire where Russell claimed he had lived in the 19th century. Here again, many of the facts Russell had given about the Harrogate area proved to be accurate; but again, the crucial facts were simply wrong. It seemed that Russell was also a liar. And so, upon investigation, was the loveable World War One veteran Harry Maddox. His accounts of World War One battles were accurate; but Harry did not exist.

Finally, Fisher took his search to Greece. In spite of his disillusion with the other guides, he had no doubt whatever that Filipa was genuine. She possessed, he states early in the book, 'more love, compassion and perspicacity than I had ever known'. The problem was that all his attempts to locate Theros—a village near the Turkish border—in atlases or gazetteers had failed. Yet that could be because it had been destroyed by the Turks in the past three centuries. But a town called Alexandroupoli, which Filipa had mentioned, still existed. After a long and frustrating search for the remains of Theros, Fisher went to Alexandroupoli, a city that he assumed had been founded by Alexander the Great. But a brochure there disillusioned him. Alexandroupoli was a mere two centuries old; it had not even existed at the time when he and Filipa were supposed to have been lovers . . . Like the others, Filipa was a liar and a deceiver.

In a chapter called 'Siren Call of the Hungry Ghosts', Fisher tries to analyse what has happened to him. And the answer seems simple. He had been involved with what Kardec called 'earthbound spirits', spirits who either do not realise they are dead, or have such a craving to remain on earth that they remain attached to it. These earthbound spirits or, in Tibetan Buddhist phraseology, *pretas* or 'hungry ghosts', are individuals whose minds, at the point of physical death, have been incapable of disentangling from desire. Thus enslaved, the personality becomes trapped on the lower planes even as it retains, for a while, its memory and individuality. Hence the term 'lost soul', a residual entity that is no more than an astral corpse-in-waiting. It has condemned itself to perish; it has chosen a 'second death'. He quotes Lt-Col.Arthur E.Powell, in a book called *The Astral Body*: 'Such spooks are conscienceless, devoid of good impulses, tending towards disintegration, and consequently can work for evil only, whether we regard them as prolonging their vitality by vampirising at seances, or polluting the medium and sitters with astral connections of an altogether undesirable kind.'

He also cites the modern American expert on 'out of the body' journeys, Robert Monroe: 'Monroe tells of encountering a zone next to the Earth plane populated by the 'dead' who couldn't or wouldn't realise they were no longer physical beings . . . The beings he perceived kept trying to be physical, to do and be what they had been, to continue physical one way or another. Bewildered, some spent all of their activity in attempting to communicate with friends and loved ones still in bodies or with anyone else who might come along.'

The conclusion would seem to be that the vampire cannot be dismissed as a myth. But the reality of vampirism has very little in common with the Dracula legend. There is no fundamental difference betwaeen vampires and poltergeists—except that, fortunately, vampire phenomena seem to be far more infrequent.

And what of the vampire's equally celebrated cousin, the were-wolf? Here, as in the case of the vampire, we have many highly circumstantial reports: in the one hundred and ten years between 1520 and 1630, there are thirty thousand in central France alone. (Here they were called *loup-garous*.) But there are also reports from Great Britain, Germany, Hungary, Spain, Holland, Belgium, Norway, Denmark, Sweden, Russia, Iceland, Lapland and Finland. So it is difficult to dismiss them, as Rossell Hope Robbins does in his *Encyclopedia of Witchcraft and Demonology*, as a sign of superstition or madness. A typical report is as follows. In 1598 a 16-year-old boy named Benoit Bidel, who lived at Naizan in the Jura region of France, was found dying from a stab wound. He claimed that he had climbed a tree and was picking fruit when his sister, who was down below, was attacked by a wolf. The boy tried to fight off the wolf with a knife, but he claimed that the wolf had snatched the knife from him—it had human hands—and stabbed him. The boy died, and a search of the area was made; a semi-imbecile girl named Perrennette Gandillon was found. Deciding that she might be the werewolf, the townspeople killed her. Then someone remembered that her brother Pierre was scarred with scratches; he was arrested, together with his sister Antoinette and his son George. All three confessed to being werewolves. Judge Henri Boguet, author of *Discourse on Sorcerers*, visited the Gandillons in jail and said that they ran around on all fours. They confessed that they had turned themselves into wolves with the aid of a witch's salve, and that they had attended 'Sabbats'. All three were sentenced to death and burned. Rossell Hope Robbins takes the commonsense view that all three were insane. Another interesting possibility is suggested by Neville Drury and Stephen Skinner in *The Search for Abraxas* (1971). Discussing Carlos Castaneda and his Don Juan books, they note that Castaneda described how the 'witch doctor' Don Juan had taught him to make a paste of the root of the datura plant, also called Devil's Weed, and how, when he rubbed it on his body, he felt he was flying at great speed through the air. Is it possible, ask the authors, that the witches' salves of past centuries were made of some similar substance that produced the hallucination that they were flying? (In fact, Lord Lytton had already made such a suggestion in his occult novel *A Strange Story*.) Of course, much of Castaneda's work has been discredited since astute critics noticed that his books were full of factual contradictions, especially regarding dates; yet this particular suggestion remains highly plausible.

In studying the reports of werewolves one thing becomes clear: the werewolf was very closely bound up with witchcraft. The Gandillon family, whether they were insane or not, believed that they had attended witches' Sabbats and that they were able to turn themselves into wolves by means of a salve. They believed that their powers came ultimately from the Devil. It is interesting to note that Pierre Gandillon fell into a trance on Maundy Thursday and, when he had recovered, claimed to have attended a Sabbat of werewolves. He believed, then, that he attended these Sabbats 'in the spirit' rather than in the flesh, a belief which ties in with theories of 'astral bodies'. Indeed according to the 19th-century French 'magician' Eliphas Lévi, a werewolf is simply the astral body of the sorcerer projected into the shape of a wolf.

It is undoubtedly true that many 'werewolves' were people who suffered from delusions. In 1603 a mentally defective youth named Jean Grenier claimed to some girls that he was a werewolf; when he was arrested, he implicated his father and a neighbour. In fact, children had been attacked in the area. But the Parlement of Bordeaux took a surprisingly reasonable view for that period and accepted the father's explanation that his son was an imbecile; Jean was placed in custody in a monastery, where he died a few years later.

In other cases, the explanation may be less simple. In the late 16th century the case of a 'werewolf' named Peter Stubbe caused a great stir all over Europe. There had been many wolf attacks in the Cologne area; after a wolf had attacked a group of children, nearly tearing the throat out of one of them, a hunt was organized; the wolf vanished, but the hunters found a man—Peter Stubbe—walking towards Cologne in the area where the wolf had apparently vanished. Under torture Stubbe confessed to being a werewolf, claiming that he was a witch and that the Devil had given him a magic belt (which was never found) which enabled him to transform himself. He admitted to incest with his sister and daughter, with whom he had had a child. He claimed that he had killed many children, as well as large numbers of sheep, lambs, and goats, over a period of twenty-five years. He was broken on the wheel, his flesh pulled off with red hot pincers, and then decapitated; his daughter and sister were sentenced to be burned.

In mediaeval Europe, wolves were the commonest and most dangerous beasts of prey, and the sexual obsessions that drove Isobel Gowdie caused sexually frustrated peasants to identify with wolves. But the most curious question is how far their obsession caused actual physical changes. William Seabrook has a remarkable description of how a Russian emigrée woman meditated on hexagram 49 from the *I Ching*, whose meaning is associated with an animal's fur, and with moulting. She imagined herself to be a wolf in the snow, then began to make baying noises, and slaver at the mouth. When one of the witnesses attempted to wake her up, she leapt at his throat and tried to bite it. In the case of Gilles Garnier, executed as a werewolf in 1574, he seems to have carried out the attacks on children either in the shape of a man or a wolf. The charge, drawn up at Dôle, alleged that he had seized a 12-year-old girl and killed her in a vineyard with his hands and teeth, then dragged her along the ground—with his teeth—into the wood at La Serre, where he ate most of her. He so enjoyed it that he took some home for his wife. (This does not indicate that she was also a *loup-garou*; three hundred years later, in the same area, a peasant named Martin Dumollard made a habit of murdering girls that he lured into lonely places, and taking their clothes to his wife. He would say, 'I've murdered another girl,' and then go off with a spade. She seems to have regarded these activities as a sign of mild eccentricity.) Garnier killed a 12-year-old boy in a wood, and was about to eat the flesh ('although it was a Friday') when he was interrupted by some men. They testified that he was in human form, and Garnier agreed. But he insisted that he was in the shape of a wolf when he strangled a 10-year-old boy and tore off the leg with his fangs; he does not explain how a wolf could strangle anybody. He also attacked another 10-year-old girl—again wearing his wolf-shape—but was forced to flee when interrupted; she died of her wounds. On this occasion, the peasants who interrupted Garnier saw him as a wolf, but nevertheless thought they recognised Garnier's face. He was sentenced to be burned alive.

The rational explanation is that Stubbe and Garnier confessed to a great deal of nonsense under torture, and this is possible.

But it is surely more significant that the great majority of werewolf reports date from the same period as the witchcraft trials in Europe, and that many 'werewolves', like the Gandillons, confessed to being witches. Our study of witchcraft has left no doubt that the majority of cases were miscarriages of justice, but that 'real witchcraft' undoubtedly existed in Europe, and that many witches had 'intercourse' with spirits they believed to be demons. We have also considered many cases of African witchcraft in which the sorcery undoubtedly worked, and even one in which a Catholic priest vouched that a man changed himself into a cassowary.

In cases of vampirism, it seems a reasonable assumption that the vampire is a 'hungry ghost' or earthbound spirit; in cases of lycanthropy, it seems clear that individuals with a taste for sorcery or witchcraft have attempted to invoke spirits in order to change into a wolf. In effect, such individuals were inviting the spirits to possess them.

And, as in the case of vampirism, there seem to be powerful sexual undertones. In discussing werewolves in *The Occult*, I have pointed out that many modern sex killers—for example, the child-murderer Albert Fish and the necrophile Ed Gein—have behaved very much like the traditional idea of the werewolf. If Fish and Gein had been 'witches', it is easy to imagine them performing rituals to invoke spirits until they genuinely felt they had been transformed into beasts of prey. But how far would this cause actual physical changes? In the Gandillon case, we note that the 16-year-old victim, Benoit Bidel, said that the 'wolf' had human hands, while in the Garnier case, Garnier confessed to *strangling* a young boy. And peasants who interupted Garnier as he was attacking a 10-year-old girl said they thought they recognised his face. It certainly sounds as if the 'wolf' remained in many respects human—rather like the upright beast into which Lon Chaney is transformed in the film of *The Wolf Man*.

In his classic work *Man into Wolf*, the Jungian psychologist Robert Eisler suggests that early man had to transform himself from a herbivorous ape into a carnivore struggling for supremacy with other carnivores, and that in the course of this battle, he deliberately acquired something of the ferocity of the wild animal. In his novel *Steppenwolf*, Hermann Hesse writes of a quiet, scholarly man who likes to imagine himself transformed into a wolf of the steppes, and who writes in a poem about attacking a girl:

> The lovely creature I would so treasure,
> And feast myself deep on her tender thigh,
> I would drink of her red blood full measure,
> Then howl till the night went by.

We should also bear in mind Allen Kardec's remark that spirits are able to 'possess' those whose affinities they share, and that many sex killers—from the 19th century American mass murderer H. H. Holmes to Peter Sutcliffe, the Yorkshire Ripper—have believed themselves possessed by the Devil. Is it not conceivable that lychanthropy, like vampirism, should be understood as a special case of 'demoniacal possession'?

As we have seen in the chapter on witchcraft, the occult tradition recognises another type of spirit, the nature spirit or 'elemental'—the psychic Geoffrey Hodson described the 'huge, crimson, bat-like thing' that he saw in the Lake District.

Like the vampire and the werewolf, the elemental can be found in all mythologies of the world. The name obviously implies that such entities are connected with the 'four elements' of the ancient philosophers—earth, air, fire and water—(respectively gnomes, sylphs, salamanders and undines). And since we now know that there are ninety-two natural elements, it would seem that we can at least dismiss this notion without fear of being accused of scientific materialism.

On the other hand, the Cambridge don Tom Lethbridge (whom we met in an earlier chapter; see Pp. 210ff) was convinced that there was some scientific foundation for the belief in elementals. When Lethbridge was eighteen, he and his mother had gone for a walk in the Great Wood near Wokingham, and, at a certain spot, had both experienced a sense of deep depression. A few days later they heard that the body of a suicide had been discovered a short distance from where they were standing.

Forty two years later, after he had retired to an old house in Devon, Lethbridge and his wife Mina went out one Sunday afternoon to collect seaweed for the garden from nearby Ladram

Bay. It was a grey, damp day in January, and almost as soon as they walked on to the beach, both felt as if they had 'stepped into a kind of blanket, or fog, of depression and . . . fear.' Mina came hurrying back from the other end of the beach, saying: 'I can't stand this place any longer. There's something frightful here.'

The following Sunday they returned to Ladram beach. Again they encountered the same 'fog of depression' at the same place. He noted that it was close to a spot where a tiny stream ran down from the cliff. When they went to the spot where Mina had experienced the depression the previous week, it was overwhelming, 'so strong as to make me feel almost giddy'. He likened it to being in bed with a high temperature when one is full of drugs. They went to the cliff top and Tom began to make a sketch while Mina wandered off. As she stood on the edge of the cliff, she experienced a sensation as if someone was urging her to jump.

Back at home, Tom thought he saw a clue. Lethbridge was an excellent dowser, so good that he often used it in his archaeological work. On one occasion, as an experiment, he had allowed a friend to blindfold him then lead him over ground that contained volcanic dykes; his dowsing-rod had located every one of them. Dowsing, he was convinced, was some kind of response to the electrical field of water. (If he had known about split-brain physiology, he might have carried his speculations further and suggested that it is the right hemisphere that responds.) But suppose this 'field' could *record* emotions? Lethbridge was not, apparently, aware of Sir Oliver Lodge's 'tape recording' theory of ghosts (see page 211), but the theory he came to formulate was in many ways similar: that when strong emotions occur in certain places, they are somehow recorded, and can be 'picked up' later by someone who is sensitive to such things. This, he thought, explained the feeling of depression in the Great Wood; the emotions of the man who had committed suicide lingered like a bad smell.

In the case of Mina's urge to jump from the cliff, Lethbridge speculated that someone had intended to commit suicide by jumping from the same spot, and that she was somehow responding to the 'recording' of his depression. At this stage, Lethbridge did not assume that the man *had* actually jumped;

he might have gone home, had a large whisky, and felt better. But he discovered later that a man had, in fact, committed suicide from the place where Mina was standing.

In his book *Ghost and Divining Rod*, Lethbridge speculates on how the classical belief in nymphs came about. Suppose a youth sits down on the bank of a stream, and falls into a vivid sexual daydream in which he imagines a girl, unaware of his presence, taking off her clothes and bathing. His excitement is so strong that his mental image of the naked girl is 'recorded' on the electrostatic field of the water. Some time later, a casual passer-by, thinking of nothing in particular (and therefore in a receptive state), catches a glimpse of a naked girl in the stream, and a moment later, she vanishes. He naturally supposes that she is a supernatural being who has made herself invisible when she sensed that she was being watched . . . Lethbridge coined the name 'naiad field' for the 'recording' medium of the water.

The Great Wood near Wokingham was not particularly damp, and this led Lethbridge to suggest that woods possess their own kind of electrical field, for which he coined the term 'dryad field', after the Greek word for a wood nymph. He went on the suggest that open places—like moors or deserts—and mountainous areas might have their own type of electrostatic field, and that this could account for similar tales of 'spectral beings' seen there. Lethbridge coined the word 'ghouls' for the kind of unpleasant feeling he experienced in the Great Wood, and applied the word 'ghost' to actual appearances—like the man in hunting kit he had seen in his friend's rooms in Cambridge.

But even Lethbridge had to admit that his neat scientific theory of 'elemental fields' failed to explain some of his own experiences. In 1924 he had visited the island of Skellig Michael off the coast of Kerry. He had climbed a hill to look at the ruins of an 8th-century monastery when he noted a heap of rubbish halfway down the cliff face. As he made his way down towards it, he was overtaken by an odd conviction that someone wanted to push him over the cliff, and the feeling was so strong that he changed his mind and went back. According to his later theory, he had experienced a 'ghoul' like the one that made Mina feel she ought to jump from the cliff. But shortly afterwards, as he walked down the hill in front of the monastery, he experienced a sensation that there was someone behind him, and he was suddenly flung flat on his face by a blow. When he sat up, he was alone on the hillside. Clearly, this was not a 'ghoul', a tape recording of negative emotions. A telegraph operator on the mainland told him that the lighthouse on the island had been haunted since a shipwreck. But Lethbridge thought that whatever had knocked him on his face was some kind of poltergeist.

In *Ghost and Ghoul* (where he tells the story), Lethbridge goes on to speculate about the nature of the poltergeist. He discusses the notion that poltergeists take their energy from disturbed adolescents, and adds that 'many still think that the mind of the individual concerned is linked with that of some sub-human personality'. But he then goes on to talk about psychokinesis, and ends by suggesting that his experience on Skellig Michael could be explained in terms of some person who saw the shipwreck, and whose shock had created some kind of delayed psychokinetic effect. He fails to explain where the 'poltergeist' had obtained the energy to knock him down. Or rather, he throws off casually the suggestion that the energy was somehow connected with the ancient religious site.

We are in a position to recognise that Lethbridge was closer to the truth when he suggested that the poltergeist is 'some sub-human personality'. His 'elemental field' hypothesis is a bold and interesting attempt to create a scientific theory that can explain 'ghosts and ghouls'. But Lethbridge lacked the actual experience of poltergeists that led Guy Playfair to recognise that, in many cases at least, they are 'spirits'. If he had, he would have recognised that his 'tape recording' theory of ghosts simply fails to cover the facts.

Elsewhere in *Ghost and Ghoul*, Lethbridge goes on the discuss the most familiar type of elemental known to folklore, the 'sith' or fairy, and he records with amusement that a Scotsman of his acquaintance, an old boatman named John M. Robertson, was a firm believer in the sith. When Lethbridge and some Cambridge friends were on the Shiant Islands, in the Hebrides, one them placed his coat and his lunch beside a rock on a hilltop. When he went back, they had vanished. The rest of the party laughed and said that a gull had probably taken them. But while a gull might well help itself to someone's lunch, it would certainly ignore a coat. His friend was so certain that no one could have taken them without being seen that he declared they had been removed by some supernatural agency. John M. Robertson agreed, declaring that the sith were the culprits. Lethbridge's later experience on Skellig Michael led him to wonder whether Robertson might not be closer to the truth than the sceptical young men from Cambridge, and that his friend's coat might have been taken by some kind of poltergeist, like the one that knocked him down on Skellig Michael. But he remained adamant that the fairies described to him by various Scottish and Irish countrymen were some form of 'mental projection'—a euphemism for hallucination.

Three decades earlier, the poet W.B.Yeats had arrived at a different conclusion. Yeats's early poems are full of fairies, but at the time Yeats was convinced that this was wishful thinking. What changed his mind was a collaboration with his friend—and patroness—Lady Augusta Gregory. In the summer of 1897, Yeats had been staying with Lady Gregory at her home, Coole Park, and the two of them began collecting fairy stories from the local peasantry. Yeats's acquaintance with the extraordinary Madame Blavatsky, founder of the Theosophical Society, had already convinced him of the existence of 'spirits'. Now the sheer factuality of so many descriptions of fairies—many of them eye-witness accounts—convinced him that they could not be dismissed as products of the 'folk imagination'.

G.K. Chesterton, who met Yeats a few years later, was impressed by his insistence on the factual reality of fairies. 'He was the real original rationalist who said that the fairies stand to reason. He staggered the materialists by attacking their abstract materialism with a completely concrete mysticism: 'Imagination!' he would say with withering contempt: 'There wasn't much imagination when Farmer Hogan was dragged out of bed and thrashed like a sack of potatoes—that they did, they had 'um out;' the Irish accent warming with scorn; 'they had 'um out and thumped 'um; and that's not the sort of thing that a man wants to imagine."

Chesterton goes on to make a point of basic importance: 'It is the fact that it is not abnormal men like artists, but normal men like peasants, who have borne witness a thousand times to such things; it is the farmers who see the fairies. It is the agricultural labourer who calls a spade a spade who also calls a spirit a spirit; it is the woodcutter with no axe to grind . . . who will say he saw a man hang on the gallows, and afterwards hang round it as a ghost.'

A few years later, Yeats was to encourage the orientalist W.Y.Evans Wentz—best known for his translation of the *Tibetan Book of the Dead*—to study the folklore of the fairies: the result was Wentz's first book *The Fairy Faith in Celtic Countries* (1911), a bulky and scholarly volume, based upon his own extensive field-work. Yeats's friend, the poet 'AE' (George Russell) contributed an anonymous piece to the book (under the title 'An Irish Mystic's Testimony') in which he describes his own fairy sightings with the factuality and precision of an anthropologist describing primitive tribes: shining beings, opalescent beings, water beings, wood beings, lower elementals . . . 'The first of [the fairies] I saw I remember very clearly . . . there was first a dazzle of light, and then I saw that this came from the heart of a tall figure with a body apparently shaped out of half-transparent or opalescent air, and throughout the body ran a radiant electrical fire, to which the heart seemed the centre. Around the head of this being and through its waving luminous hair, which was blown all about the body like living strands of gold, there appeared flaming wing-like auras. From the being itself light seemed to stream outwards in every direction; and the effect left on me after the vision was one of extraordinary lightness, joyousness or ecstasy.'

Wentz concludes that the factual and scientific evidence for the existence of fairies is overwhelming. 'There are hundreds of proven cases of phenomena . . .'

But AE's fairies were essentially 'visions', and could therefore be classified with unicorns or centaurs. Nine years after Wentz's book appeared, the British public was intrigued to learn of new scientific evidence which seemed to place belief in 'the little people' on an altogether more solid foundation.

The story began on a Saturday afternoon in July 1917, when an engineer named Arthur Wright, went into the dark room to develop a photograph taken earlier in the day by his 16-year-old daughter Elsie. As the plate began to develop, Wright saw vague white shapes appearing—he took them for birds. But when the picture became clear, he was startled to see that they were fairies. The picture showed a serious-faced little girl—Elsie's cousin Frances Griffiths, aged 11—standing behind a bush, her chin propped on her hand. And in front of her, dancing on top of the bush, were four neat little female figures with wings and diaphanous garments, one of them playing a pan-pipe. 'What on earth are they?' said Arthur Wright to his daughter, who was standing behind him. 'Fairies,' she said, matter-of-factly.

Now working-class Yorkshiremen tend to be phlegmatic and down-to-earth. Arthur Wright did not press his daughter for explanations; he merely grunted, and awaited further developments. They came a month later, when the girls again borrowed his camera. Elsie and Frances scrambled across the deep stream —or 'beck'—that ran at the bottom of the garden, and went to the old oaks in the dell beyond. And when Arthur Wright later developed the plate, it showed Elsie sitting on the grass, holding her hand out to a gnome who was apparently about to step up on to her dress.

This time, Arthur and his wife Polly looked through the bedroom of the girls, hoping to find cut-out pictures that would explain the photographs. They found nothing. Arthur Wright became mildly exasperated when both girls insisted there had been no trickery—that there really *were* fairies at the bottom of their garden. He told Elsie she couldn't use the camera again until she told him the truth.

In November 1917, Frances wrote a letter to a friend in South Africa enclosing one of the photographs, and remarking casually that it 'is me with some fairies up the beck . . .'

These events took place in the village of Cottingley, in Yorkshire, on the road from Bradford to Bingley. It has long since ceased to be a separate village, and has become a part of the urban sprawl; but the Fairy Dell still exists.

In the summer of 1919, Polly Wright, Elsie's mother, went to a meeting of the Theosophical Society in Bradford. She was interested in 'the occult', having had experiences of astral projection and memories of past lives. The lecture that evening was on fairies—for it is the position of the Theosophical Society that fairies are simply a type of 'elemental spirit'—nature spirits

—that can manifest themselves to people with second sight or 'clairvoyance'. Naturally, Mrs Wright could not resist mentioning her daughter's 'fairy photographs' to the person sitting next to her. As a result, Arthur Wright made prints of the two photographs, and they were passed from hand to hand at the Theosophists' conference at Harrogate a few weeks later, and finally made their way to London, and into the hands of Edward Gardner, who was the president of the London branch of the Theosophical Society. Gardner was familiar with faked photographs of ghosts and spirits, and decided that these looked doubtful. He asked his correspondent if he could let him see the negatives. When these arrived a few days later, Gardner was surprised to find no evidence of double exposure or other cheating. He took the negatives to a photography expert named Snelling, who examined them carefully under a powerful lens, and announced that it was undoubtedly *not* a double exposure. Nor were the dancing fairies made of paper, or painted on to a sheet of glass. They had *moved* during the exposure. A week later, after enlarging the photographs, Snelling announced that, in his opinion, they were not faked. They were ordinary open-air shots.

It so happened that Sir Arthur Conan Doyle, the creator of Sherlock Holmes, had agreed to write an article on fairies for the Christmas number of the *Strand Magazine* (in which Holmes first appeared). When he heard about the photographs, he contacted Gardner and asked if he could see them. The two men met, and agreed that the pictures were too good to be true—the waterfall in the background (which looked like a painted backcloth), the highly appropriate toadstools . . . Gardner agreed to go to Cottingley to see the girls, and to find out whether they were hoaxers. Mr and Mrs Wright were startled to hear that the experts thought the photographs genuine. And Gardner was startled when he walked up the glen with Elsie, and saw the scene exactly as she had photographed it, complete with waterfall and toadstools—although without fairies.

Gardner decided to test the girls. Two cameras were bought, and the film-plates were sealed so they could not be tampered with. In due course, the negatives were returned to Gardner, and the factory that had produced them verified that they were still sealed. One showed Frances with a fairy leaping close to her face, another showed a fairy offering a flower to Elsie, while the third showed two fairies in the middle of a bush. In the centre of the picture there is an object that looks rather like a bathing costume hung on a line. Elsie apparently had no idea what this was; but Gardner, with his wider knowledge of fairy lore, identified it as a 'magnetic bath' which fairies weave in dull weather. (It had rained continually that August.)

Once more, the experts got to work to try to discover if the photographs had been faked; again, they concluded that they were genuine. That Christmas, Doyle's article on the fairies appeared in the *Strand Magazine* and caused a sensation. Inevitably, the majority of people thought it was a hoax; yet no expert on photography was able to say anything conclusive about how it might have been done. A reporter on the *Westminster Gazette* learned the true identities of the girls (Conan Doyle had used pseudonyms to protect them from publicity) and went to see them. He concluded that everyone seemed honest and genuine, and there was no evidence of trickery. Arthur Wright was baffled by it all, and deeply disappointed that Conan Doyle was naive enough to be taken in, 'bamboozled by our Elsie, and her at the bottom of her class'. Conan Doyle was himself puzzled and critical; yet he could not discount the possibility that these were real fairies, nature spirits of some kind. He contacted a well-known clairvoyant named Geoffrey Hodson, and Hodson went to Cottingley, talked to the girls, and went to the dell with them. He also saw fairy forms. We have met Hodson in connection with a 'bat-like' elemental.)

By the end of 1921, most people had lost interest in the fairies. Conan Doyle was to write a book about the case, called *The Coming of the Fairies*, which came out in 1922; but there was no re-investigation.

In 1965, Elsie, then in her 60s, was tracked down in the Midlands by a *Daily Express* reporter Peter Chambers. His own conviction was that the pictures were faked; and Elsie's comment that people should be left to make up their own minds on the subject only deepened his scepticism. Elsie made the curious remark:

'As for the photographs, let's say they are pictures of figments of our imagination, Frances' and mine, and leave it at that.'

In 1971, Elsie was asked by the BBC's *Nationwide* programme, if her father had had a hand in the taking of the photographs; she replied: 'I would swear on the Bible that father didn't know what was going on.' But when asked if she would swear on a Bible that the photograph were not tricks, she replied after a pause: 'I'd rather leave that open if you don't mind . . . but my father had nothing to do with it, I can promise you that.' Again she seemed to be coming close to admitting that there was some kind of fraud.

On the other hand when Frances was asked by Yorkshire Television if the photographs were fabricated, she replied: 'Of course not. You tell us how she could do it—remember she was 16 and I was 10. Now then, as a child of 10, can you go through life and keep a secret?'

This, it seemed was the chief argument in favour of the fairy photographs; that it seemed unlikely that Francis and Elsie would and could keep such a secret for so long.

Frances made this comment in 1976; the occasion was a television programme about Frances and Elsie, which had been suggested by the Yorkshire psychical investigator Joe Cooper. Which is why, on September 10, the two women turned up at a house on Main Street, Cottingley, opposite the house where the Wright family had lived half a century earlier. During that time, Elsie had lived in India with her husband Frank Hill, a Scots engineer; Frances had married a soldier, Frank Way, and had spent much time with him abroad.

Joe Cooper describes Frances as 'a bespectacled woman of middle class and height wearing fashionable denim clothes but with a dash of red and black about the scarf and blouse'. Elsie, when she arrived, looked a good ten years younger than her 75 summers, dressed in fashionable slacks and 'mod' gear, with a black billycock hat. During the day Cooper became friendly with the two women, even carrying Elsie over a stile. The camera team interviewed locals—who all expressed extreme scepticism about the photographs—and filmed the women down by the beck. Interviewer Austin Mitchell made no secret of believing that the case of the Cottingley fairies had started as a joke, then got out of hand. Cooper was inclined to believe them. On camera, Elsie and Frances identified the place where they had seen a gnome, and flatly denied that they had fabricated the photographs. 'Of course not!' said Frances. And interviewed by Mitchell, Joe Cooper stated his view that the girls had seen an 'elemental form of fairy life'—that is to say, nature spirits. After all, W. B. Yeats and thousands of his fellow countrymen were quite certain about the existence of fairies . . .

In 1977, there was an interesting development. A researcher named Fred Gettings, working on 19th century fairy illustrations, came upon *Princess Mary's Gift Book*, published during the First World War to make money for the 'Work for Women' fund. It contained a poem called 'A Spell for a Fairy' by Alfred Noyes, and this was illustrated by Claude Shepperson. And two of the fairies in his illustration were virtually identical with the fairies in the first Cottingley photograph, showing Frances looking over the heads of five prancing fairies. Their positions had merely been reversed.

In August 1978, *The New Scientist* reported that the magician James Randi ('The Amazing Randi') and the Committee for the Scientific Investigation of Claims of the Paranormal (CSICOP) had put the photographs through an image-enhancement process, and found that this revealed strings holding up the fairies. When Joe Cooper told Elsie about the article, she merely laughed and pointed out that there was nowhere in the region of the beck where string could be strung. After a TV play about the fairies had been broadcast in October 1978, Randi expressed indignation that the BBC had failed to state clearly that the photographs had been proved to be fakes.

In 1981, Joe Cooper was writing a book on telepathy, and had some correspondence with Frances—who now lived in Ramsgate—about it. In September 1981, she asked him to go to see her, telling him that there were 'some things he should know'. When he arrived, she was still not ready to specify what these were. But the following day, she asked him to drive her to Canterbury; once there, she asked him to wait for her while she went into the cathedral. When she returned, they sat in a coffee bar, and she asked him what he thought of the first fairy photograph. He commented that it has been greatly touched up. Then Frances dropped her bombshell:

'From where I was, I could see the hatpins holding up the figures. I've always marvelled that anybody ever took it seriously.'

'Why are you telling me?' asked the flabbergasted investigator.

'Because Elsie has already told Glenn'—(Glenn was Elsie's son).

'What about the other four? Are they fakes?'

Her answer was, in its way, as astonishing as the original admission.

'Three of them. The last one's genuine.'

Cooper and Frances now discussed writing a book together, and giving Elsie a share of the proceeds; Frances was adamant that Elsie should play no part in writing the book. Cooper went to London to talk to his publisher. Unfortunately, the publisher was not particularly interested in a 60-year-old story about fairies, particularly since it ended so anticlimactically.

The present writer had also got involved. I had met Joe Cooper at a weekend conference on parapsychology (at the Swanwick Conference Centre in Derbyshire) in 1980, and he told me he had written a book on the Cottingley fairies—this, of course, was a year before Frances told him the true story. He sent me the typescript, and I found it fascinating. I had also come across people who claimed to have seen fairies—one of them a hard-headed Scottish TV interviewer—and I was simply not willing to rule out the possibility that 'Nature spirits' might exist. Joe's own researches into the paranormal had convinced him that 'elementals' could not simply be ruled out as an absurdity.

In fact, I was on my way to Yorkshire to research the 'Black Monk of Pontefact' (see Appendix), an investigation that led me—as I shall describe—to accept the notion that poltergeists are 'spirits', and not simply a form of RSPK (recurrent spontaneous psychokinesis). So it was hardly logical for me to deny the existence of 'Nature spirits' on the grounds that only a child could believe in them.

But even in its original version, the problem with Joe Cooper's book was obviously that the story was too slight—it could be told in fifty pages. The rest had to be some kind of 'padding'. And since, at that point, both Frances and Elsie were still insisting that the photographs were genuine, there was no real conclusion.

I tried to find a publisher for the book, but was unsuccessful. And at this point, Joe said he wanted to rewrite it anyway; and there the matter rested.

It was in the following year that Frances finally 'came clean'. Oddly enough, Joe was excited that the case had finally reached a definite conclusion. When he told me about Frances's confession, I was less optimistic. If the book ended with Frances's confession, it would be a damp squib.

Joe Cooper came to the same conclusion. Late in 1982, a partwork called *The Unexplained*, on which I was a consultant editor, published his article: 'Cottingley: At Last the Truth', in which he revealed that the fairies in the first four photographs were cut-outs stuck to the branches with hatpins. Understandably, this upset both Frances and Elsie. When Frances called Joe's wife on New Year's Day, 1983, and Joe answered the phone, she called him a traitor and hung up. She died in 1986. Elsie died in 1988, maintaining to the end that she did not believe in fairies.

Which seems to be the end of the story. Or is it? Certainly the sceptics are justified in regarding the case as closed. Possibly they are correct. Yet before we make up our minds, there is a great deal more to be said.

What Frances is asking us to believe is this. She came to England from South Africa in 1917, when she was ten, and went to stay with her 16-year-old cousin Elsie in Cottingley. Elsie had always been fascinated by fairies, and claimed to have had some odd ghostly experiences—she insisted that when she was 4 she was regularly visited in bed by a woman in a tight dress buttoned up to her neck. And when she was 6, she woke up one night and called for a drink. When no one replied, she went downstairs, and found a strange man and woman in the house. She asked where her parents were, and was told they had gone out to play cards with the neighbours. When Elsie said she wanted to go and find them, the man opened the front door for her. Her parents—who were, in fact, playing cards with the neighbours—were greatly alarmed to hear about the man and woman, for they had left the house empty. But when they went to investigate, the house was empty.

Frances had had no 'psychic' experiences. But in the spring of 1918, she saw her first gnome. She had gone down to the beck after school when she noticed a phenomenon she had often observed before: a single willow leaf began to shake on the tree by the stream. Then a small man, all dressed in green, was standing on the branch. Frances watched, breathless, terrified of disturbing him. Then the little man looked straight at her, and disappeared. After that, she claimed, she often saw little men wearing coats of greyish green and matching caps by the beck. She gradually reached the conclusion that the little men were engaged in some kind of purposeful activity, perhaps associated with helping plants to grow. Later, she began to see fairies, with and without wings; these were smaller than the elves, with white faces and arms, and often seemed to be holding some kind of meeting. Elsie, she insists, never saw the fairies or little men.

It was after falling in the stream yet again that Frances admitted that she went to the beck to see fairies. And it was the total scepticism of the adults that led Elsie to decide to take some fairy photographs. This was not a simple desire to deceive. Elsie believed Frances when she said she saw fairies; her own psychic experiences made it quite plausible. She wanted to shake the credulity of the grown-ups. So the photographs were taken with cut-outs propped up by hatpins.

When the world suddenly became interested in their fairies, they were in a difficult position. The photographs were fakes, but the fairies really existed. If the whole thing had been a hoax, it would have been easier to confess. But it was not a hoax—not totally, anyway. They were in an embarrassing and anomalous position. If they admitted that the photographs were fakes, they would be implying that the whole affair was nothing but a hoax. And that would be untrue as continuing to maintain the the photographs were genuine. So they kept silent.

When the whole affair blew up again in 1965, the situation was more or less unchanged. Elsie, now a hard-headed woman in her 60s, was no longer so convinced that Frances had seen fairies; yet she was absolutely certain that she had had 'psychic' experiences, and was therefore prepared to be open-minded. As to Frances, she *had* seen fairies and had nothing to retract. In a letter to Leslie Gardner, the son of Edward Gardner, Elsie remarked that after her interview with Peter Chambers (in 1965), in which she had declared that people must judge for themselves, and that the pictures were of 'figments of our imaginations', Frances had said indignantly: 'What did you say that for? You know very well that they were real.'

Frances had always maintained that the fairies were real. In November 1918 she sent the first fairy photograph to a friend in South Africa, and scrawled on the back: 'Elsie and I are very friendly with the beck Fairies. It's funny I never used to see them in Africa. It must be too hot for them there.'

In his original typescript of the Cottingley book, Joe Cooper had included a chapter called 'Other Sightings', consisting of accounts of fairies related to him by other people, and it makes clear why he believed Frances. One man, a healer, told how he was sitting with a girl in Gibraltar, eating a sandwich, when it was snatched from him by 'a little man about eighteen inches high'. An 80-year-old officer of the Theosophical Society insisted that when he was a small boy, he was often visited in bed by a green-clad gnome. Another old man described seeing a green-clad gnome, about two feet high, walking along a path in a cornfield. Some young male students told how, when walking in a wood near Bradford, they saw fairies who were 'circling and dancing', but who were invisible to the direct gaze: they could only be seen 'out of the corner of the eye'. An elderly lady showed Cooper a photograph of a gnome seen through a frosty window; she claimed that she had come down one morning, seen the gnome, and rushed upstairs to get her camera. The photograph also shows diminutive white rabbits.

In his book *Modern Psychic Experiences*, Joe Cooper publishes most of these accounts, together with many more. A New Zealand medium named Dorothy described how she used to play with a 'spirit' girl called Mabel as a child, and how she had first seen fairies, who came from under plants. One day she came home to find her father unconscious on the floor—a gastric ulcer had perforated—and the fairies took charge and escorted her to the door of the doctor. Joe Cooper's own niece Jo, in her thirties, described how, at the age of 16, she had seen three small men crouching on top of a wall.

When I wrote about the Cottingley fairies in *Poltergeist*, I also went to some trouble to find accounts of 'real fairies'. I describe being interviewed on television at the 1978 Edinburgh Festival by a man called Bobbie (whose surname I forgot to note in my journal): in the pub next door he told me casually that the had once seen a gnome standing on the pavement outside a convent gate, and that it had 'scared the hell out of him.'

My friend Marc Alexander, author of many books on the paranormal, told me a story of a friend in New Zealand called Pat Andrew, who claimed to have seen a pixie when he was 6. Years later, after seeing a stage hypnotist, Marc and Pat Andrew began experimenting with hypnosis on one another. Marc had no doubt that Pat Andrew was genuinely hypnotised, and one day decided to try and 'regress' him to the age at which he saw the pixie. The result was an amazing one-sided conversation that left Marc in no doubt whatever that, whether Andrew had really seen a pixie or not, he undoubtedly *believed* he had.

One of the most circumstantial accounts I know of an encounter with a pixie is recounted by another friend, Lois Bourne, in her book *Witch Among Us*. Lois is a 'witch' in the sense of possessing odd psychic powers, of whose reality I have not the slightest doubt. She is an extremely sensible and down-to-earth lady. And in her book, among many stories that psychical researchers will find credible enough, she tells a story that will obviously cause most readers to doubt her truthfulness. Staying on holiday at a cottage at Crantock, in Cornwall, she met another member of a 'wicca' coven, and spent an evening at her home. The woman's husband, Rob, asked her if she would like to see a goblin. One appeared among the rushes of the millstream at Treago Mill, Cuberts Heath, every morning at sunrise, and if she wanted to see him, she had to be up early. The next morning Lois and her husband Wilfred joined Rob at the mill gate, and they crept up to the stream. 'I have never been able to decide, and still cannot decide, whether I really saw that goblin, or if Rob made me see it . . . Whatever it was, there, sitting on a stone calmly washing his socks, was an elfin creature with a red hat, green coat and trews, one yellow sock on, and one in his tiny hands in the process of being washed. I remember thinking at the time in my sleepy befuddled but practical way 'what an atrocious colour combination'. Suddenly he saw us and he disappeared . . . 'Now do you believe me?' asked Rob.'

I have known Lois for years. I may be gullible and she may be a liar, but I believe her. She is not the type to invent such a silly story. And her husband Wilfred—who also saw it—is not the type to support a downright lie.

As already mentioned, the poet W. B. Yeats had been convinced of the existence of fairies ever since he and Lady Gregory went from door to door collecting information from the local peasants. They recorded these interviews in a book called *Visions and Beliefs* in 1920. Evans Wentz concludes his *Fairy Faith in Celtic Countries* by acknowledging: 'we seem to have arrived at a point . . . where we can postulate scientifically . . . the existence of such invisible intelligences as gods, genii, daemons, all kinds of true fairies, and disembodied man . . .' (By the latter he means ghosts). And he goes on to cite the very sound evidence for the existence of the poltergeist. George Russell (AE)—and Wentz—emphasise that these entities are seen only by 'psychics', and Russell believes that such beings are not 'individuals' in the human sense. 'Theirs is a collective life, so unindividualised and so calm that I might have more varied thoughts in five hours than they would have in five years.'

When all this is taken into account, we may feel that the notion that Frances really saw fairies by the beck in Cottingley no longer seems quite so absurd.

15.
Standing Stones and Space Men

LETHBRIDGE, AS WE HAVE SEEN, was fascinated by the problem of 'earth forces', and the notion that they are responsible for the 'sacredness' of religious sites. He comments again and again on the fact that so many Christian churches are built on ancient pagan sites, and on that curious directive issued by Pope Gregory the Great that where possible, Christian churches should be built in these places. It could be, of course, that he was simply trying to recruit converts who happened to be attached to the 'Old Religion' of the witches. But there was almost certainly a second reason: that he recognised that certain places were chosen because the *ground itself* was 'sacred. Stonehenge is an example; so is the Cornish circle of standing stones known as the Merry Maidens. In both these places, Lethbridge's dowsing-rod detected powerful forces. When he placed his hand on a stone at the Merry Maidens, while he was using a dowsing pendulum with the other hand (a pendulum can be more sensitive than a dowsing-rod), he experienced a tingling force, not unlike an electric shock. He theorised that ancient priests had recognised this force in the earth, and had ordered the stones to be placed there to conduct the force—rather as an acupuncturist places the needles at the crossing points of certain 'meridians' in the body.

It is a pity that Lethbridge was unaware of the work of his predecessor Alfred Watkins, a Hereford brewer who had also been intrigued by 'sacred places'. Half a century earlier, on June 30, 1921, Watkins was riding his horse across the hills near Bredwardine, and as he paused on a hilltop, he noticed something that excited him. He could see a number of straight tracks and ancient footpaths running across the countryside, and he now observed that they seemed to connect up old churches, standing stones and ancient mounds (known as tumps or tumuli). It struck him that what he was looking at was ancient man's equivalent of a telecommunications system. Some of these tracks, he thought, were simply trade routes, while others must have some religious significance, since they connected sacred sites. He decided to call them 'ley lines', from the old word for an enclosed field.

It is, in fact, fairly easy to create a straight line that runs for miles across country, even if it has to go up hill and down dale. The technique is known as 'ranging a line', and it requires only three staves. The man constructing the path drives the first staff into the ground, and then closes one eye and looks beyond it to the hilltop—or whichever point he wishes to go towards. An assistant then places a second staff in line with the first. The third staff is placed further along still, in such a position that it is blotted out by the second. Then the first staff is pulled up, and the process continues.

The men who originally marked out these 'old straight tracks' were—Watkins thought—probably of priestly rank, and would carry a staff as a badge of office. This may explain the great hillside figure called the Long Man of Wilmington, who seems to be holding a long staff in either hand . . .

Watkins's suggestion led to the formation of an 'Old Straight Track' club, whose members spent their weekends looking for new ley lines.

One of its members made an interesting and puzzling observation in the late 1930s—that, very often, *two* tracks ran parallel. But why should there be two tracks—like railway lines—when one would suffice? A retired solicitor named Guy Underwood found what he thought was the answer. He spent his retirement dowsing around stone circles, and he noticed that his dowsing-rod often showed two parallel tracks of some underground force running for miles. And when he examined 'holy sites'—like Stonehenge—he found many of these 'double' tracks (named by him 'aquastats'). They seemed to be lines of some kind of magnetic force.

Watkins had never suspected that his straight tracks were anything but trade routes or tracks between churches. Now Underwood was suggesting that they followed lines of underground force. Moreover, at sacred sites, he found that these lines often formed a spiral. Ancient rock carvings all over the world display the same spiral pattern. Could this be because it is the obvious symbol for this sacred earth force?

In the 1960s—when the 'occult revival' was in full swing—another student of ancient monuments, John Michell, revived Watkins' now forgotten 'ley lines'. Oddly enough—or perhaps not so oddly, as it turned out—Michell began as a student of the strange phenomenon known as flying saucers or UFOs. These had leapt to international prominence in the late 1940s, after a businessman named Kenneth Arnold, flying his private aeroplane near Mount Rainier, in Washington State on June 24, 1947, had sighted nine shining disc-like objects flying in V formation. Other sightings poured in, and in Kentucky in January 1948, Captain Thomas Mantell, piloting a Mustang, tried to follow a 'flying saucer' to twenty thousand feet and fell out of the sky. From then on, there were thousands of UFO sightings, and books about them poured off the presses—to the disgust of orthodox scientists, who regarded it all as mass hysteria.

What John Michell noted was that many of the places where flying saucers were reported were also 'places of ancient sanctity', and that in many cases their flight path seemed to follow ley lines. This led Michell to re-examine the evidence of Watkins and Underwood. He also noticed that in Ireland ley lines are called 'fairy paths', and have been known since time immemorial. His views were first propounded in a book called *The Flying Saucer Vision* (1967), and then, two years later, in *A View Over Atlantis*. It suggested that the religions of ancient man were based upon a recognition of the magnetic forces of the earth, which were closely connected with its fertility. Ancient man, he believed, had his own form of non-technological civilisation based upon these sacred forces. Glastonbury was one of the sites of this ancient religion.

But why Atlantis? The Atlantis of legend was an ancient civilisation described by Plato, an enormous island in the Atlantic ocean which had been swallowed up by some gigantic catastrophe nine thousand years earlier. Scholars had dismissed it as a myth, although one modern archaeologist, Professor A.G. Galanopoulos, had suggested that Atlantis was really the island of Santorini, north of Crete, which had been destroyed in a gigantic volcanic explosion about 1500 BC; Galanopoulos thought that the Egyptian priests from whom Plato got the story had accidentally multiplied all their figures by ten, including the date of the catastrophe. What Michell was suggesting is that the story of Atlantis indicates that there *had* been a complex civilisation long before those that are known to history, and that folk memories of this civilisation survive in legends of the 'Golden Age'. Primitive religions were an *interaction* between man and nature, an interaction that modern man has totally forgotten.

One effect of Michell's book was to turn Glastonbury into a place of pilgrimage for hippies; another was to create a new interest in ley lines and 'earth magic'.

Lethbridge, living quietly in Devon, knew none of this. Yet his own studies had brought him remarkably close to the same ideas. He had noticed, to begin with, how often churches called after St Michael are found along the lines that join sacred places. This, he believed, was because the Christians had taken over pagan sites, and replaced the Celtic god Lugh (or Lucifer), the sun god and light-bringer, with Lucifer's traditional enemy St Michael.

Lethbridge's interest in St Michael and in the standing stones that so often seemed to be associated with him (or with the sun god) led him to wonder about another ancient mystery: the legends of the great 'war in heaven' between St Michael and the 'dragon'. Was it possible that this was also something more than a primitive myth?

Lethbridge began from the same question that had intrigued John Michell: *why* were there legends of a 'golden age'? What made men of the bronze or iron age—who were, after all, so much better off than their forefathers – look back nostalgically to some idyllic past?

He was also fascinated by the passage in the sixth chapter of Genesis about the sons of God finding the daughters of men desirable, and fathering children on them. It adds that 'there were giants in the earth in those days', and that the daughters of men bore children to them. And, since he was so interested in the question of St Michael and his enemy the dragon, he wondered about the passage in Revelation 12 about a 'war in heaven', when Michael and his angels fought against the dragon.

The solution that suggested itself to him struck him as so preposterous that he delayed publishing it for a long time. It was that the 'sons of God' were visitors from space, and that the 'war in heaven' had actually taken place, and that an atomic bombardment accounted for the heavy cratering of Mars and the moon. As to the standing stones—like Stonehenge and the Merry Maidens: was it not possible that they might have served as 'beacons' for the space craft to home in on?

In short, what Lethbridge suggests is that the 'golden age'—Michell's Atlantis—was an age in the remote past when visitors from space had landed on earth and taught human beings a great deal about the use of technology. The result was a diffusion of this knowledge over the surface of the earth, which accounted for the similarity of artifacts found all over the world.

Because Lethbridge was such a loner, he was unaware that he had simply tuned in to the 'spirit of the age', and was raising questions that had occurred to other speculative thinkers. Lethbridge was, in fact, devastated to discover just before his death that his 'space men' idea had been suggested by the Swiss writer Erich von Daniken, in a book called *Memories of the Future* (1967) and translated as *Chariots of the Gods?*, which suggested that all kinds of ancient artifacts and monuments—including the Great Pyramid—were the work of space men. In fact, as early as 1958, a writer named George Hunt Williamson had written a book called *Secret Places of the Lion*, in which he declared that visitors from space had landed eighteen million years ago, and had dedicated themselves since then to the evolution of mankind. Pauwels and Bergier repeated the suggestion in their *Morning of the Magicians* (1960). The same idea was given popular currency in 1968 in Stanley Kubrick's film *2001: A Space Odyssey*.

If Lethbridge had had time to study Daniken more carefully, he would have felt less chagrined. Although Daniken achieved international best-sellerdom with his books on 'space visitors', scholarly analysis revealed that most of his ideas were simply absurd guesses or distortions of fact. *Chariots of the Gods?* describes how, in the Assyrian *Epic of Gilgamesh*, there is an episode in which the hero Enkidu is borne upward in the claws of the sun god, so that his body feels as heavy as lead; he then flies for four hours in the talons of an eagle. These episodes, Daniken suggests, are really accounts of a trip in a space craft. A door that speaks with a human voice is obviously a loudspeaker . . . In fact, a careful perusal of the *Epic of Gilgamesh* reveals that these events do not occur.

Von Daniken also suggests that the Great Pyramid must have been built by ancient astronauts because rope was not known in Egypt at the time it was built; in fact, many tomb paintings depict men using ropes. (Von Daniken also manages to multiply the weight of the pyramid by five.) He insists that the statues on Easter Island must have been built by space men, because carving them and moving them was beyond the technology of the Easter Island natives; but modern Easter Islanders disproved that by carving and erecting a statue for the benefit of the explorer Thor Heyerdahl. The lines drawn on the flat surface of the desert in Peru—known as the Nazca lines—were, according to Daniken, intended as landing strips for space ships; he ignores the obvious fact that the turbulence created by any large craft would destroy the lines, which have remained unchanged since 500 AD only because the desert is windless.

In a later book, *Gold of the Gods*, Daniken indulges in actual deceit. He describes in detail how he descended into a vast underground cave system in Ecuador, and examined an ancient library of strange metal leaves engraved with unknown characters. Later exploration of the caves revealed no such library, and when Daniken's companion revealed that Daniken had not even ventured underground, Daniken himself admitted that this was true, but explained that the writers of books like *Gold of the Gods* are permitted to embroider their facts.

The result of all this is that Daniken has now been totally discredited, and that the 'ancient astronaut' theory associated with his name has few serious supporters. This is a pity, for there is far more convincing evidence than that presented by Daniken. An impeccably scholarly book, *The Sirius Mystery* by Robert Temple, examines the question of how an African tribe called the Dogon came to know that Sirius is a double star, (since this can only be perceived through an astronomical telescope), and that its companion (Sirius B) is a white dwarf—a 'collapsed' star of tremendous density, which rotates on its axis and revolves around Sirius A every fifty years. Temple argues that the Dogon derived their knowledge from ancient Egyptians, who in turn must have learnt it from 'space visitors'. Opponents of the theory have argued that early white missionaries may have brought astronomical knowledge to the Dogon, but there is not the slightest scrap of evidence for this. The Dogon themselves insist that their knowledge of the Digitaria star (as they call it) is part of their ancient tradition.

More interesting evidence can be found in another scholarly study, *Maps of the Ancient Sea Kings* (1966), subtitled 'Evidence of Advanced Civilisation in the Ice Age', by Professor Charles Hapgood. In 1956, a Turkish naval officer presented a copy of an ancient map to the US Navy Hydrographic Society. A student of old maps, Captain Arlington Mallery, concluded that it showed the Antarctic coast of Queen Maud Land in the days before its bays were covered over by ice—about six thousand years ago. Hapgood decided to recruit his students at Keene State College into the project, and got them studying the Piri Reis maps: Piri Reis was not (as Pauwels and Bergier state) a 19th century naval officer, but a Turkish pirate of Greek nationality who was beheaded in 1554, and whose seafaring maps had been preserved in the Topkapi Palace in Istanbul. These also showed Antarctic bays that have been frozen over for six thousand years; yet seafaring began only about 2,000 BC.

The obvious conclusion seemed to be that a seafaring civilisation existed in 4,000 BC. This, admittedly, is hardly proof of Lethbridge's space visitors – perhaps men built ships two thousand years earlier than anyone suspected, at the time the Sumerians were creating the earliest known civilisation in Mesopotamia (and, of course, before the birth of writing). What seems altogether odder is the evidence of another map—the Hamy-King chart—which showed a land bridge across the Bering Straits which has not existed for twelve thousand years.

Hapgood argued that all this seemed to show that a worldwide civilisation with a powerful navy probably existed twelve thousand years ago—at a time when, according to historians, the earth was inhabited only by primitive Stone Age hunters, and the earliest farmers had not yet appeared.

All this naturally excited devotees of the legend of Atlantis, (not to mention Mu, a similar civilisation which was supposed to have existed in the Pacific in an earlier epoch). The publication of Daniken's *Chariots of the Gods* in the following year poured cold water on all this excitement, much as the birth of Spiritualism had caused the eclipse of Buchanan's psychometry; Hapgood found himself tarred with the same brush and labelled a crank. Yet republication of his book, in a revised edition, in 1979, left no doubt that his theory of an ancient worldwide civilisation must be taken seriously.

All this, of course, is still no proof of Lethbridge's space men theory. In his book *Timescale*—a narrative 'map' of world history—Nigel Calder refers to our Cro-magnon ancestors, who replaced the more ape-like Neanderthal Man around thirty-four thousand years ago, as a 'race of supermen, created by mutations among the highbrow subspecies living in warm regions'. This race of supermen survived the last great Ice Age, starting twenty-eight thousand years ago, and when the thaw began, about fourteen thousand years ago, nothing seems more likely than that they quickly learned to take advantage of the seas with their teeming fish population. So it may be that we merely have to revise our notions of history to accommodate the idea of a Stone Age civilisation with seagoing vessels. But it is far more difficult to believe that these Stone Age seafarers created complex maps—even if they scratched them on bark. Hapgood's evidence suggests that we may have to choose between the legend of Atlantis, and the notion of ancient astronauts.

In *Legend of the Sons of God*, Lethbridge is inclined to accept both. Atlantis, he thinks, may be a 'garbled memory' of the exploits of the Megalith bullders. But he is also inclined to believe that flying saucers may also be the vehicles in which the 'sons of God' originally came to earth. Lethbridge had seen something that might have been a flying saucer in 1931—a shining disc like a large balloon floating down towards the road. (Nicholas Roerich, who designed Stravinky's *Rite of Spring* ballet, saw one in 1926, when he and a party of travellers were making their way across the Himalayas from Mongolia to India; this one behaved like the traditional flying saucer in moving at a great speed and then suddenly changing direction). After discussing flying saucers at some length, he suggests that they could either be 'space visitors', or beings from some other dimension. (Lethbridge's studies with the pendulum had convinced him of the reality of 'other dimensions'[1]) But he is inclined to believe that the solution to the mystery lies in what he calls 'bio-electronics', the study of the living forces of the earth, which ancient man seems to have understood so well. Like John Michell, he believes that there is some connection between UFOs and the 'magnetic' forces of the earth. He also believes that there is a connection between these magnetic forces and the human mind. He goes on to suggest that 'out of the body' experiences are a proof of the human mind's ability to escape our earthly 'vibration rate' and move to a higher one. (His neighbour at Branscombe—the 'witch'—convinced him of this by paying an 'astral' visit to his bedroom one night, and later describing what she saw there.)

Lethbridge died in September 1971, before publication of *Legend of the Sons of God*. What is clear from that book—and from his final posthumous work *The Power of the Pendulum*—is that he was experiencing a problem that seems to haunt all investigators of the paranormal. They begin by studying some phenomenon that personal experience led them to accept (as Buchanan's experiences with his students convinced him of the reality of psychometry), and they propound some basically commonsense theory to explain it in scientific terms. Then more evidence turns up that contradicts the theory—like Buchanan's discovery that psychometry worked just as well on a newspaper photograph that had not been in contact with its original. The theory is then expanded slightly to try to accommodate the problem—at which point some new anomaly makes its

1. See my book *Mysteries*, Chapter 1.

appearance . . . And so on, until it is clear that no purely rational theory can accommodate all the facts.

Many who have decided to look into 'flying saucers' have encountered the problem. One of these was an American journalist named John Keel, who had prepared a radio documentary as early as 1952, and decided that the evidence for UFOs could not be dismissed.

Like so many others, John Keel was also mildly sceptical about flying saucers until he tried the unusual expedient of studying the subject instead of passing a priori judgements. In 1952 he prepared a radio documentary on things seen in the sky, and came to believe that—even then—there had been too many sightings of flying saucers to dismiss them as mistakes or lies. In 1953, in Egypt, he saw his first UFO, a metallic disc with a revolving rim, hovering over the Aswan dam in daylight. Yet even so, it was not until 1966 that he decided to undertake a careful study of the subject, and subscribed to a press-cutting bureau. What then staggered him was the sheer number of the sightings—he often received 150 clippings in a day. (In those days press clippings were only a few pence each; twenty years later, at about a pound each, the experiment would be beyond the resources of most journalists.) Moreover, it soon became clear that even these were only a small percentage of the total, and that thousands of sightings were going unrecorded. (This is in fact the chief disadvantage of a chapter like this one; it cannot even begin to convey the sheer volume of the sightings. Any sceptic should try the experience of reading, say, a hundred cases, one after the other, to realize why the 'delusion' theory fails to hold water.) What also fascinated Keel was that so many witnesses who had seen UFOs from their cars had later seen them over their homes; this suggested that the 'space men' were not merely alien scientists or explorers, engaged in routine surveying work.

In the following year, 1967, Keel was driving along the Long Island Expressway when he saw a sphere of light in the sky, pursuing a course parallel to his own. When he reached Huntington he found that cars were parked along the roads, and dozens of people were staring at four lights that were bobbing and weaving in the sky; the light that had followed Keel joined the other four. Keel was in fact on his way to interview a scientist, Phillip Burckhardt, who had seen a UFO hovering above some trees close to his home on the previous evening, and had examined it through binoculars; he had seen that it was a silvery disc illuminated by rectangular lights that blinked on and off. The nearby Suffolk Air Force Base seemed to know nothing about it.

Keel was impressed by the witnesses he interviewed; most were ordinary people who had no obvious reason for inventing a story about UFOs. His study of the actual literature convinced him that it was 98 per cent nonsense; but most individual witnesses were obviously telling the truth. Keel had soon accumulated enough cases to fill a 2,000-page typescript; this had to be severely truncated before it was published under the title *UFOs: Operation Trojan Horse*.

As his investigation progressed, Keel became increasingly convinced that UFOs had been around for thousands of years, and that many biblical accounts of fiery chariots or fireballs are probably descriptions of them. In 1883 a Mexican astronomer named Jose Bonilla photographed 143 circular objects that moved across the solar disc. In 1878 a Texas farmer named John Martin saw a large circular object flying overhead, and actually used the word 'saucer' in a newspaper interview about it. In 1897 people all over American began sighting huge airships—cigar-shaped craft. (This was before the man-made airship had been invented.) Dozens of other early 'UFO' sightings have been chronicled in newspaper reports or pamphlets; Chapter 26 of Charles Fort's *Book of the Damned*—written thirty years before the UFO craze—is devoted to strange objects and lights seen in the sky.

Keel was also interested by the parallels between reports of 'space men' and descriptions by people who claim to have had supernatural experiences. The 'angel' that instructed Joseph Smith—founder of the Mormons—to go and dig for engraved gold tablets sounds very like the kind of space visitor described by Adamski and so many others. During the First World War three children playing in meadows near Fatima, Portugal, saw a shining globe of light, and a woman's voice spoke from it. (Only two of the three heard it, although all saw it, suggesting that it was in their minds rather than in the objective world.) Crowds began to visit the spot every month where the 'Lady of the Rosary' (as she called herself) appeared to the three children—only the children were able to see and hear her. But on October 13, 1917, when the Lady had announced that she would provide a miracle to convince the world, the rainclouds parted, and a huge silver disc descended towards the crowd of seventy thousand people. It whirled and bobbed—exactly like the UFOs Keel had seen- and changed colour through the whole spectrum; all watched it for ten minutes before it vanished into the clouds again. Many other people in the area saw it from their homes. The heat from the 'object' dried the wet clothes of the crowd. Keel cites this and other 'miracles' (such as one that occurred in Heede, Germany), and argues that they sound curiously similar to later UFO accounts.

There also seemed to be a more sinister aspect to the UFO affair: witnesses began to report that 'government officials' had called on them and warned them to be silent; these men were usually dressed in black, although sometimes they wore military uniforms. No government department had—apparently—ever heard of them. Albert K.Bender of Bridgeport, Connecticut, suddenly closed down his International Flying Saucer Bureau in 1953, and declared that three dark-skinned men with glowing eyes had pressured him into abandoning his researches. Most UFO enthusiasts blamed the government; but when Bender published his full account ten years later it was obvious that something much stranger was involved; the three men materialised and dematerialised in his apartment, and on one occasion had transported him to a UFO base in Antarctica. Jacques Vallee, another scientist who had become interested in the UFO phenomenon, noted the similarity between this story and medieval legends about fairies and 'elementals'.

When Keel began to investigate sightings in West Virginia of a huge winged man who seemed to be able to keep up with fast-moving cars, he himself began to encounter vaguely hostile entities. A photographer took his picture in an empty street, then ran away. Just after arranging to meet another UFO expert, Gray Barker, a friend revealed that she had been told about the meeting two days ago- before Keel had even thought of it. 'Contactees' would ring him up and explain that they were with someone who wished to speak to him; then he would have conversations with men who spoke in strange voices. (He sometimes got the feeling he was speaking to someone in a trance.) Keel would be instructed to write letters to addresses which upon investigation proved to be non-existent; yet he would receive prompt replies, written in block letters. On one occasion, he stayed at a motel chosen at random, and found a message waiting for him at the desk. He says (in *The Mothman Prophecies*): 'Someone somewhere was just trying to prove that they knew every move I was making, listened to all my phone calls, and could even control my mail. And they were succeeding.' The entities also made many predictions of the assassination of Martin Luther King, of a planned attack on Robert Kennedy, of an attempt to stab the pope; but they frequently seemed to get the dates wrong. Keel concluded that 'our little planet seems to be experiencing the interpenetration of forces or entities from some other space-time continuum'.

But this is enough to remind us that, according to Kardec, this has been happening throughout human history. Stone Age shamans performed their magic ritual dances to enlist the aid of the spirits in hunting game. Bronze Age priests performed their religious ceremonies to ensure a good harvest. Devotees of the witch-goddess Aradia performed their nature rituals to enlist the aid of the moon goddess to aid the poor against the rich. Mediaeval witches invoked the Devil to make their spells effective. Upper-class Frenchwomen in the age of Napoleon indulged in 'table turning'—and later in automatic writing—to interrogate the denizens of the spirit world . . . And fifty years later, Spiritualists learned to 'contact the dead' through the agency of mediums. It is arguable that they were all doing much the same thing—achieving contact with various bodiless entities who may or may not be what they claim to be.

In the light of this recognition, we can begin to understand the strange experiences of a contemporary scientist, Dr Andrija Puharich, who has also been drawn into the bewildering world of the paranormal. Puharich started life as a nerve specialist who became interested in the phenomenon of telepathy—apparently the most innocuous and scientifically explainable of all paranormal phenomena. He began a series of experiments with the well-known medium Eileen Garrett, who was placed in a Faraday cage (an electrified cage) to test whether telepathy is some kind of electromagnetic radiation like radio waves. Apparently it was not: Mrs Garrett was able to tell Puharich that his friend Henry Wallace wanted to reach him urgently while she was in the Faraday cage. Minutes later, Puharich's secretary came in to tell him that Henry Wallace was on the telephone. Puharich's book *Beyond Telepathy* (1974) was to become a classic of parapsychology.

Now Puharich became interested in a young Dutch sculptor named Harry Stone, who, when examining an ancient Egyptian pendant, fell into a trance and began drawing hieroglyphics. An expert on Egyptology confirmed them to be genuine hieroglyphics of the period of the Pharaoh Snofru. They identified the writer as a scribe called Ra Ho Tep, who mentioned that his wife was called Nefert; both identifications proved to be historically correct. Puharich watched with fascination as Stone went into a trance and wrote out messages in ancient Egyptian—and learned from them of a 'cult of the sacred mushroom', of which historians had never heard. Another acquaintance also fell into a trance, identified herself as someone born in ancient Syria, and also spoke of the cult of the mushroom called amanita muscaria, which was claimed to cause 'out of the body experiences'. Puharich had his one-and-only such experience during the investigation. Ra Ho Tep demanded a sacred mushroom while Stone was in trance, and applied it ritualistically to his tongue and the top of his head. In a subsequent ESP test, Stone scored 100 per cent, and was able to see through a brick wall.

Soon after this, a Hindu scholar, Dr D.G. Vinod, went into a trance while visiting Puharich, and speaking in a deep, sonorous voice quite unlike his own high pitched tones, identified himself as M, a representative of 'the Nine'—short for Nine Principles and Forces, superintelligences whose purpose was to help the human race. If Puharich had known anything about the history of witchcraft and Spiritualism, he would probably have told M to get lost. As it was, he felt highly privileged and awaited further developments, which were not slow in coming. Vinod relayed more messages from the Nine, and materialised a ball of cotton; and a couple named Laughead, whom Puharich had met by chance, also delivered messages from the Nine which were consistent with previous ones, convincing Puharich of the genuineness of the space people . . .

Next Puharich investigated a Brazilian 'psychic surgeon' called Arigo, and watched him performing delicate operations with a kitchen knife, cutting open patients, removing tumours with his hands, then sealing the incision by pressing its edges together with his fingers. But when Puharich was informed of Arigo's death in a car crash—by telephone—he learned that he had received the message *before* Arigo crashed.

In 1971, Puharich heard about a young Israeli psychic named Uri Geller, and hurried off to Tel Aviv to meet him. He watched Geller perform successful feats of mind reading, saw him break a ring which a woman held in her clenched fist merely by placing his own hand above it, and bend spoons by gently rubbing them with his finger. One day, Geller fell into a trance and told Puharich how, at the age of 3, he had fallen asleep in a garden, and been awakened by a space craft which had knocked him down with a beam of light. Then a strange metallic voice, speaking from the air above Geller's head, informed Puharich that it was a 'space being' who had programmed Geller at the age of three, and that its purpose was to help Geller avert an immensely destructive war. The same 'space man' later identified himself as one of the Nine. Whenever these beings communicated, they caused the tape recording to dematerialise.

The strange series of events that followed are described in detail in Puharich's book *Uri: A Journal of the Mystery of Uri Geller*, yet are so bewildering and preposterous that they caused the book to be received with extreme hostility. The Nine stopped cars and started them again, made UFOs appear overhead, 'teleported' various objects (and even Geller himself), and performed so many other bizarre miracles that the reader is finally left in a state of punch-drunk indifference. (When I met Puharich, he told me that he had deliberately left out some of the more preposterous events for fear of creating incredulity; when he described some of them to me, I saw his point.) The book, which the publishers had expected to become a bestseller, was a flop.

Geller and Puharich parted; Geller grew tired of being subjected to endless tests. But the 'space intelligences' were apparently enjoying themselves too much to allow Puharich to get back to science. When Puharich went to investigate a medium named Bobby Horne in Florida, they lost no time in re-establishing contact, and telling him that his purpose now was to prepare mankind for a mass landing of space ships on planet earth during the next year or two. Another medium, Phyllis Schlemmer, also began relaying messages from the space intelligences. (One of the space beings, a man called Tom, explained that the first civilisation on earth was founded by space visitors in the Tarim Basin in China thirty-two thousand years ago.) Stuart Holroyd, an English writer who became involved with the group, subsequently wrote a book called *Prelude to a Landing on Planet Earth* which describes the amazing goings-on that followed. They are too bewildering to describe in detail: what happened basically was that Puharich, Holroyd, Phyllis Schlemmer and another Englishman named Sir John Whitmore rushed around the Middle East, holding seances in hotel rooms and praying for peace; Tom periodically assured them that they had just saved mankind. By 1975, the landing on planet earth had failed to materialise, and Holroyd settled down to writing his book. His own theory is that the unconscious minds of the people involved were responsible. He cites a curious work called *From India to the Planet Mars*, in which a French psychologist, Theodore Flournoy, investigated the mediumship of an attractive girl named Catherine Muller, who described her past incarnation as the wife of a prince in 15th century India, and the civilisation of the planet Mars. The Indian incarnation is convincing; she appeared to know all kinds of details about 15th century India, and the prince to whom she was married, Sivrouka Nakaya, proved to be a real historical personage. But the Martian details—which many accepted as genuine—were finally disproved in 1976 when a Viking spacecraft finally landed on Mars and revealed it to be an airless desert.

The unconscious deception hypothesis would be more convincing if Catherine Muller had not displayed genuine psychic powers—for example, she could read Flournoy's mind, and various 'apports' appeared while she was in trance, including Chinese artifacts and roses and violets (in midwinter). As it is, it is difficult to avoid the conclusion that Flournoy, like Catherine Muller, was the victim of the astral confidence tricksters that Joe

Fisher has called 'hungry ghosts'. And the same explanation seems to cover the weird events described in *Prelude to a Landing on Planet Earth*.

But perhaps the best example of the problems encountered by unwary investigators of the paranormal is furnished by the career of the late F.W.Holiday, a naturalist whose modest aim was merely to establish (or disprove) the existence of the Loch Ness monster. Sightings of the monster—a kind of long-necked dinosaur—began in 1933, soon after the completion of a road along the northern shore of Loch Ness, Britain's largest and deepest lake. A couple saw it surging across the loch, and another couple saw it on land—a strange grey creature with a long neck like a serpent. It was even photographed later the same year. In 1961, an engineer named Tim Dinsdale took a cine-film of the monster swimming across the loch. In the following year, Holiday stood beside the loch on a clear morning and saw a black, glistening shape like a hippopotamus rise out of the water, then dive below the surface; he estimated it at about 45 feet long. Holiday saw it twice more, and wrote a book called *The Great Orm of Loch Ness* (1968), arguing that it was a kind of giant slug. But Holiday was much intrigued to learn that Boleskine House, on the southern shore of the loch, had been tenanted by Aleister Crowley, and that Crowley had performed rituals to summon up 'spirits'. He began to entertain a cautious suspicion that the 'monster' had been conjured up by Crowley. This was not as absurd as it sounds. After his Loch Ness investigations, Holiday went to Ireland to try to photograph lake monsters seen in a number of loughs (the Irish version of lochs) in Galway. The reports of sightings by various witnesses were totally convincing; yet what puzzled Holiday was that the loughs were obviously too small to support a large mammal. This led him to wonder whether the 'peiste' (as the Irish call the monsters) is a creature of flesh and blood, or some kind of Jungian 'projection' (i.e. illusion) of the racial unconscious. Jung had formulated this theory to explain UFOs (although he later came to accept that they were objectively real), and Holiday had also experienced UFO sightings.

And now, slowly, Holiday was coming around to the view that lake monsters are not simply 'prehistoric survivals'—that they may be somethng altogether more elusive. In the Middle Ages, 'orms' (or 'worms') and dragons had been associated with evil, and he had been struck by the number of witnesses who had experienced a sense of horror on seeing lake monsters. Could the Loch Ness monster be some kind of phantom?

By 1971 Holiday had abandoned the notion that the lake monsters are simply 'prehistoric survivals'. He was coming round to the admittedly eccentric view that there is some influence at work that actively prevents the final solution of the mystery, just as in the case of Unidentified Flying Objects. And some time in 1972 this view seemed to be confirmed when he read a newspaper controversy between an 'exorcist', the Rev. Donald Omand, and some opponent who thought the Loch Ness monster was simply an unidentified animal. Omand had inherited 'second sight' from Highland ancestors, and had no doubt of the real existence of powers of evil—or at least of mischief; he often performed exorcisms to get rid of them. He had caught his first glimpse of a lake monster in Loch Long in Ross-shire in 1967. In June 1968, in a boat in Norway's Fjord of the Trolls, he saw another, which came straight towards them; the Norwegian captain who was with him told him not to be afraid: 'It will not hurt us—they never do.' And in fact the monster dived before it reached their boat. But the Captain, Jan Andersen, was convinced that the monsters were basically evil, that in some way they could do harm to men's characters (or, as Omand would have said, their souls). In 1972 Omand attended a psychiatric conference at which an eminent Swedish psychiatrist read a paper on the monster of Lake Storsjön, and said that he was convinced that the monsters had a malevolent effect on human beings, especially those who hunted them or saw them regularly. He thought their influence could cause domestic tragedies and moral degeneration. So Omand began to consider the theory that perhaps lake monsters are not real creatures, but 'projections' of something from the prehistoric past.

Holiday wrote to Omand, and the odd result was that in June 1973 Holiday and Donald Omand rowed out into the middle of Loch Ness, and Omand performed an exorcism of the loch. Holiday said they both felt oddly exhausted when it was over. And his suspicion that he was stirring up dangerous forces seemed to be confirmed two days later when he went to stay the night with a retired Wing-Commander named Carey. Holiday was telling Mrs Carey about a Swedish journalist called Jan-Ove Sundberg who had been wandering through the woods behind Foyers when he had seen a strange craft in a clearing, and some odd-looking men; the craft had taken off at a great speed, and after his return to Sweden, Sundberg had been plagued by 'men in black'—people claiming to be officials who often seem to harass UFO 'contactees'.

Holiday said he intended to go and look at the place where the 'UFO' had landed, and Mrs Carey warned him against it. At this moment there was a rushing sound like a tornado outside the window and a series of violent thuds; a beam of light came in through the window, and focused on Holiday's forehead. A moment later, all was still. The odd thing was that Wing-Commander Carey, who had been pouring a drink only a few feet away from his wife, saw and heard nothing. The next morning, as Holiday was walking towards the loch, he saw a man dressed entirely in black—including helmet and goggles—standing nearby; he walked past him, turned his head, and was astonished to find that the man had vanished. He rushed to the road and looked in both directions; there was nowhere the man could have gone. One year later, close to the same spot, Holiday had a heart attack; as he was being carried away he looked over the side of the stretcher and saw that they were just passing the exact spot where he had seen the 'man in black'. Five years later, in 1978, Holiday died of a heart attack.

Perhaps a year before his death, Ted Holiday sent me the typescript of his book *The Goblin Universe*, in which he attempted to justify the rather strange views he had gradually developed since starting his hunt for the Loch Ness monster. He had already discussed them in his second book *The Dragon and the Disc*, in which he linked UFOs ('discs') and 'worms' as symbols of good and evil. Then, to my surprise, he changed his mind about publishing the book.

There were, I suspect, two reasons. The team of investigators from the Academy of Applied Science at the Massachusetts Institute of Technology, led by Dr Robert H. Rines, had taken some remarkable underwater photographs in 1972 and 1975; one of the 1972 photographs showed very clearly an object like a large flipper, perhaps eight feet long, while a 1975 photograph showed very clearly a long-necked creature and its front flipper; this was particularly impressive because the sonar evidence—waves of sound reflected back from the creature—made it clear that this was not some freak of the light or piece of floating wreckage or lake-weed. By the time he was thinking about publishing *The Goblin Universe*, Holiday was probably wondering whether the book would be contradicted by some new evidence that would establish the physical reality of the monster beyond all doubt. Apart from this, the argument of *The Goblin Universe* was not quite as rigorous as it might be—he was attempting to explain why his views had changed so startlingly since 1962, and spent a great deal of time dwelling on 'the paranormal'. At all events, he decided not to publish the book, and instead wrote another typescript confined to lake monsters. I finally succeeded in finding a publisher for the book in England and America, and it has appeared in both countries.

The Goblin Universe will confirm sceptics in their view that any involvement in the paranormal is likely to result in some mild form of insanity. Without apology, he states his conclusion that both lake monsters and UFOs are 'psychic' phenomena—or, at least, have some psychic component—and that the same probably applies to such odd anomalies as phantom pumas, leopards, Bigfoots and Abominable Snowmen. It is an oddly frustrating book because he makes no attempt to advance some unifying theory that will explain these phenomena—although there are times when he seems to hint that, like John Keel, he regards them as some kind of attempt to force human beings to abandon their dogmatism and widen their mental horizons. Like so many investigators, Holiday has moved from the position of open-minded sceptic to that of a thoroughly confused believer in the paranormal. There is no reason to believe that, if he had lived, he would have become any less bewildered.

The confusion, of course, is due to his attempt to reconcile the endless contradictions that seem to arise in any serious attempt to interrogate the paranormal. We, at least, are in a slightly better position, since, like any experienced detective, we recognise that a large number of our suspects are incapable of telling the truth.

The latest—and in some ways one of the most puzzling—manifestations of 'the goblin universe' is the curious mystery of the 'crop circles'.

In early August, 1980, a Wiltshire farmer named John Scull was irritated to find three flattened circular areas in one of his oatfields. It looked as if vandals had stood in the centre, and swung around some heavy object on a long piece of rope, flattening the oats to the ground in a clockwise direction. But if this *is* how they were made, the vandal must have been a very tall and powerful man, for the circles were sixty feet in diameter. And the fact that the surrounding oats showed no sign of trespassers made it unlikely that the circles had a human origin. The *Wiltshire Times* reported the incident on August 15, adding that the circles were within the view of the famous White Horse of Westbury, the hillside figure cut into the chalk.

Close study of the three circles established that they had been formed on three different dates, probably over a period of months. One of the experts, an atmospheric physicist called Terence Meaden, stated that the likeliest explanation was summer whirlwinds. But he admitted that it was odd that each 'whirlwind' had remained stationary, instead of flattening a path through the crops.

On August 19 the following year—1981—three more circles appeared in a punchbowl formation below Cheesefoot Head, near Winchester in Hampshire. This time the pattern made whirlwinds seem unlikely. There was one central circle, about 60 feet in diameter, and two smaller ones—about 25 feet across—placed neatly on either side. Would a whirlwind 'bounce' three times?

There were a few isolated reports of incidents in 1982, but they were unspectacular, and excited little attention. As if to make up for it, a series of five-circle phenomena began in 1983, one of them again close to the White Horse of Westbury. These made it clear that whirlwinds could not be the explanation. A 'bouncing' whirlwind might make three circles in a line, but these 'fivesomes' had a central circle, with the others placed neatly around it as if at four corners. 'UFO' enthusiasts had already noted that one of the groups had appeared at the foot of Cley Hill, near Warminster, where there had been dozens of UFO sightings. Now the 'fivesomes' began to excite the attention of the national media.

When another 'fivesome' close to the Westbury Horse proved to be a hoax, paid for by the *Daily Mirror*, the sceptics said 'I told you so'. But the man who had detected the hoax was Bob Rickard, editor of an 'anomaly' magazine called the *Fortean Times*. He noted the tell-tale signs of human intruders which had not been present in any of the original circles.

From then on, circles began to multiply. The whirlwind theory remained the chief standby of the experts. As if to disprove this, the circles began to increase in complexity. Anti-clockwise flattenings began to appear, and some of the circles had a larger ring outside them—some as many as three rings. This was getting preposterous. At Oadby, near Leicester, three circles appeared in neat triangle formation around a larger ringed crop circle in 1988. On Charity Down, near Goodwood Clatford (Hampshire), a remarkable 'Celtic Cross' appeared in August of the same year—a double circle with four symmetrical circles in its outer rim. When the circle expert, Dr Terence Meaden published a book explaining the circles in terms of an 'electromagnetic plasma vortex', and pointing out that successive rings in ringed circles caused flattening in opposite directions, a circle that contradicted all his theories promptly appeared at Cheesefoot Head, reminding students of poltergeist phenomena that poltergeists often show the same sensitivity to comments made about them. But when a group of UFO enthusiasts suggested that the circles were made by UFOs landing, another circle quickly appeared under a power cable, where a landing would have been virtually impossible.

Crop circle experts now called themselves 'cereologists', and they also noticed that the phenomena seemed to respond to human ideas. An aerial photographer named Busty Taylor was returning home from a day of photographing circles when he remarked that he would like to see one in the form of a Celtic Cross; the next day, a Celtic Cross circle had appeared at the spot he was flying over at the time.

The circles went on becoming increasingly complex, ruling out most 'natural' explanations. In 1990, an extraordinary pattern of six elaborate circles—in a straight line—appeared near Alton Barnes, in Hampshire, with a number of key-like objects sticking out of the sides of three circles, producing the effect of ancient pictograms.

There have been a number of eye-witness accounts of the formation of the circles. Typical of these is one reported from Scotland in August 1989 by a Mr Sandy Reid. Meaden reports: 'For half a minute as he watched, at a distance of 15 metres, the wind was violently rustling the corn over a circular area, all the time making a strange noise, but where he stood there was *no wind at all*. Then suddenly a 'force' shot downwards and a circle appeared almost instantaneously. This was a good observation of the vortex-breakdown of a standing eddy vortex.'[1]

Here are a number of other eye-witness descriptions, compiled by Bob Rickard:

'Suddenly the grass began to sway before our eyes and laid itself flat in a clockwise spiral . . . A perfect circle was completed in less than half a minute, all the time accompanied by a high-pitched humming sound . . . My attention was drawn to a "wave" coming through the heads of the cereal crop in a straight line . . . The agency, though invisible, behaved like a solid object . . . When we reached the spot where the circles had been, we were suddenly caught up in a terrific whirlwind . . . [The dog] went wild . . . There was a rushing sound and a rumble . . . then suddenly everything was still . . . It was uncanny . . . The dawn chorus stopped; the sky darkened . . .'

All that seems clear at the time of writing (1991) is that the circles cannot be explained in 'natural' terms, although it is still just conceivable that they might have been made by some brilliant hoaxer flying a tiny helicopter. In a book called *The Crop Circle Enigma* (1990), an article by John Michell points out that the phenomena bring to mind John Keel's descriptions of his own experiences with UFO phenomena—that 'strange ideas and experiences force their way into the lives of all who enquire into such subjects'. 'Like many other cereologists, and like Keel, Shuttlewood and ufologists before them, they admit that their lives, minds and outlooks have been radically changed by their investigations.' And he adds the significant evalaluation: 'On one level the change is philosophical; after honest appraisal

---

1. *The Crop Circle Enigma*, edited by Ralph Noyes, Gateway Books, 1990, p. 83.

of ufology and crop circle data, it is impossible to maintain the rationalistic world-view on which modern science and education are founded. One is led into unfamiliar channels of thought, which point away from structured theories and hard-and-fast beliefs towards a more mystical view of reality and, eventually, towards the greater mysteries of divinity and the living universe.'

He goes on to elaborate:

'Reviewing the evidence in this field, Devereux was struck by an observation which repeatedly occurs in reports by witnesses to mysterious light phenomena, that their experience of reality is somehow affected. Some tell of visions and psychic revelations, and a common feature is that witnesses feel aware of a mental link between themselves and the phenomena. In his category of earth lights Devereux includes manifestations which are recognised by science, though not fully explained or understood, such as will-o'-the-wisps and ball lightning. Such things certainly seem to be related to the earth's energy field, but their behaviour is unpredictable, and they often give the impression of acting in an intelligent or purposeful way towards those who see them. Devereux's conclusion, forced upon him by the overwhelming weight of evidence, is that the Earth's vital energies have a component of intelligence, similar to our own intelligence and capable of interacting with it.'

And he summarises:

'There is little doubt, especially as the astonishing events of 1990 continue to unfold, that the patterns in the corn have a meaning, and the meaning of such things is to be found in the way people are affected by them. Jung discerned the meaning of UFOs as agents and portents of changes in human thought patterns, and that function has clearly been inherited by crop circles, which are a continuation—a solidification, one might say—of the UFO phenomenon. We have seen earlier how exposure to the influence of crop circles has changed the attitudes and mentalities of many investigators. Such changes, if they are in accord with the spirit of the times, are both permanent and contagious. Judging by what has happened so far, there seems to be every justification for extending Jung's characterization of UFOs to crop circles, and thus for regarding them as signs of 'great changes to come which are compatible with the end of an era'.'

If Ted Holiday had lived for another decade, he would undoubtedly have changed his mind about his decision not to publish *The Goblin Universe*. From the point of view of the last decade of the 20th century, it seems more relevant than ever.

16.
The Expansion of Consciousness

AT THE BEGINNING of this book we spoke of Ouspensky and
his obsession with 'secret knowledge'. Now, at the end, we must
return to him.

Pyotr Demianovitch Ouspensky was born in Moscow on March
5, 1878, the son of a government official and a talented artist, and
his earliest experience of mystery came from sudden flashes of the
feeling: 'I have been here before', which began when he was six.
When he discovered the writing of Nietzsche, he concluded that his
'I have been here before' feeling was what Nietzsche's Zarathustra
meant by 'Eternal Recurrence', the notion that human beings live
their lives over and over again. And when, at the age of 18, he lost
his mother, he decided to travel to foreign countries in search of
the 'hidden knowledge' which he was certain existed. His travels
took him around Russia, Europe and India in search of 'masters'
who could teach him the meaning of life. He wrote a rather gloomy
novel called *The Strange Life of Ivan Osokin* about a character who
has to keep on reliving his life. (To do Ouspensky justice, he did
not believe that the repetition is identical; rather, our lives are like
a play which has to follow the script, but which the actor himself
can turn into a triumph or a flop.)

Back in Russia, he wrote a remarkable work called *Tertium Organum* (which was quoted in the first chapter). This work was later to make him famous in the west, for at the end of the First World War, it was read by a young Russian, Nicholas Bessarabov, who lived in America, and was published by a writer and architect called Claude Bragdon. It was an instant success, with the result that Bragdon tried to contact the author to send him his royalties. His letter caught up with Ouspensky in Constantinople; Ouspensky had fled from the Russian Revolution and was virtually destitute when the money arrived. He asked Bragdon if he could help him to emigrate to England. A few weeks later, with the help of another Ouspensky admirer, Lady Rothermere—wife of the newspaper magnate—Bragdon was able to send Ouspensky the money to travel to London. There he discovered that *Tertium Organum* had already gone into a second edition, and that a circle of admirers was waiting eagerly to learn what he had to teach them.

What he had to teach them was—as we know from the twelfth chapter of this book—what Gurdjieff had taught him in Russia: that human consciousness is a form of *sleep*, and that our problem is to awaken. Ouspensky remained identified with the teaching of Gurdjieff—who quickly became as well known in Europe as Ouspensky himself—and is still generally labelled a 'Gurdjieff disciple'. This is a major mistake. If Ouspensky had died after he had written *Tertium Organum*, he would still be recognised as a thinker of remarkable freshness and originality. And if he had died after he had written his second book, *A New Model of the Universe*—still before he met Gurdjieff—he would be known as one of the most original thinkers of the 20th century. In a sense, his meeting with Gurdjieff, which was the most important event of his life, was also a misfortune which prevented his own genius from being recognised.

In fact, in 1910, soon after he returned from India, Ouspensky began a series of 'experiments' in mysticism that brought him some of the profoundest insights of his life. They deserve to be regarded not merely as a watershed in Ouspensky's life, but as a watershed in the history of human consciousness.

It is a pity that Ouspensky refuses to go into the techniques he used for achieving 'mystical' states of consciousness. This, I suspect, is because he was ashamed of them. I believe he simply used the gas that dentists used to use for putting their patients to sleep: nitrous oxide. It was discovered in 1795 by a young chemist called Humphry Davy, who was heating a mixture of damp iron filings and nitric acid, and, as he sniffed it, experienced a pleasant sensation of dizziness and a tremendous gaiety, so that he burst out laughing. Then he lost consciousness. When he woke up he exclaimed: 'What a wonderful discovery—laughing gas.'

The philosopher William James remarked: 'Nitrous oxide and ether, especially nitrous oxide, when sufficiently diluted with air, stimulate the mystical consciousness in an extraordinary degree. Depth beyond depth of truth seem revealed to the inhaler. This truth fades out, however, or escapes, at the moment of coming to; and if any words remain over in which it seemed to clothe itself, they prove to be the veriest nonsense. Nevertheless, the sense of profound meaning having been there persists; and I know more than one person who is persuaded that in the nitrous oxide trance we have a genuine metaphysical revelation.'[1]

Ouspensky had also undergone training in yoga, and it may be that this was why he was able to cling on to so much of the revelation, instead of losing it as he returned to consciousness.

Significantly, Ouspensky mentions James's remarks on mysticism and the use of narcotics at the beginning of his chapter 'Experimental Mysticism' in *A New Model of the Universe*.

What Ouspensky discovered was that as soon as he began the experiment, a change in his state of consciousness began to occur. The problem was that this state offered so much that was new and unexpected, and these insights flashed by so quickly, 'that I could not find words . . . which would enable me to remember what had occurred even for myself, still less to convey it to somebody else.'

The first sensation, he says, was an odd sense of duality, *as if he had become two people*. This, I suspect, was an activation of both sides of the brain, so that his 'I' became double. The right side had the mystical experience; the left did its best to observe and remember it.

But now he makes his most important observation: that the

1. *Varieties of Religious Experience*, chapter 16, p. 378.

problem in describing this state is that *everything is linked together*. To describe something, we need a starting-point. Ouspensky found that 'in order to describe the first impressions, the first sensations, it is necessary to describe *all* at once. The new world with which one comes into contact has no sides, so that it is impossible to describe first one side and then the other. All of it is visible at every point.'

In other words, what he saw in this state is that *everything is connected with everything else*, so that trying to describe it is like trying to pick up a heap of chain when you have no idea where to find its beginning . . .

In fact, we are all familiar with this experience. When you listen to a piece of music for the first time—particularly if it is a complex piece of music, like a symphony—you only 'register' small parts of it. The more often you hear it, the more these parts come together, until finally you have the whole work 'in your head'. A young child listening to a symphony simply fails to understand it; it sounds like an incomprehensible jumble of notes. But when the child is old enough to understand and enjoy the symphony, he still could not explain it to his younger brother. He could only say: 'Ah yes, now I *see*.'

Ouspensky offers an example of the way in which he actually 'saw' the connectedness:

'I remember once sitting on a sofa smoking and looking at an ashtray. It was an ordinary copper ash-tray. Suddenly I felt that I was beginning to understand what the ash-tray was, and at the same time, with a certain wonder and almost with fear, I felt that I had never understood it before and that we do not understand the simplest things around us.

'The ash-tray roused a whirlwind of thoughts and images. It contained such an infinite number of facts, of events; it was linked with such an immense number of things. First of all, with everything connected with smoking and tobacco. This at once roused thousands of images, pictures, memories. Then the ash-tray itself. How had it come into being? All the materials of which it could have been made? Copper, in this case—what was copper? How had people discovered it for the first time? How had they learned to make use of it? How and where was the copper obtained from which this ash-tray was made? Through what kind of treatment had it passed, how had it been transported from place to place, how many people had worked on it or in connection with it? How had the copper been transformed into an ash-tray? These and other questions about the history of the ash-tray up to the day when it had appeared on my table.

'I remember writing a few words on a piece of paper in order to retain something of these thoughts on the following day. And next day I read:

'"*A man can go mad from one ash-tray*."

'The meaning of all that I felt was that in one ash-tray it was possible to know *all*. By invisible threads the ash-tray was connected with everything in the world, not only with the present, but with all the past and with all the future. To know an ash-tray meant to know all.

'My description does not in the least express the sensation as it actually was, because the first and principal impression was that the ash-tray was alive, that it thought, understood and told me all about itself. All I learned from the ash-tray itself. The second impression was the extraordinary emotional character of all connected with what I had learned about the ash-tray.

'"Everything is alive," I said to myself in the midst of these observations; "there is nothing dead, it is only we who are dead. If we become alive for a moment, we shall feel that everything is alive, that all things live, think, feel and can speak to us."'

This sensation was intensified when he tried his 'experiments' when walking down the street:

'On such occasions the whole of the ordinary world changed in a very subtle and strange way. Everything became different, but it is absolutely impossible to describe what happened to it. The first thing that can be said is that there was nothing which remained indifferent for me. All taken together and each thing separately affected me in one way or another. In other words, I took everything emotionally, reacted to everything emotionally. Further, in this new world which surrounded me, there was nothing separate, nothing that had no connection with other things or with me personally. All things were connected with one another, and not accidentally, but by incomprehensible chains of causes and effects. All things were dependent on one another, all things lived in one another. Further, in this world there was nothing dead, nothing inanimate, nothing that did not think, nothing that did not feel, nothing unconscious. Everything was living, everything was conscious of itself. Everything spoke to me and I could speak to everything. Particularly interesting were the houses and other buildings which I passed, especially the old houses. They were living beings, full of thoughts, feelings, moods and memories. The people who lived in them were their *thoughts, feelings, moods*. I mean that the people in relation to the "houses" played approximately the same rôle which the different "I"s of our personality play in relation to us. They come and go, sometimes live in us for a long time, sometimes appear only for short moments.

'I remember once being struck by an ordinary cab-horse in the Nevsky, by its head, its face. It expressed the whole being of the horse. Looking at the horse's face I understood all that could be understood about a horse. All the traits of horse-nature, all of which a horse is capable, all of which it is incapable, all that it can do, all that it cannot do; all this was expressed in the lines and features of the horse's face. A dog once gave me a similar sensation. At the same time the horse and the dog were not simply horse and dog; they were "atoms", conscious, moving "atoms" of great beings—"the great horse" and "the great dog". I understood then that we also are atoms of a great being, "the great man". Each thing is an atom of a "great thing". A glass is an atom of a "great glass". A fork is an atom of a "great fork".'

He records many other strange insights in his 'mystical' states, including one that seems typical of their paradoxical nature:

'I will try to describe in short what I met with in this strange world in which I saw myself.

'What I first noticed, simultaneously with the "division of myself into two", was that the relation between the objective and the subjective was broken, entirely altered, and took certain forms incomprehensible to us. But "objective" and "subjective" are only words. I do not wish to hide behind these words, but I wish to describe as exactly as possible what I really felt. For this purpose I must explain what it is that I call "objective" and "subjective". My hand, the pen with which I write, the table, these are objective phenomena. My thoughts, my mental images, the pictures of my imagination, these are subjective phenomena. The world is divided for us along these lines when we are in our ordinary state of consciousness, and all our ordinary orientation works along the lines of this division. In the new state all this was completely upset. First of all we are accustomed to the constancy of the relation between the subjective and the objective—what is objective is always objective, what is subjective is always subjective. Here I saw that the objective and the subjective could change places. The one could become the other. It is very difficult to express this. The habitual mistrust of the subjective disappeared; every thought, every feeling, every image, was immediately objectified in real substantial forms which differed in no way from the forms of objective phenomena; and at the same time objective phenomena somehow disappeared, lost all reality, appeared entirely subjective, fictitious, invented, having no real existence.

'This was the first experience. Further, in trying to describe this strange world in which I saw myself, I must say that it resembled more than anything a world of *very complicated mathematical relations*.

'Imagine a world in which all relations of quantities, from the simplest to the most complicated, have a form.

'Certainly it is easy to say "imagine such a world".

'I understand perfectly well that to "imagine" it is impossible. Yet at the same time what I am saying is the closest approximation to the truth which can be made.

'"A world of mathematical relations"—this means a world in which everything is connected, in which nothing exists separately and in which at the same time the relations between things have a real existence apart from the things themselves; or, possibly, "things" do not even exist and only "relations" exist.'

Equally fascinating is his observation that, in this state of intense excitement (he also mentions that he was seething with a sense of sheer joy and delight), time seemed to *slow down*. It became impossible to communicate with anyone because his mind was moving so much faster than his words:

'I tried my experiments under the most varied conditions and in the most varied surroundings. Gradually I became convinced that it was best to be alone. Verification of the experiments, that is, observation by another person, or the recording of the experiences at the very moment they took place, was quite impossible. In any case I never obtained any results in this way.

'When I tried having someone near me during these experiments, I found that no kind of conversation could be carried on. I began to say something, but between the first and second words of my sentence such an enormous number of ideas occurred to me and passed before me, that the two words were so widely separated as to make it impossible to find any connection between them. And the third word I usually forgot before it was pronounced, and in trying to recall it I found a million new ideas, but completely forgot where I had begun. I remember for instance the beginning of a sentence:

'"I said yesterday" . . .

'No sooner had I pronounced the word "I" than a number of ideas began to turn in my head about the meaning of the word, in a philosophical, in a psychological and in every other sense. This was all so important, so new and profound, that when I pronounced the word "said", I could not understand in the least what I meant by it. Tearing myself away with difficulty from the first cycle of thoughts about "I", I passed to the idea "said", and immediately found in it an infinite content. The idea of speech, the possibility of expressing thoughts in words, the past tense of the verb, each of these ideas produced an explosion of thoughts, conjectures, comparisons and associations. Thus, when I pronounced the word "yesterday" I was already quite unable to understand why I had said it. But it in its turn immediately dragged me into the depths of the problems of time, of past, present and future, and before me such possibilities of approach to these problems began to open up that my breath was taken away.

'It was precisely these attempts at conversation, made in these strange states of consciousness, which gave me the sensation of change in time which is described by almost everyone who has made experiments like mine. This is a feeling of the extraordinary lengthening of time, in which seconds seem to be years or decades.

'Nevertheless, the usual feeling of time did not disappear; only together with it or within it there appeared as it were another feeling of time, and two moments of ordinary time, like two words of my sentence, could be separated by long periods of another time.

'I remember how much I was struck by this sensation the first time I had it. My companion was saying something. Between each sound of his voice, between each movement of his lips, long periods of time passed. When he had finished a short sentence, the meaning of which did not reach me at all, I felt I had lived through so much during that time that we should never be able to understand one another again, that I had gone too far from him. It seemed to me that we were still able to speak and to a certain extent understand one another at the beginning of this sentence, but by the end it had become quite impossible, because there were no means of conveying to him all that I had lived through in between.'

It is worth mentioning, at this point, the experiences of another 'experimental mystic', R.H. Ward, the author of a remarkable work called *A Drug-Taker's Notes*. The book is mainly devoted to his accounts of 'controlled' experiments with LSD; but, in an earlier chapter, he also describes an earlier experience under dental gas—nitrous oxide:

'On this occasion it seemed to me that I passed, after the first few inhalations of the gas, directly into a state of consciousness already far more complete than the fullest degree of ordinary waking consciousness, and that I then passed progressively upwards (for there was an actual sensation of upward movement) into finer and finer degrees of this heightened awareness. But although one must write of it in terms of time, time had no place in the experience. In one sense it lasted far longer than the short period between inhaling the gas and "coming round", lasted indeed for an eternity, and in another sense it took no time at all. In terms of time, however, the first phase of the experience was comparatively brief (though perhaps it would be more exact to say that it was comparatively unimportant): a confusion of sensations in which, while I was already hardly aware of my body, I was still able to think in the ordinary way, and with some surprise that I was not being made unconscious by the gas I was inhaling, but very much the reverse. For already

I knew, I understood, I actually was, far more than I normally knew, understood and was. I put it in this way because I had no impression of suddenly receiving new knowledge, understanding and being. Rather I felt that I was rediscovering these things, which had once been mine, but which I had lost many years before. While it was altogether strange, this new condition was also familiar; it was even in some sense my rightful condition. Meanwhile, what was becoming unreal, slow and clumsy was the ordinary world which I was leaving behind, but of whose shadowy existence I was still vaguely aware; indeed it presented itself to me as being like the receding shadow which fades across a landscape when the sun comes out.'

Like Ouspensky, Ward records the sheer happiness of the experience, its emotional richness:

'As for the emotional tone of this phase of the experience, I can only describe it as being compounded of wonder, joy, and a wholly peaceful *inevitableness* for which there is no name. This sensation, which yet had nothing to do with my already anaesthetized senses, had an emotional depth which does not belong to waking sensation, and to which our waking word-values do not belong, so that it is all but indescribable. Meanwhile, the extraordinary feeling of *the rightness of things* increased, became more poignant, and was accompanied as it did so by a peculiar sensation of upward and bodiless flight. This sense of upward movement continued until it seemed to me that I was rapidly passing through what I afterwards told myself was a "region of ideas". The emphasis had shifted, that is to say, from the emotional to the intellectual.'

It is clear that this 'region of ideas' corresponds to Ouspensky's world of mathematical relations. Ward compares it to Plato's world of forms or ideas—recalling Ouspensky's comment that 'a fork is an atom of a Great Fork'.

Both Ouspensky and Ward describe the disappointment of returning to ordinary consciousness. This is Ward:

'Thereafter the upward flight became a downward flight; whereas one had risen into the pure light of the sun, now one fell again towards the shadows of earth. I was once more aware of being in the "region of ideas", and this time, as consciousness diminished towards the consciousness of everyday life (or, paradoxically, as my anaesthetized body "regained consciousness"), the "region of ideas" took form; on its nether fringes the symbols we need in the waking state if we are to comprehend "intuition" were supplied. In a flash, as it seemed to me, *I saw the meaning*; the meaning, that is, of the universe, of life on earth, and of man. As the darkness of what we flatter ourselves is consciousness closed in upon me, and even as I began dimly to be aware that I was "coming to", the sum of things appeared before my inward eyes as a *living geometrical figure*, an infinitely complicated and infinitely simple arrangement of continually moving, continually changing golden lines on a background of darkness. ("Geometry," it has often been recorded, is a common form for such visions to take.)' [We note here again the need to fall back on a mathematical analogy.]

Ouspensky expresses an even stronger sense of rejection of 'normal consciousness':

'The strangest thing in all these experiences was the coming back, the return to the ordinary state, to the state which we call life. This was something very similar to dying or to what I thought dying must be.

'Usually this coming back occurred when I woke up in the morning after an interesting experiment the night before. The experiments almost always ended in sleep. During this sleep I evidently passed into the usual state and awoke in the ordinary world, in the world in which we awake every morning. But this world contained something extraordinarily oppressive, it was incredibly empty, colourless and lifeless. It was as though everything in it was wooden, as if it was an enormous wooden machine with creaking wooden wheels, wooden thoughts, wooden moods, wooden sensations; everything was terribly slow, scarcely moved, or moved with a melancholy wooden creaking. Everything was dead, soulless, feelingless.

'They were terrible, these moments of awakening in an unreal world after a real one, in a dead world after a living, in a limited world, cut into small pieces, after an infinite and entire world.'

Ouspensky's own vision of an 'entire world' had been oddly reminiscent of Ward's living geometrical figure:

'Once when I was in the state into which my experiments brought me, I asked myself: "What is the world?"

'Immediately I saw a semblance of some big flower, like a rose or a lotus, the petals of which were continually unfolding from the middle, growing, increasing in size, reaching the outside of the flower and then in some way again returning to the middle and starting again at the beginning. Words in no way express it. In this flower there was an incredible quantity of light, movement, colour, music, emotion, agitation, knowledge, intelligence, mathematics, and continuous unceasing growth. And while I was looking at this flower *someone* seemed to explain to me that this was the "World" or "Brahma" in its clearest aspect and in the nearest possible approximation to what it is in reality—"If the approximation were made still nearer, it would be Brahma himself, as he is," said the voice.'

The main difference between the two accounts is that Ward describes only 'mystical' insights, while Ouspensky—no doubt because he repeated the experiment so often—also had certain experiences that are closer to some of the paranormal experiences described in this book. He heard 'voices', and was able to ask them questions. From the beginning he mistrusted the voices; but on at least one occasion, when he asked them a question about alchemy, they were able to tell him the name of the book in which, in fact, he found the answer to his question (although, he adds, 'not the complete answer'.)

In these states, Ouspensky also found that he was able, to some extent, to foresee the future—or rather, that some inner voice was able to predict it. Thinking about going to Moscow that Easter, he was suddenly 'told' that he would not be able to go, and he was able to foresee the chain of events that would prevent him from going. It was only just before Easter, when these events began to happen—and prevented him from going to Moscow—that he remembered he had known about it in advance. In states of intensified consciousness—as Alan Vaughan discovered—the mind is able to see future events.

The sense of world-rejection experienced by both Ouspensky and Ward as they returned to 'normality' raises again one of the most basic of all questions: what might be called 'the great Outsider question'. In Shaw's *John Bull's Other Island*, the mystic Father Keegan explains that he has discovered the answer to the mystery of human suffering: this world is actually Hell, and we are all here to expiate sins commited in some other existence. And for the epigraph of my first book, *The Outsider*, I had chosen another passage from the same play:

Broadbent: . . . I find the world quite good enough for me—rather a jolly place, in fact.
Keegan (looking at him with quiet wonder): You are satisfied?
Broadbent: As a reasonable man, yes. I see no evils in the world—except of course, natural evils—that cannot be remedied by freedom, self-government and English institutions. I think so, not because I am an Englishman, but as a matter of common sense.
Keegan: You feel at home in the world then?
Broadbent: Of course. Don't you?
Keegan (from the very depths of his nature): No.

This is the essence of the Romantic dilemma, the problem that caused so many of the men of genius of the 19th century to commit suicide or to die in despair—for the Romantics also experienced this same sense of revulsion on returning to the everyday world. The crucial question is therefore: *is the anticlimax necessary and inevitable*? If the answer is yes, then we are admitting that our human reality is a kind of trap, and that life is fundamentally futile.

But if life is futile, if all effort is a waste of time, then why have we devoted this book to asking so many questions and formulating answers? Why did we bother to launch into this exploration of the unknown in the first place? Is it not because, in spite of our rather unstable sense of reality, we have a curious certainty that these questions will *lead* somewhere, will provide us with answers that could transform our lives? And if that is so, then surely it means that it is possible to *do something* about human consciousness, to behave in such a way that we can live on a far higher level of happiness and purpose—in a state that is far closer to what

Abraham Maslow called 'the peak experience'?

This, I am convinced, is true. I have spent more than forty years attempting to answer this question. Now, as I approach sixty, I am certain that I know the answer. I have glimpsed it again and again, and lost it again and again. It is like trying to do an enormous jigsaw puzzle which is spread out over the whole floor of the room. You find half a dozen pieces that interlock, and you quickly fit them together. But then you pass on to another part of the puzzle in another part of the room, and the part you have 'solved' gets forgotten and buried under other pieces as you move them around. And one of the greatest problems is that this room called everyday consciousness is too small; you know that the floor is simply not big enough to hold the whole puzzle in its completed state. In an attempt to maintain some kind of order, you try classifying the 'completed' bits of the puzzle under different headings. This book, for example, contains about 25% of the bits I have labelled 'occult' or 'paranormal'. (A book with the off-putting title *Beyond the Occult*—it was imposed on me by the publisher—contains about 25% more.) Some of the most promising of the 'completed' sections are to be found in books like *The Outsider* or *The New Existentialism*, which could be labelled 'philosophy'. Oddly enough, my books on criminology also contain some of the most interesting parts, and one single page (111–12) in a book on sexual deviation called *The Misfits* contains one of the most important paragraphs in all my work:

'Our human senses show us only a small part of the world—the present. We have to *supplement* this present-awareness with memory and imagination. The reason I feel more 'alive' when I set out on holiday is that my memory and imagination are finally pulling their weight, and supplementing the present moment with all kinds of other times and places. It is as if I am in two places at once. The same is true if I am sitting in front of a blazing fire on a cold winter night, with the snow pattering against the windows. I am in two places at once; my body is in the warm room, while my imagination is out there, in the cold. But it would be a mistake to assume that we are talking about mere imagination. We are talking about something that might be called the *sense of reality*—what the psychologist Pierre Janet called 'the reality function'. Whenever the reality function is awake, we are happy.

'In short, before we can feel really alive, the mind needs to add a dimension of reality to the world of the senses. If there is such a thing as the "great secret" of human existence, this is it.'

Let me try to explain why I feel that Ouspensky's attitude about the 'wooden world' was a kind of premature defeatism, the defeatism of a man who was in some ways a great thinker, but who was also a typical 19th-century romantic.

One of my most basic insights came one day when I was reflecting upon this problem of defeatism and pessimism. I was also considering this interesting fact that any kind of *crisis* immediately arouses us to a higher level of drive and purpose, so that when it goes away, we momentarily experience a sense of total freedom. In *Crime and Punishment*, the hero Raskolnikov (who has committed a murder) realises that that he might be executed, and reflects: 'If I had to stand on a narrow ledge for ever and ever, in eternal darkness and tempest, I would rather do that than die at once.' We all know exactly what he means—that if someone placed a revolver against your head, and said: 'What is it to be: immediate death, or a narrow ledge for the rest of your life?', you would reply without hesitation: 'Narrow ledge, of course.' But consider: what would you actually *do* on a narrow ledge? What is that strange secret that you glimpse, when threatened by crisis, that convinces you that a narrow ledge is preferable to death?

These reflections led me to recognise that one of our most basic problems is what I labelled 'upside-downness'. You could say that you have three 'selves'—a physical self, an emotional self, and an intellectual (or mental) self. My physical values have a nasty habit of changing from one hour to the next; I may feel marvellous at ten in the morning, and rather depressed a few hours later merely because I am hungry or feel tired. But then, we are used to these physical ups and down, and do not let them bother us too much. Much more dangerous are our emotional ups and downs. We can have every reason for being pleased with ourselves and with life, and then some minor problem—a tax demand, someone being rude to us, a flash of alarm—can hurl us into a thoroughly negative state of mind. Emotions seem to drag us down like a heavy weight.

On the other hand, my intellect stands above these physical and emotional problems. When I am feeling angry or jealous or upset, another part of me looks down on it with cool detachment and tells me not to be such a fool. On the whole, my intellect tells me the truth—or at least, does its best. It is my emotions that often manage to creep in and distort this truth.

We might turn this insight into a Chinese parable. When the intellect is the Emperor, and emotions are the Grand Vizier, the kingdom is peaceful and happy. But when the Grand Vizier overthrows the Emperor and usurps the throne, everything becomes confused and chaotic.

In our internal political organisation, intellect was meant to be 'on top'. Emotions were intended to be the servant. What happens when we are upset is that we turn 'upside down'—almost as if our feet had turned into gas-filled balloons and made us stand on our heads. What is so dangerous is that this can happen without us even noticing it. We think we are still clear-headed and rational, but emotion has sneaked in and taken control. Without realising what has happened, a fog of depression settles over us. Life seems futile and boring. We are convinced that we have good reason for feeling that life is a cheat and that free will is an illusion. All that has happened is that we have turned 'upside down', and the world from this position looks alien and somehow frightening. I have described in *Mysteries* (and again, in *Beyond the Occult*) how, during a period of severe overwork, I began to suffer from a series of 'panic attacks' that brought me to the verge of nervous breakdown. All that had happened was that I had been overwhelmed by sheer exhaustion, and I could no longer keep my feet on the ground; every hour or so, I kept finding myself dangling upside down, seeing the world as meaningless and dangerous. Only my total *intellectual* certainty that this negative vision was an illusion allowed me to struggle 'the right way up' and stay in that position.

The real trouble is the *passivity* of human consciousness. We are like cows standing around in a field, accepting whatever happens as inevitable. Of course, as soon as some crisis arises, it has the effect of *shaking the mind awake*, and we respond magnificently. Suddenly, we recognise that we are free, and that we can change our lives. But as soon as the crisis is over, we go back to sleep again, and to chewing the cud.

To explain why this happens, I have to repeat a point I made in the first chapter. We have to recognise that we all have a robot inside us, whose job is to do things for us. I learn to type slowly and painfully; then the robot takes over and does it twice as fast as *I* could. He also drives my car and talks French for me. The problem is that he not only does the things I want, but also the things I would rather do myself. If I go for a walk with my robot switched on, I don't enjoy the walk; if I eat a meal robotically, I don't enjoy the food. Although the robot was intended to make our lives more easy and pleasant, he often goes too far and *lives* them for us.

When this happens, we *sink to a lower level of consciousness*. What is more, we assume that this lower level of consciousness is telling us the truth about the world. In fact, it is telling us lies, because it is so dim and dull. Once we begin to see this, we can also grasp that there are a number of distinct levels of consciousness that every one of us experiences during the course of a lifetime.

Let us, simply as an exercise, see if we can recognise the most fundamental of these levels. Let us start off with the basic state of non-consciousness that we experience in very deep sleep, and call this Level O. In that case Level 1 is the level we experience as we dream, and which persists in hypnagogic experiences.

Level 2 is the most basic level of waking consciousness: that is *mere awareness*. A child experiences this when he is too tired to take any interest in anything. He may be on his way home from a party but he gazes blankly at the passing world. If you were to ask, 'What have you just seen?' he would reply, 'I don't know.' His consciousness is merely a mirror reflecting the outside world. Nietzsche once said that we envy the cows their placidity, but it would be no use asking them the secret of their happiness for they would have forgotten the question before they could give the answer. This is Level 2.

At Level 3 consciousness has become self-aware but it is still dull and heavy—so heavy that we are only aware of one thing at a time: everything seems to be 'merely itself', utterly without meaning, and your own reflection in a mirror seems to be a stranger. This is the level that Sartre calls nausea.

Level 4 is the normal consciousness we experience every day. It is no longer too heavy to move: it has learned how to cope with existence yet it tends to think of life as a grim battle—possibly a losing battle. Consequently it tends to sink back easily towards Level 3 and to find experience meaningless and boring.

So far the one thing the levels all have in common is a basically *passive* attitude towards life and experience. At Level 5 this ceases to be so. This is a level that I have labelled provisionally 'spring morning consciousness' or 'holiday consciousness'. It is characterized by that bubbling feeling of happiness we experience when life suddenly becomes more interesting and exciting and all kinds of prospects seem to be opening up in front of us. Quite suddenly caution and doubt disappear; life becomes *self-evidently* fascinating and delightful. This is the feeling that Hesse's Steppenwolf experiences as he tastes a glass of wine and is reminded of 'Mozart and the stars'.

Level 6 could be labelled the 'magical level'. It is what happens to a child on Christmas Day, when everything combines to make life seem wonderful. Or imagine the consciousness of two honeymooners on their wedding night looking down from a balcony on to a moonlit lake, with the dark shapes of mountains in the distance. In such states we feel a total reconciliation with our lives. 'For moments together my heart stood still between delight and sorrow to find how rich was the gallery of my life,' says Steppenwolf. Problems seem trivial; we see that the one real virtue is courage. Consciousness has become a continuous mild peak experience, what J. B. Priestley calls 'delight'.

Level 7 is the state I have called (in *The Occult*) Faculty X – the odd ability to sense the *reality* of other times and places Proust says in *Swann's Way* I had ceased to feel mediocre, accidental, mortal. . . .' This is more than a peak experience: it is an odd sense of *mastery over time*, as if every moment of your life could be recalled as clearly as the last ten minutes. We suddenly realise that time is a manifestation of the heaviness of the body and the feebleness of the spirit. We can also see that if we could learn to achieve this condition of control permanently, time would become, in a basic sense, non-existent.

The most interesting thing about the levels beyond Level 7—the levels explored by Ouspensky and other mystics—is that they seem to *contradict* the evidence of our senses and of everyday consciousness. The inner becomes the outer, the outer becomes the inner, man is the whole universe and a mere atom, space and time are seen to be illusions and so on. Yet we can see that these contradictions are already inherent in everyday consciousness. At Level 2 consciousness has no kind of 'connectedness'; it is merely a flow of meaningless impressions. Level 3—nausea—starts to arrest this flow, to connect things together, but it keeps collapsing into a sudden perception that the world is after all quite meaningless and futile. Level 4—ordinary consciousness—'connects' things to a far higher degree, yet it still takes it for granted that life is an endless uphill struggle and that we have to make a continuous effort to see any meaning in it. At Level 5—'holiday consciousness'—all this changes: there is a sense of being able to see to distant horizons, of becoming aware of 'Mozart and the stars'. We suddenly realize that the world around us is so fascinating in itself that no effort is required. Everything makes us think of something else and so we are kept in a continuous state of interest and excitement.

At Level 6—'magic consciousness'—we seem to be floating in a sea of meaning and find it hard to understand how we could ever have been unhappy, or how anyone else could be. Even the worst experiences of the past now seem deeply interesting attempts to teach us something, essential steps on the upward path to this sense of optimism and control. The only tragedy in the universe seems to be that so many people lack the courage and sheer dogged stubbornness to *keep going* and so miss this literally 'heavenly' sense of wonder and reconciliation.

Level 7, with its sense of freedom, of mastery over time, is only a short step from the mystical level, just as Level 6—'magic'—is only a short step from Faculty X. A sudden additional effort can carry the mind over the threshold into that strange realm where 'separateness' is seen to be a delusion caused by fatigue and everything is *seen* to be connected. One of the most encouraging things about this insight into the levels is that each level is only a short and easy step away from the previous one.

Now if you look at this list you will notice an interesting thing

544

about Level 4—our ordinary everyday consciousness. At the
'bottom end' it is still dull and heavy, like waking up with a
hangover. Life is no longer horrible and meaningless, as it is
in Level 3 ('nausea'), but it is still an uphill struggle. But as
you continue to fight back, your 'engine' warms up, and you
begin to experience an increasing sense of optimism, a feeling
that obstacles are being overcome. 'Three down, seven still to
go.' And a point comes—about halfway—when suddenly you are
enjoying life, and even the struggle gives you pleasure, like a
strong swimmer who enjoys battling against a powerful current.

The turning-point is Level $3\frac{1}{2}$. And three and a half is precisely
half of seven. Until you reach $3\frac{1}{2}$, life is an uphill struggle. After
$3\frac{1}{2}$, it is all downhill. And at the top end of Level 4, we are bubbling
with optimism, and what Maslow calls the peak experience, the
experience of overflowing happiness, carries us up to Level 5,
'holiday consciousness'. You could say that the peak experience
is a spark that leaps the spark-gap between levels 4 and 5.

In other words, below $3\frac{1}{2}$ you are toiling uphill; *beyond* Level
Level $3\frac{1}{2}$, it is all downhill. The odd thing is that most healthy
people spend their days fairly close to Level $3\frac{1}{2}$. If they made a
slightly larger effort, they would be over the top of the hill.

Let me put this another way. You could say that, for practical
purposes, you are normally 50% robot, and 50% what you might
call 'real you'. When you feel tired, you sink to 51% robot, and
49% 'real you'. On the other hand, when you feel cheerful and
optimistic, you are 49% robot and 51% real you. In moods of great
optimism—setting out on holiday, for example—you become 52%
real you and only 48% robot.

That 'turning point'—the 50/50 level—is also what we have
called 'Level $3\frac{1}{2}$'.

And now it should be possible to see the answer to what
I called 'the Outsider problem' (in the first chapter of this
book). Those 19th-century Outsiders had marvellous glimpses
of sheer delight, when it seemed self-evident that the whole
universe is marvellous. Then they woke up the next morning,
and the old depression was back again. They told themelves
that the 'moments of delight' were an illusion, or that they
are bound to disappear as the 'shades of the prison house
begin to close' around us. This is why so many of them

committed suicide or died of wasting diseases that were caused by discouragement.

What we can see clearly is that they were making a simple mistake. The 'moments of delight' are not an illusion. They are a perfectly normal consequence of raising consciousness above level $3\frac{1}{2}$.

But how do we *do* that?

The answer is obvious. The romantics were defeated by their sense of gloom, by their conviction that life is a trap and that 'you can't win'. It was this conviction that kept them below Level $3\frac{1}{2}$. Notice that as soon as you *feel* optimistic, your energy levels rise. And if you were in a 50/50 state, the optimism has the effect of pushing you up to 51% 'real you' and 49% robot. The mere *knowledge* that we are so close to the 'turning point' is enough to push us 'over the top of the hill'. Maslow noticed that people who constantly had 'peak experiences' were all cheerful and healthy people. The peak experiences made them cheerful and healthy, and the health made them have peak experiences. The romantics, on the other hand, were convinced that life is one long defeat, so they immersed themselves in gloom and self-pity. There is no better formula for remaining below Level $3\frac{1}{2}$. They were in a state of 'negative feedback'.

This is the fundamental reason that I am convinced that the human race is on the point of an evolutionary leap to a higher stage. Our evolution has been brought about by the long, slow acquisition of knowledge, from the moment one of our ape-like ancestors learned to use a sharp stone as a hatchet. Now we have acquired the most important piece of knowledge of all: the knowledge of how close we are to Level $3\frac{1}{2}$. What it means, in effect, is that human beings are close to the level at which they will *recognise* that they possess the power to remain above Level $3\frac{1}{2}$.

And precisely how do we *do* this—in terms of everyday living? Again, we all know the answer without realising that we know it. When I walk out of my room and into a busy street, I am inclined to wince at the impact of 'everyday reality'. I am, in effect, 49% 'real me'. But I *can* make that small additional effort to cope with reality, to expect positive instead of negative things to happen—in short, to *push* myself up that extra 1% that will make all the difference and, having achieved it, to push myself up another 1%, beyond Level 3½.

At this point a personal experience may help to make my point. In 1987, I was on a lecture tour in Japan. I do not enjoy travel—I have the natural Outsider's preference for my own home—and I found that it was important to make a conscious effort not to allow myself to slip into a state of boredom and indifference in the crowded streets of Tokyo or Hiroshima. One evening, after a particularly crowded day, my wife and I were being taken to a theatrical performance by our interpreter. I would greatly have preferred to stay in my hotel room and rest, and have to admit that I had allowed myself to lose interest in the evening ahead. I had slipped, without noticing it, into a state of 'upside-downness'.

The theatre was in a very long street, with metal barriers on either side to force pedestrians to cross at the traffic light. But the traffic light was several hundred yards away. The street was empty, and our interpreter ducked underneath the barrier, and beckoned us to follow her. As we started to cross, the lights changed, and a sports car roared towards us at 50 miles an hour. I jerked myself out of my state of indifference, grabbed my wife's arm, and hauled her across the road as fast as I could. And that 'awakening' made me aware that I had permitted myself to slip into a state of upside-downness. As I sat in the theatre a few minutes later, I reflected that if my boredom had resulted in my wife being struck by a sports car, I would never have forgiven myself. My 'indifference' vanished, and I made a determined attempt to give my full attention to the play.

Early the next morning, we were on our way out of Tokyo, being taken to some distant place in the country; and roaring along the crowded freeway at 70 miles an hour, I reflected on the incident of the evening before, and on my recognition that it is of vital importance never to allow ourselves to sink into states of bored resentment. And now I recalled an image that I had used in the final chaper of my book *The Quest for Wilhelm Reich*. It had struck me that 'ordinary consciousness' has a substratum of boredom. It is disorganised, like billiard balls spread at random over a billiard table. As soon as something arouses our interest, we make a mental effort which pulls all the billiard balls together into the centre of the table. When we lose interest, or become tired, they spread all over the tabletop again.

If we become deeply absorbed, we make an additional effort of concentration, and this seems to have the odd effect of compressing the billiard balls still further, so they seem to climb on top of one another, forming a second tier. And at this point, I become aware of the power of my own mind. I realise that if I made a still greater effort of concentration, I could make the billiard balls climb up into a third layer, and even a fourth. What is so interesting about this procedure is that as I become increasingly 'absorbed' (T.E. Lawrence once remarked 'Happiness is absorption') my mental power seems to increase, and I can see that if I could maintain this level of energy, it should be possible to make the billiard balls form into a pyramid. It is a process of 'positive feedback', where interest releases further energy and excitement, and the excitement deepens our interest. And, that being so, the pyramid need *never collapse*. The billiard balls 'spread out' only because we lose vigilance. We *forget*. And if we could once achieve that intense level of excitement and interest, the universe would be so obviously fascinating that we would never be tempted to allow our attention to lapse.

As we drove along the Tokyo freeway, I experienced a state of intense excitement. I felt that I had achieved a 'bird's eye view' of the problem of human existence—what I sometimes call 'a hole in one'. (I do not play golf, but the analogy seems apt.) This, I saw, was *the* answer, the key to the next phase of man's evolution. And because I was able to formulate that insight so clearly *in words*, it has remained with me ever since. I recognise that this is the solution of the 'Outsider problem' that preoccupied me throughout my teens.

You may feel that this problem hardly concerns the average 'insider' who goes about his daily business. This is untrue. The Outsider problem permeates our civilisation. Every serious thinker and artist in the world has to struggle with it to some extent. And most of them are still trapped in the pessimism that led so many of the romantics to despair. Think of any 'serious' writer of the 20th century, and you will immediately recognise that basic pessimism—Proust, Joyce, Eliot, Musil, Valery, Hemingway, Sartre, Camus, Greene, Beckett, Derrida and the rest. It permeates the attitudes of philosophers, painters and musicians. When our ancestors look back on the 20th century, they will shake their heads and say: 'They lived in a negative culture'.

Consider again what happens when you have been threatened by some crisis, which is then averted. You not only experience a sense of relief. You also experience a curious sense of insight, of what G.K. Chesterton called 'absurd good news'. Hans Keller, the director of BBC music programmes, described how he had been in Germany during the late 1930s. As a Jew, he was in danger of disappearing into a concentration camp. He records that he prayed: 'O God, let me escape from Germany and I promise I will never be unhappy again for the rest of my life.' It suddenly seemed to him that it would be *so easy* to remain ecstatically happy for the rest of his life, *if only* he could escape from the Nazis. In fact, he did not keep his promise—he was generally known as a rather touchy and oversensitive little man. But then, human beings have never learned to keep that particular promise—not because they are lazy, but because they don't yet know how.

But think what happens when you are in some situation of crisis. Suddenly, you are giving your full attention to the crisis. *And you feel that, when the crisis is over, you will continue to give the same full attention to life without crisis*. This is why Keller thought it would be 'so easy' to be happy for the rest of his life.

Think of being in bed on a freezing winter morning, when you have to get up in ten minutes. The bed has never seemed so warm and comfortable. Yet on a Sunday, when you can stay in bed as long as you like, you can no longer re-create that feeling of comfort and warmth. Why?

Because when you have to get up in ten minutes, it is as if you are looking in a mirror, conscious of yourself and of your situation. It is the same for a man standing on the scaffold, waiting to be hanged. He is paying total attention to his situation.

We have returned to John Cowper Powys and the subject of Chapter One. As Wolf Solent sits in the railway carriage, he is paying total attention to his situation—to the seaside posters with their fly spots, to the telegraph poles flashing past the window. Yet he is also totally aware of himself, like a man relaxing in a warm bath.

Whenever human beings experience that deep sense of happiness and meaning, it is because they are 'paying attention'. If you eat a meal without paying attention, you do not enjoy it. But the reason that you can experience that sense of expanding happiness when setting out on a journey is that you are paying attention, and attention is somehow *expanding*, so you are aware of far more than your immediate situation. In some strange way, you are aware of other times and other places. It is almost as if you are in two places at once. This is what human consciousness *should* be like all the time. This is what it *will* be like when we have taken that next evolutionary step.

When I was a child, I was often told to chew my food properly, or it would give me indigestion. What I am now pointing out is that when we are happy, it is because we are chewing our experience properly—as you do in bed on a cold winter morning. Otherwise, we tend to swallow experience unchewed, and it does no good. This is what Socrates meant when he said: 'The unexamined life is not worth living.'

But in order for this analogy with chewing to take on its full significance, we have to suppose that if a child swallowed food without chewing it, the food would remain undigested, and would fail to have any nutritive effect whatever. For this *is* what happens with 'unchewed' experience: it passes straight through us, and contributes nothing to our growth. That is why so many unreflective people are spiritually stunted.

Human beings have to learn to become 'reflective', to chew their experience, to savour it. We see this truth every time we experience crisis and wish it would go away. We suddenly see how easy it would be to savour every moment of our lives. We have to learn to calm ourselves down, to relax, to *go inwards*. R.H. Ward said that when he tried to put the essence of his mystical experience into words, he saw it as a repetition of 'Within and within and within and within . . .' like a repeating decimal.

Although mystics have known this for centuries, it is only within the past two and a half centuries that the 'trick' has begun to spread to the rest of us—to be more specific, since 1740. I am not, of course, claiming that Richardson's *Pamela* was the first sign of this development. Throughout recorded history men have had this curious longing to escape into the world of the mind, the world of myths and stories, and that 'eternal longing' is manifested in *The Epic of Gilgamesh* and the *Odyssey* and the Greek drama and the *Canterbury Tales* and the Elizabethan drama and *Don Quixote* and Grimmelshausen's *Simplicissimus* and *Robinson Crusoe*. But because *Pamela* was the first 'soap opera', it was a watershed, somehow as different from *Don Quixote* as a steamship is from a sailing ship. It taught people to *pay attention* to their own lives instead of dreaming about mythical heroes and faraway places with strange-sounding names.

Ever since *Pamela*, man has been trying to absorb that lesson. But the industrial revolution made life far more hectic, preventing us from 'paying attention'. So we continue to swallow our experience without chewing it, and wondering why we suffer from indigestion. We have to consciously learn to make that effort to chew. The great heroes of this new phase of human evolution are not the conquerors, or even the scientists, but the men who have taught us to reflect, to 'mythologise', to go 'within and within and within . . .'

Meanwhile, we remain trapped in a negative culture, whose cult figures are artists and writers who remain convinced that life is basically meaningless or tragic. Here, for example, is a typical passage from the French philosopher and critic Roland Barthes:

'. . . the art of living has no history; it does not evolve: the pleasure which vanishes vanishes for good, and there is no substitute for it. Other pleasures come, which replace nothing. *No progress in pleasures*, nothing but mutation.'[1]

This is still the same pessimism that we can find in the Romantics, from Novalis to Verlaine. And he is clearly missing the point: that the only way of preventing experience from 'vanishing for good' is to 'permanise' it through 'attention'. This word processor on which I am writing has a key labelled 'save', and when I press it, the words I have written are transferred from the screen to the disc. Now they are recorded, fixed—as writing 'fixes' our speech. If my word processor is accidentally switched off before I have pressed the 'save' key, the words 'vanish for

1. From *Barthes by Barthes*.

good'. Barthes, like so many of his fellow romantics, has simply failed to realise that his brain has a 'save' key, and that it is because we have learned to use this key that human beings have evolved faster than any other animal.

Now it should be clear why I think that 'the paranormal' is of such immense importance. Here is one field that is untinged by contemporary pessimism. The clear message that emerges is that man possesses powers of which he is normally unaware. As Richard Church watched the gardener wielding the axe, and noticed that the sound came after the blow, he says that he experienced a marvellous sense of freedom. His enemy so far had been 'the drag of the earth'. Now he realised that he had been overestimating the enemy. It was at that moment that he made an instinctive effort and rose from the ground and glided about the room. When man can clearly recognise the existence of these powers, and incorporate that recognition into his everyday awareness—so that he is no longer subject to a permanent 'leakage' of vitality—then he will suddenly have become a totally different kind of creature.

Appendix

IT SEEMS wortwhile to explain how I came to be converted from the notion that poltergeists are simply a form of 'spontaneous psychokinesis', due to the hidden powers of the unconscious mind, to the conviction that they are independent 'spirits'. It began in 1976, when I presented the Rosenheim case on BBC television.

In 1967 the office of a lawyer in Rosenheim, Bavaria, became the scene of a number of violent poltergeist disturbances. Light tubes shattered, pictures turned on the walls and a heavy filing cabinet was moved as if it weighed only a few pounds. Moreover the telephone bill was enormous because hundreds of calls had apparently been made to the talking clock – more calls than were physically possible in the time available. The 'poltergeist' was apparently getting straight through the relays. A well-known professor of parapsychology from Freiburg, Hans Bender, went to investigate the case and soon observed that the disturbances only took place when a young girl named Anne-Marie Schaberl was in the office. Anne-Marie was a country girl who was unhappy working in a town; her family life had been difficult – her father was a strict disciplinarian – and she was mistrustful and tense. Bender took her back to his laboratory to try various tests for extra-sensory perception and she showed remarkable telepathic abilities. And while Anne-Marie was in Freiburg the disturbances in the office ceased. But they continued at the mill where she found work: when someone was killed in an accident Anne-Marie was blamed, and she left. Her fiancé broke off his engagement to her because she had such an extraordinary effect on the electronic scoring equipment at his favourite bowling alley. Finally she married and had a child, and the manifestations ceased.

Anne-Marie had no suspicion that she was the cause of the disturbances in the lawyer's office: indeed when I met him during the course of the programme Professor Bender told me that one of the first rules of poltergeist investigation is not to tell the 'disturbed adolescent' that he – or she – is the real cause of the disturbances, for it usually terrifies them.

In 1980 I heard of a poltergeist haunting that was even more astonishing than the Rosenheim case. It had taken place in Pontefract in Yorkshire and I heard about it from a friend of the family concerned, who seemed to think that it might make a book rather like the best-selling *Amityville Horror*. The poltergeist had, it seemed, wrecked practically every breakable item in the house and made such loud drumming noises at night that neighbours gathered in crowds to listen. But in this case a number of people concerned had apparently also seen the poltergeist, which took the form of a monk dressed in black. The friend of the family who contacted me was also interested in local history and told me that his researches had revealed that there had once been a gallows on the site of the house, and that a Cluniac monk had been hanged there for rape in the time of Henry VIII.

The story sounded almost too good to be true. But before deciding to write about it I asked a friend who lived in the area, Brian Marriner, to go and investigate. He wrote me a long letter in which he outlined the story of the haunting, and I was left in no doubt that this was a genuine case, not a hoax. The daughter of the family, Diane Pritchard, had been dragged upstairs by the throat by 'Black Monk' and thrown out of bed repeatedly. But the ghost also seemed to have a sense of humour. When Aunt Maude, a determined sceptic, came to see for herself, a jug of milk floated out of the refrigerator and poured itself over her head. Later what looked like two enormous hands appeared around the door: they proved to be Aunt Maude's fur gloves. As the gloves floated into the bedroom Mrs Pritchard asked indignantly, 'Do you still think it's the kids doing it?' Aunt Maude burst into 'Onward Christian Soldiers' and the gloves proceeded to conduct her singing, beating in time.

Having studied Brian Marriener's report on the case I concluded that there was not enough material there for a full-length book, but it would make an admirable centre-piece for a book on the poltergeist, on which there is an immense amount of well-authenticated material. Poltergeist cases seem to be among the most frequent of paranormal events – at any given moment there is likely to be one going on within a dozen miles of where you are now reading this book. This, I concluded, is because the world is so full of sexually disturbed adolescents. I sketched out an outline of a history of poltergeist phenomena and submitted it to my publisher, who wrote back to say he liked the idea. Then, accompanied by my wife, I set out for Yorkshire to investigate for myself.

On our way to Pontefract we stopped for a night at the Hayes Conference Centre in Swanwick, Derbyshire, where I was to lecture at a conference on the paranormal. The following afternoon, just as we were about to leave, someone mentioned that Guy Playfair was due to arrive in half an hour. He and I had corresponded but had never met. So although I was anxious to get on to Yorkshire I decided to stay around for another half hour to introduce myself. It proved to be one of those fateful decisions that exercise an immeasurable influence on the future.

Guy, I knew, had spent some time in Rio de Janeiro, where he had joined the Brazilian equivalent of the Society for Psychical Research and studied the local version of black magic, *umbanda*. I knew his book *The Indefinite Boundary*, a scientific study of the paranormal, and was impressed by its logic and detachment. I was just as impressed by Playfair himself, a quietly-spoken man whose modest utterances nevertheless carried total conviction. For half an hour or so we talked about ley lines, animal homing and telepathy. Then, just as it was about time to leave, I told him I was writing a book on the poltergeist and asked his opinion. He frowned, hesitated, then said, 'I think it's a kind of football.' 'Football!' I wondered if I'd misheard him: 'A football of energy. When people get into conditions of tension, they exude a kind of energy – the kind of thing that happens to teenagers at puberty. Along come a couple of spirits, and they do what any group of schoolboys would so – they begin to kick it around, smashing windows and generally creating havoc. Then they get tired and leave it. In fact the football often explodes, and turns into a puddle of water.'

'So you mean a poltergeist is actually a spirit?'

'That's right. I'm not saying there's not such a thing as spontaneous psychokinesis. But most poltergeists are spirits.' And he advised me to read the French spiritualist Allan Kardec.

I must admit that I found this notion hard to swallow. Ever since making the programme on the Rosenheim case I had taken it for granted that poltergeists are some kind of strange manifestation of the unconsious mind. I was not sure where the energy came from, but suspected that it was from the earth itself. I had seen a dowser standing above an underground spring, his fingers locked together and his hands pumping up and down so violently that the sweat poured down his face: he was obviously unable to stop himself while his hands were together. And at a dowsing conference I had been introduced to an old lady who sometimes picked up a large fallen branch and used it as a dowsing rod. Suspended in one hand, it would swing from side to side like a huge voltmeter needle. It seemed to me highly likely that the energy used by the poltergeist flows from the earth via the right brain of the disturbed adolescent. And now Guy Playfair was advising me to abandon these carefully constructed theories and return to a view that sounded like crude mediaeval superstition.

The following afternoon we arrived at the home of Joe and Jean Pritchard in Pontefract. It was the typically neat home of an upper-working-class family. Their nineteen-year-old son Phillip was at home, and during the course of the afternoon their daughter Diane came over with her husband to join us. These two had been the unconscious cause of the events that had caused a local sensation in 1966. I asked how the disturbances had begun. 'With these pools of water on the kitchen floor.' Joy and I looked at one another. 'Can you describe their shape?' Mrs Pritchard shook her head. 'They were just neat little pools – like overturning an ink bottle.' This, according to Playfair, was a description of the pools of water created by the explosion of the 'energy football'.

He said it was almost impossible to make them by pouring water on the floor – from a jug for example – because it splashes. These pools look as if a small cat has placed its behind close to the floor and urinated. I began to feel that there might be something in his spirit theory after all.

Mrs Pritchard said that as fast as they mopped up the pools they reappeared elsewhere. But waterboard officials could find no leak. And when the tap was turned on green foam rushed out. Then the button of the tea dispenser began to move in and out, covering the draining board with dry tea leaves; lights switched on and off and a plant-pot somehow found its way from the bottom to the top of the stairs.

This first set of manifestations occurred in 1966 and Phillip was obviously the focus since Diane way away on holiday at the time. Two days later, they ceased. But when they began again in 1968, Diane – now fourteen – had become the focus. The ghost seldom paid a visit during the day, when she was at school. But in the evening the racket would start – usually a noise like a child beating a big drum – and ornaments would levitate across the room while the lights turned erratically on and off. Yet the poltergeist did not seem malicious – rather an infuriating practical joker. After a tremendous crash all the contents of the china cabinet were found scattered around the sitting room, yet not one was even craked. When the vicar came to try to exorcise the poltergeist and told the family that he thought their trouble was subsidence, a candlestick rose from the shelf and floated under his nose. The exorcism was unsuccessful.

Diane found it frightening, yet less so than might be expected. She always had a kind of inward notification when the pranks were about to start. Hurled violently out of bed with the mattress on top of her, she was unhurt. When the hall stand – made of heavy oak – floated through the air and pinned her down on the stairs (with a sewing machine on top of it for good measure) she was unable to move and the family were unable to budge it, yet she was not even bruised. When the ghost – whom they called Mr Nobody – hurled the grandfather clock downstairs so that it burst like a bomb, no one was anywhere near.

At a fairly late stage in the haunting the ghost began to show itself. Jean and Joe Pritchard awakened one night to see a dim figure standing in the open doorway. Their next-door neighbour was standing at the sink when she felt someone standing behind her: it proved to be a tall figure in a monk's habit with a cowl over the head. It looked so solid and normal that she felt no alarm: then it vanished. Another neighbour, Rene Holden (who was a bit psychic), was in the Pritchards' sitting room when the lights went out. In the faint glow of the streetlamp that came through the curtains she saw the lower half of a figure dressed in a long black garment.

The haunting was nearing its climax. One evening when the lights went out Diane was heard to scream: the family rushed into the had and found her being dragged up the stairs. The ghost seemed to have one hand on her cardigan, which was stretched out in front of her, and the other on her throat. As Phillip and Jean Pritchard grabbed her the ghost let go, and they all tumbled down the stairs. Diane's throat was covered with red finger-marks yet Mr Nobody had not exerted enough pressure to hurt her. Soon after this Jean Pritchard came downstairs to find the hall carpet soaked in water; on the wet surface there were huge footprints.

One day Phillip and Diane were watching television when they both saw the Black Monk – or at least his shape – silhouetted on the other side of the frosted glass door that led to the dining room. As Phillip opened the door they saw his tall, black shape in the process of vanishing. It seemed to disappear into the kitchen floor. And that was the end of the Pontefract haunting. Mr Nobody disappeared and has not been heard from since.

I spent the whole of that Sunday afternoon listening to recordings of the poltergeist making violent banging noises, and questioning the family and neighbours. I also read the accounts contained in the local newspapers at the time. There could not be the slightest reasonable doubt that the haunting was genuine: there were too many witnesses.

Even if I had not met Guy Playfair some of the features of the case would have puzzled me. This poltergeist behaved more like a ghost, and its connection with the former Cluniac monastery and the local gallows was fairly well established. In that case the theory that it was a really a kind of astral juvenile delinquent from Diane's unconscious mind seemed absurd. Besides, as Diane described her feelings as she was pulled upstairs by Mr

Nobody I experienced a sudden total conviction that this was an independent entity, not a split-off fragment of her own psyche. When I left the Pritchards' house that afternoon I had no doubt whatever that Guy Playfair was right: poltergeists are spirits.

It was an embarrassing admission to have to make. With the exception of Guy Playfair there is probably not a single respectable parapsychologist in the world who will publicly admit the existence of spirits. Many will concede in private that they are inclined to to accept the evidence for life after death, but in print even that admission would be regarded as a sign of weakness. Before that trip to Pontefract I had been in basic agreement with them: it seemed totally unnecessary to assume the existence of spirits. Tom Lethbridge's 'tape-recording' theory explained hauntings; the unconsciousness' and the 'information universe' combined to explain mysteries like telepathy, psychometry, even precognition. Spirits were totally irrelevant. Yet the Pontefract case left me in no probability of some local monk who died in a sudden and violent death, perhaps on the gallows, and who might or might not be aware that he was dead. And I must admit that it still causes me a kind of flash of protest to write such a sentence: the rationalist in me wants to say, 'Oh come off it. . .' Yet the evidence points clearly in that direction and it would be simple dishonesty not to admit it.

When I returned from Yorkshire I took a deep breath and plunged into the annals of poltergeist activity with the aid of the library at the Society for Psychical Research and the College of Psychic Studies. The picture that now began to emerge made me aware of how far my preconceptions had caused me to impose an unnatural logic on the whole subject of the paranormal. It was not so much that the conceptions underlying my previous books *The Occult* and *Mysteries* were wrong as that they were incomplete. And much of the evidence required to complete them had been staring me in the face from the beginning.

Index

562

564

566